THE HANDBOOK OF JOURNALISM STUDIES

This handbook charts the growing area of journalism studies, exploring the current state of theory and setting an agenda for future research in an international context. The volume is structured around theoretical and empirical approaches, and covers scholarship on news production and organizations; news content; journalism and society; and journalism in a global context. Emphasizing comparative and global perspectives, each chapter explores:

- Key elements, thinkers, and texts
- Historical context
- Current state-of-the-art
- Methodological issues
- Merits and advantages of the approach/area of studies
- Limitations and critical issues of the approach/area of studies
- Directions for future research

Offering broad international coverage from top-tier contributors, this volume ranks among the first publications to serve as a comprehensive resource addressing theory and scholarship in journalism studies. As such, *The Handbook of Journalism Studies* is a must-have resource for scholars and graduate students working in journalism, media studies, and communication around the globe.

A Volume in the International Communication Association Handbook Series.

Karin Wahl-Jorgensen is Reader in the Cardiff School of Journalism, Media, and Cultural Studies, Cardiff University, Wales. Her work on media, democracy, and citizenship has been published in more than 20 international journals as well as in numerous books.

Thomas Hanitzsch is Assistant Professor in the Institute of Mass Communication and Media Research at the University of Zurich. He founded the ICA's Journalism Studies Division and has published four books and more than 50 articles and chapters on journalism, comparative communication research, online media, and war coverage.

INTERNATIONAL COMMUNICATION ASSOCIATION (ICA)
HANDBOOK SERIES

Robert T. Craig, Series Editor

Strömbäck/ Kaid – *The Handbook of Election News Coverage Around the World*
Wahl-Jorgensen/Hanitzsch – *The Handbook of Journalism Studies*

THE HANDBOOK OF JOURNALISM STUDIES

Edited by

Karin Wahl-Jorgensen

Thomas Hanitzsch

NEW YORK AND LONDON

First published 2009
by Routledge
270 Madison Ave, New York, NY 10016

Simultaneously published in the UK
by Routledge
2 Park Square, Milton Park, Abingdon, Oxon OX14 4RN

Routledge is an imprint of the Taylor & Francis Group, an informa business

Typeset in Times and Helvetica by EvS Communication Networx, Inc.

Library of Congress Cataloging in Publication Data
The handbook of journalism studies / [edited] by Karin Wahl-Jorgensen and Thomas Hanitzsch.
p. cm. — (ICA handbook series)
Includes index.
1. Journalism. I. Wahl-Jorgensen, Karin. II. Hanitzsch, Thomas, 1969-
PN4724.H36 2008
070.4—dc22
2008024854

ISBN10 HB: 0-8058-6342-7
ISBN10 PB: 0-8058-6343-5
ISBN10 EB: 1-4106-1806-4

ISBN13 HB: 978-0-8058-6342-0
ISBN13 PB: 978-0-8058-6343-7
ISBN13 EB: 978-1-4106-1806-1

Contents

V. JOURNALISM STUDIES IN A GLOBAL CONTEXT

Series Editor's Foreword

Robert T. Craig

Although the origins of academic research on journalism can be traced to mid-nineteenth century Europe and work on this topic developed in several disciplines through the twentieth century, especially in U.S. schools of Journalism and Mass Communication during the century's last several decades, in the perspective of the present moment journalism seems to have emerged rather suddenly on the international scene of communication research as a vibrant new interdisciplinary field. The Journalism Studies interest group of the International Communication Association, formed as recently as 2004 with 50 initial members, at this writing is one of the largest, fastest growing. and most broadly international ICA divisions with over 500 members as of mid-2008. *The Handbook of Journalism Studies*, edited by Karin Wahl-Jorgensen and Thomas Hanitzsch, is thus a timely contribution that provides a benchmark assessment and sets the agenda for future research in this burgeoning area.

The editors' introduction notes other signs of growth including several new journals and major books on Journalism Studies published in recent years. It must be acknowledged that much of what is here called Journalism Studies continues lines of research that have gone on for many years under the rubric of Mass Communication, but the shift to Journalism Studies represents more than just a new label for old work or the familiar process of a maturing sub-specialty spinning off from an overpopulated division. Rather, it marks a significant shift of focus away from the functionalist tradition in which journalism has been studied primarily with regard to abstract functions of the mass communication process like gatekeeping and agenda setting. While these and other similar lines of empirical research, as represented by excellent chapters in this volume, continue to flourish and hold an important place, the frame shift from Mass Communication to Journalism Studies inverts figure and ground. As the central focus shifts away from abstract functions of mass communication and toward journalism as, in the editors' words, "one of the most important social, cultural and political institutions," then the normative, historical, cultural, sociological, and political aspects of journalism that were formerly overshadowed emerge as primary concerns and redefine the intellectual context in which empirical studies are conducted.

The editors and authors contributing to this volume hail from 11 countries around the world and include leading scholars representing a range of disciplines. Thirty chapters review bodies of literature on diverse aspects of Journalism Studies as an academic field, practices of news production, analyses of news content, the complex relations of journalism to society, and the global context of journalism research. Internationalizing the field and developing a global perspective on journalism institutions, extending research in traditionally marginalized institutions and practices, and connecting scholarship with journalism education and professional practice are appropriately emphasized by the editors as goals for the future.

THE ICA HANDBOOK SERIES

The ICA Handbook series is a joint venture between the International Communication Association and Routledge. It will be a series of scholarly handbooks that represent the interests of ICA members and help to further the Association's goals of promoting theory and research across the discipline. These handbooks will provide benchmark assessments of current scholarship and set the agenda for future work. The series will include handbooks that focus on content areas, methodological approaches, and theoretical lenses for communication research.

We seek proposals from prospective editors of handbooks. We especially seek proposals that cross the boundaries of established disciplines and fields to address timely problems of international scope, not just representing different specialties but bringing them together collaboratively to address intersecting interests and research problems of broad interest. For example, such problems might be formulated as topical concerns (e.g., globalization, virtual environments), theoretical approaches (e.g., social cognition, critical studies), or matters pertaining to communication or communication research in general (e.g., methodological innovations, communication theory across cultures).

For more information about this series, contact:

Robert T. Craig
ICA Handbook Series Editor
Department of Communication
University of Colorado at Boulder
270 UCB
Boulder, CO 80309-0270
303-492-6498 voice
303-492-8411 fax
Robert.Craig@colorado.edu

or

Linda Bathgate
Senior Editor, Communication Studies
Routledge
270 Madison Avenue
New York, NY 10016
212-216-7854 phone
212-643-1430 fax
linda.bathgate@taylorandfrancis.com

Preface

The book that you now have before you is a product of the conviction that we should care about journalism and its study. We should care about journalism because it's central to democracy, citizenship, and everyday life, and we should care about journalism studies because it helps us understand this key social institution. We are not alone in holding this conviction: Journalism studies is one of the fastest growing areas within the larger discipline of communication research and media studies. As indicated by a serious, though not altogether coherent body of academic literature and ongoing scholarly work, the study of journalism has matured to become an academic field of its own right. We felt that the arrival of journalism studies ought to be both celebrated and solidified, and to honor this ambition, *The Handbook of Journalism Studies* was conceived as a gathering place for the varied lasting and emerging preoccupations of scholars in the field. This handbook therefore bears witness to the rapid and exciting developments within this important area of research, as well as its complexity, richness and promise in terms of theory and research. We hope the book can boost the intellectual foundations of journalism studies, providing the reader with an overview of journalism as a dynamic field of study across its diverse epistemological, theoretical and methodological traditions.

The Handbook of Journalism Studies sets out to comprehensively chart the field and define the agenda for future research in an international context. It is our hope that the handbook, when taken as a whole, provides a sense of journalism research on a global scale, covering not just the dominant Anglo-American traditions but also looking beyond this context, to Africa, Latin America, continental Europe, and Asia. Although we have sought to make journalism studies a broad church in including 30 different chapters, each covering an impressive breadth of subject matter, we do not claim to survey every key area and tradition of scholarship in journalism studies. We had to make tough choices about what we were able to include and, regrettably, what to leave out. Needless to say, it would be impossible to do complete justice to a rich, dynamic and ever-emerging field of research in only one volume, however bulky, and we are reassured that journalism studies continues to be a productive scholarly community where the debates that echo in this book and those we have been unable to reflect continue with unabated fervor. What we do hope is that *The Handbook of Journalism Studies* will be a useful compendium resource for anyone trying to get a sense of an academic field of inquiry and its past, present and future. We intend for the book to provide the starting point for further discussion and debate among scholars and students in communication and journalism studies.

The book is structured around a critical engagement with key theoretical and empirical traditions, fields of inquiry and scholarly debates in journalism studies, laid out by the foremost experts in each area. Beginning with four introductory chapters which outline more general issues in the field, the organization of the book reflects the aim of covering the broad contours of journalism studies. The volume contains four thematic sections, covering scholarship on news production and organizations, news content, journalism and society, and journalism in a global context. Within these sections, each chapter provides a systematic and accessible overview of the state of scholarship and defines key problems, but also advances theory-building and problem-solving, and identifies areas for further research.

Editing this book and working with some of the most renowned scholars of our field has been a pleasure and a privilege, but it would not have been possible without the help and dedication of many committed people. We would therefore like to express our gratitude to all contributors for their excellent chapters. We would also like to thank Linda Bathgate from Routledge and the series editor Robert T. Craig for their helpful comments on the first draft of the proposal and their help during the editing process. We are especially indebted to Hong Nga Nguyen "Angie" Vu who did an exceptional job in proofreading all chapters. Karin would like to thank colleagues in the Cardiff School of Journalism, Media and Cultural Studies for their support and advice, and Jacob Wahl-Byde for his arrival in the middle of this project, adding both endless joy and chaos. Thomas would like to thank colleagues in the Institute for Mass Communication and Media Research at the University of Zurich for their patience and support during the editing stage of the book.

Contributors

Chris Anderson is completing his doctoral studies in communication at the Columbia University Graduate School of Journalism, New York. His research focuses on new media technologies, journalistic authority and the position of journalism within the sociology of the professions. He has contributed chapters to a number of books, including *The Media and Social Theory* (Routledge, 2008), *The International Encyclopedia of Communication* (Blackwell, 2008) and *Making Our Media* (Hampton Press, 2008).

Chris Atton is Reader in Journalism at the School of Creative Industries, Napier University, Edinburgh. His research into alternative media is interdisciplinary, drawing on sociology, journalism, cultural studies, popular music studies and politics. His books include *Alternative Journalism* (Sage, 2008, with James Hamilton), *An Alternative Internet* (Edinburgh University Press, 2004), *Alternative Media* (Sage, 2002) and *Alternative Literature* (Gower, 1996). He is currently researching the nature of distributed creativity in avant-garde and experimental music; the cultural politics of post-punk fanzines; and audiences for community media in Scotland.

Kevin G. Barnhurst is Professor, Department of Communication, University of Illinois at Chicago. His studies of news consumption and critical analyses of journalism include *The Form of News: A History* (Guilford Press, 2001), with John Nerone, *Seeing the Newspaper* (St. Martin's Press, 1994), and many other articles and book chapters. He has been LSU Reilly Visiting Fellow; Distinguished Fulbright Chair, Italy; Shorenstein Fellow at Harvard; Visiting Scholar at Columbia University; and Senior Fulbright Scholar, Peru.

Lee B. Becker is a professor and Director of the James M. Cox Jr. Center for International Mass Communication Training and Research at the University of Georgia, Athens. His research focuses on a variety of topics, including news work, the interface between the journalism labor market and educational and training institutions, and the evaluation of media performance. His most recent book is *The Evolution of Key Mass Communication Concepts* (Hampton Press, 2005), edited with Sharon Dunwoody, Douglas M. McLeod, and Gerald M. Kosicki.

Daniel A. Berkowitz is Professor of Journalism and Mass Communication at the University of Iowa. His main areas of research are in sociology of news, and media and terrorism. He is the editor of *Social Meanings of News: A Text-Reader* (Sage, 1997) and has published articles in *Journalism*, *Journalism Studies*, *International Communication Gazette*, *Journalism & Mass Communication Quarterly*, *Journal of Communication*, as well as chapters in *Media and Political Violence* (Hampton Press, 2007) and in *Media Anthropology* (Sage, 2005).

S. Elizabeth Bird is Professor and Chair, Department of Anthropology, University of South Florida. Her books include *For Enquiring Minds: A Cultural Study of Supermarket Tabloids*

(University of Tennessee Press, 1992), *Dressing in Feathers: The Construction of the Indian in American Popular Culture* (Westview, 1996) and *The Audience in Everyday Life: Living in a Media World* (Routledge, 2003). She has published over 50 articles and chapters; she is currently editing a book on the anthropology of news and journalism.

Renita Coleman is Assistant Professor at the University of Texas in Austin. Her research focuses on visual communication and ethics. She is co-author of the book *The Moral Media: How Journalists Reason About Ethics* (Erlbaum, 2004, with Lee Wilkins), and has published articles in numerous journals including *Journalism & Mass Communication Quarterly*, *Journal of Communication*, and *Journalism Studies*. She is associate editor of the *Journal of Mass Media Ethics*. She was a newspaper journalist for 15 years.

Simon Cottle is Professor of Media and Communications and Deputy Head of the School of Journalism, Media and Cultural Studies at Cardiff University, Wales. His latest book is *Global Crisis Reporting: Journalism in the Global Age* (Open University Press, 2009) and recent books include *Mediatized Conflict: Developments in Media and Conflict Studies* (Open University Press, 2006) and *The Racist Murder of Stephen Lawrence: Media Performance and Public Transformation* (Praeger, 2004). He is the editor of the international Peter Lang series *Global Crises and Media*.

Robert W. Dardenne is Associate Professor of Journalism and Media Studies at University of South Florida, St. Petersburg. He co-authored *The Conversation of Journalism* (Praeger, 1996) and authored *A Free and Responsible Student Press* (Poynter Institute for Media Studies, 1996). His articles, book chapters, and newspaper op-ed pieces center on various aspects of news content, practice, and history. As a Fulbright Lecturer, he spent 1999–2000 teaching and lecturing in China and has consulted with leading print media and lectured in Nigeria. He worked 12 years as reporter and editor in newspapers and magazines.

Arnold S. de Beer is Professor Extraordinary in the Department of Journalism, Stellenbosch University, South Africa. He is managing and founding editor of *Ecquid Novi: African Journalism Studies* and director of the Institute for Media Analysis in South Africa (iMasa). De Beer edited *Global Journalism* (Allyn & Bacon, 2004, 2009), with John C. Merrill and authored or co-authored journal articles and book chapters published in the US and the UK on topics such journalism education in Africa; media and democracy, as well as and media and conflict. He is the founding editor of the *Journal of Global Mass Communication*.

William Dinan is Lecturer in Sociology at the University of Strathclyde Glasgow, where he teaches undergraduate courses on media and society, and postgraduate classes on the Masters programme in Investigate Journalism. He is an editorial board member of SpinWatch and has recently co-authored a monograph on the history of Public Relations, *A Century of Spin: How Public Relations Became the Cutting Edge of Corporate Power* (2008) and co-edited a volume on PR titled *Thinker, Faker, Spinner, Spy: Corporate PR and the Assault on Democracy* (2007, both Pluto Press, with David Miller).

Robert M. Entman is J.B. and M.C. Shapiro Professor of Media and Public and International Affairs at The George Washington University, Washington, DC. He is author or editor of *Projections of Power: Framing News, Public Opinion and US Foreign Policy* (University of Chicago

Press, 2004), *Mediated Politics: Communication in the Future of Democracy* (Cambridge University Press, 2001, with Lance Bennett) and *The Black Image in the White Mind: Media and Race in America* (University of Chicago Press, 2000, with Andrew Rojecki). His next books will be *Doomed to Repeat: Media, War and History* and *Rather Biased? A Theory of Media and Power*.

Thomas Hanitzsch is Assistant Professor in the Institute of Mass Communication and Media Research at the University of Zurich. His teaching and research focuses on global journalism cultures, comparative methodology and crisis and war communication. He has published and edited four books and more than 50 journal articles and book chapters, and is co-editor of the *Journal of Global Mass Communication*. A newspaper and radio journalist for several years, Dr. Hanitzsch has founded the Journalism Studies Division of the International Communication Association.

Tony Harcup is Senior Lecturer in the Department of Journalism Studies at the University of Sheffield, UK. He is the author of *The Ethical Journalist* (Sage, 2007) and *Journalism: Principles and Practice* (Sage, 2004), and his research on news values, ethics, and alternative media has also been published in *Journalism Studies*, *Journalism*, and *Ethical Space*. He has worked as a journalist in both mainstream and alternative media and is an active member of the National Union of Journalists and the Association for Journalism Education.

John Hartley is Australian Research Council Federation Fellow, Research Director of the ARC Centre of Excellence for Creative Industries and Innovation, and Distinguished Professor at Queensland University of Technology in Australia. He is the author of 18 books, translated into a dozen languages, including *Television Truths* (Blackwell, 2008), *The Indigenous Public Sphere* (Oxford University Press, 2000), *Popular Reality* (Arnold, 1996) and *Understanding News* (Routledge, 1982). He is editor of the *International Journal of Cultural Studies*.

Beate Josephi is in charge of Masters courses in the School of Communications and Arts at Edith Cowan University, Perth, Australia. Her research is mostly in journalism. She has published articles in *Gazette*, *Global Media and Communication*, and Australian journalism journals, and is the editor of the forthcoming book *Journalism Education in Challenging Environments* (Hampton Press), which looks at journalism education in countries that have partial or no press freedom.

Mirca Madianou is a Lecturer in Sociology at the Faculty of Social and Political Sciences, University of Cambridge and a Fellow of Lucy Cavendish College. Her main research interests are in news, and particularly news consumption; media and nationalism; new communication technologies and transnational identities; the emotional dimension of mediated communication; media ethics; comparative ethnography. She is the author of *Mediating the Nation: News, Audiences and the Politics of Identity* (UCL Press/Routledge, 2005) and is currently working on a book manuscript on news and emotion.

Jörg Matthes is a Post-doc researcher at the Institute of Mass Communication and Media Research, University of Zurich. His research focuses on processes of public opinion formation, media effects, news framing, trust in news media and empirical methods. He has published in international journals including *Journal of Communication*, *Communication Research*, *International Journal of Public Opinion Research*, *International Journal of Advertising*, *Communication Methods and Measures* and *Public Understanding of Science*.

Maxwell McCombs holds the Jesse H. Jones Centennial Chair in Communication at the University of Texas at Austin. Co-founder of the agenda-setting research tradition, his most recent book is *Setting the Agenda: The mass media and public opinion* (Blackwell, 2004). A former president of the World Association for Public Opinion Research, McCombs has received the Paul Deutschmann Award for Excellence in Research from the Association for Education in Journalism and Mass Communication the Murray Edelman Award for Distinguished Scholarship in Political Communication from the American Political Science Association.

John H. McManus is the founder of GradeTheNews.org, a Web site that evaluated the quality of news in the San Francisco Bay Area. His research explores how market forces shape news. He helped develop the online news assessment tools at NewsTrust.net. His book, *Market-Driven Journalism: Let the Citizen Beware?* (Sage, 1994) won the Society of Professional Journalists research prize in 1994.

Brian McNair is Professor of Journalism and Communication at the University of Strathclyde, Glasgow. He is the author of many books and essays on the relationship between journalism and politics, including *Journalism and Democracy* (Routledge, 2000), *An Introduction to Political Communication* (Routledge, 4th edition, 2007), *The Sociology of Journalism* (Arnold, 1998) and *Cultural Chaos* (Routledge, 2006).

David Miller is Professor of Sociology in the Department of Geography and Sociology at the University of Strathclyde in Glasgow. His recent books include *Tell Me lies: Propaganda and Media Distortion in the Attack on Iraq* (Pluto, 2004), *Arguments Against G8* (Pluto, 2005, with Gill Hubbard), *Thinker, Faker, Spinner, Spy: Corporate PR and the Assault on Democracy* (Pluto, 2007, with William Dinan) and *A Century of Spin* (Pluto, 2008, with William Dinan). He is co-founder of *spinwatch.org*.

Hallvard Moe is a PhD student at the Department of Information Science and Media Studies, University of Bergen, Norway. His research interests include media and ICT-policy, television studies and democratic theory. His work has appeared in *Media, Culture & Society*, *Television & New Media* and *Nordicom Review*.

John Nerone is Professor of Communications Research and Media Studies in the Institute of Communications Research at the University of Illinois at Urbana Champaign. He is the author of *Violence against the Press: Policing the Public Sphere in US History* (Oxford University Press, 1994); coauthor and editor of *Last Rights: Revisiting Four Theories of the Press* (University of Illinois Press, 1995); and, with Kevin Barnhurst, coauthor of *The Form of News: A History* (Guilford Press, 2001).

Deirdre O'Neill is an Associate Principal Lecturer in Journalism at Leeds Trinity and All Saints. Before joining Leeds Trinity she worked on magazines, was a college press officer and ran journalism training for the newspaper industry. Her research interests are in the field of news selection, sources, access and influence; and her work has appeared in *Journalism Studies* and *Journalism Practice*.

Lynn Pellicano is a quantitative and qualitative research analyst with APCO Insight, the public opinion research division of APCO Worldwide. Her main areas of research include framing, public opinion, mass media and political communication. She has presented manuscripts on framing effects at the Midwest Political Science Association and at the George Washington University.

Thorsten Quandt is Professor of Communication Studies at the Free University Berlin. His research and teaching fields include journalism studies, online communication, media innovation research and communication theory. He has published several books and more than 50 articles, both in international journals and edited books. He is co-author of *Journalism Studies: An Introduction* (Blackwell, forthcoming, with Thomas Hanitzsch).

Stephen D. Reese holds the Jesse H. Jones professorship and is Associate Dean for Academic Affairs in the College of Communication. He is editor of *Framing Public Life* (Erlbaum, 2001) and co-author, with Pamela Shoemaker, of *Mediating the Message: Theories of Influence on Mass Media Content* (Longman, 1991, 1996). He was area editor of the recent *ICA Encyclopedia of Communication* and has lectured internationally at universities in Mexico, Spain, Germany, Finland and The Netherlands.

Michael Schudson is Distinguished Professor of Communication at the University of California, San Diego, and Professor of Communication at the Graduate School of Journalism, Columbia University, New York. He is an authority on the history and sociology of the US news media. His books include *The Sociology of News* (Norton, 2003), *Watergate in American Memory* (Basic Books, 1992), *Discovering the News* (Basic Books, 1978) and *Why Democracies Need an Unlovable Press* (Polity Press, forthcoming).

Donald Shaw is Kenan Professor in the School of Journalism and Mass Communication at the University of North Carolina at Chapel Hill. Author, co-author, or editor of ten books, he researches media agenda setting and 19th century American newspapers. He has been visiting professor at six universities and presented papers or lectured in 20 countries. *The Emergence of American Political Issues: The Agenda Setting Function of the Press* (West Publishing, 1977), co-authored with Maxwell McCombs, was recognized as one of the top 35 books of the 20th century, while he has been identified as one of the 38 most outstanding journalism educators in the last century.

Pamela J. Shoemaker is the John Ben Snow Professor at the S.I. Newhouse School of Public Communications, Syracuse University. She has published *News Around the World: Practitioners, Content and the Public* (with Akiba Cohen, Routledge, 2006), *How to Build Social Science Theories* (with James Tankard & Dominic Lasorsa, Sage, 2004), *Mediating the Message: Theories of Influences on Mass Media Content* (with Stephen Reese, Longman, 1996) and *Gatekeeping* (Sage, 1991). She is co-editor of *Communication Research.*

Jane B. Singer is the Johnston Press Chair in Digital Journalism at the University of Central Lancashire and associate professor (on leave) at the University of Iowa School of Journalism and Mass Communication. Her research explores digital journalism, including newsroom convergence and changing roles, perceptions, and practices. Singer is the coauthor of *Online Journalism Ethics: Traditions and Transitions* (M.E. Sharpe, 2007, with Cecilia Friend). A former newspaper and digital journalist, she is the 2008–2010 national president of Kappa Tau Alpha, the US journalism honor society.

Linda Steiner is Professor of Journalism at the University of Maryland, College Park. Among her recent books are *Women and Journalism* (Routledge, 2004) and *Critical Readings: Gender and Media* (Open University Press, 2004). She has published in, among others, *Critical Studies in Media Communication* (which she served as editor), *Journalism & Mass Communication Quarterly* (having served as Associate Editor), *Journalism*, *Journalism Studies*, *Javnost* and *Journal of Mass Media Ethics*. Her research interests include ethics, feminist theorizing and journalism history.

Trine Syvertsen is Professor of Media Studies and currently Dean of the Faculty of Humanitities, University of Oslo. Her research interests include television programming, public broadcasting and media policy. She has published several books and articles in Nordic and international journals, including *Media, Culture and Society*, *Convergence*, *Javnost*, *Television and New Media* and *Nordicom Review*. She is currently participating in the collaborative research project *Participation and Play in Converging Media*.

Howard Tumber is Dean of the School of Arts and Professor of Journalism Research at City University, London. He has published widely in the field of the sociology of news and journalism and is the author, co-author/editor of eight books including *Journalism: Critical Concepts in Media and Cultural Studies* (Routledge, 2008), *Journalists under Fire* (Sage, 2006), *Media at War: the Iraq Crisis* (Sage, 2004), *Media Power, Policies and Professionals* (Routledge, 2000) and *News: A Reader* (Oxford University Press, 1999). He is a founder and co-editor of the academic journal *Journalism: Theory, Practice and Criticism*.

Teun A. van Dijk is Professor at the Universitat Pompeu Fabra, Barcelona. After earlier work on generative poetics, text grammar and the psychology of text processing, his recent research is concerned with discursive racism, news in the press, ideology, knowledge and context. His last books are *Discourse and Context* and *Society in Discourse* (both Cambridge University Press, 2008). He is founding editor of four international journals in the field of discourse studies, including the new journal *Discourse and Communication*.

Tudor Vlad is Associate Director of the James M. Cox Jr. Center for International Mass Communication Training and Research, Grady College of Journalism and Mass Communication, University of Georgia, Athens. His main areas of research are international media, the role of the press in democratization and evaluation of media assistance programs. He authored two books, *The Romanian Writers' Fascination with Film* (Centrul de Studii Transilvane, 1997) and *The Interview: From Plato to Playboy* (Dacia Publishing House, 1997) and co-edited *Copyright and Consequences* (Hampton Press, 2003, with Stephen D. Reese). He has worked as a journalist for 20 years.

Tim P. Vos is Assistant Professor at the University of Missouri School of Journalism, Columbia. He is co-author of the forthcoming book, *Gatekeeping Theory* (Routledge, 2008, with Pamela Shoemaker), author of book chapters on gatekeeping and media history, and author of conference papers on media sociology, media policy, political communication, and media history.

Karin Wahl-Jorgensen is Reader in the Cardiff School of Journalism, Media and Cultural Studies, Cardiff University, Wales. Her books include *Journalists and the Public* (Hampton Press, 2007), *Citizens or Consumers?* (Open University Press, 2005, with Justin Lewis and Sanna Inthorn) and the recent edited collection *Mediated Citizenship* (Routledge, 2008). Her work on media, democracy and citizenship has appeared in more than 20 different international journals.

Silvio Waisbord is Assistant Professor in the School of Media and Public Affairs, George Washington University, Washington, DC. His main areas of research are journalism and politics in a global context, and communication and global health. He is the author of *Watchdog Journalism in South America* (Columbia University Press, 2000), and co-editor of *Global Media, Latin Politics* (University of Texas Press, 2002) and *Media and Globalization: Why the State Matters* (Rowman and Littlefield, 2001). Dr. Waisbord is the editor of the *International Journal of Press/Politics*.

Stephen J. A. Ward is Director of the Graduate School of Journalism at the University of British Columbia, Vancouver, and Professor of Journalism Ethics. His current research is in global journalism ethics and science journalism. He is the author of *The Invention of Journalism Ethics: The Path to Objectivity and Beyond* (McGill-Queen's University Press, 2005), and his work has appeared in *Journalism Studies* and the *Harvard Journal of Press and Politics*. He is associate editor of the *Journal of Mass Media Ethics* and chair of the ethics committee for the Canadian Association of Journalists. Dr. Ward has worked as a reporter, war correspondent and bureau chief for 13 years.

Herman Wasserman is Senior Lecturer in the Department of Journalism Studies at the University of Sheffield in the UK and is Associate Professor Extraordinary in the Department of Journalism at Stellenbosch University, South Africa. He is editor of *Ecquid Novi: African Journalism Studies* and serves on the editorial boards of the *Journal of Global Mass Communication, Journal of African Media Studies* and *Journal of Mass Media Ethics*. His current research interests include popular media and citizenship in Africa and global media ethics.

David Weaver is the Roy W. Howard Research Professor in the School of Journalism at Indiana University, Bloomington. He has published a dozen books and many articles and book chapters about journalists, media agenda setting, foreign news coverage, and newspaper readership. His latest books include *Global Journalism Research* (Blackwell, 2008) and *The American Journalist in the 21st Century* (Erlbaum, 2007). He is currently working on a five-year panel study update of the 2002 American Journalist study and a 40-year replication of the original Chapel Hill agenda-setting study.

Xu Xiaoge is Assistant Professor at the Wee Kim Wee School of Communication and Information, Nanyang Technological University, Singapore. His major areas of research include modeling journalism differences in Asia, development journalism, online journalism and online communication. He has published *Demystifying Asian Values in Journalism* (Marshall Cavendish Academic, 2005) and research articles in *Journalism & Mass Communication Educator, Asian Journal of Communication, American Communication Journal, Media Asia* and *Mass Comm Review*.

Kyu Ho Youm is the Jonathan Marshall First Amendment Chair in the School of Journalism and Communication at the University of Oregon. His research interests focus on freedom of the press and mass media law. He has edited the communication law and policy area of the *International Encyclopedia of Communication* (Blackwell, 2008). As a member of the Communication Law Writers Group since 1998, he has contributed to a US media law book, titled *Communication* *and the Law* (Vision Press, 2008). His scholarly articles have been noted by American and non-American courts, including the UK House of Lords and the Australian High Court.

Barbie Zelizer is the Raymond Williams Professor of Communication and Director of the Scholars Program in Culture and Communication at the University of Pennsylvania's Annenberg School for Communication, Philadelphia. Her books include *Taking Journalism Seriously: News and the Academy* (Sage, 2004), *Journalism After September 11* (Routledge, 2002, with Stuart Allan), *Remembering to Forget: Holocaust Memory Through the Camera's Eye* (University of Chicago Press, 1998) and *Covering the Body: The Kennedy Assassination, the Media, and the Shaping of Collective Memory* (University of Chicago Press, 1992). A former journalist, Dr. Zelizer is co-editor of *Journalism: Theory, Practice and Criticism.*

I

INTRODUCING JOURNALISM STUDIES

1

Introduction: On Why and How We Should Do Journalism Studies

Karin Wahl-Jorgensen and Thomas Hanitzsch

This handbook seeks to provide a sense of what we know about one of the most important social, cultural, and political institutions: journalism.

Journalism has been around "since people recognized a need to share information about themselves with others" (Zelizer, 2004, p. 2). However, the *study* of journalism is a more recent phenomenon. There are several reasons why the study of journalism is a worthwhile endeavor for scholars. First, news shapes the way we see the world, ourselves and each other. It is the stories of journalists that construct and maintain our shared realities (cf. Carey, 1989). Because of this, news can become a singularly important form of social glue; our consumption of stories about current events large and small binds us together in an "imagined community" (Anderson, 1983) of co-readers. Through the rituals of consuming and discussing the texts of journalism we come to understand and construct ourselves as subjects within local, national and, increasingly, global contexts. In particular, journalism is seen as intrinsically tied to democracy. It plays a key role in shaping our identities as citizens, making possible the conversations and deliberations between and among citizens and their representatives so essential to successful self-governance. In short, news is "the stuff which makes political action [...] possible" (Park, 1940, p. 678).

Not all scholars share such an optimistic view of the persistence and prospects of journalism in its professional and institutionalized mode. With the advent of interactive communication technologies, journalism as we know it has been proclaimed "dead" and called a "zombie institution" (Deuze, 2006, p. 2), and researchers continue to speculate about the "end of journalism" (e.g., Bromley, 1997; Waisbord, 2001). It is especially the potential decline of traditional political journalism that raises normative concerns for many theorists, as "[i]ts loss would rob us of the centerpiece of deliberative politics" (Habermas, 2006, p. 423). However, to appropriate Mark Twain's adage, rumors of the death of journalism may be greatly exaggerated. We might be witnessing not the end of journalism but rather its re-invention (Weber, 2007).

As a textual form journalism is, as Hartley (1996, pp. 32–34) put it, the primary "sense-making practice of modernity." It advances the key narratives of modernity and provides a store for our collective memory. The texts of journalism constitute "the first draft of history." It is primarily through journalistic texts that historians and other observers of an age apprehend that age, in accounts of and reactions to events and people. Journalism is the primary means for articulating and playing out both consensus (Hall, Critcher, Jefferson, Clarke, & Roberts, 1978) and conflicts (Cottle, 2006) in society; so news stories capture the ongoing drama of the battles between the dominant ideology and its challengers.

If journalism plays such a central role in society, studying it is all the more important for anyone wishing to understand contemporary culture. Doing so has become an increasingly popular endeavor. Today, journalism studies is a fast-growing field within the communication discipline. Over the past decades, the number of scholars identifying themselves as journalism researchers has increased tremendously, helped along, among other things, by the foundation of several new journals in the area, including *Journalism: Theory, Practice and Criticism*, *Journalism Studies*, and *Journalism Practice*. The past few years have also seen the creation of Journalism Studies divisions in the International Communication Association (ICA), the International Association for Media and Communication research (IAMCR), and the European Communication Research and Education Association (ECREA). The number of regional journals covering journalism studies is constantly growing, including, for instance, the *Brazilian Journalism Research*, *Ecquid Novi: African Journalism Studies*, *Pacific Journalism Review*, as well as a significant number of semi-trade journals, such as the *British Journalism Review*, *Global Journalism Review* and the *American Journalism Review*.

As journalism studies has matured to become a field of its own, it has produced its own body of theories and literature. Books addressed to an audience of journalism researchers are increasingly appearing in the market. Recent volumes such as *Journalism* (Tumber, 2008), *Key concepts in journalism studies* (Franklin, Hamer, Hanna, Kinsey, & Richardson, 2005), *Journalism: Critical issues* (Allan, 2005), *News: A reader* (Tumber, 1999) and *Social meanings of news: A text-reader* (Berkowitz, 1997) have all helped to consolidate journalism studies as a field, with a companion to news and journalism studies (Allan, forthcoming) and an introductory textbook on journalism research (Hanitzsch & Quandt, forthcoming) underway. Yet the roots and subsequent growth of this solidifying field are diverse and complex. Here, we identify four distinct, but overlapping and co-existing phases in the history of journalism research: While the field came out of *normative* research by German scholars on the role of the press in society, it gained prominence with the *empirical turn*, particularly significant in the United States, was enriched by a subsequent *sociological* turn, particularly among Anglo-American scholars, and has now, with the *global-comparative* turn, expanded its scope to reflect the realities of a globalized world.

A BRIEF HISTORY OF JOURNALISM STUDIES RESEARCH

The Prehistory: Normative Theories

In some ways journalism studies can be seen as both a newcomer and an old hand on the stage of scholarly research. Most observers have argued that scholarly work in the field began in the early 20th century alongside the emergence of journalism as a profession and a social force. However, some have found even earlier antecedents. As James Carey (2002) and Hanno Hardt (2002) observed, many of the originating impulses behind research on communication and journalism came from Germany in the mid-19th century. As such, the "prehistory" of journalism studies research can be found in the work of critical German social theorists (Hardt, 2002, p. 1), highlighting the *normative* impulses which gave the field its founding impetus. Hanno Hardt, in his now-classic work on *Social Theories of the Press* (2002), traced affinities, continuities, and departures between and among early German and American thinkers on the press. Among 19th and early 20th century German theorists, he pinpointed the work of Karl Marx, Albert Schäffle, Karl Knies, Karl Bücher, Ferdinand Tönnies, and Max Weber as particularly influential in their conceptions of the social place of journalism (Hardt, 2002, p. 15).

Similarly, Löffelholz (2008), in tracing the German tradition of journalism studies, found the ancestry of contemporary journalism theory in the work of the German writer and literary historian Robert Eduard Prutz (1816–1872). In 1845, long before the establishment of newspaper studies ("Zeitungskunde") as a field of research, Prutz published *The History of German Journalism*. Most early German theorists looked at journalism through a historical and normative lens, based on the view that journalism is a craft of more or less talented individuals (Löffelholz, 2008). Journalism scholars were more concerned with what journalism ought to be in the context of social communication and political deliberation than with the processes and structures of news production. The engagement with journalism as seen from a macro-sociological perspective has, in many ways, endured in German communication scholarship—often at the expense of empirical research. While Max Weber, in an address to the first annual convention of German sociologists, called for a comprehensive survey of journalists as early as 1910, such a study was not carried out until the early 1990s (Schoenbach, Stuerzebecher, & Schneider, 1998; Weischenberg, Löffelholz, & Scholl, 1998).

The Empirical Turn

An interest in the processes and structures of news production, as well as the people involved, only began to emerge in the context of journalism training, first and most notably in the United States. In this sense, *empirical*, rather than normative/theoretical work on journalism probably got its start in the context of professional educators gaining an interest in sharing knowledge about their work. It is certainly the case that in the US context, the study of journalism sprang out of professional education (Singer, 2008) and was often administrative in nature. The establishment of *Journalism Quarterly* in 1924 (later to become *Journalism & Mass Communication Quarterly)*, heralded this new age of journalism scholarship. Among other things, the first issue contained an essay by University of Wisconsin's Willard "Daddy" Bleyer outlining key approaches to newspaper research (Singer, 2008). As Rogers and Chaffee (1994) pointed out, Bleyer was instrumental in initiating a new age of journalism scholarship which took journalism seriously both as a practical endeavor and an object of study. In the 1930s, Bleyer proceeded to create a PhD minor within already-existing doctoral programs in political science and sociology (Singer, 2008).

In other countries, such as the UK and Denmark, journalism education took place outside of the academy, within news organizations where journalists were trained through apprenticeships and skills-based short courses (Wahl-Jorgensen & Franklin, 2008). Under those conditions, the education of journalists was considered along pragmatic lines, so that students took courses in topics such as shorthand and journalism law. Because of the separation of journalism training from the academy, a more reflective and scholarly approach was lacking from this model, and it has meant that in countries where this has been the template for journalism training, most scholarship on journalism has come from social sciences and humanities disciplines that have taken up journalism among many other interests. This may be one of the key reasons for the historically interdisciplinary nature of journalism studies.

In the United States, the empirical study of journalism was given a renewed impetus when early communication research emerged in the 1950s. This work came out of disciplines of sociology, political science and psychology, and was spearheaded by larger-than-life figures such as Paul Lazarsfeld, Carl Hovland, Kurt Lewin, and Harold D. Lasswell. The origins within the social sciences had a profound impact on the production of knowledge about journalism. In particular, this influence solidified the empirical turn, drawing on methods such as experiments and surveys to understand the workings of news media.

While most research in this period was concerned with audiences and media effects, the emerging field of journalism studies slowly turned its attention to "news people" and their professional values, as well as to editorial structures and routines. Theories and concepts were generated by and based on empirical research, such as the gatekeeper model (White, 1950), the professionalization paradigm (McLeod & Hawley, 1964), and theories of news values (Galtung & Ruge, 1965) and agenda setting (McCombs & Shaw, 1972). The ground-breaking research of these scholars belongs to the relatively few studies in the history of journalism studies that can consensually referred to as "classics." They have generated genuine journalism theories that remain influential and important. And although many of their ideas may seem dated and have been superceded by subsequent research, they continue to be significant to the field to the extent that they have established important research traditions. These classic studies "may not be the most advanced in either theory or method, but they capture the imagination" (Reese & Ballinger, 2001, p. 642).

The Sociological Turn

The 1970s and 1980s witnessed a stronger influence of sociology and anthropology on journalism research, leading to what might be described as a *sociological turn* in the field. The focus shifted to a critical engagement with journalism's conventions and routines, professional and occupational ideologies and cultures, interpretive communities, and to concepts related to news texts, such as framing, storytelling and narrative, as well as to the growing importance of the popular in the news. The increasing attention paid to cultural issues went hand in hand with the adoption of qualitative methodologies, most notably ethnographic and discourse analytical strategies. Among the figures who have left a lasting imprint on journalism studies in this tradition are sociologists such as Gaye Tuchman, Herbert J. Gans, Philip Schlesinger, and Peter Golding, as well as cultural studies proponents such as James Carey, Stuart Hall, John Hartley, and Barbie Zelizer. This tradition of scholarship, often focused on work in and of national and elite news organizations, allowed for a greater understanding of news production processes through descriptive work, but also paved the way for a view of journalism's role in constructing and maintaining dominant ideologies (Wahl-Jorgensen & Franklin, 2008).

The Global-Comparative Turn

Finally, the 1990s have seen a *global-comparative turn* in journalism studies: While cross-cultural research was pioneered by Jack McLeod as early as in the 1960s (McLeod & Rush 1969a, b), it has taken up until the past two decades before the comparative study of journalism could establish a tradition of its own.[1] The global rise of international and comparative research has been accelerated by political changes and new communication technologies. Journalism researchers are finding more and more opportunities to meet with colleagues from afar, made possible by the end of the cold war and increasing globalization. New communication technologies have triggered the rise of institutionalized global networks of scientists, while it has become much easier to acquire funding for international studies. As journalism itself is an increasingly global phenomenon, its study is becoming an international and collaborative endeavor.

JOURNALISM STUDIES TODAY

The onward march of globalization notwithstanding, journalism studies is still an extremely diverse scholarly occupation. This diversity has been profoundly shaped by different national traditions, resulting from the fact that the field has borrowed unevenly from the social sciences and humanities (Zelizer, 2004). US scholarship stands out because of its strong empirical and quantitative focus and the use of middle-range theories, while research in the UK and Australia has unfolded within a critical tradition influenced by British cultural studies. By contrast, French journalism research draws heavily on semiology and structuralism and is largely invisible to the international academy, whereas German scholarship has a tradition of theorizing journalism on a macro scale, influenced by systems theory and other theories of social differentiation. Many journalism researchers in Asia have been educated in the United States and have therefore internalized a strong American orientation. Scholars in Latin America, on the other hand, are currently re-orienting themselves, moving away from a reliance on US examples to an orientation towards Mediterranean countries, most notably Spain, Portugal, and France.

In the face of the growing internationalization of the field, however, the key English-language journals continue to be dominated by Anglo-American scholars, though with a steadily increasing degree of international contributions. *Journalism & Mass Communication Quarterly* (*JMCQ*), which was, until recently, the most important home to publications in journalism studies, draws heavily on US contributors, so that scholarship from or about other countries is a glaring exception. The composition of the journal's editorship and editorial board bespeaks the strong American dominance, with only two out of 80 editors and board members coming from outside the United States (see Table 1.1). To be sure, *JMCQ* is published by the Association for Education in Journalism and Mass Communication (AEJMC), but the journal is extensively used as a source and reference in many journalism and communication schools around the world.

Some academic associations, including the International Association for Media and Communication Research (IAMCR) and the International Communication Association (ICA) are, however, actively supporting a more equal representation of scholars from around the world, and seeking to boost their international membership and visibility. New scholarly journals, including *Journalism: Theory, Practice and Criticism*, *Journalism Studies* and *Journalism Practice*, have deliberately positioned themselves as international in orientation by introducing greater national diversity on their editorial boards. However, most editors and editorial board members are US- and UK-based, and scholars from outside the English-speaking world are still a minority. Against this background, the findings of a recent study of contributions to *Journalism: Theory,*

TABLE 1.1
International Distribution of Editors and Editorial Board Members in Leading Academic Journals in the Field of Journalism Studies (as of March 2008)

	Editors and EB members from the U.S. and U.K.	*Editors and EB members from outside the English-speaking world*	*Total number of editors and EB members*
Journalism & Mass Communication Quarterly	78 (all U.S.)	2	80
Journalism: Theory, Practice and Criticism	42	12	58
Journalism Studies	35	18	50
Journalism Practice	16	13	31

Practice and Criticism (*JTPC*) and *Journalism Studies* (*JS)* are hardly surprising. Cushion (2008) concludes:

> The data, overall, indicates a clear North American/Euro dominance in scholarly contributions. This dominance is more apparent in *JS* where nine in ten articles published have either a US or European based author. North American Universities account for a majority of articles in *JTPC*, while European institutions are the most frequent contributors to *JS*. Less than one in ten authors lie outside US/Europe in *JS*. Contributions from Asia and Australia mean *JTPC* fairs slightly better at roughly three in twenty. Scholars from African and South American institutions have contributed little to both journals. (p. 283)

Cushion (2008) further observes that close to half of all authors in *Journalism* and over a third in *Journalism Studies* come from American universities. The geographical origins of authors are, in turn, highly predictive of the area they study, so that the work of US news organizations is extremely well charted, whereas we know excruciatingly little about what goes on in newsrooms and media content in Africa, Asia, and Latin America.

Most of the research published in these journals and elsewhere focuses on journalists, their practices and the texts they produce. For example, an examination of publications in the past 10 years in the three premier journals is revealing of the preoccupations of journalism scholars. In the US context, the paradigm of framing research gives impetus to much of the current research on journalism texts, whereas scholars elsewhere are more likely to draw on discourse and textual analysis. However, *Journalism & Mass Communication Quarterly* has traditionally drawn extensively on content analysis, so that, for example, a quarter of articles published between 1975 and 1995 used this method (Riffe & Freitag, 1997). Nevertheless, *JMCQ* features considerably more research on news audiences than the other journals, because it includes frequent contributions drawing on experimental research influenced by the effects tradition. There is a considerable number of articles on the third-person effect, as well as application of concepts such as salience and attribution. Nevertheless, the majority of contributions remain focused on the psychology and sociology of journalism.

Despite the strength of an empirical tradition that has held sway since the early years of communication research, and the growing importance of global perspectives, the field is heavily influenced by a particular set of normative presumptions that we could do well to reflect on: We assume, as implied at the beginning of this chapter, that journalism is a benevolent force of social good, essential to citizenship, and that it constitutes a "fourth estate" or plays a "watchdog role" by providing a check on excesses of state power. As such, we also assume that journalists understand themselves as defenders of free speech and as independent forces for the common good. In this, contemporary journalism studies scholars of all stripes share the concerns that drove the work of the pioneering German thinkers.

However, by drawing on these assumptions we ignore the fact that in many parts of the world outside the liberal and often libertarian Anglo-American tradition, the press has, in fact, been heavily instrumentalized. Totalitarian regimes around the world have shown a profound understanding of the power of the press, from the use of journalism to advance national socialist ideology in Nazi Germany (Weischenberg & Malik, 2008, p. 159) to China's "watchdogs on party leashes" (Zhao, 2000). We should also not ignore the fact that journalism has been used to facilitate genocide and fuel hatred and intolerance, thus powering conflict. This has been well documented, for example in the cases of Rwanda, Liberia, and Sierra Leone (M'Bayo, 2005). Relatedly, ever since the Danish newspaper *Jyllandsposten*'s controversial publication of cartoons featuring the Prophet Muhammad, it has become apparent that claims of free speech universalism rub up against cultural and religious sensibilities in a globalized world (Berkowitz & Eko, 2007).

Journalism researchers aware of these complexities are increasingly interested in tracing the consequences of profound transformations in journalism organizations, production practices, content and audiences that have come about as a result of globalization and political, economic, social, and technological change.

HANDBOOK OF JOURNALISM STUDIES: AN OVERVIEW

This handbook bears witness to such preoccupations, structured as it is around a critical engagement with key theoretical and empirical traditions, fields of inquiry and scholarly debates in journalism studies. Beginning with four introductory chapters which outline broad issues in the field, the book contains four thematic sections, covering scholarship on news production and organizations, news content, journalism and society, and journalism in a global context.

The organization of the book reflects the aim of covering the broad contours of journalism studies: First, Kevin Barnhurst and John Nerone, in their chapter on journalism history, provide a broader context in tracing the parallels between the history of journalism and journalism history scholarship. They argue that conventional histories of journalism tend "to essentialize journalism, treating what journalists do as an un-problematical set of existing practices" and that they construct "journalism itself as a universal subject position," focusing on the experiences of white male professionals. The chapters from Barbie Zelizer and Beate Josephi trace the contentious and ever-evolving relationships between and among journalism practitioners, educators and scholars. Zelizer argues that the dissonance between journalism and the academic world "echoes a broader disjunction characterizing journalism's uneven and spotty existence with the world." Josephi's chapter outlines the diversity of approaches to teaching journalism around the world, demonstrating that while the US model has been dominant in scholarship, it does little to reflect the variety of experiences and educational models that prevail worldwide.

The second part of the book picks up on the significance of understanding the work of journalists by looking at the context of news production. This section is opened by Lee Becker and Tudor Vlad's chapter on news organizations and routines which holds that while work on routines has been particularly extensive and compelling, and has drawn our attention to journalism's social construction of reality, we need to move beyond this perspective by instead paying more attention to the creative processes that underlie story ideation. The second chapter in this section takes a closer look at one of the oldest and most influential journalism theories: gatekeeping. Although the roots of the theory go back as far as to the early 1950s, it remains highly relevant, as Pamela J. Shoemaker, Tim P. Vos, and Stephen D. Reese argue, and is resurfacing as a vibrant area, in part as a result of technological change within the profession, and in part because of new approaches, such as field theory.

Michael Schudson and Chris Anderson's chapter examines another source of journalistic power: The ideal of objectivity. They suggest that objectivity serves a key role in journalistic cultures, acting "as both a solidarity enhancing and distinction-creating norm and as a group claim to possess a unique kind of professional knowledge, articulated via work." Relatedly, Daniel Berkowitz, in his chapter on journalists and their sources, demonstrates that the study of reporters and their sources needs to move towards a dynamic understanding of interaction in terms of the sustained "ability to shape ongoing meanings in a culture." And while several of the key approaches to understanding news production have ignored questions of power, Linda Steiner's chapter on gender in the newsroom warns against any essentializing claims about the nature of "feminine" news, arguing that instead we can draw on feminist perspectives to think up new journalistic genres and newsroom cultures. This call for a rethink of methodological and conceptual tools is echoed by Jane Singer and Thorsten Quandt's chapter, which suggests that the impetus to renew scholarly perspectives in the light of ongoing changes has been accelerated by the advent of journalistic convergence and cross-platform production.

The third section of the book moves on from news institutions to the content they produce, looking at the plethora of theoretical and empirical perspectives which have sought to explain the texts of journalism through the whole range of theories. Renita Coleman, Maxwell McCombs, Donald Shaw, and David Weaver open this section with their chapter on agenda-setting, one of a few mass communication theories that has had a lasting influence in other social sciences disciplines. The authors point to the difficulty of distinguishing between agenda-setting research and the more recent perspective of framing. However, as, Robert Entman, Jörg Matthes and Lynn Pellicano argue in their chapter on this topic, framing has originated a rich tradition of its own. They suggest that in political communication research, framing has been rather narrowly conceived, and that scholars could benefit from broadening the study of framing effects, while connecting them to larger questions of democratic theory.

The need for a careful reconceptualization is also evident in Deirdre O'Neill and Tony Harcup's chapter on news values, which points out that although the practice among scholars in this area has been to produce lists of news values, this practice obscures the fact that conceptions of news values are ever-contested and also change dynamically across time and place. This relationship between news texts, power and contestation has long been recognized in other domains of journalism studies: Teun van Dijk, in his chapter on news, discourse and ideology, demonstrates how scholars conceptualize the concrete ways in which the news is infused with the dominant ideology and contributes to its maintenance and reproduction. John McManus' chapter on the commercialization of news extends this view to the relationship between media and markets, concluding that "relying on unregulated markets will not render the quality or quantity of news that participatory government requires to flourish." Questions of power within the commercial press also come to the forefront in the final chapter in this section, written by S. Elizabeth Bird and Robert Dardenne, which argues that a key question for scholars of news narrative ought to be *whose* story is being told.

The fourth section of the book takes a broader view by looking at work on the relationship between journalism and society. Brian McNair's chapter on journalism and democracy points to a current pessimism about journalism's role in facilitating citizenship, but also argues that there are grounds for optimistic assessments because "there is more political journalism available to the average citizen in the average mature democracy than at any previous time in history." David Miller and William Dinan pick up on scholarly debates about the health of the public sphere, calling "for a new synthesis of theories of communication, power and the public sphere" which uses Habermas' ideas as foundation.

The "norms of responsible journalism" are the focus of Stephen Ward's chapter on journalism ethics. Ward concludes that today's journalism requires a more cosmopolitan ethics that takes both global and local contexts seriously. In a similar vein, Kyu Ho Youm's chapter on journalism law and regulation demonstrates that scholarship in this area has to contend with the challenges of the diversity of national traditions and histories that shape their conceptions of press freedom.

Another blind spot in journalism studies is the relative neglect of the audience. John Hartley, in his chapter on journalism and popular culture, argues that this disregard for the audience is the result of different models of communication, widely held among journalists on the one hand and popular activists on the other. Journalism studies, he suggests, has "fetishized the producer-provider" and "ignores the agency of the consumer." Chris Atton makes a similar point in his chapter which examines alternative and citizen journalism, often seen to provide a much-needed counterforce to the problems of mainstream journalism. He suggests that scholars of these genres, while celebrating the empowerment and participation that they embody, have yet to fully account for audience engagement with them. As Mirca Madianou argues in her contribution on news audiences, although "most research on news is ultimately concerned with its impact on society, the question of the news audience has often remained an implied category."

The book's fifth and final section honors the recent global-comparative turn in journalism studies by situating journalism studies in its global context. Simon Cottle's chapter opens this section suggesting that scholars could do well to bring politics back into the study of globalization and journalism by paying attention to the dynamic processes through which "conflicts and contention are strategically pursued and performed in the media by contending interests and across time."

One type of journalism that has always been preoccupied with conflicts and contention in a global setting is examined in Howard Tumber's chapter on covering peace and war. It demonstrates how journalism scholars have responded to changing practices of war reporting, developing approaches that tell us not only about the work of war correspondents, but also about the ideologies and power relations of the societies that wage and cover war. While commercial media tend to emphasize conflict and sensation, public service media are often believed to provide a necessary balance. In light of this normative expectation, Hallvard Moe and Trine Syvertsen, in their chapter on public service broadcasting, examine the concept of public service in terms of "forms of political intervention into the media market with the purpose of ensuring that broadcasters produce programs deemed valuable to society."

While public service broadcasting has been a key paradigm for structuring the media in Western Europe, it is equally important to look at journalistic practices beyond western contexts. One of the approaches that is particularly crucial to less developed parts of the world and which rubs up against a liberal model of the press is development journalism. Xu Xiaoge, in his chapter on this paradigm, illustrates the central position of this concept in Asia and Africa, while demonstrating that scholarly interest in development journalism practices remains under-developed.

Advocacy journalism is another important paradigm that is not equally appreciated by journalists around the world, as Silvio Waisbord argues. He sees advocacy journalism as a form of "political mobilization that seeks to increase the power of people and groups and to make institutions more responsive to human needs."

Together, these chapters highlight the fact that the internationalization of journalism research itself remains incomplete. Thomas Hanitzsch's chapter points to the centrality of comparative research of the formation of journalism studies as a truly international field. However, while increasingly practiced, it is still theoretically and methodologically underdeveloped, and its heuristic potential has not yet been fully exploited. Another problem in international journalism research is the continued Western dominance of the field, as Herman Wasserman and Arnold de Beer argue in their chapter. The authors suggest that only a redistribution of economic resources can redress the imbalances in knowledge production. For many reasons, cross-cultural research therefore remains a cumbersome endeavor. Its inherently western bias and lack of universally applicable concepts, as well as problems of establishing equivalence and case selection can only be resolved by internationally collaborative research.

THE FUTURE(S) OF JOURNALISM STUDIES

In addition to telling us about how journalism is studied here and now, this book also intends to contribute to a debate about where journalism research should be heading. Each of the chapters reflects on directions for future research, highlighting the fact that we currently live in an era where both journalism and society are undergoing profound transformations. Under such circumstances we believe that one of the greatest current challenges of journalism studies is to be reflexive about the globalized power relations that shape its interests.

Anthropologists have been critical of their field's tendency to "study down" (Nader, 1969) or focus on the lives of relatively powerless and culturally distant groups.[2] By contrast, it could be argued that journalism researchers have focused on "studying up" or engaging in "elite research" (Conti & O'Neil, 2007), by paying a disproportionate amount of attention to elite individuals, news organizations and texts. The practice of studying up has profoundly shaped which types of newswork and news texts are best documented, and which are neglected. For example, studies of news organizations have tended to focus on journalism as produced in large, often national, television and newspaper newsrooms in elite nations. Similarly, analyses of news texts either focus on major events and disasters or on the routine news processes and products of elite news organizations. However, we would like to suggest that a vibrant field of journalism studies must begin to look outside this narrow realm. This means that scholars ought to broaden the scope of research beyond mainstream journalism as well as beyond elite nations, leading news organizations and prominent journalists.

For one, journalism studies has tended to ignore the work that goes on in less glamorous journalistic workplaces which are nevertheless dominant in terms of both the number of newsworkers employed by such organizations, the quantity of content output, and the audiences for their output. This scholarly neglect of a majority of the occupation it proclaims to study is particularly problematic because the working conditions of journalists vary hugely depending on economic, political, technological and social contexts. In the absence of competing accounts, the journalism cultures that have been well-documented come to stand in as the universal(izing) and authoritative descriptions of what journalism is all about. For instance, the professional practices of local journalists have been particularly neglected even though the vast majority of journalists work in local or regional media (see, for example, Franklin, 2006).

The focus on elite, national, or metropolitan media organizations can, to some extent, be explained by the political economy of publishing and the academy: Researchers may be more likely to gain institutional approval and prestige, grant money, publications and promotions from a study of a well-known, national and elite news organization than from more marginalized media practices. Also, while the relatively small number of elite national news organizations may serve as a more comfortable basis for generalizations and statements suggesting a "shared culture" (Harrison, 2000, p. 108), such claims are much more difficult to make for the vast diversity of local, alternative or specialist media practices (cf. Kannis, 1991, p. 9).

In this respect, the neglect of journalistic practices marginalized within the newsroom is particularly alarming. Research tends to overlook particular categories of newsworkers. It predominantly charts the professional cultures of privileged full-time news reporters over casualized, multi-skilled, and free-lance journalists, to mention just a few neglected categories. This is the case despite the fact that the journalistic workforce is, in fact, increasingly based on short-term employment and a reliance on free-lancers (Bew, 2006).

Other forms of journalistic production which operate at the peripheries of the newsroom—even though they may be an integral part of the content put out by news organizations—are equally neglected by researchers in journalism studies. This is particularly true of specialist journalisms which are removed from the excitement of the newsgathering process and frequently occupy the lower rungs of the newsroom hierarchy. As a result, for example, the work of arts journalists, music journalists and features reporters has received little attention (Harries & Wahl-Jorgensen, 2007). Similarly, scholars have failed to pay attention to the large numbers of newsworkers occupied in business journalism, a specialism which is growing ever-more expansively (Journalism Training Forum, 2002) and whose success is linked to larger social trends, including the globalization of capital. Popular forms of journalism, despite their broader appeal and innovative forms of story-telling, have also received scant attention (see Hartley's chapter in this volume).

As highlighted by the increasing significance of convergence, journalism studies also ought to explore the boundaries of journalism by examining talk shows, free sheets, advertorials, "citizen journalism"/user-generated content, blogs, podcasting, and online news aggregators—and the impact of these developments on our understanding of journalism. Such liminal journalism practices have frequently been ignored because they represent marginalized news producers (see Atton's chapter in this volume), but they are nevertheless becoming increasingly visible in journalism research as scholars recognize the seismic shifts they represent. Researchers need to reassess journalism's place in an increasingly global and mutually interconnected world with new communication technologies that profoundly challenge traditional boundaries between information production and information consumption and raise new questions about journalism's identity and positioning in a mediatized society.

Similarly, journalism studies could benefit from a move away from a focus on the producers and texts of media, towards an interest in a nuanced understanding of the audiences of news. The tendency—replicated here—to separate production, content, and audiences may blind researchers to fruitful and significant avenues of inquiry. To do justice to the importance of journalism, scholars ought to model and investigate it as a complex process involving producers, content, and audiences. Researchers need to link the individual, organizational and societal influences on news production to actual news content and relate these to the effects of news coverage. Traditional metaphors of journalism as a process of transmission of information need to be rethought in terms of an understanding of journalism as a cultural practice that is essentially based on a public negotiation of meaning. If the field is committed to greater reflexivity about the power relations that underlie practices of journalism, it also ought to generate more fine-grained knowledge about the ideological structures that underlie the highly rationalized processes of news production and assess the ways in which they reproduce social and cultural inequalities—as well as the potential of journalism to challenge or at least interrogate these hegemonic structures by means of alternative journalism.

Studying the experience of journalists in under-researched media, occupational roles and regions would also contribute to challenging prevailing power relations in the world, reproduced in scholarship. As Pan, Chan, and Lo (2008, p. 197) argue, like "any discursive system, journalism research articulates with the social setting where it is conducted, drawing from it inspirations, resources, and insights, and reflecting, speaking to, as well as shaping the setting in specific ways." Instead of taking Western models and theories for granted, these models and theories ought to be challenged from a truly global perspective that does not privilege any particular local point of view (Wasserman & de Beer, in this volume).

Such a radical internationalization of the field could be achieved through more international and comparative research that incorporates cultural expertise. This impulse is certainly evident in the work represented by the global-comparative turn, and it is one that ought to be continued if journalism studies is to reach its full potential. Journalism studies must therefore become truly cosmopolitan by paying more attention to regions of the world that remain largely unattended by journalism researchers, including sub-Saharan Africa, parts of the Middle East, Asia, and South

America. For researchers in less developed regions, comparative research could also provide opportunities for academic interaction, especially by providing access to unevenly distributed knowledge. Internationalizing the world of journalism studies is all the more important as a pedagogical intervention: Many scholars teach present and future journalists from areas where journalistic work is so different that they find little to recognize in the existing literature. Journalism studies has always been an inter-discipline, encompassing work in social sciences and humanities disciplines including sociology, history, linguistic, political science and cultural studies (Zelizer, 2004). Journalism scholars have the opportunity to contribute to debates beyond the disciplines of journalism, media and communication studies.

Finally, we also ought to understand and be reflexive about the power relations between journalism studies and its related professional and scholarly fields. The relationship between journalism studies and its immediate environment—the fields of journalism practice and journalism education—has not always been an easy one. Journalism studies often finds itself in a difficult position at the intersection of three different groups with frequently clashing interests: journalists, journalism educators, and journalism scholars. As a result, their relationship is often one of uneasiness and ignorance:

> [J]ournalists say journalism scholars and educators have no business airing their dirty laundry; journalism scholars say journalists and journalism educators are not theoretical enough; journalism educators say journalists have their heads in the sand and journalism scholars have their heads in the clouds. (Zelizer, in this volume)

Journalism studies therefore needs to pay more attention to the transfer of knowledge, generated by scientific inquiry, to the fields of journalism education and practice. Finally, to do full justice to its promise, journalism studies ought to engage in more explanatory studies that go beyond mere description; and conduct more systematic and truly longitudinal studies that carefully track changes in journalism over time. Such an approach will allow us to see and analyze journalism in its historical and cultural context.

In other words, we predict that the future of journalism studies is one of understanding the discipline and its object of inquiry as deeply embedded in particular historical, political, economic and cultural contexts, and simultaneously as part of a messy global world. These complex and variegated settings where journalism is studied are subject to complex power relations which we ignore at our peril.

NOTES

1. The *World of the News* study, led by Annabelle Srebeny-Mohammadi, Kaarle Nordenstreng and Robert L. Stevenson in the 1980s, was an exception to the rule.
2. Please note that some of the ideas contained in this section were first developed in Wahl-Jorgensen (in press).

REFERENCES

Allan, S. (Ed.). (2005). *Journalism: Critical issues*. Maidenhead: Open University Press.

Allan, S. (forthcoming). *The Routledge companion to news and journalism studies*. London: Routledge.

Anderson, B. R. (1983). *Imagined communities: Reflections on the origin and spread of nationalism*. London: Verso.

Berkowitz, D. (Ed.). (1997). *Social meanings of news: A text-reader*. Thousand Oaks, CA: Sage.

Berkowitz, D., & Eko, L. (2007). Blasphemy as sacred rite/right. *Journalism Studies*, *8*(5), 779–797.

Bew, R. (2006). The role of the freelancer in local journalism. In B. Franklin (Ed.), *Local journalism and local media: Making the local news* (pp. 200–209). London: Routledge.

Bromley, M. (1997). The end of journalism? Changes in workplace practices in the press and broadcasting in the 1990s. In M. Bromley & T. O'Malley (Eds.), *A Journalism Reader* (pp. 330–50). London: Routledge.

Carey, J. W. (1989). *Communication as culture: Essays on media and society*. New York: Routledge.

Carey, J. W. (2002). Foreword. In H. Hardt (Ed.), *Social theories of the press* (pp. ix–xiv). Lanham, MD: Rowman & Littlefield.

Conti, J. A., & O'Neil, M. (2007). Studying power: Qualitative methods and the global elite. *Qualitative Research*, *7*, 63–82.

Cottle, S. (2006). *Mediatized conflict*. Maidenhead, UK: Open University Press.

Cushion, S. A. (2008). Truly international? A content analysis of *Journalism: Theory, Practice and Criticism and Journalism Studies*. *Journalism Practice*, *2*(2) 280–293.

Deuze, M. (2006, May). Liquid and zombie journalism studies. *Newsletter of the ICA Journalism Studies Interest Group*, 2–3.

Franklin, B. (Ed.). (2006). *Local journalism and local media: Making the local news*. London: Routledge.

Franklin, B., Hamer, M., Hanna, M., Kinsey, M., & Richardson, J. E. (2005). *Key concepts in journalism studies*. London: Sage.

Galtung, J., & Ruge, M. H. (1965). The structure of foreign news: The presentation of the Congo, Cuba and Cyprus Crises in four Norwegian newspapers. *Journal of Peace Research*, *2*, 64–91.

Habermas, J. (2006). Political communication in media society: Does democracy still enjoy an epistemic dimension? The impact of normative theory on empirical research. *Communication Theory*, *16*(4), 411–426.

Hall, S., Critcher, C., Jefferson, T., Clarke, J., & B. Roberts (1978). *Policing the crisis*. London: Macmillan.

Hanitzsch, T., & Quandt, T. (forthcoming) *Journalism research: An introduction*. Oxford: Blackwell.

Hardt, H. (2002). *Social theories of the press* (2nd ed.). Lanham, MD: Rowman & Littlefield.

Harries, G., & Wahl-Jorgensen, K. (2007). The culture of arts journalists: Elitists, saviors or manic depressives? *Journalism*, *8*(6), 619–639.

Harrison, J. (2000). *Terrestrial TV news in Britain: The culture of production*. Manchester: Manchester University Press.

Hartley, J. (1996). *Popular reality*. London: Arnold.

Journalism Training Forum (2002). *Journalists at work: Their views on training, recruitment and conditions*. London: NTO/Skillset.

Löffelholz, M. (2008). Heteorgenous — multidimensional — competing: Theoretical approaches to journalism — an overview. In M. Löffelholz & D. Weaver (Eds.), *Global journalism research: Theories, methods, findings, future* (pp. 15–27). New York: Blackwell.

Kannis, P. (1991). *Making local news*. Chicago: University of Chicago Press.

M'Bayo, R. T. (2005). Liberia, Rwanda & Sierra Leone: The public face of public violence. *Ecquid Novi*, *26*, 21–32.

McCombs, M., & Shaw, D. L. (1972). The agenda-setting function of the mass media. *Public Opinion Quarterly*, *36*(2), 176–187.

McLeod, J. M., & Hawley, S. E. (1964). Professionalization among newsmen. *Journalism Quarterly*, *41*(4), 529–539, 577.

McLeod, J., & Rush, R. R. (1969a). Professionalization of Latin American and U.S. journalists. *Journalism Quarterly*, *46*(3), 583–590.

McLeod, J., & Rush, R. R. (1969b). Professionalization of Latin American and U.S.journalists: Part II. *Journalism Quarterly*, *46*(4), 784–789.

Nader, L. (1969). Up the anthropologist — perspectives gained from studying up. In D. Hymes (Ed.), *Reinventing anthropology* (pp. 284–311). New York: Pantheon.

Pan, Z., Chan, J. M., & Lo, V.-h. (2008). Journalism research in Greater China: Its communities, approaches and themes. In M. Löffelholz & D. Weaver (Eds.), *Global journalism research: Theories, methods, findings, future* (pp. 197–210). New York: Blackwell.

Park, R. E. (1940). News as a form of knowledge: A chapter in the sociology of knowledge. *American Journal of Sociology, 45*(5), 669–686.

Reese, S. D., & Ballinger, J. (2001). The roots of a sociology of news: Remembering Mr. Gates and social control in the newsroom. *Journalism & Mass Communication Quarterly, 78*(4), 641–658.

Riffe, D., & Freitag, A. (1997). A content analysis of content analyses. *Journalism and Mass Communication Quarterly, 74*(4), 515–524.

Rogers, E. M., & Chaffee, S. H. (1994). Communication and journalism from "Daddy" Bleyer to Wilbur Schramm: A palimpsest. *Journalism Monographs, 148*, 1–52.

Schoenbach, K., Stuerzebecher, D., & Schneider, B. (1998). German journalists in the Early 1990s: East and West. In D. H. Weaver (Ed.), *The global journalist: News people around the world* (pp. 213–227). Cresskill, NJ: Hampton Press.

Singer, J. B. (2008). Journalism research in the United States: Paradigm shift in a networked world. In M. Löffelholz & D. Weaver (Eds.), *Global journalism research: Theories, methods, findings, future* (pp. 145–157). New York: Blackwell.

Tumber, H. (Ed.) (1999). *News: A reader*. Oxford: Oxford University Press.

Tumber, H. (Ed.). (2008). *Journalism*. New York: Routledge.

Wahl-Jorgensen, K. (in press). On the newsroom-centricity of journalism ethnography. In S. E. Bird (Ed.), *Journalism and anthropology*. Bloomington: Indiana University Press.

Wahl-Jorgensen, K., & Franklin, B. (2008). Journalism research in Great Britain. In M. Löffelholz & D. Weaver (Eds.), *Global journalism research: Theories, methods, findings, future* (pp. 172–184). New York: Blackwell.

Waisbord, S. (2001). Introduction: Journalism and new technologies. *Journalism, 2*(2), 171–173.

Weber, J. (2007). The re-invention of journalism. *Times Online*, October 1, retrieved March 13, 2008, from http://technology.timesonline.co.uk/tol/news/tech_and_web/the_web/article2569470.ec

Weischenberg, S., Löffelholz, M., & Scholl, A. (1998). Journalists in Germany. In D. H. Weaver (Ed.), *The global journalist: News people around the world* (pp. 229–255). Cresskill, NJ: Hampton.

Weischenberg, S., & Malik, M. (2008). Journalism research in Germany: Evolution and central research interests. In M. Löffelholz & D. Weaver (Eds.), *Global journalism research: Theories, methods, findings, future* (pp. 158–171). New York: Blackwell.

White, D. M. (1950). The gatekeeper: A case study in the selection of news. *Journalism Quarterly, 27*(3), 383–390.

Zhao, Y. (2000). Watchdogs on party leashes? Contexts and implications of investigative journalism China. *Journalism Studies, 1*(4), 577–597.

Zelizer, B. (2004). *Taking journalism seriously: News and the academy*. Thousand Oaks, CA: Sage.

2

Journalism History

Kevin G. Barnhurst and John Nerone

The term *journalism history* is of relatively recent coinage, more recent than the term *journalism*, of course. But the discourse now called journalism history has a longer history, one that tracks the rise of news culture as a realm of first print culture and later media culture. As each new formation of news culture appeared, new genres of doing the history of news developed. Throughout this history of journalism history, the boundary separating it from other forms of media history has been porous and blurry. Since the 1970s, journalism history has been wrestling with an identity crisis, one that in many ways anticipates the broader crisis in the identity of journalism today.

Because journalism histories are so various, the best way to map them is to historicize them. This strategy has the additional advantage of showing how the project of writing histories of journalism has been part of a larger project of defining and disciplining news culture. For many scholars today, history provides and indispensable tool for critiquing professional journalism by showing its contingency and entanglements.

Journalism history emerged from two sources. The first was a kind of general intellectual interest in the evolution of means of communication. Many scholars trace this interest back to Plato's *Phaedrus*, which discusses cognitive issues related to writing. Enlightenment thinkers in Europe were particularly attentive to how literacy, then alphabetic literacy, and finally the printing press occasioned deep structural changes in social, cultural, and political life (Heyer, 1988). Twentieth-century thinkers like Harold Adams Innis and Marshall McLuhan expressed the same outlook. In works of journalism history proper, this outlook often appears as a tendency to emphasize the importance of machines in shaping the course of journalism. Comprehensive histories often use the introduction of new technologies, like the steam press or broadcasting, as narrative turning points, and journalists' autobiographies often dwell on the changes that occurred in newsroom technology in the course of their subjects' careers.

The second source for journalism history was more occupational. As newswork developed and professionalized, it constructed a history for itself by projecting its identity backward into the past. So journalism history grew up with journalism, and its historical awareness is a feature of its actual development.

PREHISTORY

Printed newspapers first appeared in Europe at the beginning of the seventeenth century. They were a late feature of the so-called printing revolution (Eisenstein, 1979; Johns, 1998), which at first concentrated on multiplying and extending the sorts of books that had previously been reproduced by hand, and only subsequently produced newer formats that took fuller advantage of the capacities of the printing press. Newspapers were not immediately established because the uses of newspapers were not readily apparent to printers and their patrons. But, with the rise of religious controversy following the Protestant Reformation, and the appearance of new economic institutions and the rise of market society, activists and entrepreneurs developed newspapers as practical media.

Early newspapers aimed at specific readers (business proprietors, landed gentry, Calvinists). By the middle of the seventeenth century, such newspapers were common in the capital cities of Western Europe. Amsterdam, a leading city in both commerce and religious independence, was a particularly important location; in fact, the first English-language newspapers (weekly newsbooks called Corantos) were published in Amsterdam in 1620.

For the most part, not until the eighteenth century did it became normal for newspapers to target a more general readership with political concerns. The rise of a bourgeois public sphere (Habermas, 1989) transformed the newspaper from an instrument of commerce, on the one hand, and religious controversy, on the other, into an instrument of continual political argumentation and deliberation. Newspapers became central resources in the age of bourgeois revolutions. The Glorious Revolution in England, the American Revolution, and the French Revolution all produced vigorous news cultures and active combat in print.

As political systems developed in Europe and North America, norms for the conduct of politics in newspapers appeared. The newspaper became a key part of a system for representing public opinion. As newspaper discourse announced its proper role, it claimed a set of expectations for rational discourse in line with what Jürgen Habermas (1989) ascribes to the bourgeois public sphere. Historians disagree, however, on whether these norms reflected the actual sociology of the news (Lake & Pincus, 2006; Mah, 2000; Raymond, 2003). Many dispute the openness, impersonality, and rationality that Habermas attributes to eighteenth-century public discourse. But even if newspapers were partisan, impassioned, and exclusive (primarily for the propertied, white male reader), they continually appealed to norms of universal rational supervision. Prime examples of such newspaper discourse were the frequently reprinted letters of Cato (Trenchard & Gordon, 1723) and of Publius. The latter was a trio of political leaders (James Madison, Alexander Hamilton, and John Jay), who published their letters, better known as the *Federalist Papers*. Their pseudonym refers to a figure from the Roman Republic but translates literally as "public man," or citizen, a rhetorical position meant to emphasize a non-partisan concern with the common good (Furtwangler, 1984).

The eighteenth-century revolutions forged a relationship between the media and democracy. Because the basis of political legitimacy shifted from blood and God to the will of the people, the principal problem of good government became the continual generation of consent through public opinion. Political thinkers dwelt on the problem of public opinion. After some experience with the practicalities of government, they began to comment actively on the need for systems of national communication, and to encourage what we would call infrastructure development in the form of postal systems and the transportation networks they required (John, 1994; Mattelart, 1996).

Until well into the eighteenth century, regulation and censorship of news culture was typically considered appropriate and necessary. The spread of news in print had coincided with and gained impetus from the Thirty Years' War (1618–1648), and was deeply implicated in the long series of wars of religion that followed the Protestant Reformation. The states of Europe considered the control of public discussion essential to maintaining peace and legitimacy. They, along with the Vatican, developed systems of press control that included licensing and prohibition (Siebert, 1952). Printers and booksellers, meanwhile, participated in the creation of copyrights and patents. In essence, the state made grants of monopoly that assured revenue while encouraging responsible behavior (Feather, 1987; Bettig, 1996).

"Freedom of the press" became one of the common narratives for early journalism histories. During the age of Revolution, narratives of heroic publicists and propagandists struggling against censorship became themselves part of the public discourse surrounding contests over forms of government. Over the next century or so, a canon of liberal thought would be created, hailing figures like John Milton, Thomas Jefferson, and Thomas Paine into a long conversation with each other. This largely artificial discourse would form part of the shared culture of subsequent journalism histories (Peters, 2005).

The age of Revolution proposed that democratic governance should be based on public opinion generated by an arena of discussion governed by norms of impartial, rational discourse. But this theory always competed with the reality of the partisan uses of the newspaper. Much of the heat of early party politics in all the new democracies came from the questionable legitimacy of the tools of party competition, including the press.

By the beginning of the nineteenth century in most Western countries, a frankly partisan model of news culture became ascendant. Only at this point does the word *journalism* come into play. It is French in origin, and initially referred to the journalism of opinion that flourished in the years following the Revolution. The term migrated into English by around 1830, but still referred to partisan debate over public affairs and had a negative connotation, as a sign of political dysfunction.

Though never made fully respectable, partisan journalism gradually acquired a positive justification. As democratic government became the norm, the spectacle of political combat came to seem healthy. Observers argued that, like the competition of the marketplace, political dispute served to promote a general social good. And, as most of Western Europe and North America relaxed press regulation through the early to mid nineteenth century, a freer market in newspapers interacted with partisan journalism to create something like a marketplace of public opinion.

EMERGENCE

At this point the first works of what would later become journalism history appeared. Predecessors include early chronicles that recorded the growth of printing, including newspapers among other publications (e.g., Thomas, 1970 [1810]). These mostly celebratory accounts of the rise of the press were usually also patriotic, inflected by a sense of the triumph of democratic government and freedom of the press. The works fell into what historians have called the Whig theory of history, a term that refers to a grand narrative constructed around the inevitable conflict of liberty and power, featuring the progressive expansion of liberty (Butterfield, 1931). The Whig model of journalism history was to remain ascendant well into the twentieth century, even as notions of journalism and freedom of the press changed dramatically (Carey, 1974; McKerns, 1977).

Whig history leaned toward biography. Because it pivoted on the advance of a specifically liberal notion of freedom, the model tended to present narratives of strong individuals as producers of change. News organizations also tended to be personified. Examples include early biographies of newspaper publishers. An admiring former aide would set a pattern of lionizing the publisher in a popular memoir, and that view would endure, either through subsequent, expanded editions of the work or in the background of biographies by authors not associated with the prominent figure. Parton's (1855) biography of Horace Greeley established this pattern in the United States, and later writers followed it for press moguls like James Gordon Bennett (Pray, 1855; Crouthamel, 1989), Joseph Pulitzer (Ireland, 1937 [1914]; Seitz, 1970 [1924]), William Randolph Hearst (Winkler, 1928; Older, 1972 [1936]), and Edward Scripps (Gardner, 1932; Cochran, 1933).

In the middle to late nineteenth century, a mass press appeared nation by nation in the United States and Europe (Chalaby, 1998), with the timing of its appearance tied to the persistence of taxation or other forms of press regulation. This commercialized press was more reliant on advertising revenue and consequently aimed at a broader audience than the earlier, primarily political newspapers. Newspapers segmented these more inclusive audiences by gender, age, and class, deploying new kinds of content to assemble specific readerships that could in turn be sold to advertisers. The news matter in the mass circulation press included more event-oriented news, especially crime news, and also more reporting on social and cultural concerns, or so-called human interest stories.

Journalism came to acquire its modern sense, as a discipline of news reporting, around that time, when it also began to distinguish itself from its "other." As a mass audience grew, the popular press fed readers sensational stories, and acquired the reputation of social marginality. Yellow journalism, perhaps named after the cheap paper produced by the new wood pulp process, or more likely named after the yellow covers on earlier cheap crime fiction, was a transnational phenomenon. Illustrated news also became popular, first in Britain, then, in a direct line of descent, in France and Spain, and then in North America and other European countries (Martin, 2006). Along with the growth of the popular press, a politics of news quality appeared. Reformers and traditional elites complained about the impact of journalism upon public intelligence and morality. The episodic character of newspaper content was said to hamper the ability of the public to engage in sustained or complex thought or deliberation, while the general taste for scandal and sensation seemed to coarsen public mores.

Journalism thus took on the task of uplifting and policing news culture. This mission suited the purposes of public figures, who wanted more decorum in news culture. In the United States, one outcome of this dynamic was the discovery of an implied constitutional right to privacy (Warren & Brandeis, 1890). Other involved parties had other reasons to support journalists' mission to purify the news. Publishers wanted to purify their image to protect themselves from a public now inclined to think of the power of the press as a danger. Newsworkers, in turn, aspired to elevate the status of their work.

The project of improving journalism coincided with a particular sociology of newswork (Nerone & Barnhurst, 2003). Newsworkers divided into three broad sorts: editors, who compiled news and wrote opinion pieces; correspondents, who wrote long letters from distant places and generally had a voice and expressed attitudes; and reporters, who scavenged news from beats and transcribed meetings and other news events. The attempt to uplift journalism enhanced adjustments to this sociology. A proto-professional form of journalism appeared as a union of the positions of the reporter and the correspondent, coupled with the construction of walls of reified separation between them and editors on the one hand and business managers on the other. The increased autonomy that came from this redefined journalism was evident in the rise of muckraking in the United States, as well as other journalisms of exposure elsewhere.

PROFESSIONALIZATION

At the beginning of the twentieth century, journalism in the West was ready to begin a professionalization project. The process was manifest in broadly based phenomena like the founding of press clubs and associations and of schools of journalism, along with the crafting of codes of ethics. In some places, journalists formed unions; in others, governments established credentialing regimes (Bjork, 1996). In all developed countries, aspects of monopoly arose around the most industrialized elements of the news system, especially metropolitan newspapers and wire services, supporting the kinds of control that an autonomous profession might establish.

The professionalization project required a somewhat different form of journalism history. The new schools of journalism wanted a teachable history that could provide moral exemplars for aspiring professionals. The old Whig histories were somewhat useful, but only after being cleansed of their mavericks.

Teaching about the news industry also called for more awareness of the conditions for business. The countries with more commercial news arenas, especially the United States, inserted a narrative of market redemption. The history textbooks most used in U.S. journalism schools saw independent journalism as a product of the market that vanquished any partisan ties (Nerone, 1987). This view was evident not just in standard textbooks (Bleyer, 1973; Mott, 1941; Emery & Smith, 1954) but also in key essays that would become canonical in journalism history: in the United States, Walter Lippmann's *Two Revolutions in the American Press* (1931) and Robert Park's *Natural History of the Newspaper* (1923). This faith in the beneficence of market forces seems odd for a series of reasons. It seemed to require a willful forgetting of the mass market press that had given the professionalization project its urgency at the close of the nineteenth century. It also seemed to make invisible the conditions of monopoly in the wire services and in the new medium of broadcasting, which both caused the popular anxiety over media power and provided the levers for imposing standards on news culture. And it seemed to argue against the call for a "wall of separation" between the counting room and the newsroom that was a central feature of the professionalization project.

Most Western countries institutionalized journalism under the professional model in the twentieth century. The project of forming journalism schools, creating codes of ethics, setting licensing standards, and forming unions contributed to what has been called the high modernism of journalism (Hallin, 1992, 1994). The rise of broadcast journalism, especially when associated with monopolistic national broadcast authorities (like the BBC in the UK or RAI in Italy) or oligopolistic commercial systems, reinforced the professionalization of news. The twentieth century wars were especially important in raising anxieties about the power of propaganda and encouraging the creation of prophylactic notions of media responsibility. And the rise of the corporate form of ownership (and its criticism) also encouraged professionalization.

Variations existed in the West regarding the institutionalization of professional journalism. Daniel Hallin and Paolo Mancini (2004) have identified three models or "media systems": partisanism in southern Europe (represented by what they refer to as the polarized pluralist system), social democracy in northern Europe (the democratic corporatist system), and market based systems in the North Atlantic (the liberal system). But all three systems paid attention to preserving for professional journalism some measure of autonomy from existing authorities, as well as from market and party influences.

Meanwhile, the model of autonomous journalism was exported to the south and east, along with the notion of freedom of the press. In the Americas, a partisan form of journalism had taken root along with national liberation movements in the nineteenth century, but in the period following World War II, especially after the 1970s, another model of investigative journalism imported from the United States supplemented—and in some cases replaced—the partisan model (Waisbord, 2000). In Asia, and especially in China, the notion of an independent journalism was an important part of early nationalist movements in the opening decades of the twentieth century.

ALTERNATIVES

Radical political theory in the nineteenth century projected an alternative vision of journalism, with a different notion of professionalism, and inspired the media systems of the communist regimes of the twentieth century. Marxism and other materialisms challenged the autonomy of the realm of ideas. In simple terms, these philosophies understand communication, and especially mediated communication, as a form of material production. Capitalist systems of communication incorporate the class structure and reproduce the class power of capitalist society. Journalism as a work routine and as an alienated occupation mystifies class power. Post-capitalist media systems, therefore, should work to expose and then overcome class power. Such systems could re-imagine journalism in two contrasting ways. Journalism could devolve to the province of ordinary citizens, or journalism could become the mission of a vanguard. The former case would absorb journalism into daily lives of citizens (an idea to return later), but the latter case would produce the opposite: an intense professionalism of journalism practice. As it happened, the media systems of the communist countries tended toward Party vanguardism.

This understanding of journalism obviously proposed a different narrative about the origins of Western journalism, which became a feature of the rise of bourgeois class relations and part of the ideological apparatus that reproduced capitalist hegemony. The heroes of journalism were not the intrepid reporters but the principled partisans who criticized establishments from the margins. Karl Marx himself was one such journalist. During his long exile in London, he supported himself in large part by working as a correspondent on European affairs for Horace Greeley's *New York Tribune*.

At the end of World War II, a new world order embraced an ambiguous liberalism. The UN Charter embodied a notion of sovereignty based on the consent of the governed, and all new national constitutions acknowledged it. The Universal Declaration of Human Rights endorsed freedom of expression and the right to communicate. But these formulations covered a broad range of possible interpretations and systems. What Hallin and Mancini (2004) identify as the North Atlantic or liberal model interpreted the right to communicate as authorizing the expansion of U.S.-style news media and especially the wire services that supported them. Others interpreted the right to communicate as referring to rights of the people as opposed to the media, which were saddled with a "social responsibility" to service these rights. In the United States, the notion of social responsibility was embodied forcefully in the report of the Hutchins Commission (1947), a document that echoed but utterly failed to refer to a global discourse on press responsibility.

Post-war global conditions occasioned another powerful frame for journalism history based on a comparative media systems approach. The most influential exemplar of this approach was the book *Four Theories of the Press* (Siebert, Peterson & Schramm, 1956), which produced a simplified schema based on philosophical presuppositions about the nature of humanity, the state, and truth. Many critics have pointed out the shortcomings of this approach, including its unreflexive incorporation of liberal presuppositions and its implied narrative of a natural history leading toward a neoliberal model (Altschull, 1984; Nerone, 1995; Hallin & Mancini, 2004) as well as its neglect of non-Western histories and especially the global south (Park & Curran, 2000; Semati, 2004).

Post-war conditions also drew attention to the rise of a global information system. Histories of the international wire services appeared (e.g., Schiller, 1976; Nordenstreng & Schiller, 1979; Rantanen, 1990, 2002; Hills, 2002). The criticism of an unequal flow of information became part of a political movement for a New World Information and Communication Order, which took shape within UNESCO in the 1970s and reached a climax with the report of the MacBride Commission in 1980, but succumbed to a counterattack from the Western countries and then shifted to other arenas, including the GATT through the 1980s and the WTO in the 1990s. Critical histories of the geography of information responded to these dynamics, the most influential of which were by Manual Castells (2000) and David Harvey (1989).

Journalism historians often neglect the international dimension. A few exemplary works put national histories in dialog with each other (Hallin & Mancini, 2004; Martin, 2006), but most remain within national borders. The same is true for media history more generally. Because national media systems are so intimately entwined in the life of the polity, scholars tend to treat them in isolation, as the nervous system of the political organism. In addition, the collection of archival materials and the funding of scholarship are usually carried out under national auspices.

The end of the twentieth century in the modern West saw the erosion of the high modern moment. Globalization, the end of the Cold War, the rise of new digital technologies, the eclipse of public service models of broadcasting and telecommunications, and the weakening of traditional cultural support for monolithic national identities have all undermined previous models of autonomous journalism. Recent trends in news include the rise of the 24-hour television news service, of new so-called personal media like talk radio and the blogosphere, of the tabloid form and a hybrid journalism, especially in Scandinavian countries, and of a new pattern of partisan media power associated with broadcast entrepreneurs like Silvio Berlusconi and Rupert Murdoch in the West and with the post-Soviet media explosion in Eastern Europe. With the erosion of high modernism came, on the one hand, calls to rethink the role of the press as an institution within the governing process (Cook, 1998) and, on the other hand, calls for a new public journalism or citizen journalism (Downing, 2002; Atton, 2002; Rodríguez, 2001; Rosen, 1999).

SCHOLARLY APPROACHES

As journalism history followed in the tracks of the history of journalism, it also tracked developments in historical and in media scholarship. Some of the impulses from other fields influencing journalism historians include the legal-political landscape and currents among mainstream historical scholarship.

The history of law and policy is perhaps the oldest and best established scholarly tradition influencing journalism history. Besides the problematic of freedom of the press already traced here, legal and political developments have reified the professionalization project of journalism. Lawyers and legal scholars have shared with professional journalists the habit of doing the history of journalism as a history of autonomous individuals in conscious action. One outcome of this mindset has been the legal recognition of journalism itself. As a particular occupation or practice, credentialed journalists acquired rights before and during legal proceedings, as well as privileges in policy to accommodate their presence at close quarters with government activities, beyond the rights and privileges of ordinary citizenship (Allen, 2005). Communication encompasses all interactions affecting the polity, but the development of special rights and political practices around what journalists do means that, in the law, journalism has become different from communication.

The boundary that separates journalism history from the broader history of media and communication has been less defensible in other arenas. The history of technology, for instance, suggests that the same forces that impel other media practices also shape the practices of journalism. Telegraphic communication is a case in point. It is a commonplace that the telegraph transformed the space-time matrix of the nation-state (Schivelbusch, 1986; Czitrom, 1982; Carey, 1989; Peters, 2005) and simultaneously produced cooperative newsgathering (Schwarzlose, 1988–90; Blondheim, 1994). The result was a particular style of journalism, characterized by brevity and ultimately the inverted pyramid as a way of organizing news narratives (e.g., Carey, 1989, but compare Pöttker, 2003). The standard narrative of journalism history often foregrounds the transformative impact of technologies: All comprehensive journalism histories discuss the camera and the steam press; many mention as well the telephone, the typewriter, and the more recent digital technologies. In these histories, agency comes from technology (sometimes mediated through the marketplace) in addition to, or rather than residing in, individual conscious actors.

In the 1970s, a different impulse came from a movement called social history. There have been many kinds of social history, but all share an aversion to event-centered history and to so-called great man history. Common to social historians was a dedication to doing history from, in the popular phrase, the bottom up. This persuasion covered a large spectrum of strategies, from the romantic notion that ordinary people make history, most influentially expressed in E. P. Thompson's *Making of the English Working Class*, to the impersonal histories of the long flows of civilizations and regions in the work of French Annaliste historians like Fernand Braudel. For journalism historians, these impulses filtered through scholars like Robert Darnton (1975), William Gilmore-Lehne (1989), and Michael Schudson (1978). Social history challenged the uniqueness of journalism history at about the same time that newsroom ethnography challenged the intellectual roots of journalism practice (Tuchman, 1978; Gans, 1979; Fishman, 1980), and led some to conclude that "there is no such thing as journalism history" (Nerone, 1991).

GENRES

But obviously journalism history continues to exist, and as the academy has become more specialized and trade and then academic publishing has pursued marketable formulas, journalism history has subdivided into a set of genres. Most work in journalism history falls into four genres, three of them narrow and one broad, which emerged in this order: biographical, comprehensive, event-focused, and image-focused. The oldest and probably still most common genre is the biographical. Focusing on an individual actor, whether a journalist or a news organization, has two practical advantages. Such actors often produce neat bodies of primary documents, and their lives support the writing of neat chronological narratives. In any country, the dominant national news organizations, like the *Times* of London or *il Corriere della Sera* in Italy, have been the subjects of multiple biographies (Licata, 1976; Woods & Bishop, 1983).

Nearly as old as the habit of press biography is the genre of comprehensive journalism histories. These are almost always national. As already indicated, the first comprehensive histories appeared in the nineteenth century, alongside the appearance of journalism as a positively connoted term. Written to give an illustrious pedigree to the practice, comprehensive histories then became indispensable teaching tools in journalism schools. These products of professional historians usually offered progressive narratives, showing the advancing autonomy and respectability of the occupation while offering inspiration for would-be professionals (Bleyer, 1973; Mott, 1941; Emery & Emery, 1977). Usually focusing on exemplary practitioners, such histories often amount to a collective biography. More recent comprehensive histories have proposed more critical narratives (Folkerts & Teeter, 1989). A common device is to focus on a particular explanatory motif, as Michael Schudson (1978) did when he analyzed objectivity as a feature of democratic market society.

Event-oriented histories constitute a third common genre. Any particular crisis or controversy can be a useful hook for analyzing press response. The earliest of this genre grew out of journalism practice, such as the study two (later prominent) journalists conducted of World War I newspaper coverage (Lippmann & Merz, 1920). Journalists continue to produce popular histories of major events from the perspective of journalism practice. Although in the main, this genre lends itself to flat narratives of point-counterpoint, it can also afford scholars an opportunity to conduct a diagnostic exploration of the capacities or biases of a press system (Gitlin, 1980; Hallin, 1986; Lipstadt, 1986).

The image-oriented genre attempts to expand the purview of journalism history beyond media leaders and enterprises by examining larger collectivities. Image-oriented histories have limitations and affordances similar to event-oriented histories. Studies of images of groups like women or ethnic minorities, or of entities such as a nation or religion usually are flat and obvious, but have the potential to unpack and expose the cultural work of the press (e.g., Coward, 1999).

NEW DIRECTIONS

Each of these conventional genres of journalism history tends to essentialize journalism, treating what journalists do as an un-problematical set of existing practices. Another form of journalism history takes the construction of journalism itself as a problem. The construction-of-culture tendency has recently been setting an agenda for the field.

Many years ago, James W. Carey called for a history of the "form of the report" (1974, p. 5). Although this history remains unwritten, some recent contributions have explored how the form of the newspaper invites readers to participate in rituals of citizenship (Anderson, 1991; Clark, 1994; Leonard, 1995; Barnhurst & Nerone, 2001).

The analysis of the form of news suggests a different approach to the question of the power of the press. The traditional genres of journalism history equate the power of the press with the power of ideas, suggesting that the press has power to the degree that it can persuade the public by exposing audiences to true information and sound reasoning. This historical notion of the power of the press does not comport with scholarly understandings of the power of today's media, which point to agenda-setting, framing, and priming as ways that the media work to reproduce hegemony, all matters concerning which traditional journalism history is in denial.

Traditional journalism history also tends to treat journalism itself as a universal subject position. Again, this runs counter to the consensus of studies of present-day media, which detect particular racial, ethnic, gender, and class valences in media practice. Put crudely, traditional journalism history remains white even as it seeks to include nonwhites and women. To date, no exemplary history of the racing and gendering of journalism has been published, though many narratives in more or less traditional genres herald such a history (Coward, 1999, Rhodes, 1998; Tusan, 2005).

These histories will explore race and gender as aspects of newswork. Journalism history has had a tense relationship with the notion of its subjects as workers. In its first generations, journalism history sought to portray its heroes as autonomous professionals, not the sort of workers who would need to join unions or negotiate for wages and hours. For more than a decade, there have been calls to center journalism history on the concept of work (Schiller, 1996; Hardt & Brennen,

1999). This is itself a labor-intensive enterprise, and easier in countries that have powerful central journalists' unions. It should also be an international history.

Like any other kind of history, journalism history responds to its times, although, like other historical fields, it attempts to present itself as preservationist and answers to the needs of journalists and journalism education while at the same time attending to the trends and fashions of professional historians. In the future, journalism history will likely continue to do so.

REFERENCES

Allen, D. S. (2005). *Democracy, Inc.: The press and law in the corporate rationalization of the public sphere*. Urbana: University of Illinois Press.

Altschull, J. H. (1984). *Agents of power: The role of the news media in human affairs*. New York: Longman.

Anderson, B. (1991). *Imagined communities: Reflections on the origin and spread of nationalism* (rev. ed.). London: Verso.

Atton, C. (2002). *Alternative media*. London: Sage.

Barnhurst, K. G., & Nerone, J. (2001). *The form of news: A history*. New York: Guilford.

Bettig, R. V. (1996). *Copyrighting culture: The political economy of intellectual property*. Boulder, CO: Westview Press.

Bjork, U. J. (1996). The European debate in 1894 on journalism education. *Journalism and Mass Communication Educator, 51*(1), 68–76.

Bleyer, W. G. (1973[1927]). *Main currents in the history of American journalism*. New York: Da Capo.

Blondheim, M. (1994). *News over the wires: The telegraph and the flow of public information in America, 1844–1897*. Cambridge, MA: Harvard University Press.

Butterfield, H. (1931). *The Whig interpretation of history*. London: G. Bell.

Carey, J. W. (1974). The problem of journalism history. *Journalism History, 1*(3–5), 27.

Carey, J. W. (1989). Technology and ideology: The case of the telegraph. In Carey, J. W. (Ed.), *Communication as culture: Essays on media and society* (pp. 201–230). Boston: Unwin Hyman.

Castells, M. (2000). *The rise of the network society* (2nd ed.). London: Blackwell.

Chalaby, J. K. (1998). *The invention of journalism*. New York: Palgrave-MacMillan.

Clark, C. (1994). *The public prints: The newspaper in Anglo-American culture, 1665–1740*. New York: Oxford University Press.

Cook, T. E. (1998). *Governing with the news: The news media as a political institution*. Chicago: University of Chicago Press.

Coward, J. M. (1999). *The newspaper Indian: Native American identity in the press, 1820–90*. Urbana: University of Illinois Press.

Curran, J., & Park, M.-J. (Eds.). (2000). *De-westernizing media studies*. New York: Routledge.

Czitrom, D. (1982). *Media and the American mind: From Morse to McLuhan*. Chapel Hill: University of North Carolina Press.

Cochran, N. O. (1933). *E. W. Scripps*. New York: Harcourt, Brace & Co.

Darnton, R. (1975). Writing news and telling stories. *Daedalus, 104*(2), 175–94.

Downing, J. (2002). *Radical media: Rebellious communication and social movements*. Thousand Oaks, CA: Sage.

Eisenstein, E. (1979). *The printing press as an agent of change: Communications and cultural transformations in early modern Europe*. New York: Cambridge University Press.

Emery, E., & Smith, H. L. (1954). *The press and America*. Englewood Cliffs, NJ: Prentice-Hall.

Emery, E., & Emery, M. (1977). *The press and America*. Englewood Cliffs, NJ: Prentice-Hall.

Feather, J. (1987). The publishers and the pirates: British copyright law in theory and practice, 1710–1775. *Publishing History, 22*, 5–32.

Fishman, M. (1980). *Manufacturing the news*. Austin: University of Texas Press.

Folkerts, J., & Teeter, D. (1989). *Voices of a nation: A history of media in the United States*. New York: Macmillan.

Furtwangler, A. (1984). *The authority of Publius: A reading of the Federalist papers*. Ithaca, NY: Cornell University Press.

Gans, H. J. (1979). *Deciding what's news: A study of "CBS Evening News," "NBC Nightly News,"* Newsweek, *and* Time. New York: Pantheon.

Gardner, G. (1932). *Lusty Scripps: The life of E. W. Scripps*. New York: Vanguard Press.

Gilmore-Lehne, W. J. (1989). *Reading becomes a necessity of life: Material and cultural life in rural New England, 1780–1835*. Knoxville: University of Tennessee Press.

Gitlin, T. (1980). *The whole world is watching: Mass media in the making and unmaking of the new left*. Berkeley: University of California Press.

Habermas, J. (1989). *The structural transformation of the public sphere*. Cambridge: Polity Press.

Hallin, D. C. (1992). The passing of the "high modernism" of American journalism. *Journal of Communication, 42*(3), 14–25.

Hallin, D. C. (1986). *The uncensored war: The media and Vietnam*. Berkeley: University of California Press.

Hallin, D. C. (1994). *We keep America on top of the world: Television journalism and the public sphere*. New York: Routledge.

Hallin, D. C., & Mancini, P. (2004). *Comparing media systems: Three models of media and politics*. Cambridge, UK: Cambridge University Press.

Hardt, H., & Brennen, B. (Eds.). (1999). *Picturing the past: Media, history, and photography*. Urbana: University of Illinois Press.

Harvey, D. (1989). *The condition of postmodernity: An enquiry into the origins of cultural change*. Oxford: Basil Blackwell.

Heyer, P. (1988). *Communications & history: Theories of media, knowledge, and civilization*. New York: Greenwood Press.

Hills, J. (2002). *The struggle for control of global communication: The formative century*. Urbana: University of Illinois Press.

Hutchins Commission (1947). *A free and responsible press*. Chicago: University of Chicago Press.

Ireland, A. (1914). *Joseph Pulitzer: Reminiscences of a secretary*. New York: M. Kennerly.

John, R. R. (1994). *Spreading the news: The American postal system from Franklin to Morse*. Cambridge, MA: Harvard University Press.

Johns, A. (1998). *The nature of the book: Print and knowledge in the making*. Chicago: University of Chicago Press.

Lake, P., & Pincus, S. (2006). Rethinking the public sphere in early modern England. *Journal of British Studies, 45*(2), 270–292.

Leonard, T. C. (1995). *News for all: America's coming-of-age with the press*. New York: Oxford University Press.

Licata, G. (1976). *Storia del* Corriere della Sera. Milano: Rizzoli.

Lippmann, W. (1931). Two revolutions in the American press. *The Yale Review, 20*(3), 433–441.

Lippmann, W., & Merz, C. (1920). A test of news. Supplement to *The New Republic*, 23.296, Part 2, August 4, 1–42.

Lipstadt, D. E. (1986). *Beyond belief: The American press and the coming of the Holocaust, 1933–1945*. New York: Free Press.

Mah, H. (2000). Phantasies of the public sphere: Rethinking the Habermas of historians. *Journal of Modern History, 72,* 153–182.

Martin, M. (2006). *Images at war: Illustrated periodicals and constructed nations*. Toronto: University of Toronto Press.

Mattelart, A. (1996). *The invention of communication*. Minneapolis: University of Minnesota Press.

McKerns, J. P. (1977). The limits of progressive journalism history. *Journalism History, 4,* 84–92.

Mott, F. L. (1941). *American journalism: A history of newspapers in the United States through 250 years, 1690–1940*. New York: Macmillan.

Nerone, J. (1987). The mythology of the penny press. *Critical Studies in Mass Communication, 4*, 376–404.

Nerone, J. (1991). The problem of teaching journalism history. *Journalism Educator, 45*(3), 16–24.

Nerone, J. (1995). *Last rights: Revisiting four theories of the press*. Urbana: University of Illinois Press.

Nerone, J., & Barnhurst, K. G. (2003). US newspaper types, the newsroom, and the division of labor, 1750–2000. *Journalism Studies, 4*(4), 435–449.

Nordenstreng, K., & Schiller, H. (Eds.). (1979). *National sovereignty and international communication*. Norwood, NJ: Ablex.

Older, C. M. (1936). *William Randolph Hearst, American*. New York: Appleton-Century.

Park, R. E. (1923). Natural history of the newspaper. *American Journal of Sociology, 29*(3), 273–289.

Park, M.-J., & Curran, J. (2000). *De-westernizing media studies*. New York: Routledge.

Parton, J (1855). *The life of Horace Greeley, editor of the New York Tribune*. New York: Mason Brothers.

Peters, J. D. (2005). *Courting the abyss: Free speech and the liberal tradition*. Chicago: University of Chicago Press.

Pöttker, H. (2003). News and its communicative quality: The inverted pyramid: When and why did it appear? *Journalism Studies, 4*, 501–511.

Pray, I. (1855). *Memoirs of James Gordon Bennett and his times*. New York: Stringer & Townshend.

Rantanen, T. (1990). *Foreign news in imperial Russia: The relationship between international and Russian news agencies, 1856–1914*. Helsinki: Suomalainen Tiedeakatemia.

Rantanen, T. (2002). *The global and the national: Media and communications in post-communist Russia*. London: Rowman & Littlefield.

Raymond, J. (2003). *Pamphlets and pamphleteering in early modern Britain*. New York: Cambridge University Press.

Rhodes, J. (1998). *Mary Ann Shadd Cary: The Black press and protest in the nineteenth century*. Bloomington: Indiana University Press.

Rodríguez, C. (2001). *Fissures in the mediascape: An international study of citizens' media*. Cresskill, NJ: Hampton Press.

Rosen, Jay. (1999). *What are journalists for?* New Haven: Yale University Press.

Schiller, D. (1996). *Theorizing communication*. New York: Oxford University Press.

Schiller, H. I. (1976). *Communication and cultural domination*. White Plains, NY: International Arts and Sciences Press.

Schivelbush, W. (1986). *The railway journey: The industrialization of time and space in the 19th century*. Berkeley: University of California Press.

Schudson, M. (1978). *Discovering the news: A social history of the American newspaper*. New York: Basic Books.

Schwarzlose, R. A. (1988). *The nation's newsbrokers*. Evanston, IL: Northwestern University Press.

Seitz, D. C. (1924). *Joseph Pulitzer: His life and letters*. New York: Simon & Schuster.

Semati, M. (Ed.) (2004). *New frontiers in international communication theory*. Lanham, MD: Rowman & Littlefield.

Siebert, F. S. (1952). *Freedom of the press in England, 1476–1776: The rise and decline of government controls*. Urbana: University of Illinois Press.

Siebert, F. S., Peterson, T., & Schramm, W. (1956). *Four theories of the press*. Urbana: University of Illinois Press.

Thomas, I. (1970[1810]). *The history of printing in America*. Barre, MA: Imprint Society.

Trenchard, J. & Gordon, T. (1723). *Cato's letters*. London: Wilkins, Woodward, Walthoe, and Peele.

Tuchman, G. (1978). *Making news: A study in the construction of reality*. New York: Free Press.

Tusan, M. (2005). *Women making news: Gender and the women's periodical press in Britain*. Urbana: University of Illinois Press.

Waisbord, S. (2000). *Watchdog journalism in South America*. New York: Columbia University Press.

Warren, S. D., & Brandeis, L. D. (1890). The right to privacy. *Harvard Law Review, IV*(5), 193–220.

Winkler, J. K. (1928). *W. R. Hearst, an American phenomenon*. London: J. Cape.

Woods, O., & Bishop, J. (1983). *The story of* The Times. London: Joseph.

3

Journalism and the Academy

Barbie Zelizer

Journalism's place in the academy is a project rife with various and sundry complications. As the recognizable forms of journalism take on new dimensions to accommodate the changing circumstances in which journalism exists, the question of journalism's study has developed along an uneven route filled with isolated pockets of disciplinary knowledge. The result is that we have little consensus about the two key terms at the focus of our attention, agreeing only marginally about what journalism is and generating even less agreement about what the academy's relationship with it should be. This chapter discusses the various sources of existential uncertainty underlying journalism's coexistence with the academy and offers a number of suggestions to make their uneven and often symbiotic relationship more mutually aware and fruitful.

THE SHAPE OF JOURNALISM AND ITS STUDY

In an era when journalism stretches from personalized blogs to satirical relays on late night television and its study appears in places as diverse as communication, literature, business and sociology, considering journalism's place in the academy from anew might seem like an unnecessary attempt to generate alarm about the future viability of a phenomenon that seems to be everywhere. However, in being everywhere, journalism and its study are in fact nowhere. On the one hand, journalism's development has produced a long line of repetitive and unresolved laments over which form, practice or convention might be better suited than their alternatives to qualify as newsmaking convention. On the other hand, its study has not kept step with the wide-ranging and often unanticipated nature of its evolution over time.

The dissonance between journalism and the academy echoes a broader disjunction characterizing journalism's uneven and spotty existence with the world. When George Orwell added newspaper quotations to his first book, critics accused him of "turning what might have been a good book into journalism" (Orwell, 1946, cited in Bromley, 2003), and his collected works were compiled decades later under the unambivalent title *Smothered Under Journalism, 1946* (Orwell, 1999). Similar stories dot the journalistic backgrounds of literary giants like Charles Dickens, Samuel Johnson, John Dos Passos, Andre Malraux, Dylan Thomas and John Hersey. Reactions like these proliferate despite a profound reliance on journalism not only to situate us vis à vis the larger collective but to use that situation as a starting point for more elaborated ways of positioning ourselves and understanding the world.

This is curious, because much of our situated knowledge rests in part on journalism. Where would history be without journalism? What would literature look like? How could we understand the workings of the polity? As a phenomenon, journalism stretches in various forms across all of the ways in which we come together as a collective, and yet the "it's just journalism" rejoinder persists.

Journalism's coexistence with the academy rests on various sources of existential uncertainty that build from this tension. The most obvious uncertainty stems from the pragmatic questions that underlie journalism's practice, by which its very definition is tweaked each time supposed interlopers—blogs, citizen journalists, late night TV comedians or reality television—come close to its imagined borders. A second source of uncertainty draws from the pedagogic dimensions surrounding journalism and the academy. How we teach what we think we know is a question with a litany of answers, particularly as journalism's contours change. And yet those who teach what counts and does not count as journalistic practice and convention have tended to be behind rather than ahead of its rapidly altering parameters. And finally one of the most significant sources of uncertainty surrounds the conceptual dimensions of the relationship—what we study when we think about journalism. In that over the years academics have invoked a variety of prisms through which to consider journalism—among them its craft, its effect, its performance and its technology—they have not yet produced a scholarly picture of journalism that combines all of these prisms into a coherent reflection of all that journalism is and could be. Instead, the study of journalism remains incomplete, partial and divided, leavings its practitioners uncertain about what it means to think about journalism, writ broadly.

This chapter addresses these sources of uncertainty and in so doing thinks through some important challenges facing the study of contemporary journalism. It argues for a space of reflection, both about the backdrop status of journalism's practice and study and about the degree to which the default assumptions that comprise it correspond with the full picture of contemporary journalism. What about journalism and its study has been privileged, and what has been sidestepped? These questions are particularly critical when thinking about journalism studies in its global context, where variance has not been accommodated or even recognized as much as it exists on the ground.

INTERPRETIVE COMMUNITIES AND THINKING ABOUT JOURNALISM

What academics think relies upon how they think and with whom, and perhaps nowhere has this been as developed as in the sociology of knowledge. Thomas Kuhn (1964) was most directly associated with the now somewhat fundamental notion that inquiry depends on consensus building, on developing shared paradigms that name and characterize problems and procedures in ways that are recognized by the collective. On the way to establishing consensus, individuals favoring competing insights battle over definitions, terms of reference and boundaries of inclusion and exclusion. Once consensus is established, new phenomena tend to be classified by already proven lines. In other words, what we think has a predetermined shape and life-line, which privileges community, solidarity and power.

This notion goes far beyond the work of Kuhn, and it has been implicated in scholarship by Emile Durkheim (1965 [1915]), Robert Park (1940), Michel Foucault (1972), Peter Berger and Thomas Luckmann (1966), and Nelson Goodman (1978)—all of whom maintained in different ways that the social group is critical to establishing ways of knowing the world. The idea of interpretive communities, originally suggested by Stanley Fish (1980) and developed in conjunction with journalism by Zelizer (1993), Berkowitz (2000) and others, helps situate the strategies that go into the sharing of knowledge as integral to the knowledge that results. Recognizing that groups with shared ways of interpreting evidence shed light on the way that questions of value are settled and resettled, the persons, organizations, institutions and fields of inquiry engaged in journalism's analysis become central to understanding what journalism is. As the anthropologist Mary Douglas (1986, p. 8) argued, "true solidarity is only possible to the extent that individuals share the categories of their thought." Inquiry, then, is not just an intellectual act but a social one too.

What this suggests for journalism's study is an invitation to think about the forces involved in giving it shape. In this sense, no one voice in journalism's study is better or more authoritative than the others; nor is there any one unitary vision of journalism to be found. Rather, different voices offer more—and more complete—ways to understand what journalism is, each having evolved in conjunction with its own set of premises about what matters and in which ways.

As an area of inquiry, journalism's study has always been somewhat untenable. Negotiated across three populations—journalists, journalism educators and journalism scholars, the shared concern for journalism that is independently central to each group has not remained at the forefront of their collective endeavors. Rather, journalism's centrality and viability have been waylaid as lamentations have been aired contending that the others fail to understand what is most important: journalists say journalism scholars and educators have no business airing their dirty laundry; journalism scholars say journalists and journalism educators are not theoretical enough; journalism educators say journalists have their heads in the sand and journalism scholars have their heads in the clouds. As each has fixated on who will be best heard above the din of competing voices, the concern for journalism has often been shunted to the side. Underlying the ability to speak about journalism, then, have been tensions about who can mobilize the right to speak over others and who is best positioned to maintain that right.

The alternate voices in journalism's study each constitute an interpretive community of sorts. Each has defined journalism according to its own aims and then has set strategies for how to think about it in conjunction with those aims.

JOURNALISTS

Journalists are individuals who engage in a broad range of activities associated with newsmaking, including, in Stuart Adam's (1993, p. 12) view, "reporting, criticism, editorializing and the conferral of judgment on the shape of things." Journalism's importance has been undeniable, and while it has been the target of ongoing discourse both in support and critique of its performance, no existing conversation about it has suggested its irrelevance. Rather, contemporary conditions have insisted on journalism's centrality and the crucial role it can play in helping people make sense both of their daily lives and of the ways in which they connect to the larger body politic.

However, not all of journalism's potential has borne out in practice. Contemporary journalists have been under siege from numerous quarters. They live in an economic environment in which falling revenues, fragmentation, branding and bottom-line pressures keep forcing the news to act as a shaky for-profit enterprise across an increased number of outlets. These outlets have not necessarily produced a broader scope of coverage, and many journalists have taken to multitasking the same story in ways that previous generations would not recognize. In the United States, every media sector but the ethnic press—mainstream newspapers, broadcast and cable news, the alternative press—is losing its public. Entering a "new era of shrinking ambitions," contemporary journalism is no longer a dependable economic enterprise (Project for Excellence in Journalism, 2007).

Politically, journalists have come under attack from both the left and right, which have argued for different definitions of so-called journalistic performance alongside a political environment that has undercut the journalist's capacity to function in old ways. While the competing and contradictory expectations from left and right have paralyzed aspects of journalism's performance in more stable political systems, the demise of the nation-state in many areas of the world has raised additional questions regarding journalism's optimum operation. All of this has produced an untenable situation for journalists, who have been caught in various kinds of questionable embraces with government, local interests and the military and who, in the United States, have gravitated toward coverage that plays to "safe" political spaces, producing news that is characterized by heightened localism, personalization and oversimplification (State of the News Media, 2007). Journalists have learned to follow various models of practice, not always thoughtfully and none of which have been fully suited to the complexities of today's global political environments.

Technically, journalists have faced new challenges from the blogosphere and other venues, which have made the very accomplishment of newswork tenuous. How journalists cover the news has faded in importance alongside the fact of coverage. Alternative sites like late night television comedy, blogs and online sites like Global Voices have taken the lead in gatekeeping, with journalism "becoming a smaller part of people's information mix" (State of the News Media, 2007). In that regard, people watching sites like Comedy Central's *The Daily Show* have been thought to be better informed about public events than those who watched mainstream news (State of the News Media, 2007).

Lastly, moral scandals involving journalists have abounded. Incidents involving Judith Miller or Jayson Blair in the United States or the Gilligan Affair in Britain have all raised questions about the moral fiber of journalists, paving the way for an insistence on homemade media, or citizen journalism, by which journalists' function is being increasingly taken over and performed by private citizens. That same trend has also meant that the public can see journalism's limitations more easily, leading them to argue, at least in the US case, that the news media are "less accurate, less caring, less moral and more inclined to cover up rather than correct mistakes" (State of the News Media, 2007).

All of this suggests that journalists have not been as effective as they might have been in communicating to the world journalism's centrality and importance. Questions persist about changing definitions of who is a journalist: Does one include Sharon Osbourne or the Weather Channel? Questions also underlie the issue of which technologies are bona fide instruments of newsmaking: Does one include cellular camera phones or reality television? And finally, the fundamental question of what journalism is for has no clear answer. Is its function to only provide information or to more aggressively meld community and public citizenship? Journalism's different functioning in different parts of the world—as in the distinctions separating the developmental journalism prevalent in parts of Asia from the partisan models popular in Southern Europe—has made the question more difficult to answer.

Part of this has derived from the fact that there are a number of competing visions at the core of journalism's self definition. Is it a craft, a profession, a set of practices, a collective of individuals, an industry, an institution, a business or a mindset? In that it is probably a bit of all of these things, there is a need to better figure out how they work off of and sometimes against each other. This is critical, for even basic questions about journalistic tools have really never been addressed and journalism's tools have not been equally valued. Images in particular are one aspect of news that has been unevenly executed, with pictures regularly appearing without captions, without credits and with no identifiable relation to the texts at their side. Yet the turn to images in times of crisis—by which there are more images, more prominent images, bolder images, and larger images—has been poorly matched to the uneven conventions by which images act as news relays. Following both the terror attacks of September 11 and the launching of the US war on Iraq, there were two and a half times the number of photos in the front sections of a paper like the *New York Times* than it regularly featured in peacetime (Zelizer, 2004). The lack of a clear development of standards, then, is problematic, because visuals have taken over the forefront of journalism's relays even if they have not been sufficiently addressed. Moreover, because their so called "correct usage" has not been figured out, the image's presentation has become an open field, with people crying foul every time journalism's pictures grate their nerves. This means that journalism's hesitancy about doing its job has allowed others—politicians, lobbyists, concerned citizens, bereaved parents, even members of militias—to make the calls instead, and they do so in journalism's name but without journalism's sanction.

Similarly undervalued has been the degree to which crisis has become the default setting for much of journalistic practice. In that there has been much in the news that takes shape on the backs of improvisation, sheer good or bad fortune, and ennui than is typically admitted, the evolution of crisis as the rule rather than the exception of journalism suggests a need to be clearer about how such impulses play into newsmaking. For in leaving crisis out of the picture, journalism has seemed to be a far more predictable and manageable place than it is in actuality.

All of this has rendered journalists a group somewhat out of touch with itself, its critics and its public. Givens such as the needs of the audience, the changing circumstances of newsmaking or the stuff at the margins of the newsroom—like inspiration and creativity—have remained relatively unaddressed. It is no surprise, then, that in the US journalists rank at the bottom of nearly every opinion poll of those whom the public trusts.

JOURNALISM EDUCATORS

The journalism educators have come together around a strong need to educate novices into the craft of journalism. Although vernacular education has differed across locations, it has exhibited similar tendencies regardless of specific locale. In the United States, teaching a vernacular craft began in the humanities around 1900, where newswriting and the history of journalism moved from English departments into the beginnings of a journalism education that eventually expanded into ethics and the law. Other efforts developed in the late 1920s in the social sciences, where the impulse to establish a science of journalism positioned craft—commonly called "skills" courses—as one quarter of a curriculum offering courses in economics, psychology, public opinion and survey research. Journalism educators were thus caught in the tensions between the humanities and social sciences as to which type of inquiry could best teach journalists to be journalists. For many this split still proliferates, reflected in the so-called quantitative/qualitative distinction in approaches to news.

In the United Kingdom, journalism education was set against a longstanding tradition of learning through apprenticeship and a prevalent view that journalism's "technical elements" were "lacking in academic rigor" (Bromley, 1997, p. 334). Practical journalism did not appear on the curriculum until 1937 but only became a setting worthy of academic investigation once sociology and political science, largely through the work of Jeremy Tunstall (1970, 1971), arrived in the late 1960s. In Germany and Latin America, an academic interest was evident first in the social sciences, which pushed journalism education toward sociology and notions of professionalism (Marques de Melo, 1988; Weber, 1948).

In each case, the academic interest among educators helped link journalists to the outside world, but it also did enormous damage to the craft, leveling it down to what James Carey (2000, p. 21) called a "signaling system." At first offering an old-fashioned apprenticeship, journalism educators over time came to address journalism by dividing it into technologies of production, separating newspapers, magazines, television and radio from each other. Lost in this was a place where all of journalism could be thought of as a whole with many disparate parts. And the resulting curriculum, again in Carey's view, in many cases came to lack "historical understanding, criticism or self-consciousness" (p. 13). In this regard, journalism education generated dissonance across the larger university curriculum. In the humanities it came to be seen as part of "the vernacular, the vulgate" (p. 22). In the social sciences, it came to be seen as a tool for channeling public opinion but not important in and of itself.

JOURNALISM SCHOLARS

The final population of interest to journalism is the journalism scholars, who despite an enormous body of literature dealing with the values, practices, and impact of journalism, still have not produced a coherent picture of what journalism is. And yet journalism can be found literally across the university curriculum.

Journalism has come to inhabit academic efforts in communication, media studies and journalism schools, as well as the less obvious targets of composition sequences, history, sociology, urban studies, political science, and economics and business. What this means is that much of what has been laid out thus far in terms of creating a distinctive and separate interpretive community has been experienced tenfold within the academy. In that academics often function within the boundaries and confines of disciplinary communities, what they study often takes on the shape of the perspectives set forth by those communities. These disciplines, which are akin to interpretive communities, have helped determine what counts as evidence and in which ways. Similarly, they have made judgment calls about which kinds of research do not count.

How has journalism existed across the curriculum? Journalism has been approached in pockets, each of which has isolated aspects of the phenomenon from the others: Such compartmentalization has worked against a clarification of what journalism is, examining journalism's partial workings rather than its whole. The result has been a terrain of journalism study at war with itself, with journalism educators separated from journalism scholars, humanistic journalism scholars separated from scholars trained in the social sciences, and a slew of independent academic efforts taking place in a variety of disciplines without the shared knowledge crucial to academic inquiry. Alongside these efforts, journalists have long resisted the attempts to microscopically examine their work environment.

This has had problematic ramifications: One has had to do with narrowing the varieties of news. In that scholars have not produced a body of material that reflects all of journalism, they have primarily defined it in ways that drive a specific form of hard news over other alternatives. This metonymic bias of academic studies has thus pushed a growing gap between what Peter Dahlgren (1992, p. 7) called "the realities of journalism and its official presentation of self." Missing for long periods of time have been copy-editors, graphic designers, online journalists, journals of opinion, camera operators, tabloids and satirical late night shows. In other words, the academy has pushed certain focal points in thinking about journalism that do not account for the broad world of what journalism is. The diversity of news has for the most part disappeared.

A similar destiny has met the craft of journalism. The academy's move to professionalize journalists—largely driven by its sociological inquiry—has told journalists that they are professionals, whether or not they want to be, and this has raised the stakes involved in being a journalist, often to the detriment of those practicing the craft. The ramifications of this have been tangible, in that traditional notions of craft have gone under. For instance, imposing codified rules of entry and exclusion has produced an anti-professionalization position among many European journalists: In the UK, there has been an inability to accommodate the growing number of newly-educated journalists (Bromley, 1997); in France, journalists have developed an overly aggressive style of investigative reporting (Neveu, 1998). As longtime British correspondent James Cameron (1997 [1967], p. 170) put it, "it is fatuous to compensate for our insecurity by calling ourselves members of a profession; it is both pretentious and disabling; we are at our best craftsmen." And yet craft, itself the defining feature of journalism, has faded to the background of what is necessary to know.

The same narrow fate has met diverse international forms of journalism. Though the practice of journalism has taken on unique shape in the various regions in which it has been practiced, the vast majority of scholarship has focused on journalism in its US venues. In that much of this research has been US-centered, standing in as a very limited but honorific gold standard for a wide range of journalistic practices implemented around the world, this has left unaddressed those kinds of journalism practiced beyond journalism's Western core (i.e., Gunaratne, 1998; Hallin & Mancini, 2004; Zhao, 1998). It has also left unanswered the many question marks about journalism that dot the global horizon.

Equally important, though much of journalism's history has been wrapped up in the history of the nation-state, in today's global age we are hard pressed to argue that that linkage works anymore. Though one of globalization's key effects has been to undermine the nation state's centrality, what kind of alternative impulse should be behind the journalistic apparatus it creates instead? Examples here are the contrary cases of capitalism and religious fundamentalism, both of which have created new boundaries of inclusion and exclusion, thereby adjusting the answer of what journalism is for by gravitating toward modes of journalistic practice awry with the impulses for so-called free information relay.

What all of these circumstances suggest is that journalism scholars have not done enough to tend the ties that bind them back to journalism in all of its forms. This is of critical importance, in that there has developed a body of knowledge about journalism that largely preaches to the converted but does little to create a shared frame of reference about how journalism works or what journalism is for.

TYPES OF INQUIRY

Within the academy, there have been five main types of inquiry into journalism—sociology, history, language studies, political science, and cultural analysis. Proposed largely as a heuristic device that implies more mutual exclusivity than exists in real practice, these are not the only disciplines that have addressed journalism. But the perspectives they provide offer a glimpse of the range of alternatives through which journalism can be conceptualized. The underlying assumptions that each frame has imposed on its examination of the journalistic world say much about how different prisms on journalism have created a picture that is at best partial.

Each frame offers a different way to address the question of why journalism matters: sociology has addressed how journalism matters; history how it used to matter; language studies through which verbal and visual tools it matters; political science how it ought to matter; and cultural analysis how it matters differently. Lost here, or at least dropped into the backdrop of the research setting, has been the way in which each of these answers comes to bear on the larger question of why academics should be addressing journalism to begin with.

Sociology has offered the default setting for thinking about how journalism works. Largely built upon a memorable body of work called the ethnographies of news or the newsroom studies of the seventies (Fishman, 1980; Gans, 1979; Tuchman, 1978), sociological inquiry by and large has created a picture of journalism that focuses on people rather than documents, on relationships, work routines, and other formulaic interactions across members of the community who are involved in gathering and presenting news. Sociology has established the idea that journalists function as sociological beings, with norms, practices and routines (Tunstall, 1971; Waisbord, 2002; Weaver & Wilhoit, 1996), that they exist in organizational, institutional and structural settings (Breed, 1955; Epstein, 1973; McManus, 1994), that they invoke something akin to ideology in their newswork (Gitlin, 1980; Glasgow University Media Group 1976), and that their activities have effects (i.e., Lang & Lang, 1953).

In that sociology has largely favored the study of dominant practices over deviant ones and freezing moments within the news-making process for analysis rather than considering the whole phenomenon, it has created a picture of journalism from which much other inquiry proceeds. The emphasis here on behavior and effect more than meaning, on pattern more than violation, on the collective more than the individual, has helped advance a view of journalists as professionals, albeit not very successful ones (Henningham, 1985). This work has remained somewhat captured by its past, in that early canonical work has yet to address fully the more contemporary trends toward conglomeratization, corporatization, standardization, personalization, convergence, and the multiple (often differently normative) nature of journalistic work in its more recent forms (Benson & Neveu, 2004; Cottle, 2000). Moreover, this work has been primarily structured within the confines of US sociology, and its pictures of primarily mainstream news organizations in the United States have assumed a universal voice in standing for our understanding of journalism.

History and the inquiry of news have evolved largely from the earliest expansions of journalistic academic curricula. Central in establishing the longevity of journalism and journalistic practice, the history of news has used the past—its lessons, triumphs, and tragedies—as a way to understand contemporary journalism. Within this frame, what has drawn academic attention has tended to be that which has persisted. However, the picture has been a narrowly drawn one.

Largely dependent on documents rather than people, historical inquiry can be divided into three main kinds of documents—journalism history writ small, as in memoirs, biographies and organizational histories (i.e., Gates, 1978); history writ midway, organized around temporal periods, themes and events, like "the penny press" or "war journalism" (i.e., Nerone, 1994; Schudson, 1978); and history writ large, where the concern primarily surrounds the linkage between the nation state and the news media (i.e., Curran & Seaton, 1985). Each differs substantially by the country being considered, as work from Australia and France suggests (Kuhn, 1995; Mayer, 1964). Missing here has been a conscious twinning of the role that writing history plays for both journalists and the academy: The histories of journalistic practice published primarily in US journalism schools with the aim of legitimating journalism as a field of inquiry do not reflect the generalized, so-called objective histories that followed the model of German historicism (Carey, 1974; Scannell, 2002). Not enough effort has been invested in figuring out how to better combine the two. Here too a focus on largely US history (and its progressive bias) has bypassed the extremely rich and varied evolution of journalistic practice elsewhere in the world. Not surprisingly, much of this scholarship has had to wrestle with the question of who can lay claim to the past. The issue of "whose journalism history" remains to this day an underlying challenge to those doing historical inquiry.

The study of journalism's *languages* has assumed that journalists' messages are neither transparent nor simplistic but the result of constructed activity on the part of speakers. Developed primarily only during the past 35 years or so, this area has been markedly European and Australian in development (i.e., Bell, 1991; Van Dijk, 1987). The combination of formal features of language—such as grammar, syntax and word choice—with less formal ones—such as storytelling frames, textual patterns, and narratives—has grown to address verbal language, sound, still and moving visuals, and patterns of interactivity.

There have been three kinds of language study—informal study, which uses language as a backdrop without examining extensively its features, such as content analysis and semiology (Hartley, 1982; Schramm, 1959); formal study, such as sociolinguistics, discourse analysis, and critical linguistics (Fowler, 1991; Greatbatch, 1988); and the study of the pragmatics of language, as in the patterns of language use in the news that are shaped by narrative and storytelling conventions, rhetoric, and framing (Campbell, 1991; Gamson, 1989). This inquiry has gone in different directions, with framing largely focused on the political aspects of news language and narrative and storytelling targeting its cultural aspects and particularly alternative forms like tabloids or newzines (i.e., Bird, 1990; Reese, Gandy Jr., & Grant, 2001). In stressing not only the shape of language itself but also its role in larger social and cultural life, this largely microanalytic work suffers from a lack of applicability to other kinds of inquiry. At the same time, though, its beginning premise that language is ideological challenges both traditional mainstream news scholarship as well as journalistic claims that the news is a reflection of the real.

Political scientists have long held a normative interest in journalism, querying how journalism "ought" to operate under optimum conditions. Interested in examining journalism through a vested interest in the political world, an assumption of interdependency between politics and journalism motivates this inquiry. Thus, many scholars have clarified how journalism can better serve its publics. Political science inquiry has ranged from broad considerations of the media's role in different types of political systems, such as the classic *Four Theories of the Press* (Siebert, Peterson, & Schramm, 1956) to studies of political campaign behavior, journalistic models and roles and the sourcing patterns of reporters and officials (i.e., Graber, McQuail, & Norris, 1998; Sigal, 1973). Also of relevance is the extensive literature on public journalism (Rosen, 1999).

Largely US in focus, although some parallel work has been done by scholars of government and politics in the United Kingdom, Latin America and Eastern Europe (i.e., Fox, 1988; Schlesinger & Tumber, 1995; Splichal & Sparks, 1994), this work has considered journalism's larger "political" role in making news, such as journalism at its highest echelons—the publishers, boards of directors, managing editors—more often than at its low-ranking individual journalists. Many of these studies have been motivated by normative impulses and have concluded on notes of recuperation, which suggest that journalism is and should be in tune with more general political impulses in the society at large.

Finally, the *cultural analysis* of journalism has tended to see itself as the "bad boy" in the neighborhood. It has defined itself as querying the givens behind journalism's own sense of self, seeking to examine what is important to journalists themselves and exploring the cultural symbol systems by which reporters make sense of their profession. In assuming a lack of unity within journalism—in news-gathering routines, norms, values, technologies, and assumptions about what is important, appropriate, and preferred—and in its research perspective, which uses various conceptual tools to explain journalism, much of this inquiry has followed two strains, largely paralleling those evident in models of US and British cultural studies—the former focusing on problems of meaning, group identity and social change (i.e., Ettema & Glasser, 1998; Pauly, 1988; Steiner, 1992), the latter on its intersection with power and patterns of domination (i.e., Hall, 1973; Hartley, 1992). This work has looked at much of what has not been addressed in the other areas of inquiry—worldviews, practices, breaches, form, representations, and audiences—but all with an eye to figuring out how it comes to mean, necessitating some consideration of the blurred lines between different kinds of newswork—such as tabloid and mainstream (Lumby, 1999; Sparks & Tulloch, 2000), mainstream and online (Allan, 2006), newswork and the non-news world (Eason, 1984; Manoff & Schudson, 1986). The value of some of this work, however, has been challenged by the field's own ambivalence about journalism's reverence for facts, truth and reality, all of which have been objects of negotiation and relativization when seen from a cultural lens.

Each frame for studying journalism has emerged as a singular and particular prism on the news, creating a need for more explicit and comprehensive sharing across frames. Not only would such sharing help generate an appreciation for journalism at the moment of its creation, but it would offset the nearsightedness with which much scholarship on journalism has been set in place. How scholars tend to conceptualize news, newsmaking, journalism, journalists, and the news media, which explanatory frames they use to explore these issues, and from which fields of inquiry they borrow in shaping their assumptions are all questions in need of further clarity. Adopting multiple views is necessary not only because journalism scholarship has not produced a body of scholarly material that reflects all of journalism, but it has not produced a body of scholars who are familiar with what is being done across the board of scholarly inquiry. There is both insufficient consensus about journalism and about the academy that studies it. The result, then, is an existential uncertainty that draws from pragmatic, pedagogic and conceptual dimensions of the relationship between journalism and the academy.

FUTURE CORRECTIVES

Numerous correctives can help resolve journalism's existential uncertainty. Positioning journalism as the core of a mix of academic perspectives from which it can most fruitfully prosper is essential. Recognizing journalism as an act of expression links directly with the humanities in much the same way that recognizing journalism's impact links directly with the social sciences, and those alternate views need to be made explicit as equally valued but nonetheless partial prisms on what journalism is. Keeping that inquiry porous—so that it is possible to examine not only what many of us know about journalism, but how we have agreed on what we know—is no less important. Similarly, keeping craft, education and research together in the curriculum will help us understand journalism more fully. In this regard, journalism studies is about making a setting to include different kinds of engagement with journalism—both those who practice journalism, those who teach others to practice journalism, and those who teach yet others to think critically about what that practice means. None of this is a new idea: Everett Dennis (1984) made a similar call over twenty years ago, and such a notion underlies both the Carnegie-Knight Initiative on the Future of Journalism Education and the European Erasmus Mundus program in journalism and media.

In some places there has already begun to be movement toward tweaking the foundation of journalism's study. The founding of two parallel academic journals in the late 1990s—*Journalism: Theory, Practice, and Criticism* and *Journalism Studies*—reflects a need for a concentrated place to air the concerns about journalism that arose from academic inquiry. New research centers have developed that are devoted to journalism studies and to the study of certain aspects of journalistic performance—trauma, religion, and online journalism, among others. And finally, a Journalism Studies Interest Group (now Division) was recently established at the International Communication Association, with the intention of bringing together journalism theory, research and education. In all cases, these efforts have provided a corrective to the limitations of journalism's inquiry in its existing frameworks.

All of this is a long way of saying that we need to figure out how to make journalism simultaneously more of the world while keeping it at the forefront of our imagination. Finding a clearer template for the mutual engagement of journalism and the academy depends on our being ahead of journalism's development—on anticipating where it needs to go and on envisioning broad and creative ways in which it might go there. Journalism is too important to not address the issues raised in these pages, but if it does not wrestle with them quickly, it remains questionable as to what kind of a future it will face.

REFERENCES

Adam, G. S. (1993). *Notes toward a definition of journalism.* St. Petersburg, FL: Poynter Institute.

Allan, S. (2006). *Online news.* New York: Open University Press.

Bell, A. (1991). *The language of news media.* Oxford, UK: Blackwell.

Benson, R., & Neveu, E. (2004). *Bourdieu and the sociology of journalism.* Cambridge, UK: Polity.

Berkowitz, D. (2000). Doing double duty. *Journalism: Theory, Practice and Criticism, 1*(2), 125–143.

Berger, P., & Luckmann, T. (1966). *The social construction of reality.* Garden City, NJ:Anchor Books.

Bird, S. E. (1990). *For enquiring minds.* Knoxville: University of Tennessee Press.

Breed, W. (1955). Social control in the newsroom. *Social Forces, 33,* 326–335.

Bromley, M. (1997). The end of journalism? Changes in workplace practices in the press and broadcasting in the 1990s. In M. Bromley & T. O'Malley (Eds.), *A journalism reader* (pp. 330–150). London: Routledge.

Bromley, M. (2003). Objectivity and the other Orwell. *Media History, 9*(2), 123–135.

Cameron, J. (1997 [1967]). Journalism: A trade. In *Point of departure.* London: Arthur Barker; reprinted in M. Bromley & T. O'Malley (Eds.), *A journalism reader* (pp. 170–173). London: Routledge.

Campbell, R. (1991). *60 Minutes and the News.* Urbana: University of Illinois Press.

Carey, J. (1974). The problem of journalism history. *Journalism History, 1*(1), Spring, 3–5, 27.

Carey, J. (2000). Some notes on journalism education. *Journalism: Theory, Practice and Criticism, 1*(1), 12–23.

Cottle, S. (2000). New(s) times: Towards a "second wave" of news ethnography. *Communications, 25*(1), 19–41.

Curran, J., & Seaton, J. (1985). *Power without responsibility.* London: Fontana.

Dahlgren, P. (1992). Introduction. In P. Dahlgren & C. Sparks (Eds.), *Journalism and popular culture* (pp. 1–23). London: Sage.

Dennis, E. (1984). *Planning for curricular change: A report on the future of journalism and mass communication education.* Eugene: School of Journalism, University of Oregon.

Douglas, M. (1986). *How institutions think.* Syracuse, NY: Syracuse University Press.

Durkheim, E. (1965 [1915]). *The elementary forms of the religious life.* New York: Free Press.

Eason, D. (1984). On journalistic authority: The Janet Cooke scandal. *Critical Studies in Mass Communication, 3,* 429–447.

Epstein, E. J. (1973). *News from nowhere.* New York: Random House.

Ettema, J., & Glasser, T. (1998). *Custodians of conscience.* New York: Columbia University Press.

Fish, S. (1980). *Is there a text in this class?* Cambridge, MA: Harvard University Press.

Fox, E. (1988). *Media and politics in Latin America: the struggle for democracy.* Newbury Park, CA: Sage.

Fishman, M. (1980). *Manufacturing the news.* Austin: University of Texas Press.

Foucault, M. (1972). *The archaeology of knowledge.* London: Tavistock.

Fowler, R. (1991). *Language in the news.* London: Routledge.

Gamson, W. (1989). News as framing. *American Behavioral Scientist, 33*(2), 157–161.

Gans, H. (1979). *Deciding what's news.* New York: Pantheon.

Gates, G. P. (1978). *Airtime: The inside story of CBS news.* New York: Harper and Row.

Gitlin, T. (1980). *The whole world is watching.* Berkeley: University of California Press.

Glasgow University Media Group. (1976). *Bad news.* London: Routledge and Kegan Paul.

Goodman, N. (1978). *Ways of worldmaking.* Indianapolis, IN: Hackett Publishing Company.

Graber, D., McQuail, D., & Norris, P. (Eds.). (1998). *The politics of news: The news of politics.* Washington, DC: CQ Press.

Greatbatch, D. (1988). A turn-taking system for British news interviews. *Language in Society, 17*(3), 401–430.

Gunaratne, S. (1998). Old wine in a new bottle: Public journalism, developmental journalism and social responsibility. In M. E. Roloff (Ed.), *Communication Yearbook 21* (pp. 276–321). Thousand Oaks, CA: Sage.

Hall, S. (1973). The determinations of news photographs. In S. Cohen & J. Young (Eds.), *The manufacture of news* (pp. 176–190). London: Sage.

Hallin, D., & Mancini, P. (2004). *Comparing media systems: Three models of media and politics*. Cambridge University Press.

Hartley, J. (1982). *Understanding news*. London: Methuen.

Hartley, J. (1992). *The politics of pictures*. London: Routledge.

Henningham, J. (1985). Journalism as a profession: A reexamination. *Australian Journal of Communication, 8*, 1–17.

Kuhn, R. (1995). *The media in France*. London: Routledge.

Kuhn, T. (1964). *The structure of scientific revolutions*. Chicago: University of Chicago Press.

Lang, K., & Lang, E. (1953). The unique perspective of television and its effect. *American Sociological Review, 18*(1), 103–112.

Lumby, C. (1999). *Gotcha: Life in a tabloid world*. Sydney: Allen and Unwin.

Manoff, R., & Schudson, M. (1986). *Reading the news*. New York: Pantheon.

Marques de Melo, J. (1988). Communication theory and research in Latin America. *Media, Culture and Society, 10*(4), 405–418.

Mayer, H. (1964). *The press in Australia*. Melbourne: Lansdowne.

McManus, J. (1994). *Market driven journalism: Let the citizen beware*. Thousand Oaks, CA: Sage.

Nerone, J. (1994). *Violence against the press*. New York: Oxford University Press.

Neveu, E. (1998). Media and politics in French political science. *European Journal of Political Research, 33*(4), 439–458.

Orwell, G. (1946). Why I write. *Gangrel*, Summer.

Orwell, G. (1999). *Smothered under journalism, 1946*. London: Martin Secker and Warburg, LTD.

Pauly, J. (1988). Rupert Murdoch and the demonology of professional journalism. In J. Carey (Ed.). *Media, myths and narratives* (pp. 246–261). Newbury Park, CA: Sage.

Park, R. E. (1940). News as a form of knowledge, *American Journal of Sociology, 45*, March, 669–686.

Project for Excellence in Journalism. (2007). State of the news media: An annual report on American journalism. Washington, DC: Project for Excellence in Journalism.

Reese, S., Gandy Jr., O., & Grant, A. (Eds.). (2001). *Framing public life*. Mahwah, NJ: Erlbaum.

Rosen, J. (1999). *What are journalists for?* New Haven, CT: Yale University Press.

Scannell, P. (2002). History, media and communication In K. B. Jensen (Ed.), *A handbook of media and communication research* (pp. 191–205). London: Routledge,.

Schlesinger, P., & Tumber, H. (1995). *Reporting crime*. Oxford, UK: Oxford University Press.

Schudson, M. (1978). *Discovering the news*. New York: Basic Books.

Schramm, W. (1959). *One day in the world's press*. Stanford, CA: Stanford University Press.

Siebert, F., Peterson, T., & Schramm, W. (1956). *Four theories of the press*. Urbana: University of Illinois Press.

Sigal, L. (1973). *Reporters and officials*. Lexington, MA: D.C. Heath.

Sparks, C., & Tulloch, J. (2000). *Tabloid tales*. New York: Rowman and Littlefield.

Splichal, S., & Sparks, C. (1994). *Journalists for the 21st century*. Norwood, NJ: Ablex.

Steiner, L. (1992). Construction of gender in news reporting textbooks, 1890–1990. *Journalism Monographs, 135*, October, 1–48.

Tuchman, G. (1978). *Making news*. New York: Free Press.

Tunstall, J. (1970). *The Westminster lobby correspondents: A sociological study of national political journalism*. London: Routledge and Kegan Paul.

Tunstall, J. (1971). *Journalists at work*. London: Constable.

Van Dijk, T. (1987). *News as discourse*. Hillsdale, NJ: Erlbaum.

Waisbord, S. (2002). *Watchdog journalism in South America.* New York: Columbia University Press.

Weaver, D., & Wilhoit, G. C. (1996). *The American journalist in the 1990s.* Mahwah, NJ: Erlbaum.

Weber, M. (1948). Politics as a vocation. In *From Max Weber: Essays in sociology.* London: Routledge and Kegan Paul.

Zelizer, B. (1993). Journalists as interpretive communities. *Critical Studies in Mass Communication, 10*(3), 219–237.

Zelizer, B. (2004). When war is reduced to a photograph. In S. Allan & B. Zelizer (Eds.), *Reporting war.* London: Routledge.

Zelizer, B. (2004). *Taking journalism seriously: News and the academy* (pp. 115–113). Thousand Oaks, CA: Sage.

Zhao, Y. (1998). *Media, market and democracy in China: Between the party line and the bottom line.* Urbana: University of Illinois Press.

4

Journalism Education

Beate Josephi

INTRODUCTION

Journalism education is seen as improving the quality of journalism by improving the quality of journalists. It is perceived as the "one way in which society can intervene to influence the development of journalism" (Curran, 2005, p. xiv). In other words, the kind of education future journalists receive matters because journalists matter among the many factors that make up journalism.

UNESCO, in its foreword to *Model Curricula for Journalism Education for Developing Countries & Emerging Democracies* (2007, p. 5), states "that journalism, and the educational programmes that enable individuals to practice and upgrade their journalistic skills, are essential tools for the underpinning of key democratic principles that are fundamental to the development of every country."

This chapter will look at the key elements of journalism education, notably the idea of enriching journalism practice. It will go on to examine the history of journalism education as it has, for much of a century, evolved in the United States. It will review recent key texts and consider the question of professionalization, which is seen as underpinning tertiary journalism education. The chapter will then outline the discussion about what ought to be taught in journalism education and the often unacknowledged ideological assumptions underlying journalism teaching. Finally, the chapter will point to areas of future research.

LAYING FOUNDATIONS

One key element of journalism education is that it is seen as laying the foundation for the attitudes and knowledge of future journalists. However, there are manifold views on what journalists *should* be taught. There are equally many ways that journalists *are* taught.

Another key element of journalism education therefore is its great diversity. To get the picture, one only needs to be aware of the variety of journalists' educational backgrounds, and the percentages of those who studied journalism before becoming journalists. The figures, insofar as current data are available, show a decisive trend for journalists to have university or college education (Deuze, 2006, p. 22). However, only a minority has completed degrees in journalism, media or communication studies before becoming journalists.

If we take journalism to mean predominantly news journalism and look at newspapers, we also have to acknowledge that the highest proportion of these is produced in Asia (World Association of Newspapers, 2005), reflecting the ever increasing importance of Asia in population and geo-political terms. Japan has the highest circulation newspapers. According to Gaunt (1992, p. 115), the most prestigious news organizations, the *Asahi*, the *Yomiuri* and the *Mainichi*, take only graduates from elite universities who hold degrees in political science, economics or the humanities. Few universities offer media studies, and the vast majority of journalists-to-be receive on-the-job training, which has the form of a rigid apprenticeship system.

In China, in the first decade of the twenty-first century, communication and journalism are fast becoming popular areas of study. This is indicative of the rapid transformation of Chinese society and the Chinese media market. For the moment, courses combine skills classes with studies in Chinese Communist philosophy, and are seen as lagging behind the demands of the market (Yu, Chu, & Guo, 2000).

Yet, as seen in the United States and Germany, an increase in higher education offerings in media, communication or journalism studies does not translate into journalists actually taking them as pathways to their job. As Weaver, Beam, Brownlee, Voakes, and Wilhoit (2007, p. 35) found in the United States, "from 1982 to 2002, the proportion of journalism and mass communication bachelor's-degree graduates who went into mass communication jobs declined sharply from over one-half (53 percent) to about one-fourth." This has shaped journalism education in the United States into a more general mass or public communication field (ibid). On the other hand, the percentage of journalists holding a degree stands at almost 90 percent (p. 37).

Similarly in Germany, 80.5 percent of journalists hold a university degree or have spent time at university, but only 13 percent hold a major or minor in journalism and another 17 percent have done communication or media studies (Weischenberg, Malik, & Scholl, 2006, p. 353). Importantly, almost 70 percent did an internship—in the age group under 35 years it is 90 percent—and 60 percent have passed through the two-year, for graduates one-year, in-house training (ibid).

The pathways to journalism mentioned above indicate clear national preferences despite the fact that basic journalistic "working practices appear universal" (de Burgh, 2005b, p. 6; Josephi, 2001). These figures serve to illustrate that tertiary journalism education is just one way of becoming a journalist (also see Deuze, 2006, p. 22; Fröhlich & Holtz-Bacha, 2003a; Weaver, 1998, p. 459; Gaunt, 1992). This puts writing about journalism education, which comes from academia and is almost entirely confined to tertiary journalism education, out of synch with the actual situation of chiefly in-house training.

Gaunt (1992, p. 1) opens his book, *Making the Newsmakers*, with the words "Journalism training perpetuates or modifies professional practices and molds the perceptions journalists have of the role and function of the media." Journalism education, as discussed here, has the clear intent of modifying practice, enriching the quality of information produced and, with the help of this quality journalism, achieving improvement in the workings of civil society.

THE HISTORY OF JOURNALISM EDUCATION

The idea of achieving better journalism by giving journalists a college or university education was born in the United States in the second half of the nineteenth century (Weaver, 2003, pp. 49–51). For much of the twentieth century, the United States was the main site to provide journalism as a tertiary study. Only in the 1980s and 1990s did journalism become accepted as a subject field world-wide, often in new universities. One reason why the United States broke new ground was that the country not only pioneered journalism education but also news journalism. According to Chalaby (1996), journalism as we define it today is an Anglo-American invention. Journalism in continental Europe was closely linked with the literary field which demanded a different set of talents and writing skills from those of a daily rounds reporter.

The person credited with implementing the idea that future journalists should receive a college education was the losing general of the US Civil War, Robert E. Lee. As president of Washington College—today Washington & Lee University in Lexington, Virginia—he offered scholarships for journalism studies as part of a liberal arts degree as early as 1869 (Medsger, 2005, p. 205).

Already then doubts were raised about journalism as an academic discipline. Lee's initiative came at a time when newspapers were small enterprises with the editor and printer often being one and the same person. The early courses accordingly included technical printing skills as well as writing and editing rather than focusing on reporting (Johansen, Weaver, & Dornan, 2001, p. 471). Irrespective of this earlier effort, James Carey claimed that journalism education did not begin in earnest until Joseph Pulitzer pressed money into the somewhat reluctant hands of Columbia University to establish a School of Journalism (Carey, cited in Johansen et al., 2001, p. 475). The Columbia School of Journalism opened in 1912 as a graduate school rather than the undergraduate college initially envisaged by Pulitzer (Adam, 2001, pp. 318–322). Pulitzer's motive was to improve the minds of journalists at a time when many, if not most, reporters came from working-class families. He wanted to achieve this by providing them with the liberal arts education they lacked (Medsger, 2005, pp. 206–208).

Other pioneers of journalism studies took a different direction. Willard Bleyer, in the late 1920s, placed the new study within Wisconsin University's PhD programs in political science and sociology. To him, research into journalism was an essential part of journalism education. This decision to locate journalism in the social sciences had long-term implications. The "founders of many major journalism schools elsewhere came from the Wisconsin program and carried its empirical social sciences assumptions with them" (Chaffee, cited in Johansen et al., 2001, p. 471). Bleyer also played a vital part in creating

> two pillars of the journalism education establishment in the United States: the Association of Journalism Education Administrators (now also known as the Association of Schools of Journalism and Mass Communication) and the accrediting body for journalism programs (now known as the Accrediting Council on Education in Journalism and Mass Communication). (Medsger, 2005, p. 208)

Soon there were three distinct models of journalism education at the university level. These operated as independent journalistic schools at either graduate or undergraduate level, such as the program Walter Williams had established at the University of Missouri, or as separate departments within colleges of liberal arts, or the social science faculties.

A further model was added by Wilbur Schramm. Schramm was head of journalism education at the University of Iowa at the end of the Second World War and later became the founder of communication studies and communication research institutes at the University of Illinois and Stanford University (Rogers, 1994, p. 29). While Schramm initially chose to place his new communication program within the existing discipline of journalism, communication as a field study soon overtook its host, and left behind journalism education which could not shed its tag of vocational training. Unlike Pulitzer, Professors Bleyer, Williams and Schramm were interested only in journalism, not journalists. As Rogers (1994, p. 127) wrote, a "communication research institute could serve as a source of prestige for a school of journalism that may have been looked down upon by academics in other fields because of the perceived trade school nature of journalism training." This left journalism education in the uneasy spot between practical and academic studies where it still finds itself, and the discussion about the professionalization of journalism and the journalism education curriculum highlights the unresolved nature of the debate.

The United States is not the only country with a history of journalism education, but no other nation has had a similar impact on the discipline. France opened its first journalism school, L'Ecole Superieure de Journalisme, in 1899, which was attached to the Ecole de Hautes Etudes en Sciences Sociales a year later (Gaunt, 1992, p. 46). The darker side of journalism education was shown in Spain where the national school of journalism was set up in 1941 by General Franco and placed under the control of the Falangist Party (Barrera & Vaz, 2003, p. 23; Gaunt, 1992, p. 63). The national school of journalism was the most important training center in Spain, and it remained under government supervision until the early 1970s. The journalists in the major Spanish government-controlled papers had to pass through this journalism school. Similar examples of government-controlled journalism education could be found in the former states of the Eastern bloc, attesting to the fundamental idea that journalism education is an important element, if not tool, for shaping journalists and journalism.

KEY TEXTS

Given the diversity of journalism education, it is no surprise that there are no key texts as such on the topic. Deuze correctly remarked that

> journalism education literature tends to be very specific—featuring case studies of what works and what does not work in a particular curriculum, course or classroom—or wildly generic—where often senior scholars offer more or less historical accounts of their lifelong experiences in "doing" journalism education. (Deuze, 2006, p. 19)

The books that take in a wider view invariably possess a survey character, charting what is done where in journalism education. The most complete—though no longer up-to-date—survey was provided by Philip Gaunt in 1992. In his book, *Making the Newsmakers*, sponsored by UNESCO, Gaunt first assesses the differences in training systems, training needs and structures before proceeding continent by continent, country by country to detail the various nations' or regions' efforts in journalism education.

Gaunt sees the challenges and prospects for journalism education as falling into two predictable clusters (1992, p. 157): those affecting the developing world and the industrialized countries, respectively. He names government control and the lack of resources as the two main hurdles facing the developing world, and technological change as the key challenge to the industrialized world. In detailing his concerns, Gaunt (p. 158) also draws attention to the status and pay journalists receive as having a direct impact on the kinds of students and teachers drawn to journalism studies:

> In countries in which journalists are considered to be government employees, or "flacks", the profession is unlikely to attract the best and the brightest students or the most qualified teachers. In such systems, courses on ethics, professional standards, investigative reporting, press history and different aspects of communication theory have no place in the curriculum.

Though this observation still rings true in a number of nations a decade and a half later, much has shifted in the world politically and developmentally. The changes in Central and Eastern Europe had hardly begun to take effect at the time of Gaunt's writing, nor had the world taken note of the immense transformation taking place in China. The media systems of those countries, and also nations like South Africa, are today labeled "transitional." Not only their media system but also their journalism education is affected by these shifts. Furthermore, other countries that are on the "not free" list with regard to media freedom, such as Qatar, home to Al Jazeera, are now seen as contributing quality journalism backed by journalism education. The outdated dichotomous view of a world split into countries in which journalism and journalism education is either free or fully government-controlled is giving way to the recognition that countries may exercise long leashes (Zhou, 2000) or "calibrated coercion" (George, 2007) rather than suppression, and that the freedom of the media in democratic countries can come with commercial and ideological strings attached.

It is this awareness which informs Hugo de Burgh's collection, *Making Journalists* (2005a). While similar in its title to Gaunt's book, this volume's structure is different. *Making Journalists* is a collection of chapters on issues rather than a systematic appraisal of what is done where. The book's editor states categorically that "there is no satisfactory way to write a "world" account of journalism education" (2005b, p. 4). He considers the approach he has chosen as a way of "exorcising homogenisation by demonstrating that the old fallacy that all journalisms were at different stages on route to an ideal model, probably Anglophone, is passé" (2005b, p. 2). De Burgh's book leaves the details of training systems aside in favour of exploring more broadly "journalism and journalists," "journalism and the future" and "journalism and location" on most continents and the Indian subcontinent. The differences in journalism education, very deliberately embraced and emphasized in de Burgh's book, stem, according to its editor, not so much from the variances in political and legal systems as from differences in culture. De Burgh hopes to arrive at a new culturally based paradigm because to him the way "journalism operates in a society [...] is the product of culture" (2005b, p. 17). His point, enlisting Carey, "that communication is most revealingly examined as ritual rather than as transmission" (ibid) is a bold one. Emphasizing cultural rather than political, legal and economic frameworks for journalism allows de Burgh to sidestep any questions about the ideological influences on the norms and values passed on in journalism education.

Fröhlich and Holtz-Bacha's earlier book, *Journalism Education in Europe and North America: An International Comparison* (2003a), consisting of 14 contributions, has something of Gaunt's survey character. The volume divides the European countries, the United States and Canada according to their journalism education predilections, into those countries which have a long standing academic tradition, those who prefer non-tertiary journalism schools and those who have mixed forms. The possibility of an emerging European journalism is also looked at. Yet while there are common trends throughout Europe, Fröhlich and Holtz-Bacha, in their conclusion, acknowledge a wide variety of journalism education pathways: "Although this volume was limited to the Western democracies (with an outlook on the developments in Eastern Europe) and thus to similar political systems, the chapters revealed an unexpected diversity of educational philosophies" (Fröhlich & Holtz-Bacha, 2003c, p. 321). Unlike de Burgh, Fröhlich and Holtz-Bacha see the reason for these divergences mainly in political and historical differences.

A study of a different kind is Splichal and Sparks' *Journalists for the 21st Century* (1994), which examines the motivations, expectations and professionalization tendencies among first year journalism students in 22 countries from all five continents, ranging from Austria to Tanzania. Methodologically the book has its flaws. Its conjecture to view first year journalism students, who have not had any newsroom experience as "socialised" and to assume that they can give conclusive answers as to how their norms and values have been shaped by national context and political system, has to be severely doubted.

What was measured instead, it can be argued, was the relative influence of professional education in its early stages. In this, Splichal and Sparks' results are highly encouraging for journalism education. The most striking similarity that emerged was for these young people "to stress a desire for the independence and autonomy of journalism" (Splichal & Sparks, 1994, p. 179). Splichal and Sparks remark that first year students of journalism are at "the precise point in their development when one would expect to find the "idealistic" conception of journalism as a genuine profession most strongly marked" and concede that "exposure to more realities of the occupational situation would lead to a moderation of these idealistic views" (p. 182).

Splichal and Sparks' book makes an important point for journalism education: The fact that a third of these students' home countries are classified as partly free in terms of press freedom did not lessen the journalism students' desire for independence and autonomy. This leads to the assumption that the norms and values taught in semi-democratic or autocratic nations are similar to those in democratic countries. Journalism education therefore, to all intents and purposes, can be perceived as an agent of change.

JOURNALISM—TRADE OR PROFESSION?

The key question in journalism education to this day is whether journalism should be regarded as a trade or a profession (Tumber & Prentoulis, 2005, p. 58). The main distinction between the two is the implicit standing afforded to journalists and the educational background expected from them. A trade is defined as the habitual practice of an occupation. Regarding journalism as a trade would require only vocational teaching needed "to perpetuate practice" (Gaunt, 1992, p. 1), and on-the-job training without prior study would suffice.

If journalism demands to be a profession, then it would need at least a defined educational pathway to underpin this claim. However, as indicated above, journalists come to their jobs from a great variety of educational backgrounds, and most of them receive in-house training by the media organization they join. This has led to the debate about journalism education having been "framed as scholars versus practitioners" (Cunningham, 2002), and has caused a mistrust between academy and industry that shows few signs of easing. According to Deuze (2006, p. 22), "journalism education [...] must negotiate rather essentialist self-perceptions of both industry and academy." Deuze (2006, p. 22) correctly points out that this dichotomy between theory and practice "adds a level of complexity to our understanding of journalism (and its education)."

This dichotomy is also perceived as one of the key questions in journalism education in tertiary institutions, with discussion centering on the weighting of subjects either towards the scholarly or the practical. Yet this debate masks another, wider issue. When looking at the theoretical subjects that are part of journalism studies, the entrenched ideological positions of journalism education become apparent. To most in the Western world, journalism—and hence journalism education—is inextricably linked to the political form of democracy. The importance of this link is one of the as yet rarely debated key questions of journalism education. So far journalism education has been seen as the exclusive domain of democracies, but geopolitical changes and transitions in media systems will force journalism scholars and educators alike to address this hallowed view.

PROFESSIONALIZATION

The debate about professionalization is hardest fought in the English-speaking world because it is here that the notion of professions exists. Tumber and Prentoulis remark that the founding fathers of sociology, Marx, Weber and Durkheim, remain "relatively vague about the role of professions" (Tumber & Prentoulis, 2005, p. 58). The reason for this can be found in the fact the German has the term *akademische Berufe* —meaning jobs that require university study—but not a concept of what the professions are. In other words, there are differing notions of what professionalization means with regard to journalism, and the literature reflects this diversity.

Jeremy Tunstall (in Tumber & Prentoulis, 2005, p. 71) described journalism as an indeterminate occupation and "journalist" as a "label which people engaged in a very diverse range of activities apply to themselves." This non-committal remark from the doyen of British media sociology should not surprise. The United Kingdom, unlike the United States, did not have university-based journalism schools until the late twentieth century. Traditionally journalism in the UK was viewed as a craft for which the requisite skills could be taught on the job (Esser, 2003). Unsurprisingly, the major push for professionalization came from the United States, the country with the most university-based journalism schools (Weaver et al., 2007, p. 33).

One of the most wide-ranging attempts to outline what professionalization might mean to journalism is made by Hallin and Mancini in their book, *Comparing Media Systems* (Hallin & Mancini, 2004, pp. 33–41), with the arguments partially based on Hallin's earlier chapter "Commercialism and Professionalism in the American News Media" (Hallin, 1997).

Hallin's view is strongly influenced by his awareness of journalism's lack of detachment from commercial and political factors, and also by the position that journalism is "very different from the classical professions—law, medicine, architecture, engineering—in that its practice is not based on any systematic body of knowledge" (Hallin, 1997, p. 245). Yet despite these drawbacks, Hallin (p. 258) sees the potential in professionalization—i.e. formal, college-based education—to act as a shield for journalists against commercial pressures and political instrumentalization.

These ideas are carried further in *Comparing Media Systems*, where Hallin and Mancini (2004) gauge journalistic professionalism against the following criteria: autonomy, distinct professional norms and public service orientation. Measured against these criteria, Hallin and Mancini find that journalists have never achieved a degree of autonomy comparable to that of doctors and lawyers. They work in large organizations where many influences affect the production process. Yet journalists "have often been successful in achieving relative autonomy within those organizations" (p. 35). With regard to professional norms, Hallin and Mancini see important variations in the way and degree to which journalistic norms have evolved. They also argue that norms can only be established in professions that enjoy relative autonomy and suggest that journalistic practice could be considered as being too often controlled by outside actors (p. 36). Though Hallin and Mancini (2004, pp. 36–37) caution against taking journalists' claims to serve the public at face value, they do not want to dismiss this claim as "mere ideology."

> The ethic of public service may be particularly important in the case of journalism, compared with other occupations claiming professional status: because journalism lacks esoteric knowledge, journalists' claim to autonomy and authority are dependent to a particularly great extent on their claim to serve the public interest.

Public service, so vital to Hallin and Mancini, differs markedly from the American professional norm of objectivity (see Schudson and Anderson, chapter 7, in this volume). To Glasser and Marken (2005, p. 270) "being a professional means abiding by certain norms and accepting the uniformity of practice that this implies." They acknowledge, though, that such norms prove elusive in a world with diverse and often clashing ideologies and that America's "disdain for any model of journalism that violates the precepts of private ownership and individual autonomy" (ibid, p. 274) forestalls a broader agreement.

Also, the Internet has challenged conventional notions of professionalism. On one hand, an increased "communication autonomy" of citizens has cast journalistic work as an "intervention" (Bardoel, 1996, p. 290) rather than a helpful conduit to information. On the other, the professional ideals of objectivity and disinterestedness have been seen as a barrier to contentious journalism (George, 2006, p. 179). This has led to the concern that professionalization can make journalism elitist and exclusive rather than inclusive (Nordenstreng, 1998, p. 126). While in the early years of the twenty-first century the professionalization debate is less energetic than in the past, the deliberations about journalism education curricula have never ceased.

THE QUESTION OF CURRICULA

Any judgment about what is to be considered "state of the art" in journalism education is dependent on what is considered "state of the art" journalism. State-of-the-art journalism, in many people's opinion, is rarely found, thus giving journalism educators and critics ample room to step into the breech. Yet state-of-the-art-journalism in the minds of university-based educators is often incongruent with the objectives of the media industry, perpetuating the fault line between industry and educators.

News journalism was mainly an Anglo-American invention, yet interestingly, the United Kingdom and the United States went very different ways with regard to journalism education. The pathways historically chosen by the two countries can in fact be seen as the boundaries within which the discussion about the state of the art in journalism education moves. There are "those who advocate a singular focus on vocational training and those who would have journalism students follow a much broader program of study" (Skinner, Gasher, & Compton, 2001, p. 341), making the curriculum "one of the most contentious and problematic issues" in journalism education (Morgan, 2000, p. 4).

While no one doubts the necessity of imparting skills—and these are defined as interviewing, reporting, researching, sourcing, writing and editing—the relevance of the inquiry into the nature and rituals of journalism has been questioned, in particular by future employers. Their argument is not against tertiary educated journalists, but against having them educated in journalism or communication studies, rather than holding a degree in another discipline. In many Western countries journalism is therefore taught as a postgraduate degree as an addition to prior studies, for example in history, politics, laws economics or business (Fröhlich & Holtz-Bacha, 2003a). A particular challenge, therefore, is the design of undergraduate courses which make up the whole of a journalist's education (Adam, 2001, p. 318), but graduate courses also pose their difficulties.

One of the most highly regarded postgraduate schools of journalism is at Columbia University in New York. An example of how little the discussion of teaching craft or knowledge has been resolved was demonstrated in the very public debate that surrounded the search for a new vision for that school. In April 2003 Columbia University's president, Lee Bollinger (2003), announced the new vision for the school:

> A great journalism school within a great university should always stand at a certain distance from the profession itself. ... Like journalism itself with respect to the general society, journalism schools must maintain an independent perspective on the profession and the world. Among other things, they are the profession's loyal critics. The habits of mind developed in the academic atmosphere of engaged reflection will inevitably suffuse the educational process, leading to an emphasis on some aspects of professional life and the neglect of others.

Though Bollinger also said that "a professional school must instill certain basic capacities in its students" (ibid), Columbia University's president firmly decided in favor of reflective learning for its graduate students. So have most scholars, irrespective of whether designing undergraduate or post graduate journalism courses (Adam, 2001; Reese & Cohen, 2001; Skinner et al., 2001; Weischenberg, 2001; Bacon, 1999; de Burgh, 2003; Deuze, 2006).

Suggestions as to what constitutes an ideal curriculum vary in their weighting of skills and knowledge. Skinner, Gasher and Compton's integrated curriculum "*refuse[s]* to accept journalism as a simple technique and, instead, emphasize[s] that journalism is a complex professional practice" (Skinner et al., 2001, p. 349, original emphasis). Their suggestions are broadly gathered under the following heading (pp. 349–355): "Journalism as a practice of meaning production", in which it is "fundamental that students understand the signifying power of language" and grasp that "journalism is not simply "a transparent stenography of the real'" (p. 351). "Journalism within its broader cultural context" teaches students "how to deal responsibly in their work with alternative values, belief systems, social systems, traditions and histories," citing Edward Said who "assigns journalists an 'intellectual responsibility' for the depictions they produce" (p. 352). "Journalism as a practice of knowledge production" insists that "journalists become more than uncritical recorders" (p. 354). The assumption underlying these curriculum suggestions is that journalists need to be equipped with knowledge, sensitivity and "virtue" (Rosen, 2002) that will ultimately lead to an improvement in journalism.

The discussion about the state-of-the-art in journalism education is largely, but by no means entirely, carried out in Western developed nations. UNESCO (2007) has published model curricula for developing countries and emerging democracies, which have to be seen as the most concerted effort towards wide-reaching state-of-the-art journalism education curricula to date.

NOT METHODOLOGY BUT IDEOLOGY

The question of methodology in journalism education often exhausts itself in discussions about how to weigh practical and theoretical subjects. Few probe the underlying assumption that journalism—and by extension journalism education—is an invaluable pillar in the workings of democracy. But this cannot be taken for granted.

A look at twentieth century history, for example in Europe, shows numerous instances in which journalism education was used to train journalists in the service of dictatorships (Barrera & Vaz, 2003, p. 23; Fröhlich & Holtz-Bacha, 2003b, p. 198; Wilke, 1995). In variations, this instrumentalization can be seen in many countries around the globe today, given that over half of the world's nations are deemed partly free or not free in terms of press freedom (Freedom House, 2006). The norms and values underpinning journalism education in those countries have so far received scant attention.

James Curran (2005, p. xii) put it down to the American dominance in journalism scholarship that the "American model of fact-based, neutral professionalism [... and] the libertarian, market-based model of organising journalism" directs the discussions, and that alternative models rarely stand a chance of being noticed though they evidently exist. Paolo Mancini (2000, 2003), in article after article, and finally in his book with Daniel Hallin, *Comparing Media Systems* (2004), patiently points to the very different expectation of journalists in Italy:

> What counts in journalists is above all the devotion, political and ideological loyalty, and the ability to create consensus regarding clearly defined ideas advocated by the newspaper or television channel for which they work ...One becomes a professional journalist on the recommendation of a party or politicians who have direct control over a newspaper or considerable influence on its management. (Mancini, 2003, p. 97)

This shows that even among democratic countries—and few countries can boast as many elections as Italy—the spectrum stretches from the ideology of objectivity to the ideology of loyalty. For the latter, however, it is crucial to distinguish between voluntary and involuntary loyalty.

In a review of United States journalism text books, Bonnie Brennen (2000, p. 106) came to the conclusion "that all of these books address the practice of journalism from an identical ideological perspective." The constant in all of these books is the steadfast belief that journalists act as members of the Fourth Estate by providing a necessary check on other branches of government (Brennen, 2000, p. 110).

Given this emphasis on the watchdog function, investigative reporting is the most revered form of journalism in US journalism educational texts, with little consideration of how this might serve the *status quo* (Ettema & Glasser, 1998; de Burgh, 2000). Brennen (2000, p. 111) concludes that the actual role journalists "play in the late industrial capitalist society is never questioned."

The ideology of loyalty—both of the voluntary and involuntary kind—can be found in the majority of the world's nations, sometimes in interesting mixtures, where the ideology of objectivity can be a cover for loyalty, as has happened in the United States in the wake of 9/11, or, as in the Chinese case, where the ideology of loyalty can accommodate investigative reporting.

Yu et al. (2000, p. 75) show the changes in China's journalism education as "characterized by gradual movement towards the market without seriously violating traditional norms of propaganda." Market consciousness, in Yu et al.'s words, has made journalism education a testing ground for authority tolerance. However, their survey also reveals that what happens in the classroom does not necessarily transfer to the newsroom, resulting in a "disconnection between class-room teaching and real world needs" (ibid). This "disconnection," which is replicated in many countries, especially those considered "transitional" in their media system, can also be interpreted in a positive way: At least ideas can be discussed in class, even if they may only partially be implemented in the newsroom, leading in China to what Zhou has called "Watchdogs on Party Leashes" (2000).

Africa, largely characterized by partisan media, is closer to the ideology of loyalty than objectivity. All the same, this permits the press to "play a significant role as interpreter of events, and in communicating information to the public" (Rønning, 2005, p. 175). Though journalism education is on the rise in Africa, its media institutional and organizational culture and practices need to be as much transformed as journalism education expanded to bring about real change (Boezak & Ranchod, cited in Steyn & de Beer, 2004, p. 396).

South America has probably the most eclectic mix of the ideologies of objectivity and loyalty, being on the one hand within the US ambit, yet on the other having inherited the partisan, clientilistic structures of journalism from Spain and Portugal. Waisbord (2000) and Alves (2005) see the rise of investigative journalism as proof that Latin American journalists are turning from lapdogs into watchdogs. A generational split, similar to the one outlined by Barrera and Vaz for Spain (2003, p. 44), can be observed here: The older group is characterized by a more loyal ideological outlook, tending towards an interpretative kind of journalism, while the younger group places greater emphasis on impartiality and tends towards a factual journalism more inclined to criticize the power structures.

While the two ideologies, as bases for journalism teaching, are reconcilable in transitional countries, the loyalty shown to government—be it a party, a group of clerics, or royal rulers—will always be regarded with suspicion by Western democracies. This forces the question of whether there is an inextricable link between journalism and democracy, and how journalism and journalism education should be viewed in non-democratic countries.

ACADEMY VERSUS INDUSTRY

Journalism education, as increasingly provided by tertiary institutions around the globe, is seen as a preparation for and a corrective to journalism. This dual role is its strength and its weakness. It puts tertiary journalism education at arm's length to the industry but also entrenches the mistrust between academe and the media's working world. As Skinner et al. (2001, p. 356) point out, "media owners and managers do not generally welcome critical perspectives on media practices, especially if they are contrary to commercial considerations." Similarly, Cunningham (2002) regrets that the intellectual capital of journalism schools is at odds with industry: "Unlike law and business schools, they are not think-tanks for their profession."

Deuze (2006, p. 27) has put this split down to the fact that many journalism programs work "with the philosophical notion of journalism as an act of individual freedom and responsibility, rather than a social system located in and managed by corporate media." This recognition goes a long way towards explaining why the academy and industry are at odds to each other, but it is unlikely to resolve the contest for influence on journalism. Besides, it is not a level playing field. While journalism schools may well try to modify journalism as practiced, their success is measured "by the number of internship opportunities it affords and the kind of jobs graduates are able to land" (Skinner et al., 2001, p. 356). In other words, journalism schools are dependent on the industry, whereas the industry is only partially convinced of the validity and usefulness of journalism degrees.

All the same, one of the strongest arguments in favor of journalism education is that it improves journalists' lot in the workplace. What has been said about Portugal applies to many countries: "Traditionally, journalism has not been a prestigious profession. Censorship and the non-existence of specific academic qualifications made it a low-qualified and low-paid profession" (Pinto & Sousa, 2003, p. 181). While in some countries the remuneration is adequate, as for example in the United States (Weaver et al., 2007, pp. 97–106), in many countries, especially in the developing world, the pay and conditions for journalistic work are poor (International Freedom of Expression eXchange, 2006; Rønning, 2005).

For Britain, which until recently preferred on-the-job training for journalists, Delano (2000) had to conclude, "No Sign of a Better Job: 100 years of British journalism". Delano wondered why journalists had not been "able or willing to exert the influence *inside* their professional world that they are able to wield *outside* it?" (p. 271, original emphasis). But then, Britain, in contrast to the United States, only recently embraced tertiary education for journalists and the weak professional position of British journalists can in fact be used as argument in favor of university education for journalists.

FUTURE AREAS OF RESEARCH

While the "graduatization of journalism" (Splichal & Sparks, 1994, p. 114) is progressing fast, this fact should be tempered by the knowledge that only about a quarter to a third of those studying journalism take up jobs in the industry. The research into journalism education therefore needs to extend to encompass the training received in places other than tertiary institutions, such as in newsrooms or in the media industry, to complete the picture of the forces that shape journalism.

Furthermore, researchers need to recognize global geo-political shifts. The media are no longer American (Tunstall, 2007). As a list of the 100 highest circulation newspapers shows, 75 of these are Asian (WAN, 2005). In audience numbers no other continent can rival Asia. It follows that Asia, and in particular China and India, produce the largest number of journalists. Yet Asian journalism education hardly features in the discussion so far.

For historical reasons, discourses on journalism and journalism education have been American dominated (Curran, 2005, p. vi). This has led to the perception that there is only one valid form of journalism underwriting journalism education. However, future writing on journalism education will have to accept a broader range of journalisms. Even when staying within the dominant language of the discourse, that of English, adding the British model of journalism considerably widens the visions of journalism. The British model, with its dual strands of public service and commercial media, offers elements that are far more adaptable globally than the American, purely commercial, model. The Qatari channel Al Jazeera, built largely on BBC norms and practices, is a case in point (Sakr, 2005, p. 149).

Research into journalism education cannot remain confined to democratic countries only. As Splichal and Sparks' book shows, journalism education can be seen as an agent of change, and the characteristics of journalism education in partly free and not free countries need to be delved into. Only by exploring more fully the global picture can scholarship into journalism education support efforts towards an informed and deliberative society.

REFERENCES

Adam, G. S. (2001). The education of journalists. *Journalism, 2*(3), 315–339.

Alves, R. C. (2005). From lapdog to watchdog: The role of the press in Latin America's democratization. In H. de Burgh (Ed.), *Making journalists* (pp. 181–202). London: Routledge.

Bacon, W. (1999). What is a journalist in a university? *Media International Australia, 90*, 79–90.

Bardoel, J. (1996). Beyond journalism. A profession between information society and civil society. *European Journal of Communication, 11*(3), 283–302.

Barrera, C., & Vaz, A. (2003). The Spanish case: A recent academic tradition. In R. Fröhlich & C. Holtz-Bacha (Eds.), *Journalism education in Europe and North America. An international comparison* (pp. 21–48). Cresskill, NJ: Hampton Press.

Bollinger, L. (2003). *President Bollinger's statement on the future of journalism education*. Retrieved March 26, 2007, from http://www.columbia.edu/cu/news/03/04/lcb_j_task_force.html

Brennen, B. (2000). What the hacks say. The ideological prism of US journalism texts. *Journalism, 1*(1), 106–113.

Chalaby, J. (1996). Journalism as an Anglo-American invention. *European Journal of Communication, 11*(3), 303–326.

Cunningham, B. (2002). The mission. Search for the perfect j-school. *Columbia Journalism Review, 2002*(6). Retrieved 2 April, 2007, from http://www.cjr.org/issues/2002/6/school-cunningham.asp

Curran, J. (2005). Foreword. In H. de Burgh (Ed.), *Making journalists* (pp. xi–xv). London: Routledge.
de Burgh, H. (Ed.). (2000). *Investigative journalism*. London: Routledge.
de Burgh, H. (2003). Skills are not enough. The case for journalism as an academic discipline. *Journalism, 4*(1), 95–112.
de Burgh, H. (Ed.). (2005a). *Making journalists*. London: Routledge.
de Burgh, H. (2005b). Introduction: Journalism and the new cultural paradigm. In H. de Burgh (Ed.), *Making journalists* (pp. 1–21). London: Routledge.
Delano, A. (2000). No sign of a better job: 100 years of British journalism. *Journalism Studies, 1*(2), 261–272.
Deuze, M. (2005). What is journalism? Professional identity and ideology of journalists reconsidered. *Journalism, 6*(4), 442–464.
Deuze, M. (2006). Global journalism education. A conceptual approach. *Journalism Studies, 7*(1), 19–34.
Ettema, J., & Glasser, T. (1998). *Custodians of conscience: Investigative journalism and public virtue*. New York: Columbia University Press.
Esser, F. (2003). Journalism training in Great Britain: A system rich in tradition but currently in transition. In R. Fröhlich & C. Holtz-Bacha (Eds.), *Journalism education in Europe and North America. An international comparison* (pp. 209–236). Cresskill, NJ: Hampton Press.
Freedom House (2006). *Table of global press freedom rankings*. Retrieved September 5, 2006, from http://www.freedomhouse.org/uploads/PFS/ PFSGlobalTables2006.pdf
Fröhlich, R., & Holtz-Bacha, C. (Eds.). (2003a). *Journalism education in Europe and North America. An international comparison*. Cresskill, NJ: Hampton Press.
Fröhlich, R. & Holtz-Bacha, C. (2003b). Journalism education in Germany. In R. Fröhlich & C. Holtz-Bacha (Eds.), *Journalism education in Europe and North America. An international comparison* (pp. 187–205). Cresskill, NJ: Hampton Press.
Fröhlich, R., & Holtz-Bacha, C. (2003c). Summary: Challenges for today's journalism education. In R. Fröhlich & C. Holtz-Bacha (Eds.), *Journalism education in Europe and North America. An international comparison* (pp. 307–323). Cresskill, NJ: Hampton Press.
Gaunt, P. (1992). *Making the newsmakers. International handbook on journalism training*. Westport, CT: Greenwood Press.
George, C. (2006). *Contentious journalism and the Internet. Towards democratic discourse in Malaysia and Singapore*. Singapore: Singapore University Press in association with University of Washington Press.
George, C. (2007). Consolidating authoritarian rule: Calibrated coercion in Singapore. *The Pacific Review, 20*(2), 127–145.
Glasser, T., & Marken, L. (2005). Can we make journalists better? In H. de Burgh (Ed.), *Making journalists* (pp. 264–276). London: Routledge.
Hallin, D. (1997). Commercialism and professionalism in the American news media. In J. Curran & M. Gurevitch (Eds.), *Mass media and society* (pp. 243–262). London: Arnold.
Hallin, D., & Mancini, P. (2004). *Comparing media systems—Three models of media and politics*. Cambridge, UK: Cambridge University Press.
International Freedom of Expression eXchange. (2006). Majority of Indonesian Journalists vastly underpaid: Aliansi Jurnalis Independen [AJI] survey. *IFEX Communique 15*(35). Retrieved April 2, 2007, from http://www.ifex.org/en/content/view/full/76840/
Johansen, P., Weaver, D., & Dornan, C. (2001). Journalism education in the United States and Canada: Not merely clones. *Journalism Studies, 2*(4), 469–483.
Josephi, B. (2001). Entering the newsroom: What rite of passage? The induction of cadets at the *Frankfurter Allgemeine Zeitung* in comparison with young journalists' training at English language papers in Hong Kong, Singapore and Australia. *Communications: The European Journal of Communication Research 26*(2), 181–195.
Mancini, P. (2000). Political complexity and alternative models of journalism. The Italian case. In J. Curran & M.-J. Park (Eds.), *De-Westernizing media studies* (pp. 265–278). London: Routledge.

Mancini, P. (2003). Between literary roots and partisanship: Journalism education in Italy. In R. Fröhlich & C. Holtz-Bacha (Eds.), *Journalism education in Europe and North America. An international comparison* (pp. 93–104). Cresskill, NJ: Hampton Press.

Medsger, B. (2005). The evolution of journalism education in the United States. In H. de Burgh (Ed.), *Making journalists* (pp. 205–226). London: Routledge.

Morgan, F. (2000). Recipes for success: Curriculum for professional media education. *AsiaPacific Media-Educator 8*, 4–21.

Nordenstreng, K. (1998). Professional ethics: Between fortress journalism and cosmopolitan democracy. In K. Brants, J. Hermes, & L. van Zoonen (Eds.), *The media in question* (pp. 124–134). London: Sage.

Pinto, M., & Sousa, H. (2003). Journalism education at universities and journalism schools in Portugal. In R. Fröhlich & C. Holtz-Bacha (Eds.), *Journalism education in Europe and North America. An international comparison* (pp. 169–186). Cresskill, NJ: Hampton Press.

Reese, S., & Cohen, J. (2001). Educating for journalism: The professionalism of scholarship. *Journalism Studies, 1*(2), 213–227.

Rogers, E. (1994). *A history of communication study: A biographical approach.* New York: The Free Press.

Rønning, H. (2005). African journalism and the struggle for democratic media. In H. de Burgh (Ed.), *Making journalists* (pp. 157–180). London: Routledge.

Rosen, J. (2002, September 6). Taking Bollinger's course on the American press. *Chronicle of Higher Education, 42*(2), B10.

Sakr, N. (2005). The changing dynamics of Arab journalism. In H. de Burgh (Ed.), *Making journalists* (pp. 142–156). London: Routledge.

Skinner, D., Gasher, M., & Compton, J. (2001). Putting theory into practice. A critical approach to journalism studies. *Journalism, 2*(3), 314–360.

Splichal, S., & Sparks, C. (1994). *Journalists for the 21st Century.* Norwood, NJ: Ablex.

Steyn, E., & de Beer, A. (2004). The level of journalism skills in southern African media: A reason for concern within a developing democracy? *Journalism Studies, 5*(3), 387–397.

Tumber, H, & Prentoulis, M. (2005). Journalism and the making of a profession. In H. de Burgh (Ed.), *Making journalists* (pp. 58–74). London: Routledge.

Tunstall, J. (2007). *The media were American: U.S. mass media in decline.* Oxford, UK: Oxford University Press.

UNESCO (2007). *Model curricula for journalism education for developing countries & emerging democracies.* Paris: UNESCO.

Waisbord, S. (2000). *Watchdog journalism in South America. News, accountability, and democracy.* New York: Columbia University Press.

Weaver, D. (1998). *The global journalist.* Creskill, NJ: Hampton Press.

Weaver, D. (2003). Journalism education in the United States. In R. Fröhlich & C. Holtz-Bacha (Eds.), *Journalism education in Europe and North America. An international comparison* (pp. 49–64). Cresskill, NJ: Hampton Press.

Weaver, D., Beam, R., Brownlee, B., Voakes, P., & Wilhoit, G. C. (2007). *The American journalist in the 21st Century. U.S. newspeople at the dawn of a new millenium.* Mahwah, NJ: Erlbaum.

Weischenberg, S. (2001). Das Ende einer Ära? Aktuelle Beobachtungen zum Studium des künftigen Journalismus [End of an era? Topical observations about studies of future journalism]. In H. Kleinsteuber (Ed.), *Aktuelle Medientrends in den USA* (pp. 61–82). Opladen: Westdeutscher Verlag.

Weischenberg, S., Malik, M., & Scholl, A. (2006). Journalismus in Deutschland 2005 [Journalism in Germany 2005]. *Media Perspektiven, 7/ 2006*, 346–361.

Wilke, J. (1995). Journalistenausbildung im Dritten Reich: die Reichspresseschule [Journalism education during the Third Reich: The Reich press school]. In B. Schneider, K. Reumann, & P. Schiwy (Eds.). *Publizistik. Beiträge zur Medienentwicklung. Festschrift für Walter J. Schütz* (pp. 387–408). Konstanz: Universitätsverlag Konstanz.

World Association of Newspapers [WAN]. (2005). World's 100 largest newspapers. Retrieved April 2, 2007, from http://www.wan-press.org/rubrique75.html

Yu, X., Chu, L., & Guo, Z. (2000). Reform and challenge. An analysis of China's journalism education under social transition. *Gazette, 64*(1), 63–77.

Zhou, Y. (2000). Watchdogs on party leashes? Contexts and implications of investigative journalism in post-Deng China. *Journalism Studies, 1*(4), 577–597.

II

NEWS PRODUCTION

5
News Organizations and Routines

Lee B. Becker and Tudor Vlad

INTRODUCTION

Journalists and the organizations for which they work produce news. In other words, news is both an individual product and an organizational product. Even freelance journalists—journalists not employed by a media organization—were dependent until recently on media organizations for the distribution of their messages. The complex technologies that have been used to distributed media messages have required resources that few individuals controlled.

The Internet has changed much about the way news is produced and distributed. Journalists now can do their work on their own and distribute their messages on their own. While, at present, most journalists continue to work for organizations that distribute news—news organizations—it is not clear how long that will continue to be the case.

The literature on news organizations and news construction, for the most part, is grounded in the past, when the journalist was weak and the news organization was powerful. That literature is changing, however, reflecting the shifts in the relationship of the news worker to news organizations.

This chapter begins with a brief overview about how news organizations have been conceptualized and studied. It next moves to a discussion of news routines—the repeated activities of journalists who go about their work. The observation that journalists and media organizations follow identifiable routines in producing the news has had significant impact on the study of news work. The identification of these routines has contributed to a major theoretical argument in the literature, namely that news should be viewed as constructed social reality rather than a mirror image of events that have taken place.

A careful review of the initial research on news routines as well as subsequent research in this tradition, however, suggests that the concept of news routines has a significant limitation. Researchers have struggled to identify elements of the routines that vary across time, across settings, among media organizations and among journalists.

In this chapter, we have identified some routines that do vary and have provided a conceptual framework for understanding them. Drawing on the historical work on routines and our own, more recent research, we have suggested a way to view and understand the basic mandates of news work and to see how those mandates affect routines. We believe the review indicates that some aspects of routines do vary across time, across setting, among media organizations and workers.

The chapter ends with a discussion of the questions raised by this literature for future study of news construction, particularly in an environment where news work—and news routines—will not always take place in news organizations.

NEWS ORGANIZATIONS

Research on news construction has come from three perspectives, according to Schudson (2002). The political economy perspective links news construction to the structure of the state and the economy. Herman and Chomsky (1988), for example, argued that the media create news that supports state interests rather than those of the individual. A second approach draws mainly on sociology and attempts to understand news production from the perspective of organizational and occupational theory. Epstein's (1974) classic study of how television network structure influenced news is an example. The bulk of the work on news construction has come from this perspective. A third approach focuses on broad cultural constraints on news work. Chalaby's (1996) study of the development of French and American journalism, which notes the influence of the French literary tradition on its journalism, is an example. As Schudson (2002) notes, the three perspectives are not wholly distinct, and some of the key studies in the organizational tradition have strong cultural and political references as well.

Tunstall (1971) made a distinction between *news organizations*, defined as editorial departments employing primarily journalists, and *media organizations*, which are larger entities that contain more than one news organization plus other types of communication units, such as magazines and publishing houses. In Tunstall's view, these two categories of organization differ in terms of goals and bureaucracy. Media organizations will be more commercially oriented, while news organizations will have fewer routines.

Large news organizations have all of the characteristics of bureaucracies, Sigal (1973) argued. They have a division of labor along functional and geographic lines. Journalists can be differentiated in terms of whether they are reporters or editors. Reporters are differentiated between those who do general assignment and those with specialized topic areas. News organizations are organized geographically as well.

Epstein (1974), in a study of the three major television networks, focused on the way they structured their news gathering and found that there were only slight differences in the processes that those organizations employed to produce national newscasts. Epstein argued that the mirror metaphor was not an accurate model for how television news programs work. If television news was analogous to a mirror, routines of selection and production of news would be of no relevance. The metaphor suggested that all the events of significance would be reflected by television news. Network news, Epstein argued, was a limited and highly prioritizing news-gathering operation. During the period of observation, for instance, Epstein found that 90 percent of the NBC national news was produced by ten crews in five major cities because that was where they had news crews.

Warner (1969), in an earlier study of television news, found similarities between the organization structure there and in a newspaper. He concluded that the executive producer's role, for example, was similar to the role of the editor of a newspaper and that the main criteria identified by the executive producers for news selection and distribution were space, significance and political balance, much as is the case in a newspaper. Halloran, Elliot, and Murdock (1970) in their study of the coverage by British television services and national newspapers of anti-Vietnam war demonstration, found an important similarity among the media. The media all focused on the issue of violence. The authors claimed that it was less a deliberate attempt to distort the event, but the result of what those news organizations defined as newsworthy. Observed differences among the media in terms of technologies, political orientation, and newsgathering routines did not matter much in the end.

In their overview of the research on the nature of news organizations, Shoemaker and Reese (1996) defined media organizations as social, formal, usually economic entities that employ media workers to produce media content. In most of the cases, the main goal of these organizations is to generate profit, especially by targeting audiences that are attractive to advertisers. The economic pressures influence the journalistic decisions. According to the authors, other factors that affect the content and the routines utilized to generate it are the size of the media organization, the membership to a network or media group, and the ownership.

THE CONCEPT OF NEWS ROUTINES

Shoemaker and Reese (1996) defined news routines as "Those patterned, routinized, repeated practices and forms that media workers use to do their jobs" (p. 105). These routines, Shoemaker and Reese contended, are created in response to the limited resources of the news organization and the vast amount of raw material that can be made into news. More specifically, the routines are dictated by technology, deadlines, space, and norms (Reese, 2001). "The job of these routines is to deliver, within time and space limitations, the most acceptable product to the consumer in the most efficient manner," Shoemaker and Reese (1996, pp.108–109) wrote.

Tuchman (1972), drawing from the writings in the sociology of work, seems to have been the first to discuss routines in the context of journalism. She argued that a key part of news creation is a reliance on routine procedures for "processing information called news, a depletable product made every day (p. 662)." Tuchman (1973) elaborated on this theme by arguing that organizations routinize tasks because it "facilitates the control of work (p. 110)." Workers always have too much work to do, she wrote, so they "try to control the flow of work and the amount of work to be done" (p. 110).

In Tuchman's view, journalists exemplify workers with a need to control their work because journalists are "called upon to give accounts of a wide variety of disasters—unexpected events—on a routine basis" (p. 111). News work, she argued, "thrives upon processing unexpected events, events that burst to the surface in some disruptive, exceptional (and hence newsworthy) manner" (p. 111).

Tuchman (1973) compared the classification of news based on a scheme commonly used by news workers with a scheme she created based on the sociology of work. News workers classify news as "hard," "soft," "spot," "developing," and "continuing." Tuchman argued that news should be classified based on how it happens and on the requirements for the organization. This led her to classify news based on whether it was "scheduled" or "unscheduled," whether its dissemination was urgent or not, how it was affected by the technology of news work, and whether the journalists could make decisions in advance about future coverage of the event or not.

Tuchman argued that her classification of news better explained how news organizations actually work than did the category scheme of the journalists. Specifically, she said, her scheme explained how journalists and journalistic organizations control their work to allow them to process unexpected events. The journalistic category scheme, she argued, did not accomplish that goal.

This initial discussion of routines by Tuchman was important for at least two reasons. First, it suggested that news work could be understood from the broader perspective of the sociology of work generally. Second, it suggested "it might be more valuable to think of news not as distorting, but rather as reconstituting the everyday world" (p. 129). Journalists construct and reconstruct social reality, she argued. Researchers who wanted to understand news should focus on that construction, rather than on whether the end product was biased in some way.

Tuchman's initial interest in news work grew out of a concern with the use of newspaper stories by sociologists to measure community variables. In her 1972 article in the *American Journal of Sociology*, she argued explicitly that these stories should not be treated as a reflection of reality, but rather that news work constructs its own reality. In a debate published in the *American Sociological Review*, Tuchman (1976) criticized Danzger (1975), who used newspaper articles to index community conflict. She argued that news routines, such as relying on centralized sources, systematically support those with political and economic power. Power, in fact, often includes the ability to generate news.

This argument about news as the product of news workers and news organizations, rather than a reflection of some "reality," is central to three articles published during this same period by Molotch and Lester (1973, 1974, 1975). The media are "not an objective reporter of events but an active player in the constitution of events," the team argued in the first of these papers (Molotch & Lester, 1973, p. 258). The goals of the media lead them to select some events over others for inclusion in the news. News, in fact, needs to be viewed as "purposive behavior," they argued (Molotch & Lester, 1974), that is, the product of activities of the journalists and their employers that suite the needs of both. The journalists work with the raw materials largely provided to them by promoters of events to "transform a perceived set of promoted occurrences into public events through publication or broadcast" (p. 104).

Molotch and Lester (1975) differentiate this perspective from what they consider to be the normal view on the part of sociologists and others concerned with news at the time. They argued that most observers make an "assumption of an objectively significant set of happenings which can be known, known to be important, and hence reported by competent, unrestrained news professionals" (p. 235). When news deviates from this "objective" view of the happening, they argued, the usual explanation is that the reporters were incompetent, management interfered, or outsiders corrupted the process through payoffs. The result is "bias." But Molotch and Lester (1975) said they made no assumption that there is an "objective reality," but they rather saw news as the product of the processes that are used to create news.

For Molotch and Lester (1974), news "routines" are important for an understanding of that production of occurrences into news. The media need to be understood as formal organizations that use "routines for getting work done in newsrooms" (p. 105). Molotch and Lester (1975), in a study of the Santa Barbara, California, oil spill of 1969, identified some of those routines, which they say, "may become so ingrained that they become reified as 'professional norms' of 'good journalism'" (p. 255). These include the routines of covering occurrences close to when they happened and then decreasing attention over time, of concentrating news personnel in large cities, and of covering events close at hand less than those more distant.

This formative work of Tuchman, Molotch, and Lester was important for at least three reasons. First, it explained that routine behaviors help journalists create news. Second, it focused on the role of power in determining news. Third, it distinguished between the constructed reality of news and what news workers refer to as "reality."

These early writers about routines did not see these fundamental characteristics of work as variable among media organizations or media workers or across time. Rather, these "routines" were seen as defining characteristics of news work.

Eliasoph (1988) challenged this assumption that routines were universal in a study of what she termed an "oppositional radio station." What she found, however, was that the routines, in fact, did not vary. The reporters at the radio station she observed, KPFA-FM in Berkeley, California, followed the same routines as the reporters at the media studied by others. Despite this reliance on the same techniques, however, the journalists at the oppositional radio station did not produce the same type of news as the reporters at the other media. The routines were used for the same reason as at the other media—to make the work of the journalists manageable—but the relationship of the station to its audience, the social and political position of the journalists and those who controlled the newsroom shaped the characteristics of the news product.

Hansen, Ward, Conners, and Neuzil (1994) examined whether the creation of electronic news libraries for the storage and retrieval of previously printed stories influenced the news routines of newspapers. For the most part, they concluded, the routines had not changed. In a subsequent study in the same vein, Hansen, Neuzil, and Ward (1998) concluded that the creation of teams within newspaper newsrooms to focus on news topics also had not affected markedly the routines of news creation.

More recent research using the concept of news routines seems largely to have assumed the lack of variability in the concept. Cook (1998), in his analysis of the role of news media in politics, argues that news routines produce predictable news across time and similar news across news outlets. Oliver and Maney (2000), in work reminiscent of that of Danzger (1975), compared newspaper coverage of community demonstrations with police records of those demonstrations. They found discrepancies between the coverage and the police records that could be explained by what they called newspaper routines, namely a preference for stories about local leaders and those with conflict resulting for the presence of counterdemonstrators. Wolfsfeld, Avraham, and Aburaiya (2000) found evidence that cultural and political assumptions in Israeli society dictate largely fixed routines of news coverage that result in a negative presentation of its Arab citizens.

Consistent with the Wolfsfeld et al. study (2000), Bennett (1996), and Ryfe (2006b) argued that the media follow routines that are the outcome of organizational and professional rules. The use of the word "rules" is significant, for it indicates something that is not variable. For Bennett, these rules explain the consistency of news content across time and circumstances. Writing in the same vein, Sparrow (2006) did acknowledge that routines and practices of the media should vary in response to uncertainty in the environment of the media organization. The nature of the variation, however, is not specified.

The lack of variability in news routines renders the concept of limited value in news construction research. To understand the origins and the consequences of the routines, the researcher must be able to identify variability in the routines themselves. In other words, the researcher needs to find situations were the routines are not followed or in some other way are altered in order to understand why the routines are not followed or differ and to understand the consequences of the routines.

The importance of this early work on routines, in sum, rests largely on its contribution to a view of news as a construction of reality, rather than a mirror of that reality. Schudson (2002, 2005), in reviews of the literature on news routines and on news construction, has both acknowledged that contribution and expressed some concern about it. In his view, it seems that the assumption that real world events are not particularly important in determining what is news was "overstated" by scholars (Schudson, 2005, p. 181). The event that stimulates the creation of news has more impact than many of the early writers on news construction believed, in his view. "The reality-constructing practices of the powerful will fail (in the long run) if they run roughshod over the world "out there,'" Schudson wrote (2005, p. 181). As one example, Schudson pointed to the findings of Livingston and Bennett (2003). These researchers reported that the amount of news based on spontaneous activities increased dramatically on at least one cable news channel, CNN, in the 1994 to 2001 period as a result of the technological change in the industry.

THE CONCEPT OF BEATS

Integrated into the discussion of news routines is the concept of news beats. News organizations generally organize themselves so as to be able to observe events and gather the raw materials that are used to produce news.

The origins of the term "beat" as used to describe the organizational structure of news gathering are not known. One possibility is that the term is borrowed from police work, where police officers are assigned geographical areas or beats that they cover in a routine way. In fact, one dictionary definition of the word "beat" is "a habitual path or round of duty: as a policeman's beat" (*Webster's New World Dictionary*, 1964).

The literature examining the construction of news and news routines has given extensive attention to beats. For Tuchman (1978), news organizations use a "news net" as a means of acquiring the raw materials that become news. The net, she argues, was originally designed for "catching appropriate stories available at centralized locations" (p. 25). It assumes that the audiences of news are interested in occurrences at these locations, that they are concerned with the activities of specific organizations, and that they are interested in specific topics.

For these reasons, Tuchman argues, the news net is "flung through space, focuses upon specific organizations, and highlights topics" (p. 25). Of these three methods of dispersing reporters, geographic territoriality is most important. A beat, for Tuchman, is a method of dispersing reporters to organizations associated with the generation of news and holding centralized information.

Fishman (1980), in his now-classic observational study of news gathering, noted that the beat system of news coverage was so widespread when he did his study in the late 1970s that not using beats was a distinctive feature of being an experimental, alternative, or underground newspaper. In Fishman's view, the beat is a journalist's concept, grounded in the actual working world of reporters. Beats have a history in the news organization that outlives the histories of the individuals who work the beats. Superiors assign reporters to their beats, and, while the reporter is responsible for, and has jurisdiction over, covering the beat, the reporter does not own that beat. For Fishman, the beat is a domain of activities occurring outside the newsroom consisting of something more than random assortments of activities. Finally, Fishman argued, the beat is a social setting to which the reporter belongs. The reporter becomes part of the network of social relations which is the beat. In Fishman's view, beats have both a topical and territorial character. Journalists talk about their beats as places to go and people to see and as a series of topics one is responsible for covering.

For Gans (1979), the key process in news creation is story suggestion. Reporters have the responsibility for thinking up story ideas. To this end, they are required to "keep up with what is going on in the beats they patrol or in the areas of the country assigned to their bureaus, and they are evaluated in part by their ability to suggest suitable stories" (p. 87). Other staff members, including top editors and producers, are also expected to come up with story ideas, and nonjournalists are encouraged to do so as well, Gans noted.

Gans' conceptualization is informative, for it focuses on the generation of the idea that lies behind the story and links this generation of ideas to beats. In this view, raw material has the potential to become news only if it is recognized as having that potential by someone in the news construction business. Bantz, McCorkle, and Baade (1980) called this process of story idea generation "story ideation," a concept discussed in more detail below.

Beats and Television

For the most part, the literature on beats assumed their existence in news organizations. Yet there was evidence in early studies of news construction of variability regarding beats and beat structure. Specially, that early research showed that television newsrooms did not make use of beat structure as frequently as newspapers or that the beats television newsrooms used were generally not as well developed as those used by newspapers. Drew (1972), in his study of decision-making in three local television newsrooms in a medium sized midwestern market, found that some beats, specifically to cover city hall, have sometimes been used in television. Based on a study of newsgathering and production procedures at three major US television national networks, Epstein (1974), however, found that fixed beats, except for those in Washington, particularly at the White House, did "not satisfy the network's basic problem of creating 'national news'" (p. 136). As a result, correspondents were moved from one topic to another depending on availability and logistical criteria after the assignment editor decided that the specific event was worth covering.

Altheide (1976), in his classic study of a local television newsroom, found no evidence of a beat structure. The primary concern of the reporters and editors was having enough material to fill the newscasts, and they relied on wire services, newspapers, press releases, and telephone calls to get their story ideas. Thus, newspapers and wire service reporters, who largely work beats, indirectly determine what most of the newsworthy events are for television journalists, Fishman said.

McManus (1990), in a study of three television news operations, found that most reporters at the three stations were assigned to specific "areas to search for news," which he called news beats. The demands of filing daily stories assigned by the news managers, however, resulted in no more than a few minutes a day of looking for newsworthy events. At one station, reporters were supposed to have one day a week to catch up on their beats, but that day was routinely reclaimed by the assignment editor for a pressing story. The size of the station is important in the process of gathering information. A larger station will have more highly active discovery. McManus argued, however, that all television stations consume much more air time on stories discovered relatively passively than on stories resulting from active discovery.

The Concept of Story Ideation

At least part of the answer to the question of why beats are created seems to lie with the concept of story ideation. For Gans (1979), as noted, the key process in news creation is story suggestion. Bantz, McCorkle, and Baade (1980) use the term "story ideation" to describe this process of story idea generation. Something became news, they observed in the television newsroom they studied, as a result of a process that began with the story idea. Individual news workers assessed the information flowing into the newsroom from various sources, such as press releases, general mail, newspapers, magazines, reporter tips, police-fire-FBI radios, and phone calls to determine what could be a story. These story ideas were then discussed in the daily story "budget" meeting, where decisions were made on which of the raw material would become news.

Television organizations, it seems, have found other techniques to generate story ideas. Unlike newspapers, television news operations cannot afford to produce more stories than they will use because of the high production costs and limited number of staff members. As a result, assignment editors disperse their staffs so as to maximize the probability of generating a story.

Some of the techniques used in television news as an alternative to traditional beats are similar to beat structures in that reporters are expected to generate ideas on a specific topic, and some are not. What all these techniques have in common, however, is that they produce the ideas that satisfy the needs of the media organization. While most of the existent literature on news construction sees beats as ways of structuring news gathering, they should rather be seen as one way of generating story ideas.

The Concept of News Philosophy

If story ideation is a defining characteristic of news, meaning that all news organizations need story ideas, and if there are multiple ways for media organizations to generate story ideas, what is required is some understanding of why a particular media organization would employ one technique for story ideation over another. In the terminology of Hage (1972), what is needed is an action premise, specifying when one mechanism for story ideation will be used rather than another.

Recent research on how media organizations respond to market pressures offers at least one suggestion. Media organizations in commercial systems create an identity for their product, or what marketers call a brand. The identity, or brand, specifies characteristics of the news product. This forces media managers to develop what they calls a news philosophy, or a view about the nature of the news product the organization will offer. That news philosophy can be expected to shape the techniques for story ideation used by the media organization.

Branding in media industries, and particularly among television stations, only recently has received attention by media scholars. Atwater (1984) found that television news operations do differentiate their product to compete more successfully in a competitive market. Specifically, stations used more or less soft news stories as a way of distinguishing their offering from that of other stations. Such product differentiation is often achieved through branding, or the development and maintenance of sets of product attributes and values appealing to customers.

What media organizations often brand, either explicitly or implicitly, is "news philosophy" (Connolly, 2002). This is the organization's general approach to the news product (Chalaby, 2000). Organizations make decisions to reflect some aspects of their communities and reject others, to provide a mix of news that is more serious or more entertaining, to downplay or play up news of conflict and news about crime. These decisions are market driven, for they are used to differentiate competitive news products. In radio and television, where competition, at least in the United States, is great, organizations opt for different "news philosophies" and then promote those differences, i.e., brand their products accordingly.

Additional Functions of Beats

This discussion of the concepts of news philosophy and story ideation provides the needed action premise to explain the use of beats in some media organizations and not in others. As market competition increases, media organizations would be expected to be more differentiated in terms of news philosophy, and, consequently, more differentiated in terms of use of story ideation techniques.

While the literature on news construction focuses on the utility of beats as a means of gathering news, research also shows that beats may serve additional functions for newsrooms. Becker, Lowrey, Claussen, and Anderson (2000), in fact, have argued that are at least three different ways in which beats can be viewed. In one view—the view of the literature on news construction reviewed—beats exist in news organizations because they are efficient—if not essential—tools for gathering news. From the perspective of the sociology of organizations literature, Becker and his colleagues argued, beats are a form of job differentiation. That is, they are a way of putting people into positions in which they can most efficiently operate for the betterment of the overall organization. In this view, newsrooms would be expected to create beats as they increased in size for the simple reason that job differentiation allows an organization to function more efficiently. Finally, beats can be viewed as part of the managerial reward structure. Beats may be ranked hierarchically and, as a result, used to reward those who have performed well and punish or discipline those who have not.

These three definitions of a beat are not in conflict. Beats can serve as the means of generating story ideas as gathering news. They also can reflect job differentiation and be used as a reward structure. Becker and his colleagues (2000) found little evidence in their newspaper newsroom study that beats are used for this third function. Beat structure did vary by size of organization however, though it retained its basic fabric as it grew in complexity, consistent with the view that beats are tools of news construction.

Clearly, then, beats can have consequences beyond those intended by their creators. For example, some have commented on the consequences of the relationships that develop in beats. For Breed (1955), the importance of beats is the power it gives to reporters. He concluded that beat reporters gained the "editor" function. Eliasoph (1988) says that reporting on beats does not necessarily have to be uncritical, depending on the power relations between reporter and source. Soloski (1989) noted that beat reporters are drawn into a "symbiotic relationship" of mutual obligations with their sources. This both facilitates and complicates their work. Donohue, Olien, and Tichenor (1989) argued that writers who regularly covered a beat share a system of meaning, so that stories could be produced efficiently with generally similar results.

ILLUSTRATIVE STUDY

A study we conducted provides tentative support for the posited relationship between news philosophy, story ideation, and adoption of story ideation strategies (Becker et al., 2001). Researchers spent two days observing the newsrooms in two television stations and a newspaper within a medium-sized metropolitan community in the southeastern United States. The television stations were chosen because they were roughly comparable in newsroom size and number of newscasts produced per week, with similar network-related resources. But there was reason to expect differences in approaches to the final news product. The newspaper represented the single daily newspaper for the metropolitan area. The researchers also conducted informal interviews with newsroom managers and journalists. The newscasts and the newspapers created during the time of observation were viewed/read and analyzed.

Some simple answers to the questions posed about the importance of beats emerge from this study. First, though the television newsrooms did not have as obvious of a specialization structure as the newspaper, they did have specialists. For example, specialists covered weather, sports, consumer news, and health. These specialists were responsible for generating story ideas and stories or other content in their special areas. The observations indicate that the television newsrooms did not have the elaborate beat structure of the newspaper newsroom simply because the television newsrooms did not need such an elaborate structure. The television newsrooms need fewer stories than the newspapers, and they could generate the story ideas and the stories from scanners, from the casual observation of their general assignment reporters, from web sites, from press releases, and from listings of community activities that were readily available to them. The study showed that when news organizations decided they needed specialized kinds of content on a regular basis, they created a system to generate it. This was done by designating an individual whose job it was to create this type of content. At one of the television stations studied, these specialists were called "franchise" reporters. Their job was to generate story ideas and then report and produce stories about such topics as consumer news and health issues. Though the sports reporter or even the weather person was not called a "franchise" reporter, she or he functioned in the same way. The station decided it needed a steady diet of sports and weather, and it also decided the best way to get that was to have a specialist whose job it was to create it.

At the newspaper studied, the editors had decided they needed a steady stream of copy from a geographic area outside the metropolitan area, so they created a beat for that area. The creation of a geographic beat at the paper served a very specific need for the newspaper studied. The paper wanted copy from that region, because it wanted to increase its circulation in the region. In addition, the newspaper wanted to satisfy the internal desire to be regional in focus. The reporter assigned to the beat was expected to regularly suggest story ideas, and to regularly send in stories.

The two television stations studied differed in terms of how they generated story ideas. The smaller of the stations relied more on its reporters and producers, while the larger of the two stations relied more on the talents, expertise, and organizational skills of the key assignment person. The differences seem to reflect differences in news philosophy at the two stations. Clearly a major difference between the newspaper and the television stations was reflected in news philosophy. Conversations in the newspaper newsroom reflected an interest in comprehensiveness, completeness of news coverage, and breadth of topics covered. In the television newsrooms, the focus was much narrower. In both cases, the news directors recognized the limited scope of what they could do in a newscast. Fundamentally, they were interested in a newscast that was interesting to the audience, rather than a newscast that reflected even the major features of the activities of the community. The data are rather clear in differentiating story ideation and creation in the daily newspaper from story ideation and creation at the television stations. They provide less clarity regarding the differences between the television stations. Those differences were small, but they seemed to be significant, in part because they seemed to reflect differences in news philosophy.

The findings of these case studies are consistent with the basic premises generated from the news construction literature in this chapter. Each of the news organizations observed began each news day with a need for raw materials, namely, the ideas to be used to generate news stories. The organizations had limited resources available for the acquisition of these materials, and they developed routines or procedures to guarantee their availability. For the newspaper, these involved beats. For the television stations, they involved less elaborate specialization, but specialization nonetheless. The television stations assigned individuals to produce "packages" on a routine basis, and they assigned individuals within the organization the specific task of creating, assembling and organizing story ideas. Anticipated consumer demand helped shape the characteristics of the news product. Each of the media organizations seemed to have a news philosophy, or a sense of its mission that was shaped by what was successful in the market. They sought to "brand" their products accordingly.

CONCLUSIONS

Ryfe (2006a), in the introduction to a special issue of the journal *Political Communication* dealing with news, argues that the research on news media has produced one largely consistent finding: news is extraordinarily homogeneous. The research also offers an explanation for this homogeneity: news is the product of a set of organizational routines that do not vary across time, place, or organization.

Most of the research on routines is based on the study of American media, Ryfe acknowledges, and it is an open question as to whether routines differ in other parts of the world as well as to whether they have varied across time and can be expected to change in the future. Bourdieu (2001) argues that sameness of content is a feature of French media as well. Shoemaker and Cohen (2006) found more similarity than dissimilarity in the topics in the news in a composite week of newspapers, radio broadcasts and television broadcasts across 10 countries from around the world. Donsbach (1995), however, found that US journalists have a higher level of division of labor than journalists in four European countries studied for comparison. The US journalists also are more likely to have their stories edited for the sake of accuracy than are journalists in the other countries. Esser (1998), in a detailed analysis of newsroom structure in German and British newspapers, found huge differences in terms of role differentiation; the German newsrooms had almost none, while the British newsrooms were highly role structured. Weaver (1998), in a study of journalists from 12 different national states, found large differences in terms of the roles the journalists say they should play in society. Esser (1998) concluded that the existing scholarship is naive in not recognizing differences in structure and routines, perhaps because that research has focused on the gross similarities in content.

Cook (1998), in a critique of the organizational approach to the study of news, argued that this perspective produced evidence of the necessity of routines but gave little information about those routines. Cook argued that the news media in the United States are more than a series of organizations. The similarities of news content and of the process that produces that content suggest that the news media should be analyzed as a single institution, he contends.

The focus of Cook (1998) and, at nearly the same time, Sparrow (1999) on an institutional approach to news has generated new interest in news routines. Essays and reports by Benson (2006), Cook (2006), Entman (2006), Kaplan (2006), Lawrence (2006), Lowrey (forthcoming), Ryfe (2006b), and Sparrow (2006), most published in the special issue of *Political Communication*, attest to that fact.

Lowrey (forthcoming), drawing on the sociological literature (particularly Meyer & Rowan, 1977) argues that the "new institutional" approach is a reaction to traditional research and theorizing on organizational behavior. That research has viewed humans and their organizations as purely calculating and goal-oriented, and it has not seen their actions in context. The institutionalists have focused on the power of habits, norms and unquestioned typifications in decision making and on the environment of the organizations. The policies and practices of the institutions acquire unquestioned status. Organizations follow them without concern for their effectiveness.

At this point, it is unclear how much difference this new approach is going to make in research on news production. Sparrow (2006) argues, based on new institutionalism, that news media develop standard routines in response to three kinds of uncertainty: over profits, legitimacy and raw materials. The first and third of these are central issues in the media economics literature, which argues that media organizations are fundamentally economic in nature (Alexander et al., 2004; Croteau & Hoynes, 2001; Doyle, 2002; Hoskins et al., 2004; McManus, 1994). Entman (2004) argues that news institutionalism alone will not explain media coverage of foreign policy and suggests an integration of it and insights from the media and foreign policy literature (Entman, 2004).

As we have explained above, we believe the organization perspective continues to have merit. In our view, a defining characteristic of news organizations is their need for story ideas, as these ideas are the raw material of news. The structure of the organizations and their routines result from this need, and these structures and routines, in turn, shape the final news product.

The historical literature has given less focus to story ideation than would seem to be ideal. The result is that the multiple ways in which stories can be generated is not known. Clearly beats, which have been a historical concern in the news construction literature, play a key role in generating story ideas. Other techniques exist as well.

The literature on news routines seemed to have stagnated, because the notion of routines was not seen as variable. This new focus on variations in techniques for story idea generation offers a fresh avenue for exploration. Similarly, the antecedents of variation in story ideation techniques are worthy of exploration. Here news philosophy is identified as one such antecedent. Others are likely to present themselves as well. An examination of variability in story ideation techniques may suggest differences in media content, particularly on the local level, that much of the existing research has missed.

Consistent with Ryfe (2006a), we expect routines to vary across time. We also think that the uncoupling of journalism from media organizations will have a large amount of impact on how news is produced. Preliminary research (Project for Excellence in Journalism, 2007) has shown that the news agenda of use-driven web sites is strikingly different from that of the mainstream press. It seems likely that citizen journalists, that is, journalists working without special training in journalism and/or working without the constraints of the traditional media, also will generate different story ideas than journalists working for the media. The routines for generating those ideas are likely to be different as well, since they will have little or no link to the present practice of journalism.

Story ideation will almost certainly remain the key process in news production. For that reason, it is where future research can be directed most profitably.

REFERENCES

Alexander, A., Owers, J. Carveth, R., Hollifield, C. A., & Greco, A. (Eds.). (2004). *Media economics: Theory and practice* (3rd ed.). Mahweh, NJ: Erlbaum.

Altheide, D. L. (1976). *Creating reality: How TV news distorts events*. Beverly Hills: Sage.

Atwater, T. (1984, Winter). Product differentiation in local tv news. *Journalism Quarterly, 61*, 757–762.

Bantz, C. R., McCorkle, S., & Baade, R. C. (1980). The news factory. *Communication Research, 7*(1), 45–68.

Becker, L. B., Lowrey, W., Claussen, D. S., & Anderson, W. B. (2000). Why does the beat go on? An examination of the role of beat structure in the newsroom. *Newspaper Research Journal, 21*, 2–16.

Becker, L. B., Edwards, H. H., Vlad, T., Daniels, G. L., Gans, E. M., & Park, N. (2001). Routinizing the acquisition of raw materials: A comparative study of news construction in a single community. Paper presented to the Midwest Association for Public Opinion Research, Chicago.

Bennett, W. L. (1996). An introduction to journalism norms and presentations in politics. *Political Communication, 13*, 373–384.

Benson, R. (2006). News media as a "journalistic field": What Bourdieu adds to new institutionalism, and vice versa. *Political Communication, 23*, 187–202.

Bourdieu, P. (2001). Television. *European Review, 9*, 245–256.

Breed, W. (1955). Social control in the newsroom. *Social Forces, 33*, 326–355.

Chalaby, J. K. (1996). Journalism as an Anglo-American Invention. *European Journal of Communication, 11*, 303–326.

Chalaby, J. K. (2000). "Smiling pictures make people smile": Northcliffe's journalism. *Media History, 6*(1), 33–44.

Connolly, P. (2002). Stars in eyes turn to tears. *The Halifax Daily News*, June 22, 2.

Cook, T. E. (1998). *Governing the news*. Chicago: University of Chicago Press.

Cook, T. E. (2006). The news media as a political institution: Looking backward and looking forward. *Political Communcation, 23*, 159–172.

Croteau, D., & Hoynes, W. (2001). *The business of media*. Thousand Oaks, CA: Pine Forge Press.

Danzger, M. H. (1975). Validating conflict data. *American Sociological Review, 40*(5), 570–584.

Donohue, G. A., Olien, C. N., & Tichenor, P. J. (1989). Structure and constraints on community newspaper gatekeepers. *Journalism Quarterly, 66*, 807–812.

Donsbach, W. (1995). Lapdogs, watchdogs and junkyard dogs. *Media Studies Journal, 9*, 17–30.

Drew, D. G. (1972). Roles and decision making of three television beat reporters. *Journal of Broadcasting, 16*(2), 165–173.

Doyle, G. (2002). *Understanding media economics*. London: Sage.

Eliasoph, N. (1988). Routines and the making of oppositional news. *Critical Studies in Mass Communication, 5*, 313–334.

Entman, R. M. (2004). *Projections of power*. Chicago: University of Chicago Press.

Entman, E. M. (2006). Punctuating the homogeneity of institutionalized news: Abusing prisoners at Abu Ghraid versus killing civilians at Fallujah. *Political Communication, 23,* 215–224.

Epstein, J. (1974). *News from nowhere*. New York: Vintage Books.

Esser, F. (1998). Editorial structures and work principles in British and German newsrooms. *European Journal of Communication, 13*, 375–405.

Fishman, M. (1980). *Manufacturing the news*. Austin: University of Texas Press.

Gans, H. J. (1979). *Deciding what's news*. New York: Random House.

Halloran, J. D., Elliot, P., & Murdock, G. (1970). *Demonstrations and communication: A case study.* Middlesex, UK: Penguin Books.

Hage, J. (1972). *Techniques and problems of theory construction in sociology*. New York: John Wiley.

Hansen, K. A., Ward, J., Conners, J. L., & Neuzil, M. (1994). Local breaking news: Sources, technology, and news routines. *Journalism Quarterly, 71*(3), 561–572.

Hansen, K. A., Neuzil, M., & Ward, J. (1998). Newsroom topic team: Journalists' assessments of effects on news routines and newspaper quality. *Journalism & Mass Communication Quarterly, 75*(4), 803–821.

Herman, E. S., & Chomsky, N. (1988). *Manufacturing consent*. New York: Pantheon Books.

Hoskins, C., McFadyen, S., & Fin, A. (2004). *Media economics: Applying economics to new and traditional media.* Thousand Oaks, CA: Sage.

Kaplan, R. L. (2006). The news about new institutionalism: Journalism's ethic of objectivity and its political origins. *Political Communication, 23*, 173–186.

Lawrence, R. G. (2006). Seeing the whole board: New institutional analysis of news content. *Political Communication, 23*, 225–230.

Livingston, S., & Bennett, W. L. (2003). Gatekeeping, indexing, and live-event news: Is technology altering the construction of news? *Political Communication, 20*, 363–380.

Lowrey, W. (Forthcoming). Institutional roadblocks: Assessing journalism's response to changing audiences. In M. Tremayne (Ed.), *Journalism and citizenship: New agendas*. London: Taylor & Francis.

McManus, J. (1990). How local televison learns what is news. *Journalism Quarterly, 67*(4), 672–683.

McManus, J. (1994). *Market-driven journalism*. Thousand Oaks, CA: Sage.

Meyer, J. W., & Rowan, B. (1997). Institutionalized organizations: Formal structure as myth and ceremony. *The American Journal of Sociology, 83*, 340–363.

Molotch, H., & Lester, M. (1973). Accidents, scandals and routines: Resources for insurgent methodology. *Critical Sociology,* 25(2/3), 247–259.

Molotch, H., & Lester, M. (1974). News as purpose behavior: On the strategic use of routine events, accidents, and scandals. *American Sociological Review, 39*(1), 101–112.

Molotch, H., & Lester, M. (1975). Accidental news: The great oil spill as local occurrence and national event. *American Journal of Sociology, 81*(2), 235–260.

Oliver, P. E., & Maney, G. M. (2000). Political processes and local newspaper coverage of protest events: From selection bias to triadic interactions. *American Journal of Sociology, 106*(2), 463–505.

Project for excellence in journalism. (2007). Retrieved on September 12, 2007, from http://www.journalism.org/node/7493

Reese, S. D. (2001). Understanding the global journalist: A hierarchy-of-influences approach. *Journalism Studies, 2*(2), 173–187.

Ryfe, D. M. (2006a). Guest's editor introduction: New institutionalism and the news. *Political Communication, 23,* 135–144.

Ryfe, D. M. (2006b). The nature of news rules. *Political Communication, 23*, 203–214.

Schudson, M. (2002). The news media as political institutions. *Annual Review of Political Science, 5,* 249–269.

Schudson, M. (2005). Four approaches to the sociology of news. In J. Curran& M. Gurevitch (Eds.), *Mass media and society* (4th ed., pp. 172–197). London: Hodder Arnold.

Sigal, V. S. (1973). *Reporters and officials*. Lexington: DC Heath.

Shoemaker, P., & Reese, S. (1996). *Mediating the message*. White Plains, NY: Longman.

Shoemaker, P. J., & Cohen, A. A. (2006). *News around the world*. New York: Routledge.

Soloski, J. (1989). News reporting and professionalism. *Media, Culture & Society, 11*, 207–228.

Sparrow, B. H. (1999). *Uncertain guardians: The news media as a political institution*. Baltimore: The Johns Hopkins University Press.

Sparrow, B. H. (2006). A research agenda for an institutional media. *Political Communication, 23*, 145–157.

Tuchman, G. (1972). Objectivity as strategic ritual: An examination of newsmen's notions of objectivity. *American Journal of Sociology, 77*(4), 660–679.

Tuchman, G. (1973). Making news by doing work: Routinizing the unexpected. *American Journal of Sociology, 79*(1), 110–131.

Tuchman, G. (1976). The news' manufacture of sociological data. *American Sociological Review, 41*(6), 1065–1067.

Tuchman, G. (1978). *Making news*. New York: Free Press.

Tunstall, J. (1971). *Journalists at work*. Beverly Hills, CA: Sage.

Warner, M. (1969). Decision-making in American T.V. political news. *The Sociological Review monograph, 13*, 169–179.

Webster's New World Dictionary of the American Language College Edition. (1964). New York: World Publishing.

Weaver, D. H. (Ed.) (1998). *The global journalist*. Cresskil, NJ: Hampton Press.

Wolfsfeld, G., Avraham, E., & Aburaiya, I. (2000). When prophesy always fails: Israeli press coverage of the Arab minority's Land Day protests. *Political Communication, 17*, 115–131.

6

Journalists as Gatekeepers

Pamela J. Shoemaker, Tim P. Vos, and Stephen D. Reese

Journalists are bombarded with information from the Internet, newspapers, television and radio news, news magazines, and their sources. Their job of selecting and shaping the small amount of information that becomes news would be impossible without gatekeeping. It is the process of selecting, writing, editing, positioning, scheduling, repeating and otherwise massaging information to become news. Since gatekeepers provide a picture of the world for the rest of us, it is vital for scholars to understand the gatekeeping process and its impact on the reality presented to the public.

Gatekeeping is one of the oldest social science theories adapted and developed for use in the study of news[1] and has been used by communication scholars continuously since the 1950s. This chapter defines the central elements of gatekeeping theory, the leading thinkers and leading texts of gatekeeping, the current state of gatekeeping research, critical issues in theorizing about gatekeeping, methodological issues and concerns, and, finally, considerations for future gatekeeping scholarship.

KEY ELEMENTS

Items, those bits of information that are rejected or selected, shaped and scheduled, are the focus of all gatekeeping studies. Tracking the flow of items dates back to Kurt Lewin's (1947) social psychological theory of how people's eating habits could be changed. In his theory, items were food products. Figure 6.1 illustrates a world of items that may enter the gatekeeping process. Not all items are selected. Some make their way into channels, which are sometimes divided into sections, each of which can be entered only by passing through a gate. Forces facilitate or constrain the flow of items through gates, by varying in magnitude and valence direction and by working on either or both sides of the gate. Figure 6.1 shows three channels and many information items, but only one item makes its way through a channel and is transmitted to one or more audiences. Negative or weak forces keep some items from progressing through the channels, and it is important to note that forces exist both before and after gates. For example, the expense of microwave remote equipment is a negative force in front of the gate, slowing a television station's ability to cover live events, but once the equipment is purchased and passes the gate, the purchase has a positive force, leading the news producer to use it often to justify the expense. The final element shown in Figure 6.1 is the outcome of the gatekeeping process, not only the

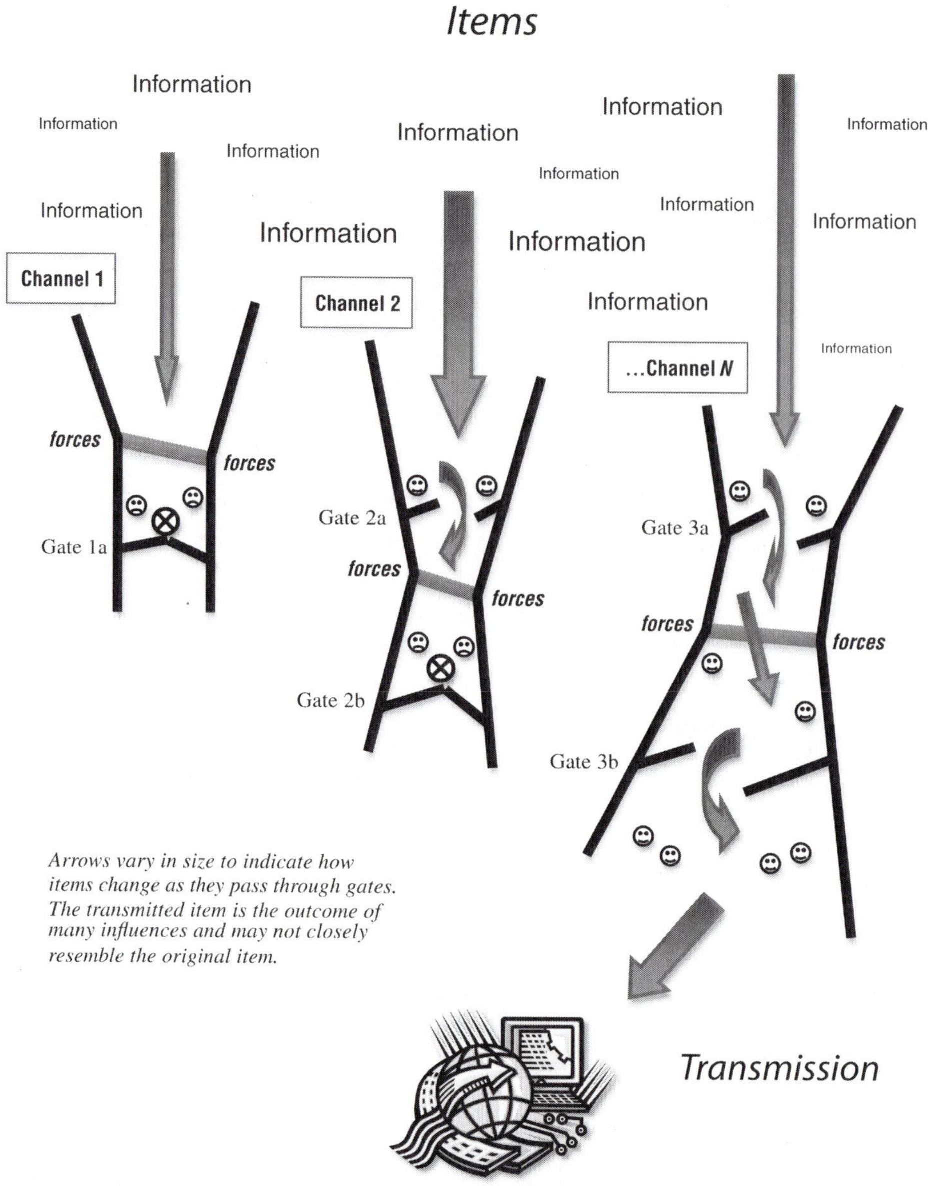

Items

Information Information Information Information Information Information Information Information Information Information Information Information Information Information

Channel 1 Channel 2 ...Channel *N*

forces forces Gate 1a Gate 2a forces forces Gate 2b Gate 3a forces forces Gate 3b

Arrows vary in size to indicate how items change as they pass through gates. The transmitted item is the outcome of many influences and may not closely resemble the original item.

Transmission

FIGURE 6.1 The basic elements of gatekeeping studies.

result of being selected, but also the outcome of many influences on the item as it passes through channels, sections, and gates.

Two important elements are hidden in Figure 6.1. The gatekeeper controls whether information passes through the channel and what its final outcome is. Gatekeepers take many forms, for example: people, professional codes of conduct, company policies, and computer algorithms. All gatekeepers make decisions, but they have varying degrees of autonomy. Autonomy varies from an individual's idiosyncratic whims to sets of unbreakable rules interpreted by computer programs. The information management company Google uses algorithms—sets of formula that translate the company's gatekeeping policies into computer instructions—to select news items for readers of the news Web page news.google.com. Google's selections are presented as current news to its many readers, and it might seem that the human gatekeepers have no autonomy; however, algorithms are the product of many decisions from the level of management to code writers. Google News is the outcome of this process, representing a seemingly objective picture of the day, but this objectivity is a characteristic of humans and their understanding of the world, not of computer programs.

In early gatekeeping studies about news events (e.g., Buckalew, 1968; Donohew, 1967; Gieber, 1956; Jones, Troldahl, & Hvistendahl, 1961; White, 1950), the gate was understood to be an in/out decision point, with little or no concern for other aspects of the gatekeeper's job. Donahue, Tichenor, and Olien (1972), however, emphasize that gatekeeping is a more complex process, involving decisions about the amount of time/space allotted to a news event, where within a publication or news program the story is placed, the use of graphics, and number of stories about the event on one day or across days, and whether the story returns in a cyclical pattern. In other words, journalists can frame the story (Entman, 1993).

EARLY INFLUENCES

Although the field of communication research has been dominated by issues of audience and effects, gatekeeping has continually reminded us of the importance of institutional, organizational and professional factors in understanding the media landscape. One of the earliest theories in the field, gatekeeping is associated with one of the "four founders" of the field as identified by Berelson (1959) and one of the key "forerunners" nominated by Rogers (1994): Kurt Lewin. The influence of the gatekeeping tradition, like any model, has been to direct attention to certain phenomena in a compelling manner. As a result, a number of research questions across a wide domain of communication activity have been guided by this major concept, taking it far beyond the original sense of the one coined by Lewin, a social-psychologist but trained as a physicist. He sought to apply the principles of physical science to human behavior by identifying channels and gates controlling what passed through them.

This simple but compelling model, applicable across a number of domains, served to clarify the seemingly infinite number of influences and individuals operating within a communication setting. Believing that psychological "forces" could be studied mathematically, Lewin's thinking resembled that of other early figures, such as Claude Shannon (1949) and Norbert Wiener (1948), who developed unifying "engineering" models that could be applied across mass and interpersonal communication regardless of "channel."

One key influence of Lewin was on former journalist David Manning White, an assistant of Lewin's at the University of Iowa and a student of Wilbur Schramm. As White recalled it:

> One day I happened to run across a paper by Kurt Lewin in which he coined the term "gatekeeper." I thought that the complex series of "gates" a newspaper report went through from the actual criterion event to the finished story in a newspaper would make an interesting study, and thus pursued it. (cited in Reese & Ballinger, 2001, p. 646)

White's 1949 study of a news editor helped apply the concepts of Lewin to a journalistic setting and launch a tradition of research into the media "gatekeepers." His work tackled the intuitively obvious question of how news organizations solve the problem of so much information and so little space. Titled, "The 'Gatekeeper': A case study in the selection of news," White's widely reprinted and cited article in *Journalism Quarterly* in 1950, which called it "one of the first studies of its kind," examined the reasons expressed by a news editor for accepting or rejecting a list of potential news items. Although it addressed the decisions of only a single person, the model proved highly influential.

In reviewing the reasons given for selecting one-tenth of the wire stories for inclusion in the *Peoria Star*, White observed "how highly subjective, how reliant upon value judgments based on the 'gatekeeper's' own set of experiences, attitudes and expectations the communication of 'news' really is" (1950, p. 386). His adaptation of Lewin was firmly individualistic, placing more emphasis on the gatekeeper than the channel, and subsequent studies followed suit, identifying journalist selectivity as the main source of news "bias." In White's recollection of his own earlier professional work, he had a similar insight:

> I quickly became quite aware of my antipathy to the incoming columns of Westbrook Pegler, but I tried to edit his vitriolic prose with objectivity. One afternoon, though, the paper's managing editor called me into his office and said, "David, I've noticed lately that Pegler's columns are considerably shorter these past few weeks."...Either subconsciously or with palpable awareness I had been cutting out sentences or whole paragraphs of vintage Pegler. (p. 647)

The model strongly suggests that the main reason for media distortion is the need to narrow a multitude of happenings in the world to a modest number that eventually make the news. That implies that were that less the case and editors better able to choose appropriately, then news selection would be less problematic. Furthermore, the gatekeeping model includes room for a number of decision makers along the path of selection, but the tendency of many studies, including White's, is to focus on one section of that process. "Mr. Gates" was perhaps given too much credit for wielding influence, given that he did not have at his command an entire selection of the day's happenings. And his job was mainly to choose from among stories in the major wire services, which were largely comparable, meaning his selections were from among a narrow range of choices to begin with (as advanced later by Gieber, 1964).

Although not a "gatekeeping" study as such, Warren Breed's (1955) research on social control in the newsroom is a close contemporary of White's and often mentioned together. In "Social control in the newsroom: A functional analysis," Breed—also a former newspaper reporter—interviewed a sample of newsmen at medium-sized newspapers to determine how they discerned the appropriate way to handle their story selection. Breed, in a sense, identified newspaper publishers as the de facto gatekeepers who operate through indirect means to ensure that only news consistent with organizational policy gets through. The relevant gatekeeping issue for Breed was that "policy news may be slanted or buried so that some important information is denied the citizenry" (p. 193).

Breed's contribution was to show how the most important gatekeeper may not be the one who is most immediately involved in the selection, but may reside elsewhere within more influential levels of the organization. If news is what the journalist says it is, the subjectivity of the gatekeeper would seem to profoundly problematize the news process, and yet the field was slow to follow up on this key insight. Reese and Ballinger (2001) argue that the reason lay in the expectation that acting adequately on behalf of the community, the gatekeeper "sees to it (even though he may never be consciously aware of it) that the community shall hear as a fact only those events which the newsman, as the representative of his culture, believes to be true" (White, 1950, p. 390). Like White, Breed implied (as did subsequent interpretations by field synthesizers) that the gatekeeping process could work to the satisfaction of the community via journalistic codes and other guidance, were the undue influence of publishers to be curtailed. According to these views, then, as long as gatekeepers remained faithful cultural representatives, the society need not fear their decisions.

This benign view of gatekeepers worked to suppress attention to this important process for many years, until relative outsiders to the field of communication brought newsroom decisions back into scrutiny. If Breed's view placed gatekeeping control with the publisher, and White with the editor's subjective judgment, later work, a decade or more later, in media sociology placed it at the level of the organization. The highly influential book of sociologist Herbert Gans (1979), identified sources of power within the organization, and the incentives journalists have to conform to group norms and follow practical considerations. In a valuable corrective, this approach embeds gatekeeping in the ongoing and functional activities of organizations. Gans locates the construction of news not in the journalist, the publisher, or in the gatekeeping editor, but in the process by which all parts, routines, and arrangements of the organization are engaged for the creation of news. This helps direct blame for distortion away from the individual journalists.

For Gans (1979) the news process is the process of solving the problems involved in packaging the daily flow of events into a marketable product for audiences. For the solution, journalists use "considerations" to aid in the decision making process, which must be applicable without too much deliberation. They must help avoid excessive uncertainty, be flexible, easily rationalized or explainable to others, and efficient, guaranteeing the best results for the least effort. The news equation is based on efficiency and power, which are closely connected.

The clearest demonstration of the fact that these considerations are not automatically applied, are the competitive factors. If considerations were automatic, news media would not need to look to each other for confirmation. Journalists in the ambiguous world of news strive to know what others are doing (*Time* with *Newsweek*, CBS with NBC, in this study). Journalists use the competition to judge their own performance. One of Gans's most insightful observations is the way journalists depend on the *New York Times*. The networks and newsmagazines need an arbiter that is presumed to transcend medium considerations and act as the trend setter. If it did not exist, it would have to be invented.

Consistent with the influence gatekeeping ascribes to journalists, Gans gives the news its own autonomy by observing that "the news is not simply a compliant supporter of elites or the Establishment or the ruling class; rather, it views nation and society through its own set of values and with its own conception of the good social order" (1979, p. 62). In this approach, gatekeeping decisions are made that help solve practical problems, rather than on individual subjectivity. But do these decisions act to systematically create a predictable range of news products? Gans correctly notes that, especially in television with its limited space, the final product is the highlight of the highlights. This leaves unanswered, of course, the question of on what basis the highlighting is made, which features of reality become most exaggerated?

The Gatekeepers

Although it leaves room for channels and external pressures, the gatekeeping tradition has by its nature, focused research attention on the individuals controlling the gates: "Mr. Gates." A major line of research has been devoted to describing the characteristics of these individuals, in an attempt to better understand what decisions they will be likely to make. Recent theorizing has had to grapple with the very definition of "who is a journalist," but gatekeeping implicitly locates that definition squarely with the professionals working within news organizations:

> those who have editorial responsibility for the preparation or transmission of news stories or other information, including full-time reporters, writers, correspondents, columnists, news people, and editors. (Weaver, Beam, Brownlee, Voakes, & Wilhoit, 2007, p. 3)

Weaver and colleagues have pursued this track most extensively, identifying the kinds of professional attitudes guiding journalist gatekeepers, extending the two categories of "neutral" and "participant," proposed by the original work of Johnstone, Slawski and Bowman (1976, p. 256) to include "disseminator," "adversarial," "interpretive," and, with a nod to the public journalism movement, "populist mobilizer" (Weaver & Wilhoit, 1996). The most recent national survey by Weaver et al. (2007) continues two prior efforts that described the personal and professional traits of these journalists, comparing them to the public in general. Thus, along with the numerous and less scientifically detached surveys of journalists purporting to show individual bias, these reports are premised on the importance of the some 120,000 individuals making up this professional group. Their makeup matters more, the authors argue, precisely because of their power to shape our perspectives on the world (Weaver et al., 2007).

STATE OF THE ART

A review of communication journals and books would suggest that the evolution of gatekeeping research slowed in the 1980s, only to see a resurgence in empirical studies in the last decade. The dearth of gatekeeping scholarship in the 1980s followed the sociological turn in journalism scholarship signaled by Gans's (1979) and others (e.g., Tuchman, 1978). The sociology of news work has steered the field toward studying gatekeepers in their organizational context. White's (1950) take on gatekeeping, which emphasized the agency of individual gatekeepers in selecting news, has fallen out of favor.

Gatekeeping research has also moved forward since the 1980s by revisiting previous studies to account for the changing face of journalism. As noted above, Weaver and his colleagues (2007, 1986, 1996) have tracked many of the changing demographics and practices of journalism. They are not alone. Bleske (1991), in keeping with the growing number of women in journalism, explored how gatekeeping changed, or did not change, when the gatekeeper was a woman instead of a man. Liebler and Smith (1997) found that the gender of the gatekeeper made little difference in news content. Others have explored the role of race in the selection and construction of news (Gant & Dimmick, 2000; Heider, 2000). Weaver et al. (2007) have explored how the public or civic journalism movement of the 1990s has expanded journalistic role conceptions, influencing how gatekeepers understand their work.

However, it has been the arrival of technological and accompanying institutional changes that has spurred new waves of gatekeeping research. For example, while early studies examined gatekeeping at newspapers, Berkowitz (1990) explored how the gatekeeping process worked in local television news. Abbott and Brassfield (1989) compared gatekeeping at print and electronic media and found some similarity in their decision making. Attention has more recently shifted to the online environment in which news is constructed. The common thread in this line of research is that technological changes will produce changes in what news organizations do and how they function. As Singer puts it, "Unlike the print newspaper, the Web is not a finite, concrete media form; instead, its form is simultaneously fluid and global and supremely individualistic" (2001, p. 78).

The initial studies of online news vary in their conclusions—some trumpeting the collapse of organizational influences on gatekeeping in the new media environment (Williams & Carpini, 2004), some finding little difference in gatekeeping functions between older and newer media (Cassidy, 2006). Singer (1997, 2005) explores how traditional print-based news organizations have adapted to functioning in a world of online news and suggests that print-based routines remain powerful in the new setting (see also Arant & Anderson, 2001). Even so, some news

Web sites have embraced the interactivity of the Internet, creating a forum for engagement with readers (Singer, 2006). Singer concludes that even though the gatekeeping function is changing in the online news environment, "it seems unlikely to lose all relevance any time soon" (Singer, 1998).

As the demographic profile of gatekeepers, the routines of news work, and the context of news work have changed, empirical research has emerged to understand how those changes have led to the news we see and hear each day. These studies have typically relied on earlier theorizing about the mechanisms of gatekeeping. For example, the concept of the news subsidy, articulated by Gandy (1982) and others (e.g., VanSlyke Turk, 1986), has been used to study new forms of subsidy, such as the emergence of video news releases aimed at electronic news organizations (e.g., Cameron & Blount, 1996; Machill, Beiler, & Schmutz, 2006). The vibrancy of gatekeeping comes in part from a body of scholarship that has kept pace with changes in journalism.

Meanwhile, the relative dearth of gatekeeping scholarship in the 1980s may have also come from the general acceptance of the gatekeeping concept as it has been more broadly defined. Gatekeeping, as noted above, is no longer understood as solely a matter of selection; nor is it understood as the action of a singular, powerful agent. A broader understanding of gatekeeping has paved the way for gatekeeping scholarship to be absorbed into the domain of media sociology (Schudson, 2003) and thus to regain theoretical relevance.

This movement toward a sociological orientation was less a bold step forward than a bold step backward. In fact, gatekeeping's continued relevance has come from a return to its roots. Lewin (1951), the father of gatekeeping research, had emphasized the place of the gatekeeper within a "field." According to Lewin's "field theory," gatekeeping emerged from an interaction of factors within a social field. Lewin's field theory was rooted in what he called "psychological ecology" (1951, p. 170), which became associated with ecological systems theory and human ecology theory. Individuals were to be understood within the context of four systems: a microsystem (immediate context), mesosystem (nexus of immediate contexts), exosystem (external institutions), and macrosystem (culture or social system) (Bronfenbrenner, 1979). These systems roughly corresponded with what Shoemaker and Reese (1991/1996) identified as five levels of analysis (also see Reese, 2001). These five levels, which are elaborated below, include the individual journalist level, the routines or practices of journalism level, the organizational level, the extra-media level, and the social system level. This analytical framework has led to greater precision and greater scope in theorizing about the construction and selection of news. For example, Shoemaker, Eichholz, Kim, and Wrigley (2001) compared factors across levels of analysis to better understand the factors that shape news on federal legislation.

Theorizing about gatekeeping also stands to gain from renewed examinations of field theory. While original gatekeeping research grew out of Lewin's (1951) concept of the "field," more recent efforts have examined the field theory of Pierre Bourdieu (1998, 1993). It is beyond the scope of this chapter to delve into the intricacies of Bourdieu's theorizing or to catalog the many ways in which Bourdieu's field theory speaks to journalistic gatekeeping—much of that work has been done by Benson and Neveu (2005). A couple of significant contributions will be noted here. First, Bourdieu's field theory addresses the relationship among levels of analysis. "(F)ield theory is concerned with how macrostructures are linked to organizational routines and journalistic practices, and emphasizes the dynamic nature of power" (Benson & Neveu, 2005, p. 9). The agency of individuals is bound by those macrostructures, organizational routines, and journalistic practices. However, this is not strictly a hierarchical model where macrostructures, for example economic structures, dictate routines and practices. As influential as economic factors are to most Western media, journalism still maintains some degree of autonomy, rooted in "the specific capital unique to that field" (Benson & Neveu, 2005, p. 4). In other words, the institutional characteristics and routines of the news media provide gatekeepers some insulation from the power of outside influences.

Second, since the field is an interrelated nexus of factors, studying isolated factors can prove problematic. Benson and Neveu conclude that "the 'field' opens up a new unit of analysis for media research: the entire universe of journalists and media organizations acting and reacting in relation to one another" (2005, p. 11). Benson (2004) puts forward a number of hypotheses for empirical study, few of which seem to address the field itself as a unit of analysis. For example, he offers: "Greater dependence on advertising is likely to contribute to more positive (and less negative) coverage of business, more critical (or sparse) coverage of labor unions, as well as a pro-consumerist depoliticization and ideological narrowing of news" (Benson, 2004, p. 282). Regardless, Bourdieu's field theory provides new impetus to theorizing about the relationship among levels of analysis in a gatekeeping model.

CRITICAL ISSUES

Although gatekeeping research has a long track record in the journalism discipline, some critical issues remain. One of those critical issues has been explored above—how we theorize about the different levels of analysis for the journalistic field. If gatekeeping is ultimately controlled by ideological factors for example, as Herman and Chomsky (2002) have argued, then we need to be precise about why it is worthwhile to study other levels of analysis. One other critical issue will be considered here: the so-called "forces" at the gates in the gatekeeping process.

As noted above, Lewin (1951) held that forces at the gate determine which items become news and which do not. These forces limit the autonomy of individual gatekeepers and shape the news in consistent ways. Although some of Lewin's gatekeeping theory invoked metaphors, such as channels and gates, "force" apparently has some ontological substance. At least there are pressures on gatekeepers to select or not select information. But what are those forces? For the most part, gatekeeping theorizing and research have skirted that question. However, for a variety of reasons, it is a question worth asking and worth answering. First, to the extent that society is not satisfied with the news that journalistic gatekeepers produce, we should empower practitioners to alter institutional practices or alignments. That will take knowledge of the forces that have shaped or empowered those practices and alignments in the first place. Second, the way that Lewin used "force" can obscure the nature and use of coercive "power" in the gatekeeping process. Hegemonic elites may exert power over the journalism field in ways that are not completely apparent to those with little power. Thirdly, theorizing requires a consistent set of propositions (Shoemaker, Tankard, & Lasorsa, 2004). But without articulating the nature of the force at the gate, we may hold contradictory assumptions, for example, about the nature of human rationality. Or we may rely on functionalist assumptions that do not hold up to empirical scrutiny. Gans, for example, acknowledged the empirical limitations of functional analysis, calling even his own observations "speculative" (1980, p. 291).

Although little has been done in the way of systematically examining the nature of the "forces" at the gate, it would appear that they vary depending on the level of analysis. At the individual level for example, research has shown that not all decision making is driven by conscious reflection—it can just as easily result from subconscious factors, such as an availability or representativeness heuristic (Nisbett & Ross, 1980). At the social system level, meanwhile, social institutions create "constraints and opportunities to which media organizations and actors respond" (Hallin & Mancini, 2004, p. 296). These constraints and opportunities emerge based on the contemporaneous development of economic, political, and media institutions. News content is similar in a social system because actors respond rationally to the same constraints and opportunities. To the extent that the institutional environment may produce more than one rational path, we might expect variation even among rational actors.

METHODOLOGICAL ISSUES

Today, we understand gatekeeping to be a complex theory, and one that can be tested using a variety of methodological and statistical procedures. Many research methods have been used in gatekeeping studies: case studies (e.g., White, 1950), participant observation (e.g., Gans, 1979), content analysis (e.g., Singer, 2001), surveys (e.g., Berkowitz, 1993), and experiments (e.g., Machill, Neuberger, Schweiger, & Wirth, 2004). Some studies use more than one method (e.g., Machill et al., 2006). Each method tackles a different aspect of gatekeeping.

Analysis: Levels Versus Units

Specifying the level of analysis and the unit of analysis are the most important decisions made in designing a gatekeeping study. A study's variables are characteristics of the unit of analysis. It is the thing being measured. In a data file, each case represents one unit of analysis, for example, Web pages, magazine stories, television news shows, the front pages of several newspapers, reporters, editors or producers, and company codes of ethics. The level of analysis of a study is more theoretical: What is the theory about? What is hypothesized about? What is the degree of aggregation of certain phenomena? Levels of analysis divide the world into parts for theorizing, from micro (e.g., individuals) to macro (e.g., social systems).

These aspects of the study cause more confusion than any other, partially because people sometimes use the terms synonymously. This is the result of the fact that most quantitative communication research uses survey and experimental methods—the level of analysis is generally the individual, as is the unit of analysis. We gather data about individual people in order to test theories about them. Gatekeeping studies, however, often use content analysis methodology, and the unit of analysis often differs from the level of analysis. Shoemaker and Reese (1996) propose that five levels of analysis are appropriate to the study of communication content: the individual, media routines, organization, extramedia, and ideological levels. More than one unit of analysis can be studied on each level of analysis. Often, explanation is offered at one level by reference to data gathered at a different level. This may lead to the "ecological fallacy" when, for example, conclusions are drawn about news professionals based on the organization to which they belong.

In individual-level studies, micro units are studied, but these are not limited to individual people. For example, other individual-level units of analysis could include news stories, television news shows, blogs, or photographs, as well as reporters, producers or even audience members. Whether the newspaper or the day (date on which the newspaper is published) is the unit of analysis is an important decision. If the newspaper is the unit of analysis (in a study of major newspapers around the world), then we are working at the organizational level of analysis. On the individual level of analysis, variables are characteristics of individual people.

Studies that look at routine practices of communication work have units of analysis that are the routines with which work is accomplished. For example, a scholar interested in looking at the effects of ethics on gatekeeping decisions could study individuals, or television organizations' codes of ethics. The code of ethics becomes the unit of analysis, with variation found across news organizations. It is possible that journalists may be subject to more than one code of ethics, such as from a professional organization and the government. In this case, each code of ethics would be a separate case in the data file, not each newspaper. Variables are characteristics of each code of ethics, such as topics covered, date revised or degree of specificity.

Many gatekeeping studies use the organizational level of analysis, in which newspaper chains or separate newspapers, blogs, television networks or stations become the unit of analysis, and all variables are characteristics of them. Variables might include hits per day, number of responses, topics of blog entries, and so on. If radio stations are the units of analysis, then the variables would be characteristics of each station, such as profitability, signal coverage, or percentage of the coverage area that is of Asian ethnic origins.

The social institution level of analysis includes units of analysis such as governments, interest groups, or religious organizations. These are also organizations, but, unlike the organizational level of analysis, looking at non-media social institutions allows us to assess their separate influence on the gatekeeping process. Variables are characteristics of these units, such as the number of public relations people employed, the budget for outside public relations services, or the total expenditures on public relations efforts last year.

Finally at the macro level, we look at variables that are characteristics of social systems. The social system is the base on which all other levels rest. Social system units of analysis include cities, countries, continents, and political alliances. Variables describe the units being studied, such as the political system, amount of imports, exports, population size, or number of ethnic groups.

Crossing Levels of Analysis

Many aspects of the gatekeeping process range across levels of analysis, and this complexity may have encouraged communication scholars to adopt the case study as the first method of choice. Case studies allow the scholar to collect many types of information that is analyzed inductively, with the data being used by the scholar to build theory. Although the studies of Mr. and Ms. Gates (Bleske, 1991) concentrated on the decisions made by individuals, it was clear from the beginning that these editors did not select news items totally according to personal whims, but also were following the standards of news ethics as interpreted by the profession generally and by their employers (organizational level) specifically.

Thus, the gatekeeper's personal likes and dislikes are variables on the individual level of analysis, and the question becomes: What characteristics of individual people can explain likes and dislikes? Deadlines and a predilection against the repetition of information about the same topic fall on the level of analysis covering routine practices of communication workers. News values that are common across news organizations are also among routine practices, but it is also possible that the organizations or managers promote their own preferences to include or exclude stories about topics of interest to them. When such preferences become organizational policy, written or unwritten, then the organizational level of analysis is also being studied.

Items are also influenced by social institutions and by the social system. Although media organizations are themselves social institutions, studying them apart from other institutions allows us to look both at variations between media organizations and at the relationships between media companies and other social institutions. Government, interest groups, advertisers, and religious groups are a few institutions that interact with the mass media.

When gatekeeping studies theorize about units on different levels of analysis, confusion is certain and incorrect conclusions probable. Scholars often avoid theorizing about one level of analysis and collecting data about units of analysis from another level, but it can be done. For example, Shoemaker, Eichholz, Kim, and Wrigley (2001) investigated the relative influences of variables from the individual and routine practice levels of analysis on the content of newspaper stories about 50 Congressional bills. The scholars conducted two surveys and a content analysis. The first survey went to the newspaper reporters who wrote articles about the 50 bills and the other to their editors. Reporters were asked only about their personal characteristics, including gender and political ideology. Editors were only asked to rate each of the 50 bills' newsworthiness.

Because the data were collected from three different units of analysis, creating the final data file (with each case a newspaper article) required merging data from the two surveys with data about the newspaper articles. Such complexity is common in gatekeeping studies. The editors' ratings of the newsworthiness of each bill were averaged and assigned to each story about the bill in the final data file, as were the characteristics of the reporter for each story. Statistical analysis revealed that the routine "news values" was a better predictor of how prominently the bills were covered than the characteristics of the people who wrote them.

Newer statistical procedures, such as hierarchical linear modeling, allow the scholar to assess quantitative data from more than one level of analysis. The major advantage of this is the extra precision gained by using data on lower levels as they were gathered instead of averaging or otherwise combining them in the data set to form aggregation at a higher level of analysis.

DIRECTIONS FOR FUTURE RESEARCH

Media environments are always changing and the body of knowledge about the gatekeeping process must stay current. Bourdieu argues that the journalistic field is "constantly being modified" (Benson & Neveu, 2005, p. 3). Gans reminds us that ideology "changes somewhat over time" (1980, p. 68). A promising new line of research has explored the dynamics of gatekeeping in the new media environment, but other new lines of research also need to be explored.

Gatekeeping research has been slow to explore differences and similarities in gatekeeping across social-systems. According to Schudson, understanding journalism in the context of the social system "should be not the closing line of a sermon but the opening of an inquiry into how different political cultures and institutions shape and structure different news cultures and institutions" (2003, p. 166). Benson and Neveu make the same point: "Certain types of variation—especially at the broad system level—only become visible via cross-national research" (2005, p. 87). And while we need to look for differences across systems, we also need to explore similarities. Shoemaker and Cohen (2006) have examined similarities in how news is defined in ten different countries—similarities explained in part by human evolutionary biology (see also Shoemaker, 1996).

Similarities can also come from the forces of globalization. Gatekeeping research must increasingly accommodate the realities of globally interconnected news work, coordinated across organizational boundaries. The "global newsroom" metaphor helps describe how this coordination occurs across national boundaries, particularly among cooperating broadcast organizations. In the largest such exchange, for example, Geneva-based Eurovision, decision making is not concentrated by virtue of common ownership but rather shared among "distributed" gatekeepers in a way that leads to consensus over a commonly available pan-national agenda of television stories. Cohen, Levy, Roeh, and Gurevitch (1996) examined this coordination of the supply and demand for news in the form of requests and offers from member news organizations. Story lineups, largely event-driven, were marked by consensus on top stories, and diversity among the others. The authors found in this "newsroom" a dynamic culture showing attempts to achieve consensus on appropriate news, while calling into question the particularistic news judgments of individual national news services. National news professionals offered and requested stories that they were socialized into perceiving as having universal interest, because they had to be agreed to by a group judgment (Reese, 2008).

Future research must better understand the institution of journalism as a historical creation, not just an economic, rational institution. Much research, even when it is critical of such efforts, focuses on how news organizations respond to the market imperatives (e.g., McChesney, 2004). For example, in Turow's (1992) consideration of news media he highlights their utility maximizing behaviors. Media develop coping routines such as track record talent, entertaining news story forms, and market research as a rational means to achieve predetermined goals. For example, "news executives act to cultivate audience belief in the journalistic integrity of their products while pursuing a strategy of linking news and entertainment organizations for the parent firm's profit" (Turow, 1992, p. 173). Media organizations no doubt seek to maximize efficiency and profitability—that is not in dispute. However, we must be careful if we assume that this explains all journalism routines and all organization practices.

The theories of new institutionalism (see for example, Hall & Taylor, 1996; Pierson, 2004) require us to consider that institutional behavior emerges from a historical context that may not maximize utility and may in fact emerge as an unintended consequence. Bourdieu argues that the gatekeepers in a particular institution are constrained by "the possibilities bequeathed by previous struggles, a space which tends to give direction to the search for solutions and, consequently, influences the present and future of production" (quoted in Benson & Neveu, 2005, p. 95).

Although new institutionalism may point to new areas of empirical investigation, its worth is ultimately in helping us theorize about the interconnectedness of the journalistic field. A possible example is the way in which the journalistic role conception of the disseminator, which remains the soul of US journalism practice even as some have pushed alternatives (Weaver et al., 2007), not only serves the interests of organizations (Berkowitz, 1987; Sigal, 1973), but also the interests of powerful elites (Bagdikian, 2004). The explanation does not start with powerful elites—they do not simply dictate news coverage. The disseminator role is a historical creation (Schudson, 1978) that audiences have come to expect and that expectation is a powerful path dependent force that limits what journalistic organizations can do. No one factor explains the outcome—the journalistic field is an interaction of factors that emerge in concrete temporal settings.

Other areas for future research could be pursued—some theoretical (the possibilities of Giddens' (1979) structuration theory for theorizing about the role of gatekeepers), some methodological (the need for more studies that connect gatekeeping with content analysis), and some empirical (the value of looking more for interaction effects among factors). Gatekeeping theory, even though it has one of the longest histories in mass communication research, continues to hold much potential for a substantive research program.

NOTE

1. Psychologist Kurt Lewin coined the word gatekeeping in the 1940s, and his theory was adapted by David Manning White for his 1950 study of news transmission. Their contemporaries were Harold Lasswell, Paul Lazarsfeld and Karl Hovland, all bringing other theories from the social sciences to create the new discipline of mass communication research.

REFERENCES

Abbott, E. A., & Brassfield, L. T. (1989). Comparing decisions on releases by TV and newspaper gatekeepers. *Journalism Quarterly, 66,* 853–856.

Arant, M. D., & Anderson, J. Q. (2001). Newspaper online editors support traditional standards. *Newspaper Research Journal, 22*(4), 57–69.

Bagdikian, B. H. (2004). *The new media monopoly.* Boston: Beacon Press.

Benson, R. (2004). Bringing the sociology of media back in. *Political Communication, 21*(3), 275–292.

Benson, R., & Neveu, E. (2005). *Bourdieu and the journalistic field.* Malden, MA: Polity.

Berelson, B. (1959). The state of communication research. *Public Opinion, 23,* 1–5.

Berkowitz, D. (1987). TV news sources and news channels: A study in agenda-building. *Journalism Quarterly, 64*(2), 508–513.

Berkowitz, D. (1990). Refining the gatekeeping metaphor for local television news. *Journal of Broadcasting & Electronic Media, 34*(1), 55–68.

Berkowitz, D. (1993). Work roles and news selection in local TV: Examining the business-journalism dialectic. *Journal of Broadcasting & Electronic Media, 37*(1), 67–83.

Bleske, G. L. (1991). Ms. Gates takes over: An updated version of a 1949 case study. *Newspaper Research Journal, 12*(3), 88–97.

Bourdieu, P. (1998). *On television.* New York: New Press.

Bourdieu, P., & Johnson, R. (1993). *The field of cultural production: Essays on art and literature.* New York: Columbia University Press.

Breed, W. (1955). Social control in the newsroom: A functional analysis. *Social Forces, 33,* 326–335.

Bronfenbrenner, U. (1979). *The ecology of human development: Experiments by nature and design.* Cambridge, MA: Harvard University Press.

Buckalew, J. K. (1968). The television news editor as a gatekeeper. *Journal of Broadcasting, 13,* 48–49.

Cameron, G. T., & Blount, D. (1996). VNRs and air checks: A content analysis of the use of video news releases in television newscasts. *Journalism & Mass Communication Quarterly, 73*(4), 890–904.

Cassidy, W. P. (2006). Gatekeeping similar for online, print journalists. *Newspaper Research Journal, 27*(2), 6–23.

Cohen, A., Levy, M., Roeh, I., & Gurevitch, M. (1996). *Global newsrooms, local audiences: A study of the Eurovision News Exchange.* London: John Libbey.

Donohew, L. (1967). Newspaper gatekeepers and forces in the news channel. *Public Opinion Quarterly, 31,* 61–68.

Donahue, G. A., Tichenor, P. J., & Olien, C. N. (1972). Gatekeeping: Mass media systems and information control. In F. G. Kline & P. J. Tichenor (Eds.), *Current perspectives in mass communication research* (pp. 41–70). Beverly Hills, CA: Sage.

Entman, R. M. (1993). Framing: Toward clarification of a fractured paradigm. *Journal of Communication, 43*(4), 51–58.

Gandy, O. H., Jr. (1982). *Beyond agenda setting: Information subsidies and public policy.* Norwood, NJ: Ablex.

Gans, H. J. (1979). *Deciding what's news.* New York: Pantheon.

Gant, C., & Dimmick, J. (2000). African Americans in television news: From description to explanation. *The Howard Journal of Communications, 11,* 189–205.

Giddens, A. (1979). *Central problems in social theory: Action, structure, and contradiction in social analysis.* Berkeley: University of California Press.

Gieber, W. (1956). Across the desk: A study of 16 telegraph editors. *Journalism Quarterly, 33,* 423–432.

Gieber, W. (1964). News is what newspapermen make it. In L. A. Dexter & D. M. White (Eds.), *People, society and mass communication.* New York: Free Press.

Hall, P. A., & Taylor, R. C. R. (1996). Political science and the three new institutionalisms. *Political Studies, 44*(5), 936–957.

Hallin, D. C., & Mancini, P. (2004). *Comparing media systems: Three models of media and politics.* New York: Cambridge University Press.

Heider, D. (2000). *White news: Why local news programs don't cover people of color.* Mahwah, NJ: Erlbaum.

Herman, E. S., & Chomsky, N. (2002). *Manufacturing consent: The political economy of the mass media.* New York: Pantheon Books.

Johnstone, J., Slawski, E., & Bowman, W. (1976). *The news people: A sociological portrait of American journalists and their work.* Urbana: University of Illinois Press.

Jones, R. L., Troldahl, V. C., & Hvistendahl, J. K. (1961). News selection patterns from a state TTS-wire. *Journalism Quarterly, 38,* 303–312.

Lewin, K. (1947). Frontiers in group dynamics: Concept, method and reality in science; social equilibria and social change. *Human Relations, 1,* 5–40.

Lewin, K. (1951). *Field theory in social science: Selected theoretical papers.* New York: Harper.

Liebler, C. M., & Smith, S. J. (1997). Tracking gender differences: A comparative analysis of network correspondents and their sources. *Journal of Broadcasting & Electronic Media, 41*(1), 58–68.

Machill, M., Beiler, M., & Schmutz, J. (2006). The influence of video news releases on the topics reported in science journalism. *Journalism Studies, 7*(6), 869–888.

Machill, M., Neuberger, C., Schweiger, W., & Wirth, W. (2004). Navigating the internet: A study of German-language search engines. *European Journal of Communication, 19*(3), 321–347.

McChesney, R. W. (2004). *The problem of the media: U.S. communication politics in the twenty-first century.* New York: Monthly Review Press.

Nisbett, R., & Ross, L. (1980). *Human inference: Strategies and shortcomings of social judgment.* New York: Prentice-Hall.

Pierson, P. (2004). *Politics in time: History, institutions, and social analysis.* Princeton, NJ: Princeton University Press.

Reese, S. D. (2001). Understanding the global journalist: A hierarchy of influences approach. *Journalism Studies, 2*(2), 173–187.

Reese, S. D. (2008). Theorizing a globalized journalism. In M. Löffelholz & D. H. Weaver (Eds.), *Global journalism research: Theories, methods, findings, future* (pp. 2982–2994). Malden, MA: Blackwell.

Reese, S. D., & Ballinger, J. (2001). The roots of a sociology of news: Remembering Mr. Gates and social control in the newsroom. *Journalism and Mass Communication Quarterly, 78*(4), 641–658.

Rogers, E. M. (1994). *A history of communication study: A biographical approach.* New York: The Free Press.

Schudson, M. (1978). *Discovering the news: A social history of American newspapers.* New York: Basic Books.

Schudson, M. (2003). *The sociology of news.* New York: Norton.

Shannon, C. E., & Weaver, W. (1949). *The mathematical theory of communication.* Urbana: University of Illinois Press.

Shoemaker, P. J. (1991). *Gatekeeping.* Newbury Park, CA: Sage.

Shoemaker, P. J. (1996). Hardwired for news: Using biological and cultural evolution to explain the surveillance function. *Journal of Communication, 46*(3), 32–47.

Shoemaker, P. J., & Cohen, A. A. (2006). *News around the world: Content, practitioners, and the public.* New York: Routledge.

Shoemaker, P. J., Eichholz, M., Kim, E., & Wrigley, B. (2001). Individual and routine forces in gatekeeping. *Journalism and Mass Communication Quarterly, 78*(2), 233–246.

Shoemaker, P. J., & Reese, S. D. (1996). *Mediating the message: Theories of influences on mass media content* (2nd ed.). White Plains, NY: Longman.

Shoemaker, P. J., Tankard, J. W., & Lasorsa, D. L. (2004). *How to build social science theories.* Thousand Oaks, CA: Sage.

Sigal, L. V. (1973). *Reporters and officials: The organization and politics of newsmaking.* Lexington, MA: D.C. Heath.

Singer, J. B. (1997). Still guarding the gate?: The newspaper journalist's role in an on-line world. *Convergence: The Journal of Research into New Media Technologies, 3*(1), 72–89.

Singer, J. B. (1998). Online journalists: Foundations for research into their changing roles. *Journal of Computer Mediated Communication, 4*(1). Retrieved July 28, 2008, from http://www.jcmc.indiana.edu/col4/issue1/singer/html.

Singer, J. B. (2001). The metro wide web: Changes in newspapers' gatekeeping role online. *Journalism and Mass Communication Quarterly, 78*(1), 65–81.

Singer, J. B. (2005). The political j-blogger: "Normalizing" a new media form to fit old norms and practices. *Journalism, 6*(2), 173–198.

Singer, J. B. (2006). Stepping back from the gate: Online newspaper editors and the co-production of content in campaign 2004. *Journalism & Mass Communication Quarterly, 83*(2), 265–280.

Tuchman, G. (1978). *Making news: A study in the construction of reality*. New York: Free Press.

Turow, J. (1992). *Media systems in society: Understanding industries, strategies, and power.* New York: Longman.

VanSlyke Turk, J. (1986). Information subsidies and media content: A study of public relations influence on the news. *Journalism Monographs, 100.*

Weaver, D. H., Beam, R. A., Brownlee, B. J., Voakes, P. S., & Wilhoit, G. C. (2007). *The American journalist in the 21st century: U.S. news people at the dawn of a new millennium.* Mahwah, NJ: Erlbaum.

Weaver, D. H., & Wilhoit, G. C. (1986). *The American journalist: A portrait of U.S. news people and their work.* Bloomington: Indiana University Press.

Weaver, D. H., & Wilhoit, G. C. (1996). *The American journalist in the 1990s: U.S. news people at the end of an era.* Mahwah, NJ: Erlbaum.

White, D. M. (1950). The "gate keeper:" A case study in the selection of news. *Journalism Quarterly, 27,* 383–390.

Wiener, N. (1948). *Cybernetics, or control and communication in the animal and the machine.* Cambridge, MA: The Technology Press/Wiley.

Williams, B. A., & Carpini, M. X. D. (2004). Monica and Bill all the time and everywhere: The collapse of gatekeeping and agenda setting in the new media environment. *American Behavioral Scientist, 47*(9), 1208–1230.

7

Objectivity, Professionalism, and Truth Seeking in Journalism

Michael Schudson and Chris Anderson

The field of journalism studies and the subfield of sociology that examines professionalization and professional systems—the sociology of the professions—have coexisted in a state of mutual indifference for decades. Few of the classic professional studies in the sociology of professions hazard even a guess as to journalism's professional status, preferring for the most part to focus on the traditional professions of medicine and law (see, for example, Bledstein, 1976; Dingwall & Lewis, 1983; Freidson, 1970; Haskell, 1984); most studies of journalistic professionalism, on the other hand, forego engagement with the bulk of the sociological literature on professional occupations and systems. (For a rare exception, see Tumber & Prentoulis, 2005.) At a time when many of the most important scholarly questions about journalism revolve around issues of the occupation's power, authority, and professional status, there is much to be gained, it would seem, from revisiting questions of journalism and professionalization from an explicitly sociological angle—articulating a deeper understanding of journalism's troubled professional project, the relationship between the objectivity norm and that project, and the manner in which journalists attempt to forge a journalistic jurisdiction out of the link between their everyday work and their heavily qualified claim to possess a form of professionalized knowledge.

To draw these journalistic and sociological perspectives on professionalization into dialog, we begin this chapter with an overview of Weberian studies of the professions, carried out in the late 1970s and 1980s, including a discussion of Abbott's (1988) influential analysis of "professional jurisdiction." We then examine the two major strands of scholarship that have emerged within the field of journalism studies. The first strand, emerging from journalism itself (for example, Weaver, Beam, Brownlee, Voakes, & Wilhoit, 2007), tends not to worry about whether journalism produces authoritative knowledge or possesses professional traits; for researchers in this line of work, the importance of journalism is self-evident and not dependent on its status in a hierarchy of occupations. The emphasis in this line of work is to measure the degree to which journalism has achieved professional status, often through occupational or educational surveys. A second strand of work comes from the sociology of news organizations (Fishman, 1980; Gans, 2004; Schudson, 1978; Tuchman, 1978) and media studies (Zelizer, 1992) and focuses on the character of journalistic knowledge or claims to knowledge and thus on the standing of journalism's "cultural authority" in Paul Starr's (1984) terms. While the first strand suffers from its (probably unconscious) adoption of the "trait perspective" on the professions, the second strand confuses journalistic objectivity with journalistic professionalism per se. As Hallin and Mancini's (2004) recent work demonstrates, objectivity is not the definitive professional norm in many non-American media systems where professionalism, nonetheless, exists.

In our conclusion, we advance the argument that a productive mode of analysis of journalistic objectivity, professionalism, and truth seeking would continue to build on the best work of the two strands noted above while adopting a modified version of Abbott's (1988) framework. For Abbott, the study of the professions begins with the study of professional work, and "the central phenomenon of professional life is thus the link between a profession and its work" that Abbott calls "jurisdiction." Jurisdiction refers to the day-to-day manner in which a profession both concretizes and displays its base of "abstract knowledge" or, in the peculiar case of journalism, knowledge real and expert but by no means abstract. We seek to integrate Abbott's analysis with the two streams of research mentioned above, apply it to current controversies surrounding journalistic professionalism, and outline an agenda for future research.

FROM OCCUPATIONAL TRAITS TO OCCUPATIONAL STRUGGLE

The most productive era within the subfield of sociology dedicated to professionalization research begins with the widespread abandonment of the "trait approach" of occupational analysis, an approach that dominated the field for decades and whose more extreme normative tendencies defined a profession as a model of occupational autonomy and self-regulation worthy of imitation (Carr-Saunders & Wilson, 1993; Tawney, 1920). Key to the trait approach was an attempt to isolate certain professional characteristics and then to determine the degree to which various occupational categories fulfilled them. No single overview stands out as authoritative, but lists generally include the following features: work based on scientific or systematic knowledge, formal education, self-governing associations, codes of ethics, a relationship of trust between professional and client (as opposed to a strictly market-based relationship), licensing or other barriers to entry to the field, and widely recognized social status or social esteem. In the 1960s and 1970s, taking their cue from Everett C. Hughes and inspired by Max Weber's work on status and authority, sociologists abandoned the trait approach, passing "from the false question 'Is this occupation a profession' to the more fundamental one 'What are the circumstances in which people in an occupation attempt to turn it into a profession and themselves into professional people'" (Hughes, 1963, p. 655). In the forty years since Hughes' challenge, the study of the profession as an idealized structural-functionalist category has been replaced in much of sociology by the more Weberian study of professionalization and the "professional project."

One of the first explicitly Weberian professionalization theorists, Magali Sarfatti Larson argues in her analysis of the "professional project" that "ideal typical constructions do not tell us what a profession is, only what it pretends to be." We should ask instead, she argued, "what professions actually do in everyday life to negotiate or maintain their special position." (1977, p. xii). In MacDonald's (1995, p. 7) formulation, the word "'profession' is a lay or folk term, and [...] assessing whether an occupation is or is not a profession, is a semi-profession, or is more or less professional than other occupations is what the 'folk' do. It is not the task of sociology to do it for them scientifically." As Freidson (1983, p. 27), finally, summarizes the point:

> If "profession" may be defined as a folk concept then the research strategy appropriate to it is phenomenological in character. One does not attempt to determine what a profession is in an absolute sense so much as to how people in society determine who is professional and who is not, how they "make" or accomplish professions by their activities.

Initially advanced by Sarfatti Larson (1977), the theory of the professional project has remained at the center of much of the most important work in the sociology of the professions for the past several decades. The concept represents a fusion of Freidson's early, groundbreaking work on the medical field with Weber's classic analysis of the attempts of occupational groups to link economic class and social status. For Sarfatti Larson, professions are neither naturally existing occupational categories nor the bearers of socially functional "traits"; rather, they are collective social actors who "attempt to translate one order of scarce resources—special knowledge and skills—into another—social and economic rewards." This effort is what Sarfatti Larson calls "the professional project" and which she describes as a collective intention with coherence and consistence even though the "goals and strategies pursued by a given group are not entirely clear or deliberate for all the members" (p. xiii).

Framed in this manner, certain aspects of the professional project assumed key roles in the Weberian analysis of professional struggle that prevailed in the late 1970s. These aspects included: a profession's attempt to create organizational monopoly on a socially useful body of abstract knowledge; the need for a market in which to transact the exchange of the technical utilization of that knowledge; the relationship between a profession's monopolization of knowledge and its members' social status; the mutual interdependency of the profession's drive for social mobility and market control; attempts to convert economic power to social status (and vice versa); the ultimate dependence of this knowledge monopoly on the sanction of the state; and, finally, the need for a profession to "produce its producers" via schooling, credentialism, codes of ethics, etc. (Collins, 1979). Indeed, much sociological writing about professions was related to and inspired by sociological studies of education and higher education as a system for the orderly reproduction of a class system and the legitimation of class inequality. Neo-Marxist studies emphasized the place of education not in training individuals to acquire technical knowledge or skills fit for the modern economy but to acquire cultural capital to justify their high standing in the social order (Bourdieu, 1984; Collins, 1979; Ehrenreich & Ehrenreich, 1979; Karabel & Halsey, 1977). Early criticism of the ideal of objectivity in US journalism drew on this work or shared in the same intellectual mood skeptical of the authority of professions and inclined to see claims to neutrality, detachment, or dispassion as a veil for power. (Debates over objectivity in US journalism arising in the Vietnam war years are summarized in Schudson, 1978; a spirited defense of objectivity as a journalistic ideal is Lichtenberg, 1989.)

From this disciplinary reorientation, it follows that any investigation into issues of professionalism, objectivity, and truth seeking in journalism specifically should move from the question of whether journalism is or is not a profession to the more interesting analysis of the circumstances in which journalists attempt to turn themselves into professional people. Rather than outlining the traits that best characterize professionals, and then assessing the degree to which journalists attain them, we can analyze the social process through which journalists struggle to claim professional status. This research agenda places the study of journalism within the sociological study of the professions, and can cast new light on many of the classic institutional histories of journalism, including those that ignore or discount a sociological lens.

PROFESSIONAL RESEARCH AND JOURNALISM

How has this disciplinary transition from "traits" to "struggle" played out within the field of journalism studies? It would be an exaggeration to say that developments in sociology proper have had no effect on studies of journalistic professionalism. Arguably, however, the relationship has been indirect. Much of this can perhaps be attributed to the general decoupling, over the past two and a half decades, of sociology and media research tout court; on the side of journalism studies, as Zelizer (2004, p. 80) notes, "despite the auspicious beginnings of sociological inquiry into journalism, much contemporary work on journalism no longer comes from sociology per se." Or as Klinenberg (2005, p. 28) argues from the perspective of a sociologist:

> A paradox of contemporary sociology is that the discipline has largely abandoned the empirical study of journalistic organizations and news institutions at the moment when the media has gained visibility in political, economic, and cultural spheres, [and] when other academic fields have embraced the study of media and society.

The paradox is at least partially explained by the migration of sociologists to the burgeoning communications and media departments. Sociologists including Rodney Benson, Todd Gitlin, Michael Schudson, and Silvio Waisbord have primary or exclusive appointments in communication rather than sociology departments. The work of these scholars has found an audience in communication and media studies more than in sociology. Some sociologists, to be sure—the work of Steven Clayman and his colleagues stands out—still speak primarily to an audience inside sociology, even if it is in the subfield of sociolinguistics and conversational analysis.

In the absence of work that explicitly links the sociology of the professions to journalism, two strands of analysis have emerged within journalism studies. The first, encompassing what might be termed institutional research, usually seeks quantitative data on journalists' employment, education levels, adherence to ethical codes, etc. Such research has most often been initiated by the news industry itself, or by academics with close ties to professional journalism. In the United States, the Annual Survey of Journalism and Mass Communication Graduates has provided regularly updated statistics on the employment prospects of recent journalism school graduates. In other countries, as well as in the United States, additional surveys and employment analyses have been conducted to "measure" the degree to which professionalization has occurred within journalism, at least along the axis of higher education credentialing. The data presents something of a mixed picture. In the United States, for the twenty years from 1982 to 2002, the number of journalism and mass communication bachelor's-degree graduates who went into degree-related jobs declined from one-half to one-quarter (Weaver et al., 2007, p. 37). At the same time American newspaper editors mouth verbal support to the importance of a journalism or communications degree, even though a substantial minority (32 percent) from the 1995 survey contends that the degree of an entry-level hire is irrelevant. While the value of a "journalism degree" may be open to question, the importance of higher education is not; over 90 percent of journalists hold a degree (Weaver et al., 2007, p. 37). The situation is similar in other countries with established media systems: a greater hiring emphasis is placed on higher education in general than on the possession of specific "communication" degrees.

For journalism, it is tempting to turn to talk of a "quasi," "pseudo," or "failed" profession and to echo Weaver and Wilhoit's (1986, p. 145) contention that journalism "is *of* a profession but not *in* one." Indeed, many of the investigations of journalistic professionalism have halted at this point. Basic institutional research echoes (probably unconsciously) the older body of "trait theory" and stops the investigation before it truly begins. This first strand of journalism studies, in short, largely avoids the deeper questions surrounding journalism's unsettled occupational status. Rather than placing journalism somewhere on the professional spectrum between plumbers and neurosurgeons, it would be far more productive to inquire why and how the occupations of reporting and news editing achieved the professional status they did and how journalism may be attempting (or not, as the case may be) to raise that status. This removes us by one step from the rather arid analysis of employment data and forces us to consider the history, theory, and practice of journalism. Such questions have been dealt with most explicitly by authors working within the second strand of journalism studies, a strand that we might label cultural histories of professional objectivity.

CULTURAL THEORIES OF PROFESSIONALISM AND OBJECTIVITY

Schudson (1978, p. 151), in *Discovering the News*, identifies Walter Lippmann as "the most wise and forceful spokesman for the ideal of objectivity." Journalists, according to Lippmann, should "develop a sense of evidence and forthrightly acknowledge the limits of available information; ... dissect slogans and abstractions, and refuse to withhold the news or put moral uplift or any cause ahead of veracity." In short, Lippmann urged reporters to fuse their professionalism with claims to objectivity. The link between professionalism, objectivity, and truth seeking would come to be accepted, not only by journalists themselves in the form of an occupational ideology but by media researchers and journalism scholars as a related series of problems susceptible to historical and sociological investigation. Understanding the emergence of objectivity would, in short, provide the key to understanding the emergence of professionalism.

Kaplan (2002) has provided one of the most recent overviews of the social histories of the American press. Following and expanding on his lead, we can speak here of at least five orientations to this history. *First,* progressive historiography, which closely tracked the development of journalism's own occupational ideology, has depicted journalism as moving inevitably toward social differentiation, occupational autonomy, and professional freedom. By this account, objectivity serves as a normative endpoint, one enabled by modernization and the growing social differentiation among politics, business, and journalism; it is seen not as a tool, or a claim, but as a goal, a "best practice" made possible by historical progress. A *second*, related understanding of the relationship between objectivity and professionalism, though one not discussed by Kaplan, is the "technological" explanation for the emergence of objective journalism. This explanation, which most recent historical scholarship dismisses (though one can see glimpses of its return, in an inverted form, in some of the more utopian writings on the Internet), sees objectivity as a literary form fostered by technological developments.

A *third* strand of scholarship points to economic developments that fuel commercialism (and by implication, a misleading, ideological claim to impartiality called "objectivity"). Kaplan singles out Baldasty's *The Commercialization of News in the 19th Century* as an especially forceful, carefully documented, and ultimately wrongheaded argument about the relationship between commercialism and professionalization. "In Baldasty's theory, news content and indeed 'journalistic visions' followed from the [capitalistic] funding mechanism" (Kaplan 2002, p. 8) and produced a journalism that saw the public as consumers rather than citizens.

A *fourth* strand of research on the rise of journalistic objectivity in the United States begins with Schudson's *Discovering the News* (1978), which, along with his later work (2001), moved away from seeing the emergence of objectivity as an "inevitable outcome" of wide-scale social processes and changes—whether social, economic or technological—and linked the emergence of journalistic professionalism to questions of group cohesion, professional power, social conflict, and the cultural resonance of claims to occupational authority. Schudson's original move in *Discovering the News* was to seek the origins of professional objectivity in the nexus of developments that built a "democratic market society" rather than in technological developments or in a "natural" evolutionary progress. Schudson distinguishes journalistic beliefs of the 1890s—naïve empiricism, or a faith in "the facts"—from the more modern, early 20th century view of objectivity, which takes norms of objective reporting to be a set of defensive strategies rooted in the "disappointment of the modern gaze"—the understanding that true objectivity is impossible. Many authors—primarily historians of journalism—have followed Schudson in discussing the emergence of a professional class of reporters in the context of the development of professional objectivity (most notably Banning, 1999; Dicken-Garcia, 1989; Summers, 1994; Tucher, 2004). For these authors, and many others, objectivity continues to be the *sine qua non* of journalistic professionalization: explain the reasons behind the emergence of objectivity as an occupational practice, fix a date at which it first emerged, and you have gone a long way towards uncovering the "secret" of professional journalism.

Recent scholarship, however, calls into question the strong linkage this work implies between objectivity and professionalism. At the very least, objectivity cannot be seen as the *only* occupational norm to both emerge from and buttress the professional project, and in some cases, it may not even be the *most important* norm. Chalaby (1998) has called journalism as a "fact-based discursive practice" rather than a literary, philosophical, or political commentary on current affairs, an "Anglo-American invention." Ramaprasad's extensive surveys of non-Western journalism do not even include adherence to "objectivity" as a major characteristic of newswork in Egypt (Ramaprasad & Hamdy, 2006), Tanzania (Ramaprasad, 2001), or Nepal (Ramaprasad & Kelly, 2003), and the new notion of "contextual objectivity" has emerged to explain the editorial policies of non-Western cable news channels like al-Jazeera (Berenger, 2005). Donsbach and Patterson (2004) have argued that a commitment to objectivity still distinguishes American from European newsrooms. Their extensive survey of German, Italian, Swedish, British, and American journalists, both print and broadcast, finds that US journalists almost uniformly report that their political views have no relationship to the views of their employers. Italian and German journalists at national newspapers say that their political views are close to their papers' editorial position. Schudson also now argues that the journalism he took to be "modern" is more appropriately judged "American," and some of its distinctive features have more to do with American cultural presuppositions than a universal modernism. This is notably the case with the American invention of interviewing as a standard journalistic tool, one judged by many European observers at the time (the late 19th century) as a particularly rude and presumptuous way of doing business (Schudson, 1995, 2005).

It is Hallin and Mancini, however, who make the strongest case for severing the link between objectivity and professional standing in the world of journalism. For them, professionalism is defined less in terms of educational barriers to entry, a lack of state regulation, or the ideal of "objectivity"; rather, it is viewed primarily in terms of "greater control over [one's] own work process" (Hallin & Mancini, 2004, p. 34), the presence of distinct professional norms (p. 35), and a public service orientation (p. 36). Different media systems vary in their levels of professionalization, they argue. The Mediterranean model of journalism maintains a fairly weak level of professionalization; the North Atlantic model (America and Britain) and North/Central European model (Germany, Scandinavia) are both highly professionalized. However, being a "professional" in the democratic corporatist countries does not necessarily mean being committed to objectivity or being free from political party ties. Rather, journalists in democratic corporatist states (generally speaking, northern European countries) judge journalistic autonomy to be compatible with active and intentional intervention in the political world. In these terms, journalists in Germany are as "professional" as those in the United States. The social bases of their professionalism, however, and the specific content of their values are different.

In a later argument that amounts to an elaboration and generalization of his thesis in *Discovering the News,* Schudson (2001) has contended that the "objectivity norm" in American journalism ultimately provides some sort of benefit to the group that articulates it, either by stimulating social cohesion (in a Durkheimian sense) or social control (in a Weberian one).

Ethics and norms exist for ritualistic reasons, helping to provide internal solidarity and cohesion to a particular group; they also can also represent a way of defining a group in relation to other groups. Weberian explanations for the emergence of occupational norms, on the other hand, imply that they provide a measure of hierarchical control over social groups. The needs of superiors (editors) to control their subordinates (reporters) within large organizations mandates the adoption of a kind of "overt ethical reinforcement" that helps steer individuals in a rational, predictable manner.

Schudson's essay focuses on the social functions of the objectivity norm in American journalism, but it acknowledges that "a variety of moral norms could achieve the ends of providing public support and insulation from criticism" (p. 165). Journalists in Germany or China might work with norms other than objectivity, Schudson notes, and indeed they do. If, as Hallin and Mancini argue, professionalism implies the existence of an occupational autonomy undergirded by distinct professional norms, professional journalism might have different bases cross-culturally, historically, and even in the future. The end of objectivity, even if it arrives, may not signal the end of professional journalism.

Kaplan (2002), *fifth* and finally, argues for the contingency of the development of objectivity as the American professional norm and for seeing it as a product of the distinctive shape of the US "public sphere." Previous theories of the rise of objectivity in American journalism are insufficient, Kaplan argues, because they ignore the role played by political contention in American history. These theories often assume, incorrectly, that a social consensus around notions of political liberalism and economic capitalism has been the driving force in press history. Kaplan's own empirical contribution is to show for Detroit newspapers (1880–1910) that Progressive Era politics, including the weakening of the authority of political parties through primary elections and other reforms, and the specific political consequences of the election of 1896, helped propel among publishers, editors, and reporters a vision of "public service" via impartial and independent reporting.

We have seen, in these various cultural histories of journalistic objectivity in the United States, a productive focus on the manner in which journalists "turn themselves into a profession and themselves into professional people" (Hughes 1963, p. 655). Informed by comparative studies of journalism, the best of these studies recognize that a variety of professional norms might provide public support and critical insulation for professional projects in journalism in other countries, while the most recent historical surveys have usefully re-interrogated the relationship between professional norms, journalistic style, and the authority conferred by the public sphere. Scholars of journalistic professionalism are at least indirectly rediscovering a key insight articulated by Hughes and advanced initially by the Weberian professionalization theorists—that journalism's authority, status, occupational norms, and claims to expertise can be analyzed as facets of a professional project, of an inter- and intra-group struggle.

A large question remains: what exactly is the nature of this struggle? What, exactly, is the object over which this struggle is waged? And further: what are the dynamics of conflict and cooperation through which this struggle unfolds? In sketching out the answers to these questions we argue, first, that professional expertise (or rather, an odd form of specifically journalistic expertise) and the linking of this expertise to work serves as a lever by which occupational jurisdictions are created and seized by contending occupational groups. Second, we contend that the dynamics of this struggle are marked out by an odd fusion of overlapping networks and sharply defined boundary lines, and that a primary tactic in the struggle to define "who is a journalist" is to simultaneously sharpen and blur the lines between professional "insiders" and paraprofessional "outsiders."

JURISDICTION, NETWORKS, EXPERTISE, AND AUTHORITY

Following the lead of the professionalization theorists, then, over what social markers would we expect to see occupations struggle as they advance their "professional project"? For Sarfatti Larson, groups seeking professional status must organize themselves to attain market power—they must fight to first constitute and then control the market for their services. They must, as marketers of human services, "produce their producers" through training and education; they must attain state sanction for their occupational monopoly; they must ratify this monopoly through "the license, the qualifying examination, the diploma" (1977, p. 15).

Sociologist Andrew Abbott's (1988) work in *The System of the Professions* shares much with Sarfatti Larson's, but is a substantial refinement. In addition to criticizing Larson for her overemphasis on economic power as the ultimate basis of journalistic authority (rather than seeing professional power as emerging from mixture of economic control, political power, social status, and cultural authority), Abbott's most important advance over the 1970s' work is to argue that study of the professions must begin with a focus on professional *work* rather than the *occupational group* and the structural markers of professionalism as a distinct object of analysis. The key aspect of professional struggle, argues Abbott, is the struggle over jurisdiction, or the struggle over the link between knowledge and work. Abbott views the professional field as a terrain of competition, though in this instance as a competition over jurisdiction rather than the structural emblems of professionalism. As it claims jurisdiction, a profession asks society to recognize its cognitive structure (and thus the authority conferred by that recognition) through exclusive rights. "Jurisdiction has not only a culture, but also a social structure," Abbott argues (p. 59), a structure emerging out of this societal recognition. Doctors and lawyers, for instance, not only claim jurisdiction over specific areas of work but gain enforceable legal and political rights through state intervention. Even journalists, who lack many of the structural advantages granted to other professional groups, have achieved some level of juridical recognition via shield laws, for example, and privileged access to political leaders.

For Abbott, establishing professional jurisdiction requires more than simply labor; instead, the jurisdictional process refers to the day-to-day manner in which a profession both concretizes and displays its base of "abstract knowledge." According to Abbott, what differentiates professional knowledge from mere occupational knowledge in general is "a knowledge system governed by abstractions, a knowledge system that can redefine its problems and tasks, defend them from interlopers, and seize new problems" (p. 93). At the same time, this knowledge must be displayed via work. Or as Fournier (1999, p. 74) describes the link between knowledge and work in Abbott's theoretical scheme:

> Abbott uses [the] notion of cultural work to refer to the strategies that the professions deploy to manipulate their systems of [abstract] knowledge in such a way that they can appropriate various problems falling under their jurisdiction [...] Abbott's suggestion that professions engage in cultural *work* to establish their exclusive claim of competence over a particular "chunk of the world" emphasizes the active work that professionals have to put in to maintain the boundaries defining their jurisdiction.

By shifting his focus from "the structure(s) of professionalization" to an analysis of jurisdictional disputes concerning the relationship between abstract knowledge and work, Abbott allows us to expand our discussion of knowledge-based occupations outside the "traditional" professions, and also helps us to conceive of a new way in which occupational groups struggle over social and cultural status.

Conveniently for us, Abbott devotes substantial space to a discussion of journalists. In Abbott's account, journalism, at least in the United States, has claimed jurisdiction over the collection and distribution of qualitative, current information about general events. Journalism in general, and US journalism in particular, also displays an internal differentiation in which journalists who cover politics or other topics that bear on political democracy have the highest professional standing and an especially marked cultural authority. This close link to democratic politics gives journalism its closest relationship to recognition by the state, but a paradoxical recognition in that the First Amendment prohibits state regulation rather than requiring it (as in the case of state-regulated licensing of lawyers and doctors and a number of other professional occupations). US journalism's claim to objectivity—i.e., the particular method by which this information is collected, processed, and presented—gives it its unique jurisdictional focus by claiming to possess a certain form of expertise or intellectual discipline. Establishing jurisdiction over the ability to objectively parse reality is a claim to a special kind of authority.

In sum, journalistic objectivity operates as *both* an occupational norm and as object of struggle within the larger struggle over professional jurisdiction. "Expert" professionals—in this case, journalists—seek, via occupational struggle, to monopolize a form of journalistic expertise, which itself is discursively constructed out of various journalistic practices and narratives, including the claim to professional objectivity.

And yet, this very notion of journalistic expertise makes journalism an unusually fascinating case within the sociological analysis of the professions. The very notion of journalistic expertise is doubly problematic. Professions, argues Abbott, are "somewhat exclusive groups of individuals applying somewhat abstract knowledge to particular cases" (Abbott, 1988, p. 8). Yet most segments of the journalism profession are not exclusive (and with the arrival of on-line journalism becoming progressively less so); nor is journalistic knowledge abstract. Journalism seems to simultaneously make a grandiose knowledge claim (that it possesses the ability to isolate, transmit, and interpret the most publicly relevant aspects of social reality) and an incredibly modest one (that really, most journalists are not experts at all but are simply question-asking generalists). Abbott's framework, with its focus on knowledge and jurisdiction, helps us see immediately what makes journalism a sociologically anomalous profession.

If professional struggles are, in part, struggles over a definition of and jurisdiction over particular forms of expertise, what, exactly, is the nature of this struggle? Several answers common to both the sociological and journalism studies literature suggest themselves, each of which place an emphasis on the drawing of boundary lines and the creation of insiders and outsiders. In an important 1983 essay, Thomas Gieryn (1983) advanced the concept of "boundary work," the process by which divisions between fields of knowledge are delimited, attacked and reinforced. Specifically addressing the separation of religion from science in 19th century England, Gieryn argued that the emerging distinctions between "science" and "non-science" were partially constructed, and stemmed from the self-interested rhetorical maneuvers of scientists. In effect, the very act of answering the question "what is science" helped to shape the modern notions of science, defining it by both what it was and what it was not. For Gieryn, the struggle over the definition of scientist was a rhetorical struggle over boundaries.

A decade later, Zelizer (1992) echoed Gieryn's notion of boundary-work in her discussion of journalism. Specifically rejecting the paradigm of professionalization, Zelizer instead identifies journalists as an "interpretive community" whose authority stems from discursive sources operating both inside and outside the professional sphere. In her case study of media coverage of the John F. Kennedy assassination, Zelizer details how one emerging group, TV journalists, imposed themselves on the profession via both their coverage of Kennedy's murder and, just as importantly, the stories they later told one another about the killing. Zelizer agues that journalists use narrative to strengthen their position as an "authoritative interpretive community," using narrative to both consolidate their "truth-telling" position *vis-à-vis* other interpretive groups and to maintain internal group coherence (p. 197). As Zelizer emphasizes, the process of journalistic legitimization is primarily a rhetorical one, carried out through strategies such as synecdoche, omission, and personalization:

> The ability of journalists to establish themselves as authoritative spokespersons for the assassination story was predicated on their use of narrative in deliberate and strategic ways. Journalists' claims to legitimacy were no less rhetorically based than their narrative reconstructions of the activities behind the news [...] *While all professional groups are constituted by formalized bodies of knowledge, much of journalists' interpretive authority lies not in what they know, but in how they represent their knowledge.* (p. 34, original emphasis)

The claim that journalistic professionalism is established as much by the *representation* of knowledge as by the actual *possession* of knowledge would not, in and of itself, be a controversial theoretical claim; indeed, arguments about the constructed nature of professional expertise predate the post-structuralist critique and can be found in sociological scholarship as far back as Elliot Freidson. What is important and original is the emphasis on the rhetorical dimension of constituting the cultural authority of journalists. Where Zelizer's *Covering the Body* falls short is in its almost exclusive focus on the rhetorical dimension. Eyal's (2005, p. 16) recent critique of Gieryn is applicable to Zelizer as well:

> The first, and obvious [problem with Gieryn's notion of boundary work], is the fact that boundary work is limited to rhetoric. The social mechanisms that limit the number of authoritative speakers, that assign their statements with differential values, that close off certain topics and devices from non-expert inspection, that characterize something as "calculable" or "not calculable," etc., these mechanisms are far more robust than mere rhetoric. Rhetoric alone would never have been able to produce the relational reality of science or the economy, or politics, etc.

It is possible that journalists define themselves rhetorically more than do other professions—their rhetoric is not only about their work, it *is* their work. And where doctors and lawyers have, with government assistance, considerable control over the gates of entry to their fields, and hence have market power, journalists have no such autonomy in their work. They are almost always hired hands, not independent operators.

Struggle over the journalistic jurisdiction, then, includes, but cannot be limited to, "rhetorical" conflict. Once again, this key line from Abbott: "Jurisdiction has not only a culture, but also a social structure" (Abbott, 1988, p. 59). Zelizer's conception of journalistic authority, almost entirely cultural, is important but incomplete. How else might the struggle over journalistic expertise be framed, in a way that more productively incorporates the profession's social structure, as well as the "external" structures that impact upon the profession itself?

One possibility, gaining a following in recent years, would be to rethink journalism as a journalistic "field" in the terms of Pierre Bourdieu. Bourdieu envisions modern society as highly differentiated, composed of different spheres or "fields," each relatively autonomous and operating to some degree by a logic of its own. These fields include domains of art, politics, academia, and, most importantly for our purposes, journalism. Among communications scholars, Rodney Benson and Eric Neveu (2005) have led the way in applying Bourdieu's field concepts to journalism studies. In the same volume, Klinenberg has spoken of alternative youth media attempts to "channel into the journalistic field," and a few other researchers (Atton, 2002; Benson, 2003; Couldry & Curran, 2003) have used field concepts to explore the relationship between professional and non-professional media systems.

Nevertheless, as Chris Atton (2002) notes, it is difficult to fit alternative media into Bourdieu's conceptual frame since, almost by definition, they claim journalistic status by challenging mainstream journalism's norms and practices. The field concept may theorize well about highly structured and fairly unchanging social-cultural constellations (fields) but is less supple at explaining the spaces between fields, the competition between fields, and the edges of fields. When Bourdieu himself wrote about journalism as a field, he expressed alarm that it might subordinate itself to the political or economic fields. But full autonomy from these other fields is scarcely conceivable and perhaps not even desirable (Schudson, 2006); the political and the economic are incorporated inside journalism. If this were not so, the inclination of journalists to solipsism rather than to engagement with a large democratic public might prove irresistible. The concept of "field" does not seem to offer leverage for analyzing fringes, spaces, or competition.

Consider the difficulty in conceptualizing blogging in relation to journalism. Boundary lines between "insider and outsider," "professional and non-professional," "journalist and blogger" are blurred today and growing ever more fuzzy. Instead of a sharply defined boundary line we might better imagine a thick, poorly defined "border zone" made up of proliferating hybrids, shifting social and occupational roles, and networks of expertise (Eyal, 2005). Bloggers, once interlopers whose claim to journalistic jurisdiction mainstream journalist rejected, now receive press credentials. Longtime *Philadelphia Inquirer* reporter Dan Rubin goes from being a journalist to full-time (paid) blogger to journalist again. Vast numbers of amateurs with camera phones are spread across the world, far outnumbering professional news photographers, and so have access to many events of the moment the professionals do not—a subway commuter, for instance, provided key photos of the 2005 London subway bombings that news organizations around the world printed.

The boundary-maintaining problem this creates for journalism is apparent when an organization like World Press Photo, an international organization of professional photojournalists based in the Netherlands, selected its best photos of the year in 2005—choosing to eliminate from competition the photos at Abu Ghraib or in the wake of the tsunami because, even though they appeared in mainstream news publications, they were produced by amateurs (Livingstone, 2007). In an era of cell phone, camera phone, and blog, jurisdictional questions will be legion. Meanwhile, other developments in portable and efficient information transmission alter the character of how journalistic claims to authority are articulated. In television, the growing use of live "two way" interactions between a studio-based news presenter and a field-based reporter lend a growing air of informality to on-air discourse, a style that affords the reporters in the field leeway to distance themselves from a commitment to the factuality of their pronouncements, as Montgomery observes. Montgomery (2006), in a study of the BBC, sees an increase in reporters' use of terms like "probably" and "perhaps," "certainly" and "actually," and "I think" or "my instinct is," introducing a personal rather than institutional voice into the discourse of news. In a sense, this style of work maintains journalistic authority by removing it from its pedestal.

This does not deny that social actors still find a *rhetorical* value in fixing their own borders. Journalists, bloggers, citizen journalists, activist reporters all find it useful to define themselves and others as insider or outsider, as part of "our" or "the other" group. This is where the Bourdieuean notion of the field is valuable, perhaps not as a description of actually existing social reality, but at least as a term that points to the cultural construction of boundaries to which conventional journalists and their various competitors are emotionally invested. With the categories flexible and challenged, the rhetoric defining insider and outsider in flux, the deployment of the rhetoric is both strategic and essential to the identity of the various social actors involved.

CONCLUSION

We have argued, building on earlier work (Schudson, 2001), that objectivity acts as both a solidarity enhancing and distinction-creating norm and as a group claim to possess a unique kind of professional knowledge, articulated via work (Abbott, 1988). This knowledge claim, in the case of journalism, is an odd one: unlike most scientific or legal claims to possess the occupational ability to discern the "objective truth" about reality, journalists do not argue that they possess esoteric or uniquely complex expertise. Rather, journalism makes a claim that has been simultaneously grandiose (jurisdiction over the collection and distribution of information about current events of general interest and importance) and modest (in the US case, gathering information less on the basis of expertise than of attitude, a capacity to and willingness to subordinate the views of the journalist to the voices of their sources).

The question of the manner by which objectivity (or other journalistic norms and knowledge claims) function within a larger occupational, political, and economic social structure is more complicated and difficult to discern. On the one hand, professional claims obviously serve to draw boundary lines between those on the "inside" and "outside" of the profession. On the other hand, several decades of science studies have warned us to be wary of assuming that the *rhetorical* claims made about boundaries, claims often put forth by occupational groups themselves mirror the actual reality by which professional power, knowledge, and authority operate. In short, claims to knowledge and professional power are often contradictory and incoherent.

We have not tried to formulate any grand theoretical statement regarding the operation of professional power, authority, and expertise. For now, the following simple propositions are worth keeping in mind: any empirical investigation into the status of journalism should be sensitive to the importance of journalistic expertise (in the form of objectivity claims and in other forms) along with the contradictory nature of that claim; simultaneously, any analysis of journalism should keep in mind the complex and, once again, contradictory nature of claims to be "inside" and "outside" an occupational system of power.

REFERENCES

Abbott, A. D. (1988). *The system of professions: An essay on the division of expert labor.* Chicago: University of Chicago Press.

Atton, C. (2002). *Alternative media.* London: Sage.

Banning, S. A. (1999). The professionalization of journalism: A nineteenth-century beginning. *Journalism History, 24*(4), 157–160.

Benson, R. (2003). Commercialism and critique: California's alternative weeklies. In N. Couldry & J. Curran (Eds.), *Contesting media power: Alternative media in a networked world* (pp. 111–127). New York: Rowan & Littlefield.

Benson, R., & Neveu, E. (2005). *Bourdieu and the journalistic field.* Cambridge, MA: Polity.

Benson, R., & Saguy, A. (2005). Constructing social problems in an age of globalization: A French-American comparison. *American Sociological Review, 70*, 233–259.

Berenger, R. (2005). Al Jazeera: In Pursuit of "Contextual Objectivity," Transnational Broadcasting Studies Journal, 14, Retrieved June 7, 2006, from http://www.tbsjournal.com/Archives/Spring05/Reviews-Berenger.html

Bledstein, B. J. (1976). *The culture of professionalism: The middle class and the development of higher education in America.* New York: Norton.

Bourdieu, P. (1984). *Distinction: A social critique of the judgment of taste.* Cambridge, MA: Harvard University Press.

Carr-Saunders, A. M., & Wilson, P. A. (1993). *The professions*. Oxford: Clarendon Press.

Chalaby, J. (1998). *The Invention of journalism*. London: MacMillan.

Collins, R. (1979). *The credential society*. New York: Academic Press.

Couldry, N., & Curran, J. (2003). *Contesting media power: Alternative media in a networked world.* New York: Rowan & Littlefield.

Dicken-Garcia, H. (1984). *Journalistic standards in the 19th century*. Madison, WI: University of Wisconsin Press.

Dingwall, R., & Lewis, P. (Eds.). (1983). *The sociology of the professions: Doctors, lawyers, and others.* New York: St. Martin's.

Donsbach, W., & Patterson, T. E. (2004). Political news journalists. In F. Esser & B. Pfetsch (Eds.), *Comparing political communication: Theories, cases, and challenges* (pp. 251–270). Cambridge: Cambridge University Press.

Ehrenreich, B., & Ehrenreich, J. (1979). The professional-managerial class. In P. Walker (Ed.), *Between labor and capital* (pp. 5–45). Boston, MA: South End Press.

Eyal, G. (2005). Spaces between fields. Paper presented at the conference on "Bourdieuian Theory and Historical Analysis," at The Center for Comparative Research, Yale University, New Haven, CT, April 28.

Fishman, M. (1980). *Manufacturing the news*. Austin: University of Texas Press.

Fournier, V. (1999). The appeal to "professionalism" as a disciplinary mechanism. *Social Review, 47*(2), 280–307.

Freidson, E. (1970). *Profession of medicine: A study of the sociology of applied knowledge*. New York: Dodd, Mead.

Freidson, E. (1983). *Professional powers: A study of the institutionalization of formal knowledge*. Chicago: University of Chicago Press.

Gans, H. J. (2004). *Deciding what's news: A study of CBS Evening News, NBC Nightly News, Newsweek, and Time.* New York: Pantheon Books.

Gieryn, T. (1983). Boundary work and the demarcation of science from non-science: Strains and interests in professional ideologies of scientists. *American Sociological Review, 48*, 781–795.

Hallin, D., & Mancini, P. (2004). *Comparing media systems: Three models of media and politics*. Cambridge: Cambridge University Press.

Haskell, T. L. (1984). Professionalism versus capitalism: R. H. Tawney, Emile Durkheim, and C. S. Peirce on the Disinterestedness of Professional Communities. In T. L. Haskell (Ed.), *The authority of experts: Studies in history and theory* (pp. 180–225). Bloomington: Indiana University Press.

Hughes, E. C. (1963). "Professions." *Daedalus, 92*, 655–658.

Karabel, J., & Halsey, H. (Eds.). (1977). *Power and ideology in education.* New York: Oxford University Press.

Kaplan, R. (2002). *Politics and the American press: The rise of objectivity, 1865–1920*. Cambridge: Cambridge University Press.

Klinenberg, E. (2005). Convergence: New production in a digital age. *Annals of the American Political Science Association, 59*(7), 48–68.

Lichtenberg, J. (1989). In defense of objectivity. In J. Curran & M. Gurevitch (Eds.), *Mass media and society* (pp. 216–231). London: Arnold.

Livingstone, S. (2007). The "Nokia Effect": The reemergence of amateur journalism and what it means for international affairs. In D. D. Perlmutter & J. M. Hamilton (Eds.), *From pigeons to news portals: Foreign reporting and the challenge of new technology* (pp. 47–69). Baton Rouge: Louisiana State University Press.

MacDonald, K. M. (1995). The sociology of the professions. London: Sage.

Montgomery, M. (2006). Broadcast news, the live "two-way" and the case of Andrew Gilligan. *Media, Culture & Society, 28*, 233–259.

Ramaprasad, J. (2001). A profile of journalists in post-independence Tanzania. *Gazette, 63*(6), 539–555.

Ramaprasad, J., & Kelly, J. (2003). Reporting the news from the world's rooftop: A survey of Nepalese journalists. *Gazette, 65*(3), 291–315.

Ramaprasad, J., & Hamdy, N. (2006) Functions of Egyptian journalists: Perceived importance and actual performance. *Gazette, 68*(2), 167–185.

Sarfatti-Larson, M. (1977). *The rise of professionalism: A sociological analysis.* Berkeley: University of California Press.

Schudson, M. (1978). *Discovering the news: A social history of American newspapers.* New York: Basic Books.

Schudson, M. (1995). *The power of news.* Cambridge, MA: Harvard University Press.

Schudson, M. (2001). The objectivity norm in American journalism. *Journalism: Theory, Practice & Criticism, 2*(2), 149–170.

Schudson, M. (2005). Four approaches to the sociology of news. J. Curran & M. Gurevitch (Eds.), *Mass media and society* (pp. 172–197). London: Arnold.

Schudson, M. (2006). Autonomy from what? In R. D. Benson & E. Neveu (Eds.), *Bourdieu and the journalistic field* (214–223). Cambridge, MA: Polity.

Starr, P. (1984). *The social transformation of American medicine.* New York: Basic Books.

Summers, M. W. (1994). *The press gang: Newspapers and politics (1865–1878).* Chapel Hill: University of North Carolina Press.

Tawney, R. H. (1920). *The acquisitive society.* New York: Harcourt, Brace & Company.

Tucher, A. (2004). Reporting For duty: The Bohemian brigade, the Civil War, and the social construction of the reporter. Revised version of a paper presented to the Organization of American Historians, March 2004.

Tuchman, G. (1978). *Making news: A study in the construction of social reality.* New York: Free Press.

Tumber, H., & Prentoulis, M. (2005). Journalism and the making of a profession. In H. de Burgh (Ed.), *Making Journalists* (pp. 58–74). London: Routledge.

Weaver, D. H., & Wilhoit, G. C. (1986). *The American journalist: A portrait of newspeople and their work.* Bloomington: University of Indiana Press.

Weaver, D. H., Beam, R. A., Brownlee, B. J., Voakes, P. S., & Wilhoit, G. C. (2007). *The American journalist in the 21st century.* Mahwah, NJ: Erlbaum.

Zelizer, B. (1992). *Covering the body: The Kennedy assassination, the media, and the shaping of collective memory.* Chicago: University of Chicago Press.

Zelizer, B. (2004). *Taking journalism seriously: News and the academy.* Thousand Oaks, CA: Sage.

8

Reporters and Their Sources

Daniel A. Berkowitz

The study of reporters and their news sources draws its roots from questions about bias, power, and influence. Couched in an atmosphere of adversarial conditions, a key question in the early literature concerned whether reporters or sources exert greater influence in shaping the news. One extension of this question asks how journalists' use of news sources leads toward a particular news agenda that either favors or excludes some issues over others. A second extension asks if source power provides the ability to subsidize the time and effort required for reporting.

In essence, the relationship between reporters and their sources has long been depicted as a battle for power over public opinion and public consent (Anderson, Peterson, & David, 2005; Blumler & Gurevitch, 1981; McQuail, 2000; Sallot & Johnson, 2006). Journalists end up in a role of protecting society from corruption, while officials in government and business take on the task of protecting their own interests at all costs. But these kinds of power only represent something ephemeral, that is, the ability to shape the outcome of specific issues and policies. Once the outcome is resolved, the power battle begins anew.

This chapter argues that more is at stake between journalists and their sources than the short-term power to sway public opinion. Instead, the interaction between these two parties represents a long-term, yet dynamic influence on society: the ability to shape ongoing meanings in a culture. Also called into question is the Western grounding for much of this research. In particular, press systems and political systems both vary across regions and countries, as does the social status of journalists, so what might appear to a Western perspective as co-optation, just as likely reflects the pragmatics of journalistic and, more broadly, cultural realities.

It is important to mention here that the term "source" is used only to refer to the people who reporters turn to for their information, often officials and experts connected to society's central institutions. Another use of the term is applied to news agencies (see, for example, Boyd-Barrett & Rantanen, 2004), organizations such as the Associated Press that provide news content to newspapers, broadcast outlets and websites: that second use of the term is not part of the scope of this discussion.

The chapter begins with a sociological perspective for the relationship between reporters and their sources, providing a framework for understanding the positions of their interaction. It then embarks from an initial depiction of an adversarial relationship, grounded in attempts to influence public opinion, to a more neutral exchange between two parties who each have something to gain, and finally, to a negotiation over long-term cultural meanings and ideological power. With these elements in place, the chapter then takes what is essentially a Western research discourse and begins to place it into broader global settings. The question of voice and empowerment—of both reporters and sources—is then introduced as a key mediating factor. Finally, the chapter gains closure on the overall argument, briefly touching on the role of evolving media technologies in reshaping the nature of journalist-source interaction.

A SOCIOLOGICAL PERSPECTIVE ON THE REPORTER-SOURCE RELATIONSHIP

The shape of the reporter-source relationship grows from core tenets of journalism's professional ideology (Deuze, 2005; Hackett, 1984; Roshco, 1975; Schudson, 2002). To understand the relationship, then, requires stripping away—at least temporarily—this ideology to see what lies within. Two dimensions need to be addressed: First, the basic demands of the ideology, and second, the procedures that journalists apply to accomplish their work and produce their product.

The ideology of the profession represents a paradigm, a method for accomplishing a task in a prescribed way. If journalists adhere to this paradigm, the desired result is expected to follow (Ericson, 1999). Essentially, journalism's paradigm follows a science-like model, where reporters gather authoritative data and then present it without explicitly taking a side in the discourse. Experts and officials—as sources—become the providers of this data, so that reporters become beholden to them for the raw materials of news (Herman & Chomsky, 1988). On their own, reporters are not allowed to provide an opinion—even when reporting on an event—so that interpretation is limited to such things as crowd-size estimates, descriptions of settings, depictions of how people appeared, and what those people said. By following this source-driven process, reporters become society's scientists and the news they produce becomes their "scientific report"—their truth (Ericson, 1999).

On the face of it, this paradigm would seem to work effectively, but that ignores the fact that news sources usually have a vested interest in journalists' reports, linking news content to public opinion, and ultimately, their own success (Griffin & Dunwoody, 1995; Herman & Chomsky, 1988; Reich, 2006). For authority figures, keeping public opinion in their favor enhances the ability to remain in that position of authority. For elected authority figures, the imperative to favorably influence public beliefs becomes even stronger: at stake is their ability to remain in office and implement their desired policies. For leaders of organizations and businesses, what news says about them helps maintain social permission to continue their current course of doing business: losing public favor can require a change of course.

In all, both reporters and sources have a lot at stake. Reporters put their credibility and believability on the line with each news item they write. Likewise, sources regularly risk their career success. Putting both parts of this equation together suggests that the interaction between reporters and their sources is a delicately negotiated relationship, with each party hoping to achieve their goals and maintain their organizational and societal status. As Sigal (1986, p. 29) asserted:

> News is, after all, not what journalists think, but what their sources say, and is mediated by news organizations, journalistic routines and conventions, which screen out many of the personal predilections of individual journalists.

This depiction of news and the reporter-source relationship highlights the second dimension that journalists face, that news is a product with organizational expectations, and that reporters must develop strategies and procedures to help ensure they will produce their product on time and in a form that their peers will judge as "good" (Tuchman, 1973). News becomes a construction, and the interaction of reporters and sources is how that construction comes to be (Ericson, 1999).

Nearly every vocation and profession faces that same challenge, at least in the abstract: a business must hire a workforce, workers need to apply their skills strategically to meet production quotas given their available resources, and ultimately, consumers must be satisfied with the product they receive, both in terms of timeliness and quality (McManus, 1994).

In practical terms, reporters manage their organizational limitations by routinizing their tasks (Ericson, 1999). Although they need to contact multiple sources for writing stories, their reconnaissance process needs boundaries. Sources are not always instantly available, so that scheduling of interviews becomes a task that demands time to accomplish and cuts into total working time until deadline. A basic collection of known sources helps make this task easier, but sometimes new sources must be found (Berkowitz, 1987; Berkowitz & Adams, 1990; Brown, Bybee, Wearden, & Straughan, 1987; Gant & Dimmick, 2000; Roshco, 1975). Adding to complications, some sources might not be cooperative for some stories or might not be available when needed. Some sources, too, might want to jump into the fray unexpectedly and reporters must deal with their input. Making things more complicated yet, unspoken, socially-learned organizational "policy" can sometimes dictate the routes that reporters must take and the sources and topics that are off limits.

Once reporters meet up with their sources, whether face-to-face or electronically, a second negotiation process takes place (Ericson, Baranek, & Chan, 1989; Reich, 2006). There, reporters attempt to glean the maximum amount of information from their sources, taking their conversation in directions that a source might not always want to go (Awad, 2006). Sources, in turn, attempt to maintain the information-gathering effort in line with the information they are willing to provide, generally details that are neutral, that can further their own cause, or in some cases, that can damage the cause of an opponent (Gans, 1980). But reporters do not always lead the way, because sources often proactively try to influence what becomes news through news releases, news conferences, planned events, and leaks that can jump-start the reporting process. Sources can even attempt to promote their cause by bringing attention to occurrences that may have happened naturally, such as crises and disasters involving others (Gandy, 1982; Molotch & Lester, 1974). A very large proportion of news originates from sources' efforts, and sources who can provide reporters with easily assembled news have a greater chance of making their voices heard (Curtin, 1999; Gandy, 1982; Turk, 1985). Over time, much of the news originates from savvy sources who understand reporters' needs and can deliver information regularly; paradoxically, much of what sources deliver overall tends to miss the mark and lose a place in the news (Berkowitz, 1992).

In sum, the work of a journalist becomes an everyday task of scheduling: sources are what must be scheduled. For some stories, scheduling becomes more complicated, either because of limited deadline time or source availability. Reporters learn how to find sources that can readily be scheduled and who will provide the kinds of information they seek in a concise and manageable way. Once the scheduling of sources and their interviews has taken place, reporters can then shift to a new work mode, interpreting the information they have received, privileging some sources' information over others, and crafting a news story that corresponds to the rules of the paradigm.

FROM A POWER PERSPECTIVE TO A FOCUS ON CULTURAL MEANING-MAKING

If a central element of journalistic ideology is the media's watchdog role over government and big business, then reporters' struggles to gather important information from sources become crucial. This could be characterized as a power struggle, with reporters constantly digging for information and sources working to prevent what could be perceived as overzealous journalistic inquiry (Kaniss, 1991). If a source has a high level of power, reporters' efforts to gather information can be thwarted. Conversely, high power reporters have the ability to gather more information from more sources (Reese, 1991). Part of the question, then, is "What determines the power of journalists and sources?" A related question asks, "What does this power affect?"

Turning to the first question, "What determines power?" offers different answers for reporters and their sources. For reporters, the question comes down to attributes of the reporter and attributes of the reporter's organization (Herman & Chomsky, 1988). Regarding the reporter, three aspects stand out. The first is experience, so that a reporter with longevity in the profession gains status over the years. Longevity alone does not equate with power, however. For example, a long-time society reporter would have little power in relation to national, state, or even local news sources. A second factor shaping a reporter's power, then, is his or her track record for writing stories of impact, an impact known by the news sources that reporter encounters on the job. A third factor is intra-organizational power: if a reporter has more autonomy within an organization, then deadline pressure can be lessened and there will be more opportunity to develop a story.

The reporter's organization also influences power, although this is not an absolute designation. For example, news organizations with a broader scope of operation—nationally or internationally—generally have greater power when they face news sources. Previous reputations for publishing or airing influential news stories enhance and solidify that power. For example, a quality broadsheet newspaper and a popular tabloid would have different levels of power within the same range of sources and audience: here, the influence they wield closely links to their power differential (Berkowitz & TerKeurst, 1999). However, when a news organization from a larger sphere covers news in a smaller sphere, that large-scale power might be irrelevant. For example, a national media organization covering news that mainly impacts a small geographic community would not necessarily have much power if the local residents in that area were not part of the media organization's audience. There, the local media organization might turn out to have more influence in the outcome of an issue or event.

Source power is somewhat simpler to assess. Sources located within a power structure, who have both authority of knowledge and autonomy to speak about that knowledge, tend to be most powerful (Ericson, 1999). Sources with the ability to promote an occurrence to the media under certain circumstances could have temporary power, such as promoting an environmentalist position to the media after an oil spill (Molotch & Lester, 1974). Reese (1991) suggests that the perceived power levels that reporters and their sources bring to a specific interaction have an important impact on the news outcome. This balance can also shape the nature of the relationship, making interactions more symbiotic and cooperative when power levels between journalists and sources are approximately equal but more adversarial when one of the two parties is perceived to have the upper hand.

Altogether, this discussion suggests that the relationship between reporters and their sources is a dynamic phenomenon, depending on the context of a specific occurrence as well as the perceived power that each party brings to the relationship. This power balance also shapes how interactions between reporters and sources unfold and which party can lead the negotiation for information that turns into news reports. That brings up the second question: "What does this power affect?"

Conventionally, the answer to this question has been cast in terms of power over public opinion and influence over the news agenda (Kaniss, 1991; Curtin, 1999). For public officials and business leaders, daily life is a matter of maintaining positive public opinion. Thus, at the simplest level, power for a source translates to the ability to have a voice in an ongoing debate in the news agenda (Berkowitz & TerKeurst, 1999). A somewhat more powerful position for sources is not only to be able to speak to an issue on the news agenda, but to be able to influence the shape of an issue that gains a place on the agenda and then form the initial discussion about that issue. More powerful yet is the ability to influence whether an issue will reach the news agenda and gain public discussion: keeping something away from the public eye amounts to the ability to make decisions impacting society without having to gain public consent.

For journalists, power translates to a mirror image of these levels. Being able to gain source information that broadens public debate represents a basic level of power. Being able to draw attention to issues and begin public dialogue among news sources becomes a more powerful position. There is no clear analog to the third level of power, however, because reporters would rarely want to hide a story from public view.

But the power of journalists and sources to control an ongoing news agenda is ephemeral, depending on the fluctuating tides of those who are in charge and the social world in which they interact (Fico & Balog, 2003). When a new administration gains power, the lasting ability of the news agenda becomes up for grabs. Some issues would linger, while others would disappear. Public opinion for an out-of-office official becomes largely irrelevant unless it has some impact on those who have moved in. In sum, focusing only on public opinion when considering the relationship between reporters and their sources is to overlook some of the more long-term, lasting impact. It thus becomes important to shift the discussion to culture and the meanings it contains.

The concept of framing is one way to consider the impact of reporters and their sources on meanings (Pan & Kosicki, 2001). Thinking of news meanings like this suggests that issues can be discussed in specific ways, with specific boundaries applied to which meanings are included in the discussion and which are beyond its scope. When reporters or their sources rein in an issue this way, certain depictions become the dominant way of thinking as the issue runs its course. A weakness of the approach, however, is that the larger implications of framing often do not get considered. That is, to say that an issue, an event, or a social group was "framed" in such-and-such way mainly plays off of specific norms. From a journalism studies perspective, it is always easy to find how news framing misses a norm and therefore can be considered an "unfair" depiction. But the implications can be taken much deeper, from an argument about whether reporters or their sources have more power in the relationship, to the more macro-level perspective of what long-term societal impact this framing has for the political power of certain groups, administrations, or interests over others. Thus when the interface between reporters and their sources produces and reproduces a specific frame, a specific vantage point on the social order is propagated and maintained: the meaning of occurrences and issues is one of the implications of the reporter-source relationship that impacts ideology itself (Coman, 2005).

Another perspective on meanings connected to the reporter-source relationship comes from sources' responsiveness to their *interpretive community* (Berkowitz & TerKeurst, 1999; Zelizer, 1993). An interpretive community represents a cultural location where meanings are constructed, shared, and reconstructed during the course of everyday life. Interpretive groups can be formed by a physical place, an organization, a virtual online gathering and other social collectives. Members of an interpretive community interact by internalizing taken-for-granted shared meanings and draw on those meanings as a guide to their values and interpretations of issues and occurrences.

Reporters find themselves in a duality of meanings, from both their professional interpretive community and the interpretive community of their sources (Berkowitz & TerKeurst, 1999). There are four main dimensions of reporters' professional interpretive community. First, reporters are guided by their professional ideology, taking professional ideals into consideration, such as objectivity, independence, fairness, and a watchdog role. Second, reporters keep in mind the interpretive community of their media organization, the "policy" that they have socially learned through everyday life on the job. This second interpretive community might conflict with the first, providing subtle guidance about favoring certain sources and organizations over others, going easy on some sources while reporting aggressively on others. The third and fourth interpretive communities appear through Zelizer's concept of *double time*, where reporters consider both present-day localized meanings for occurrences and issues, and a broader historical reference point that provides constant comparison between what has happened in the past and what is happening in the present (Zelizer, 1993).

Sources' interpretive communities face up against these four reporter dimensions. When an event occurs, when an issue is raised, sources have a goal of bringing forward one dominant meaning from among the possible interpretations. For corporate, government, and special interest sectors, the ultimate objective is to protect and strengthen their social position and power through interpretations that facilitate acceptance of the meanings they prefer (Berkowitz & TerKeurst, 1999). For both reporters and their sources, adoption of these meanings does not necessarily become a conscious or purposively strategic act. Instead, they turn into tacit understandings, with meanings growing from group (and cross-group) interactions over time. In addition, although these meanings generally have short-term consistency, they are gently dynamic as well.

In sum, these two sites of meaning making—journalistic practice and source communities—show how news content is not shaped by the classic vision of socially autonomous journalists acting as watchdogs or by short-term battles between reporters and their sources. Instead, journalists are beholden to four dimensions of their interpretive community. Likewise, news sources live within their own competing interpretive communities, responding to the preferred meanings that they have learned.

PLACING THE REPORTER-SOURCE RELATIONSHIP INTO A GLOBAL CONTEXT

Much of the research about reporters and their sources has been based on Western press systems and even more specifically, on how the relationship surfaces in the United States (Josephi, 2005). A question needs to be addressed, however: How far can we take this knowledge in order to understand other press systems? Two extensions of the basic question go to opposite poles (Reese, 2001). One extended question asks how differences *between* press systems should be weighed into our understandings; a second question asks how much attention should be paid to differences *within* a single press system (Hanitzsch, 2006).

These are not easy questions to answer, and yet, it would be equally difficult to assert that there is a *global* journalism that blurs many of the long-standing distinctions between nations and their press systems. Many anecdotal examples are available to show how one system's norms become another system's aberrations (Schudson, 2003, pp. 134–153). An appropriate level of analysis for understanding these examples is not obvious. Although the extra-media or societal levels stand out as most likely, care must be taken to avoid over-reducing a single system's homogeneity (Hanitzsch, 2006; Reese, 2001). In the end, we are left with that same big question: How does the reporter-source relationship influence the news? We are, however, left floundering for precise answers once leaving the comfort of a single home base for study.

Examples of a Portable Relationship

The basic relationship between reporters and their sources can thus be seen as "portable," that is, the relationship exists in all press systems, from the most authoritarian to the most libertarian, if in different forms (Josephi, 2005). Even when examining the same situation, what might be seen as an element of freedom through one lens of journalistic professionalism might be viewed as rather constrained through another. In every case, a fundamental belief of journalists is that they cannot simply make up news but instead must rely on what they have been told by somebody holding a perceived level of authority (Hanitzsch, 2006).

For example, the relationship between reporters and officials is highly controlled at Japanese Kisha clubs, while foreign affairs reporters in the Netherlands enjoy a high degree of freedom from official sources because they face little imperative to produce news (Schudson, 2003, pp. 138–139; Zelizer, 2004, p. 152). In the Japanese case, news becomes largely what officials say, while in the Netherlands, reporters are essentially in charge, with subjective output as an accepted norm. In other systems, sources pay reporters for coverage, an extremely unethical situation for American reporters, but taken as part of the "envelope journalism" system by Mexican reporters (and those in several other countries) to subsidize their low wages in a way similar to restaurant waiters (Schudson, 2003, pp. 149–150; Zelizer, 2004, p. 152).

Other comparisons highlight differences that emerge from a combination of professional and societal cultures. For example, when comparing American and Israeli reporters through their responses to a set of hypothetical scenarios, those from the United States were much less likely to negotiate with a source, although both groups expressed similar views about protecting source confidentiality (Berkowitz, Limor, & Singer, 2004). In Korea, several studies have found that the relationship becomes more personal than is typical in the West, yet sources are not attempting to co-opt reporters through friendly interactions: this kind of close friendship is instead a key element of Korean culture overall (Berkowitz & Lee, 2004; Kim & Bae, 2006; Shin & Cameron, 2003). In a study of Swedish/Danish media, a high degree of symbiosis was found between political-economic elites and journalists working for regional media (Falkheimer, 2005). This contrasts with the situation found in Russia, where autonomous sources have emerged only recently, so that conflict underlies an ongoing battle, with sources vying to promote their vested interests and journalists working to maximize their new-found power (Koltsova, 2001). In New Zealand, the situation appears more congenial, yet sources still tend to dominate, serving in a role closer to what Schudson (2003) called the para-journalist who provides "favourable facts" rather than a more neutral representation of information (Rupar, 2006). A study of journalists in Britain and Spain found that the element of crisis created a special case for the journalist-source relationship, with sources attempting to gain journalists' favor in order further their agendas and damage their opponents, through what has been called "ventriloquist journalism" (Sanders & Canel, 2006).

Learning from the Global Base of Research

These examples suggest some commonalties for the reporter-source relationship across countries, with both subtle and significant variations appearing in the extra-media and societal levels. The clearest commonalties link within similar locations on the authoritarian-libertarian continuum, where similar degrees of reporters' autonomy shape the boundaries of the relationship. Altschull's (1995) vision of press systems recasts the situation yet again, so that reporters facing constraints from a pro-development stance become self-limiting in their demands on official sources in the name of national growth.

One position to take in applying research from one system to another would be to argue that findings from one cannot be generalized to another, no matter how similar they appear. A second, more productive position would be to adopt the concept of transferability (Denzin & Lincoln, 2005) that identifies contextual and structural similarities and contrasts between two cases, and then adjusts the findings from one to better inform the other. This second stance avoids a reductionist approach that overlooks key differences, while also avoiding an absolutist view suggesting that very little can be moved from one situation to the next.

An advantage of transferability and comparison is that the contrasting cases can more clearly highlight the salient characteristics of each. For example, contrasts between cultures' interpersonal relationships in general can be used as a basis for understanding differences in synergistic or conflictual levels between reporters and officials across systems. Similarly, considering cultures' gender equity positions, especially in relation to the gender makeup of the journalistic workforce, can highlight subtle- and not-so-subtle nuances of the power that officials wield over reporters (Lachover, 2005; Robins, 2001).

Overall, the key point for global understanding is to stay alert to the context of research about reporters and their sources when developing a conceptual framework for new research, and to maintain an awareness of the boundaries of interpretation when that existing lens is then applied.

WHO GETS A VOICE?—GENDER, ETHNICITY, AND THE JOURNALIST-SOURCE RELATIONSHIP

A central point of concern for the relationship between reporters and sources is that, if the journalistic paradigm calls for turning to authoritative news sources, then those believed to possess authority will have a better chance of getting a voice in the news. When high prestige official sources appear in the news, the reporter-source relationship tends to legitimate or even reify the power structure of society (Manning, 2001; Sigal, 1973; Soloski, 1989). This occurs because the job of journalists is to produce news content that bears the aura of factuality: the statements of credible sources can be taken as fact, certifying the news without the need to research the veracity of that "fact" (Ericson, 1999). In most societies, fact bearers live in the ideologically dominant mainstream, representing that mainstream's dominant ideological institutions and presenting their dominant frame (Hertog & McLeod, 2001). Most often, sources tend to be male authority figures and do not belong to one of their society's minority groups (Allan, 1998; Kitzinger, 1998; Ross, 2007).

In relation to the reporter-source relationship, then, an important question asks, "Who gets a voice?" That is, to what degree do dominant mainstream voices control the information that journalists get and how much opportunity do women and minorities have to appear in the news and shape its meanings? Of course, the answers do not literally have fixed quantitative parameters, but they nonetheless can be addressed from that perspective. A second—and less obvious—question must also be raised: How does the gender and ethnicity of *reporters* shape the kinds and quantities of "facts" that can be obtained?

If reporters' choice of news sources tends to be male officials from the mainstream, it is useful to consider the circumstances where women gain voice and take an active role in the relationship. One central question that has been studied involves the interaction between female reporters and female news sources (Armstrong, 2004; Freedman & Fico, 2005; Van Zoonen, 1998; Zeldes & Fico, 2005). The main direction of inquiry in this vein asks whether female reporters are more likely to draw on female news sources when the opportunity arises. The logic here is that female reporters will be less ingrained in the male power structure and they will feel more comfortable interviewing female sources, a sort of gender-based camaraderie that would not exist with male sources, who might also have the upper hand in terms of socio-political power.

Zeldes and Fico (2005) explored this notion through a study of gender and race of reporters and sources appearing on network newscasts during the 2000 presidential election. They found that stories by women and minority reporters were indeed linked to more diverse source use. This finding also appeared in several other studies, but to a lesser degree. Freedman and Fico (2005) examined sources—particularly source expertise—in news coverage of a state governor race and found that stories with the byline of a female reporter had a greater tendency to cite female non-partisan sources. However, the overwhelming majority of non-partisan sources were still male, and female non-expert sources appeared far less often than their proportion in the overall population. A study by Armstrong (2004) had a similar result, finding that male sources received more mention and were placed more prominently. Again, female reporter bylines were a predictor of more frequent use of female news sources. Ross (2007) addressed the gender question within the context of local British newspapers and found the same patterns held true, with male sources still dominating the news, even when the reporters were women.

In part, the degree of difference in these findings is tempered by broader organizational and professional expectations, with newsroom norms and practices operating as a conformity mechanism, especially at larger newspapers (Rogers & Thorson, 2003). These expectations from newsroom colleagues would rein in female reporters' boundaries for broadening the news, particularly where newsrooms are dominated by male leadership (Weaver et al., 2007). It is possible, however, that for certain genres of news, female sources are somewhat more likely to appear (Armstrong, 2006). And as a counter-force, some news organizations have established formal policy encouraging a greater use of diverse news sources (Mohamed & Fleming-Rife, 2002).

Research related to source gender also informs the use of news sources from ethnicities and races outside the mainstream. In the United States, for example, Latinos, Asian Americans, Native Americans rarely serve as news sources. African Americans appear somewhat more frequently, especially when another source appears in a news item (Poindexter, Smith, & Heider, 2003). Even in cases with explicit organizational policy for drawing on minority news sources, the mix of news sources appears much the same (Mohamed & Fleming-Rife, 2002).

Extending the concept of source diversity further, some news organizations see themselves as alternative or oppositional: an expectation for their news would be to include a greater proportion of ordinary citizens as sources. Surprisingly, oppositional news also emphasizes elites rather than citizens, although these elites come from outside the dominant mainstream. This was found in a study of an activist newspaper in the UK (Atton & Wickenden, 2005) as well as in an oppositional radio station in the US (Eliasoph, 1988). In either case, the answer is simple: reporters need to gather their information from authoritative sources whom audiences will view as legitimate bearers of "facts." The real difference in these cases is that alternative media draw on authoritative sources more closely aligned with their own ideological positions. In contrast, a mainstream news organization faced with choosing between a mainstream official source or an expert located in an oppositional camp will choose the mainstream official source as a means of producing ideological consistency (Coleman, 1995).

Switching the Power Relationship: Female Reporters and Male Sources

The preceding discussion has shown how mainstream sources tend to dominate the news and how the majority of those sources tend to be male officials. This situation gives sources a socially powerful position. The US newsroom gender balance includes approximately one-third women overall, and slightly more than one-half of new journalists are women. This gender balance tapers off significantly when power, expertise and authority are taken into account (Weaver et al., 2007). Among those with at least fifteen years of experience in the journalistic workforce, only about one-quarter are women. In sum, female reporters enter the journalist-source relationship in a lower status position and often do not increase their status as much over time as do their male counterparts.

A study of female journalists and male sources in Israel bears out this imbalance, identifying the gendered tone of reporter-source interactions (Lachover, 2005). There, male sources were sometimes found to draw on the power imbalance to sway a female reporter, yet sometimes male sources became more cooperative than usual in order to impress a female reporter. Women reporters, aware of the sexualized relationship with their male sources, admitted, though, that they sometimes took advantage of the situation by flirting or feigning weakness to gain more from their sources. A similar situation was found in a study of female reporters in Tanzania (Robins, 2001), even though male sources were often guilty of sexual harassment.

In all, this discussion suggests some clear imbalances in the reporter-source relationship, constructing a gendered and ideological representation of society and its voices. Although much of the literature discussed here is drawn from US-based studies, there are clear implications for understanding the power balance and meaning-making implications that are involved. Most simply, not all sources are equal in their relationships with reporters, with women and minorities tending to have the weaker position, whether as a journalist or as a source.

CONCLUSIONS

This chapter began with the premise that the study of reporters and their sources has been cast in terms of two polar dimensions: the adversarial position, with journalist as watchdog, and the symbiotic position, where both reporters and their sources give up something and gain something in return. Both positions have been drawn from a Western perspective, often an American one.

Three problems underlie these positions. First, the situation is not an either/or outcome. Instead, the elements of adversarial and symbiotic interaction appear on a continuum, with the perceived power of each party constantly shifting. The reporter-source relationship, then, is a constantly negotiated one. Second, the relationship is context dependent. Its nature depends on the context of the times, of course, but also on the issues under consideration, the press system where journalists and sources meet, and even the gender and ethnicity of each party involved. Third, much of the research has overlooked the "So what?" question. That is, why do we care which party is in charge? The short-term answer is easier: controlling the face of the news provides shape over public opinion and the ability to exert power over social issues and social debate.

But the short-term answer is not enough: the ability to influence the news also equates to long-term control over cultural meanings. Although meanings are dynamic, they do not move nearly as quickly as public opinion. When a reporter or a source can influence a long-term news discourse over meanings, they have influence over dominant ideological positions, those "common sense" understandings about individuals, institutions, and occurrences. Key terms at the center of discussion also load up with ideological meaning, turning into ideographs with essentially uncontested attributes. Ideographs then become the tools of everyday conversation, with meanings taken for granted when they are drawn into use. For example, "terrorism" after events in the United States, England, Spain, and Russia began to automatically include specific social groups, specific political positions, specific issues, and even specific regions of the world. As further social dialog continued, the meanings became more-and-more natural and the separation between "us" and "the other" became taken for granted. The term "democracy" lands in a similar position.

Related to this influence over meanings, two mediating factors were introduced: the influence of culture and the role of identity. The country where reporters interact with their sources does make a difference, partly because of press system differences, but also partly because of the role that media play in a specific culture. Similarly, gender and ethnicity bring attributes of social meaning to journalists and sources that both limit and enable the extent of their roles. Female sources often have less ability to access journalists and less ascribed power to influence the direction of their interactions once they do gain access. The case is much the same for sources outside a culture's dominant ethnicities. Female reporters end up in a similar role problem, too, with less power and influence than male reporters.

One other factor—technology—comes into play as well. Television news, for example, has become "more opinionated and less densely sourced," so that it can be considered a "soft discourse" that allows journalists to distance themselves from source-based facts (Schudson & Dokoupil, 2007). Convergence, likewise, has changed the situation, with less face-to-face or voice-to-voice communication between reporters and their sources, and email filling the gap. Even further, blogs have begun to blur the line about who is a journalist and who is a source, and the role of sourcing has become equally ambiguous as a result (Pavlik, 2004). Finally, the practice of obtaining sources second-hand from the Internet has complicated questions about which sources count and what degree of sourcing is sufficient (Ruggiero, 2004).

Regardless of these mediating factors, sourcing in some form or another will remain a crucial tenet of the strategic ritual of "doing journalism." As long as reporters need to write beyond their opinions alone, as long as they see themselves as conveyers of information rather than interpreters of issues and occurrences, they will need to rely on sources. Sources, although usually deemed authoritative, speak from vested positions in their organizations and from ideological positions in their cultural worlds. In the short-term balance hangs ephemeral social power, while in the long-term, the interaction between reporters and their sources—and the media accounts that result—have the potential to shape people's taken-for-granted assumptions about how their world revolves.

REFERENCES

Allan, S. (1998). (En)gendering the truth politics of news discourse. In C. Carter, G. Branston, & S. Allan (Eds.), *News, gender and power* (pp. 121–140). London: Routledge.

Altschull, J. (1995). *Agents of power: The media and public policy, 2nd ed.* White Plains, NY: Longman.

Anderson, A., Peterson, A., & David, M. (2005). Communication or spin? Source-media relations in science journalism. In S. Allan (Ed.), *Journalism: Critical issues* (pp. 188–198). Berkshire & New York: Open University.

Armstrong, C. (2004). The influence of reporter gender on source selection in newspaper stories. *Journalism & Mass Communication Quarterly, 81*(1), 139–154.

Armstrong, C. (2006). Story genre influences whether women are sources. *Newspaper Research Journal, 27*(3), 66–81.

Atton, C., & Wickenden, E. (2005). Sourcing routines and representation in alternative journalism: A case study approach. *Journalism Studies, 6*(3), 347–359.

Awad, I. (2006). Journalists and their sources: Lessons from anthropology. *Journalism Studies, 7*(6), 922–939.

Berkowitz, D. (1987). TV news sources and news channels: A study in agenda-building. *Journalism Quarterly, 64*, 508–513.

Berkowitz, D. (1992). Who sets the media agenda? The ability of policymakers to determine news decisions. In J. D. Kennamer (Ed.), *Public opinion, the press, and public policy* (pp. 81–102). Westport, CT: Praeger.

Berkowitz, D., & Adams, D. (1990). Information subsidy and agenda-building in local television news. *Journalism Quarterly, 67* (Winter), 723–731.

Berkowitz, D., & Lee, J. (2004). Media relations in Korea: *Cheong* between journalist and public relations practitioner. *Public Relations Review, 30,* 431–437.

Berkowitz, D., & TerKeurst, J. (1999). Community as interpretive community: Rethinking the journalist-source relationship. *Journal of Communication, 49*(3), 125–136.

Berkowitz, D., Limor, Y., & Singer, J. (2004). A cross-cultural look at serving the public interest: American and Israeli journalists consider ethical scenarios. *Journalism: Theory, Practice, & Criticism, 5*(2), 159–181.

Blumler, J., & Gurevitch, M. (1981). Politicians and the press: An essay on role relationships. In D. Nimmo & K. Sanders (Eds.), *Handbook of political communication* (pp. 467–493). Newbury Park, CA: Sage.

Boyd-Barrett, O. & Rantanen, T. (2004). News agencies as news sources: A re-evaluation. In C. Paterson & A. Sreberny (Eds.), *International news in the twenty-first century* (pp. 31–45). London: John Libbey.

Brown, J., Bybee, C., Wearden, S., & Straughan, D. (1987). Invisible power: Newspaper news sources the the limits of diversity. *Journalism Quarterly, 67*, 45–54.

Coleman, C. (1995). Science, technology and risk coverage of a community conflict. In D. Berkowitz (Ed.), *Social meanings of news: A text-reader* (pp. 483–496). Thousand Oaks, CA: Sage.

Coman, M. (2005). Cultural anthropology and mass media: A processual approach. In E. Rothenbuhler & M. Coman (Eds.), *Media anthropology* (pp. 46–55). Thousand Oaks, CA: Sage.

Curtin, P. (1999). Reevaluating public relations information subsidies: Market-driven journalism and agenda-building theory and practice. *Journal of Public Relations Research, 11*(1), 53–90.

Denzin, N., & Lincoln, Y. (2005). Introduction: The discipline and practice of qualitative research. In N. Denzin & Y. Lincoln (Eds.), *The Sage handbook of qualitative research, 3rd ed.* (pp. 1–32). Thousand Oaks, CA: Sage.

Deuze, M. (2005). What is journalism? Professional identity and ideology of journalists reconsidered. *Journalism: Theory, Practice & Criticism, 6* (4), 442–464.

Eliasoph, N. (1988). Routines and the making of oppositional news. *Critical Studies in Mass Communication, 5,* 313–334.

Ericson, R. (1999). How journalists visualize fact. *The Annals of the American Academy of Political and Social Science, 560*(1), 83–95.

Ericson, R., Baranek, P., & Chan, J. (1989). *Negotiating control: A study of news sources.* Toronto: University of Toronto.

Falkheimer, J. (2005). Formation of a region: Source strategies and media images of the Sweden-Danish Oresund region. *Public Relations Review, 31*(2), 293–297.

Fico, F., & Balog, O. (2003). Partisan sources receive more space in conflict issues. *Newspaper Research Journal, 24*(4), 22–35.

Freedman, E., & Fico, F. (2005). Male and female sources in newspaper coverage of male and female candidates in open races for governor in 2002. *Mass Communication & Society, 8*(3), 257–272.

Gandy, O. (1982). *Beyond agenda setting: Information subsidies and public policy.* Norwood, NJ: Ablex.

Gans, H. (1980). *Deciding what's news.* New York: Vintage Books.

Gant, C., & Dimmick, J. (2000). Making local news: A holistic analysis of sources, selection criteria, and topics. *Journalism & Mass Communication Quarterly, 77*(3), 628–638.

Griffin, R., & Dunwoody, S. (1995). Impacts of information subsidies and community structure on local press coverage of environmental contamination. *Journalism & Mass Communication Quarterly, 72*(2), 271–284.

Hackett, R. (1984). Decline of a paradigm? Bias and objectivity in news media studies. *Critical Studies in Mass Communication, 1,* 229–259.

Hanitzsch, T. (2006). Mapping journalism culture: A theoretical taxonomy and case studies from Indonesia. *Asian Journal of Communication, 16*(2), 169–186.

Herman, E., & Chomsky, N. (1988). *Manufacturing consent: The political economy of the mass media.* New York: Pantheon.

Hertog, J., & McLeod, D. (2001). A multiperspectival approach to framing analysis: A field guide. In S. Reese, O. Gandy, & A. Grant (Eds.), *Framing public life* (pp. 139–161). Mahwah, NJ: Erlbaum.

Josephi, B. (2005). Journalism in the global age: Between normative and empirical. *Gazette: The International Journal for Communication Studies, 67*(6), 575–590.

Kaniss, P. (1991). *Making local news.* Chicago: The University of Chicago.

Kim, Y., & Bae, J. (2006). Korean practitioners and journalists: Relational influences in news selection. *Public Relations Review, 32*, 241–245.

Kitzinger, J. (1998). The gender-politics of news production: Silenced voices and false memories. In C. Carter, G. Branston, & S. Allan (Eds.), *News, gender and power* (186–203). London: Routledge.

Koltsova, O. (2001). News production in contemporary Russia: Practices of power. *European Journal of Communication, 16*(3), 315–335.

Lachover, E. (2005). The gendered and sexualized relationship between Israeli women journalists and their male news sources. *Journalism: Theory, Practice & Criticism, 6*(3), 291–311.

Manning, P. (2001). *News and news sources: A critical introduction*. London: Sage.

McManus, J. (1994). *Market-driven journalism: Let the citizen beware*. Thousand Oaks, CA: Sage.

McQuail, D. (2000). *McQuail's mass communication theory, 4th ed.* London: Sage.

Mohamed, A., & Fleming-Rife, A. (2002, August). Use of minority sources in news. Paper presented to the annual convention of the Association for Education in Journalism & Mass Communication, Miami, FL.

Molotch, H., & Lester, M. (1974). News as purposive behavior: On the strategic use of routine events, accidents and scandals. *American Sociological Review, 39*, 101–112.

Pan, Z., & Kosicki, G. (2001). Framing as a strategic action in public deliberation. In S. Reese, O. Gandy, & A. Grant, *Framing public life* (pp. 35–65). Mahwah, NJ: Erlbaum.

Pavlik, J. (2004). A sea-change in journalism: Convergence, journalists, their audiences and sources. *Convergence, 10* (4), 21– 29.

Poindexter, P., Smith, L., & Heider, D. (2003). Race and ethnicity in local television news: Framing, story assignments, and source selections. *Journal of Broadcasting & Electronic Media, 47*(4), 524–536.

Reese, S. (1991). Setting the media's agenda: A power balance perspective. In J. Anderson (Ed.), *Communication Yearbook 14* (pp. 309–340). Beverly Hills, CA: Sage.

Reese, S. (2001). Understanding the global journalist: A hierarchy-of-influences approach. *Journalism Studies, 2*(2), 173–187.

Reich, Z. (2006). The process model of news initiative: Sources lead first, reporters thereafter. *Journalism Studies, 7*(4), 497–514.

Robins, M. (2001). *Intersecting places, emancipatory spaces: Women journalists in Tanzania.* Trenton, NJ: Africa World Press.

Rogers, S., & Thorson, E. (2003). A socialization perspective on male and female reporting. *Journal of Communication, 53*(4), 658–675.

Roshco, B. (1975). *Newsmaking*. Chicago: The University of Chicago.

Ross, K. (2007). The journalist, the housewife, the citizen and the press: Women and men as sources in local news narratives. *Journalism: Theory, Practice & Criticism, 8*(4), 449–473.

Ruggiero, T. (2004). Paradigm repair and changing journalistic perceptions of the Internet as an objective news source. *Convergence, 10*(4), 92–106.

Rupar, V. (2006). How did you find that out? Transparency of the newsgathering process and the meaning of news: A case study of New Zealand journalism. *Journalism Studies, 7*(1), 127–143.

Sallot, L., & Johnson, E. (2006). Investigating relationships between journalists and public relations practitioners: Working together to set, frame and build the public agenda, 1991–2004. *Public Relations Review, 32*, 151–159.

Sanders, K., & Canel, M. (2006). A scribbling tribe: Reporting political scandal in Britain and Spain. *Journalism: Theory, Practice & Criticism, 7*(4), 453–476.

Schudson, M. (2002). The objectivity norm in American journalism. *Journalism: Theory, practice & criticism, 2*(2), 149–170.

Schudson, M. (2003). *The sociology of news*. New York: W. W. Norton.

Schudson, M., & Dokoupil, T. (2007, January/February). Research report: The limits of live. *Columbia Journalism Review*, *45*(5), 63.

Shin, J., & Cameron, G. (2003). The interplay of professional and cultural factors in the online source-reporter relationship. *Journalism Studies, 4*(2), 253–272.

Sigal, L. (1973). *Reporters and officials: The organization and politics of newsmaking.* Lexington, MA: D.C. Heath.

Sigal, L. (1986). Who? Sources make the news. In R. Manoff & M. Schudson (Eds.), *Reading the news* (pp. 9–37). New York: Pantheon Books.

Soloski, J. (1989). Sources and channels of local news. *Journalism Quarterly, 66,* 864–870.

Tuchman, G. (1973). Making news by doing work: Routinizing the unexpected. *American Journal of Sociology, 79*(1), 110–131.

Turk, J. (1985). Information subsidies and influence. *Public Relations Review, 11*(3), 10–25.

Van Zoonen, L. (1998). One of the girls?: The changing gender of journalism. In C. Carter, G. Branston, & S. Allan (Eds.), *News, gender and power* (pp. 33–46). London: Routledge.

Weaver, D., Beam, R., Brownlee, B., Voakes, P., & Wilhoit, G. (2007). *The American journalist in the 21st century: U.S. news people at the dawn of a new millennium.* Mahwah, NJ: Erlbaum.

Zeldes, G., & Fico, F. (2005). Race and gender: An analysis of sources and reporters in the networks' coverage of the 2000 presidential campaign. *Mass Communication & Society, 8*(4), 373–385.

Zelizer, B. (1993). Journalists as interpretive communities. *Critical Studies in Mass Communication, 10,* 219–237.

Zelizer, B. (2004). *Taking journalism seriously: News and the academy.* Thousand Oaks, CA: Sage.

9

Gender in the Newsroom

Linda Steiner

Without necessarily using the precise language of "gender," discussions of "gender in the newsroom" date to the late nineteenth century, when, to support themselves and their families, women began entering UK and US newsrooms in great numbers. A worried UK woman's magazine reader responded, "Our girls will rush into journalism, teaching or the stage, three professions already overstocked, and neglect really useful branches of employment, by which they might earn a steady, if not luxurious livelihood" (in Onslow, 2000, pp. 15–16). Enraged by women's invasion, men said newswork would defeminize and even desex women. These continued assertions, muted only during world wars, had little to do with beliefs about women's inherent inability to report. Instead, such claims betrayed the marginality of women readers and men's interest in preserving a monopoly on high status work. In any case, these diatribes indicate that women were managing to compete in this masculine space. Women continued to demand newsroom jobs, despite their oft-expressed complaint that male editors, colleagues and sources refused to take them seriously and relegated them to the women's angle.

During much of the twentieth century, the "gender" debate among both working journalists and scholars focused on women. In part this shows the residue of maleness as the "unmarked" standard, and the "Otherness" of women. It also rests on a notion of men and women as polar opposites, with femininity as the problem. Scholarship on gendered practices in journalism rarely challenges assumptions about gender or sex differences per se. Instead, gender and women are conflated as a distinctive, fixed, and self-evident category and then deployed to examine women's status. Only recently has attention turned to shifting formations of masculinity and the role of men's magazines in producing or reproducing various forms of masculinity (Beynon, 2002). The constructed relationship of femininity and masculinity is rarely studied. Whether the newsroom is treated as a literal site, an institution, or a set of cultural practices, gender has largely been invoked to raise one question: could or should women reporters try to act like men, or would they (and journalism) be better served if women produced distinctive forms?

At least until the 1950s, newsmen reserved their highest compliments for a very few women whose work was "just like men's." The *New York Tribune* crime reporter Ishbel Ross herself was praised by her editor Stanley Walker as the paragon of newspaperwomen precisely for achieving this standard. Ross's *Ladies of the Press* (1936), the first book-length history of women reporters, acknowledged that even successful front-page girls had not revolutionized newsrooms. The few women who wrote journalism textbooks aimed at women took a practical view and encouraged women to do the same. Ethel Brazelton (1927), who taught journalism for women at Northwestern University, insisted: "The fact of sex, the "woman's angle," is the woman writer's tool, but it must never be her weapon.... But being a woman, she is possessed of a real advantage in the business of doing, recording, interpreting women's interests, ways and work" (p. 8). Otherwise, since the 1900s, women reporters' autobiographies and other self-reports increasingly emphasize how they avoided becoming "sob sisters" or "agony aunts," regardless of pay. Thus, in blunt terms, summarizing the ancient history of gender in the newsroom involves tracing a shift from initial agreement among women and men journalists that women's role was to write with a woman's "touch" about women for women readers, whose interests were seen as dichotomously different from men's; to a claim by women that they could produce the same "unmarked" journalism as men, who in turn disputed these claims to protect their status, jobs, and salaries. Women's topics were initially women's entry point: Pauline Frederick, for example, first covered women's topics for radio; later ABC hired her to interview political candidates' wives. But it was not women's goal. Women understood that such women's forms—explicitly marked as female—represented professional ghettoes, not socialization, much less natural instincts.

The story grew more complicated and contested over the twentieth century. So now, at least officially, men assert that gender is irrelevant in contemporary newsrooms, which they see as changed (and challenged) by new economic constraints, technologies, audiences, norms of professionalism, and by the pronounced presence of women themselves. Recent complaints about the feminization of newsrooms, ironically, may be reactions to new feminine forms. Alternatively, they may reflect how women are overrepresented on camera, or are remembered more because of their (re-made) appearance. Perhaps it stems from backlash against feminism. Meanwhile, women journalists themselves largely, but not unanimously, agree with men that gender is a minor issue. Women and other "minorities"—defined by race, ethnicity, sexual orientation and class or hyphenated combinations of these—challenge employment discrimination on the basis of merit, of professional status. Relying on different logics, scholars have abandoned naturalized definitions of women but continue to treat gender as inherently and eternally significant. Scholars, then, argue that inclusion is necessary because distinct standpoints matter; they assume that women and men journalists work differently and/or that they should. The literal or perceived absence of women (or people of color or gays and lesbians) in the newsroom means, they assert, that such groups will not be "well" reported in terms of quantity or quality.

The controversy emerged in 2005, when Susan Estrich, a law professor and free-lance opinion writer, condemned a male editor for not running enough columns by women. Estrich said even the few women who do produce columns "don't count as women because they don't write with 'women's voices'" (Applebaum, 2005). Anne Applebaum (2005), a regular *Washington Post* columnist, called Estrich's complaint "bizarre" and "seriously bad" for women: "Possibly because I see so many excellent women around me at the newspaper, possibly because so many of *The Post*'s best-known journalists are women, possibly because I've never thought of myself as a 'female journalist.'" Nor did Applebaum think other women regarded themselves as female journalists with special obligations to write about women's issues.

THE IMPACT OF THE WOMEN'S LIBERATION MOVEMENT

Both the structure of the US news media and the refusal of the women's liberation movement to identify spokespeople worked against publicity for that movement (Tuchman, 1978b), although sympathetic women reporters, by virtue of sounding objective to their sexist male editors, managed in the 1960s to insert some women's issues, such as rape laws, into the women's pages. The National Organization for Women worked hard to mobilize news media and to cultivate relationships with women journalists. Whether because of the proactive information subsidies by women's organizations (Barker-Plummer, 2002) or agitprop efforts of radical feminists (Bradley, 2003), the movement was covered. And the women's movement had major consequences for newsrooms. First, inspired and emboldened by the movement, women journalists used regulatory and legal channels to challenge exclusionary hiring and promotion practices at several news organizations. Each victory further opened doors for women.

The long-term consequences for content are less clear. A *Los Angeles Times* reporter claims the resulting increased presence of women reporters had an important, positive impact (Mills, 1990). Women reporters are said to report on social issues and subjects that interest women and to use more women, feminist organizations, and "ordinary people" as sources; the resulting diversity benefits newsrooms. Certainly women acted to dismantle women's pages, first at *The Washington Post* and other elite papers and, later, at smaller papers. Since the 1890s, when Jane Cunningham Croly created a women's page for the *New York Daily World*, both mainstream and African-American newsrooms had hired women as editors of these pages. In the 1950s and 1960s some women's page editors had tried to expand the political and social scope of these sections, as well as their racial scope; but these efforts were limited and inconsistent. Again, newly-emboldened second-wave feminists attacked these sections for trucking in "symbolic annihilation" equivalent to other sexist forms that condemned or trivialized women (Tuchman, 1978a). As underscored in several oral histories sponsored by the Washington Press Club Foundation (available at http://npc.press.org/wporal) eliminating women's pages had the immediate effect of eliminating the single editorial slot reserved for women. A similar dynamic came into play in Ireland, where "real reporters" regarded women's pages with contempt (Maher, 2003) until the late 1960s, when the *Irish Times* let women revamp the women's pages to incorporate "serious" reporting. The section was soon killed off; Maeve Binchy, its second editor and now a blockbuster novelist, said women don't need a special place. Ironically, in the 1980s, to please advertisers some US papers reintroduced women's pages (Harp, 2007). Both experiments reveal not women's distinct values, but how marketing concerns drive the sex-binary packaging of news and the construction of women (readers and reporters) as interested in lifestyle issues and domesticity.

The second wave of the women's movement also inspired women to enter the academy and pursue their interests in women's history; it encouraged research on women's culture and work and created an audience for that research. Marzolf's (1977) path-breaking history brought long-forgotten women "Up from the Footnote." The next step was, as another title put it, *Great Women of the Press* (Schilpp & Murphy, 1983) and full-bore biographies of single individuals. Eventually scholars moved to more specialized categories—black women (Streitmatter, 1994), war reporters (Elwood-Akers, 1988), and sob sisters (Abramson, 1990) as well as theoretically-sophisticated histories of women's journalism around the world.

More importantly, scholars reconsidered the assumption that newsroom practices are the direct inevitable result of professional routines and socialization, with management defining the skills and talents they want in terms of what previously enhanced circulation and status. New thinking about how journalists' gendered identity matters influenced both explanations for why newsroom diversity is important (one can only understand someone if one has walked in the subject's shoes) and the research agenda itself. This led to reconceptualizing how women respond to newsroom dynamics and structures, including what constitutes news or newsrooms.

WOMEN'S ALTERNATIVE MEDIA

One key research area for the second-wave generation was the women-led news media, beginning with mid-nineteenth century periodicals by young US textile workers, perhaps the first consistent efforts by women to produce their own news and thereby redefine themselves. Of continuing interest are periodicals of the women's movement, given their importance in explaining, justifying, and sustaining women's liberation; and in debating new models for womanhood. Suffrage journals addressed not only voting but larger issues, including health, law, politics, and labor. Their editors were active in other reform movements and periodicals, and formed their own community (Steiner, 1992). Their periodicals can also be analyzed in terms of newsroom policies, including their approach to accommodating family responsibilities, and commitment to journalism training and to reforming journalism along feminist lines. Thus, the 150 women-run UK political papers published 1856–1930 facilitated the growth of a gendered community of activists who convinced women that they could "affect social change by creating a new gender-based political culture" that commandeered public space (Tusan, 2005, p. 4).

Twentieth-century feminist periodicals are likewise important fora. *Time and Tide* (1920–1977), for example, was established out of frustration with both UK mainstream newspapers, which belittled women, and advocacy papers narrowly fixated on women (Tusan, 2005). Feminist periodicals that proliferated in the US in the 1970s were narrower in scope than the earlier US and UK papers; they were for, about, and generally by a niche: ecofeminists, prostitutes, celibates, older women, Marxists, feminist witches, and a host of other interests and professions. They were also more self-consciously experimental in rejecting conventional definitions of newsworthiness and newsroom structures, and loudly denounced sexist stereotypes (Endres & Lueck, 1996; Steiner, 1992). Since 1970 *off our backs* has been published by a collective that continues to operate by consensus. It eschews conventional principles: "We intend to be just; but we do not pretend to be impartial" (February 1970, p. 1).

Women producing women's movement organs of the second-wave type have primarily been activists, reformers, and crusaders wholly uninterested in profit. *Ms.*, since 1972 the "mouthpiece" of popular feminism in the US, is the exception that proves the rule. *Ms.* has been treated as a corrupt hybrid, "always firmly enmeshed in a commercial mass media matrix" (Farrell, 1998, p. 9), although *Ms.* refused to publish "complementary copy" for advertisers and for many years gave up advertising altogether. Otherwise, the leaders of feminist newsrooms lacked commercial journalism experience and did not identify themselves foremost as journalists. Yet, they provided both professional and industrial opportunities, including in journalism. Amelia Bloomer, for example, was willing to postpone production of *The Lily*, which she began in 1849 as "a medium through which woman's thoughts and aspirations might be developed," in order to train her own women printers. They limited advertising to what they deemed appropriate and kept subscription prices accessible to unpaid or low-paid women. Thus, criticisms of alternative media certainly apply to feminist political papers, given their amateurish writing, inattention to aesthetics, lack of long-range business strategies, and inefficiency caused by collective or horizontal organization and obsession with principle (see Atton, chapter 19, this volume; Winship, 1987).

These critiques open up for research the possibilities of new media, including satellite radio, public access cable channels, and Internet zines, for covering on a global scale issues difficult to discuss elsewhere. Even in mainstream and commercial radio, women's voices were once assumed to irritate audiences and so were not heard, except on shows aimed at helping women with domestic work. Women are now prominent as reporters, news shows hosts, and interviewers. More to the point, feminist public affairs programs and even women-run radio stations operate with varying degrees of feminist commitment in several countries. Feminist International Radio Endeavor (FIRE) creates an Internet-based global news flow; WINGS (Women's International News Gathering Service) furnishes feminist news to radio stations. Moreover, third-wave feminists operate by seemingly wholly new principles.

EMPIRICAL EVIDENCE OF GENDER DIFFERENCES IN VALUES

According to national surveys (Delano & Henningham, 1995; Weaver & Wilhoit, 1996), gender is not a reliable predictor of differences in professional practices. Men and women conceive the role of news and evaluate the ethics of reporting methods in similar ways; they show similar (declining) levels of job satisfaction. On the other hand, feminist theorizing suggests that ways of thinking and knowing are highly influenced by social identity, in turn, affected by inherently gendered experiences, differences in socialization, and social history. Rogers and Thorson (2003) contend that "men and women socialize differently into the workplace because men and women have different values and priorities" (p. 659). Since men and women have distinct identities they had predicted that, "like females in other professions," women reporters would have unique values, interests, and priorities that would affect how stories are researched, sourced, framed, and written. As it turns out, Rogers and Thorson's content analysis of three newspapers found that women drew upon a greater variety of female and ethnic sources, especially in positive stories, but women at the large paper sourced and framed stories much like their male counterparts. Van Zoonen (1998) concludes that, overall, women journalists, with their distinctive "womanview," tend to be more interested in their audience, more concerned about context. She says women challenge male journalists' detachment, believing that men use objectivity as a shield against the sensitivity and sympathy that journalism requires.

Given its hazards and the risk of fatal injury, but also the potential for career-making reputation, war reporting arguably continues to be the most contested beat for women, with audiences criticizing women, especially mothers, for putting their bodies in danger. War reporting has also provoked unusually intense debate among audiences, journalists, and scholars regarding whether women and men report differently. The Vietnam War was the first war that women covered in significant numbers. Some women found that their very visibility meant they were noticed at press conferences; their questions were answered first. Even when they were paid to write from and about the woman's angle, however, women faced prejudice and suspicion from the American military, the Vietnamese forces and male reporters. Some women hated doing human interest war stories, precisely because they knew the stereotype that women were more attuned to the "human side" of the war, and these stories were more likely to be cut. That is, the numbers of women who refused to write as women or complained about being assigned according to sex stereotype suggest that the problem was sexism, not sex differences. Liz Trotta (1991), the first woman to report on Vietnam for television, speculated that male colleagues felt threatened by having to compete with women. In any case, men and women wrote substantially similar kinds of stories (Elwood-Akers, 1988).

Smaller studies of gender produce contradictory and inconclusive results. Women activists and scholars are the most likely to find that gender "matters" or that it should "matter" more. According to informal surveys by the International Women's Media Foundation (www.iwmf.org), women believe female journalists offer a different, "more human perspective" to the news, although some women asserted that "news is news" and ethics are ethics. Likewise, the 22 women members of an advocacy group responding to a questionnaire split over whether women report women's issues differently (Ross, 2001). Many women said that they react differently from men to stories because they have more sympathy for women and emphasize personal and emotional dimensions; a majority said men still dominate the professions. But three-quarters do not incorporate feminism into their reporting, and many agreed that women managers are even more macho than men. Ross regards many of her respondents as blind to gender issues, having normalized male-identified concerns and incorporated into what is a male profession. At the least, women's considerable ambivalence and lack of consensus cast doubt on hopes that a "critical mass" of women will transform the newsroom. Margaret Gallagher (2001), having published crucial comparative research on the global exclusion of women, argues that gender still needs to be addressed—indeed, in new, creative ways—as a professional issue. But her Global Media Monitoring projects argue against assuming that the increasing entry of women into journalism in most countries will radically transform content. Women form no unitary bloc. Many are unsympathetic to feminism as a movement and are insensitive to historical changes accomplished by feminists. In sum, women recognize that many of their male colleagues are sexist, but they largely adopt journalism's structures as part of the profession and choose to embrace its reward system. Gender socialization theory, moreover, cannot explain why some women escape their gender. It accounts for the chicken/egg argument on the domestic front no more than it settles the question at the battle front, largely because it ignores the key way to understand gender—not as a role, much less a static and dichotomous set of differences between women and men, but as a performance, a relational act (Butler, 1990). Men and women perform gender, sometimes creatively and often uncreatively, and provoke others to perform gender.

MANAGEMENT

In the 1970s Marlene Sanders, one of the first female network news correspondents, became the first woman named as a network vice president on the news side. But until recently, little work was available about or by those few women who made it to the top. This makes Katharine Graham (1997) notable for her candid description of becoming *Washington Post* publisher: although her father had owned the paper, her involvement was minimal—primarily social—until the suicide of her husband in 1963. More critically, world-wide, corporations, including news organizations, have been and remain reluctant to promote women to executive positions. No wonder that Hemlinger and Linton's (2002) report on newsrooms' gendered glass ceiling was subtitled *Still Fighting an Uphill Battle*. In the US, in 2006, 18 percent of large newspaper publishers were women. Women held 30 percent of all executive jobs at daily newspapers, concentrated in a few chains, and are 35 percent of television news managers. Women are 20 percent of the top executives at network news companies and only 12 percent of the boards of directors of news and entertainment companies, according to Annenberg's study "No Room at the Top" (available at http://www.appcpenn.org). Yet, it is potentially contradictory to complain that 46 percent of female executives in the media/entertainment companies and 38 percent of the female news executives are in communications/marketing/PR, human resources or government relations (i.e., seen collectively as "woman's sphere") but also to justify, as the report does, women's executive potential in terms of their distinctive communication skills and knowledge of the female market.

The suggestion that women and men "execute" leadership differently parallels other dichotomized notions: "feminine" management style is more interpersonal, democratic, constructive, collaborative; while "masculine management is more autocratic, competitive, defensive. In any case, statistically men run most papers in both categories (Arnold & Nesbitt, 2006).

At a minimum, the attention to management betrays dissatisfaction with the argument about the impact of women reporters. For example, women are editors of 19 percent of New Zealand's newspapers, but nearly 50 percent of the reporters. Judy McGregor (2006), the first woman to edit a major paper in New Zealand and now an Equal Employment Opportunities Commissioner, asserts that representing women's distinctive perspective and undoing the male-ness of news requires women in top management. Notably, during the years (1999–2003) the *Sarasota Herald Tribune* had women as its publisher, executive editor, managing editor, and two assistant managing editors, it carried the same content as other papers, with same percentage of female sources. But that paper's all-female management team was perceived as offering, as promised, an atmosphere of openness and transparent decision making (Everbach, 2006).

TELEVISION REPORTING

The continuing emphasis on women's physical appearance cannot be ignored here. Nancy Dickerson, whose five minute afternoon newscast in 1963 made her the first woman to host a news show, was also the first to be promoted as an attractive woman, but certainly not the last. Networks have promoted attractive women not ready for big-time prominence, such as Sally Quinn, a *Washington Post* writer who quickly failed as a CBS co-anchor in 1973. A journalistically-inexperienced Jessica Savitch was promoted when market researchers found that she "scored as high with men, who saw her as a sex object, as with women, who saw her as a role model" (Blair, 1988, p. 168). Two decades later, BBC war reporter Kate Adie complains that even female war correspondents, including her, are judged by their appearance; she says TV management prefers women with "cute faces and cute bottoms" to those with journalistic experience. And women's attractiveness has limited shelf life, as Christine Craft (1986) demonstrated. Having been "made over" as a platinum blonde for CBS, Craft was demoted after eight months in 1981 as co-anchor for an ABC affiliate. The reason was focus group data indicated she was "too old, too unattractive and wouldn't defer to men."

Beginning in 1968 the US Federal Communications Commission encouraged broadcasters to hire more women; but this took time. In 1971 five of the 60 on-air correspondents in NBC's news division were women and all off-air women were secretaries, researchers, or assistants, "dead-end" jobs to which no men were assigned. Now that women hold about 40 percent of US network news jobs (Bulkeley, 2004), the issue is network status, the ultimate mark of status in television. Having been hired and promoted for their good looks, do women now have the gravitas—or whatever ratings systems measure—required to anchor high status shows? In 2007 Katie Couric became the first woman to anchor, solo, a network evening newscast. Much of Couric's potential rides on appearance—in her case, visibly remade. Granted, pushed by the "hard" numbers of focus groups, appearance is becoming increasing important for men. Nonetheless, extraordinary, albeit contradictory, amounts of public criticism have been directed at Couric's hair, clothes, and make-up. The *New York Times* announced its conclusion in a typical headline (July 12, 2007): "Now the News: Couric Still Isn't One of the Boys." Narrowly defined standards for appearance continue to be crucial in determining who gets hired, how they are used, and how long they last on television.

SEX AND SEXUAL HARASSMENT

Among the most studied newsroom topics is the journalist-source relationship. When the journalist is female—because most sources are people in power and most people in power are male—the relationship is particularly fraught. Many women journalists believe that manipulating their sexuality gives them an edge with their sources (Chambers et al., 2004; Robertson, 1992). Male reporters resent their female colleagues for enjoying what men are convinced is a competitive edge. On the other hand, deploying sexuality can backfire against women, as seen in 2007, when Univision demoted a television anchor for her relationship with the mayor of Los Angeles, and a Chicago anchor was fired for an inferred relationship with a male source. Meanwhile, sex and sexuality are remarkably understudied—referring here to relationships among journalists and to sources, to the relevance of journalists' and public's attitudes about sex, and to the possible impact of sexuality and sexual orientation (i.e., whether this matters in ways equivalent to gender.)

If women reporters long avoided making allegations of sexual harassment, the 1990s saw dramatic increases in harassment complaints and new legal remedies. Reporters continued to imply either that they transcend their bodies or that their embodied experiences never influence them. Still, a 1992 Associated Press Managing Editors survey found that about 2 percent of men and 11 percent of women journalists said sexual harassment or fear of it had affected their work; nearly 30 percent of women journalists surveyed said they had been sexually (non-physically) harassed by co-workers (Walsh-Childers, Chance, & Herzog, 1996).

After a flurry of attention, the controversy abated. Perhaps the trend toward professionalism and middle-class respectability slightly dented the bohemian "pub culture," long seen as inherent to journalism and much romanticized by male journalists. But more than one-third of 32 women journalists in Israel, where approximately 37 percent of newspaper staffs are female, reported experiencing either sexual harassment (mainly verbal) or sexist contempt from sources (Lachover, 2005). Notably, these women rarely described themselves as victims or even defined the behavior as sexual harassment; they ignored it, in the name of professionalism. The willingness to flirt with men who treat women as sexual objects is seemingly evident around the world, especially among sports journalists, who also may consistently endure the most overt non-sexual harassment, from athletes and male sports reporters (Chambers et al., 2004). Most, but not all, women accept the sexual attentions of co-workers or sources as part of journalism culture.

MAGAZINES

Beasley (2001) calls for evaluating women journalists with broader criteria than applied to men. She would extend the definition of journalism to embrace informative material with wide popular appeal and include as journalists talk show hosts, advice columnists, and public relations professionals. The idea has had little take up, perhaps because redefining publicists and occasional columnists as journalists may fuel suspicions of women reporters. But Beasley's point bears on the question of women's magazines. Journalists and feminists world-wide have disdained and distanced themselves from women's magazines. Nonetheless, for centuries avid readers have regarded women's magazines as providing useful information. Women's magazines have understood their scope, albeit perhaps less in recent decades, to embrace social and political controversies, including birth control, food safety legislation, and child labor. Not unimportantly, the popularity of women's magazines proved to newspaper executives and advertisers that women were desirable consumers (Zuckerman, 1998). Many women's magazines in the US, Europe, and Asia were at least initially published and/or edited by men. Yet, eventually these became sites where women could achieve high levels of responsibility, even if women editors adopted and promoted sexist stereotypes.

As with newspaper reportage on women and women's issues, magazine content was long assumed to influence (i.e., to limit) how women see themselves and how society views women.

More recent scholarship emphasizes the potential for playful counter-hegemonic or oppositional readings by readers. Both approaches ignore magazines' newsroom policies and processes. Among the exceptions, Ferguson (1983) found that UK women's magazine editors defined themselves as professionals and defined professional success in economic/monetary terms. A generation later, editors may describe themselves in similar language, as "high priestesses" who know what is best and deserve the "divine right" to autonomy. But motivational research and, more recently, life-style research are increasingly powerful; they determine how women's magazines (similar to women's pages) construct and attract readers (Winship, 1987; Gough-Yates, 2003). In highly parallel ways, new markets of masculine readers are jointly co-constructed by publishers, journalists, and advertisers (Nixon, 1996).

METHODS AND PROBLEMS FOR FUTURE RESEARCH

Lerner (1975) argued against the notion that any single framework or factor, or even eight-factor explanation, can describe the history of women. She famously described "compensatory" and "contribution" history, which judge women by male standards, as merely the first two stages in women's history. Notably, of 76 books and articles about women journalists, 71 were categorized as compensatory or contribution history; five developed new categories, periodization systems, concepts, and methods (Mitchell, 1990). Gender history is still at this transitional stage. More contextualized historical research on how men and women work, including how maleness and femaleness has figured in the newsroom, will contribute to the synthesis Lerner called for; research may get at successes and failures in attempts to challenge conventional definitions of professionalism, including how gender can work, or be worked against, in the newsroom. Untapped documentary sources for individuals and organizations are far-flung and often difficult to locate but do exist; some archival sources are even available electronically.

Feminist methods suggest, inter alia, expanding the scope of research materials. Journalists' autobiographies, memoirs, and oral histories are inherently unreliable as research materials, given the form itself and the fact that these texts are edited for a public audience; but they are no more unreliable than other forms. They are especially useful when analyzed collectively (Steiner, 1997). Autobiographies and oral histories allow reporters to be self-reflective and self-critical, and to explain why they entered or quit the newsroom. If our behaviors reflect our sense of what others expect of us, then popular culture representations of journalists are also worth investigating, especially newsroom-set novels written by women reporters. *The Image of the Journalist in Popular Culture* project (http://www.ijpc.org) maintains an extensive bibliography.

Ethnographic fieldwork that is informed by feminist theorizing and methodology is difficult but important in analyzing informal practices and cultures of mainstream and alternative newsrooms. Gough-Yates's (2003) plan for fieldwork on women's magazines floundered when insiders, perhaps suspecting that her feminist politics would lead to yet another hatchet job, refused her access. Nonetheless, fieldwork may help explain newsroom culture and the intersections of work and family responsibilities. Whether ambitious women reporters remain less apt than other women, and far less than male colleagues, to marry or to stay married requires more study. In the absence of total restructuring of all workplaces and of the stubbornly persistent expectations that women must be the primary care-takers, women—but also men—may have useful proposals for helping newsrooms to accommodate and support healthy interpersonal relationships, families, and working parents. The most effective suggestions will emerge from fieldwork.

Conversely, interviews and surveys are relatively straight-forward, cheap, and popular but over-used and decreasingly productive methods. Even focus groups do not successfully prod respondents to confront thorny issues that warrant continued attention, such as women's networking or sexual harassment. Content analyses of published or broadcast stories produces at best inconclusive, shallow data, given that journalism is a complicated, institutional, thoroughly mediated and partly anonymous process. Therefore, and since even bylines may be non-gendered or pseudonyms, most large-scale studies of news representations of "gender" (again, that is, women) ignore who specifically produces that news. Lavie and Lehman-Wilzig (2005) properly describe data from their study of Israel's two major public radio stations as internally and externally inconsistent. Their content analyses found "gender otherness" in topic selection, with male editors preferring "hard" news while women tended to emphasize soft news; but their questionnaire yielded minimal differences in how male and female editors defined the functions of news. The paradoxical results required considerable explanation by the authors. For example, since the gap between declared news values and actual editorial behavior was wider among female editors than men, they suggest that women, being newer to journalism, are more ambivalent about new trends toward more feminine journalism. They conclude that women must "overcome their 'professional-psychological block' about being true to their innate value system" (p. 84). Alternatively, we might abandon the notion of an innate gender value system.

Crucial for a robust useable understanding of gender in the newsroom are transnational approaches, despite the difficulties of language skills and other resources necessary for scholarly attention to newsrooms around the world. Survey data is fragmentary, outdated, and cannot be reliably compared. That said, 1990s data collected in Weaver (1998) and other sources suggest that women are about 33 percent to 38 percent of the journalism workforce (but then journalists are only 10 to 15 percent of newspaper employees) in many countries, including China, Australia, and Hungary. Women are 15 percent in Korea; 25 percent to 42 percent in Britain and Spain, Canada, Germany, and Brazil; and nearly 50 percent in Finland, Estonia, and Lithuania. Nearly everywhere these percentages are significantly higher among journalists under 30. That is, as decades go by, more (new) women are being hired, although whether this evinces continuing intolerance of older women, presumed to be less attractive, or women's movement into jobs permitting greater stability is unclear.

Apart from such demographic data, internationalized discussions of newsrooms in countries outside the US or UK often ignore gender. Very little, at least of what is published in English, is comparative (Robinson, 2005). The parallels around the world in sexism and gender are remarkable, as are global shifts toward new technologies, to celebrity and lifestyle reporting, and decision making by marketing and advertising. Research is necessary to determine whether terms such as sexism and gender have consistent meanings across countries and cultures, as well as over time. Persuasive discussions of gender identities at work in newsrooms in various countries (for example, see deBruin and Ross, 2004) take gender as a persistent, universalizable issue; but, geographical and cultural differences referenced in those small-scale studies also suggest the need for much larger scale, comparative research. At a minimum, issues of national ideology would complicate the question of whether newsroom routines represent professional norms or a specifically white male prism.

More to the point, numbers do not explain where or how gender is meaningful, when and how women have cracked the glass ceiling in terms of senior-level management, how gender compounds (or does not) problems of castes, ethnicity, religion, marital or domestic status. How does color bear on the career trajectories of journalists? What about marital status? In Sweden, where women are almost 50 percent of journalists but 26 percent of senior managers, female top managers were more likely than men to marry other senior managers (i.e., gained professional and economic capital through marriage); and had more mentors (Djerf-Pierre, 2005). That is, although Toril Moi (1999) generally assumed that female gender capital is negative and maleness is positive capital, these Swedish women countered the negative gender capital by amassing social capital. When must women adopt distasteful professional values for the sake of career advancement, and when can these norms be challenged or transformed? What are the consequences for resistance? Why do so many women journalists distance themselves from the feminist movement? Conversely, what are the important features of distinct cultural and geographic arenas?

CONCLUSION

Covert (1981) was among the first to observe that journalism history celebrated independence and individual autonomy, thereby ignoring the influences of family and friendship networks. Journalism itself was written in terms of conflict, controversy, and competition, which Covert took to reflect men's interest in winning. Covert contrasted this masculine language to women's values: concord, harmony, affiliation, and community. But well before Covert's provocative and fruitful essay, the debate has been whether sexual identity (i.e., of women) trumped professionalism, meaning that, at least with sufficient numbers, women would change the newsroom.

While this continues to drive considerable research, claims about women's distinct news values have become internally and externally contradictory. First, the claim constructs women journalists as ever and always sharing a fixed standpoint as homemakers and parents. It ignores how gender may go in and out of focus. It ignores contemporary differences in experience and standpoint by virtue of race, sexual orientation, and religion. Decrying the lack of women covering politics, Anna Ford, an outspoken BBC newscaster, said: "We might have put different questions from those of the middle-aged, middle-class, white, Anglo-Saxon Protestant men" (in Sebba, 1994, p. 249). This counterposes a singular "we" to men correctly treated as speaking through sex as well as class, race, age, ethnicity.

Rush (2004) asserts that women always and everywhere get what is left over—this amounts to one-quarter to one-third—of symbolic representation, status, and salary. Similarly, Melin-Higgins (2004) quotes a European journalist who argues that newsrooms are so wracked by gender-based power, conflict, and culture clashes that they require guerilla warfare. Women journalists can take on the role of the "woman journalist" as defined by the dominant culture; challenge male supremacy by becoming one of the boys; or challenge the very "doxa" of journalism by becoming one of the girls, making journalism more feminine. But, in the twenty-first century women are no longer always confined to a woman's ghetto or called unfeminine if they infiltrate the newsroom. Rush's "Ratio of Recurrent and Reinforced Residuum" no longer holds. Moreover, not only have feminists changed newsrooms and privileged soft news and women's forms, but the very forms that Melin-Higgins promotes as oppositional are precisely the ones marketers seek. Historical work must take seriously how women have changed journalism, in part, by inventing forms never before credited to women. Perhaps once these softer forms became normalized and "hardened," they were redefined as conventional: sob sisters and front-page stunt girls morphed over the century into civic journalists and enterprise journalists. Even discarding the essentializing and universalizing dynamic, to conclude from data showing few sex differences that organizational constraints force women to reproduce existing masculinist practices ignores widespread social changes, including in journalism, where hard/soft binaries have been radically blurred. Claims about gender differences in reporting and editing are caught in philosophical, empirical, and methodological traps. Put bluntly, the solution is not multi-method approaches to gender effects in the newsroom, but asking new questions.

Gender remains an important issue, from war reporting (where the stress of putting bodies on the line is marked by problems in intimate relationships and substance abuse among men and women) to political cartooning (where, women remain under 5 percent of those employed). Lingering gender effects need to be addressed as they intersect with other structural problems, such as newsroom fiscal policies that compound the likelihood of exploitation of women. For example, the increase in the women, who are especially likely to be stringers or freelancers even as foreign correspondents, may reflect a profit-driven shift to cheaper workers. Certainly sexism and using women sexually continues in society and in newsrooms. Indeed, accusing women of reproducing masculinist assumptions does not solve the problem of using women on air to add spice, drama, and sex appeal as well as encouraging newswomen to express disdain for women (say, for their dress or sexuality) and feminism. That is, because men can no longer get away with crude sexism, at least in the elite press and network news, women are providing intellectual "cover" for news organizations.

Some of the gender logic is self-fulfilling, as when data showing that women are less likely (45 percent as opposed to 55 percent) to read newspapers are said to show women's inability to find stories relevant to their interests; but a circulation drop under female-led management is attributed to over-all circulation declines (Everbach, 2006). The notion that women and men are opposites is even more misguided when women are associated with all "good" qualities, here referring to suggestions that women journalists tend to privilege readers' needs, prefer nuance, emphasize contexts, and cover a broader agenda than men, who engage in pack journalism because they are worrying about their competitors (Christmas, 1997). Celebrating women's styles as if women can do no wrong overstates women's preference for consensus and concord. Insisting that women express such sentiment is potentially distorting, both methodologically and affectively. Feminine is not always the opposite of masculine. It ignores crucial feminist insights on the arbitrary constructedness of gender.

Indeed, dichotomous thinking is unproductive. Instead of describing a female journalism, which depends on hard/soft and neutrality/subjectivity binaries, we might imagine a feminist journalism. Feminist theorizing suggests the value of more contextual and situated journalistic forms that get at reasons, consequences, impacts; and of collaborative, non-competitive, horizontal work structures that allow for integrating domestic responsibilities. Encouraging journalists to revise, if not reinvent, ways of understanding and representing human action is commendable. New kinds of newsrooms and new forms of print, broadcast, and online journalism require a new political sensibility and feminist epistemology, not women's innate values. Experiments in newsroom structures, content, policy and decision-making emerging from feminist theorizing and critique are necessary if journalism is to serve the ongoing political and social needs of people who are embodied, and who may be particularly disadvantaged by class and race.

REFERENCES

Abramson, P. L. (1990). *Sob sister journalism*. Westport, CT: Greenwood Press.

Applebaum, A. (2005, March 16). Writing women into a corner. *The Washington Post*, p. 23.

Arnold, M., & Nesbitt, M. (2006). *Women in media 2006: Finding the leader in you*. Evanston, IL: Media Management Center at Northwestern University.

Barker-Plummer, B. (2002). Producing public voice: Resource mobilization and media access in the National Organization for Women. *Journalism & Mass Communication Quarterly, 79*(1), 188–205.

Beasley, M. (2001). Recent directions for the study of women's history in American journalism. *Journalism Studies*. *2*(2), 207–220.

Beynon, J. (2002). *Masculinities and culture*. Buckingham, UK: Open University Press.

Blair, G. (1988). *Almost golden: Jessica Savitch and the selling of television news*. New York: Simon and Schuster.

Bradley, P. (2003). *Mass media and the shaping of American feminism, 1963–1975.* Jackson: University Press of Mississippi.

Brazelton, E. M. Colson. (1927). *Writing and editing for women.* New York: Funk & Wagnalls.

Bulkeley, C. C. (2004). Whose news? Progress and status of women in newspapers (mostly) and television news. In R. R. Rush, C. E. Oukrop, & P. J. Creedon (Eds.), *Seeking equity for women in journalism and mass communication education: A 30-Year Update* (pp. 183–204). Mahwah, NJ: Erlbaum.

Butler, J. (1990). *Gender trouble: feminism and the subversion of identity.* London: Routledge.

Chambers, D., Steiner, L., & Fleming, C. (2004). *Women and Journalism.* London: Routledge.

Christmas, L. (1997). *Chaps of both sexes? Women decision-makers in newspapers: Do they make a difference?* London: WIJ/BT Forum.

Covert, C. L. (1981). Journalism history and women's experience: A problem in conceptual change. *Journalism History, 8,* 2–6.

Craft, C. (1986). *Too old, too ugly, not deferential to men.* New York: St. Martin's.

deBruin, M., & Ross, K. (Eds.), *Gender and newsroom cultures: Identities at work.* Cresskill, NJ: Hampton.

Delano, A., & Henningham, J. (1995). *The news breed: British journalists in the 1990s.* London: London College of Printing and Distributive Trades

Djerf-Pierre, M. (2005). Lonely at the top: Gendered media elites in Sweden. *Journalism 6*(3), 265–290.

Elwood-Akers, V. (1988). *Women war correspondents in the Vietnam war, 1961–1975.* Metuchen, NJ: Scarecrow Press.

Endres, K L., & Lueck, T. L.(Eds.). (1996). *Women's periodicals in the United States: Social and political issues.* Westport, CT: Greenwood Press.

Everbach, T. (2006). The culture of a women-led newspaper: An ethnographic study of the *Sarasota Herald-Tribune. Journalism & Mass Communication Quarterly, 83*(3), 477–493.

Farrell, A. E. (1998). *Yours in sisterhood: Ms. magazine and the promise of popular feminism,* Chapel Hill: University of North Carolina Press.

Ferguson, M. (1983). *Forever feminine: Women's magazines and the cult of femininity.* London: Heinemann.

Gallagher, M. (2001). *Gender setting: New agendas for media monitoring and advocacy.* London: Zed.

Gough-Yates, A. (2003). *Understanding women's magazines: Publishing, markets and readerships.* London: Routledge.

Graham, K. (1997). *Personal history.* New York: A.A. Knopf.

Harp, D. (2007). *Desperately seeking women readers: U.S. newspapers and the construction of a female readership.* Lanham, MD: Lexington Books.

Hemlinger, M. A., & Linton, C. C. (2002). *Women in newspapers 2002: Still fighting an uphill battle.* Evanston, IL: Northwestern University.

Lachover, E. (2005). The gendered and sexualized relationship between Israeli women journalists and their male news sources. *Journalism, 6,* 291–311.

Lavie, A., & Lehman-Wilzig, S. (2005). The method is the message: Explaining inconsistent findings in gender and news research. *Journalism, 6*(1), 66–89.

Lerner, G. (1975). Placing women in history: Definitions and challenges. *Feminist Studies, 3*(1/2), 5–15.

Maher, M. (2003). Coming of age with a vengeance. In E. Gillespie (Ed.), *Changing the times: Irish women journalists 1969–1981* (pp. 11–12). Dublin: Lilliput Press.

Marzolf, M. (1977). *Up from the footnote: A history of women journalists.* New York: Hastings House.

McGregor, J. (2006). The pervasive power of man-made news. *The Pacific Journalism Review, 12*(1), 21–34.

Melin-Higgins, M. (2004). Coping with journalism: Gendered newsroom culture. In M. de Bruin & K. Ross (Eds.), *Gender and newsroom cultures: Identities at work* (pp. 195–220). Cresskill, NJ: Hampton.

Mills, K. (1990). *A place in the news: From the women's pages to the front page.* New York: Columbia University Press.

Mitchell, C. C. (1990). The place of biography in the history of news women. *American Journalism, 7*(1), 23–31.

Moi, T. (1999). *What is a woman? And other essays.* Oxford, UK: Oxford University Press.

Nixon, S. (1996). *Hard looks: Masculinities, spectatorship and contemporary consumption.* New York: St. Martin's Press.

Onslow, B. (2000). *Women of the press in nineteenth-century Britain.* New York: St. Martin's Press.

Robertson, N. (1992). *The girls in the balcony: Women, men and the New York Times.* New York: Fawcett Columbine.

Robinson, G. J. (2005). *Gender, journalism and equity: Canadian, US and European perspectives.* Cresskill, NJ: Hampton Press.

Rogers, S., & Thorson, E. (2003). A socialization perspective on male and female reporting. *Journal of Communication, 53*(4), 658–675.

Ross, I. (1936). *Ladies of the press.* New York: Harper & Brothers

Ross, K. (2001). Women at work: journalism as en-gendered practice. *Journalism Studies, 2*(4), 531–544.

Rush, R. (2004). Three decades of women and mass communications research. In R. R. Rush, C. E. Oukrop, & P. J. Creedon (Eds.), *Seeking equity for women in journalism and mass communication education: A 30-year update* (pp. 263–274). Mahwah, NJ: Erlbaum.

Schilpp, M. G., & Murphy, S. M. (1983). *Great women of the press.* Carbondale: Southern Illinois University Press.

Sebba, A. (1994). *Battling for news: The rise of the woman reporter.* London: Hodder & Stoughton.

Steiner, L. (1992). The history and structure of women's alternative media. In L. Rakow (Ed.), *Women making meaning: New feminist directions in communication* (pp.121–143). New York: Routledge.

Steiner, L. (1997, Spring). Gender at work: Early accounts by women journalists. *Journalism History,* 2–12.

Streitmatter, R. (1994). *Raising her voice: African-American women journalists who changed history.* Lexington: University Press of Kentucky.

Trotta, L. (1991). *Fighting for air: In the trenches with television news.* New York: Simon & Schuster.

Tuchman, G. (1978a). Introduction: The symbolic annihilation of women by the mass media. In G. Tuchman, A. K. Daniels, & J. Benet (Eds.), *Hearth and home: Images of women in the mass media* (pp. 3–38). New York: Oxford University Press.

Tuchman, G. (1978b). The newspaper as a social movement's resource. In G. Tuchman, A. K. Daniels, & J. Benet (Eds.), *Hearth and home: Images of women in the mass media* (pp. 186–215). New York: Oxford University Press.

Tusan, M. E. (2005). *Women making news: Gender and journalism in modern Britain.* Urbana: University of Illinois Press.

Van Zoonen, L. (1998). One of the girls? On the changing gender of journalism. In C. Carter, G. Branston, & S. Allan (Eds.), *News, gender and power* (pp. 33–56). London: Routledge.

Walsh-Childers, K., Chance, J., & Herzog, K. (1996). Sexual harassment of women journalists. *Journalism & Mass Communication Quarterly, 73*(3), 559–581.

Weaver, D. H., & Wilhoit, G. C. (1996). *The American journalist in the 1990s: U.S. news people at the end of an era.* Mahwah, NJ: Erlbaum.

Weaver, D. H. (Eds.). (1998). *The global journalist: News people around the world.* Cresskill, NJ: Hampton.

Winship, J.(1987). *Inside women's magazines.* London: Pandora Press.

Zuckerman, M. E. (1998). *A history of popular women's magazines in the United States, 1792–1995.* Westport, CT: Greenwood Press.

10

Convergence and Cross-Platform Content Production

Thorsten Quandt and Jane B. Singer

The buzzword "convergence" has become a synonym for rapid developments in media technology, markets, production, content, and reception. The term broadly refers to the blending or merging of formerly distinct media technologies, mainly based on digitization processes, though the issues extend beyond those raised by the technology itself. Journalism researchers have primarily focused on "newsroom convergence," particularly in relation to changes in work routines and organizational structures connected to the production of content across media platforms. A related, and more recent, focus of investigation has expanded the meaning of the term to include a convergence of the roles of journalists and audience members within a networked digital environment.

This chapter begins by defining convergence and outlining some of its overall effects within the newsroom. We then turn to several key branches of convergence research, involving newsroom roles and routines, journalistic content, and the contributions of online users. We consider technological, social, and ethical aspects of convergence, concluding with suggestions for future research.

BEHIND THE BUZZWORD: APPROACHES TO CONVERGENCE

Over the past twenty years, far-reaching transformations have rocked modern societies around the globe. Many of the changes have been linked to rapid developments in computer technology and communication networks affecting nearly all aspects of social life, including the economy, politics, science, and the arts. The organization of public communication has been undergoing an especially dramatic shift. The once-stable system of mainstream mass media now faces competition from multi-faceted, constantly mutating information and entertainment sources, to which people connect through interactive technologies such as computers, mobile phones, personal digital assistants (PDAs), and gaming consoles. The term "convergence"—which originally meant simply an increasing correspondence between two phenomena or entities, such as two media technologies, that might come together at some future point—has been stretched to cover all these connotations.

The variety of possible interpretations led to the conclusion that "Convergence is a dangerous word!" as early as the mid-1990s (Silverstone, 1995)—and the discussion has not become much more focused since. "Convergence" has been used to describe the blurring of boundaries between fixed and mobile communications; broadcast, telephone, mobile, and home networks; media, information, and communication; and most notably, telecommunications, media, and information technology. In its media context, the term has also been applied to technological developments such as the integration of video on the Internet, marketing efforts involving cross-promotion of media partners, and corporate mergers.

Although differing in many aspects, all of the approaches to convergence incorporate the notion of a process, and most stress the technological basis of developments. This has led to the common misunderstanding that technology "drives" media change, a technological determinism that ignores social factors. Social scientists have instead stressed the human aspects of technological development, for instance describing how people use and make sense of new tools. Journalism practitioners and journalism studies scholars have concentrated primarily on the production of content for multiple media platforms and the associated changes in work routines, skills, and newsroom culture. For those in the field of journalism, then, the term "convergence" has a particular specialized and socially relevant meaning (Quinn, 2005a).

However, some variations exist here, as well. In the United States, "converged" news organizations have been defined mainly as those in which newspaper staff members create content for television and vice versa, typically with both also contributing to an associated Web site. The partnerships have generally resulted in something less than full convergence, which ideally entails planning and producing stories based on use of each medium's strengths. Instead, most involve cross-promotion of the partnered products but retain elements of competition among journalists in the different newsrooms (Dailey, Demo, & Spillman, 2005). This basic type of cross-media production can be witnessed around the globe as a relatively cautious attempt to cope with technological change and associated user expectations. The question of how to do journalism in a networked digital environment has been especially important for large media companies, which often have material for various media platforms—for instance, television and print—and are interested in developing synergistic strategies for using it. The simplest solution is to "shovel" content from one platform to another.

A more common—and more sophisticated—convergence approach has been to produce parallel content for two media platforms, of which one is digital. With this cross-platform content production, journalists are moving away from creating stories for a single medium; instead, they are gathering information in a content pool and disseminating it in a variety of formats, including not only the Internet but, increasingly, portable devices such as cellular phones and PDAs (see Figure 10.1). Journalists thus must learn to communicate effectively using a more multi-faceted vocabulary of media technologies than they did in the past.

Despite these substantial changes in the news production process, this model of convergence continues to depend on a central institution to collect and disseminate information. In many ways, this remains a "mass media," top-down approach to publishing. However, convergence of media formats around an online delivery platform opens up the journalists' work to the other core characteristic of the Internet: Not only is it based on digital information, and therefore capable of supporting multiple types of content, but it is, of course, also a network—not just technologically but also in a social sense of connecting communicative agents, both individuals and institutionalized actors.

This latter change has far-reaching implications. Networks are not necessarily based on centralization; although they typically have central and peripheral parts, and are subject to power laws that affect information distribution, their structure is not hierarchical in the traditional sense (Monge & Contractor, 2003; Scott, 2000). Thus a "converged" digital news product can also include information, in various formats, from users—people who in the past were a more or less

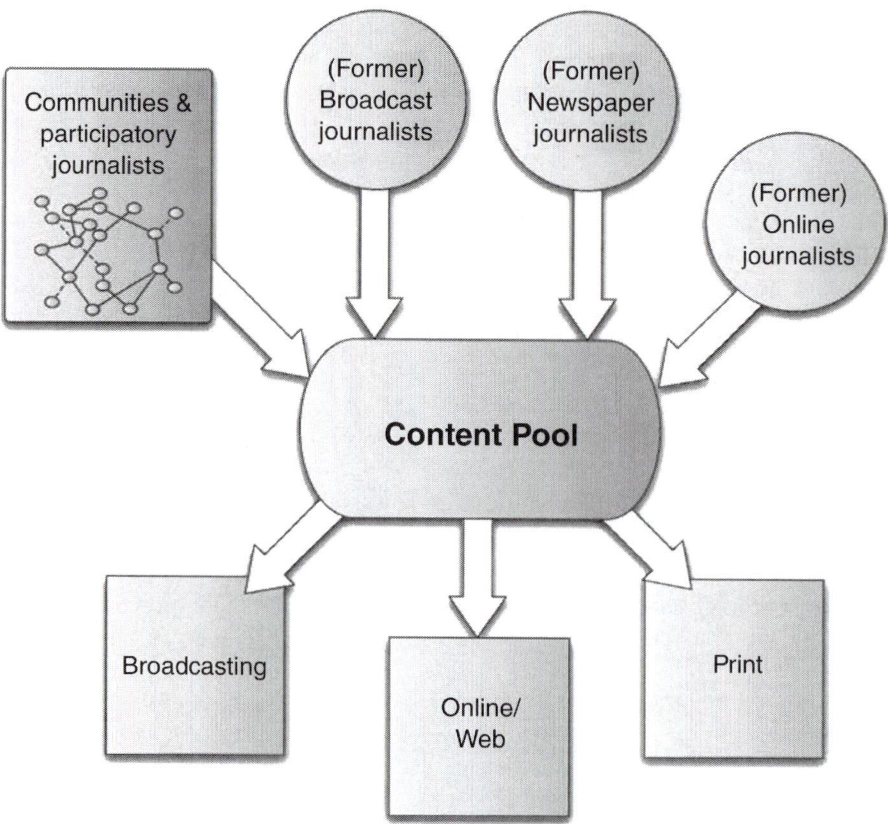

Figure 10.1 Converged production via central content pool.

passive audience for journalistic output. This broadening of the media space through user and community participation represents a form of convergence that is likely to be an even greater challenge to journalists than the one posed by the need to master new tools and techniques.

Since the Internet is both a technological and a social network, information can circulate from one communicator node to many others without the help of an institutional "mass medium" (see Figure 10.2). As a result, convergence between producers and consumers creates what Bruns (2005) calls "produsage." This shift affects not just the way journalists go about their jobs but also the way they conceptualize those jobs and their roles within society. The nature of public communication also is subject to change, with the potential for greater inclusion of individuals and communities.

Some researchers envision a society in which institutionalized media have a diminishing role or even disappear altogether once every citizen in the network can obtain a personalized set of information from every possible source without the need for an institutionalized pre-selection authority called "journalism" (Deuze, 2006a, 2006b; Haas, 2005; Hartley, 2000; Jenkins, 2006; Nip, 2006). Others question whether most people want such a radical model (Hanitzsch, 2006; Schönbach, 1997); after all, institutionalized forms of journalism guarantee a certain product quality, reduce the complexity of social communication and the work necessary to create it, and offer society a shared meaning in the form of content that reaches mass audiences. Indeed, empirical signs of a very limited acceptance of participatory forms throughout many Western countries

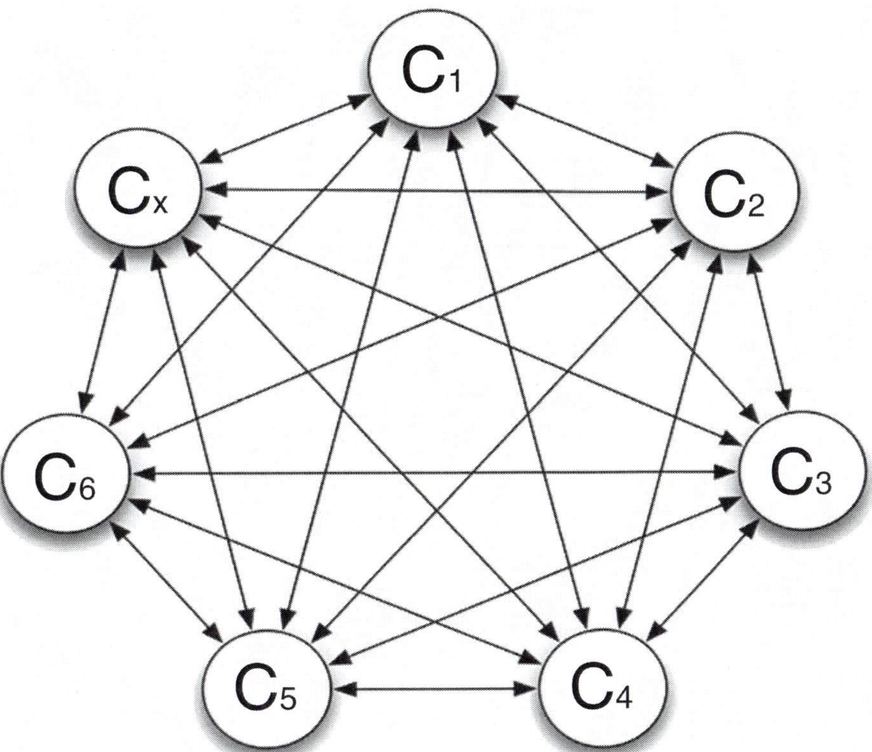

FIGURE 10.2 Network communication.

seem to support a critical position (Paulussen, Heinonen, Domingo, & Quandt, 2007), as does a long-standing pattern of unfulfilled hopes that new media technologies will significantly expand participation in civic affairs (McQuail, 2000, p. 160). Whether today's digital technologies will produce different social effects remains to be seen.

Regardless of what the future holds, the changes within journalism clearly are substantial, and recent developments that stress user input and the role of communities only increase the challenges. Scholarly investigation of journalistic convergence has therefore been multi-faceted. The following section looks more closely at research into three central aspects of convergence that directly affect journalists and journalism: its effects on newsroom roles and routines, as well as on the content that journalists create, and the implications of online users' participation in content production.

CONVERGENCE RESEARCH: STUDIES AND PERSPECTIVES

Processes of media convergence are neither new nor exclusive to the Internet: Many leaps in media technologies over the years have led to integration of formerly distinct media products and functions. However, the pervasive nature of the current shift, as well as the maturation of journalism studies as a field of inquiry, means that digital media have been scrutinized extensively and intensively throughout their development. For scholars, the result has been something of a paradigm shift, with rapidly evolving frames of reference and objects of observation. For journalists who until very recently produced content for a single media product that they alone controlled and to which they alone contributed, ongoing changes have meant new outlets, production structures, and work rules.

The impact of these changes has been both significant and variable. Indeed, convergence is best seen as what Boczkowski (2004) calls "a contingent process in which actors may follow diverging paths as a result of various combinations of technological, local, and environmental factors" (p. 210). This section looks at scholarly research into these trends and factors. We begin with studies that have explored the effects of cross-platform production on journalists' roles and routines.

Inside the Newsroom: Roles and Routines

Much of the scholarly examination of convergence has focused on its effects on the way journalists "make news" (Bardoel & Deuze, 2001; Singer, 2004b). It builds on an extensive body of work in the sociology of news that has yielded insights into how journalists go about turning occurrences and, to a lesser extent, ideas and issues into a news product ready for dissemination to the public.

A related area of academic exploration has focused on journalists' societal roles, particularly in providing the information that citizens in a democracy need for effective self-government (Gans, 2003; Kovach & Rosenstiel, 2001). The gatekeeping role has perhaps been the one most explicitly affected by technological developments, as the Internet and associated digital technologies take control over at least some news gathering and selection routines out of journalists' hands. In a traditional media environment, the journalist selects a relatively limited number of stories for dissemination and rejects the rest, seeing to it that "the community shall hear as a fact only those events which the newsman, as the representative of his culture, believes to be true" (White, 1950, p. 390). But in an environment in which anyone can publish virtually anything, the concept of discrete gates through which information must pass ceases to be a useful conceptualization of how "news" reaches the public—and if there are no gates, there can be no gatekeepers (Williams & Delli Carpini, 2000). Related media roles, such as that of agenda setters, are similarly contested as the mass media audience has fragmented at the same time as the number of information providers has expanded exponentially. Moreover, the journalistic norms that have evolved to safeguard such roles, notably the fiercely guarded ethic of professional independence, are open to challenge in a participatory, networked information environment.

A number of studies of newsroom convergence have examined its effects on these roles and routines. The dominant methodologies have been ethnographic observations, typically in the form of case studies of selected news organizations, and questionnaires. One of the most consistent findings has been that many, though not all, journalists have approached convergence with considerable trepidation. A relatively early move toward convergence by the BBC in Britain was met with resentment and frustration from journalists who felt that their special skills were valued less highly than before and that the accompanying changes within the newsroom had unsettled "professional status, traditional hierarchies, (and) career opportunities," among other negative effects (Cottle & Ashton, 1999, p. 39). In Germany, early approaches to converging newsrooms led to professional and sometimes even personal differences between journalists with varying backgrounds. Some of the efforts to bundle the production for several media in one company or even an integrated newsroom resulted in severe organizational problems and subsequent economic failure; the "electronic media" plans for the national German daily FAZ were one example

(Quandt, 2005). In the United States, a national survey of newsroom managers and staffers in 2002 indicated that journalists saw media companies, rather than practitioners or the public, as the biggest beneficiaries of convergence (Huang, Davison, Shreve, Davis, Bettendorf, & Nair, 2006).

There is a systemic reason for such problems with acceptance in the newsrooms: Convergence suggests a potential business model in which multi-skilled journalists produce more content for little or no increased cost to the organization (Quinn, 2005b). In general, journalists, trained to be skeptical, tend to distrust organizations where the benefits of required change are unclear (Killebrew, 2003) or even, to some, downright suspect.

It remains to be seen whether such critical or even oppositional perspectives represent merely initial, temporary skepticism or a lasting problem. In her case studies of converged newsrooms in the United States, Singer found that although some journalists were unhappy with specific aspects of convergence, they generally supported the idea and even believed converged operations could enhance their public service mission (Singer, 2004a, 2004b, 2006). Bressers and Meeds (2007), focusing on the convergence of newspaper and online operations, suggest four areas that might help predict levels of integration: organizational and management issues, communication and attitudinal issues, physical proximity and equipment-sharing issues, and workflow and content issues. Taken together, these suggest a potentially significant shift in newsroom culture, and other scholarly investigation also has highlighted the importance of this change; the blending of cultural dynamics specific to individual media is seen as key to the success of convergence (Lawson-Borders, 2003).

Differing media routines, particularly those of print and broadcast journalists, have the potential to lead to problems including stereotyping, conflicts over staffing and time management, and difficulties related to news flow (Silcock & Keith, 2006). Singer (2004a) suggested that convergence was propelling print journalists, in particular, to undergo a process of resocialization, though many still thought of online and broadcast counterparts as distinctly separate and had little communication with them. Moreover, newsroom routines and structures did not translate seamlessly across platforms, and competitive tendencies could block even low-impact requests for cooperation or information sharing among convergence partners. A survey-based study by Filak (2004) indicated that print journalists saw their professional culture as superior to that of broadcast journalists—and broadcast journalists similarly saw their own culture as superior to that of print; moreover, these inter-group biases tended to be commonly held and believed by members of each news culture. The author emphasized the need for news organizations seeking to converge their newsrooms to involve both groups in planning, in order to minimize the likelihood that the impetus is perceived as coming from an outgroup and thus rejected.

Scholars studying these and other complexities of managing this cultural change have argued that organizations must demonstrate their commitment to convergence as part of their mission and philosophy, making it simply part of the way they conduct business (Lawson-Borders, 2003). Clear communication from management that convergence is both supported and expected is essential (Quinn, 2005b). More specifically, Killebrew's (2003) overview of issues facing managers of converged newsrooms emphasized the need for thorough and specific staff training; a carefully designed action plan to foster understanding across all levels of the organization; and open, ongoing conversation to address any value discrepancies and dispel corporate myths.

Empirical studies have both underlined these needs and documented the not-infrequent failure to address them. A survey of US newspaper executives highlighted the importance of inclusiveness of online staff at daily news planning sessions, as well as the use of a central news desk to handle stories for multiple platforms—something a majority of news operations did not yet actually have (Bressers, 2006; Bressers & Meeds, 2007). Singer (2004b) identified a perceived lack of training as a barrier to convergence, mainly because it fostered fear about the perceived complexity of the tools needed for cross-platform content production. Her studies also highlighted the importance of open interpersonal communication channels, particularly among journalists in partnered newsrooms, and described management attempts to alleviate concerns about motives and values by allowing journalists to define the extent of their own involvement—which tended to result in relatively low levels of participation in convergence activities, particularly in larger newsrooms.

One significant sticking point has involved compensation—or more accurately, the lack of it. Not surprisingly, news staffers who responded to Huang et al.'s (2006) national survey in the United States thought they should be paid for producing stories for different media platforms, but their newsroom bosses disagreed. Singer's case studies also indicated that resentment of what journalists saw as extra work for no extra pay affected both overall morale and openness to convergence in some newsrooms (Singer, 2004b). Unions representing journalists have raised concerns about convergence in several countries, including the United States (Glaser, 2004) and Great Britain; in the latter, the National Union of Journalists (2007) has negotiated "enabling agreements" with media companies and issued convergence guidelines that address, among other issues, pay, time demands, and training.

Content Considerations: Multi Format Story Telling

Another, related strand of research has sought to understand the effect of newsroom convergence on content, drawing primarily on a series of content analyses. Early research on the impact of the Internet as a "unified" publication channel with multimedia capacities and interactivity potential implied that journalists would be free from the constraints of print and broadcasting, and thus able to invent new ways to tell stories that fully used the new medium's potential (Heinonen, 1999; Hibbert, 1998; Kimber, 1997; Newhagen & Levy, 1998; Pavlik, 1999). However, when newsrooms actually began wrestling with convergence, concerns emerged about a decline in the quality of both reporting and disseminating the news due to time constraints, lack of adequate experience or training with new tools, and, ultimately, a decrease in staffing levels.

Attempts to empirically assess these concerns have yielded mixed results. Some findings support the fears. For instance, online journalists have to work in considerably shorter production cycles than their newspaper peers because of continuous deadlines and the pressure from competing news organizations for constantly updated news (Quandt, 2005). Since the fastest media outlet affects update cycles of the others, this "turbo journalism" can influence news partners in converged environments. Furthermore, qualification levels in online journalism seem to be lower than in traditional print media, at least in some countries (Quandt et al., 2006).

A content analysis by Huang, Rademakers, Fayemiwo, and Dunlap (2004) assessed the "quality" of the *Tampa Tribune*, the newspaper partner in a pioneering US convergence effort, across dimensions of enterprise, significance, fairness and balance, authoritativeness, and localization. The researchers found that three years into its convergence experiment, the paper had not suffered a loss of quality. However, *Tribune* journalists were not engaged in significant amounts of cross-platform reporting at the time of their study in 2003; rather, most of the convergence efforts involved sharing tips and information, as well as cross-promoting the television and online partner. Huang et al.'s national study (2006) indicated nearly 40 percent of US journalists believed quality would decline—but the same number thought it would not. The researchers concluded that there was no reason to be concerned that future journalists trained on multiple media platforms would be jacks of all trades but masters of none or would produce worse reporting.

A recent content analysis of both mainstream print and online publications of German media, along with a companion study of international websites in four countries, hinted at a very limited use of interactive or multimedia elements even in a "converged" online environment. In the international comparison, only the BBC's content included and unified film, audio, and print elements—perhaps due to the existence of these files in the BBC content pool and not merely as a result of converged production. Furthermore, the online news products were limited in scope, focusing on national political news and influenced by national news specifics. These mainstream products did not fulfill the hopes that a converged technological platform would facilitate the disappearance of communicative limitations and cultural borders (Quandt, 2008). Similarly, an earlier study found that national boundaries and language zones were still structuring factors on the Internet (Halavais, 2000).

These findings echo those from several earlier studies of online content. For example, studies in the 1990s found that media organizations were not effectively exploiting opportunities to increase interactivity (Schultz, 1999), nor were they significantly incorporating links, graphics or audio (Neuberger, Tonnemacher, Biebl, & Duck, 1998). These criticisms also remained in studies conducted several years later (Oblak, 2005; Rosenberry, 2005; for a longitudinal study with a more positive verdict, see Greer & Mensing, 2004).

However, some of this criticism is based on problematic assumptions. Much of the research on online content has focused on the sites' formal characteristics, asking questions about the nature and amount of technological interactivity or multimedia elements. The underlying premise of such an approach implies an optimal use of the options inherent in the technology: The more communicative channels and capacities are fully exploited, the "better" the medium's use. Yet previous communication research has shown this assumption to be wrong. Media effects research indicates that media with a limited number of communication channels (such as newspapers) can be superior in many respects to multi-channel media (such as television). Similarly, media richness theory implies that the medium's communicative capacities must match tasks or communicative problems in order to be optimally effective, so maximizing the options is not necessarily the best approach (Daft & Lengel, 1984, 1986). These findings suggest that the somewhat limited use of "converged" multimedia and interactive options in online journalism may be an economically and socially sensible choice, in line with market conditions and user expectations, rather than an indication of lagging development.

The discussion also neglects other developments of interest, such as the ways in which advances in media technologies might change the context of media use. For example, mobile Internet access could have an impact on the integration of media into everyday routines, influencing the reception of journalistic content. The so-called "triple play" integration of telecommunications, broadband applications, and entertainment media can be extended to "quadruple play" with the addition of mobile services. In addition, companies such as Apple and Microsoft are trying to combine entertainment and media functions with computer applications in domestic networks, where a "digital hub" seamlessly connects a range of devices and information sources—a revival of earlier "smart home" ideas (Aldrich, 2003; Harper, 2003). This change of domestic environments and information channels will likely change the way users think about content.

Moreover, the availability of computer and network technology in the domestic space gives users another opportunity to produce and distribute content themselves. We will look at the implications of this "user generated content" in more detail next.

User Generated Content: The (Hyper)Active Audience Tevisited

As described above, much of the literature on convergence has focused on the newsroom, considering the people and the products associated with conventional journalism produced by mainstream news organizations. But the changes instigated by the shift to a networked digital media environment are more complex. A consideration of convergence would be incomplete without acknowledgement of the fact that not only are journalists producing content for multiple platforms, but users are, too—and some of that user-generated content is being disseminated through traditional media outlets. Journalists and media organizations migrating online must also deal with this fundamental change.

Growth of the Internet, along with advances both in broadband technology and user-friendly web production software, means more people have attained the tools to produce content with relative ease. An early sign of this enhanced accessibility was the emergence of the weblog or blog. Blogs were initially regarded as a "diary" format of no journalistic interest, but their larger implications and impact on public communication became apparent during crises, wars, and political contests in the early to mid-2000s. Bloggers began reporting directly from places where events occurred; they also contributed to political debates, both as information sources and public voices.

Discussion is ongoing about the overlap between blogs and journalism, and between bloggers and journalists (Bruns, 2005; Lowrey, 2006; Neuberger, Nuernbergk, & Rischke, 2007; Nip, 2006). Findings on the relationship between blogs and journalism are widely inconsistent (Neuberger et al., 2007). Bloggers are seen as sources for journalists and as competition; blogs are portrayed as everything from a complementary function to an irrelevant phenomenon to a danger because of the lack of quality control, the possibility of manipulation, and so on. However, there seems to be some consensus that blogs are distinct from professional journalism and that although they are unlikely to replace journalism, they are likely to alter it. Elements advanced by bloggers and of increasing importance to mainstream journalists include a conversational writing style, immediacy, and a direct connection to readers. Yet few bloggers seek to reach a mass audience or to be journalists themselves; their motivations tend to be more personal (Neuberger et al., 2007). Little of the information they provide is exclusive; most of it comes from elsewhere on the Internet, commonly from mainstream media. Still, blogs can be influential and can even fulfill an agenda-setting function for both journalists and members of the public (Haas, 2005).

In addition to blogs, other forms of collaborative or user-generated content have drawn increasing public and scholarly recognition of their importance to journalism. The shift from institutionalized control over the publishing processes to user-driven offerings has been noted for some time, but it became a focal point of interest with the advent of the "Web 2.0" idea (O'Reilly, 2005). Web 2.0 emphasizes social aspects in the latest generation of Web applications, including social networking software and collaborative formats. This socio-technological convergence brings together an older tradition of participatory, activist media and Internet publishing, pushed both by the user's expectations and technological advances. Collaborative formats include *Wikipedia*, *YouTube*, *Flickr*, and *MySpace*, which are not necessarily journalistic in nature, and user-driven online news such as *OhMyNews*, *Indymedia*, and *Wikinews*. These social network news services offer much broader content than individual blogs.

By the mid-2000s, some mainstream media were beginning to include user-generated content in their own online news sites; and a few launched experimental platforms that were mostly or fully community based, such as *HasseltLokaal* in Belgium. However, as of this writing, the overall adoption of collaborative formats is generally low in the United States and many parts of Europe (Domingo, Quandt, Heinonen, Paulussen, Singer, & Vujnovic, 2008).

Yet as outlined above, striking possibilities exist for a truly participatory media culture that breaks the publication monopoly of institutionalized media. All stages of the communicative process can be taken over by citizens, at least in principle. Access to information is much more open, and selection and filtering mechanisms are widely available. Processing, editing, and writing tools are inexpensive and easy to obtain, as are the hardware and software needed for publishing and distribution. Participation can happen during the news gathering and writing process, in the organization and display of news, in the coordination and control of the editorial processes, and in the technological delivery of information. As of the mid-2000s, most participation was occurring at the levels of news commenting, gathering, and writing, but examples also had begun to appear of moderators or communities taking over coordination and control functions, for instance with the help of reputation systems.

Observers have wondered whether these trends toward socially converging media environments mean more democracy and public inclusion in the decision-making and communication processes (Jenkins & Thorburn, 2003). This question has to be tackled in the context of societal developments, and points beyond our discussion of changes inside journalism triggered by convergence.

BEYOND THE MIDDLE RANGE: SOCIAL AND ETHICAL IMPLICATIONS

The issues of adoption and implementation described above fall mostly within the theoretical "middle range" (Merton, 1957, p. 5) of concepts grounded in data analysis and lying between minor working hypotheses and grand theoretical speculation. But many aspects of convergence, such as the generation of journalistic content for multiple media platforms and the incorporation of content created by people who are not journalists, raise broader issues. Convergence thus not only affects the inner workings of journalism; it also has an impact on other societal spheres—including political, economic, and cultural ones—that influence and are influenced by the existence and functions of journalism.

For example, like all Internet users, political and economic actors—from candidates to corporations—can bypass journalists in order to communicate directly with others in the network. Similarly, journalists have expanded and now have easier access to original source materials. This access can speed up the journalistic process and foster openness. However, it can also have negative effects; lazy journalists may simply copy and paste online information, and if "googling" counts for fact-checking, the door is open for manipulation and an erosion of quality standards. Furthermore, economically driven downsizing of newsroom staff can lead to news production that is no longer based on original investigation.

These potential dangers hint at possible changes in journalistic ideologies, which can also be discussed in the context of the broader cultural sphere (Allan, 1999; Chalaby, 2000; Hanitzsch, 2007; Hartley, 1996). For instance, there is an ongoing discussion about copyright issues and intellectual property in converging information environments. Collaborative Web sites such as *YouTube* and *Wikipedia* contain material that has been copied from other sources; the large scale of these copyright breaches and the vast amounts of readily available free online content raise the possibility of a growing tolerance for copy and paste as a valid means of content production.

Indeed, political, economic, and cultural changes raise a host of ethical issues. We briefly turn to a few that involve journalistic ethics, which guide their relations to the broader society. While ethics can be "a flag behind which to rally the journalistic troops in defense of commercial, audience-driven or managerial encroachments" as well as an emblem of legitimacy (Deuze, 2005, p. 458), the normative principles that guide practitioners remain important criteria for evaluating ongoing change.

Although all journalists emphasize public service as an overarching ethical norm and professional commitment, observers have expressed concerns about the potential of convergence to undermine this journalistic mission. Among the issues raised have been conflicts of interest created by new corporate partnerships (Davis & Craft, 2000), a blurring of boundaries between commercial and editorial operations (Williams, 2002), and an overemphasis on cross-promotion rather than enhanced news coverage (Ketterer, Weir, Smethers, & Back, 2004).

Journalists themselves do not necessarily share these concerns. Singer's case studies in 2003 indicated that many practitioners see newsroom convergence as facilitating the expression and even expansion of their public service role by enabling the audience to get news in multiple, complementary ways and to obtain a richer account informed by more resources. However, there were doubters. Some journalists said reduced competition diminished their incentive to hustle to get a story; others feared a drift toward overly sensationalistic or entertainment-oriented news judgment and an excess amount of time or space devoted to promotional efforts rather than civically desirable information (Singer, 2006).

In addition to concerns associated with converged newsrooms, the transition to a converged information space—a network in which everyone has the ability to produce and disseminate content—also raises a number of ethical issues. Journalistic autonomy, particularly over determining the appropriateness of practitioners' behavior, is called into question in a media environment filled with people more than eager to serve as watchdogs on the watchdogs (Singer, 2007). Similarly, the nature of journalistic accountability changes. A request that the public simply trust the journalist's claims to be accurate, complete, and even-handed in gathering and presenting the news shifts to an expectation, if not a demand, that the journalist use the capabilities of the network to provide evidence for those claims (Hayes, Singer, & Ceppos, 2007). More broadly, the transition from a gatekeeping role to a place within a network entails a change in the rationale behind such journalistic norms as truth-telling and fairness. These ethical principles no longer can be based on a belief that without the journalist, the public will not receive truthful or unbiased information and thus will necessarily be misinformed. Rather, these ethical principles are vital because they form the foundations of social relationships—and a network is constituted by such relationships (Nel, Ward, & Rawlinson, 2007; Singer, forthcoming).

OUTLOOK: TECHNOLOGY, CONVERGENCE, AND THE FUTURE OF JOURNALISM

The converging media environment thus poses a number of challenges and opportunities for journalism practitioners and scholars, who face both methodological and conceptual issues. For instance, the standard tool of content analysis becomes far more complicated not only because of the dynamic nature of the medium but also because of the inclusion of many more types of sources than in the past—including users as well as journalists. Network analysis offers fruitful avenues for exploration of all forms of digital communication (Tremayne, 2004) but to date has been used by relatively few journalism scholars. In general, new or significantly revised research methods will be needed to explore and understand the different forms of news and the sorts of sources providing it.

Major conceptual work is also needed. Journalism researchers will need to define new roles and new stages in the communication process to accommodate an expanded range of information collectors, editors, and disseminators. Scholars who focus on media audiences also must revise their thinking as lines separating information producers and consumers continue to blur. Some members of the audience will become increasingly involved in the news-making process, but others will remain relatively passive consumers of information. In general, definitions of audiences that are simultaneously more inclusive and more finely tuned will need to be developed and tested.

Ongoing industry changes also affect journalism at a structural level in ways that need to be more clearly understood. Journalism organizations are reconfiguring or even reinventing themselves as multimedia companies with different patterns of information gathering and dissemination than in the past. At a broader level, the function or role of journalism in society is open to redefinition as practitioners wrestle with issues of identity and occupational turf (Lowrey, 2006) in the new media environment. Longitudinal studies would be particularly valuable in tracing the implementation and effects of fundamental industry and ideological change.

Indeed, the concerns of journalism scholars are necessarily interwoven with those of practitioners. For instance, a world in which anyone can be a publisher necessarily raises the question of whether anyone can also be a journalist. Both practitioners and scholars thus are wrestling with distinctions between bloggers and journalists, between "citizen journalism" and professional journalism, and between news aggregators such as Google News and mainstream media outlets that produce their own information packages. Even within the more narrow definition of "convergence," one that focuses on the technological and cultural changes taking place within established newsrooms, concerns have arisen about pressures on both time and resources necessary to produce quality content.

We suggest that journalism in the future is both distinct from other forms of digital content and integrated with those forms to a far greater extent than in either the past or the present. It will be distinct to the extent that journalists can adhere to professional norms such as a commitment to fairness and independence from faction (Kovach & Rosenstiel, 2001), as well as the extent to which media organizations can continue to provide the resources to support original information-gathering. Amid a cacophony of voices, mainstream news organizations still wield enormous power through both the collective capabilities of their staffs and their own economic heft within their communities—professional and commercial power that individuals simply do not possess and, as individuals, will not possess in the foreseeable future. Producing news across a range of platforms, as almost certainly will be required of journalists sooner rather than later, will enhance both the strength of the stories being told and the reach of those stories.

However, in order for this to happen, journalism of the future also must integrate new formats and new voices to a far greater extent than is currently the case. Journalists in today's converged newsrooms are only beginning to realize the opportunities of this multimedia environment, let alone to harness the capabilities inherent in the various technologies now available to them. In many places, they are still at the stage of learning how to use animation tools or edit video. A new generation of "digital native" journalists who are fluent in the languages of multiple communication technologies will need to apply their skills and knowledge in ways that can match the needs of particular stories and particular media platforms.

More important, tomorrow's journalists will need to integrate the voices and viewpoints of others within the network to a far greater extent than is currently the case. Journalists will never again control the flow of information in the way they once did; a media environment in which only a very few voices had an opportunity to be heard—and those only with the permission of a media gatekeeper—is gone for good. Journalists in a network must acknowledge that they will retain power only to the extent that they share it; without facilitating the broad exchange, and not merely the delivery, of information, they will find themselves becoming increasingly irrelevant to the conversation taking place around them. The real power of convergence is in relinquishing the power of controlling information and fostering the power of sharing it.

REFERENCES

Aldrich, F. K. (2003): Smart homes: Past, present and future. In R. Harper (Ed.), *Inside the smart home.* London: Springer, pp. 17–36.

Allan, S. (1999). *News culture.* Buckingham, UK: Open University Press.

Bardoel, J., & Deuze, M. (2001). "Network Journalism." Converging competencies of old and new media professionals. *Australian Journalism Review 23* (2): 91–103.

Boczkowski, P. J. (2004). The processes of adopting multimedia and interactivity in three online newsrooms. *Journal of Communication 54* (2): 197–213.

Bressers, B. (2006). Promise and reality: The integration of print and online versions of major metropolitan newspapers. *The International Journal on Media Management 8* (3): 134–145.

Bressers, B., & Meeds, R. (2007). Newspapers and their online editions: Factors that influence successful integration. Web Journal of Mass Communication Research 10. Retrieved 6 June 2007 from http://www.scripps.ohiou.edu/wjmcr/vol10/

Bruns, A. (2005). *Gatewatching: Collaborative online news production.* New York: Peter Lang.

Chalaby, J. K. (2000). Journalism studies in an era of transition in public communications. *Journalism 1* (1): 33–39.

Cottle, S., & Ashton, M. (1999). From BBC Newsroom to BBC Newscentre: On changing technology and journalist practices. *Convergence: The International Journal of Research into New Media Technologies 5* (3): 22–43.

Daft, R. L., & Lengel, R. H. (1984). Information richness: A new approach to managerial behavior and organizational design. In L. L. Cummings & B. M. Staw (Eds.), *Research in organizational behavior 6*. Homewood, IL: JAI Press, pp. 191–233.

Daft, R. L., & Lengel, R. H. (1986). Organizational information requirements, media richness and structural design. *Management Science 32* (5): 554–571.

Dailey, L., Demo, L., & Spillman, M. (2005). The convergence continuum: A model for studying collaboration between media newsrooms. *Atlantic Journal of Communication 13* (3): 150–168.

Davis, C., & Craft, S. (2000). New media synergy: Emergence of institutional conflicts of interest. *Journal of Mass Media Ethics 15* (4): 219–231.

Deuze, M. (2006a). Participation, remediation, bricolage: Considering principal components of a digital culture. *The Information Society* 22: 63–72.

Deuze, M. (2006b). Ethnic media, community media and participatory culture. *Journalism* 7 (3): 262–280.

Deuze, M. (2005). What is journalism? Professional identity and ideology of journalists reconsidered. *Journalism: Theory, Practice and Criticism 6* (4): 442–464.

Domingo, D., Quandt, T., Heinonen, A., Paulussen, S., Singer, J. B., & Vujnovic, M. (2008). Participatory journalism practices in the media and beyond: An international comparative study of initiatives in online newspapers. *Journalism Practice 2* (3): 326–342.

Filak, V. F. (2004). Cultural convergence: Intergroup bias among journalists and its impact on convergence. *Atlantic Journal of Communication 12* (4): 216–232.

Gans, H. J. (2003). *Democracy and the news.* New York: Oxford University Press.

Glaser, M. (2004, April 7). Lack of unions makes Florida the convergence state. *Online Journalism Review.* Retrieved 6 June 2007 from http://www.ojr.org/ojr/glaser/1081317274.php

Greer, J., & Mensing, D. (2004). The evolution of online newspapers: A longitudinal content analysis, 1997–2003. *Newspaper Research Journal 25* (2): 98–112.

Haas, T. (2005). From "public journalism" to the "public's journalism"? Rhetoric and reality in the discourse on weblogs. *Journalism Studies 6* (3): 387–396.

Halavais, A. (2000). National borders on the World Wide Web. *New Media & Society 2:* 7–25.

Hanitzsch, T. (2007). Deconstructing journalism culture: Towards a universal theory. *Communication Theory 17*(4): 367–385.

Hanitzsch, T. (2006). What is journalism, and what is not.... *Journalism Studies at ICA (Newsletter)* 1: 3.

Harper, R. (Ed.). (2003). *Inside the smart home*. London: Springer UK.

Hartley, J. (2000). Communicational democracy in a redactional society: The future of journalism studies. *Journalism: Theory, Practice, Criticism 1* (1): 39–47.

Hartley, J. (1996). *Popular reality: Journalism, modernity, popular culture.* London: Arnold.

Hayes, A., Singer, J. B., & Ceppos, J. (2007). Shifting roles, enduring values: The credible journalist in a digital age. *Journal of Mass Media Ethics 22* (4), 262–279.

Heinonen, A. (1999). *Journalism in the age of the net: Changing society, changing profession.* Tampere: University of Tampere.

Hibbert, B. (1998). Publishing and the media industries in the digital age. *Info: The Journal of Policy, Regulation and Strategy for Telecommunications, Information and Media 1*: 393–403.

Huang, E., Davison, K., Shreve, S., Davis, T., Bettendorf, E., & Nair, A. (2006). Facing the challenges of convergence: Media professionals' concerns of working across media platforms. *Convergence: The International Journal of Research into New Media Technologies 12* (1): 83–98.

Huang, E., Rademakers, L., Fayemiwo, M. A., & Dunlap, L. (2004). Converged journalism and quality: A case study of *The Tampa Tribune* news stories. *Convergence: The International Journal of Research into New Media Technologies 10* (4): 73–91.

Jenkins, H. (2006). *Convergence culture: Where old and new media collide.* New York: New York University Press.

Jenkins, H. & Thorburn, D. (Eds.) (2003). *Democracy and new media.* Cambridge: The MIT Press.

Ketterer, S., Weir, T., Smethers, J. S., & Back, J. (2004). Case study shows limited benefits of convergence. *Newspaper Research Journal 25* (3): 52–65.

Killebrew, K. C. (2003). Culture, creativity and convergence: Managing journalists in a changing information workplace. *International Journal on Media Management 5* (1): 39–46.

Kimber, S. (1997). The message is (still) the medium: The newspaper in the age of cyberspace. *Information Processing & Management* 33: 595–597.

Kovach, B., & Rosenstiel, T. (2001). *The elements of journalism: What newspeople should know and the public should expect.* New York: Crown Publishers.

Lawson-Borders, G. (2003). Integrating new media and old media: Seven observations of convergence as a strategy for best practices in media organizations. *The International Journal on Media Management 5*(2): 91–99.

Lowrey, W. (2006). Mapping the journalism-blogging relationship. *Journalism 7* (4): 477–500.

McQuail, D. (2000). *McQuail's mass communication theory* (4th ed.). London: Sage.

Merton, R. K. (1957). *Social theory and social structure* (revised and enlarged edition). New York: Free Press of Glencoe.

Monge, P., & Contractor, N. (2003). Emergence of communication networks. In F. Jablin & L. Putnam (Eds.), *The new handbook of organizational communication.* Thousand Oaks, CA: Sage, pp. 440–502.

National Union of Journalists. (2007, April). *Integration & convergence: Newspapers, video and the internet; Interim guidelines from the NUJ.* Retrieved 6 June 2007 from: http://www.nuj.org.uk/inner.php?docid=1704

Nel, F., Ward, M., & Rawlinson, A. (2007). Online journalism. In P. J. Anderson & G. Ward (Eds.), *The future of journalism in advanced democracies.* Aldershot, UK: Ashgate Publishing, pp. 121–138.

Neuberger, C., Nuernbergk, C., & Rischke, M. (2007). Weblogs und Journalismus: Konkurrenz, Ergänzung oder Integration (Weblogs and journalism: Competition, supplement or integration?). *Media Perspektiven* (2): 96–112.

Neuberger, C., Tonnemacher, J., Biebl, M., & Duck, A. (1998): Online—the future of newspapers? German dailies on the World Wide Web. *Journal of Computer Mediated Communication, 4* (1). Retrieved 2 September 2008 from: http://www3.interscience.wiley.com/cig-bin/fulltext/120837748/htmlstart

Newhagen, J. E., & Levy, M. R. (1998). The future of journalism in a distributed communication architecture. In D. L. Borden & H. Kerric (Eds.), *The electronic grapevine: Rumor, reputation and reporting in the new online environment.* Mahwah, NJ: Erlbaum, pp. 9–21.

Nip, J. M. (2006). Exploring the second phase of public journalism. *Journalism Studies 7* (2): 212–236.

Oblak, T. (2005). The lack of interactivity and hypertextuality in online media. *Gazette* 67: 87–106.

O'Reilly, T. (2005, September 30). *What is Web 2.0? Design patterns and business models for the next generation of software.* Retrieved 17 June 2007 from: http://www.oreillynet.com/pub/a/oreilly/tim/news/2005/09/30/what-is-web-20.html

Paulussen, S., Heinonen, A, Domingo, D. & Quandt, T. (2007). Doing it together: Citizen participation in the professional news making process. *Observatorio (OBS*) Journal 3*: 131–154.

Pavlik, J. V. (1999). New media and news: Implications for the future of journalism. *New Media & Society 1*: 54–59.

Quandt, T. (2006). (No) News on the World Wide Web? A comparative content analysis of onlinr news in Europe and the United States. *Journalism Studies 9* (5): 717–738.

Quandt, T. (2005). *Journalisten im Netz (Journalists in the net).* Wiesbaden: Verlag für Sozialwissenschaften.

Quandt, T., Löffelholz, M., Weaver, D., Hanitzsch, T. & Altmeppen, K.-D. (2006). American and German online journalists at the beginning of the 21st century: A bi-national survey. *Journalism Studies 7* (2): 171–186.

Quinn, S. (2005a). *Convergent journalism.* New York: Peter Lang.

Quinn, S. (2005b). Convergence's fundamental question. *Journalism Studies 6* (1): 29–38.

Rosenberry, J. (2005). Few papers use online techniques to improve public communication. *Newspaper Research Journal* 26 (4): 61–73.

Schultz, T. (1999): Interactive options in online journalism: A content analysis of 100 U.S. newspapers. *Journal of Computer Mediated Communication 5* (1). Retrieved 6 July 2007 from: http://jcmc.indiana.edu/vol5/issue1/schultz.html

Schönbach, K. (1997). Das hyperaktive Publikum—Essay über eine Illusion (The hyperactive audience—Essay on an illusion). *Publizistik 42* (3): 279–286.

Scott, J. (2000). *Social network analysis. A handbook.* London: Sage.

Silcock, B. W., & Keith, S. (2006). Translating the tower of Babel? Issues of definition, language and culture in converged newsrooms. *Journalism Studies 7* (4): 610–627.

Silverstone, R. (1995). Convergence is a dangerous word. *Convergence: The Journal of Research into New Media Technologies 1* (1): 11–14.

Singer, J. B. (forthcoming). The journalist in the network: A shifting rationale for the gatekeeping role and the objectivity norm. Accepted for publication in *Tripodos: Llenguatge, Pensament, Comunicacion.*

Singer, J. B. (2007). Contested autonomy: Professional and popular claims on journalistic norms. *Journalism Studies 8* (1): 79–95.

Singer, J. B. (2006). Partnerships and public service: Normative issues for journalists in converged newsrooms. *Journal of Mass Media Ethics 21* (1): 30–53.

Singer, J. B. (2004a). More than ink-stained wretches: The resocialization of print journalists in converged newsrooms. *Journalism & Mass Communication Quarterly 81* (4): 838–856.

Singer, J. B. (2004b). Strange bedfellows? The diffusion of convergence in four news organizations. *Journalism Studies 5* (1): 3–18.

Tremayne, M. (2004). The web of context: Applying network theory to the user of hyperlinks in journalism on the web. *Journalism & Mass Communication Quarterly 81* (2): 237–253.

White, D. M. (1950). The 'gate keeper': A case study in the selection of news. *Journalism Quarterly 27* (3): 383–390.

Williams, B., & Delli Carpini, M. (2000). Unchained reaction: The collapse of media gatekeeping and the Clinton-Lewinsky scandal. *Journalism: Theory, Practice and Criticism 1* (1): 61–85.

Williams, D. (2002). Synergy bias: Conglomerates and promotion in the news. *Journal of Broadcasting & Electronic Media 46* (3): 453–472.

III

NEWS CONTENT

11

Agenda Setting

Renita Coleman, Maxwell McCombs, Donald Shaw, and David Weaver

INTRODUCTION

Agenda setting is the process of the mass media presenting certain issues frequently and prominently with the result that large segments of the public come to perceive those issues as more important than others. Simply put, the more coverage an issue receives, the more important it is to people. Since this first simple definition of the phenomenon, agenda setting has expanded from a theory describing the transfer of issue salience from the news media to the public to a broader theory that includes a "second-level" describing the transfer of attribute salience for those issues and many other "objects" such as political figures. Also, inter-media agenda setting explains how elite media transmit their agenda of important issues to other media. Agenda-setting research has stimulated debates about priming and framing; explications of obtrusiveness and the "need for orientation" that defines the conditions under which agenda-setting effects are enhanced or diminished; and, most recently, explorations of the implications of agenda-setting effects for attitudes and opinions and observable behavior. Agenda setting has proved to be a theory that is both deep and wide, applicable for more than the 30-year lifespan that is the mark of a useful theory. It has been called the theory "most worth pursuing" of mass communication theories (Blumler & Kavanagh, 1999, p. 225).

Agenda setting is one of the few theories created by mass communication scholars and adopted subsequently by many other disciplines, including health communication, political communication, business, and more. The intellectual roots of this mass communication theory have been credited to journalist Walter Lippmann, whose book, *Public Opinion,* argued that the news media construct our view of the world. That was in 1922, but it was 50 years later that Maxwell McCombs and Donald Shaw gave the now-familiar name to the phenomena Lippmann described, and since then agenda setting has become one of the major research themes in our field.

No dip into agenda-setting waters would be complete without reading the seminal 1972 *Public Opinion Quarterly* piece by McCombs and Shaw, "The Agenda Setting Function of Mass Media," which reported how undecided voters in Chapel Hill, North Carolina, used media in the 1968 presidential election. For a contemporary introduction to agenda setting, *Setting the Agenda: The Mass Media and Public Opinion* (McCombs, 2004) has been described as the *Gray's Anatomy* of the theory by John Pavlik (McCombs, 2004, p. xii). An important point in the book is that agenda setting is not the result of any diabolical plan by journalists to control the minds of the public, but "an inadvertent by-product of the necessity to focus" the news (McCombs, 2004, p. 19). Newspapers, magazines, radio, and television have a limited amount of space and time, so only a fraction of the day's news can be included. It is this necessary editing process, guided by agreed-upon professional news values, that results in the public's attention being directed to a few issues and other topics as the most important of the day. Since McCombs and Shaw set the game afoot with the Chapel Hill study, many scholars across the world have joined in the effort. The references here—and in McCombs' *Setting the Agenda*—provide a comprehensive bibliography of this research over the past 40 years. Additional important sources include James Dearing and Everett Rogers' (1996) history of the early decades, *Agenda Setting*; the book-length reports of the 1972 and 1976 US presidential elections, respectively, *The Emergence of American Political Issues* (Shaw & McCombs, 1977), and *Media Agenda Setting in a Presidential Election* (Weaver, Graber, McCombs, & Eyal, 1981); Wayne Wanta's (1997) creative studies in *The Public and the National Agenda*; and Stuart Soroka's (2002), *Agenda Setting Dynamics in Canada*.

HISTORICAL EVOLUTION

Agenda setting owes its original insight to Lippmann (1922), who discussed how media messages influence the "pictures in our heads," but contemporary scholars have greatly expanded on that idea. Ironically, Lippmann was not optimistic about journalism's ability to convey the information that citizens needed to govern themselves effectively. Twenty years later, research into the effects of mass communication also painted a dismal picture. Study after study showed that mass media had little to no effect on people (Berelson, Lazarsfeld, & McPhee, 1954; Lazarsfeld, Berelson, & Gaudet, 1948). This was the era of the "limited media effects" paradigm, a major shift from earlier belief in the power of the press, a time when propaganda was thought to work like a "magic bullet" to change people's attitudes, beliefs, and even behavior. The later emergence of evidence for an agenda-setting role of the media was one important link in a chain of research that would signal a paradigm shift in the way we look at the effects of mass media.

The initial studies of agenda setting took place during three consecutive US presidential elections, a useful place to begin because of their "natural laboratory" setting—campaigns feature a continuous set of political messages that stop on Election Day. The original study, which found a nearly perfect correlation between the media's agenda of issues and the public's agenda of issues, was conducted among undecided voters during the 1968 presidential election (McCombs & Shaw, 1972). This study has been called one of the 15 milestones in mass communication research (Lowery & Defleur, 1995). With high correlations between the media and public agendas established, the next step was to show a causal connection and the time sequence. Were the media setting the public agenda, or the public setting the media agenda?

The second major project was a panel study conducted in Charlotte, North Carolina, during the 1972 presidential election that found a +.51 correlation over time from the media to the public, but only a +.19 correlation from the public to the media (Shaw & McCombs, 1977). The third study in the opening triumvirate was an exhaustive look at the entire 1976 election year in three cities (Weaver et al., 1981). Nine waves of panel interviews explored how people learned about issues in tandem with content analyses of the media messages.

Among the intriguing findings in the Chapel Hill study was the high degree of correspondence among different media outlets. Newspapers, TV, and magazines all gave similar coverage to the same issues, a situation that initiated research on inter-media agenda setting and demonstrated the importance of elite news organizations, particularly the *New York Times*, in setting the media agenda. The proliferation of media outlets on cable and the Internet encourages continuing research on inter-media agenda setting. The 1972 Charlotte study also was a harbinger of research on the differences among media in influencing the public agenda. In Charlotte, TV news had greater short-term effects on voters than newspapers. But this effect is far from consistent. Over the years, the evidence shows that about half of the time, there is no difference in impact between TV and newspapers; the other half of the time, newspapers tend to be more powerful.

Another important insight generated by the early studies was the limited number of issues the public considered important at any point in time. From dozens of issues competing for public attention, only a few rise to importance due to the limits on the public's attention, time, and ability to focus on more than five to seven issues at a time. Nevertheless, the agenda-setting role of the news media plays an important part in focusing people's attention on the problems that government and public institutions *can* work to resolve. Without agreement on what is important, societies would struggle to accomplish public good.

Beyond the Election Studies

Moving beyond elections, Eaton (1989) examined 11 issues, including unemployment, nuclear disaster, poverty, and crime, over 41 months in the late 1980s and found similar agenda-setting effects. Among the earliest of the non-election topics studied was the civil rights movement (Winter & Eyal, 1981). Twenty-three years of the ebb-and-flow of news coverage and the corresponding changes in public opinion provided powerful evidence that agenda setting occurred in arenas other than elections. Other issues that reflect media agenda setting include the federal budget deficit (Jasperson, Shah, Watts, Faber, & Fan, 1998); the economy (Hester & Gibson, 2003); environmental issues (Salwen, 1988; Chan, 1999); and health issues, including HIV/AIDS (Pratt, Ha, & Pratt, 2002) and smoking (Sato, 2003). Agenda setting also has been documented for local issues (Palmgreen & Clarke, 1977; Smith, 1987), not just national ones.

Is agenda setting a uniquely American phenomena? Not at all. Agenda setting has been confirmed across the world at national and local levels, in elections and non-elections, with newspapers and television. This research includes Spain (Lopez-Escobar, Llamas, & McCombs, 1998), Japan (Takeshita, 1993), Argentina (Lennon, 1998), Israel (Sheafer & Weimann, 2005), and Germany (Brosius & Kepplinger, 1990). The appearance of agenda-setting effects does require reasonably open political and media systems, however. In countries where the media are controlled by the government and one political party dominates, agenda setting by the media does not occur. In Taiwan in 1994, this happened with the broadcast media; all three TV stations were government-controlled. This was not the case, however, for the two independent daily newspapers in the same election (King, 1997). This comparison of media systems, with other factors remaining constant, is a powerful endorsement of the public's ability to sort out what news is real and what is not.

A Second Level of Agenda-Setting Effects: Attribute Agenda Setting

The original concept of agenda setting, the idea that the issues emphasized by the media become the issues that the public thinks are important, is now referred to as the "first level" of agenda setting. Whereas first-level agenda setting focuses on the amount of media coverage an issue or other topic receives, the "second-level" of agenda setting looks at how the media discuss those issues or other objects of attention, such as public figures. Here the focus is on the attributes or characteristics that describe issues, people or other topics in the news and the tone of those attributes. The general effect is the same: the attributes and tone that the media use in their descriptions are the attributes and tone foremost in the public mind.

The first level of agenda setting is concerned with the influence of the media on which objects are at the center of public attention. The second level focuses on how people understand the things that have captured their attention. Using Lippmann's phrase "the pictures in our heads," first-level agenda setting is concerned with what the pictures are about. The second level is literally about the pictures. The two dimensions of the second level are the substantive and affective elements in these pictures. The substantive dimension of attributes helps people discern the various aspects of topics. For example, in news coverage of political candidates, the types of substantive attributes include the candidates' ideology, qualifications, and personality.

Particular characteristics often arise in specific campaigns; for example, corruption was important in the 1996 Spanish election (McCombs, Lopez-Escobar, & Llamas, 2000); ability to get things done and cutting taxes were key issues in the 2000 US presidential election primaries (Golan & Wanta, 2001). Even non-election issues can show differences in attributes at different times. In the case of issues, on the topic of the economy, for example, inflation is important some times, while unemployment or budget deficits may be more salient at others.

Within these substantive characteristics, each can take on an emotional quality, an affective tone that can be positive, negative, or neutral. It is important to know whether a particular candidate is described positively, negatively, or neutrally on substantive attributes such as morality and leadership ability, not just how often those substantive elements are mentioned in connection with a candidate.

Much support has been found for these second-level attribute agenda-setting effects. McCombs, Lopez-Escobar, & Llamas (2000) found second-level agenda-setting effects regarding the qualities of the candidates in the 1996 Spanish national election. In a laboratory experiment in the United States, Kiousis, Bantimaroudis, and Ban (1999) found that the public's perceptions of candidates' personalities and qualifications mirrored the manipulated media portrayals used in the study. Support for second-level effects also has been found for a variety of public issues, such as economic issues (Hester & Gibson, 2003; Jasperson, Shah, Watts, Faber, & Fan, 1998) and the environment (Mikami, Takeshita, Nakada, & Kawabata, 1994).

Comparison with Framing

There is considerable debate in scholarly circles about the differences between attribute agenda setting and framing. Some say they are different; others say they are not. Framing has been defined as "the way events and issues are organized and made sense of, especially by media, media professionals, and their audiences" (Reese, 2001, p. 7). To frame is "to select some aspects of a perceived reality and make them more salient [...] to promote a particular problem definition, causal interpretation, moral evaluation, and/or treatment recommendation" (Entman, 1993, p. 52). Both framing and attribute agenda setting call attention to the perspectives of communicators and their audiences, how they picture topics in the news and, in particular, to the special status that certain attributes or frames can have in the content of a message. If a frame is defined as a dominant perspective on the object—a pervasive description and characterization of the object—then a frame is usefully delimited as a very special case of attributes.

In another approach based on a hierarchical conceptualization in which frames are macro-categories that serve as bundling devices for lower-order attributes, Takeshita (2002) found a close correspondence between media coverage and public perceptions of Japan's economic difficulties at both levels of analysis. Yet other approaches to framing examine the origins and use of broad cultural and social perspectives found in news stories and among members of the public, approaches that have little relationship to agenda-setting theory.

Theoretical efforts to demarcate the boundary between agenda setting and framing (Price &

Tewksbury, 1997; Scheufele, 2000) on the basis of the two aspects of knowledge activation—the concepts of accessibility (linked theoretically to agenda setting) and applicability (linked theoretically to framing)—have found only limited success. Focusing specifically on the accessibility of issue attributes, Kim, Scheufele, and Shanahan (2002) found that accessibility did increase with greater newspaper use, but that the resulting attribute agenda among the public bore no resemblance to the attribute agenda presented in the news and did not replicate attribute agenda-setting effects found across four decades by previous studies. What emerged was a different version of media effects in which the relative amount of increased salience for the attributes among newspaper readers, when compared to persons unaware of the issue, largely paralleled the media agenda.

Consequences of Agenda Setting

Other studies have looked at the consequences of agenda setting for the public's opinions, attitudes, and behavior—the "so what" question. As part of this effort, scholars have linked agenda-setting research with studies of "priming" that examine the effects of media agendas on the public's opinions as well as the public's concerns. This focus on the consequences of agenda setting for public opinion can be traced back at least to Weaver, McCombs, and Spellman (1975, p. 471), who speculated in their 1972–73 panel study of the effects of Watergate news coverage that the media do more than teach which issues are most important—they also may provide "the issues and topics to use in evaluating certain candidates and parties, not just during political campaigns, but also in the longer periods between campaigns."

Their speculation was supported a decade later when Iyengar and Kinder (1987), in controlled experiments, linked television agenda-setting effects to evaluations of the US president in a demonstration of what some cognitive psychologists have called "priming"—making certain issues or attributes more salient and more likely to be accessed in forming opinions. Weaver (1991) also found that increased concern over the federal budget deficit was linked to increased knowledge of the possible causes and solutions of this problem, stronger and more polarized opinions about it, and more likelihood of engaging in some form of political behavior regarding the issue, even after controlling for various demographic and media use measures.

Willnat (1997, p. 53) argued that the theoretical explanations for these correlations, especially between agenda setting and behavior, have not been well developed, but the alliance of priming and agenda setting has strengthened the theoretical base of agenda-setting effects by providing "a better understanding of how the mass media not only tell us 'what to think about' but also 'what to think'" (Cohen, 1963).

Not all scholars agree that priming is a consequence of agenda setting. Some have argued that both agenda setting and priming rely on the same basic processes of information storage and retrieval where more recent and prominent information is more accessible. Regardless of these debates, it seems likely that an increase in the salience of certain issues, and certain attributes of these issues, does have an effect, perhaps indirect, on public opinion. Son and Weaver (2006) confirm that media attention to a particular candidate, and selected attributes of a candidate, influences his standing in the polls cumulatively rather than immediately. This finding has been replicated with data from Mexico and Canada by Valenzuela and McCombs (2007).

Media emphasis of some issues also can affect public behavior. Extensive news coverage of crime and violence, including a murder and rapes, on the University of Pennsylvania campus contributed to a significant drop in applications by potential first-year students, predominantly women, according to the university's dean of admissions (*Philadelphia Inquirer*, 1996). This decline occurred when other comparable universities experienced an increase in applications during the same period.

Roberts (1992) found further evidence of a link between agenda setting and behavior in the 1990 election for governor of Texas. Issue salience was a significant predictor of actual votes in this election, with 70 percent of the respondents' actual reported votes for governor correctly predicted by the level of issue concern over time, controlling for demographics and media reliance and attention.

In one of the most dramatic revelations of the behavioral influence of news media emphasis, Blood and Phillips (1997) carried out a time series analysis of *New York Times* headlines from June 1980 to December 1993 and found that rising numbers of unfavorable economic headlines had an adverse effect on subsequent leading economic indicators (average weekly hours for manufacturing, average weekly initial claims for unemployment, new orders of consumer goods and materials, vendor performance, contracts and orders for plant and equipment, building permits, etc.) rather than vice-versa. Blood and Phillips (1997, p. 107) wrote that their findings "suggest that the amount and tone of economic news exerted a powerful influence on the economic environment and further, that the economic news agenda was generally not being set by prevailing economic conditions."

STATE OF THE ART

Once the basic relationship between the media agenda and the public agenda was established, a second phase of research began—the exploration of factors that weaken or strengthen agenda-setting effects. The search for these contingent conditions that modify agenda-setting effects is broadly divided into two groups: audience characteristics and media characteristics, such as the differences between TV and newspapers discussed previously. Here we emphasize the individual differences found among audience members.

Need for Orientation

"Need for orientation," a psychological concept that describes individual differences among people in their desire to understand a new environment or situation by turning to the media, was introduced in the 1972 Charlotte presidential election study. Need for orientation is defined in terms of two lower-order concepts, relevance and uncertainty. Relevance means that an issue is personally or socially important. Uncertainty exists when people do not feel they have all the information they need about a topic. Under conditions of high uncertainty and high relevance, need for orientation is high and media agenda-setting effects tend to be very strong. The more people feel that something is important, and they do not know enough about it, the more attention they pay to news stories. Conversely, when the relevance of a topic is low, and people feel little desire for additional information, need for orientation is low and media agenda-setting effects typically are weak (Takeshita, 1993). Recently, the concept of need for orientation has been expanded by Matthes (2006) to explicitly measure both orientation toward topics, the first level of agenda setting, and orientation toward aspects (or attributes) of those topics, the second level of agenda setting.

One situation where agenda setting might have occurred but did not because people felt the issue was not important or relevant was the Bill Clinton-Monica Lewinsky scandal. When President Clinton was revealed to have had a sexual relationship with a White House intern—in fact, when it was merely rumored—press coverage was incessant. Some described it as "all Monica, all the time." Given the amount of coverage of this issue and how high it was on the *media's* agenda, it might have been expected to have major *public* agenda-setting effects. While the scandal was fascinating, even shocking and reprehensible, it did not generate heavy public outrage (Yioutas & Segvic, 2003). Members of the public are not slaves to the media agenda.

Need for orientation is related to another individual difference—education. Individuals with higher levels of education are more likely to experience greater need for orientation. From the many demographic characteristics studied, formal education consistently emerges as related to agenda setting. Higher education typically increases interest in public issues, and those with more education are more likely to mirror the media's agenda.

Obtrusive Issues

The media, of course, are not the only source of information people have about public affairs. Personal experience and conversations with other people are two other important sources. For most of the issues discussed so far, people have no direct experience. Unless you have been a soldier in Iraq, you have to depend on the media for your information about conflict in that country. But not all issues are this out-of-reach. Anyone who has ever been laid off from a job does not need the media to know something about unemployment. When people have direct, personal experience with an issue, that issue is said to be "obtrusive" for them, and they usually do not need more information from the media (Zucker, 1978). Unobtrusive issues, those with which people have little to no personal experience, are the ones most likely to become important to people if they are high on the media's agenda.

The same issue can be obtrusive for some people and unobtrusive for others; the unemployment issue, for example. For obtrusive issues that people experience in their daily lives, media coverage does not have much power to set an agenda, but for issues with which people do not have direct personal experience media coverage is much more influential in determining how important the issues are to those people. Some issues are mostly obtrusive or unobtrusive for everyone. Foreign affairs, the environment, energy, government spending, drug abuse, and pollution are unobtrusive for most people, for example, whereas local road maintenance, the cost of living, and taxes are largely obtrusive. Other issues, such as unemployment, are somewhere in the middle, and the strength of agenda setting depends on whether a person has ever been unemployed or known someone who has. These middle-range issues underscore the importance of measuring obtrusiveness on a continuum rather than as a dichotomous variable.

New Arenas

While elections and political campaigns are prominent settings for agenda-setting studies, there is considerable evidence for agenda-setting effects in many other settings. These range from business news (Carroll & McCombs, 2003), religion (Harris & McCombs, 1972), foreign relations, (Inoue & Patterson, 2007), and healthcare (Ogata Jones, Denham, & Springston, 2006). Some studies have extrapolated an agenda-setting effect from news to entertainment media (Holbrook & Hill, 2005). Almost any topic you can think of can be studied from an agenda-setting perspective.

Most agenda-setting studies examine the content of the media as defined by words. However a few have included visuals, such as photographs or television video, and found evidence for visual agenda-setting effects. In Wanta's (1988) first-level analysis, the size of a photograph was found to influence readers' perceptions of importance. Coleman and Banning (2006) examined the second-level effects of television images of the candidates and found significant correlations between television's visual framing of George W. Bush and Al Gore and the public's affective impressions of them in the 2000 election. This study was replicated and extended in the 2004 election (Coleman & Wu, 2006). Furthermore, the presence or absence of pictures can have profound implications. Famines, starvation, and drought in 1984 in Ethiopia and Brazil were roughly comparable, but compelling photographs and video were widely available only for Ethiopia, which then benefited from massive coverage and international relief efforts (Boot, 1985).

Agenda Melding

There is growing evidence that audiences mix agendas from various media—meld them—and so are influenced by a mixture of agendas. Agenda setting establishes a connection between medium and audience but scholars recently have moved to incorporate audiences and the media choices they make within the general hypothesis of agenda setting. Audiences have choices and those choices rise from their own established values and attitudes and, as we have seen, their need for orientation. Audiences use general news media, and they also use a variety of specialized media that fit their personal lifestyles and views, such as talk radio or television shows. Agenda-setting research has established that journalists and editors have great power to shape the main topics of importance to audiences, along with many details of those topics. But we also know that many people use Web sites or other news sources to supplement that initial picture and to find views on events that fit their own expectations. This effort, from the point of view of the audience, is called agenda melding.

How does agenda melding work? Recently Ericson and colleagues (2007) sorted the descriptive vocabulary used by the *Charlotte Observer* and the *New York Times* to describe the 21–year career of NASCAR driver Dale Earnhardt, Sr., who died in a crash in 2001. The descriptive language used in the early, middle, and end of his career were different, with only a few descriptions constant throughout his career. Examples of early descriptions were "the boy," "Jaws II," "aggressor," and "youngster." Middle-of-career descriptions were "The Intimidator," "ironhead," and "dominator," and toward the end of the career, "the man in black," "carburetor cowboy," and "the big E." A follow-up experimental study to this content analysis discovered that subjects were quite responsive to the variations in this vocabulary, especially regarding the affective dimension of the attribute agenda. This suggests the importance of audience involvement to complete the message. The audience melds personal feelings associated with certain language elements with the message itself. The media set the agenda, but the audience also melds with the agenda in conformance with their established values and attributes. Agenda-melding suggests the important role of audiences in blending, adapting, and absorbing messages.

METHODOLOGICAL ISSUES

Public Opinion Polls Plus Content Analysis

Often overlooked are the methodological contributions of the first agenda-setting study in Chapel Hill. This 1968 study combined two methods, a content analysis and a survey of public opinion, and it established the idea of a time-lag. Agenda-setting studies today still routinely measure and rank-order the number of stories on specific issues in the media using content analysis, then survey the public to ascertain their views on what are the "Most Important Problems" of the day—the MIP question—which also are rank-ordered. Using Spearman's rank-order correlation coefficient, the media's agendas of most important issues are correlated with the public's agendas of important issues. Time and again, in countries around the world, the rankings are highly significant and strong—typically around +.55 or greater (Wanta & Ghanem, 2000).

Establishing Causality

One of the frequent criticisms of the content analysis plus survey method of studying agenda setting is that a one-time correlational study cannot definitively show causality. Even though the early studies were careful to measure the media content before the public opinion surveys, questions still remain about which came first, public opinion that influenced what the media covered, or media coverage that influenced public opinion. Thus, agenda setting has looked to two other methods to supplement its basic research by establishing a cause-and-effect sequence. Both longitudinal studies and experiments satisfy the necessary condition for demonstrating time-order.

Longitudinal studies consist of several waves of public opinion surveys and content analyses. For example, the 1976 election panel study involved nine waves of interviewing (Weaver, Graber, McCombs, & Eyal, 1981). The civil rights study involved 27 replications over a 23-year period (Winter & Eyal, 1981). This type of evidence is grounded in "real world" data using the general public's opinions about actual issues in the news, but it still suffers from a myriad of uncontrollable factors. To definitively say that media coverage can set the public's agenda, researchers turned to controlled experiments.

While laboratory experiments lack the external validity of field studies grounded in survey research and content analysis, they are seen as necessary complements to traditional agenda-setting studies, even those that use longitudinal designs. Only laboratory experiments can document a causal relationship unaffected by extraneous factors between the media agenda and public agenda. Evidence of causality exists for both first- and second-level agenda setting. A classic set of first-level agenda-setting experiments by Iyengar and Kinder (1987) systematically manipulated the frequency of topics in TV news programs. A second-level agenda-setting experiment by Kiousis, Bantimaroudis, and Ban (1999) systematically manipulated the characteristics of a fictitious political candidate. Usually, even brief exposure to news articles in a laboratory setting results in significant agenda-setting effects.

Lag Time

Additional methodological research investigates the time lag—that is, the optimal time that an issue must be covered in the media before the public considers it as important. Research has identified a variety of lag times for different issues—one month was the optimal time for the civil rights issue (Winter & Eyal, 1981), but Wanta, Golan, and Lee (2004) used a 9-1/2-month time lag for their study of international news because stories about foreign countries are found less frequently than stories of domestic issues. Differences in individual issues are important, of course, but the optimum range of time for the media agenda to influence the public agenda is one to eight weeks, with a median of three weeks. Longer is not always better when it comes to the amount of time required for the media agenda to influence the public agenda, however. Agenda-setting effects, of course, also decay, taking anywhere from eight to 26 weeks to disappear entirely (Wanta & Hu, 1994).

Measuring Object and Attribute Salience

The now-classic agenda-setting question, the "Most Important Problem," was born in the 1930s when the Gallup organization began asking Americans to name the most important problem facing the country. This open-ended question provides a convenient way for scholars to assess the salience of the problems on the public agenda. Typically, no more than five to seven issues, those with the greatest number of people saying they were the most important, end up being used in agenda-setting studies; issue categories ranked lower tend to have too few people for any meaningful analysis. One frequently used threshold for an issue's inclusion is that 10 percent or more of the public surveyed identify it as a "most important problem."

Min, Ghanem, and Evatt (2007) compared the traditional MIP question with one designed to measure *personal* salience rather than *social* salience, asking, "What is the most important problem that is personally relevant to you?" No differences were found in the issues named. Even though question wording sometimes can strongly affect the outcome of a survey, the assessment of issue salience appears very robust, and the use of creative alternatives for measuring the public's most important issues have not been discouraged. Rather, using different questions to measure the same construct is seen as expanding our knowledge about agenda setting through replication and diversity of measures.

Recognition and recall are two other prominent alternatives to the MIP (Althaus & Tewksbury, 2002). Closed-ended questions also are popular. Some survey respondents have been asked to select the most important issues from a list; others have been asked sets of questions using 5-point scales on the importance of an issue, extent of discussion with friends, and need for more government action (Wang, 2000). Similarly, sets of bipolar semantic scales have been used in experiments (Evatt & Ghanem, 2001).

Attribute agendas also have been measured with both closed- and open-ended questions. A widely used open-ended question for attribute agenda-setting studies is, "Suppose you had some friends who had been away for a long time and were unfamiliar with the presidential candidates [or other public figures]. What would you tell them about [person X]?" Closed-ended questions also abound, such as rating how honest, sincere, and trustworthy a candidate is, typically with 5- or 7-point rating scales. One of the most unusual measures used non-response as an inverse measure of salience (Kiousis, 2000). That is, the smaller the number of people who hold no opinion, the greater the salience of a candidate or issue.

Historical Analysis

Surveys that asked people about the most important problems facing the country only date back to the 1930s, yet there is evidence of historical agenda-setting effects dating as far back as the founding of the British colonies (Merritt, 1966) and the Spanish-American War (Hamilton, Coleman, Grable, & Cole, 2006). Given the strong evidence from the 1960s on, even historians feel comfortable extrapolating to the past.

DIRECTIONS FOR FUTURE RESEARCH

The rise in popularity of the Internet is the most obvious and important new frontier for agenda-setting research. Little is known so far about the effect of Web sites, blogs, and social networking sites on the public agenda of important issues. Some speculate that with the Internet come more diverse sources of news with little consensus on issues, a situation that could alter agenda setting as we know it. Couple that with the explosion of cable TV and radio channels via satellite, and the predictions seem dire.

There is, quite simply, not much original journalism being conducted in the online environment. Bloggers and blogging have been receiving considerable publicity. But are they reporting or repeating? Murley and Smith (2004) found that about one-half of bloggers scavenge their news from newspapers, and another fifth purloin it from other bloggers, who may have lifted it from newspapers.

Yu and Aikat (2005) looked at the *New York Times* and the *Washington Post* as representatives of online newspapers, *CNN* and *MSNBC* for online TV, and *Yahoo News* and *Google News* as online news services. They examined two weeks in 2004 and found a remarkable correlation of +.51 to +.94 of all the news on the opening or home pages of those online publications. The media correlation was +.77. They also looked at just the top three news stories and found a range of +.53 to +.99 with a +.82 median correlation. This power over the wider media agenda may explain why the agendas of leading newspapers at least, despite slipping readership, are still so strongly correlated to the national agenda.

Other studies, however, reveal less agreement. Song's (2007) study of a particular news event in Korea revealed stark differences in coverage by online news sites and traditional newspapers. But another study, also in Korea, found that online newspapers influenced the agendas of the online wire services (Lim, 2006).

In an early study of electronic bulletin boards during the 1996 US election, three issues correlated significantly with traditional media coverage; only one, abortion, showed no agenda-setting effects (Roberts, Wanta, & Dzwo, 2002). The authors surmise that traditional media provide people with information they use in their online discussions. In more recent studies of blogs and traditional media, both liberal and conservative blogs covered the 2004 US election issues in the same way as the mainstream media. Liberal blogs issues agendas correlated +.84 with the mainstream media agenda, and conservative blogs correlated +.77 (Lee, 2006). Using state-wide surveys in Louisiana and North Carolina to investigate variations in agenda-setting effects by Internet use and age, Coleman and McCombs (2007) found that while agenda-setting effects were somewhat weaker for both heavy Internet users and younger people, they still were significant. The issue agendas in traditional news media correlated +.80 for young adults in one state and +.90 for young people in the other; for the heaviest Internet users their issue agenda correlated with the media's at +.70. They conclude that use of the Internet did not eliminate the agenda-setting influence.

With an expanding media landscape as well as new theoretical domains to explore, the theory of agenda setting can look forward to at least another 30 years of fruitful exploration in cyberspace.

REFERENCES

Althaus, S. L., & Tewksbury, D. (2002). Agenda setting and the "new" news. *Communication Research, 29*, 180–207.

Berelson, B., Lazarsfeld, P., & McPhee, W. (1954). *Voting*. Chicago: University of Chicago Press.

Blood, D. J., & Phillips, P. C. B. (1997). Economic headline news on the agenda: New approaches to understanding causes and effects. In M. McCombs, D. Shaw, & D. Weaver (Eds.), *Communication and democracy: Exploring the intellectual frontiers in agenda-setting theory* (pp. 97–113). Mahwah, NJ: Erlbaum.

Blumler, J. G., & Kavanagh, D. (1999). The third age of political communication: Influences and features. *Political Communication, 16*, 209–230.

Boot, W. (1985, March–April). Ethiopia: Feasting on famine. *Columbia Journalism Review*, 47–48.

Brosius, H.-B., & Kepplinger, H. M. (1990). The agenda setting function of television news: Static and dynamic views. *Communication Research, 17*, 183–211.

Carroll, C., & McCombs, M. (2003). Agenda setting effects of business news on the public's images and opinions about major corporations. *Corporate Reputation Review, 6*, 36–45.

Chan, K. (1999). The media and environmental issues in Hong Kong 1983–95. *Intenational Journal of Public Opinion Research, 11*(2), 135–151.

Cohen, B. (1963). *The press and foreign policy*. Princeton, NJ: Princeton University Press.

Coleman, R., & Banning, S. (2006). Network TV news' affective framing of the presidential candidates: Evidence for a second-level agenda-setting effect through visual framing. *Journalism & Mass Communication Quarterly, 83*(2), 313–328.

Coleman, R., & McCombs, M. (2007). The young and agenda-less? Exploring age-related differences in agenda setting on the youngest generation, baby boomers, and the civic generation. *Journalism & Mass Communication Quarterly, 84*(3), 495–508.

Coleman, R., & Wu, H. D. (2006). *Affective priming of the 2004 presidential candidates: Exploring the second-level agenda-setting effect through visual information.* Paper presented at the AEJMC, San Antonio, TX.

Dearing, J., & Rogers, E. (1996). *Agenda setting*. Thousand Oaks, CA: Sage.

Eaton, H. (1989). Agenda setting with bi-weekly data on content of three national media. *Journalism Quarterly, 66*, 942–948.

Entman, R. M. (1993). Framing: Toward clarification of a fractured paradigm. *Journal of Communication, 43*(4), 51–58.

Ericson, B., Sherine El-Toukhy, S., Terry, T., & Shaw, D. (2007). *The "Intimidator's" final lap: Newspaper evaluations of Dale Earnhardt's career*. Unpublished paper, University of North Carolina at Chapel Hill.

Evatt, D., & Ghanem, S. (2001). *Building a scale to measure salience.* Paper presented at the World Association for Public Opinion Research. Rome, Italy.

Golan, G., & Wanta, W. (2001). Second-level agenda setting in the New Hampshire primary: A comparison of coverage in three newspapers and public perceptions of candidates. *Journalism and Mass Communication Quarterly, 78*(2), 247–259.

Hamilton, J. M., Coleman, R., Grable, B., & Cole, J. (2006). An enabling environment: A reconsideration of the press and the Spanish-American War. *Journalism Studies, 7*(1), 78–93.

Harris, J., & McCombs, M. (1972). The interpersonal/mass communication interface among church leaders. *Journal of Communication, 22*, 257–262.

Hester, J. B., & Gibson, R. (2003). The economy and second level agenda setting: A time-series analysis of economic news and public opinion about the economy. *Jounalism & Mass Communication Quarterly, 80*(1), 73–91.

Holbrook, A., & Hill, T. G. (2005). Agenda-setting and priming in prime time television: Crime dramas as political cues. *Political Communication, 22*, 277–295.

Inoue, Y., & Patterson, D. (2007). News content and American's perceptions of Japan and U.S.-Japanese relations. *Harvard International Journal of Press/Politics, 12*(1), 117–121.

Iyengar, S., & Kinder, D. R. (1987). *News that matters: Television and American opinion*. Chicago: University of Chicago Press.

Jasperson, A. E., Shah, D. V., Watts, M. D., Faber, R. J., & Fan, D. P. (1998). Framing and the public agenda: Media effects on the importance of the federal budget deficit. *Political Communication, 15*(2), 205–224.

Kim, S.-H., Scheufele, D. A., & Shanahan, J. (2002). Think about it this way: Attribute agenda-setting function of the press and the public's evaluation of a local issue. *Jounalism & Mass Communication Quarterly, 79*(1), 7–25.

King, P.-T. (1997). The press, candidate images, and voter perceptions. In M. McCombs, D. L. Shaw, & D. Weaver (Eds.), *Communication and democracy* (pp. 29–40). Mahwah, NJ: Erlbaum.

Kiousis, S. (2000). *Beyond salience: Exploring the linkages between the agenda setting role of mass media and mass persuasion.* Unpublished dissertation, University of Texas, Austin, TX.

Kiousis, S., Bantimaroudis, P., & Ban, H. (1999). Candidate image attributes: Experiments on the substantive dimension of second-level agenda setting. *Communication Research, 26*(4), 414–428.

Lazarsfeld, P., Berelson, B., & Gaudet, H. (1948). *The people's choice*. New York: Columbia University Press.

Lee, J.-K. (2007). The effect of the Internet on homogeneity of the media agenda: A test of the fragmentation thesis. *Journalism & Mass Communication Quarterly, 84*(4), 745–760.

Lennon, F. R. (1998). *Argentina: 1997 elecciones. Los diarios nacionales y la campana electoral* [The 1997 Argentina election. The national dailies and the electoral campaign]. Report by The Freedom Forum and Austral University

Lim, J. (2006). A cross-lagged analysis of agenda setting among online news media. *Journalism & Mass Communication Quarterly, 83*(2), 298–312.

Lippmann, W. (1922). *Public opinion*. New York: Macmillan.

Lopez-Escobar, E., Llamas, J. P., & McCombs, M. (1998). Agenda setting and community consensus: First and second level effects. *International Journal of Public Opinion Research, 10*(4), 355–348.

Lowery, S., & Defleur, M. (1995). *Milestones in mass communication research: Media effects, 3rd ed.* White Plains, NY: Longman.

Matthes, J. (2006). The need for orientation towards news media: Revising and validating a classic concept. *International Journal of Public Opinion Research, 18*, 422–444.

McCombs, M. (2004). *Setting the agenda: The mass media and public opinion*. Cambridge, UK: Polity Press.

McCombs, M., Lopez-Escobar, E., & Llamas, J. P. (2000). Setting the agenda of attributes in the 1996 Spanish general election. *Journal of Communication, 50*(2), 77–92.

McCombs, M., & Shaw, D. L. (1972). The agenda-setting function of the mass media. *Public Opinion Quarterly, 36*(2), 176–187.

Merritt, R. (1966). *Symbols of American community, 1735–1775*. New Haven, CT: Yale University Press.

Mikami, S., Takeshita, T., Nakada, M., & Kawabata, M. (1994). *The media coverage and public awareness of environmental issues in Japan*. Paper presented at the International Association for Mass Communication Research. Seoul, Korea.

Min, Y., Ghanem, S., & Evatt, D., (2007). Using a split-ballot survey to explore the robustness of the "M.I.P." question in agenda-setting research: A methodological study. *International Journal of Public Opinion Research, 19*, 221–236.

Murley, B., & Smith, K. (2004). Bloggers strike a nerve: Examining the intersection of blogging and journalism. Unpublished paper, University of South Carolina, Columbia.

Ogata Jones, K., Denham, B. E., & Springston, J. K. (2006). Effects of mass and interpersonal communication on breast cancer screening: Advancing agenda-setting theory in health contexts. *Journal of Applied Communication Research, 34*(1), 94–113.

Palmgreen, P., & Clarke, P. (1977). Agenda setting with local and national issues. *Communication Research, 4*, 435–452.

Philadelphia Inquirer (1996, December 27), pp. A1 & 18.

Pratt, C. B., Ha, L., & Pratt, C. A. (2002). Setting the public health agenda on major diseases in Sub-Saharan Africa: African popular magazines and medical journals, 1981–1997. *Journal of Communication, 52*(4), 889–905.

Price, V., & Tewksbury, D. (1997). News values and public opinion: A theoretical account of media priming and framing. In G. A. Barnett & F. J. Boster (Eds.) *Progress in communication sciences: Advances in persuasion* (pp.173–212). Greenwich, CT: Ablex.

Reese, S. D. (2001). Prologue—Framing public life: A bridging model for media research. In S. D. Reese, O. H. Gandy, & A. E. Grant (Eds.), *Framing public life: Perspectives on media and our understanding of the social world* (pp. 7–31). Mahwah, NJ: Erlbaum.

Roberts, M. S. (1992). Predicting voting behavior via the agenda-setting tradition. *Journalism Quarterly*, 69, 878–892.

Roberts, M., Wanta, W., & Dzwo, T.-H. (2002). Agenda setting and issue salience online. *Communication Research, 29*(4), 452–466.

Salwen, M. (1988). Effects of accumulation of coverage on issue salience in agenda setting. *Journalism Quarterly, 65*, 100–106, 130.

Sato, H. (2003). Agenda setting for smoking control in Japan, 1945–1990: Influence of the mass media on national health policy making. *Journal of Health Communication, 8*(1), 23–41.

Scheufele, D. A. (2000). Agenda-setting, priming, and framing revisited: Another look at cognitive effects of political communication *Mass Communication & Society, 3*(2&3), 297–316.

Shaw, D. L. & McCombs, M. (Eds.). (1977), *The emergence of American political issues: The agenda-setting function of the press*. St. Paul, MN: West.

Sheafer, T., & Weimann, G. (2005). Agenda building, agenda setting, priming, individual voting intentions, and the aggregate results: An analysis of four Israeli elections. *Journal of Communication, 55*(2), 347–365.

Smith, K. (1987). Newspaper coverage and public concern about community issues. *Journalism Monographs, 101,* 1–32.

Son, Y. J. & Weaver, D. H. (2006). Another look at what moves public opinion: Media agenda setting and polls in the 2000 U.S. election. *International Journal of Public Opinion Research*, 18 (2), 174–197.

Song, Y. (2007). Internet news media and issue development: A case study on the roles of independent online news services as agenda-builders for anti-US protests in South Korea. *New Media & Society, 9*(1), 71–92.

Soroka, S. N. (2002). *Agenda setting dynamics in Canada*. Vancouver: UBC Press.

Takeshita, T. (1993). Agenda-setting effects of the press in a Japanese local election. *Studies of Broadcasting, 29*, 193–216.

Takeshita, T. (2002). *Expanding attribute agenda setting into framing: An application of the problematic situation.* Paper presented to the International Communication Association. Seoul, Korea.

Valenzuela, S., & McCombs, M. E. (2007). *Agenda-setting effects on vote choice: Evidence from the 2006 Mexican Election*. International Communication Association. San Francisco. May, 2007.

Wang, T.-L. (2000). Agenda-setting online. *Southwestern Mass Communication Journal, 15*(2), 59–70.

Wanta, W. (1988). The effects of dominant photographs: An agenda-setting experiment. *Journalism Quarterly, 65*(1), 107–111.

Wanta, W. (1997). *The public and the national agenda*. Mahwah, NJ: Erlbaum.

Wanta, W., & Ghanem, S. (2000). Effects of agenda-setting. In J. Bryant & R. Carveth (Eds.), *Meta-analyses of media effects* (Chapter 4). Mahwah, NJ: Erlbaum.

Wanta, W., Golan, G., & Lee, C. (2004). Agenda-setting and international news: Media influence on public perceptions of foreign nations. *Journalism & Mass Communication Quarterly, 81*(2), 364–377.

Wanta, W., & Hu, Y. (1994). Time-lag differences in the agenda-setting process: An examination of five news media. *International Journal of Public Opinion Research, 6*(3), 225–240.

Weaver, D. (1991). Issue salience and public opinion: Are there consequences of agenda-setting? *International Journal of Public Opinion, 3,* 53–68.

Weaver, D., Graber, D., McCombs, M., & Eyal, C. (1981). *Media agenda setting in a presidential election: Issues, images and interest*. New York: Praeger.

Weaver, D., McCombs, M., & Spellman, C. (1975) Watergate and the media: A case study of agenda-setting. *American Politics Quarterly*, 3, 458–472.

Willnat, L. (1997). Agenda setting and priming: Conceptual links and differeneces. In M. McCombs, D. L. Shaw, & D. Weaver (Eds.), *Communication and democracy: Exploring the intellectual frontiers in agenda-setting theory* (pp. 51–66). Mahwah, NJ: Erlbaum.

Winter, J., & Eyal, C. (1981). Agenda setting for the civil rights issue. *Public Opinion Quarterly, 45*, 376–383.

Yioutas, J., & Segvic, I. (2003). Revisiting the Clinton/Lewinsky scandal: The convergence of agenda setting and framing. *Journalism & Mass Communication Quarterly, 80*(3), 567–582.

Yu, J., & Aikat, D. (2005). *News on the web: Agenda setting of online news in web sites of major newspaper, television and online news services.* Unpublished paper, University of North Carolina at Chapel Hill.

Zucker, H. G. (1978). The variable nature of news media influence. *Communication Yearbook, 2*, 225–240.

12

News Values and Selectivity

Deirdre O'Neill and Tony Harcup

Ideas about what news is and how it is selected have long fascinated the practitioners and scholars of journalism alike, although they tend to use very different language when discussing the subject. Legendary newspaper editor Harold Evans (2000, p. 2, 9) writes that "a sense of news values" is the first quality required of copy editors—those "human sieves of the torrent of news" who select and edit material for publication—more important even than an ability to write or a command of language. But when it comes to defining this sense of news values, "journalists rely on instinct rather than logic," according to veteran television reporter John Sergeant (2001, p. 226). In contrast, academics have described the production of news as "the passive exercise of routine and highly regulated procedures in the task of selecting from already limited supplies of information" (Golding & Elliott, 1979, p. 114).

This chapter will explore the tension between practitioner and academic accounts of news selection, beginning with a description of several of the many practitioner definitions of news and news values before moving on to chart some of the key ways in which such "common sense" explanations have been critiqued from within the academy. There have been a number of attempts at cataloguing news values and selection criteria, and these taxonomies of news values will be explored in the following section, which will also include consideration of some of the ways in which news values may be perceived to differ in different media, in different geographical or social contexts, and over time. The chapter will then move on to examine some of the ways in which the usefulness of this taxonomy approach has been questioned by scholars. After a brief observation that mainstream news values have themselves been challenged by journalistic practitioners within alternative media, the chapter will conclude with a consideration of the value of the news values concept itself.

WHAT IS NEWS?

News, according to Jackie Harrison (2006, p. 13), is that which "is judged to be newsworthy by journalists, who exercise their news sense within the constraints of the news organisations within which they operate." This judging process is guided by an understanding of news values—a "somewhat mythical" concept, according to John Richardson (2005, p. 173)—which is "passed down to new generations of journalists through a process of training and socialisation" (Harrison, 2006, p. 153). Such news values work, as Jerry Palmer (2000, p. 45) notes, as "a system of criteria which are used to make decisions about the inclusion and exclusion of material" and about which aspects of selected stories to emphasise. In this sense, they "transcend individual judgements, although of course they are to be found embodied in every news judgement made by particular journalists" (Palmer, 2000, p. 45).

Analysis of the values and processes involved in the selection of news is one of the most important areas of journalism studies as it goes to the heart of what is included, what is excluded, and why. As we shall see, it is also claimed that by shedding light on the values inherent in news selection we can help illuminate arguments about the wider role(s) and meaning(s) of journalism within contemporary society.

NEWS VALUES: A "SLIPPERY CONCEPT"

Journalists tend to acquire their news values from the College of Osmosis, argues Harold Evans (2000, p. 3); meaning that journalists sit around newsrooms "long enough to absorb the essentials." However, new recruits to journalism may be surprised on their arrival in the newsroom that they are unlikely to witness many lengthy debates about the relative merits of news stories, notes David Randall (2000, p. 24), another experienced practitioner:

> Instead they see a lot of news judgements being made swiftly and surely and seemingly based on nothing more scientific than gut feeling. The process is, however, a lot more measured than that. It just appears to be instinctive because a lot of the calculations that go into deciding a story's strength have been learnt to the point where they are made very rapidly—sometimes too rapidly.

Exhaustive newsroom discussions about news values may be rare but that does not mean that journalists are unable to understand or articulate their reasons for selecting one story over another, observe Peter Golding and Philip Elliott (1979, p. 114):

> Indeed, they [news values] pepper the daily exchanges between journalists in collaborative production procedures [...T]hey are terse shorthand references to shared understandings about the nature and purpose of news which can be used to ease the rapid and difficult manufacture of bulletins and news programmes.

According to the National Council for the Training of Journalists, the accrediting body for vocational training in print journalism within the UK, "news is information—new, relevant to the reader, topical and perhaps out of the ordinary." Similar definitions are to be found in numerous practitioner accounts of the journalistic craft. The key consideration when selecting a story is usually very simple, argues former Fleet Street editor Alastair Hetherington (1985, pp. 8–9). It boils down to the question: "Does it interest me?" For Evans, meanwhile, "news is people" (as cited in Watson & Hill, 2003, p. 198). Not, however, all of the people all of the time, but people *doing* things (Harcup, 2004, p. 31). What sort of things? "The unexpected and dramatic, not the run-of-the-mill," answers *Times* journalist Mark Henderson (2003). Yet news can also be predictable (Harcup, 2004). For David Randall (2000, p. 23), news is "the fresh, unpublished, unusual and generally interesting." However, the operation of news values should not be compared with a scientific process, and Randall acknowledges that news selection is subjective; indeed, that subjectivity "pervades the whole process of journalism."

News values are a slippery concept, but that has not prevented practitioners from grappling with them nor academics from attempting to pin them down via a succession of taxonomical studies such as those discussed later in this chapter. Whilst such sets of news values may be "predictive of a pattern" of which events will make the news and which will not, they cannot provide a complete explanation of all the irregularities of news composition (McQuail, 2000, p. 343). And, as John Hartley points out, identifying the news values within a story may tell us more about *how* that story has been covered than about *why* it was selected for coverage in the first place (Hartley, 1982; also see Palmer, 2000). Yet, despite offering only an incomplete explanation of the processes at work in news journalism, the study of news values is regarded as an important area of exploration within journalism studies scholarship because it is a way of making more transparent a set of practices and judgements which are otherwise shrouded in opacity, as Stuart Hall (1973, p.181) argues:

> "News values" are one of the most opaque structures of meaning in modern society [...] Journalists speak of "the news" as if events select themselves. Further, they speak as if which is the "most significant" news story, and which "news angles" are most salient are divinely inspired. Yet of the millions of events which occur daily in the world, only a tiny proportion ever become visible as "potential news stories": and of this proportion, only a small fraction are actually produced as the day's news in the news media. We appear to be dealing, then, with a "deep structure" whose function as a selective device is un-transparent even to those who professionally most know how to operate it.

In their classic study of news values—discussed in more detail later—Galtung and Ruge (1965) argued that the more clearly an event could be understood and interpreted unambiguously, without multiple meanings, the more likely it was to be selected as a news story. But it is not necessarily the event itself that is unambiguous, and a subsequent study of the UK press found "many news stories that were written unambiguously about events and issues that were likely to have been highly ambiguous" (Harcup & O'Neill, 2001, p. 270). According to Nkosi Ndlela (2005, p. 3), by selecting and shaping news, media represent the world rather than reflect it, leading to stereotyped frames: "Media representations reduce, shrink, condense and select/repeat aspects of intricate social relations in order to represent them as fixed, natural, obvious and ready to consume." For James Curran and Jean Seaton (2003, p. 336), news values allow journalists to "translate untidy reality into neat stories with beginnings, middles, and denouements," and in the process such values tend to "reinforce conventional opinions and established authority." Furthermore, they argue, "many items of news are not 'events' at all, that is in the sense of occurrences in the real world which take place independently of the media." This question of the definition of events is central to consideration of news values, argues Joachim Friedrich Staab (1990, pp. 430–431), and it hinges on "how a recognizing subject relates to a recognized object":

> [E]vents do not exist per se but are the result of subjective perceptions and definitions [...] Most events do not exist in isolation, they are interrelated and annexed to larger sequences. Employing different definitions of an event and placing it in a different context, news stories in different media dealing with the same event are likely to cover different aspects of the event and therefore put emphasis on different news factors. (p. 439)

Similarly, Denis McQuail (1994, p. 270) observes that lists of news values seem to be based on the presumption that a given reality exists "out there" which journalists acting as gatekeepers will either admit or exclude. Yet, for Jorgen Westerstahl and Folke Johansson (1994, p. 71), the journalistic selection process involved in news reporting is itself "probably as important or perhaps sometimes more important than what 'really happens'."

TAXONOMIES OF NEWS VALUES

Lists of news values—sometimes labelled as news factors or news criteria—such as those drawn up by Galtung and Ruge (1965) and Harcup and O'Neill (2001)—have been described as "useful as an ad hoc set of elements with a partial explanatory value," although such lists "probably cannot constitute a systematic basis for the analysis of news" (Palmer, 2000, p. 31). The problem with such lists of news values, argues John Richardson (2005), is that they downplay the issue of ideology: "Illustrating that ephemeral issues are newsworthy, for example, does little to explain *why* this is the case, nor to interrogate whether it is in the public interest to pander persistently to 'what interests the public'" (p. 174; emphasis in original).

News values, then, are "far from a unified entity" because "they are divided by medium and by format" as well as by the "title identity" of the news organisation and by the "local" context within which news judgements are made (Palmer, 2000, pp. 45, 58).

Johan Galtung and Mari Ruge were arguably the first to provide a systematic list of news values (Palmer, 1998, p. 378) in a paper presented at the first Nordic Conference on Peace Research in Oslo in 1963, and published in 1965. More than four decades on Galtung and Ruge's study remains the starting point for the discussion of news in numerous journalism textbooks (see, for example, Sissons, 2006; McKane, 2006). Their paper has long been regarded as *the* study of news values: Bell (1991, p. 155) described the work as "the foundation study of news values," McQuail (1994, p. 270) as the "most influential explanation" of news values, and Tunstall (1970, p. 20) believed it could be the classic answer to the question "what is news?" For Barbie Zelizer (2004, p. 54), Galtung and Ruge were responsible for "perhaps the single piece of research that most cogently advanced a general understanding of news selection processes" that "remains even today one of the most influential pieces on news making."

Given its subsequent influence, it is ironic that Galtung and Ruge's paper was not primarily concerned with identifying news values. Their article critiqued the reporting of three major foreign crises in the Norwegian press, and proposed some alternative approaches to reporting conflict. As part of this process they asked, "How do events become news?" It was in an effort to answer this question that Galtung and Ruge presented 12 factors (summarized below) that they intuitively identified as being important in the selection of news:

- *Frequency:* An event that unfolds within a publication cycle of the news medium is more likely to be selected than a one that takes place over a long period of time.
- *Threshold:* Events have to pass a threshold before being recorded at all; the greater the intensity (the more gruesome the murder or the more casualties in an accident), the greater the impact and the more likely it is to be selected.
- *Unambiguity:* The more clearly an event can be understood and interpreted without multiple meanings, the more likely it is to be selected.
- *Meaningfulness:* The culturally familiar is more likely to be selected.
- *Consonance:* The news selector may be able to predict (due to experience) events that will be newsworthy, thus forming a "pre-image" of an event, which in turn increases its chances of becoming news.
- *Unexpectedness:* Among events meaningful and/or consonant, the unexpected or rare event is more likely to be selected.
- *Continuity:* An event already in the news has a good chance of remaining in the news (even if its impact has been reduced) because it has become familiar and easier to interpret.
- *Composition:* An event may be included as news less because of its intrinsic news value than because it fits into the overall composition or balance of a newspaper or news broadcast.

- *Reference to elite nations:* The actions of elite nations are seen as more consequential than the actions of other nations.
- *Reference to elite people:* Again, the actions of elite people, likely to be famous, may be seen by news selectors as having more consequence than others, and news audiences may identify with them.
- *Reference to persons:* News that can be presented in terms of individual people rather than abstractions is likely to be selected.
- *Reference to something negative:* Bad events are generally unambiguous and newsworthy.

Galtung and Ruge (1965, pp. 64–65) stated at the outset: "No claim is made for completeness in the list of factors or 'deductions'." And they concluded with the following warning: "It should be emphasised [...] that the present article hypothesises rather than demonstrates the presence of these factors, and hypothesises rather than demonstrates that these factors, if present, have certain effects among the audience" (pp. 84–85).

Winfried Schulz (1982) developed the work of Galtung and Ruge by carrying out a content analysis of newspapers, examining domestic and apolitical news, as well as foreign news. He proposed six different dimensions to news selection, which he further broke down into 19 news factors: *status* (elite nation, elite institution, elite person); *valence* (aggression, controversy, values, success); *relevance* (consequence, concern); *identification* (proximity, ethnocentrism, personalization, emotions); *consonance* (theme, stereotype, predictability); and *dynamics* (timeliness, uncertainty, unexpectedness).

The issue of whether news values are universal for all news media, or whether certain values dominate in certain types of media, was raised during studies of television news. For instance, in his 1978 study of BBC news (updated in 1987), Schlesinger noted that broadcast news set out to use the media values of television to create its "own set of news values" where visuals dominate and the "light tail-piece" was developed (Day, as cited in Schlesinger, 1987, p. 41). Schlesinger also highlighted technical imperatives which, in broadcast news, he argued, dominated news selection more than "substantive news judgements" (p. 51). For Schlesinger, the driving forces behind news values contained assumptions about audience interest, professional duty, and actuality (or a pictorial imperative whereby picture value is a selection criterion, making TV a strong news medium by virtue of its ability to depict events as they happen or have happened).

This approach was also taken by Golding and Elliott (1979) who argued that news values were often imbued with greater importance and mystique than they merit. For them, news values derived essentially from occupational pragmatism and implicit assumptions, which they described as *audience*, *accessibility*, and *fit*. This involved consideration of whether an event/issue was important to the audience, would hold their attention, be understood, enjoyed, registered or perceived as relevant; the extent to which an event was known to the news organisation and the resources it would require to obtain; and whether the event fitted the routines of production and made sense in terms of what was already known about the subject.

Informed by this analysis, Golding and Elliott suggested the following selection criteria (pp. 115–123):

- *Drama:* This is often presented as conflict, commonly as opposing viewpoints.
- *Visual attractiveness:* They discuss this in terms of images for television though, of course, images are also relevant to newspapers. "A story may be included simply because film is available or because of the dramatic qualities of the film" (p. 116).
- *Entertainment:* In order to captivate as wide an audience as possible, news producers must take account of entertainment values that amuse or divert the audience. This includes

"human interest" stories and the actors in these whimsical and bizarre events may be celebrities, children and animals.

- *Importance:* This may mean the reported event is greatly significant for a large proportion of the audience, but it also explains the inclusion of items that might be omitted on the criteria of other audience-based news values.
- *Size:* The more people involved in a disaster, or the bigger the "names" at an event, the more likely the item is to be on the news agenda.
- *Proximity:* As with size, this derives partly from audience considerations and partly from accessibility since there is cultural *and* geographical proximity. The first depends on what is familiar and within the experience of journalists and their audience, while the second may depend on where correspondents are based. As a rule of thumb, nearby events take precedence over similar events at a distance.
- *Negativity:* "Bad news is good news... News is about disruptions in the normal current of events [...] not the uneventful" (p. 120). Such news provides drama and shock value which attracts audiences.
- *Brevity:* A story that is full of facts with little padding is preferred (particularly important for broadcast news).
- *Recency:* Competition between news outlets puts a "premium" on exclusives and scoops. Also daily news production is within a daily time frame so that news events must normally occur within the 24 hours between bulletins (or newspaper editions) to merit inclusion.
- *Elites:* Clearly big names attract audiences, but there is a circularity in that big names become famous by virtue of their exposure.
- *Personalities:* Since news is about people, this is reflected in the need to reduce complex events and issues to the actions of individuals.

An essentially similar definition of newsworthiness in terms of the "suitability" of events was produced by Herbert Gans (1980). Allan Bell (1991) went further and argued for the importance to story selection of co-option, whereby a story only tangentially related could be presented in terms of a high-profile continuing story; predictability, whereby events that could be pre-scheduled for journalists were more likely to be covered than those that arrived unheralded; and pre-fabrication, the existence of ready-made texts, such as press releases.

Sigurd Allern (2002, p. 145) arrived at similar criteria by distinguishing between "traditional" news values and what he described as "commercial" news values. He suggested that traditional news values do not, in themselves, explain the selection process and, since "news is literally for sale," they need to be supplemented with a set of "commercial news criteria." The market is crucial to the output of any news organisation, yet this is not usually made explicit or taken into account when discussing the selection and production of news. This means news must be selected and packaged in a format that is audience-orientated and commercial by being entertaining and reflecting popular tastes. But it is also more than this: for Allern there are three general factors that govern the selection and production of news, one of which is *competition.* The second concerns the *geographical area of coverage and type of audience.* For Allern, this is more than just *proximity*, whereby events nearby are more interesting than distant ones. "Certain English-language elite papers, such as the *Financial Times* and *Herald Tribune*, have market-based reasons to carry considerably more international politics, etc, than newspapers that address a national readership" (p. 143). And he emphasises the role of advertisers in this process: "[E]vents that take place outside a paper's home market, even dramatic ones, may be considered non-events simply because they occur outside the area [or social class/niche interest] where the medium has its audience (and its advertisers)" (ibid, our addition). The third of Allern's general factors is *the budget allotted to news departments*, which is an expression of the company's financial objectives. The reality—rarely acknowledged in journalism textbooks—is that budget constraints mean that managers are far more often focussed on financial control than winning professional recognition. The cheapest type of news is that produced by what BBC journalist Waseem Zakir coined as "churnalism"—rewrites of press releases, press statements, copy from news agencies and from organised bureaucratic routine sources such as regular calls to the police, fire service, courts, local government and other public bodies (Harcup, 2004, pp. 3–4). A recent academic study of "converged" digital newsrooms within the UK regional press, in which newspaper journalists produce audio-visual material as well as text for their company's online presence, has found that this trend towards cheap and recycled news is likely to continue unless managements adopt an alternative model of investing in journalism (Williams & Franklin, 2007).

Informed by such factors, Allern presented a supplementary list of commercial news values:

- The more resources it costs to follow up a story or expose an event/issue, the less likely it will become a news story.
- The more journalistically a potential news item is prepared/formatted by the source or sender, the greater the likelihood that it will become news.
- The more selectively a story is distributed to news organisations, the more likely it will become news.
- The more a news medium's strategy is based on sensationalist reporting in order to attract public attention and the greater the opportunity for accentuating these elements in a potential story, the more likely a story is to be used.

In examining news, scholars have often found it necessary to distinguish between news appearing in different sections of the media market. Whilst differences in the style and content of, for instance, the popular and quality press have been eroded in recent years (Franklin, 1997), in a UK analysis of newspapers Palmer found broad agreement about what constitutes the main story or stories of the day, but found less foreign news in popular papers. In general, the treatment of stories differed, with the quality press concentrating on policy, background and a wider range of reactions and the popular press on human interest angles (Palmer, 2000).

If the audience and market forces should be part of the equation in any study of news values (Allern, 2002), then the influence on news values of the economic, cultural and social changes which affect the audience and the market—such as the promotion of individualism or the rise and rise of "celebrity culture"—must also be explored. To investigate such changes in news values over time, Harcup and O'Neill (2001) carried out an empirical study of the UK press by applying Galtung and Ruge's 12 news factors to 1,200 news stories to see how relevant they remained nearly 40 years on. While some of their findings had similarities with Galtung and Ruge's factors, there were some notable problems and differences. For example, "elite people" was too vague a category, with no distinction made between a pop star and the President of the United States. There were a surprising number of stories that were not concerned with elite countries or people but with elite institutions (for instance, the Bank of England, the Vatican, the United Nations). Some of Galtung and Ruge's factors could have more to do with news treatment, rather than selection (unambiguity or personification may have less to do with the intrinsic subject matter than how journalists are required to write up stories). Going against conventional wisdom, there were a surprising number of "good news" stories, as well as stories with no clear timescale or which did not appear to unfold at a frequency suited to newspaper production.

From the national newspapers examined, Harcup and O'Neill (2001, p. 279) proposed a new set of news values. They found that news stories must generally satisfy one or more of the following requirements to be selected:

- *The Power Elite:* Stories concerning powerful individuals, organisations or institutions.
- *Celebrity:* Stories concerning people who are already famous.
- *Entertainment:* Stories concerning sex, show business, human interest, animals, an unfolding drama, or offering opportunities for humorous treatment, entertaining photographs or witty headlines.
- *Surprise:* Stories that have an element of surprise and/or contrast.
- *Bad News:* Stories with particularly negative overtones, such as conflict or tragedy.
- *Good News:* Stories with particularly positive overtones such as rescues and cures.
- *Magnitude:* Stories that are perceived as sufficiently significant either in the numbers of people involved or in the potential impact.
- *Relevance:* Stories about issues, groups and nations perceived to be relevant to the audience.
- *Follow-up:* Stories about subjects already in the news.
- *Newspaper Agenda:* Stories that set or fit the news organization's own agenda.

All such taxonomies of news values must "remain open to inquiry rather than be seen as a closed set of values for journalism in all times and places" (Zelizer, 2004, p. 55); and further research is needed to measure the extent to which the above news values apply to other forms of media, in different societies, and how they may change over time.

NEWS VALUES: CONTEXT AND LIMITATIONS

Exploration of news values may help us to answer the question, "What is news?," but it has frequently been argued that the concept of news values offers only a partial explanation of the journalistic selection process. Whilst acknowledging that a set of common understandings exists among journalists, Lewis (2006, p. 309) believes that any rationale for what makes a good story has an arbitrary quality, because journalism requires comparatively little training and no depth of understanding. News values are therefore often contradictory and incoherent. It is also argued that news values tend to retrospectively endow judgments made by journalists with legitimacy. "News values exist and are, of course, significant," write Golding and Elliott. "But they are as much the resultant explanation or justification of necessary procedures as their source" (Golding & Elliott, 1979, pp. 114–115).

As outlined in the previous section, news selection is not based merely on intrinsic aspects of events, but also on external functions, including occupational routines and constraints, and ideology whereby news is "a socially determined construction of reality" (Staab, 1990, p. 428). Staab asserted that most studies of news values do not in fact deal with the actual process of news selection, but with news *treatment.* He went on to question their objectivity and causal role, as well as the problem of defining events themselves. Since news values have limited validity, he argued for a functional model that takes into account the intentions of journalists.

For Wolfgang Donsbach (2004), understanding the psychology of news decisions by journalists is key to understanding news selection. Evaluative judgements such as news values by definition lack objective criteria—they are based on value judgements which can neither be verified nor falsified. Nor can the role of ideology in news selection be underestimated, argue Westerstahl and Johansson (1986, 1994). They distinguish between news values—generally static and informed by audience taste—and news ideologies, which they perceive as born out of a desire to inform or influence the audience and which are shifting over time. "In our view ideologies are the main source of deviations in news reporting from a standard based on more or less objectified news values" (1994, p. 77).

Other academics argue that news values themselves can be seen as an ideologically loaded way of perceiving—and presenting—the world. For Hall (1973, p. 235), although the news values of mainstream journalism may appear to be "a set of neutral, routine practices," they actually form part of an "ideological structure" that privileges the perspectives of the most powerful groups within society. Robert McChesney (2000, pp. 49–50, 110) highlights the way in which a journalistic emphasis on individual "events" and "news hooks" results in less visible or more long-term issues being downplayed, with individualism being portrayed as "natural" and more civic or collective values being treated as "marginal."

In their "propaganda model," Edward Herman and Noam Chomsky ([1988] 1994, p. 298) go further, suggesting that "selection of topics" is one of the key ways in which the media fulfil their "societal purpose" of inculcating "the economic, social, and political agenda of privileged groups that dominate the domestic society and the state." According to their model, five filters—identified as the concentration of media ownership; the influence of advertising; the over-reliance on information from the powerful; "flak" against transgressors; and an ethos of anti-communism—combine to produce "the news fit to print" (p. 2). Debate and dissent are permitted, but only within a largely internalised consensus.

Studies of news coverage of marginalised groups such as trade unionists would appear to confirm this (Beharrell & Philo, 1977; Jones, Petley, Power, & Wood, 1985; Greenberg, 2004; O'Neill, 2007). However, in her study of a national firefighters' strike, Deirdre O'Neill also found that by appealing to human interest news values the union was able to achieve publication of a number of news stories that highlighted its members' case, thus, to some extent, militating against the dominance of establishment views (O'Neill, 2007).

UNIVERSAL NEWS VALUES?

Studies have also examined the universality of news values: are they changed by socio-economic, cultural and political differences? For example, a study of male and female editors in seven Israeli papers found that both sexes applied broadly similar criteria to news selection and practice, with little in the way of gender distinctions (Lavie & Lehman-Wilzig, 2003). In the same way that news values were adhered to by both sexes, news values appeared to drive French television coverage of the 2002 presidential elections, rather than any party political bias of newsroom staff (Kuhn, 2005). News values were also found to dominate professional practice in a study of long-term trends in campaign coverage in the German press. Wilke and Reinemann (2001) found that German political journalists used the same news values in or out of election campaigns.

Investigating news values in different countries, Chaudhary (1974) compared the news judgements of American and Indian journalists. Despite being culturally dissimilar, journalists of English language newspapers in democratic countries used the same news values. However, Lange (1984) found that the socio-political environment in which journalists operated—including the severe sanctions for criticizing the government that some Third World journalists face—did affect their news values. He found that the less developed a nation, the more emphasis on direct exhortations in the news, the more emphasis on news stories set in the future, the more emphasis on news stories about co-operation and the more emphasis on positive evaluations of the news subjects—the type of reporting often described as development journalism (Rampal, 1984; Chu, 1985).

In a study of the role of national identity in the coverage of foreign news in Britain, the United States and Israel, news values became subordinate to national loyalties (Nossek, 2004). The closer journalists were to a news event in terms of national interest, the less likely they were to apply professional news values. Zayani and Ayish (2006, p. 494) found that the news values of Arab satellite channels covering the fall of Baghdad in 2003, while generally professionally driven, "were also tainted to various degrees with cultural, political and historical considerations."

While there is an assumption that adherence to news values is implicitly more "professional," eliminating bias, political or otherwise, this can be problematic in that news values may create uniformity, negativity and reduction to stereotypes (Ndlela, 2005), as well as presenting obstacles for non-Western journalists. A study of journalism training in Tunisia, Algeria, Morocco and Libya (Rampal, 1996) found that an emphasis on what could be described as Western professional news values did not reflect the realities for graduates facing severe political and legal constraints. Rampal (1996, p. 41) argues for a curriculum that teaches "a journalistic philosophy—and concomitant news values—that is compatible with the political and legal orientation of a given country, yet helps in improving the quality of journalism."

Lee, Maslog, and Kim (2006) believe that traditional news values, which focus on conflict, are a barrier to what they term peace journalism, a journalism that explores the causes of and alternatives to conflict. In a study of the Zimbabwean crisis as reported in the Norwegian press, Ndlela (2005) found that coverage primarily fitted with Galtung and Ruge's negativity factor, leading to stereotyped frames and unbalanced reporting which presented the crisis as a racial one, rather than a political one. Subsequent reporting treated developments as isolated events, which lacked an historical or wider context. Chu (1985, p. 6) also notes an emphasis on conflictual criteria and bizarre and exceptional events in Western news values, and calls for the "gradual institutionalisation of an additional value" that allows for development news which reflects and mobilizes the process of social, cultural and political change. Finally, in examining determinants of international news coverage in 38 countries, Wu (2000) found that news values alone could not explain coverage—economic interest, information availability and production cost of international news were also at work in determining the volume of information from abroad.

AN ALTERNATIVE APPROACH

Having studied the operation of news values, Galtung and Ruge (1965) suggested that journalists should be encouraged to counteract the prevailing news factors by, among other things: including more background and context in their reports; reporting more on long-term issues and less on "events"; paying more attention to complex and ambiguous issues; giving more coverage to non-elite people and nations. Such a desire to counter—or subvert—prevailing news values has been one of the motivating factors behind the production of what have been termed "alternative media" (Atton, 2002; Harcup, 2005, 2006; Rodriguez, 2001; Whitaker, 1981).

In an attempt at promoting an alternative approach to international news, and to counter stereotypical and simplistic depictions of people from developing countries, a set of alternative criteria has been produced by a group of European charitable and non-governmental organisations. Their recommendations to journalists amount to a critique—and a rejection—of the news values that have traditionally guided much Northern news coverage of the South:

- Avoid catastrophic images in favour of describing political, structural and natural root causes and contexts.

- Preserve human dignity by providing sufficient background information on people's social, cultural, economic and environmental contexts; highlight what people are doing for themselves.
- Provide accounts by the people concerned rather than interpretations by a third party.
- Provide more frequent and more positive images of women.
- Avoid all forms of generalisation, stereotyping and discrimination. (NGO-EC Liaison Committee, 1989)

Such an alternative approach to news values may operate at the margins of journalism—and, indeed, may occupy a marginal position within journalism studies (Keeble, 2005)—but that does not mean it has no significance. Rather, it has been argued that the issues raised by the existence of alternative media highlight important questions about "what news is, for whom it is intended, and about whether mainstream news values serve the democratic participation and civic engagement of citizens as well as they might" (Harcup, 2007, p. 56).

CONCLUSION

The concept of news values, then, can help us to understand the ways in which some phenomena become identified as "events" and the ways that some of those "events" are then selected to become "news." The concept of news values also helps us to explore the ways in which certain elements of the selected "events" will be emphasised whilst others will be downplayed or excluded. In this sense, discussion of news values sometimes blurs distinctions between news *selection* and news *treatment*.

Definitions of news are not fixed. Many lists of news values have been drawn up, and news values can change over time, from place to place, and between different sectors of the news media. For example, Galtung and Ruge put great emphasis on the "frequency" with which events occur; yet, as technology changes many of the ways in which news is produced and received, criteria such as "frequency" may become increasingly irrelevant in the world of continuous deadlines required by the production of online and 24-hour news. For these news media, however, "recency" (Golding & Elliot, 1979) and "competition" (Gans, 1980; Bell, 1991; Allern, 2002) may become more dominant selection criteria, as well as the "type of audience" (Golding & Elliott, 1979; Gans, 1980; Allern, 2002) in an increasingly fragmented news market. This and other perceived changes in news values suggest that the topic will remain a fruitful one for journalism scholars for many years to come. For, whatever the technology and media involved—and notwithstanding the growth of user-generated content, blogs, and online news aggregators—the process of news journalism will still involve selection. And, although many journalists tend to refer to the need for an instinctive "nose" for news selection, most academic researchers in the field would argue that it is probably not possible to examine news values in a meaningful way without also paying attention to occupational routines, budgets, the market, and ideology, as well as wider global cultural, economic and political considerations.

News values will continue to be subjected to scrutiny by academic researchers for the reasons indicated above. Future research projects could usefully explore the impact of online journalism, mobile telephony and podcasting on decisions about news selection and, indeed, on definitions of news. Technological developments mean that news producers can now more accurately gauge the relative popularity of particular stories online; the ways in which such knowledge may impact upon news selection should be an area of increasing critical scrutiny. Many scholars are already turning their attention to the role of so-called "citizen journalism" or "user-generated content" within the media, and a fruitful area of research is likely to be the ways in which the availability of such material results in variations in news values. At the same time, continuing study of the news values of 24-hour broadcast news (itself a relatively recent phenomenon) will help shed further light on the changing journalistic environment of the 21st century. However, "old media" such as newspapers are likely to remain fertile areas of study, including comparisons of local, regional, national and international news outlets; comparisons between genre and/or different delivery platforms. Historical comparisons of news values could help inform what has come to be known—in the UK at least—as the "dumbing down" debate. There is also a great deal of potential in extending the study of news values and selection decisions to incorporate other areas of research, such as the potential impact on news of changes in the journalistic workforce in terms of gender, race or social class. Another area ripe for further investigation is the interaction between news selection and the sources used or privileged in news production; this issue could also usefully include exploration of the claims of alternative media to offer alternatives both to mainstream news values and to the mainstream cast of sources.

An understanding of news values is clearly of importance for practitioners and scholars of journalism; but they are not the only ones to grapple with the question of what news is. Public relations professionals and "spin doctors" use their knowledge of news values to place or influence stories in the news media. Critics of mainstream media use an understanding of news values either to urge changes in such values or to inform the creation of alternative forms of media with an alternative conception of news values. Groups who find their viewpoints marginalized in mainstream media, such as environmental groups or unions, can use an understanding of mainstream news values to obtain some access for their message (Manning, 2001; O'Neill, 2007). And, last but by no means least, a society's citizens can benefit from the increase in media literacy that may potentially result from the efforts of journalism studies scholars to scrutinize, unpick and explain the ways in which news is selected and constructed.

REFERENCES

Allern, S. (2002). Journalistic and commercial news values: News organizations as patrons of an institution and market actors. *Nordcom Review, 23*(1–2), 137–152.

Atton, C. (2002). *Alternative media*. London: Sage.

Bell, A. (1991). *The language of news media*. Oxford: Blackwell.

Beharrell, P., & Philo, G. (Eds.). (1977). *Trade unions and the media*, London: Macmillan.

Chaudhary, A. (1974). Comparative news judgment of Indian and American journalists. *International Communication Gazette, 20*, 233–248.

Chu, L. L. (1985). An organizational perspective on international news flows: Some generalizations, hypotheses, and questions for research. *International Communication Gazette, 35*, 3–18.

Curran, J., & Seaton, J. (2003). *Power without responsibility: The press, broadcasting, and new media in Britain*. London: Routledge.

Donsbach, W. (2004). Psychology of news decisions: Factors behind journalists professional behaviour. *Journalism, 5*(2), 131–157.

Evans, H. (2000). *Essential English for journalists, editors and writers*. London: Pimlico.

Franklin, B. (1997). *Newszak and news media*. London: Arnold.

Galtung, J., & Ruge, M. (1965). The structure of foreign news: The presentation of the Congo, Cuba and Cyprus crises in four Norwegian newspapers. *Journal of International Peace Research 1*, 64–91.

Gans, H. J. (1980). *Deciding what's news*. London: Constable.

Golding, P., & Elliott, P. (1979). *Making the news*. London: Longman.

Greenberg, J. (2004). Tories, teachers and the media politics of education reform: News discourse and the 1997 Ontario teachers' strike. *Journalism Studies, 5*(3), 353–371.

Hall, S. (1973). The determinations of news photographs. In S. Cohen & J. Young (Eds.), *The manufacture of news: Deviance, social problems and the mass media* (pp. 226–243). London: Constable.

Harcup, T. (2004). *Journalism: Principles and practice*. London: Sage.

Harcup, T. (2005). "I'm doing this to change the world": Journalism in alternative and mainstream media. *Journalism Studies, 6*(3), 361–374.

Harcup, T. (2006). The local alternative press. In B. Franklin (Ed.), *Local journalism and local media: Making the local news* (pp. 129–139). London: Routledge,.

Harcup, T. (2007). *The ethical journalist*. London: Sage.

Harcup, T., & O'Neill, D. (2001). What is news? Galtung and Ruge revisited. *Journalism Studies, 2*(2), 261–268.

Harrison, J. (2006). *News*. London: Routledge.

Hartley, J. (1982). *Understanding news*. London: Methuen.

Henderson, M. (2003, September 20). Junk medicine: Don't believe the hype. *Times*, Body and Soul, p. 4.

Herman, E., & Chomsky, N. [1988] (1994). *Manufacturing consent: The political economy of the mass media*. London: Vintage.

Hetherington, A. (1985). *News, newspapers and television*. London: Macmillan.

Jones, D., Petley, J., Power, M., & Wood, L. (1985). *Media hits the pits: The media and the coal dispute*. London: Campaign for Press and Broadcasting Freedom.

Keeble, R. (2005). Journalism ethics: towards an Orwellian critique. In S. Allan (Ed.), *Journalism: Critical issues* (pp. 54–56). Maidenhead: Open University Press.

Kuhn, R. (2005). "Be very afraid': Television and l'insecurite in the 2002 French presidential election. *European Journal of Communication, 20*(2), 181–198.

Lange, J. C. (1984). National development and news values: The press in the third world and the west. *International Communication Gazette, 33*, 69–86.

Lavie, A., & Lehman-Wilzig, S. (2003). Whose news? Does gender determine the editorial product? *European Journal of Communication, 18*(1), 5–29.

Lee, S. T., Maslog, C. C., & Kim, H. S. (2006). Asian conflicts and the Iraq War. *International Communication Gazette, 68*, 499–518.

Lewis, J. (2006). News and the empowerment of citizens. *European Journal of Cultural Studies, 9*(3), 303–319.

McChesney, R. (2000). *Rich media, poor democracy: Communications politics in dubious times*. New York: The New Press.

McKane, A. (2006). *News writing*. London: Sage.

McQuail, D. (1994). *Mass communication theory*. London: Sage.

McQuail, D. (2000). *McQuail's mass communication theory*. London: Sage.

Manning, P. (2001). *News and news sources: A critical introduction*. London: Sage.

Ndlela, N. (2005). The African paradigm: The coverage of the Zimbabwean crisis in the Norwegian media. *Westminster Papers in Communication and Culture*, 2 (Special Issue November 2005), 71–90.

NGO-EC Liaison Committee. (1989). *Code of conduct: Images and messages relating to the Third World*. Retrieved July 18, 2008, from http://www.globalnews.org.uk/teacher_values.htm

Nosseck, H. (2004). Our news and their news: The role of national identity in the coverage of foreign news. *Journalism, 5*(3), 343–368.

O'Neill, D. (2007). From hunky heroes to dangerous dinosaurs: Journalism-union relations, news access and press coverage in the 2002–3 British Fire Brigades Union dispute. *Journalism Studies, 8*(5), 813–830.

Palmer, J. (1998). News production, news values. In A. Briggs & P. Cobley (Eds.), *The media: An introduction* (pp. 117–132), Harlow: Longman.

Palmer, J. (2000). *Spinning into control: News values and source strategies*. London: Leicester University Press.

Rampal, K. R. (1984). Adversory vs developmental journalism: Indian mass media at the crossroads. *International Communication Gazette, 34*, 3–20.

Randall, D. (2000). *The universal journalist*. London: Pluto.

Richardson, J. (2005). News values. In B. Franklin, M. Hamer, M. Hanna, M. Kinsey & J. Richardson (Eds.), *Key concepts in journalism studies* (pp. 173–174). London: Sage.

Rogriquez, C. (2001). *Fissures in the mediascape: An international study of citizens' media.* Creskill, NJ: Hamton Press.

Schlesinger, P. (1987). *Putting reality together*. London: Methuen.

Schulz, W. F. (1982). News structure and people's awareness of political events. *Gazette, 30*, 139–153.

Sergeant, J. (2001). *Give me ten seconds*. London: Macmillan.

Sissons, H. (2006). *Practical journalism: How to write news*. London: Sage.

Staab, J. F. (1990). The role of news factors in news selection: A theoretical reconsideration. *European Journal of Communication, 5*, 423–443.

Tunstall, J. (Ed.). (1970). *Media sociology*. London: Constable.

Watson, J., & Hill, A. (2003). *Dictionary of media and communication studies*. London: Arnold.

Westerstahl, J., & Johansson, F. (1986). News Ideologies as moulders of domestic news. *European Journal of Communication, 1*, 133–149.

Westerstahl, J., & Johansson, F. (1994). Foreign news: News values and ideologies. *European Journal of Communication, 9*, 71–89.

Whitaker, B. (1981). *News Ltd: Why you can't read all about it.* London: Minority Press Group.

Wilke, J., & Reinemann, C. (2001). Do the candidates matter? Long-term trends of campaign coverage—A study of the German press since 1949. *European Journal of Communication, 16*(3), 291–314.

Williams, A., & Franklin, B. (2007). *Turning around the tanker: Implementing Trinity Mirror's online strategy*. Cardiff: School of Journalism, Media and Cultural Studies, Cardiff University.

Wu, H. D. (2000). Systemic determinants of international news coverage: A comparison of 38 countries. *Journal of Communication, 50*, 110–130.

Zayani, M., & Ayish, M. I. (2006). Arab satellite TV and crisis reporting: Covering the fall of Baghdad. *International Communication Gazette, 68*, 473–447.

Zelizer, B. (2004). *Taking journalism seriously: News and the academy*. London: Sage.

13

Nature, Sources, and Effects of News Framing

Robert M. Entman, Jörg Matthes, and Lynn Pellicano

INTRODUCTION

Framing is arguably a victim of its own success. In research practice, it means too much, with scholars applying an unruly mélange of concepts under the framing rubric to a vast array of contexts and issues. Yet, perhaps directed in part by the ready availability of opinion effects data from survey and lab experiments, framing in political communication research also means too little, and focuses too narrowly. Although there are some notable exceptions, most of the framing literature, empirical and theoretical, implies that what matters above all are the effects of single framing messages on individual citizens' opinions about one policy or candidate.

Of course, framing is an individual psychological process, but it is also an organizational process and product, and a political strategic tool. Therefore, the main argument of this chapter is that framing scholars need to focus on the political sources of frames and the full range of their effects, including the feedback of initial impacts on further frame production. To pursue this argument, the chapter is organized as follows: After clarifying the terms *frames* and *framing*, we present a diachronic process model of political framing that expands framing theory beyond the focus on individual effects. Based on these insights, the chapter then provides a systematic overview of the state of scholarship in framing research. The major focus of this part is on the psychology of framing effects. It is concluded that, while further developing micro-level understanding of framing's impacts on individual opinions, we also need an effort to develop an integrated theory of frame construction, circulation, impact and reaction; one that accounts for the larger flow of communication and influence among elites, media and public.

CLARIFYING FRAMES AND FRAMING

It comes as no surprise that social scientists are very far from consensus on what exactly "frame" and "framing" mean. Examining the framing literature, we can find many different uses of the concept. There are two basic genres of definition. Some define framing in very general terms, roughly following Gamson and Modigliani's frequently quoted definition of framing as the "central organizing idea or story line that provides meaning to an unfolding strip of events" (1987, p. 143). However, to treat a frame as a central idea or a story line provides an insufficient basis for consistent measurement or theory. The second genre of definition specifies what frames generally do, especially issue frames. This includes defining problems, making moral judgments, and supporting remedies (Entman, 1993, 2004). Drawing on functional specifications seems preferable because it enables analysts to draw clearer measurements and inferences that distinguish framing from themes, arguments, assertions, and other under-theorized concepts.

One useful suggestion when using the more fine-grained genre is distinguishing between issue-specific frames and generic frames (de Vreese, 2005). Issue-specific frames are pertinent only to specific topics or events; that means every issue has different issue-specific frames. Examples are Reese and Buckalew's (1995) in-depth analysis of local television coverage about the Persian Gulf War, or Shah, Watts, Domke and Fan's (2002) computer-aided content analysis of the Monica Lewinsky debate. Moreover, the attributes in second level agenda setting can also be understood as issue-specific frames (McCombs, 2005).

Generic frames transcend thematic limitations as they can be identified across different issues and contexts. Prime examples of generic frames are Iyengar's (1991) episodic and thematic frames. When news is framed episodically, social issues are constructed around specific instances and individuals. There is no broader context provided in order to steer attention away from public solutions. For example, Iyengar's experiments show that viewers of episodic coverage were more likely to attribute responsibility to the individual for his or her plight (such as blaming poverty on an individual's lack of motivation). In contrast, thematic framing emphasizes broader trends or backgrounds of issues. Iyengar found that viewers of thematic coverage were more likely to make societal attributions (such as blaming poverty on economic hardships). Semetko and Valkenburg's study of European politics (2000) suggested five generic frames: conflict, human interest, economic consequences, morality, and responsibility. Other suggestions include Entman's (2004) differentiation between substantive and procedural framing, with the latter focused on evaluating political strategy, "horserace" and power struggles among elites, rather than on the substantive nature and import of issues, events and actors.

Framing processes occur at four levels: in the culture; in the minds of elites and professional political communicators; in the texts of communications; and in the minds of individual citizens (Entman, 1993, 2004). An initial graphic overview of the political framing process appears in Figure 13.1.

Culture is the stock of schemas commonly found in the minds of a society's individuals, and the stock of frames present in the system's communications, including literature, entertainment, news, conversations and other political discourse. By definition, these common schemas are the ones that form the basis for most individuals' reactions to framing communications. Elites do not have unlimited autonomy but are constrained to choosing from this cultural stock, which records the traces of *past* framing. So any larger *political* theory of framing in politics must take into account t-1, t1, t2 and more—it must be diachronic. Figure 13.1 suggests how the framing process moves from initial responses at time 2 to a new issue or event that occurred at time 1, to framing responses at time 3 that are based on time 2 anticipations of the future.

Framing *in communication texts* arises from *networks of professional communicators* who engage in framing, defined as *selecting some aspects of a perceived reality and constructing messages that highlight connections among them in ways that promote a particular interpretation.* "Framing" (or "to frame") is the verb form of the concept, as distinct from the noun form defined below. Some communicators engage in framing strategically, seeking to exert power over outcomes by inducing target audiences to accept interpretations that favor their interests or goals. These include politicians, bloggers, political satirists, editorial writers and pundits. Other communicators, most importantly reporters and news editors in mainstream national news media, normally engage in framing without intending to push any particular policy or political goal (with

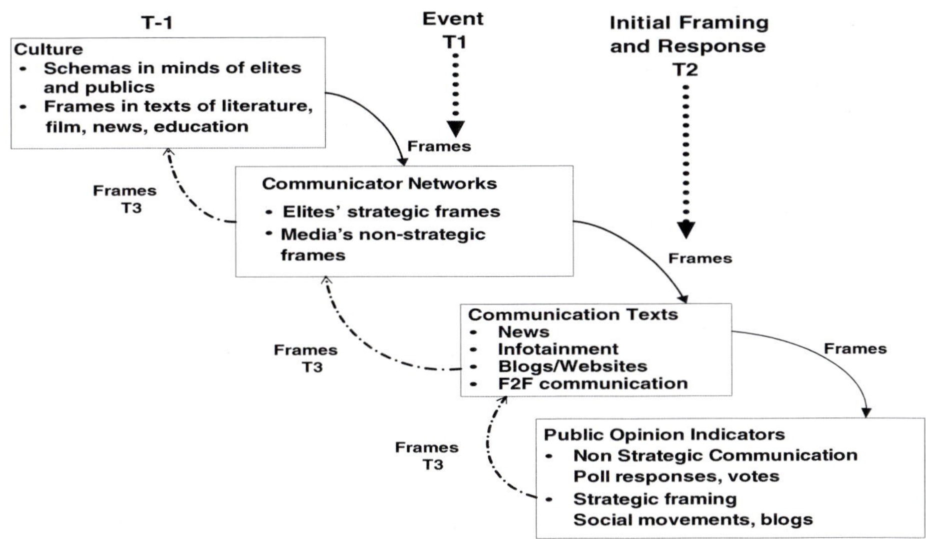

FIGURE 13.1 The political framing process.

the exception of certain party-affiliated newspapers and government-owned broadcast newscasts in Europe (cf. Hallin & Mancini, 2004)).

What Is a "Frame"?

What differentiates a framing message, or "frame" in a communication from a plain persuasive message or simply an assertion? A frame *repeatedly invokes the same objects and traits, using identical or synonymous words and symbols in a series of similar communications that are concentrated in time. These frames function to promote an interpretation of a problematic situation or actor and (implicit or explicit) support of a desirable response, often along with a moral judgment that provides an emotional charge.* Here again framing is distinguished from other communication by its diachronic nature. A framing message has particular cultural resonance; it calls to mind currently congruent elements of schemas that were stored in the past. Repeating frames over time in multiple texts gives a politically significant proportion of the citizenry a chance to notice, understand, store and recall the mental association for future application. Framing is thus diachronic in the sense that exposure during a given period is presumed to increase probabilities of particular responses during a future period, while diminishing the probability of thinking about other potentially relevant objects or traits. Finally, once a frame has appeared enough to be widely stored in the citizenry's schema systems, it no longer needs to be repeated in concentrated bursts, nor must it be fully elaborated; citizens can summon the stored associations years later in response to a single vivid component ("9/11" or "Berlin Wall").

If a communication does not exhibit repeated words and symbols that connect with the cultural associations of many citizens, then by these standards, it is not a frame. This is not to suggest that aspects of political communication not possessing these traits are unimportant, only that progress in framing research requires specifying what "frame" and "framing" mean, and using those concepts consistently.

The conception put forth in this chapter suggests that framing effects occur more widely throughout the political process than is typically recognized (for a partial exception see Hsiang

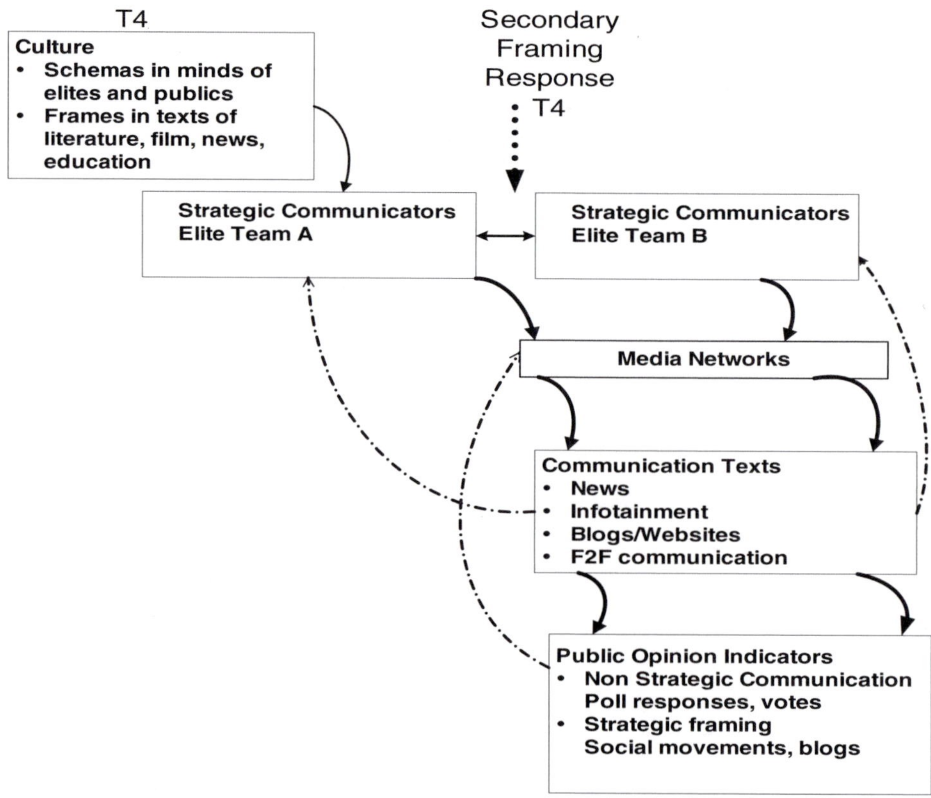

FIGURE 13.2 The diachronic political framing process.

& McCombs, 2004). Figure 13.2 extends Figure 13.1 in time, further illustrating the diachronic nature of the framing cycle and indicating the many junctures at which framing occurs and might be investigated. It highlights the possibility—if not the likelihood—that by time 4 a competition over framing will break out among elites, diversifying media content and yielding important potential impacts on politics and policy. This model also suggests that surveys or lab experiments, with their essentially synchronic structures and focus on members of the mass public, may tap only a restricted range of real world framing effects.

FRAMING: THE RESEARCH LITERATURE

Having put forth the context for an improved understanding of framing, let us step back to review the course and literature of framing research. What follows is a survey of the different forms of framing in politics that have been investigated. We begin with the origins of framing research, followed by a review of research about strategic framing, journalistic framing, frames in media content, and framing effects.

Origins of Framing Research

Walter Lippmann, arguably the progenitor of framing theory, observed that for most people, "the world that [they] have to deal with politically is out of reach, out of sight, out of mind" (Lippmann, 1922, p. 18). Citizens, in other words, do not acquire much of their political knowledge from personal experience. Instead, they get most of their information from the media and the elites the media portray. As the chief means of symbolic contact with the political environment, the media wield significant influence over citizens' perceptions, opinions and behavior.

The idea that framing and frames are primary means through which people make sense of a complicated world got its modern impetus from two scholars, Gregory Bateson and Erving Goffman. As Bateson puts it, "definitions of a situation are built up in accordance with principles of organization which govern events—at least social ones—and our subjective involvement in them; frame is the word [...] to refer to such of these basic elements" (1954, pp. 10–11). Goffman (1974), who cites Bateson several times in formulating his own definition of framing, claims that frames are cognitive structures that guide the representation of everyday events.

Given that ordinary persons use frames to organize their thoughts on the world's simple daily events, it is no surprise that they will respond to framing when it comes to the more distant, complicated events of politics. As Lippmann (1922) observed, "Of public affairs, each of us sees very little, and therefore, they remain dull and unappetizing, until somebody, with the makings of an artist, has translated them into a moving picture" (p. 104).

Strategic Framing

As suggested above, political leaders recognize the power of framing to strategically shape public discourse and public understanding, and try to exploit it to their own advantage, especially to promote a future course of action (Benford & Snow, 2000). According to this view, framing involves both the strategic communication of one's own frame, and competition with other communicators' frames. Fröhlich and Rüdiger's study of German political public relations (PR) indicates that framing plays an integral role in professional practice, as "bringing their frames unaltered into the media is an indicator of PR success" (Fröhlich & Rüdiger, 2006, p. 19; see also Hallahan, 1999). Most PR studies compare practitioners' preferred frames to frames in the news (e.g., Fröhlich & Rüdiger, 2006; Kiousis, Mitrook, Wu, & Seltzer, 2006). Likewise, social movement theorists understand framing as a strategy for social movements to mobilize the public. In this context, frames are defined as "action oriented sets of beliefs and meanings that inspire and legitimate the activities and campaigns of a social movement organization" (Benford & Snow, 2000, p. 614). As Snow and Benford (1992) argue, successful frames must diagnose a problem (diagnostic framing), propose solutions and tactics (prognostic framing), and motivate for action (motivational framing). Frames are not understood as individual schemas, but as collectively shared patterns of a social group. These collectively shared frames are identified by the analysis of movement documents, interviews with movement members, or an analysis of media content (Johnston, 1995).

Journalistic Framing

In contrast to research on strategic framing, less is known about the professional frames that guide informational processing and text production by journalists. A professional journalistic frame is a "schema or heuristic, a knowledge structure that is activated by some stimulus and is then employed by a journalist throughout story construction" (Dunwoody, 1992, p. 78). These frames are central to the tradecraft of journalism and should be differentiated from frames in media texts; such professional frames are more akin to scripts or menus that guide selections of issues and construction of news reports (Dunwoody, 1992). Tuchman (1976) describes journalistic frames as useful tools that journalists apply in order to cope with the tide of information. As Scheufele

(2006) explains, journalistic frames can be described on an individual level (i.e., the individual frame of a journalist), and on a newsroom level (i.e., frames shared by journalists in a newsroom). Framing scholars argue that journalists prefer information that is consistent with their journalistic frames (Scheufele, 2006). In times of routine coverage, journalistic frames are applied to incoming information. As a consequence, frame-consistent information is more likely to be used for the construction of a news report than inconsistent information. However, key events can shift existing journalistic frames and even replace these frames. Therefore, in contrast to other influences on news selection and news construction (e.g., news values), journalistic frames can be shifted and changed after the occurrence of key events (Scheufele, 2006; Brosius & Eps, 1995).

Frames in Media Content

Frame analysis has become a very lively and important methodology. In essence, frame analysis examines the selection and salience of certain aspects of an issue by exploring images, stereotypes, metaphors, actors and messages. However, studies differ in their ways of extracting frames from the media content. Four broad approaches can be roughly distinguished (Matthes & Kohring, 2008): a qualitative approach, a manual-holistic approach, a manual-clustering approach, and a computer-assisted approach.

Qualitative Approach. A number of studies try to identify frames by providing an interpretative account of media texts (Downs, 2002; Reese & Buckalew, 1995). Rooted in the qualitative paradigm, these studies are based on relatively small samples that should mirror the discourse of an issue or event. Typically, frames are described in-depth, and little or no quantification is provided. Pan and Kosicki's (1993) approach to frame analysis can be considered a subclass of qualitative studies. In these linguistic studies frames are identified by analyzing the selection, placement and structure of specific words and sentences in a text (see also Esser & D'Angelo, 2003). Usually, the unit of analysis is the paragraph, not the article. Researchers have to construct a data matrix for each individual news text. In this matrix the signifying elements for each individual proposition are analyzed. The basic idea is that specific words are the building blocks of frames (Entman, 1993). Pan and Kosicki distinguish structural dimensions of frames: metaphors, examples, key sentences, and pictures.

Manual-Holistic Approach. The essence of this method is that frames are manually coded as holistic variables in a quantitative content analysis, whether inductively or deductively. In inductive manual-holistic studies, frames are first generated by a qualitative analysis of some news texts and then coded as holistic variables in a manual content analysis. For instance, Simon and Xenos (2000) conducted a thorough analysis of a sample of newspaper articles in the first step in order to generate six working frames. Subsequently, these frames were defined in a codebook and coded in a quantitative content analysis. In a similar vein, Husselbee and Elliott (2002) coded several frames in their study about the coverage of two hate crimes. Examples of deductive manual-holistic measurement are Iyengar's (1991) episodic and thematic frames and Pfau et al.'s (2004) one-item measure to assess the extent to which an article embodied episodic framing.

Manual-Clustering Approach. These studies manually code single variables or frame elements in standard quantitative content analysis. These variables are subsequently factor- or cluster-analyzed. In other words, rather than directly coding the whole frame, splitting up the frame into separate variables or elements is suggested. Following this process, a factor or cluster analysis of those elements should reveal the frame. In a study by Semetko and Valkenburg (2000), each news story was analyzed through a series of twenty questions to which the coder had to answer "yes" or "no." A factor analysis of those twenty items revealed five factors that were interpreted as frames. Matthes and Kohring (in press) proposed a method of frame analysis that codes the single frame elements as defined by Entman (1993) in a standard content analysis. After that, a cluster analysis of these elements reveals the frame.

Computer-Assisted Approach. In contrast to the manual-clustering and the manual-holistic approach, neither holistic frames nor single frame elements or variables are manually coded in the computer-assisted studies. As a prime example of computer-assisted frame analysis, Miller, Andsager and Riechert (1998) suggest frame mapping. Based on the notion that frames are manifested in the use of specific words, the authors seek to identify frames by examining specific vocabularies in texts. Words that tend to occur together in texts are identified with the help of a computer. For example, the words charity, charities, charitable, and money form the "charity-frame" (Miller et al., 1998). In fact, there is no manual coding at all. A few other studies have advanced computer-assisted content analysis by moving beyond the grouping of words. For instance, Shah et al. (2002) used a computer program to create comparatively sophisticated syntactic rules that capture the meaning of sentences. In other words, their study enabled an analysis of meaning behind word relationships.

Framing Effects

Public opinion scholar James Druckman (2001b) emphasizes two types of frames—frames in communication and frames in thought—that work together to form a framing effect. Both are concerned with variations in emphasis or salience. Frames in communication—often referred to as "media frame"—focus on what the speaker or news text says; such as how an issue is portrayed by elites, while frames in thought focus on what an individual is thinking; such as the value judgment of an issue. It might be preferable to use "schemas" to refer to frames in thought, to minimize confusion with frames in communication. Frames in communication often play an important role in shaping frames in thought. For example, the considerations that come to mind after exposure to a media frame may affect how individuals form their opinion on a given issue. This is what Druckman defines as a framing effect. He identifies two distinct types of framing effects; equivalency framing effects and emphasis (or issue) framing effects.

Equivalency framing: Equivalency framing effects cause people to alter their preferences when presented with different, but logically equivalent, words or phrases. Such framing effects have been largely the province of psychological research. Kahneman and Tversky's (1984) "Asian disease problem" offers perhaps the most widely cited example of equivalency framing effects. The authors asked experimental subjects to choose between two programs for the treatment of the disease, one framed as a risk-averse choice because it yields a certain outcome ("200 [out of 600] people will be saved"), the other as a risk-seeking choice since the outcome is uncertain ("there is a 1/3 probability that 600 people will be saved and a 2/3 probability that no people will be saved"). Although the two outcomes are logically equivalent, 72 percent of the respondents chose the risk-averse option. Kahneman and Tversky demonstrated similarly dramatic effects using other experimental variations. For instance, when the same problem was re-framed in terms of the number of people who will *die* rather than be *saved*, 78 percent of respondents chose the risk-*seeking* (less certain) outcome.

Levin, Schneider and Gaeth (1998) refer to equivalency framing effects as valence framing effects, that is, wherein a frame casts the same information in either a positive or negative light. They develop a typology to distinguish among what they believe are three types of valence framing effects: risky choice framing, attribute framing, and goal framing. For risky choice framing, they borrow the model from Kahneman and Tversky's original experiment and explore other authors' modifications of the "Asian disease problem" that involve different levels of risk. They find that the likelihood of choice reversals was directly related to the similarity between features of a given study and features of the original "Asian disease problem." For example, when risky choice dealt with bargaining behaviors, settlement (a risk-averse choice) was more likely when outcomes were expressed as gains, and negotiation (a risk-seeking choice) was more likely when framed as losses (Neale & Bazerman, 1985).

In attribute framing, Levin, Schneider and Gaeth (1998) describe that only a single attribute within any given context is the subject of the framing manipulation. Because of its simplicity, they argue that attribute framing is the most straightforward test of valence framing effects. One study of attribute framing was conducted by Levin and Gaeth (1988). They showed that individuals evaluate the quality of ground beef on how the beef is labeled (e.g., "75 percent lean" or "25 percent fat"). They found that a sample of ground beef was rated as better tasting and less greasy when it was labeled in a positive light rather than in a negative light, regardless of the fact that these two choices are logically equivalent.

Finally, goal framing refers to manipulating a goal of an action or behavior to affect the persuasiveness of the communication. Goal framing, they argue, can be used to focus on a frame's potential to provide a benefit or gain, or on its potential to prevent or avoid a loss. Both the positive and negative frame should enhance the evaluation of the issue. Goal framing, however, is concerned with which frame will have the greater persuasive impact on achieving the same end result. Multiple studies have shown that a negatively framed message emphasizing losses tends to have a greater impact on a given behavior than the logically equivalent positively framed message emphasizing gains (e.g., Meyerowitz & Chaiken, 1987).

Emphasis (or Issue) Framing: Druckman (2001a, 2001b) argues that an "(emphasis) framing effect is said to occur when, in the course of describing an issue or event, a speaker's emphasis on a subset of potentially relevant considerations causes individuals to focus on these considerations when constructing their opinions" (2001a, p. 1042). Although both equivalency and emphasis framing effects cause individuals to focus on certain aspects of an issue over others, the information subsets presented in emphasis framing are not logically identical to one another. Nelson, Oxley and Clawson (1997) argue that issue frames tell people how to weight the often conflicting considerations that we face on a daily basis. Frames, therefore, have the best possibility to affect public opinion when emphasizing a subset of different and potentially relevant considerations. By offering a way of thinking about an issue and omitting opposing frames, this tool can be used to activate certain preferences over others (Feldman & Zaller, 1992; Price & Tewksbury, 1997) and declare certain frames as more important than others (Iyengar, 1991; Nelson, Oxley, et al., 1997; Nelson & Oxley, 1999). Emphasis framing, therefore, is concerned with increasing or decreasing the salience of an issue or consideration when formulating an opinion.

Sniderman, Brody and Tetlock (1991) provide a clear example of the power of omission in framing, in their surveys of public opinion around AIDS, in which some aspects of an issue are highlighted and others omitted. They found that a majority of the public supports the rights of a person with AIDS when the issue is framed in consideration of civil liberties, and supports mandatory testing when the issue is framed in consideration of public health. The text of the survey question supplies most subjects with the considerations they use when thinking of AIDS testing. Often a potential counterframing of the issue is absent from the text, as is the case here, when subjects are only exposed to one side of the frame that emphasizes specific considerations over others (Entman, 1993).

In another example, Sniderman and Theriault (2004) show that when government spending for the poor is framed as enhancing the chance that poor people can get ahead, individuals tend to support increased spending. However, when such government spending is framed as increasing taxes, individuals tend to oppose government spending to help the poor. Once again, these examples show that emphasizing certain considerations over others can produce different opinions on the same issue.

PSYCHOLOGY OF FRAMING

Since the literature has shown that framing can have a significant effect on how people make decisions and formulate opinions on any given issue or event, it is important to understand the psychological processes that underlie such effects.

Framing as Persuasion

Some of the existing literature on framing suggests that such effects occur via persuasion. As limited-capacity information processors (Fiske & Taylor, 1991), individuals cannot possibly consider everything they know about an issue or event at any given moment. This allows room for persuasion, a process that takes place when a communicator successfully revises or alters the content of one's beliefs by providing them with new information or additional considerations that replace or supplement favorable thoughts with unfavorable ones, or vice versa (Nelson & Oxley, 1999). However, according to Nelson and Oxley (1999, p. 1043), such an understanding of framing effects casts "some doubt on the claim that framing is a distinct contribution to communication and persuasion theory."

Framing as an Extension of Priming

Other research suggests that framing is an extension of the priming literature, with accessibility as the main psychological mechanism underlying framing effects (e.g., Zaller, 1992; Kinder & Sanders, 1996). Since people cannot consider everything they know about an issue or event at any given moment, they will consider a subset of all potentially relevant information by relying on what is accessible, easily retrieved, or recently activated in their minds, according to the "cognitive accessibility model" (Zaller, 1992). Cognitions that are accessible will be "top of the head," and therefore are more likely to influence opinion than inaccessible cognitions. It is in this sense that Kinder and Sanders (1996) suggest framing works through the temporary activation and enhanced accessibility of concepts and considerations in memory. They state that the extent to which a consideration is accessible can alter the criteria by which people can render judgments about an issue, person or event.

The recent framing literature stresses the importance of three attributes for a notable framing effect to occur: availability, accessibility, and applicability (Chong & Druckman, 2007a, 2007b; Price & Tewksbury, 1997). First, a given consideration, such as the freedom to choose in the evaluation of a mother's right to abortion, needs to have already been stored in memory to be available for retrieval and use. If an individual cannot comprehend this concept in the first place, a frame emphasizing this consideration would have no effect on the individual's opinions (Chong & Druckman, 2007a, 2007b).

Second, a consideration must be accessible. This refers to the likelihood that an already available consideration will be retrieved and activated for use from storage in long-term memory. One way in which accessibility may increase is through recent or consistent exposure to a frame in communication that emphasizes a particular consideration (Chong & Druckman, 2007a, 2007b). The potential ramifications of using accessibility to guide thoughts and opinions are discussed later.

Last, the impact of an available and accessible consideration may depend on how applicable it is to the individual. The perceived applicability of a media frame increases with perceptions of its strength, relevance, or persuasiveness. The consideration emphasizing a woman's right to choose whether or not to have an abortion may be available and accessible, but if it does not hold any weight in the individual's mind, it may not be effective in producing the desired outcome from the media frame (Chong & Druckman, 2007a, 2007b).

Framing and Schema Theory

Many scholars have stressed the importance of schemas in the information-processing routines as guides to recall, which can determine how accessible ideas and feelings are in our memory (Entman, 1989, 1993, 2004; Fiske & Taylor, 1991). Schemas allow us to simplify reality and function in a social world that would otherwise be too complex to handle. Schemas fit new thoughts to an existing organization of knowledge. Fiske and Taylor (1991) define schemas as "cognitive structures that represent knowledge about a concept or type of stimulus, including its attributes and the relations among attributes" (p. 131). Information is thus stored in an abstract form. People's prior knowledge allows them to decide what information is relevant to a given schema in order that they may make sense of specific new encounters.

A common theme in schema research is that people remember information that confirms their existing schemas, and forget information inconsistent with them. However, although schema-consistent information is favored by normal retrieval routes, this does not mean people will automatically disregard inconsistent information. Indeed, it may depend on whether sufficient time is allowed to remember and process inconsistent information, or people may very well try to make the inconsistent information fit into an existing schema (Fiske & Taylor, 1991).

Schemas can be thought of as resting in an inactive state waiting to be changed to active status. A schema's activation is partly determined by how recently it has been activated. Thus, a frequently activated schema has a higher probability of being recently activated at any given time (Fiske & Taylor, 1991). In this sense, schemas may act as heuristics, or mental shortcuts, making rapid information processing possible. Fiske and Taylor suggest the availability heuristic, for example, is used to evaluate the potential activation of knowledge on the basis of how quickly instances or associations come to mind.

Citizen Incompetence?

The cognitive accessibility model could be read as painting a pessimistic picture of citizens as basing their political opinions on arbitrary or elite-manipulated information (Druckman, 2001b). However, evidence indicates that public opinion is not shaped only by "mere accessibility." Nelson and colleagues (Nelson, Clawson, et al., 1997; Nelson & Oxley, 1999; Nelson, Oxley, et al., 1997) are the leading proponents of the argument that framing is about more than just accessibility. According to this line of research, frames do more than make certain considerations accessible; they suggest which of the many, possibly conflicting, considerations should predominate when forming opinions on an event or issue. For example, Nelson and Oxley

(1999) presented differing welfare reform frames to subjects, either a "personal responsibility" frame or a "threat to children" frame. When subjects were given the "threat to children" frame, they were more likely to think about considerations such as the importance of protecting poor children, and to express opposition to new limits on welfare. When presented with a "personal responsibility" frame, subjects were more likely to think of women on welfare as not exhibiting adequate responsibility, which increased support for the restrictive policy. The authors infer that importance judgments derive from both citizens' own predispositions and more malleable impressions of an issue—and that therefore citizens do reason with some autonomy and competence. On the other hand, the prior dispositions themselves might be heavily influenced by earlier framing, as suggested by the diachronic perspective, so the matter of citizen competence remains unresolved.

FRAMING EFFECTS: A CRITIQUE AND NEW SYNTHESIS

This section elaborates on the points that have been the focus of the most recent research on framing effects: whether strong prior attitudes preclude significant framing effects on public opinion; whether competition between frames logically entails minimal framing consequences; and whether framing messages can still have major political influence even without affecting individuals' opinions.

Framing Effects and Prior Attitudes

Scholars interested in framing focus especially on the way it influences individual citizens' policy and candidate preferences. On this matter, the literature *appears* more split than it actually is; between those advocating consistently large framing effects and those advocating weaker impacts. The latter sometimes exaggerate their differences with the former, by claiming that those who believe in strong effects overlook contingency and individual agency in citizens' arriving at their preferences, and further arguing that strong framing effects imply citizen incompetence. Yet strong effects are not logically incompatible with variation in individual responsiveness to various framing messages, nor are they axiomatically incompatible with democracy.

However, the more important point for a political theory of framing is that weak framing effects can have outsized political consequences. This might suggest caution in drawing inferences about real world political effects even when data show, as they often do, that the presence of strong prior attitudes or frame competition prevents framing messages from influencing most people's opinions.

Findings about the moderating effects of prior attitudes and frame competition may not actually indicate that framing has minimal consequences for most individuals. Chong and Druckman (2007b) found that after a strong frame has diffused and increased the chronic accessibility of a consideration, it more or less automatically applies to future communication about the framed object, working through low-effort "peripheral" processing rather than more cognitively demanding central processing. This diffusion of a strong frame, they say, leads to "diminished framing effects," but more precisely the finding shows that framing has diminished effects at time 2 because framing at time 1 was successful (Chong & Druckman, 2007b, p. 110). If, as Chong and Druckman put it, strong prior attitudes will attenuate framing effects at the time of measurement, then, this does not tell us that framing in general has weak effects, since the strong prior attitudes may have themselves resulted from previous diffusion of a strong frame (Chong & Druckman, 2007a, p. 107; see also Matthes, 2007). It would appear almost axiomatic that the attitudes people have today, which may impel them to reject a framing message, are built upon the frames that influenced them in the past.

Competition of Frames

Once we start looking more diligently for framing effects, we must confront, as always, measurement and data issues. Thus, in an important advance in framing research, Sniderman and Theriault (2004) and Chong and Druckman (2007a), among others, urge that scholars consider the effects of framing more realistically, by including not just a simple one-sided framing stimulus in experiments, but competing frames. Competition complicates matters considerably.

Some researchers conclude from these studies that frame competition diminishes the effects of framing. This appears to be a logically flawed inference. Instead, frame competition studies actually demonstrate that (quite naturally) framing effects are distributed differently when audiences are exposed to two competing frames than when they are exposed to only one frame. Only if we assume that in the real world a framing competition could pit a framed message against an unframed (i.e., exhaustively complete) version of reality, does it make sense to say frame competition can attenuate framing effects. What competition does, again, is *complicate* framing effects.

For instance, Chong and Druckman isolate seventeen different conditions that might apply to framing effects under competition, based on whether the subject is exposed to two strong frames, two weak frames, or some combination, on both the pro and con side of an issue. Then there is the fact that framing in real world news reports and other texts rarely comes in the neatly symmetrical or asymmetrical packages supplied by experimenters and that it entails multiple exposures spread out over time. Literally hundreds of different conditions might be required to construct an experiment that truly replicates framing in the real world. To make matters still worse, individuals are free to accept different parts of framing communications and combine them in idiosyncratic ways. For instance, they can accept different problem definitions yet coalesce on the same remedy.

Framing and Public Opinion

When elites engage in a contest to shape frames in the media, it is often as a way of influencing other elites' perceptions and predictions of public opinion and thus their political calculations. This influence of media frames works along at least three different paths: through effects on citizens' responses to pollsters' questions about the matter (not necessarily on citizens' actual attitudes); through elites using news frames directly to draw inferences about the current and likely future state of public opinion; and through elite assessments of how competing elites will react to all of this. For instance, if elites at time 2 believe that one frame will dominate the competition, they will anticipate significant time 3 effects on public opinion, if not on actual individual opinions, then on the public opinion that is perceived by the rest of the elite class. Frame contestation is thus quite a complicated chess game, offering much grist for future research.

Elite competition is not merely designed to affect individual citizens' issue and candidate opinions, but equally or perhaps more importantly, to influence aggregate indicators of public opinion embodied in what can be called polling opinion (majority responses to widely publicized surveys), perceived public opinion and anticipated majorities (Entman, 2004). Framing messages can still have major political influence even without affecting individuals' opinions, because those messages can affect elites' perceptions of public opinion, their assessments of the political environment and the calculations of political benefits and threats that shape their rhetoric and decisions. Public opinion is subject to framing in measurement as well as transmission (from publics to elites and the reverse path as well). The aggregation of actual public perceptions, emotions, and preferences that are encompassed by the concept "public opinion" should not be confused with the manifestations of them that are available to public officials or journalists.

Public opinion itself is a framed phenomenon and elites compete over framing it. The Arrow impossibility theorem (which demonstrates that stable majority rule is unattainable in practice) and other difficulties in aggregating individual opinion into a determinate public will are well known (e.g., Riker, 1996), as are problems with survey methods and sampling, with non-attitudes, and the list goes on. All of these dilemmas confront political elites no less than political communication scholars. The result is that elites who seek to represent public opinion, whether for altruistic or selfish political reasons, have no alternative but to employ a framed version that is a selective interpretation. We can expect politicians to be especially concerned with predicting both the direction and the intensity of opinion in the future, when the next election occurs, and with how both media treatment and public opinion will react at that future time to what the politician does and says today.

All this suggests limitations in applying results of experiments to real world framing effects. Another non-obvious drawback in relying too heavily on experiments is that the non-academic survey interview experience differs substantially from the situation in which we place experimental subjects. Yet those surveys by media organizations and pollsters can be highly politically influential. If survey responses are the politically significant signaling devices to policymakers and politicians, then the effect of framing on these in the real world, rather than on opinions expressed in experiments, demands as much attention as the effect on actual individual opinion. Frame messages can affect responses to survey questions in real world survey interview interactions, without necessarily affecting the individual's true opinions. Those opinions might be more accurately assessed in a typical framing experiment by a social scientist than by a commercial pollster's question. Even if social scientists' experiments get at the true opinions of subjects and surveys do not, researchers must be equally concerned with the effects of framing on survey responses in the real world, because these are what matter to politics when it comes to publicized policy opinions (polling majorities) to publicized evaluations of presidents, and to voting plans.

At the same time, the idea that public opinion as perceived or anticipated by elites constrains their options for framing their own strategic messages must be understood as itself limited by elites' ability to heavily influence if not determine the frames that will reach publics and shape their responses. The flow of power is two way, but most evidence suggests the elites have by far the upper hand. Where elites disagree, though, no single "elite position" may dominate the widely circulated framing of an event or issue, opening up the possibility of more autonomous citizen deliberation.

CONCLUSION

Framing research has continually raised critical concerns about the ability of elites to manipulate the public, as well as the possibility of democracy itself. For instance, Entman (1993, p. 57) argues:

> If by shaping frames elites can determine the major manifestations of "true" public opinion that are available to government (via polls or voting), what can true public opinion be? How can even sincere democratic representatives respond correctly to public opinion when the empirical evidence of it appears to be so malleable, so vulnerable to framing effects?

To the extent that elites have no way of determining precisely what "real" public opinion is, they must rely on shorthand indicators such as polls and news texts that are themselves susceptible to framing effects. Regardless of whether framing truly affects actual majority opinion—or whether true public opinion is manipulated by elites—framing is likely to have political effects through the impacts of framing on poll responses and on the emphases of the media. These observations suggest that direct framing effects on individuals' opinions may not yield the most relevant data for drawing inferences about the quality of democratic citizenship. Therefore, the literature would gain greatly from expanding the purview of framing beyond the focus on individual opinions to framing as a larger diachronic and socio-political process.

These observations are not meant as suggestions to abandon the study of framing effects on individual policy opinions. Instead, they point to a need to broaden the study of framing effects, while connecting them to larger questions of democratic theory. These include but also transcend questions around whether subjects who resist framing messages prove their competence as democratic citizens. Research should focus as much on frame quality and elite quality as citizen quality. We could devote more attention to whose frames are most available, under which conditions, and how framing both guides elites' responses to indicators of public opinion, and helps elites shape those manifestations. Such research would illuminate the production and circulation of frames and the feedback loops that trace the flow of political power among competing media, competing elites, and mass publics.

REFERENCES

Bateson, G. (1954). A theory of play and fantasy. *Psychiatric Research Reports, 2,* 39–51.

Benford, R. D., & Snow, D. A. (2000). Framing processes and social movements: An overview and assessment. *Annual Review of Sociology, 26,* 611–639.

Brosius, H.-B., & Eps, P. (1995). Prototyping through key events: News selection in the case of violence against aliens and asylum seekers in Germany. *European Journal of Communication, 10,* 391–412.

Chong, D., & Druckman, J. N. (2007a). A theory of framing and opinion formation in competitive elite environments. *Journal of Communication, 57,* 99–118.

Chong, D., & Druckman, J. N. (2007b). Framing theory. *Annual Review of Political Science, 10,* 103–126.

de Vreese, C. H. (2005). News framing: Theory and typology. *Information Design Journal + Document Design, 13,* 51–62.

Downs, D. (2002). Representing gun owners. Frame identification as social responsibility in news media discourse. *Written Communication, 19,* 44–75.

Druckman, J. N. (2001a). On the limits of framing effects: Who can frame? *The Journal of Politics, 63,* 1041–1066.

Druckman, J. N. (2001b). The implications of framing effects for citizen competence. *Political Behavior, 23,* 225–256.

Dunwoody, S. (1992). The media and public perceptions of risk: How journalists frame risk stories. In D. W. Bromley & K. Segerson (Eds.), *The social response to environmental risk: Policy formulation in an age of uncertainty* (pp. 75–100). Boston: Kluwer.

Entman, R. M. (1989). How the media affect what people think: An information processing approach. *Journal of Politics, 51,* 347–370.

Entman, R. M. (1993). Framing: Toward clarification of a fractured paradigm. *Journal of Communication, 43,* 51–58.

Entman, R. M. (2004). *Projections of power: Framing news, public opinion, and U.S. foreign policy.* Chicago: University of Chicago Press.

Esser, F., & D'Angelo, P. (2003). Framing the press and the publicity process: A content analysis of metacoverage in campaign 2000 network news. *American Behavioral Scientist, 46,* 617–641.

Feldman, S., & Zaller, J. (1992). Political culture of ambivalence: Ideological responses to the welfare state. *American Journal of Political Science, 36*, 268–307.

Fiske, S. T., & Taylor, S. E. (1991). *Social cognition* (2nd ed.). New York: McGraw Hill.

Fröhlich, R., & Rüdiger, B. (2006). Framing political public relations: Measuring success of strategies in Germany. *Public Relations Review, 32*, 18–25.

Gamson, W. A., & Modigliani, A. (1987). The changing culture of affirmative action. In R. G. Braungart & M. M. Braungart (Eds.), *Research in political sociology* (pp. 137–177). Greenwich, CT: JAI Press.

Goffman, E. (1974). *Frame analysis: An essay on the organization of experience.* New York: Harper & Row.

Hallahan, K. (1999). Seven models of framing: Implications for public relations. *Journal of Public Relations Research, 11*, 205–242.

Hallin, D. C., & Mancini, P. (2004). *Comparing media systems: Three models of media and politics.* New York: Cambridge University Press.

Hsiang, I. C., & McCombs, M. (2004). Media salience and the process of framing: Coverge of the Columbine school shootings. *Journalism and Mass Communication Quarterly, 81*, 22–35.

Husselbee, L. P., & Elliott, L. (2002). Looking beyond hate: How national and regional newspapers framed hate crimes in Jasper, Texas, and Laramie, Wyoming. *Journalism & Mass Communication Quarterly, 79*, 833–852.

Iyengar, S. (1991). *Is anyone responsible? How television frames political issues.* Chicago: University of Chicago Press.

Johnston, H. (1995). A methodology for frame analysis: From discourse to cognitive schemata. In E. Laraña, H. Johnston, & J. R. Gusfield (Eds.), *Social movements and culture* (pp. 217–246). Minneapolis: University of Minnesota Press.

Joslyn, M., & Haider-Markel, D.(2002). Framing effects on personal opinion and perception of public opinion: The cases of physician-assisted suicide and social security. *Social Science Quarterly, 83*, 690–706.

Kahneman, D., & Tversky, A. (1984). Choices, values and frames. *American Psychologist, 39*, 341–350.

Kinder, D., & Sanders, L. (1996). *Divided by color: Racial politics and democratic ideals.* Chicago: University of Chicago Press.

Kiousis, S., Mitrook, M., Wu, X., & Seltzer, T. (2006). First- and second-level agenda-building and agenda-setting effects: Exploring the linkages among candidate news releases, media coverage, and public opinion during the 2002 Florida gubernatorial election. *Journal of Public Relations Research, 18*, 265–285.

Levin, I., & Gaeth, G. (1988). Framing of attribute information before and after consuming the product. *Journal of Consumer Research, 15*, 374–378.

Levin, I., Schneider, S., & Gaeth, G. (1998). All frames are not created equal: A typology and critical analysis of framing effects. *Organizational Behavior and Human Decision Processes, 76*, 149–188.

Lippmann, W. (1922). *Public opinion.* New York: Free Press.

Matthes, J. (2007). Beyond accessibility? Toward an on-line and memory-based model of framing effects. *Communications: The European Journal of Communication Research, 32*, 51–78.

Matthes, J., & Kohring, M. 2008). The content analysis of media frames: Toward improving reliability and validity. *Journal of Communication, 58*, 258–278.

McCombs, M. (2005). A look at agenda-setting: Past, present and future. *Journalism Studies, 6*, 543–557.

Meyerowitz, B., & Chaiken, S. (1987). The effect of message framing on breast self-examination attitudes, intentions, and behavior. *Journal of Personality and Social Psychology, 52*, 500–510.

Miller, M. M., Andsager, J., & Riechert, B. P. (1998). Framing the candidates in presidential primaries. *Journalism & Mass Communication Quarterly, 75*, 312–324.

Neale, M. A., & Bazerman, M. H. (1985). The effects of framing and negotiator overconfidence on bargaining behaviors and outcomes. *Academy of Management Journal, 28*, 34–49.

Nelson, T. E., Clawson, R. A., & Oxley, Z. M. (1997). Media framing of a civil liberties conflict and its effect on tolerance. *American Political Science Review, 91*, 567–583.

Nelson, T. E., & Oxley, Z. M. (1999). Issue framing effects on belief importance and opinion. *The Journal of Politics, 61*, 1040–1067.

Nelson, T. E., Oxley, Z. M., & Clawson, R. A. (1997). Toward a psychology of framing effects. *Political Behavior, 19*, 221–246.

Pan, Z., & Kosicki, G. M. (1993). Framing analysis: An approach to news discourse. *Political Communication, 10*, 55–76.

Pfau, M., Haigh, M. M., Gettle, M., Donnelly, M., Scott, G., & Warr, D. (2004). Embedding journalists in military combat units: Impact on newspaper story frames and tone. *Journalism & Mass Communication Quarterly, 81*, 74–88.

Price, V., & Tewksbury, D. (1997). News values and public opinion: A theoretical account of media priming and framing. In G. Barnett & F. J. Boster (Eds.), *Progresses in the Communication Sciences* (pp. 173–212). Greenwich, CT: Ablex.

Reese, S. D., & Buckalew, B. (1995). The militarism of local television: The routine framing of the Persian Gulf War. *Critical Studies in Media Communication, 12*, 40–59.

Riker, W. (1996). *The strategy of rhetoric: Campaigning for the American constitution.* New Haven, CT: Yale University Press.

Scheufele, B. (2006). Frames, schemata and news reporting. *Communications: The European Journal of Communication Research, 31*, 65–83.

Semetko, H. A., & Valkenburg, P. M. (2000). Framing European politics: A content analysis of press and television news. *Journal of Communication, 50*(2), 93–109.

Shah, D. V., Watts, M. D., Domke, D., & Fan, D. P. (2002). News framing and cueing of issue regimes. Explaining Clinton's public approval in spite of scandal. *Public Opinion Quarterly, 66*, 339–370.

Simon, A. F., & Xenos, M. (2000). Media framing and effective public deliberation. *Political Communication, 17*, 363–376.

Sniderman, P., & Theriault, S. (2004). The structure of political argument and the logic of issue framing. In P. M. Sniderman & W. W. Sarris (Eds.), *Studies in public opinion: Gauging attitudes, nonattitudes, measurement error, and change* (pp. 133–165). Princeton, NJ: Princeton University Press.

Sniderman, P., Brody, R., & Tetlock, P. (1991). *Reasoning and choice: Explorations in Political Psychology.* Cambridge, UK: Cambridge University Press.

Snow, D. A., & Benford, R. D. (1992). Master frames and cycles of protest. In A. D. Morris & C. McClurg Mueller (Eds.), *Frontiers in social movement theory* (pp. 133–155). New Haven, CT: Yale University Press.

Tuchman, G. (1976). Telling stories. *Journal of Communication, 26*(4), 93–97.

Zaller, J. R. (1992). *The nature and origins of mass opinion.* Cambridge, UK: Cambridge University Press.

14

News, Discourse, and Ideology

Teun A. van Dijk

INTRODUCTION

One of the fields where the studies of discourse and communication overlap is the theory and analysis of news. Research in communication studies has increasingly realized that its objects of study should also be examined as forms of socially situated text or talk. This new focus has especially been applied to the study of news in the press.

Although linguistics, semiotics and discourse studies have paid attention to news discourse since the 1970s, their orientation used to be limited to news structures, thereby ignoring many of the relevant contextual dimensions of communication, such as the sociology and economy of news production and the way recipients understand, memorize and integrate information and knowledge from news.

In this chapter we shall, on the one hand, review some earlier work on news, and, on the other hand, sketch how this important cross-disciplinary approach to news may benefit from other developments in the humanities and social sciences.

Since this integrated study of news-as-discourse-in-communication is still a vast field, this chapter shall specifically deal with one major dimension of such an approach: the *ideological* nature of news in the press. This perspective will be developed within the broader framework of a new multidisciplinary approach to the study of ideology in the social sciences.

DISCOURSE STUDIES

Before we deal with news and ideology, let me briefly recapitulate the theoretical and disciplinary background and some basic principles of a discourse analytical approach to news (see, e.g., Van Dijk, 1997). The new cross-discipline of *discourse studies* has developed since the mid-1960s in most of the humanities and social sciences. This development has taken place more or less at the same time as, and closely related to, the emancipation of several other new interdisciplines in the humanities, such as semiotics, pragmatics, sociolinguistics, and psycholinguistics. Yet, although initially "discourse analysis," just like semiotics, was based on concepts from various strands of structural and functional linguistics, its later developments were inspired by new developments in the social sciences. Thus, anthropology began to pay attention to complex units such as "communicative events," a direction of research commonly referred to as "the ethnography of speaking," particularly influential within linguistic anthropology. Sociology made a profound impact on the study of discourse within its ethnomethodological paradigm, focusing especially on the analysis of conversation and other forms of everyday interaction. And finally, as we shall see below in more detail, discourse studies have since the 1980s been increasingly applied in the field of communication in general and of mass communication in particular.

Although a vast cross-discipline such as discourse studies can hardly be summarized, some of its main tenets are as follows (for details and a wealth of further references, see Schiffrin, Tannen, & Hamilton, 2001; Van Dijk, 1997, 2007):

1. Contrary to traditional linguistics, the study of discourse is not limited to formal grammars or abstract sentences, but focuses on *natural language use* of real language users in real social situations of interaction and communication.
2. The unit of analysis is no longer the word or sentence, as in traditional grammars, but the structures and strategies of "whole" written or spoken *discourses* or *communicative events*.
3. Discourses, analyzed as complex phenomena in their own right (as is also the case for communication), are described at *many levels of structure* and made explicit in terms of a large variety of theories and (sub) disciplines, such as discourse grammar, semantics, stylistics, rhetoric, conversation analysis, narrative analysis, argumentation analysis, pragmatics, semiotics, and so on. These levels may be described by more local, micro-level analyses, on the one hand, and by more global, macro-level analyses, on the other. One basic principle of these analyses is that of *sequentiality*: Each unit at each level (word, sentence, meaning, speech act, turn, etc.) of discourse is produced, interpreted and analyzed as being conditioned by previously interpreted units. As we shall see, this also applies to the analysis of news reports.
4. Discourses are not limited to a "verbal" dimension only, but also have paraverbal and non-verbal dimensions, such as intonation, gestures and facework, on the one hand, and other "semiotic" dimensions such as sounds, music, images, film and other multimodal aspects, on the other hand. In other words, discourse is now understood as a complex multimodal event of interaction and communication.
5. Discourses as language use also presuppose cognitive aspects of production and comprehension, involving various kinds of mental strategies, knowledge, mental models and other representations in memory.
6. Discourses are studied in relation to various kinds of "situation," such as interactional, social, communicative, political, historical and cultural frameworks, interpreted by the participants as relevant "contexts."
7. Discourses are also being studied in the social sciences as social practices that play a crucial role in the reproduction of society in general, and of social communities or groups and their knowledge and ideologies, in particular. As such, discourse analysis has also contributed to the study of the reproduction of racism and other forms of domination and social inequality in society. Indeed, large domains of society, such as politics, the mass media, education, science and law, largely consist of many discourse genres and communicative events in their respective contexts. Thus, scholars in the social sciences often study text or talk, sometimes without awareness of the discursive nature of their data.

We see that the scope of (the objects of) discourse studies has been gradually extended in the last decades, from words to sentences and from sentences to discourses; from syntax to semantics to pragmatics; from microstructures to macrostructures, from monological texts to talk in interaction; from verbal text and talk to multimodal communicative events, from text (and talk) to context, from social discourse and interaction to underlying cognitive processes and representations, and from individual discourse to social systems and domains of discourse and communication.

IDEOLOGY

Many of the observations made above for the complex object of discourse, also apply to the concept of ideology, which equally needs a multidisciplinary approach. This approach may be summarized in the following points (for detail, see Van Dijk, 1998):

1. The original notion of ideology as a "science of ideas" (proposed by Destutt de Tracy at the end of the 18th century) soon received a *negative connotation,* reflected also in the vague concept of "false consciousness" used by Marx and Lenin. This negative meaning has dominated both the study as well as the political applications of the concept of ideology until today, as we know from the work of Mannheim, Lukács, Althusser, Hall, Thompson and Eagleton, among many others.
2. Traditional approaches to ideologies largely ignored the *discursive* and *cognitive* dimension of ideology, despite the fact that ideas (beliefs) and hence ideologies are mental representations, and that ideologies are largely (re)produced by text, talk and communication.
3. A new, *multidisciplinary approach to ideology* should integrate a theory of ideology as a form of *social cognition* (as is also the case for knowledge), a theory of the role of *discourse* in the expression and reproduction of ideology, and a theory of the functions of ideology in *society*, for instance in the (re)production of social *groups* and *group relations.*
4. Such a theory should not define ideologies as inherently negative, because ideologies as socially shared by groups are not only used to legitimate power abuse (domination), but also to bolster resistance, as is the case for the socialist, feminist or pacifist movements.
5. Ideologies are not just any kind of social beliefs, but the fundamental, *axiomatic beliefs* underlying the social representations shared by a group, featuring fundamental *norms* and *values* (such as those of freedom, justice, equality, etc.) which may be used or abused by each social group to impose, defend or struggle for its own *interests* (e.g., freedom of the press, freedom of the market, freedom from discrimination, etc.).
6. Ideologies may be seen as the basis of the (positive) *self-image of a group*, organized by fundamental categories such as the desired (valued, preferred) identity, actions, norms and values, resources and relations to other groups. Characteristic of such ideological structures is the polarization between (positive) Us (the ingroup), and (negative) Them (the outgroup). Thus, journalistic (professional) ideologies are defined in terms of typical actions of newsmaking, values such as press freedom, objectivity, fairness or the protected resource of information, as well as the relations to the readers, sources, news actors and the state.
7. Ideologies control more specific socially shared *attitudes* of groups (for instance, a racist ideology may control racist attitudes about immigration, integration, legislation, and so on).
8. Attitudes (such as those on immigration, divorce, abortion, death penalty, and other important social issues) are general and abstract, and may be more or less known and shared by their members who may "apply" them to form their own *personal opinions* about specific social events. These opinions may however be influenced by various (sometimes contradictory) ideologies as well as by personal *experiences.* That is, unlike relatively stable social group attitudes, personal opinions are unique and contextual: They always depend on the person and the situation at hand.

9. Ideologically influenced personal opinions about concrete events (such as the war in Iraq, or a terrorist bomb attack) are represented in *mental models,* held in Episodic Memory (part of Long Term Memory, as part of people's personal experiences).
10. These *ideologically biased mental models are the basis of ideological discourse,* and may influence all levels of such discourse, from its sounds or visuals, to its syntax, topics, meanings, speech acts, style, rhetoric or interactional strategies.
11. Since the underlying ideologies (and the social attitudes and personal opinions influenced by them) are generally *polarized,* this also tends to be the case for ideological discourse, typically organized by emphasizing the positive representation of Us (the ingroup) and the negative representation of Them (the outgroup)—and its corollary (mitigating the negative representation of Us and the positive representation of Them). We call this combination of general discursive strategies the "Ideological Square."
12. Discourse usually does not express ideologies directly, but via specific group attitudes about social issues and personal opinions about specific events, and under the influence of the communicative situation as subjectively defined by the speakers or writers, that is, by their personal *context models.* Such context models may block or modify (mitigate or amplify) underlying ideological beliefs, when language users adapt to the situation, the audience, and so on. This also explains why ideologies are not always detectable in specific situations (Van Dijk, 2008, 2009).

NEWS AS DISCOURSE

The contemporary study of news has some parallels with the study of ideology: After and besides the more anecdotal accounts of news making and journalistic experiences, the modern study of news was originally mainly oriented toward social dimensions of news, such as news gathering routines and journalistic interactions as well as the organization of newspapers, rather than by cognitive and discursive approaches. The first systematic discursive and cognitive approaches to news structures, news production and news comprehension did not appear until the 1980s.

Thus, based on his earlier work on discourse structure and discourse processing, Van Dijk (1988a, 1988b) proposed a multidisciplinary theory of news, featuring a theory of news schemata defined by conventional categories of news discourse as a genre and social practice: Summary (Headline, Lead), New Events, Previous Events, Context, Commentary, and related categories that globally organize the (macro-level) topics of news reports in the press.

Bell (1991) in his book on language of news media adopted some of these categories, but added—correctly—the Attribution category, in which the writer or source (such as the reporter and his or her byline, the newspaper department, an international agency or a correspondent) may be mentioned, together with the date and place. Also, he mentions the category of Follow-Up as the category that organizes the information of events occurring after the major news event. He also connects such news schema categories with the well-known categories of conventional conversational stories, as investigated by Labov and Waletzky (1967) in their seminal article.

While "news stories" seem to be "stories," they do not have the same schematic (superstructural) organizations as do everyday stories told in conversation: Everyday stories are more or less chronological, whereas news reports are organized by other principles such as relevance, importance and recency. What comes first is the headline and lead, the most important information of the discourse, a summary, as in many conversational stories, but then the story in a news report is delivered in installments—the most important information of each category comes first, followed by the less important information of each category. Also, the *formal* ("syntactic") categories of a news schema (such as Summary or Commentary) should not be confused with the semantic categories of news discourse (such as action, actor, etc.), because this would mean that news discourse has a segment in which only information about an actor is given, which is usually not the case: such information is provided together with information about events or actions.

Specifically relevant for this chapter is Bell's contribution to the study of the ideological dimension of news in the press, for instance with a systematic analysis of how the news may "mis-report" or "mis-represent" events. He emphasizes that such studies should go beyond earlier content analyses, critical linguistics and semiotic analyses by developing more explicit linguistic discourse analysis. He summarizes an earlier study of climate change coverage, in which news reports were sent back to (expert) sources with the request to indicate (in)accuracy. It was found that only 29 percent of the stories were absolutely accurate, 55 percent slightly inaccurate and 16 percent inaccurate (Bell, 1991, p. 217). Besides these quantitative measures of mis-representation, interesting for an ideological analysis of news is especially also *how* the news distorts the "facts" (as defined by the original sources!). Thus, one typical transformation is overstatement, which is of the same general category as overgeneralization as we know it from stereotypes and prejudices or "extreme case" formulations in conversations. In addition to a change of semantic content or meaning, such a structural transformation relation between source discourse and news discourse may also be called *rhetorical*, since rhetoric deals with the way information (meaning, content) is emphasized or de-emphasized—for various reasons. This may be to emphasize the bad characteristics of outgroups or the good ones of ingroups, as we shall see below, but also for dramatic effect: where scholarly discourse tends to hedge, media discourse tends to be much more categorical and exaggerated—with the tacit assumption that readers will be more interested in, or will better remember the "exaggerated" news. Besides misrepresentation, Bell also found various forms of misquotations and misattributions, as well as various forms of mis-editing.

NEWS AS IDEOLOGICAL DISCOURSE

News structure analysis shows us *where* and *how* ideologies preferably manifest themselves in news reports. We have seen above that our new sociocognitive approach explains how underlying ideologies control more specific group attitudes and how personal mental models of journalists about news events control activities of news making, such as assignments, news gathering, interviews, news writing, editing and final make up.

These newsmaking activities are ultimately controlled by the specific, ongoing context model of the journalists about the relevant aspects of the social and political situation. Such context models of newsmaking include current setting (location, deadlines, etc.), news participants (reporters, editors, news actors, sources, etc.) and their roles, as well as current aims, and the social knowledge and ideologies of the participants. This also means that whatever other professional and social ideologies (including norms, news values, etc.) may be at work in news production, the constraints of the now relevant context, as defined by the participants, are the crucial filter that makes news more or less appropriate in the current social and political situation.

IDEOLOGY IN CLASSICAL STUDIES OF NEWS

Given the predominantly social approaches to news discourse, one would expect a vast literature on the ideological nature of news. Surprisingly, nothing is less true. Among the many thousands of articles on media and news in the database of the Social Science Citation Abstracts (World of Knowledge), there are at present (July, 2007) only a dozen titles that feature both keywords "news" and "ideology." And even the few articles whose titles suggest ideological news analysis, hardly deal with ideological news structures in much detail.

What about books? Some of the classical books on news and newsmaking published since the end of the 1970s do feature sections on ideology, but in those studies such accounts of ideology are more general—typically summarizing (neo) Marxist approaches and their influences, rather than integrating the notion in detailed and systematic ideological analyses of news in the press. This is not surprising, because classical theories of ideology were never developed, whether theoretically or practically, to account for language use, discourse and communication.

Interestingly, these pioneering theoretical and empirical studies of news (such as Chibnall, 1977; Fishman, 1980; Gans, 1979; Glasgow University Media Group, 1976, 1980; Golding & Elliott, 1979; Tuchman, 1978) appeared more or less at the same time, nearly thirty years ago, as the first book in critical linguistics, edited by Roger Fowler and his associates (Fowler, Kress, Hodge, & Trew, 1979). This book may be considered as the first study of what later would be called, more broadly, Critical Discourse Analysis (CDA). Fowler is also the author of one of the very few books that would later explicitly deal with news and ideology (Fowler, 1991). In other words, the end of the 1970s appears to be a fertile period of innovation, both in communication studies and in language and discourse studies. This is the period of consolidation of more social scientific and critical approach to language, discourse and communication that had been prepared in the 1970s.

Probably the most detailed, systematic and influential studies of news and ideology of the last decades may be found in the books by the Glasgow University Media Group about television news on industrial strikes (1976, 1980, etc.)—and later on other topics. From the start, this vast empirical project established a link between communication and discourse studies. Thus, in their *More Bad News* (1980) study, the authors emphasize the importance of new developments in linguistics, discourse and conversation analysis: News talk should be studied as a special case of talk in general, and language should not (only) be studied in abstract terms, as is the case of Chomskyan grammars, but should be seen as part of social life. The authors correctly observe that the formal linguistics of the time was hardly prepared to study ideology, and they therefore suggest that we look for inspiration in sociolinguistics, especially as developed by Bernstein, as well as to Sinclair and Coulthard's (1975) ground-breaking book on discourse studies. To the Glasgow Group authors, news making is based on cultural routines and professional practices that are taken for granted and hence implicit and hard to observe directly. Analysis of news talk is therefore able to reveal the (usually not explicit or intentional) ideologies of journalists. However, the authors stress that industrial news does not simply reproduce ruling class propaganda, but is usually open to various interpretations. Despite this ideological ambiguity, a "preferred reading" of actions and events that is inimical to the interests of labour usually emerges. Such preferences are part of a general formula, frame or "restricted code" of reporting social conflicts that implies an ideological defense of the legitimacy of the status quo. The study examines how various properties of television news show both such underlying professional routines and social ideologies. For instance, both in words ("disruption," "strike") and in images, striking workers may be represented negatively, or as a problem for the citizens, but no such negative representation is given of the "actions" of employers (p. 177).

One of the classical studies that pays extensive attention to the role of ideologies in news rooms and news reports is Gitlin's (1980) analysis of media coverage of the students' movement in the United States. Unlike most other US researchers of the same period, he explicitly opts for a neo-Marxist, Gramscian framework, as exemplified by the (then still rather unknown) work of Stuart Hall in the UK, to explain his data. Gitlin, thus, is interested in hegemony in journalism:

> By socialization, and by the bonds of experience and relationships—in other words, by direct corporate and class interests—the owners and managers of the major media are committed to the maintenance of the going system in its main outlines: committed, that is to say, to private property relations which honor the prerogatives of capital; committed to a national security State; committed to reform of selected violations of the moral code through selective action by State agencies; and committed to approving individual success within corporate and bureaucratic structures. (p. 258)

Gitlin, like Gans, finds that the ideologies of editors and reporters are quite similar, as is the case for journalists and most of their sources. In case of conflict, hegemonic boundaries are not overstepped: As he argues, the "work of hegemony, all in all, consists of imposing standardized assumptions over events and conditions that must be "covered" by the dictates of the prevailing in news standards" (p. 264).

Just like the other classical (sociological) books on news of the same period, Gitlin's study emphasizes the routines of newsmaking which make reporting less burdensome. However, to remain credible and responsible in times of social upheaval, journalists may need to cover alternative groups (students, feminists) and thus be partly pulled to an alternative ideological direction. In this way, hegemonic frames may slowly shift if such coverage wants to be credibly consistent with how the world is perceived.

We may conclude from this brief review of the account of ideology in some of the classical books on news of the late 1970s and early 1980s that they *do* pay attention to ideology, but that such attention is largely limited to a relatively brief account of ideologies in the newsroom and of journalists, rather than of the properties of the coverage itself. Also, such an account is given in very general terms, and is not based on a detailed study of the ideologies of journalists. Fieldwork observations are the basis of the account of the general ideological consensus in the newsroom, and of the boundaries of possible variation under hegemonic influence of the newspaper as a bureaucracy and a business enterprise. These newsroom observations remain rather general, and hardly inquire into the ideological details of news values, news beats, interactions with sources, news formats, styles and contents, among other aspects of news making. In that sense, most investigations are contemporary studies of the sociology of bureaucratic and organizational routines and taken for granted knowledge and values. They do not provide sociocognitive and discursive analyses of the details of professional and other social ideologies, and how these impact on news production and news discourse.

CONTEMPORARY STUDIES OF NEWS AND IDEOLOGIES

The ideological backlash in the America of presidents Reagan and Bush—father and son—during the 1980s and 1990s was soon disturbed by the Gulf War and then 9/11 and the Iraq war—giving rise to renewed ideological critique of the news media. Whereas communism and anticommunism defined the ideologies of the Cold War, and the media had to confront the new ideologies of resistance, namely those of feminism, antiracism and pacifism, the last decade has seen the substitution of anticommunism by a compound mixture of antiterrorism and anti-Islamism, with a continuing undercurrent of old anti-Arab racism. Such ideologies were not just those of radical neo-liberal hawks, but due to the tragic events of 9/11 could be spread and inculcated among many ordinary people as well, not least in the media. Nationalism, patriotism and jingoism thus combined with the ideologies mentioned above to form the basis of an obsession with "homeland security" on the one hand, and the legitimation of the Iraq war, on the other. The media, as well as their contemporary critics, thus faced an ideological situation that was more complex than that of straightforward anticommunism, and that had only marginally gone beyond the standard dominant ideologies of race, gender and class challenged by the civil rights and feminist movements of the 1960s and 1970s.

Whereas classical studies focus on newsmaking, contemporary studies also pay attention to the effects and consequences of news. Van Dijk (1988b) presented a general theory of news structures, as organized by specific news schemas, as well as a theory of news production as special forms of (source) discourse processing.

Further, he also offered a series of critical case studies, including one of international news and local opposition groups, such as squatters in Amsterdam (Van Dijk, 1988a). The same book also features a vast case study for UNESCO of the international coverage in hundreds of newspapers in dozens of languages covering co-occurring major events of mid-September 1982 (the assassination of president-elect Bechir Gemayel of Lebanon, the occupation of Beirut by Israel and the accidental death of the Princess of Monaco, Grace Kelly). The results first of all showed that ideological differences in the accounts were less stark than expected. For instance, the coverage of the assassination of Gemayel in (then) communist *Pravda* of Moscow, *Renmin Ribao* (*People's Daily*) in China or *Granma* of Cuba, and in much of the (anticommunist) western press, showed many more similarities than ideologically based differences. It was concluded that the (Western) international news agencies on which most of these stories were based seem to successfully promote a global story format for the coverage of such events. The ideological slant of the communist papers was clearly against (the role of) Israel, but such a bias merely showed in a few negative labels such as "Zionist" to refer to Israeli forces. Similarly, arch conservative Chilean *El Mercurio* (supporting Pinochet's military regime) hardly reported negatively on the (violent) history of Falangist Gemayel. Overall, differences in style and content were more marked by other ideological dimensions, such as those between popular and quality newspapers within the same country.

The 1990s also witnessed the publication of some more specific articles on news and ideology. Meeuwis (1993) examined nationalist ideologies in reporting on the war in Yugoslavia—and especially focused on the unchallenged beliefs about ethnicity and interculturality. Kitis and Milapides (1997) advocated a detailed critical analysis of (also) the higher levels of news texts instead of a focus on local grammar or on production conditions of news. In a detailed analysis of a *Time* article about Greece, they show how one metaphor may dominate many of the syntactic and semantic properties of that article. Kuo and Nakamura (2005) compared how two ideologically different papers in Taiwan gave a different account of the same event, namely an interview with the Taiwanese First Lady. Although based on the same text in English (occasioned by her visit to the United States), the newspapers produced systematically distinct translations of the First Lady's interview in headlines; what is included or excluded, as well as differences of lexical choice, among other discourse properties. The authors show that such specific linguistic differences of news report may be explained in terms of the re-unification vs. independence ideologies of the two newspapers.

Van Dijk (1995) examined the relations between discourse semantics and ideology. In this contribution he provided a detailed analysis of news articles in the *New York Times* and *The Washington Post* and showed how various aspects of discourse semantics, such as topic, focus, propositional structures, local coherence, level of description, lexical items, implications and macrostructure may be influenced by underlying ideologies in the United States, for instance on Arabs. Following the overall strategy of the ideological square, the latter may be described in *New York Times* editorials as "terrorists," a description never used to describe Israelis killing Palestinians. Such polarized hyperboles for one side of the conflict, as well as the use of mitigated expressions for the description of friends, allies or other ingroup members, also extend to the pragmatic level, where friendly regimes who abuse human rights are typically *recommended* to mend their ways in the softest of speech acts. In a systematic analysis of an op-ed article on Gadhafi by Jim Hoagland in the *Washington Post*, the author showed how various semantics structures, such as focus, topic-comment, foregrounding-backgrounding and related strategies of information distribution in discourse are influenced by the (conservative, anti-Arab, etc.) ideologies of the writer. Thus, not only are the negative actions of the Libyan "tyrant" and his "megalomania" highlighted in this article, his agency and responsibility are also pointed out through various strategies of foregrounding.

Scholars have already suggested that dominant political ideologies in various countries, as shared by the media, also explain differences in the account of international events: Enemy states and friendly states or allies are of course systematically covered in a different way, as Herman and Chomsky (1988) have shown. Fang (1994) shows this for *Renmin Ribao* and its coverage of riots and violence in countries that have friendly or inimical relations with China. For instance, opposition in countries that are inimical to China may typically be represented as "demonstration," "struggle" or "protest," whereas such mass action in friendly countries tends to be described as "clashes" or "riots." Such tendencies may even be more pronounced in syntactic structure: Police action in inimical countries is largely described in the active voice, thus emphasizing the responsibility of the police (violence), whereas the passive voice tends to be used for police action in non-hostile countries inculcated thus reducing the active responsibility of the police.

NEWS PRODUCTION AND IDEOLOGICAL CONTROL

Not only is there a lack of an explicit theory of ideology, but we do not have at our disposal a detailed theory of discourse and a sociocognitive theory that explains how ideologies control processes of news production. Whatever the value of existing studies for our understanding of news production routines, news values or power relationships, they remain theoretically incomplete when it comes to providing a detailed account of the ideologies involved and the structures of news that are controlled by them. Given the aims of this chapter and this section, we shall now focus more on ideologically controlled news structures in general terms, rather than on the nature of the ideologies themselves, or on the (vast quantity of) individual authors and studies.

Racism and the News

International research on racism and the mass media has consistently shown that despite considerable variation among countries, periods and newspapers, the press continues to be part of the problem of racism, rather than its solution. These ideological influences of racism on newsmaking may be summarized by the following main findings of research (for details, see, e.g., Bonnafous, 1991; Cottle, 2000; Hartmann & Husband, 1974; Henry & Tator, 2002; Husband, 1975; Jäger & Link, 1993; Martindale, 1986; Richardson, 2004; Ruhrmann, 1995; Said, 1981; Smitherman-Donaldson & Van Dijk, 1987; Ter Wal, 2002; Van Dijk, 1991, 1993; UNESCO 1974, 1977; among many other books and a vast number of articles):

1. *Hiring:* Many forms of ethnic bias defined below are crucially influenced by the fact that in *all* white-dominated societies, ethnic journalists are discriminated against in hiring, so that most newsrooms are predominantly white. And those (few) minorities being hired will tend to be recruited not only for their outstanding professionalism, but also because their ethnic ideologies (and especially their moderate antiracism) do not clash with those of the editors.

2. *News values:* Events are attributed higher news values if they are about "our own" people or when "our own" people are involved, whether or not these are "closer" geographically.
3. *Beats and sources:* In ethnic or racial conflicts, white elite sources are consistently given priority, attributed higher credibility, found more reliable and (hence) are more likely to be quoted as such.
4. *Selection:* Available news stories are more likely to be selected for inclusion not only if they are about people like us (see News values), but also when they are consistent with prevalent ethnic and racial stereotypes, as is the case for rioting blacks in the UK, black dictators in Africa or the terrorism of (Arab) Islamists.
5. *Salience* (placement and lay-out): News stories about ethnic-racial Others (minorities, immigrants, refugees, etc.) are distributed over the newspaper and the page not only by criteria of relative social or political importance or relevance, but also by ethnic-racial criteria: As a general rule, news about bad actions of Them, especially against (people like) Us, is more salient than the reverse.
6. *Topics:* Whereas (people like) Us may be represented as actors in virtually all kinds of news stories and on a large variety of social, political and economic topics, the coverage of Them tends to be limited to a few issues and topics, such as immigration, integration and race relations, crime, violence and deviance, cultural conflicts and entertainment (music, sports).
7. *Perspective:* Another global constraint on news stories is the ethnocentric perspective in the description of news events. Ethnic conflicts, problems of integration and cultural differences, for instance, tend to be represented from "our" (white) perspective, for instance in terms of Them not being able or wanting to adapt to Us, instead of vice versa.
8. *Formats, order and foregrounding:* Whereas topics are the global meaning of discourse, schemas define their overall format and order, such as the distinction between Headlines, Leads, and other categories of news (Main Events, Context, Background, History, Reactions, etc.). We find that negative actions and events of ethnic minorities or other non-European Others, for example, are not only preferably placed in the prominent positions of Headlines and Leads (because they are defined as topics), but also foregrounded in the overall order and categories of news reports.
9. *Quotation:* Given the ethnic bias of beats and source selection and evaluation, it may be predicted that those who are quoted as reliable sources or spokespersons tend to be Our (white) elites, rather than Their elites or spokespersons.
10. *News actor and event description:* Ethnic Others tend to be described more often in negative terms, whereas people like Us tend to be described positively or more neutrally, even when engaging in negative actions.
11. *Style:* At the more manifest levels of style, such as the selection of words, sentence syntax and other variable expressions of underlying global topics and local meanings, we find that lexical items used to describe Others and their actions tend to have more negative connotations.
12. *Rhetoric:* All properties of news described above may be emphasized or de-emphasized by well-known rhetorical figures, such as metaphors, hyperboles and euphemisms. Thus, the arrival of Others in Our country is consistently represented in terms of large quantities of threatening water: *waves*, *floods*, etc. and Their immigration as *invasion*, etc. On the other hand, Our racism will usually be described in terms of mitigating euphemisms, for instance in terms of *popular discontent* or as political *populism*, or reduced to less negative notions such as *discrimination*, *national preference* or *bias*.

Nationalism in the News

Journalists often identify not only with a language but also with a nation state, and in nationalist ideologies, the positive self-image is in terms of *Us* in our country, on the one hand, and *Them* in (or from) other countries, on the other hand, as we also have seen for racist ideologies, with which nationalist ideologies are closely related. In nationalist ideologies, identity is crucial, and associated with a complex system of positive characteristics about how we are, about our history and habits, our language and culture, national character, and so on (Wodak, de Cillia, Reisigl, & Liebhart, 1998).

As suggested above, nationalist ideologies also influence news and newsmaking, especially when journalists write about "foreign" events and people or about situations of wars, conflicts, terrorist attacks and international competitions. It is well-known that wars are not covered in terms of a mere conflict, but in strongly polarized terms, between (good) Us and (bad) Them, as soon as "our" country is at war, and "our" soldiers' are involved (Adams, 1986; Glasgow University Media Group, 1985 ; Hutcheson, Domke, Billeaudeaux, & Garland, 2004; Lewis, 2005; Morrison & Tumber, 1988; Schechter, 2005; Zelizer & Allan, 2003).

The norms and values associated with nationalism are those of patriotism and loyalty—especially made relevant in times of crisis or war. And the typical ("good") actions recommended by nationalist ideologies is to defend the nation against invaders and foreign influences, both military and economic as well as cultural (language, arts, etc.). The most precious resource of the nationalist, thus, is on the one hand, "our land," territory, etc., and on the other hand the symbolic resources of "our" culture, language, etc.

Nationalism is not merely manifested in times of war or serious conflicts, but also in many everyday news events. Thus, the nation may be "flagged" in many mundane ways in everyday discourse and also in the media (Billig, 1995). This may happen in the coverage of the actions of "our" politicians in international affairs, beauty contests reference to well-known national businesses and their products, as well as other symbols of "our" nation or culture: movies, film stars, writers, painters, and of course, in some countries, the Royal Family (Billig, 1992, 1995). Specifically prone to nationalist coverage in the mass media is that of international sport (Blain, Boyle, & O'Donnell, 1993).

Sexism and the News

Much of what has been said above regarding racist ideologies and their influence on the news also applies to patriarchal gender ideologies such as sexism or male chauvinism. By definition, the structure of the dominant ideology of sexism as an ideology is also polarized, as between Us (men) and Them (women), and especially between Us ("real" men) and Them (feminists). However, sexist ideologies are not limited to men, but may also be shared by those women who agree with (at least some) sexist attitudes. The structures of sexist ideologies are thus polarized between positive self-descriptions of men (e.g., as strong, independent, etc.) and other-descriptions of women (e.g., as weak, dependent, etc.), hence defining opposed identities, the characteristic activities of men vs. women, different norms and values, and different resources that define the power position of men in society.

Few of the studies of gender and news specifically focus on underlying ideologies. Rather, classical news values are discussed as the basis for discrimination in the newsroom, assignments and beats, sources and quotations, the style of coverage (objective vs. emotional), the type of stories, and so on. It is not easy to infer a detailed ideological system from such discussions, but the following gender-ideological propositions seem to have inspired these classical news values, the hierarchy of newspapers as organizations, the organization of beats and assignments, as well as the overall topics and style of representing women and men (see, among many other references, the following books: Beyerly & Ross, 2006; Carter, Branston, & Allan, 1998; Cole & Henderson Daniel, 2005):

- Men are stronger (tougher, etc.) than women.
- Men are more competent than women.
- Men are more reliable than women.
- Men are more objective than women.
- Men's issues are more important than women's issues.
- Women (e.g., feminists) actively resisting the dominant patriarchal order are bad women.
- Women who directly compete with men (such as political candidates) are a threat to male domination.
- Women as victims are "good" women only if they have behaved appropriately, if not they are "bad girls" who deserve what they get.
- Men as perpetrators of violence against women have been provoked by women, or are victims of circumstances beyond their control.

CONCLUSIONS

As is the case for most public discourse, the news is imbued with ideologies. A detailed study of such ideologies in the mass media and other forms of public elite discourse contributes to our insights into their very reproduction in society. The review of theoretical and empirical research in this chapter leaves no doubt about the prominent role of the news media in the (re)production of ideologies in society. The evidence shows that on the whole, despite some variation between different (liberal vs. conservative, and popular vs. elite) newspapers, these dominant ideologies are associated with the very position and power of white, male, middle class journalists working within a corporate environment. Women, poor people, workers, black people, immigrants, and all those who have no access to, and control over public discourse are thus largely ignored, or represented negatively when seen as a problem or a threat to the social mainstream. To sustain existing powers, polarized (Us vs. Them) ideologies are necessarily aligned along fundamental dimensions of society, such as those of class, gender, and race (and the same is true for age and sexual orientation, not dealt with in this chapter). The elites that control the access to, and the contents and structures of public discourse, and that of the mass media, in particular, thus also are able to control the formation and reproduction of the very ideologies that help to sustain their power.

Such a conclusion is hardly new. However, so far it was rather a general assumption than proven in detail by a theoretically based analysis of ideologies, on the one hand, and of news reports, on the other hand. The study of social cognition, as well as the explicit analysis of text and talk was hardly mainstream in the social sciences in general and in communication and journalism studies in particular. This chapter has shown that a more sophisticated, multidisciplinary theory of news production, news structures and news reception, combined with new theories of ideology as social cognition and of news reports and news production as specific social and discursive practices, is able to account for the detailed mechanisms of the reproduction of ideologies by the mass media in general and by daily news reports in particular.

Unfortunately, most of the studies reviewed in this chapter (as well as in other chapters of this book) are not yet formulated in such a broad, explicit and multidisciplinary framework and limited to more traditional methods, such as content or frame analysis. Yet, even so they provide sufficient evidence for our general conclusions about the role of news in the reproduction of sexism, racism, classism, and nationalism. Future studies will then be able to provide even more detailed and explicit analyses of news production routines and news report structures that provide insight into the deeper mechanisms of ideological reproduction in public discourse.

REFERENCES

Adams, V. (1986). *The media and the Falklands campaign.* London: Macmillan.

Bell, A. (1991). *The language of news media.* Oxford, UK: Blackwell.

Beyerly, C. M., & Ross, K. (2006). *Women & media: A critical introduction.* Oxford: Blackwell.

Billig, M. (1992). *Talking of the royal family.* London: Routledge.

Billig, M. (1995). *Banal nationalism.* London: Sage.

Bonnafous, S. (1991). *L'immigration prise aux mots.* Paris: Éditions Kimé.

Carter, C., Branston, G., & Allan, S. (Eds.). (1998). *News, gender, and power.* London: Routledge.

Chibnall, S. (1977). *Law-and-order news: An analysis of crime reporting in the British press.* London: Tavistock.

Cole, E., & Henderson Daniel, J. (Eds.). (2005). *Featuring females: Feminist analyses of media.* Washington, DC: American Psychological Association.

Cottle, S. (Ed.). (2000). *Ethnic minorities and the media.* Buckingham, UK: Open University Press.

Fishman, M. (1980). *Manufacturing the news.* Austin: University of Texas Press.

Fowler, R. (1991). *Language in the news. Discourse and ideology in the British press.* London: Routledge.

Fowler, R., Kress, G., Hodge, B., & Trew, T. (1979). *Language and control.* London: Routledge & Kegan Paul.

Gans, H. J. (1979). *Deciding what's news. A study of CBS evening news, NBC nightly news, Newsweek, and Time.* New York: Pantheon Books.

Gitlin, T. (1980). *The whole world is watching: Mass media in the making & unmaking of the New Left.* Berkeley: University of California Press.

Glasgow University Media Group. (1976). *Bad news.* London Boston: Routledge & Kegan Paul.

Glasgow University Media Group. (1980). *More bad news.* London: Routledge & Kegan Paul.

Golding, P., & Elliott, P. (1979). *Making the news.* London: Longman.

Hartmann, P. G., & Husband, C. (1974). *Racism and the mass media: A study of the role of the mass media in the formation of white beliefs and attitudes in Britain.* Totowa, NJ: Rowman & Littlefield.

Henry, F., & Tator, C. (2002). *Discourses of domination. Racial bias in the Canadian English-language press.* Toronto: University of Toronto Press.

Herman, E. S., & Chomsky, N. (1988). *Manufacturing consent: The political economy of the mass media.* New York: Pantheon Books.

Husband, C. (1975). *White media and black Britain: A critical look at the role of the media in race relations today.* London: Arrow.

Hutcheson, J., Domke, D., Billeaudeaux, A., & Garland, P. (2004). US national identity, political elites, and a patriotic press following September 11. *Political Communication, 21*(1), 27–50.

Jäger, S., & Link, J. (1993). *Die vierte gewalt. Rassismus und die medien* (The fourth power. racism and the media). Duisburg, Germany: DISS.

Kitis, E., & Milapides, M. (1997). Read it and believe it: How metaphor constructs ideology in news discourse: A case-study. *Journal of Pragmatics, 28*(5), 557–590.

Kuo, S. H., & Nakamura, M. (2005). Translation or transformation? A case study of language and ideology in the Taiwanese press. *Discourse & Society, 16*(3), 393–417.

Labov, W., & Waletzky, J. (1967). Narrative analysis. Oral versions of personal experience. In J. Helm, (Ed.), *Essays on the verbal and visual arts* (pp. 12–44). Seattle: University of Washington Press,

Lewis, J. (2005). *Shoot first and ask questions later. Media coverage of the 2003 Iraq war.* New York: Peter Lang.

Martindale, C. (1986). *The white press and Black America.* Westport, CT: Greenwood Press.

Meeuwis, M. (1993). Nationalist ideology in news reporting on the Yugoslav crisis: A pragmatic analysis. *Journal of Pragmatics, 20*(3), 217–237.

Morrison, D. E., & Tumber, H. (1988). *Journalists at war: The dynamics of news reporting during the Falklands conflict*. London: Sage.

Richardson, J. E. (2004). *(Mis)representing Islam. The racism and rhetoric of British broadsheet newspapers*. Philadelphia: John Benjamins.

Ruhrmann, G. (Ed.). (1995). *Das Bild der Ausländer in der Öffentlichkeit. Eine theoretische und empirische Analyse zur Fremdenfeindlichkeit* (The image of foreigners in the public sphere. A theoretical and empirical analysis of xenophobia). Opladen, Germany: Leske.

Said, E. W. (1981). *Covering Islam: How the media and the experts determine how we see the rest of the world*. New York: Pantheon.

Schechter, D. (2005). *When news lies. Media complicity and the Iraq war*. New York: SelectBooks.

Schiffrin, D., Tannen, D., & Hamilton, H. E. (Eds.). (2001). *The handbook of discourse analysis*. Malden, MA: Blackwell.

Sinclair, J., & Coulthard, M. (1975). *Towards an analysis of discourse: The English used by teachers and pupils*. London: Oxford University Press.

Smitherman-Donaldson, G., & Van Dijk, T. A. (Eds.). (1987). *Discourse and discrimination*. Detroit, MI: Wayne State University Press.

Ter Wal, J. (Ed.). (2002). *Racism and cultural diversity in the mass media. An overview of research and examples of good practice in the EU member states, 1995–2000*. Vienna: European Monitoring Center on Racism and Xenophobia.

Tuchman, G. (1978). *Making news: A study in the construction of reality*. New York: Free Press.

UNESCO. (1974). *Race as news*. Paris: Unesco.

UNESCO. (1977). *Ethnicity and the media*. Paris: Unesco.

Van Dijk, T. A. (1988a). *News analysis: Case studies of international and national news in the press*. Hillsdale, NJ: Erlbaum

Van Dijk, T. A. (1988b). *News as discourse*. Hillsdale, NJ: Erlbaum.

Van Dijk, T. A. (1991). *Racism and the press*. London: Routledge.

Van Dijk, T. A. (1993). *Elite discourse and racism*. Newbury Park, CA: Sage.

Van Dijk, T. A. (1995). Discourse semantics and ideology. *Discourse & Society, 6*(2), 243–289.

Van Dijk, T. A. (1998). *Ideology. A multidisciplinary approach*. London: Sage.

Van Dijk, T. A. (2008). *Discourse and context. A sociocognitive approach*. Cambridge, UK: Cambridge University Press.

Van Dijk, T. A. (2009). *Society in discourse. How context controls text and talk*. Cambridge, UK: Cambridge University Press.

Van Dijk, T. A. (Ed.). (1997). *Discourse studies. A multidisciplinary introduction* (2 vols.). London: Sage.

Van Dijk, T. A. (Ed.). (2007). *Discourse studies* (5 vols.). London: Sage.

Wodak, R., de Cillia, R., Reisigl, M., & Liebhart, K. (1998). *The discursive construction of national identity*. Edinburgh: Edinburgh University Press.

Zelizer, B., & Allan, S. (Eds.). (2003). *Journalism after September 11*. London: Routledge.

15

Rethinking News and Myth as Storytelling

S. Elizabeth Bird and Robert W. Dardenne

In 1988, we explored the idea that news is not merely objective reporting of fact, but also a form of storytelling that functions in a mythological way (Bird & Dardenne, 1988). We argued that journalists operate like traditional storytellers, using conventional structures to shape events into story—and in doing so define the world in particular ways that reflect and reinforce audiences' notions of reality. Journalism, more than myth, is part of rational discourse that facilitates informed citizenship; nevertheless, we argued that we must better understand the narrative construction and mythological function of news to fully comprehend the ideological way in which it operates in any culture. We built on earlier work by journalism scholars such as Schudson (1982), who interrogated the core journalistic concept of objectivity. Here, we trace the context of scholarly interest in journalism as myth and storytelling, address how it has been applied through the last several decades, and offer suggestions for future research. Such scholarship, it should be noted, has consistently applied an interpretive approach, following the tradition of anthropologists like Geertz (1973), rather than that of journalism scholars working in a social scientific tradition.

THE CONTEXT

Journalism scholars critique news in many ways, but a central thread involves questions around truth and accuracy. The ideal of objectivity holds that particular journalistic techniques can produce accurate, if not necessarily complete, accounts of events. News "bias" suggests that a "true" account potentially exists, but that various influences lead journalists to produce other than objective reports. Journalistic ideals of objectivity differ from those of positivistic social sciences, but the philosophical approach is similar. We see journalism studies operating within that larger context in the 1960s, 1970s, and into the 1980s, which saw an increase in critiques of positivism and increased doubts about the possibility of reaching truth through empirical description. Berger and Luckmann (1967) popularized the concept that reality is socially constructed, a notion that spread through the social sciences and humanities. Historians such as Mink (1987) rejected the idea that history is "out there" waiting to be described, instead asserting that historians produce history through narrative art. White (1980) and Fisher (1987) suggested that the impulse to tell stories is a universal human characteristic, and the notion of *homo narrans*, or "man the storyteller," permeated scholarship across disciplines (Mechling, 1991).

Clifford and Marcus (1986) integrated threads of a growing movement in anthropology that became known as the "crisis of representation," which argued that ethnography, rather than being a scientific account of culture, is another form of constructed narrative. In the 1980s and 90s, post-modernist theorists attempted to deconstruct the nature of truth and reality, and within this context journalism scholars seriously approached news as a form of constructed reality (although Lippmann [1922] had explored this idea earlier). Simultaneous with this ferment came increasing interest in the study of myth as a particular kind of narrative. The Jungian-inspired writings of Campbell (e.g., 1949), which focused on universal archetypes, spurred huge popular interest, manifested in such popular culture icons as *Star Wars*, video games, and countless other phenomena. Scholarly work on myth flourished in the prolific writing of Eliade (e.g., 1963) and Lévi-Strauss (e.g., 1968), while Barthes (1972), bridging popular and scholarly discourse, drew much-needed attention to myth's ideological function.

NEWS AS MYTH

We distinguish between the two clearly related ideas of "news as myth" and "news as storytelling." Myth has been defined in hundreds of ways, although all definitions address the functional role of myth in providing enduring narratives that help maintain a sense of continuity and order in the world, regardless of whether these narratives describe fantastical gods and creatures, or "real" people. Individual news stories don't function like individual myths, but as a communication process, news as a body may function like myth. As we wrote in 1988, "Myth reassures by telling tales that explain [...] phenomena and provide acceptable answers; myth does not necessarily reflect an objective reality, but builds a world of its own" (p. 70). For example, one function of myth is to explain that which cannot be easily explained—the rise and fall of the stock market and the economy, or even the weather—as well as more intangible things, such as notions of morality, appropriateness, and fairness. This, we argued, was a function of people's intolerance for randomness, inexplicability and ambiguity. The same impulses that drove the shaman to create stories to explain events, and people to need such stories, drive journalists and their audiences today. In the sense that myth comforts, news also comforts, and provides a sense of control.

In the 1980s, Knight and Dean (1982) looked at the mythical structure of news, and the seminal work of Carey (1975) established the need to view news as a whole, with significant ritual functions, rather than seeing each story as distinct. Later, Kitch (2000; 2003) demonstrated persuasively the role of news in "civil religion," during which journalists and the public converge in ritualistic moments, such as mourning after September 11, 2001. Her analysis of post-September 11 news magazines suggests that the story assumed the three-stage structure of a funeral, in which millions of Americans participated through national news media, making it "an 'American' story in symbolic ways that went beyond the fact of war" (2003, p. 222).

Discussion of the mythological frame focuses on universalities, which helps advance an understanding of the communal, celebratory role of news. News plays a cultural role analogous to that of myth by using familiar, recurring narrative patterns that help explain why it seems simultaneously novel, yet soothingly predictable. Lule (2001) elaborately developed the idea by tracing a series of mythical archetypes in the *New York Times*. He argued (again) for understanding news as recurring myth, and made journalists' role as "scribes" analogous to ancient bards: "The daily news is the primary vehicle for myth in our time" (p. 19). Like others (e.g., Langer, 1998; Corcoran, 1986) he describes how hero, trickster, good mother, and flood archetypes play out in news stories, couched in familiar and comfortable formulae. We agree that this is an important point, yet it has significant limitations.

At least in Lule's case, we think one problem is the dependence on such popular thinkers as

Campbell. We agree with Levi-Strauss (1968) and others that near-universal themes in folklore and myth exist in different times and places throughout the world, as perusal of the folk tale type and motif indexes confirm (Aarne, 1928; Thompson, 1975). However, scholars, even those who study folklore, rarely use these indexes other than to note that a familiar theme has popped up in yet another narrative. This still interests, but theoretically, it no longer advances discussion, which we think can be accomplished by asking how a given narrative speaks to and about the specific circumstances in which we now find it. The "universalist" approach pays scant attention to differences in time and place that produce particular cultural moments and narratives, rooted in particular histories. As Scherr (2004) comments, Lule's "mythic model often employs generalities that obscure as much as they explain" (p. 430). How does it help us, for example, to see Mike Tyson as an archetypal trickster (Lule, 2001), especially when, as Coman (2005) writes, he could as easily be seen as an archetypal scapegoat? We agree with Coman that while "the investigations into the relationship between myth and news story [...] are often persuasive and exciting [...] they have not generated a complete theory [...] or an intense and homogeneous current of research" (p. 119).

NEWS AS STORYTELLING

Appreciation of news as myth provides a framework to attain a deeper cultural understanding of news if we root analyses in the particular. The universal impulse toward story or storytelling seems as strong as ever in contemporary culture. Consider professional wrestling, which enhanced its popularity and involved fans in interactive debate by adding sometimes elaborate storylines to its conventional conflict between two simplistically "good" or "evil" protagonists (McBride & Bird, 2007). Video games, once mostly testing players' abilities to search and destroy, and the hugely popular Massive Multiplayer Online Role-Playing Games (MMORPG's), now allow players to participate in often complex storylines frequently drawn from cultural stocks of mythological themes. And in journalism, although the conventional inverted pyramid remains dominant, reporters make extensive use of story, especially with the ubiquitous anecdotal lead (Black, 2001) or in more consciously narrative writing that draws on the traditions of "new" or "literary" journalism and fiction (see Boyton, 2005; Kerrane & Yagoda, 1998). Reality television, which grew out of "tabloid TV" news, seeks to engage viewers by employing essentially a series of mini-stories, which, like news, bask in the aura of "truth." A "story" is different from a simple chronological account, because it seeks coherence and meaning; a story has a point, and it exists within a cultural lexicon of understandable themes.

Scholars have long analyzed news as a form of storytelling. Several authors note that as a genre, news is indebted to oral traditions, popular ballads, broadsheets, and so on (Bird, 1992; Dardenne, 1990, 1998; Ettema & Glasser, 1988). Early attempts to explore these ideas included Hughes' (1968) pioneering study of the human interest story, in which she noted that particular stories, such as that of "the lost child," recur, each feeding into those that follow and determining perception and development of "the story." In 1975, Darnton wrote an oft-cited essay of his experience in a *New York Times* newsroom showing how journalists used mythic themes and providing a personal example of how they obtained quotes for particular, standard stories: "When I needed such quotes I used to make them up, as did some of the others [...] for we knew what the bereaved mother and the mourning father should have said, and possibly even heard them speak what was in our minds rather than in theirs" (p. 190).

By the 1980s, many writers were exploring ideas of news as narrative, both in academic and professional publications. For example, Sibbison (1988) concluded that mainstream publications like *Newsweek*, the *Los Angeles Times*, and the *Boston Globe* consistently cover medical stories according to the conventions of the "medical breakthrough story" even when not justified by the facts. Barkin (1984) sketched out the basic claim that journalists are bardic storytellers. Ettema and Glasser (1988, p. 11) applied the theories of Mink and White to conclude that

> investigative journalism defends traditional virtue by telling stories of terrible vice [...]Investigative journalism maintains and sometimes updates consensual interpretations of right and wrong, innocence and guilt, by applying them to the case in hand, though it seldom analyzes or critiques such interpretations.

Ettema and Glasser's work was important in underlining the idea that news is a "moralizing" form of discourse that can actually be damaging to rational and deliberative consideration of significant social issues. The same year, we attempted to bring together most of the current scholarship on news as narrative, offering what we hoped was a coherent theoretical framework for the understanding of news as storytelling, and suggesting, like Ettema and Glasser, that the impulse to tell stories may lead journalists to frame the world in conventional ways that often reinforce existing ideologies.

The "journalism as story" concept resonated across disciplines. In public health, Golden (2000) analyzed consequences of a news story about a bartender refusing to serve alcohol to a pregnant woman. A major public debate centered on the responsibilities of women and society over fetuses, with large narrative arcs developing about victims (women or fetuses?) and villains (women or repressive moralists?). She took myth and story beyond identification of over-arching themes into analyses of how those themes operate in specific cases, and how this affects people's lives and public policy. Similarly, Bird (2003) looked at the life cycle of a story about a supposed mystery woman deliberately infecting men with AIDS. The story, which had huge impact at the peak of fear about AIDS in the mid-1990s, evoked archetypical themes that have surfaced throughout history—the exotic and dangerous woman, the power of the seductress. Much of its power derived from ancient stereotypes and fears; however, immediate circumstances of the early 1990s attributed just as significantly to its impact. It did active cultural work at that moment, in that place, speaking to that time period's fears about race, gender, and sexual practices.

Cross-cultural comparisons benefit from close analysis of narrative technique when the question becomes: How are the stories of one culture different from one another, rather than the conventional: How are we all the same? Wardle (2003) compares numerous journalistic narratives about Theodore Kaczynksi (the US "Unabomber") and David Copeland (the UK "Nailbomber")—both diagnosed as paranoid schizophrenics and tried for similar crimes in widely covered trials. Wardle concludes that British news coverage privileged the "story of the crime," while US news focused on "the story of the trial," with neither exploring significant issues of mental illness the cases raised. Wardle's exemplary study moves from detailed analysis of individual stories to interpret "the story" of the events, but without asking the next logical question—*Why* the difference between the two cultural contexts? This area holds great potential for narrative analysis, which could explore central themes distinct to particular cultural contexts. However, scholars rarely analyze news across cultures, in part because of the daunting task of describing "news" in more than one culture and linking it to known cultural themes. Occasionally, anthropologists touch on these questions. Kottak (1990) contrasts Brazilian and US national television news, showing how each focuses on civics, the nation-state, and international affairs, but balances them differently. Brazilian news often plays up stories focusing on US technologies (reproductive, for example) that are viewed as hostile to traditional local values. He argues that this theme confirms for Brazilians "the stereotype of American society as developed but flawed

[...] American culture sometimes carries its know-how and inventiveness to inhumane extremes" (p. 92). Analyses like this could go further, linking identified themes to larger and more deep-rooted characteristics of specific cultures.

WHOSE STORY?

Whose story is being told? Archetypal, mythic analysis cannot answer that question because it assumes that at some level they are all "our stories." Effective news speaks to the audience through story frames that resonate. News/myth, in invoking ancient characters and themes, clearly unifies people around shared values. Mythological analyses almost by definition affirm the status quo, because that is what myth does. And here lies the danger of journalists functioning like bards, who themselves served those in power. Ettema (2005) discusses journalistic accounts of a homeowner gunning down a trick-or-treating Japanese exchange student he thought was an intruder. The story resonated in Japan as a representation of horrific American violence, and in the United States as a gun rights issue. Eventually, Ettema argues, the US press and government effectively "normalized" the killing, fitting it within expected narratives of right and wrong.

Stories help construct the world, and those in power benefit from constructing the world in specific ways—engaging the audience, but also overshadowing or eliminating competing narratives. We don't mean to suggest, along the lines of the Frankfurt School, that government deliberately provides "bread and circuses" to keep us from thinking about important issues. Nevertheless, some huge and arguably frivolous narratives that dominate the media could be said to serve that purpose. Stories about Anna Nicole Smith, the "runaway bride," and the tribulations of Brittney Spears or Paris Hilton produce massive amounts of attractively open-ended speculation that makes such tales gripping. And such stories sometimes interrogate morality, while evoking time-honored formulae (Bird 2003). Editors find these stories easy, cheap, and popular. It may not be a conspiracy, but in this competitive, digital environment in which news organizations struggle to maintain independence and profit levels, the cheap, easy, and popular story often wins out over the expensive, difficult, and less popular one.

Some stories, however, actively feed the agendas of those in power, and more acute danger comes from conscious manipulation by those who supply the motifs upon which journalists build those narratives. High profile narratives of terrorism and war provide dramatic examples. Those in power desperately need to define the story of the deeply contested Iraq war and their skill in framing it in familiar, resonant themes greatly increases their chances of success. The first Bush administration succeeded in the first Gulf War (e.g., Hallin & Gitlin, 1994) with widely repeated comparisons of Saddam Hussein to Hitler, for example, and with carefully crafted narratives of freedom, scientific mastery, and heroism. The US government succeeded in framing the Iraq War similarly, at least in the early stages (Compton, 2004; Kellner, 2005). "For American viewers [...] the portrait of the war offered by the networks was a sanitized one free of bloodshed, dissent, and diplomacy, but full of exciting weaponry, splashy graphics, and heroic soldiers (Aday, Livingston, & Hebert 2005, p. 18). In other countries, even when nations ostensibly supported the war, "the story" was framed differently. Ravi (2005) provides a telling comparison of news coverage in the United States, United Kingdom, India, and Pakistan, concluding that "newspaper coverage seems to reflect notions, values, and ideas that resonate within particular societies" (p. 59), a point echoed by Dimitrova and Strömbäck (2005), comparing Sweden and the United States. News organizations in several countries used the US government frame of "shock and awe" in the initial bombings of Baghdad, but not in the same ways. For instance, after the first bombs dropped in Baghdad on March 22, 2003, the British press framed the attack as catastrophic, destructive, and essentially outrageous. US media played up the awe-inspiring power the attack represented, and both TV and print journalists appeared to revel in the aesthetic spectacle. TV journalists described the scene with breathless stories of unabashed admiration, and used the pronoun "we" in their stories, directly inviting audience complicity (Aday et al., 2005; Compton, 2004).

After the initial bombardment, stories continued to diverge. US media stories—until the Abu Ghraib scandal—emphasized military competence and success (although some coverage highlighted increasing problems with the inability of Iraqi police and military to maintain order) and most human interest stories focused on soldiers and the families they leave behind. European stories and those of the Arab press consistently concentrated on civilian casualties, presenting powerful images of burned children and heartbreaking accounts of families torn apart. The US press showed few images of either Iraqi deaths or US casualties, following government directives (Aday et al., 2005). The European media often seemed to contest their governments' stated support of the war, while in the United States, only one major news organization, Knight-Ridder (now McClatchy) consistently produced articles that questioned the reasons for going to war with Iraq (Ritea, 2004). Even the *New York Times* covered the lead-up to the war as the government presented it and, since then has apologized for not being more skeptical.

The US government's success in providing terms and frames that journalists found compelling helped form the backbone of the "story" of the war. The press used them so consistently that they become "natural" and therefore "true." The first was the incredibly successful "weapons of mass destruction," an imprecise term that essentially created its own story of fear, not only that Iraq had such weapons, but that they could and would use them against the United States. The term (now part of our everyday language), and the stories it evoked, proved so compelling that virtually all mainstream news media used it repeatedly, essentially co-habiting with the administration to promote the war. The government's equally successful term, "shock and awe," populated countless news articles and television broadcasts and journalists built their accounts around it. This, along with government-supplied notions of "smart bombs" from the first war and the reluctance to provide images of "collateral damage" resulted in a particular and narrow "story" of a clean and successful war, established early in 2003 and built carefully since (Compton, 2004; Kellner, 2005).

Indeed, the press typically adopts government-defined story frames especially in times of war or after catastrophic events such as the September 11 attacks (Zelizer & Allan, 2002), where journalists feel intense pressure to "pull together" and repair familiar myths. Easy narratives of heroism immediately deploy. Not all are provided by government sources; they may materialize virtually out of thin air, as in the widely circulated stories of the firefighter who "rode" the rubble down through one of the Twin Towers as it collapsed (Bird, 2003). Everyone needed heroes, and the media eagerly anointed them, even if they did not exist. Conversely, we witnessed the later-discredited news stories of rape, mayhem, and social collapse that immediately followed the Hurricane Katrina disaster, which pulled from much older narratives of the out-of-control racial "other" (see Salkowe, Tobin, & Bird, 2006), and also seemed profoundly "natural."

However, when those in power feed existing narrative impulses, the problem is compounded. For instance, it took some years for the truth to emerge about the "heroic" death in Afghanistan of former National Football League star Pat Tillman on April 22, 2004. Most stories relied on a military spokesman, who said that Tillman was killed "in a firefight at about 7 p.m. on a road near Sperah, about 25 miles southwest of a US base at Khost" (NBC, MSNBC News Services). Reports of Tillman's patrol in a heroic battle were steeped in the American cultural resonance of football and war, and received eagerly. Later, the "story" unraveled into a tale of military bungling and bureaucratic cover-up of a sorry "friendly fire" incident. A similar unraveling occurred in the Jessica Lynch story, originally presented as a tale of the teenage "girl soldier," captured while fighting "like a man," only to be rescued by brave troops. Later, Lynch herself repudiated the heroic nature of the tale. Kumar (2004, p. 297) argues that "constructed as hero, Lynch became a symbol of the West's "enlightened" attitude toward women, justifying the argument that the United States was "liberating" the people of Iraq. At the same time, the story evoked the cultural lexicon of "captivity narratives," involving fair, lovely young women actually or potentially brutalized by dark, menacing savages. The story, in other words, was especially powerful (and dangerous) because it perfectly meshed existing, culturally resonant images with the needs of the US administration to create specific heroic tales, and, no doubt, the needs of the people to have such tales. These instances point to the danger of familiar story frames, which provide easy narrative structures to the uncritical journalist. Compton (2004) characterizes contemporary media coverage as "integrated spectacle," and exhaustively describes how journalists enthusiastically jump on verbal and visual images provided for them by those in power.

Such frames exist outside war coverage. For instance, the history of US press coverage of China, at least from the early 1900s, consistently reflects official US policy toward China. Overall, news about China is mostly negative, but during periods when US-China relations are favorable, the US press writes more positively, and during periods when US-China relations are unfavorable, the press writes more negatively (Dardenne, 2005). The fundamental "reality" of China changes less than the stories created about China.

Story is compelling, not only for readers but also for the press. Any government administration finds it easier to frame stories to its advantage than to win over the press and the people with analysis and reason. This is politics, and it is what governments do. But this does not explain why the press often uncritically accepts those framings; after all, one might argue that the duty of the press is to resist them. But, the pull of "weapons of mass destruction," or "shock and awe," or "surge," or a homespun hero is powerfully compelling and comforting for journalists and audiences alike.

Having said this, the press, usually in retrospect, may counteract the myths, or offer alternatives. The *Washington Post* uncovered the more truthful story of Pat Tillman, and many media dissected the story of Jessica Lynch, and the larger stories of weapons of mass destruction and the US entry into the second Iraq war. Government-provided stories and press reports aren't always perfect fits. However, the power of the comforting narrative is clear in the way large sections of public opinion pillory the press for giving comfort to the enemy when newer narratives conflict with older ones. A newer story—of government ineptitude and dishonesty—also has cultural resonance, but by no means comforts.

WHERE DO WE GO FROM HERE?

Story, we have discovered after two decades, is not less complex. Scholars productively explored myriad texts to discover image, representation, mythic and traditional theme, and other qualities of myth and story. As Zelizer (2004, p. 132) points out, journalism scholars have found narrative approaches fruitful "in the mainstream press, on television news, and in the alternative journalistic forms of tabloids, reality television, and the internet." This interesting and important work (only a fraction referenced here) can propel us toward further significant findings valuable to both news and society.

A better understanding of the future of journalism's narrative role requires consideration of the greatly changed news environment. Even into the first decade of the 21st century, most people continue to get most of their news through mainstream corporate media, and those media appear to adopt official government narratives more than counter them. However, proliferation of cable

TV, the Internet, cell phones, citizens' news sites, and alternative and independent (indy) news sources drastically changed the media landscape, making Lule's picture of the *New York Times* setting the mythical agenda for the nation already seem quaint.

Robinson (2007) explores this change in her case study of the Spokane, Washington, *Spokesman Review's* coverage of a pedophilia scandal involving its mayor. She described a coherent, conventional story that fit many familiar narrative frames emerging over the course of a months-long investigation. However, simultaneous with the printed story, a "cyber newsroom" on the paper's own Web site made available interviews, documents, and multiple forms of information, and people dissected and analyzed the information, often offering their own sometimes radically different versions of the "official" stories. Readers, interacting with journalists, the news content, and other readers, helped form an online news narrative:

> If readers took issue with the coverage, they had the newspaper's own space to criticize the journalism [...] Like reporters, readers utilized quotation marks and hyperlinks to source the material [...] This sharing of information production changed the dynamics of the journalism resulting in a re-negotiation of the news paradigm within cyberspace. (p. 34)

A cacophony of narratives increasingly compete with mainstream journalism to define the day's stories. News audiences pick and choose stories they want to attend to and believe, and choose from a seemingly endless supply of information to assemble their own stories. Further, they produce and disseminate those stories on blogs, wikis, and personal Web sites. Nolan (2003, p. 4) notes that connectivity means that journalists become "less of an authority and more of a guide" and that journalism hasn't come to terms with that change. Many news purveyors from CNN to Fox have simply shouted more loudly that they have the truth. From Cronkite's parting, "That's the way it was," to the *Tampa Tribune* slogan, "Life. Printed daily," to the *New York Times* slogan, "All the news that's fit to print," the press claims to have "all" people need to know, emphasizing the thoroughness and truthfulness of their reports and the compelling nature of their stories, but rarely acknowledging news is part of a conversation (Anderson, Dardenne, & Killenberg, 1994).

Some see the new news environment as threatening the basis of journalism (Henry, 2007). Scholars find news reception more difficult to handle ethnographically than reception of say, soap operas, as news is imprecisely defined and people attend to it sporadically and from multiple sources. News reception is about process, not text, as "the story" emerges in conversation with the news narrative as framing structure. In making sense of news, we involve others in the negotiation of meaning and its cultural significance emerges through everyday interaction (Bird, 2003). We believe this has always been the case, but the contemporary, interactive world accentuates it. Indeed, the audience role in news storytelling is under-researched. We know little about how journalism narratives enter daily life and consciousness. We may argue, for example, that the European press framed the Iraq War in terms of civilian tragedy rather than heroic military success, because scholars find it in the texts. But is that translated by those who use the media into everyday perceptions, and more important, into action? If so, how and with what result?

Hill's (2005) longitudinal work on response to factual and reality programming and other studies begin to reposition audience's role in both responding to and creating "the story" that plays out in everyday life. A preliminary but provocative study by Gray (2007) positions online news consumers as "fans" who bring news stories to life in lively discussions centering on hard, political news. Politics, Gray writes, "must matter to the individual and must be consumed emotively to some degree if it is to become meaningful to its viewers" (p. 80). Gray's study shows that audiences see "the story" as being about more than the specific "news" events, but also about newscasters, politicians' appearances, and competing views of other audience members. Thus "the news fans showed the ability for fan-like engagement and civic duty to work together" (p. 85). Artificial separation of news as story and news as information hinders rather than clarifies our understanding of news (Bird & Dardenne, 1988, 1990) and the Gray study confirms the importance of realizing how news stories entwine emotional and informational functions.

A related topic ripe for renewed scholarly attention is audience interpretation and use of visual images, which always played key roles in defining journalistic narratives, from Matthew Brady's Civil War photos and those from Vietnam and Iraq, to the Rodney King video, images of Tiananmen Square defiance, the fireman holding a lifeless child in the Oklahoma City bombing, planes striking the twin towers, and the toppling of a statue of Saddam Hussein. In this evermore visual age, professionals as well as citizens easily create, manipulate, and instantaneously transport digital images across the world through various and ubiquitous technologies (Taylor, 2000). What story would have emerged from Abu Ghraib without digital snapshots taken by amused soldiers with cell phones? What are the consequences of "protecting" Americans from horrifying images, common elsewhere in the world, of mutilated Iraqi children? How did the YouTube video of presidential candidate John Edwards primping before a mirror combine with accounts of his $400 haircuts result in a story that could have narrated him out of the running? Creation, manipulation, and dissemination of images; their combination with words; the public's interpretation of them; and their roles in the way "the story" gains ascendancy offer enormous potential for important, interesting, and necessary research.

Newer technologies, their incorporation of images, and the public's negotiation of meanings through them provide fresh perspectives on story and the mythic qualities of story. These technologies and the journalism they allow or even mandate develop and transform, and therefore reposition citizens who attend to the news and journalists who produce it. The digital environment embraces increasing numbers of people who participate and produce rather than just receive and consume. This changes definitions, interpretations, and consequences of news. Scholars therefore need to consider: What is the role of story and myth in such an environment? While these new developments in technology and news production have not overtaken traditional news media, they confront them. Bloggers and other online commentators supplement, dissect, question, analyze, and sometimes condemn mainstream news daily. Traditional journalists never exclusively owned "the truth," but now what they do own, that is, their story, rarely goes unchallenged.

Prior to blogging, wikis, and other newer technologies, citizens got opportunities to contribute to and even create stories when in the mid-1990s, some news organizations adopted "public" journalism, in which news media invited citizens to participate in defining potential news issues and themes. Whether formally for or against the concept, many news media embraced one or more public journalism approaches, including citizen forums, parties and other gatherings hosted by journalists, reader advocates, public members of editorial boards, news organizations' active civic engagement, and innovative ways to get public voices in the news. Among public journalism's passionate advocates and critics, some claimed that journalists maintained too much control over the creation of the final narrative (Woodstock, 2002) and others claimed journalists gave up too much (Merrill, Gade, & Blevens, 2001; Merritt, 1995). Parisi (1997, p. 682) feared that news in a public journalism environment would not move beyond "conversation," and that focusing on community resources "leaves established structures of political power and economic interest [...] unexamined." Keen (2007, p. 80) argued that the rise of the amateur, online journalist is disastrous, stripping journalists of authority to shape stories, which creates a relativistic world devoid of "the telling of common stories, the formation of communal myths, the shared sense of participating in the same daily narrative of life."

Journalists risk ceding their crucial role in "speaking truth to power." Leaving the powerful unexamined abdicates journalism's major reason for existing. However, the greater danger lies not in giving more access to the public, but in the enormous access already provided to government. Further, with increasing merger and consolidation, corporate media are already themselves powerful economic institutions with less and less incentive to carefully examine the system that nourishes them. As their stories increasingly correspond to the powerful interests of which they are a part, citizens' news could contribute greatly to the alternative stories we think journalists are obligated to provide. Despite the more extreme postmodernist position that news has no claims on truth, a notion rightly critiqued by Windschuttle (1998), journalists remain obligated to make the best possible efforts to report and make sense of the world, an obligation that endures through all technological developments and academic interpretations. Journalists are obligated not to simply serve their corporate masters, by telling the government story, but to tell the most truthful story or stories that best serve citizens. Waisbord (1997, p. 191) notes the easy temptation to simply tell good stories; he shows how even an investigative story of government corruption in Brazil ended up conforming to standard narratives of personal morality, but "failed to address larger issues that could have helped to understand better the causes of corruption or to debate the ethical dimensions of Brazilian politics." Resende (2005), invoking Barthes and other narrative theorists, argues that a journalists' role must be to offer powerful "narratives of resistance" to counter and fundamentally interrogate the official ones.

Stories are powerful. That's why governments, corporations, and special interests employ legions of people to create the right ones and alter, or alter our perceptions of, all the others. And that's why so many people, including alternative and independent media activists, find the Internet so crucial. They see it as the best hope to get competing stories in circulation if journalists today do not have the will to do it, or if the corporate and other owners don't provide the resources to do it.

We don't accuse the press of never offering competing narratives. Resende (2005), for example, offers a Brazilian example in the highly personal story of a homeless street child, countering the official stories that erase the experience of such marginalized people. Leon Dash's 1994 *Washington Post* series about an African-American family on the fringes of American society, which later became a book (Dash, 1997), chronicles lives filled with drugs, abuse, AIDS, prostitution, crime and despair, and many letter writers criticized the *Post* for publishing it. But like the story of the Brazilian boy, it countered "official stories" in which such people are invisible or seen as less than human. While the story is at times ugly, Dash, by spending so much time with the family, learns enough to portray them as human beings rather than stereotypes, offers hope in showing how two sons escaped the poverty and crime, and provides a compelling story that most people never otherwise see. And, as both Lorenz (2005) and Clark (2000) discuss, literary, narrative writing techniques should not be dismissed as fake, but (if done with integrity) can be the tools that make the story real.

This kind of journalism underlies the philosophy of "new journalism," muckraking, and investigative reporting. These reporters use narrative journalism to tell stories of consequence that otherwise go untold and that resist government- and corporate-provided terms and themes. These stories require time, resources, and skills, but they help meet journalism's obligations to do more than narrate the increasingly inconsequential tide of amusement and diversion that pervades the news media. With newspaper readership and network news viewership in decline, the rise of Internet alternatives, and the domination of news by conglomerate interests, can authoritative journalistic narratives break through the media clutter, engage the reader to think, and perhaps even inspire action?

Exploring that is perhaps the greatest challenge both to journalism scholarship and to journalism itself.

REFERENCES

Aarne, A. A. (1928). *The types of the folktale: A classification and bibliography*. Helsinki: Academia Scientarum Fennica.

Aday, S., Livingston, S., & Hebert, M. (2005) Embedding the truth: A cross-cultural analysis of objectivity and television coverage of the Iraq War. *The Harvard International Journal of Press/Politics, 10*(1), 3–21.

Anderson, B., Dardenne, R. W., & Killenberg, G. M. (1994). *The conversation of journalism: Communication, community and news*. Westport, CT: Praeger.

Barkin, S. M. (1984) The journalist as storyteller: An interdisciplinary perspective. *American Journalism, 1*(2), 27–33.

Barthes, R. (1972). *Mythologies* New York: Hill and Wang,

Berger, P. L., & Luckmann, T. (1967). *The social construction of reality: A treatise in the sociology of knowledge*. New York: Anchor Books.

Bird, S. E. (1992) *For enquiring minds: A cultural study of supermarket tabloids*. Knoxville: University of Tennessee Press.

Bird, S. E. (2003). *The audience in everyday life: Living in a media world*. New York: Routledge.

Bird, S. E., & Dardenne, R. W. (1988). Myth, chronicle, and story: Exploring the narrative qualities of news. In J.W. Carey (Ed.), *Media, myths, and narratives* (pp. 67–87). Beverly Hills, CA: Sage.

Bird, S. E., & Dardenne, R. W. (1990). News and storytelling in American culture: Reevaluating the sensational dimension. *Journal of American Culture, 13*(2), 38–42.

Black, J. (2001). Hardening of the articles: An ethicist looks at propaganda in today's news. *Ethics in Journalism, 4*, 15–36.

Boyton, R. (2005). *The new new journalism: conversations with America's best nonfiction writers on their craft*. New York: Vintage.

Campbell, J. (1949). *The hero with a thousand faces*. New York: Pantheon.

Carey, J. W. (1975). A cultural approach to communication. *Communication* 2, 1–22.

Clark, R. P. (2000). The false dichotomy and narrative journalism. *Nieman Reports* (Fall), 11–12.

Clifford, J., & Marcus, G. (1986). *Writing culture: The poetics and politics of ethnography.* Berkeley: University of California Press.

Coman, M. (2005). News stories and myth: the impossible reunion? In E. W. Rothenbuhler & M. Coman (Eds.), *Media anthropology* (pp. 111–119).Thousand Oaks, CA: Sage.

Compton, J. R. (2004). *The integrated news spectacle: A political economy of cultural performance*. New York: Peter Lang.

Corcoran, F. (1986). KAL-007 and the evil empire: Mediated disaster and forms of rationalization. *Critical Studies in Mass Communication*, 3, 297–316.

Dardenne, R. (1990). *Newstelling: Story and themes in the Hartford Courant, 1765 to 1945*. Unpublished doctoral dissertation, University of Iowa.

Dardenne, R. (1998). The news as a narrative. *Contemporary media issues*. Westport, CT: Greenwood.

Dardenne, R. (2005). Image of China in U.S. news since 9-11. Paper presented at Fourth Annual International Conference of Asian Scholars, Shanghai, China, August 22..

Darnton, R. 1975. Writing news and telling stories. *Daedalus,* 104, 175–94.

Dash, L. (1997). *Rosa Lee: A mother and her family in urban America*. New York: Plume.

Dimitrova, D. V., & Strömbäck, J. (2005). Mission accomplished? Framing of the Iraq War in the elite newspapers in Sweden and the United States. *International Communication Gazette, 67*(5), 399–417.

Eliade, M. (1963). *Myth and reality*. New York: Harper and Row.

Ettema, J. S. (2005). Crafting cultural resonance: Imaginative power in everyday journalism. *Journalism, 6*(2), 131–152.

Ettema, J. S., & Glasser, T. L. (1988). Narrative form and moral force: The realization of innocence and guilt through investigative journalism. *Journal of Communication, 38*(3), 8–26.

Fisher, W. R. (1987). *Human communication as narration: Toward a philosophy of reason, value, and action*. Columbia: University of South Carolina Press.

Geertz, C. (1973). *The interpretation of cultures.* New York: Basic Books.

Golden, J. (2000). "A tempest in a cocktail glass": Mothers, alcohol, and television, 1977–1996. *Journal of Health Politics, Policy, and Law, 25*(3), 473–498.

Gray, J. (2007). The news: You gotta love it. In In C. Sandvoss, L. Harrington, & J. Gray (Eds.), *Fandom: Identities and communities in a mediated world* (pp. 75–87). New York: New York University Press.

Hallin, D. C., & Gitlin, T. (1994). The Gulf War as popular culture and television drama. In W. L. Bennett & D. L. Palet (Eds.), *Taken by storm: The media, public opinion, and policy in the Gulf War* (pp. 149–163). Chicago: University of Chicago Press.

Henry, N. (2007). *American carnival: Journalism under siege in an age of new media.* University of California Press.

Hill, A. (2005). *Reality TV: Factual entertainment and television audiences.* London: Routledge.

Hughes, H. M. (1968). *News and the human interest story.* Chicago: University of Chicago Press.

Keen, A. (2007). *The cult of the amateur: How today's internet is killing our culture.* New York: Doubleday.

Kellner, D. (2005). *Media spectacle and the crisis of democracy: Terrorism, war, and election battles.* New York: Paradigm.

Kitch, C. (2003). "Mourning in America": Ritual, redemption, and recovery in news narrative after September 11. *Journalism Studies, 4*(2), 213–224.

Kitch, C. (2000). "A news of feeling as well as fact": Mourning and memorial in American newsmagazines. *Journalism: Theory, Practice, and Criticism, 1*(2), 175–195.

Kerrane, K., & Yagoda, B. (1998). *The art of fact: A historical anthology of literary journalism.* New York: Scribner.

Knight G., & Dean T. (1982). Myth and the structure of news. *Journal of Communication, 32,* 144–161.

Kottak, C. P. (1990) *Prime time society: An anthropological analysis of television and culture.* Belmont, CA: Wadsworth.

Kumar, D. (2004). War propaganda and the (ab)uses of women: Media construction of the Jessica Lynch story. *Feminist Media Studies, 4*(3), 297–313.

Langer, J. (1998). *Tabloid television: Popular journalism and the "other" news.* London: Routledge.

Levi-Strauss, C. (1968). *Structural anthropology.* New York: Bantam Books.

Lippmann, W. (1922). *Public opinion.* New York: MacMillan.

Lorenz, A. (2005). When you weren't there: How reporters recreate scenes for narrative. *River Teeth, 71,* 71–85.

Lule, J. (2001). *Eternal stories: The mythological role of journalism.* New York: Guilford.

McBride, L. B., & Bird, S. E. (2007). From smart fan to backyard wrestler: Ritual, performance, and pain. In C. Sandvoss, L. Harrington, & J. Gray (Eds.), *Fandom: Identities and communities in a mediated world* (pp. 165–178). New York: New York University Press.

Mechling, J. (1991). *Homo narrans* across the disciplines. *Western Folklore, 50,* 41–52.

Merrill, J. C., Gade, P. J., & Blevens, F. R. (2001). *Twilight of press freedom: the rise of people's journalism.* Hillsdale, NJ: Erlbaum.

Merritt, D. (1995). *Public journalism and public life: Why telling the news is not enough.* Hillsdale, NJ: Erlbaum.

Mink, L. O. (1978/1987). Narrative form as a cognitive instrument. In B. Fay. E. O. Golob, & T. T. Vann (Eds.), *Louis O. Mink: Historical understanding* (pp. 182–203). Itaca, NY: Cornell University Press.

NBC, MSNBC News Services (2004). April 26, Ex-NFL star Tillman makes "ultimate sacrifice," April 26. retrieved August 5, 2007, from http://www.msnbc.msn.com/id/4815441

Nolan, S. (2003). Journalism online: The search for narrative form in a multilinear world. Proceedings of MelbourneDAC, the 5th International Digital Arts and Culture Conference, retrieved September 1, 2007, from http://w3c.rmit.edu.au/dac/papers/Nolan.pdf

Parisi, P. (1997). Toward a "philosophy of framing": News narratives for public journalism. *Journalism and Mass Communication Quarterly, 74,* 673–686.

Ravi, N. (2005). Looking beyond flawed journalism: How national interests, patriotism, and cultural values shaped the coverage of the Iraq War. *The Harvard International Journal of Press/Politics, 10*(1), 45–62.

Resende, F. (2005). Journalism discourse and narratives of resistance. *Brazilian Journalism Research, 1*(1), 177–194.

Ritea, S. (2004). Going it alone. *American Journalism Review*, August/September, 16–17.

Robinson, S. (2007). The cyber newsroom: A case study of the journalistic paradigm in a news narrative's journey from a newspaper to cyberspace. Paper presented at the International Symposium on Online Journalism. March 30–31, 2007, retrieved September 1, 2007, from http://journalism.utexas.edu/onlinejournalism/2007/papers/Robinson.pdf

Salkowe, R., Tobin, G. A., & Bird, S. E. (2006). Calamity, catastrophe and horror: Representation of natural disaster, 1885–2005. *Papers of Applied Geography Conferences, 29*, 196–205.

Scherr, A. (2004). Review of Lule, J. *Eternal stories: The mythological role of journalism. The Midwest Quarterly, 45*, 428–431.

Schudson, M. (1982). The politics of narrative form: The emergence of news conventions in print and television. *Daedalus, 111*, 97–112.

Sibbison, J. (1988). Covering medical "breakthroughs." *Columbia Journalism Review, 27*(2): 36–39.

Taylor, J. (2000). Problems in photojournalism: Realism, the nature of news, and the humanitarian narrative. *Journalism Studies, 1*(1), 129–143.

Thompson, S. (1975). *Motif-index of folk-literature: A classification of narrative elements in folktales, ballads, myths, fables, mediaeval romances, exempla, fabliaux, jest-books, and local legends* (3rd ed). Bloomington: Indiana University Press.

Waisbord, S. (1997). The narrative of exposés in South American journalism: Telling the story of Collorgate in Brazil. *Gazette, 59*(3), 189–203.

Wardle, C. (2003). The "Unabomber" vs. the "Nailbomber": A cross-cultural comparison of newspaper coverage of two murder trials. *Journalism Studies, 4*(2), 239–251.

White, H. (1980). The value of narrativity in the representation of reality. *Critical Inquiry, 7*(1), 5–27.

Windschuttle, K. (1998). Journalism versus cultural studies. *Australian Studies in Journalism, 7*, 3–31.

Woodstock, L. (2002). Public journalism's talking cure: An analysis of the movement's "problem" and "solution" narratives. *Journalism, 3*(1), 37–55.

Zelizer, B. (2004). *Taking journalism seriously: News and the academy*. New York: Sage.

Zelizer, B., & Allan, S. (Eds.). (2002). *Journalism after September 11*. New York: Routledge.

16

The Commercialization of News

John H. McManus

INTRODUCTION

One day in early March 2005, Anna Ayala's husband brought home the tip of a co-worker's finger that had been severed in a work accident. Anna soon put the decaying digit to use, dropping it in her steaming bowl of chili at a Wendy's restaurant in San Jose, California. Feigning revulsion, Anna threatened to sue Wendy's claiming that the fast food chain was cutting corners with the *con carne* in its chili. She protested that she hadn't ordered finger food.

Although it appeared to be a scam rather than a public health threat from the start, the *San Jose Mercury News*—once ranked among the ten best newspapers in the United States in a poll of editors—ran developments in the finger-in-the-chili-bowl story 11 times on its front page during the 33-day career of the story. During that month, from when the hoax was first reported until Ms. Ayala's arrest, the paper ran exactly one story about the US war in Iraq on 1A.[1]

Some would argue that a brutal war killing hundreds of thousands of Iraqis and displacing millions more, not to mention costing thousands of American lives and more than a billion dollars a week at the time merited the front page more than the saga of a small-bore grifter. But they would be thinking of journalism as a public trust rather than a profit-maximizing business.

This chapter briefly examines the commercialization of news: its historical context, how scholars have described it, what they have learned about its causes, processes and effects, the strengths and weaknesses of their analyses, and some ideas for future research.

DEFINING COMMERCIALIZATION

Claims of commercialization are almost as old as the practice of making money by selling news. Most have occurred in the United States, where news has been produced by business enterprises for more than a century and a half, and where almost all news is produced to earn a profit. In Eastern Europe, where the state once controlled media, commercialization is a new concern. In China, it is perhaps a future concern. In Western Europe where Karl Marx's thinking was incorporated into media scholarship by Antonio Gramsci, the "Frankfurt School" scholars, and later the Cultural Studies movement, commercialization was seen as contributing to a larger evil—class domination or hegemony. More recently, post-modernism and active audience theories have weakened the neo-Marxist assumption that all media are tools of class domination.[2] As European governments have begun to permit commercial broadcasting over the past two decades, commercialization has become a top concern of scholars.

To commercialize denotes making something into a business. But the word connotes corruption, meaning "to emphasize the profitable aspects of, especially by sacrificing quality or debasing inherent nature" (Random House, 1999). To be concerned with commercialization implies that absent such taint, profit-seeking news media can act in the public interest. So a definition of commercialization carries with it the controversial assumption that business-based journalism can, in fact, serve the public under certain conditions.

Making that assumption, I will define the commercialization of news as *any action intended to boost profit that interferes with a journalist's or news organization's best effort to maximize public understanding of those issues and events that shape the community they claim to serve.*[3] The *Mercury News'* priorities for its most read page during March 2005 seem much more oriented toward maximizing profit than public sense-making. The war in Iraq was both an issue and a series of events with far greater impact on the South San Francisco Bay region than one woman's failed scam, no matter how bizarre or entertaining.

To put this definition to practical use, it is helpful to have some understanding of the logic of commercial enterprises, market economics. In fact, I would argue that you cannot make sense of the evolution of journalism in the final quarter of the 20th century and at the beginning of the 21st without taking economics into account, particularly as it interacts with technological developments, such as the Internet, and government policy. Economics is important both to the diagnosis of contemporary journalism's shortcomings and to their solutions.

HISTORICAL CONTEXT

As Marion Marzolf's (1991) lively history of American press criticism describes, the conflict between the public service goals most news media proclaimed as their mission, and the demand of their owners for the greatest return on their investment has existed since the early days of the Penny Press in the middle of the 19th century. That was when business took over sponsorship of news from political parties and small printers. Commercialism ebbed over much of the 20th century as codes of ethics were adopted and the education levels and professional aspirations of journalists rose. But during the last two decades, and particularly during the last several years, as competition for readers and advertisers on the Internet has intensified, commercial interference appears to be rising, at least in American news media.

Since the mid-1980s the corporations that produce news in the United States have begun to treat it less as a public trust and more as a commodity, simply a product for sale (Auletta, 1991; Bagdikian, 1992; Downie & Kaiser, 2002; Hamilton, 2004; Kaniss, 1991; Lee & Solomon, 1991; McManus, 1994; Merritt, 2005, Patterson, 2000; Squiers, 1993; Stepp, 1991; Underwood, 1993). This *economic rationalization* of journalism has been exacerbated by the splintering of mass audiences as consumers took advantage of emerging news and entertainment choices offered first by cable and satellite television, and later by the Internet. Paradoxically, at the same time as these new technologies open a cornucopia of content from comedy to Congressional hearings, and democratize expression by offering almost everyman (and woman) a chance to express themselves to almost everyone, they undermine the financial foundation of the news providers democracy requires, especially in the United States.

As a consequence, we are in the greatest period of change—turmoil really—in journalism since the dawn of the Penny Press more than a century and a half ago. As we begin the 21st century with declining numbers of paid journalists (Project for Excellence in Journalism, 2007), an economic analysis of news predicts a temporary decline of journalism's expensive but vital watchdog function, less diverse coverage of a professional caliber as fewer owners exercise greater economies of scale over more newsrooms, and an erosion of ethical standards as public relations copy and advertising are "repurposed" as news. But if we understand how market forces shape news, we can propose remedies to ensure a steady supply of the kind of journalism participatory government requires.

HIGHLIGHTS OF THE LITERATURE OF COMMERCIAL NEWS BIAS

The Social Critics

The first to decry commercial contamination of news were social critics. Many were themselves journalists. Edward Ross in 1910, Will Irwin in 1911, and Upton Sinclair in 1920 decried the fakery, sensation and bias of the Yellow Press. The founder of German newspaper research, Karl Bücher (1926), described the influence of advertising in US newspapers. Later George Seldes (1938), at mid-century A. J. Leibling (1961) , and more recently Robert Cirino (1971) and Edward Jay Epstein (1973) documented structural business interference in the practice of journalism.

Perhaps the clearest assessment of an inherent conflict of interest between the economic and public service aspects of news media came from the Hutchins Commission (1947), assembled and funded by *Time Magazine* publisher Henry Luce after World War II: "The press [...] is caught between its desire to please and extend its audience and its desire to give a picture of events and people as they really are" (p. 57).

Although the Hutchins Commission warned of the concentration of newspaper ownership, the news media were to become much larger in the second half of the 20th century, incorporating broadcasting, book publishing and non-media enterprises in vast international conglomerates like Disney, News Corporation, and Time-Warner. During this period, they would also begin to seek cash for expansion from Wall Street investors. Former *Washington Post* ombudsman Ben Bagdikian chronicled the rise and risk of these corporations in *The Media Monopoly*, which has gone through seven editions since its first publication in 1983. In almost every iteration, the number of global firms controlling most informational media drops. Ownership is critical, Bagdikian (1992, p. xxxi) argues:

> Many of the corporations claim to permit great freedom to the journalists, producers and writers they employ. Some do grant great freedom. But when their most sensitive economic interests are at stake, the parent corporations seldom refrain from using their power over public information.

Another former journalist, Doug Underwood, warned of the economic rationalization of newspapers in the 1980s. He described the changes in newsroom management and news content as "green eyeshade" journalists were displaced by managers with business degrees in *When MBAs Rule the Newsroom* (1993). In interviews with hundreds of journalists, Underwood documented numerous cases of pandering to readers rather than informing them, of new advertiser-friendly policies and greater reliance on public relations to discover and report the news.

The Media Economists

While each of these social critics examined economic pressures on news, none used economics as a tool or developed theories of commercial bias. For those we have to look on campus. During the second half of the 20th century, as communication departments proliferated on university campuses, their faculty began to study news using techniques of social sciences, including economics.

Most of their economic research was designed not to critique media performance, however, but to assist and train managers for the industry (Underwood, 1993). In fact, until very recently economics was generally not seen as a useful tool for analyzing journalistic responsibility. Former Stanford media economist James N. Rosse put it bluntly in 1975:

> Although I have been a serious student of the economics of mass media for more than a decade, I have assiduously avoided the issue of media responsibility until now. The issue raises questions that do not lend themselves well to economic analysis. (p. 1)

In 1989, Robert Picard wrote a helpful primer called *Media Economics* that applied basic economic principles to media, particularly newspapers. It also focused on managerial questions rather than how markets and monopolies affect the quality of journalism. More recently Picard (2004, p. 61) has turned to commercialism of news as more newspaper companies have raised capital in the stock market and tried to satisfy investors' demands for rising profits:

> The primary content of newspapers today is commercialized news and features designed to appeal to broad audiences, to entertain, to be cost effective and to maintain readers whose attention can be sold to advertisers. The result is that stories that may offend are ignored in favor of those more acceptable and entertaining to larger numbers of readers, that stories that are costly to cover are downplayed or ignored and that stories creating financial risks are ignored.

Perhaps the most prolific media economist, at least in the United States, is Stephen Lacy. His research focuses on newspapers and is rigorously statistical. During the last decade and a half, Lacy has measured newspaper quality and its relationship to circulation and advertising revenues, as well as whether greater newsroom investment builds the bottom line.

Particularly relevant is his recent research with René Chen and Esther Thorson (2005). They examined data between 1998 and 2002 from hundreds of small and mid-size newspapers. (Larger papers did not report sufficient data to be included.) The research team found that those newspapers that invested more in their newsrooms outperformed other papers in revenues per copy from circulation and advertising as well as pre-tax profit. Combined with an earlier study (Lacy & Martin, 1998) of the failed Thomson newspaper chain, whose CEO bragged about cutting newsroom costs, Lacy and his colleagues argue that "the failure to invest in the newsroom could be a form of slow-motion suicide, where a company's disinvestment gradually alienates core readers and reduces the attractiveness of newspapers as advertising outlets" (Chen, Thorson, & Lacy, 2005, p. 527).

Lacy isolates three trends that have boosted commercialism during the past half century:

1. The decline of newspaper competition;
2. The growth of alternative information and advertising sources in the form of cable television and the Internet;
3. The growth of public [stock] ownership of news media.

Trend one has affected local markets. Trends two and three have affected both local and national markets. At the local level, starting in the late 1980s and early 1990s, trend three has put pressure to maintain high consistent profits. In some markets, competition (direct, umbrella and intercity) helped to counteract that pressure, but as competition disappeared in most larger cities and clustering ended the competition within counties—at first between dailies and later between dailies and weeklies—the counterbalance affected fewer and fewer markets.[4]

The Political Economists

During the 1970s, a new way of examining news commercialism was emerging. It focused on the intersection of politics and media and came to be known as the political economy of the media. According to Graham Murdock and Peter Golding (1997), who developed the approach in England along with Nicholas Garnham (1990) and James Curran (2004), this type of analysis was pioneered by Canadian economist Dallas Smythe (cf. *Dependency Road*, 1981) and his American student Herbert Schiller (cf. *Culture Inc.*, 1989).

From Gramsci (1971) through "Frankfurt School" theorists Theodor Adorno and Max Horkheimer (1972) to the "cultural studies" approach of Stuart Hall and Raymond Williams, European scholars puzzled over why poor and working class people would support leaders whose policies kept them down. Political economists pointed to the media as a prime suspect.

In an influential 1974 essay, Murdock and Golding wrote, "The part played by the media in cementing the consensus in capitalist society is only occasionally characterized by overt suppression or deliberate distortion" (p. 228). Rather, the routines of news work lead to systematic distortions that label anything threatening to the status quo as illegitimate or ephemeral. Journalistic objectivity, they argued, narrowed the margins of most debates to just two alternatives, neither of which threatened existing class relationships. "Most generally," they wrote, "news must be entertainment; it is, like all media output, a commodity, and to have survived in the market-place must be vociferously inoffensive in the desperate search for large audiences attractive to advertisers" (p. 230).

In the UK, Garnham (1990) reinterpreted the transformational thinking of the German social philosopher Jurgen Habermas. Habermas argued (1989) that in the 18th century bourgeois society in Western Europe had created a "public sphere" in newspapers and other publications, in coffee houses and at social gatherings that influenced government policy, leading to parliamentary rule. This public sphere was characterized by rationality, diverse viewpoints and a goal of the public good. However, in Habermas' view, modern corporate and state-controlled media undermined the public sphere. Garnham helped popularize Habermas by taking the ideal of the public sphere and proposing it as a model for democratic media that might be achieved by state-sponsored media such as the BBC and even by corporate newspapers and broadcasters under the right conditions (Curran, 2004).

At the same time in the United States, Edward Herman and the linguist Noam Chomsky (1988) postulated an influential theory that commercial news media operate both to maximize profit and to "manufacture consent" for policies that support the status quo. Reports of each day's "raw events" must pass through five filters before they can be published. Their "propaganda model" looks like this:

World of raw events	Will it sell as news? Yes → No ☹	Will advertisers support it? Yes → No ☹	Was it provided by inexpensive, establishment sources? Yes → No ☹	Will it cost money to defend? Yes ☹ No →	Does it promote Communism or attack private wealth? Yes ☹ No →	*The public*

THE STATE OF THE ART

A number of scholars worldwide constitute the state of the art in understanding commercial pressures on news. Rather than giving a few paragraphs to each, it may be more coherent to concentrate on key contributions of four researchers who have made a career examining the commercialization of news. I chose Robert McChesney, Leo Bogart, and Edwin Baker. Brazenly, I added theoretical aspects of my own work partly because I know it best.

McChesney uses political economy as a frame for critiquing the global media sphere. Bogart eschews any formal methodology. As a newspaper advertising executive, he provides a business view of news commercialization. Baker is a lawyer, yet creatively uses microeconomics to explain the failures of news media. My research combines my background as a journalist with my education as a social scientist. It poses a dynamic tension between the norms of socially responsible journalism and those of basic market economics to explain the daily workings of reporters and editors.

The Political Economy Critique

If anyone has donned the mantle of Ben Bagdikian as he has moved into retirement, it is Robert McChesney. He combines Bagdikian's flair for writing with a historian's passion for detail and documentation. McChesney has also become an activist, co-founding the progressive government watchdog Web site *FreePress.org*.

In *Rich Media, Poor Democracy* (1999), McChesney describes two contradictory trends: the increasing size and public acceptance of media conglomerates like Disney, General Electric and Bertelsmann on the one hand, and the decline of political participation on the other. Globally, he argues, "the wealthier and more powerful the corporate media giants have become, the poorer [are] the prospects for participatory democracy" (p. 2).

A major culprit, he writes, is the global rise of "neoliberalism"—a "market knows best" philosophy that leaves as much as possible to markets and corporations and minimizes the role of non-market institutions like government.

> The media, McChesney holds, are both a product of this way of thinking and promoters of it. As a consequence, we think we live in a world of informational plenty—the market provides hundreds of television channels, thousands of magazines and books and millions of Web sites. But of all these seemingly independent outlets, most of those attracting the largest audiences are owned by a few transnational companies and serve a commercial purpose, selling audience eyeballs to advertisers. Not surprisingly, content that empowers citizens and reports critically on government—and particularly corporate—power is rare. What media cover least, he says, is their own concentrated ownership and hypercommercialism.

McChesney doubts that the Internet will break the media oligopoly. As a historian, he sees a parallel with how radio, the radical new technology of the early 20th century, came to be dominated by a few large commercial interests despite its many channels, democratic potential and early use by citizen-broadcasters. As with radio, public debate over the new technology's most productive uses is being stifled. The successors of the corporate powers that dominated radio and later TV have so much influence in the US Congress, he writes, that they have already engineered a consensus that corporations, not universities, other non-profit organizations or government, should operate the Internet. Thus, making money is to be the primary concern.

The remedy, he argues, must come from the political left, particularly organized labor, and media reform must be central to its agenda. McChesney's prescription includes teaching news literacy to the public, taxing broadcasters for currently free use of public airwaves in order to fund public broadcasting, and labor creating its own news outlets.

In *The Problem of the Media* (2004), McChesney builds on his argument that media reform is primarily a political problem. He argues that government policies have encouraged exploitive media to flourish and that new policies are needed to create media supportive of democracy. To do so, he must dismantle the dominant neoliberal myth that profit-seeking corporations operating in "free" markets are the natural, ideal, even inevitable producers of news in a democracy.

That myth rests on two propositions, one political and one economic:

- Government should not be involved in creating or regulating news media because it might use this power for propaganda and censorship. The American Founding Fathers recognized this conflict and forbade it in the First Amendment guaranteeing freedom of the press from Congressional control. Thus "free enterprise" should operate news media with minimal or no regulation.
- Businesses compete in free markets, so they must give the public what it wants or suffer a loss of audience to others who will.

To the first proposition, McChesney responds that the authors of the First Amendment *were* concerned with government censorship of news, but were *not* attempting to restrict news to the private sector. The press of the day, he notes, was run by political parties and small printers. "The notions of entrepreneurs and free markets were almost entirely absent in the early republic," he writes, "as was the idea that the press was or should be a commercial activity set up solely to meet the needs of press owners" (p. 30). The First Amendment was meant to protect robust public discussion of important ideas and events, not to create a franchise for corporations to do whatever they wish.

McChesney responds to the proposition that markets give people what they want in five ways:

> First, he says, it is based on a flawed premise—that there is robust competition among media. Rather than engage in the competition Adam Smith envisioned, media and other businesses attempt to buy out, merge, or partner with competitors to the extent government anti-trust regulators permit. They also try to erect barriers to market entry by forming chains, as in newspapers and broadcast networks, or large conglomerates that can bring the resources of many industries down on any new competitor.
>
> Second, McChesney casts advertisers, not consumers, as the media's most important customers. "This changes the logic of media markets radically, since the interests of consumers must be filtered through the demands of advertisers" (p. 189). Third, he argues that markets encourage uniformity; every producer plays to the lowest common denominator of consumer preferences in order to maximize audience. This is problematic for news, which should seek out diverse perspectives. Fourth, consumers can only value what they are offered. "Media markets may 'give the people what they want,' but will do so strictly within the limited range of fare that can generate the greatest profits" (p. 199).
>
> Finally, McChesney argues, markets are inherently undemocratic; they always favor the wealthy over other strata of society. The more money consumers have, the greater their choices and ability to purchase quality goods. In a democracy, every citizen should have equal access to civic information.

Next, we will examine Leo Bogart's warning of an increasingly commercialized and anti-democratic media culture. It carries additional weight because it comes from an insider—the former executive vice-president of the Newspaper Advertising Bureau.

A Business Critique

In *Commercial Culture: The Media System and the Public Interest* (2000), Bogart rejects the argument that the shortcomings of the media can be blamed on the public because the market gives people what they want. Like McChesney, he urges a federal media policy that makes greater room for democratic processes than the current market arrangement.

> The individual means of mass communication—from the book to the compact disk—have been submerged into an interlocked system dominated by a disturbingly small number of powerful organizations [...] Entertainment increasingly overshadows information, blurring the difference between what is real and what is not, and thus weakening the public's will and capacity to confront the world and its problems. (p. 4)

Because all of these formerly separate media—TV, radio, newspapers, books, magazines, movies, video disks and tapes—are expected to promote each other, Bogart maintains, the independence of news departments in such conglomerates has been compromised. Bogart's career gives him particular insight into advertising's distortion of culture:

> Contemporary American culture is commercial because, overwhelmingly, it is produced for sale to meet marketing requirements [...] Commercial culture assigns no value or meaning to communications apart from their market value—that is, the price that someone is willing to pay for them. (p. 66)

Advertising's hyperbole and distorted world view—of well-off, handsome actors gaining happiness from consuming products—affect all social and political discourse, Bogart argues. Advertising pulls our attention away from common issues—clean air and water, affordable housing and transportation—and focuses it on personal possessions. When not selling, Bogart writes, the media do two things: They inform and they entertain. But even when trying to inform, the emphasis is on entertainment, he argues, because that generates a larger audience than information.

> With all its great resources and formidable talent, television journalism has been forced to conform to the rules of show business. It gives us a vivid first-hand view of great events, but that view is often fragmentary and distorted. (p. 175)

As Bagdikian also noted, advertising has undermined local competition among newspapers. Because newspapers are based on economies of scale, bigger ones can offer advertisers more readers at a lower cost per thousand. As the percentage of newspapers' revenue from advertising grew, competing local papers became scarce. The loss of that competition, in turn, diminished newspapers' variety and quality, ultimately diminishing readership, Bogart argues. "Competition sets higher editorial standards and makes for greater quality than can be achieved in a monopoly paper by even the highest-minded management and most dedicated staff" (p. 199).

To McChesney's rebuttal of the neoliberal myth of markets "giving people what they want," Bogart adds a further point: The banality, sensationalism and overused formulas of media content are not the result of public taste, but of manipulation by the media. Social scientists have demonstrated that people gravitate toward what's familiar. "What is easily accessible and heavily promoted becomes familiar," he writes. "Tastes are neither spontaneous nor immutable; they are provided to the public ready-made. Media's content reflects what their managements choose to offer rather than instinctive public preferences" (p. 221). "The first step" toward a solution, he concludes, "is to recognize that a problem exists, and that market forces cannot solve it" (p. 324).

The next step is to explain why market forces alone do not work. In the following section I use economic theory to explain why market-driven journalism is an oxymoron.

Commercial Logic vs. Public Service Logic

Inspired by theories of news selection beginning with Galtung and Ruge (1965), Joseph Turow (1992), Robert Entman (1989), Herman and Chomsky (1988), and Pamela Shoemaker and Stephen Reese (1991), I constructed a model of market forces shaping news content produced by commercial news corporations (1995).

This model postulates a "news production environment" constituted by national and regional culture, laws and regulations, and available technology. Within that, the news departments of media firms compete in four key markets:

- for *investors/owners* who trade capital for profit and perhaps influence over content.
- for *advertisers* who trade money for public attention to their wares.
- for *consumers* who trade subscription fees or simply "pay" attention for desirable content.
- for *sources* who supply the raw material of news—information—in return for public attention (which might yield influence) and influence over content.

I examined how each of these markets function compared to the conditions Adam Smith (1776) and his modern followers list as necessary to activate "the invisible hand" that spins the lead of self-interest into the gold of public benefit. Four conditions must be met:

1. Buyers and sellers both act rationally in their self interest; *and*
2. Buyers can distinguish between high and low quality; *and*
3. The market offers real alternatives; *and*
4. The transaction generates no negative externalities—harm to parties outside the transaction.

In *Market-Driven Journalism: Let the Citizen Beware?* (1994) I argued that the markets for investors, advertisers and sources all serve both themselves and the media firm. But the market for consumers fails to meet Smith's standards, resulting in a negative consequence for society—news that is often unequal to the demands of a participatory form of government.

First, research suggests that consumers are not as rational as economists have long assumed (Kahneman & Tversky, 1973). And even when they are, it may be rational to be ignorant (Downs, 1957) because the benefit to an individual for the daily work of keeping informed is miniscule—one vote in thousands or millions—compared to the cost in time.

Second, because news is a credence good consumed more on faith than experience or inspection (McManus, 1992), even rational consumers have trouble discerning its quality. Rarely can the audience be sure media reports are accurate or complete representations of issues and events. More importantly, consumers cannot tell whether what is presented really comprises the most important events and issues of the day. Third, the closer the event to one's own neighborhood, the less choice the consumer enjoys among professional news providers. As a consequence, consumers are vulnerable to exploitation when owners/investors seek to maximize their returns.

What kind of exploitation? In three of the markets public attention is traded, but not necessarily attention to what the Hutchins Commission would consider news. Since entertainment has historically generated a larger audience than information, and consumers are poor at evaluating news quality, there is economic pressure to generate newspapers, newscasts and Web sites that look newsy, but entertain as much or more than they inform.[5]

Two theories of news selection flow from this model. The first follows the norms of socially responsible journalism (Hutchins, 1947). The second maximizes return to shareholders/owners; it is essentially a cost-benefit analysis for various types of news stories. The probability of an event or issue becoming news in a *socially responsible* news outlet is:

- Proportional to the expected consequence of the story in terms of helping people make sense of their environment, and
- Proportional to the size of the audience for whom it is important.

Under an *economic* selection model, however, the probability is:

- Inversely proportional to harm the information might cause major advertisers or the parent corporation, and
- Inversely proportional to the cost of uncovering it, and
- Inversely proportional to the cost of reporting it, and
- Directly proportional to the expected breadth of appeal of the story to audiences advertisers will pay to reach.

These two selection logics conflict more than coincide as they shape the organizational culture of a given newsroom. Where managers can moderate profit demands of owners/investors, journalism norms do better. In others, economic demands prevail. The more the economic, or market, model of news selection is followed, the less valuable the news becomes as a resource for citizens because:

- What is most expensive to uncover and report—sometimes because those in power want it hidden—is often what is most newsworthy.
- News departments not only suffer pressure to avoid negative reporting on large advertisers—auto dealers, real estate developers, grocery chains, etc.—there is positive pressure to increase ad revenue by creating content designed to whet consumers' appetites—sections and segments about new cars, home and garden improvements, food, travel, night life, etc.
- Rich and poor, young and old, all citizens deserve coverage of issues affecting them. But rational advertisers seek the upscale and those in prime buying years. Market-driven editors will commit scarce reporting resources to please those groups at the expense of the others because advertisers contribute about 80% of paid newspaper revenues and 100% of free paper and broadcast revenues.

In the next section, Edwin Baker will use the same tool, market economics, to arrive at a similar conclusion about commercially produced journalism. But he will employ a completely different set of propositions.

The Economics of Quality Journalism

C. Edwin Baker teaches law at the University of Pennsylvania, but thinks like a media economist. Like all of the authors above, Baker takes aim at the core proposition of market-based news media—that they give the people what they want. But Baker adds four unique arguments in his 2002 book *Media, Markets and Democracy*:

Expanding on Bogart's argument about media *setting* audience preferences rather than *satisfying* them, Baker argues that people use media to discover and develop content preferences as much as to express already formed preferences. For that to occur they must first be exposed to diverse offerings—content they may not yet know they value. To the extent the market restricts choices to the content most profitable for advertisers and media owners, it does not give people what they want.

Baker's most striking contribution has to do not with the negative externalities of market-driven journalism, but with the failure of society to adequately compensate news media for positive externalities. Apathetic citizens consume little or no news. So they contribute almost nothing to the bottom line of media companies. Yet they reap vast benefits from quality journalism.

> Individuals are tremendously benefited or harmed if the country makes wise or stupid decisions about welfare, warfare, provision of medical care, the environment, and a myriad of other issues. These harms or benefits depend on the extent and quality of *other* people's political participation. The media significantly influence this participation. (p. 45)

One of the greatest of these positive outcomes of quality journalism for consumers and non-consumers alike is the deterrence of corruption among government officials who fear being exposed in the media. "'Deterrence' means, however, that the media has [sic] no 'exposé'—no product—to sell to its audience and hence no opportunity to internalize the benefits it produces" (p. 49).

Economic theory predicts that when a producer is not able to capture some of the value of the product, it is under-produced. Since deterrence of corruption is entirely uncompensated, and what builds deterrence—investigative reporting—is very expensive and little compensated as competitors are able to offer the revelations almost immediately, economic theory provides an explanation of why it is so rare.

A second insight into the economics of journalism follows Oscar Gandy's (1982) work conceptualizing public relations as an "information subsidy." Baker argues that journalism is skewed towards topics and viewpoints of those individuals and institutions able to afford public relations representation and away from those unable to afford to subsidize newsgathering. Public relations provides one pervasive and largely hidden content-shaping subsidy; advertising provides another. Baker argues that advertising subsidizes the cost of content of interest to its potential customers.

> An affluent person may be charged \$.40—or nothing—for a media product that costs \$1 because advertisers will pay the extra \$.60. Because poor people have less to spend on the advertisers' products, their value to advertisers is less. Thus media enterprises must charge much closer to the full cost for media products directed at the poor. (p. 75)

When media cannot charge for the product directly, as in broadcast news, they produce more of the advertiser-subsidized content and less of the unsubsidized. "This skewed subsidy is strikingly unfair," he writes, "especially if media content involves a person's role as a citizen and not merely as a consumer" (p. 76).

Baker's innovative use of economic theory undermines the neoliberal reliance on unregulated markets as the optimal mechanism for providing news. It also provides a basis for seeking government support for the kind of journalism the market does not encourage—investigative reporting and coverage of politically significant topics, especially those affecting citizens with interests unsubsidized by advertisers or public relations practitioners.

METHODOLOGICAL TRAPS IN CONCEPTUALIZING AND MEASURING COMMERCIALISM

Every research viewpoint has its blind spots. Because economics usually tries to explain consumer and producer behaviors by itself, there is a tendency to over-rely on it. This seems inappropriate when trying to explain journalism, which, although increasingly dominated by economic concerns, still retains vestiges of a professional ethos.

An example can be found in James T. Hamilton's *All the News That's Fit to Sell: How the Market Transforms Information Into News* (2004). Hamilton uses economics alone to explain media bias. He contends that American news media exhibit liberal bias in order to attract 18- to 34-year-old women, the group advertisers will pay the most to reach because they tend to make most family buying decisions.

> When individuals are asked to place themselves on a scale of liberalism and conservatism, those 18–34 are more liberal than those 50+, women are more liberal than men, and women 18–34 report the highest ratings as liberals. If a media outlet selects or covers issues to attract younger or female viewers, one can expect that content will on the margin relate to liberal concerns. Survey responses again bear out these predictions. Younger viewers and female viewers are less likely to report that they see political bias in news coverage. Women 18–34 are the least likely to report that that they see political bias, which is what one would expect if some news outlets were shaping content to attract these particular viewers. (p. 72)

It is certainly possible that media adopt a liberal perspective to reach the viewers advertisers most desire, but if indeed most news outlets are liberal it could also be explained by noneconomic factors, such as liberal bias among journalists. Or it could be that news media are not liberal. Young women may notice little political bias because they pay little attention, according to Hamilton's data, to any political news.

A second methodological trap is that it can be easy to ascribe economic motives to contradictory media behaviors. If concentrated ownership of newspapers, for example, leads to sameness of editorial products in a region, we can claim the owner is optimizing profit. One reporter's story can run in a dozen nearby papers because the owner saves money by reducing "redundant" coverage and staff. Owning all the papers in the region, the owner need not worry about consumers purchasing another paper.

But economic theory would also support the notion that without competition a single owner can optimize profit by providing *different* content for each segment of the audience. One-size-suits-all stories may be cheaper to produce, but multiple stories serving various segments of the audience will generate greater sales because they will please more consumers. One strategy may be more profitable than the other, but to decide you would have to know whether additional staff costs were greater or less than additional sales that might be generated by satisfying audience segments. The lesson? Predictions of news behavior based on economic theory have to be carefully specified.

DIRECTIONS FOR FUTURE RESEARCH

If we have learned anything from recent research, it is that relying on unregulated markets will not render the quality or quantity of news that participatory government requires to flourish. Here, I suggest two major directions for research: 1) exploration of non-market, or at least non-profit, financial models for news providers; and 2) analyses leading to remedies for the infirmities of markets for news products.

The breakdown of the business model of mainstream media, the rapid adoption of broadband Internet connections in developed nations and the development of low cost digital broadcast equipment creates an exciting opportunity for establishing new low cost news media because it:

- Eliminates the need for multi-million dollar presses, increasingly expensive paper, and fleets of delivery trucks—which together consume about two thirds of the average newspaper's revenues;
- Eliminates the requirement for a government license and a multi-million dollar transmitter to disseminate news in video and audio format;
- Reduces the cost of news-gathering and presentation.

Thus the time may be ripe for non-profit institutions such as foundations and perhaps universities to consider alliances with public broadcasters to fill the increasing gaps in commercial news production. But how should such partnerships be optimally funded and structured?

In *We the Media* (2006) Dan Gillmor lays out a hopeful vision of "citizen journalists" providing much more community-tailored and diverse news reports than mainstream media offer. The prospect raises a host of research questions: Will amateur reporting find enough of an audience to reward the person(s) producing it? How can consumers identify reliable information when such journalists may have hidden conflicts of interest? Should there be state or professional licensing? How might labor-intensive depth or investigative reporting be organized among a network of citizens with limited spare time? Which models of cooperation between citizens and paid journalists (such as South Korea's Web-based *Oh My News*) yield optimal results?

The second general research agenda would aim at ameliorating infirmities of the various markets shaping news.

My own project, *gradethenews.org*, has tried to enhance the ability of consumers to discriminate between "junk journalism" and more nutritious fare. By educating consumers, we have tried to make the former less profitable and the latter more. We have celebrated some success. But consumer education loses effectiveness as choice diminishes. In the United States, newspapers are increasingly forming geographic clusters with one owner/operator.

Even though consumers could not punish the cluster owner by choosing an alternate paper, research documenting gaps between the news provider's performance and public service standards it boasts might strengthen consumer demands for quality by shaming owners. Such evidence might include content analyses showing: 1) neglect of important issues and the perspectives of certain communities, such as ethnic minorities and labor groups; 2) preference for articles that promote interest in advertised products over stories of civic value; 3) violations of the standards of ethical journalism, such as disguising advertisements as news, inaccuracies, protection of sacred cows, etc.

The *market for news consumers* would work better if citizens become educated about the value of news and standards for judging it. As of this writing, a comprehensive book on *news* literacy has yet to be published. Web-based algorithms that assist consumers in evaluating news quality have yet to be developed. If we had "Nielsen ratings" for *news quality*, rather than just *audience quantity*, we might have a basis for rewarding or subsidizing the kind of journalism that makes a civic contribution.

Baker's research raises a similar question: Are there ways of quantifying the positive externalities of good journalism that might form the basis of government support? There is precedent: The US government has long subsidized postal rates and more recently relaxed anti-trust provisions such as joint operating agreements. The Swedish government supports ideologically competing local newspapers.

Little research has been conducted into altering the *market for investors* to make it more supportive of quality journalism. Some intriguing ideas have been introduced, such as Mathewson's (2005) arguments for adjusting tax law to permit newspapers to convert to non-profit status to reduce both excessive profit demand and federal tax liability. Employee-ownership models have been proposed by the Newspaper Guild. But a great deal of research is needed to learn how such general proposals might best be structured.

The *market for sources* might operate more in the public interest if reporting costs were minimized. Given the increasing power exercised by corporations, how might government increase corporate reporting requirements to allow journalists greater opportunities to hold the private sector to account? As Baker suggests, might federal shield laws be enacted that would increase the supply of whistle-blowers by allowing reporters to protect their identities? If public relations subsidizes reporting on issues of interest to those who can afford such representation, might such efforts be taxed to generate press subsidies for societal interests that cannot afford PR?

The *market for advertisers* might operate more in the public interest if methods were developed to weaken its influence over content. Bagdikian has suggested a tax on all media advertising, for example, which might be used to subsidize public affairs reporting. McChesney has advocated a strong journalists' union that might resist ethical violations such as running ads as news. Such ideas require elaboration.

Sad to say, there has not been as favorable a time to study the commercialization of news since the Yellow Press around the turn of the 20th century. Instances abound. On a more hopeful note, the revolution in digital communication technologies makes this the most exciting time to study the economics and regulation of news media. The business models underpinning virtually all mainstream news media are breaking down. What could be more rewarding than figuring out how to fix or replace them?

NOTES

1. Retrieved July 14, 2007, from http://www.gradethenews.org/commentaries/finger.htm
2. A recent example is Jesper Stromback's "Marketplace of ideas and marketplace of money," *Nordicom Review Jubilee Issue, 2007* (pp. 51–62), which argues that news media both make money *and* foster democracy by helping citizens cast informed votes.
3. "Boosting" profit, implies an effort to earn more than is necessary to ensure the long-term capability of the news-providing firm to produce high quality journalism (Picard, 2005).
4. Personal communication to the author, June 19, 2007.
5. They must *seem* informative to distinguish themselves from the much larger and more competitive "pure" entertainment market.

REFERENCES

Adorno, T., & Horkheimer, M. (1972). The culture industry: Enlightenment as mass deception. In *The dialectics of enlightenment*. New York: Herder and Herder.

Auletta, K. (1991). *Three blind mice*. New York: Random House.

Bagdikian, B. H. (1992). *The media monopoly* (4th ed.). Boston: Beacon Press.

Baker, C. E. (2002). *Media, markets and democracy*. Cambridge, UK: Cambridge University Press.

Bogart, L. (2000). *Commercial culture: The media system and the public interest.* New Brunswick, NJ: Transaction Publishers. (Original work published 1995)

Bücher, K. (1926). *Das Zeitungswessen*. In Bucher, K., *Gesammelte Aufsätze zur Zeitungskunde, Tübingen, 21.*

Chen, R., Thorson, E., & Lacy, S. (2005, autumn). The impact of newsroom investment on newspaper revenues and profits: small and medium newspapers 1998–2002, *Journalism & Mass Communication Quarterly, 82,* 516–532.

Cirino, R. (1971). *Don't blame the people.* Los Angeles: Diversity Press.

Curran, J. (2004). The rise of the Westminster school. In Calabrese, A. & Sparks, C. (Eds.), *Toward a political economy of culture.* New York: Rowman and Littlefield.

Downie, L., & Kaiser, R. G. (2002) *The news about news: American journalism in peril.* New York: Knopf.

Downs, A. (1957). *An economic theory of democracy*. New York: Harper & Row.

Entman, R. M. (1989). *Democracy without citizens.* New York: Oxford University Press.

Epstein, E. J. (1973). *News from nowhere.* New York: Random House.

Galtung, J., & Ruge, M. H. (1965). The structure of foreign news. *Journal of Peace Research, 1*, 64–91.

Gandy, O. H. (1982). *Beyond agenda-setting: Information subsidies and public policies.* Norwood, NJ: Ablex.

Garnham, N. (1990) *Capitalism and communication.* London: Sage.

Gillmor, D. (2006) *We the media.* Sebastopol, CA: O'Reilly.

Gramsci, A. (1971 translation). *Selections from the prison notebooks.* New York: International.

Habermas, J. (1989 translation). *The structural transformation of the public sphere.* Cambridge, UK: Polity.

Hamilton, J. T. (2004). *All the news that's fit to sell: How the market transforms information into news.* Princeton, NJ: Princeton University Press.

Herman, E. S., & Chomsky, N. (1988). *Manufacturing consent: The political economy of the mass media.* New York: Pantheon.

Hutchins, R. M., & the Commission on Freedom of the Press (1947). *A free and responsible press: A general report on mass communication: Newspapers, radio, motion pictures, magazines and books.* Chicago: University of Chicago Press.

Irwin, W. (January to July, 1911). The American newspaper. *Colliers.*

Kahneman, D., & Tversky, A. (1973). On the psychology of prediction. *Psychological Review, 80*(4), 237–251.

Kaniss, P. (1991). *Making local news.* Chicago: University of Chicago Press.

Lacy, S., & Martin, H. (1998, summer). High profits and declining circulation: A study of Thomson newspapers during the 1980s," *Newspaper Research Journal, 19*(3), 63–76.

Lee, M. A., & Solomon, N. (1991) *Unreliable sources: A guide to detecting bias in news media.* New York: Carol.

Liebling, A. J. (1975). *The press.* New York: Pantheon. (Original work published 1961)

Marzolf, M. T. (1991). *Civilizing voices: American press criticism, 1880–1950.* White Plains, NY: Longman.

Mathewson, J. (2005, Dec. 8). Newspaper saved! Newspaper saved! Read all about it! *Editor and Publisher-Online, retrieved July 10, 2007* http://www.editorandpublisher.com/eandp/columns/shoptalk_display.jsp?vnu_content_id=1001657297" \t "_blank

McChesney, R. W. (2004). *The problem of the media: U.S. communication politics in the 21st century.* New York: Monthly Review Press.

McChesney, R. W. (1999). *Rich media, poor democracy.* Urbana: University of Illinois Press.

McManus, J. H. (1992). What kind of commodity is news? *Communication Research, 19*(6), 787–805.

McManus, J. H. (1994). *Market-driven journalism: Let the citizen beware?* Thousand Oaks, CA: Sage.

McManus, J. H. (1995). A market-based model of news production. *Communication Theory, 5*(4), 301–338.

Merritt, W. D. (2005). *Knightfall.* New York: AMACOM.

Murdock, G., & Golding, P. (1974). For a political economy of mass communications. In R. Miliband & J. Saville (Eds.), *The socialist register 1973* (pp. 205–234). London: Merlin Press,.

Murdock, G. & Golding, P. (Eds.). (1997). *The political economy of the media I,* Cheltenham, UK: Elgar.

Patterson, Thomas E. (2000). The United States: News in a free-market society. In R. Gunther. & A. Mughan (Eds.), *Democracy and the media: A comparative perspective.* New York: Cambridge University Press.

Picard, R. G. (1989). *Media economics.* Beverly Hills, CA: Sage.

Picard, R. G. (2004). Commercialism and newspaper quality. *Newspaper Research Journal, 25*(1), 54–65.

Picard, R. G. (2005). Money, media and the public interest. In G. Overholser & K. H. Jamieson, (Eds.), *The press* (pp. 337–350). New York: Oxford University Press,.

Project for Excellence in Journalism (2007). *The state of the news media 2007,* retrieved July 10, 2007, from http://www.stateofthenewsmedia.com/2007

Random House Webster's college dictionary (1999). New York: Random House.

Ross, E. A. (1910, March). The suppression of important news. *Atlantic Monthly, 105*, 303–311.

Rosse, J. N. (1975). Economic limits of press responsibility. *Studies in Industry Economics* No. 56. Stanford, CA: Department of Economics, Stanford University.

Schiller, H. I. (1989). *Culture Inc.* New York: Oxford University Press.

Seldes, G. (1938). *The lords of the press.* New York: Julian Messner..

Shoemaker, P., & Reese, S. (1991). *Mediating the message.* New York: Longman.

Sinclair, U. (1920). *The brass check: A study of American journalism.* Pasadena, CA: author.

Smith, A. (1937 translation). *An inquiry into the nature and causes of the wealth of nations.* New York: Random House. (Original work published 1776)

Smythe, D. W. (1981) *Dependency road: Communications, capitalism, consciousness and Canada.* Norwood, NJ: Ablex.

Squiers, J. D. (1993) *Read all about it.* New York: Random House.

Stepp, C. S. (1991, April). When readers design the news. *Washington Journalism Review, 13*(3), 20–25.

Turow, J. (1992). *Media systems in society.* New York: Longman.

Underwood, D. (1993). *When MBAs rule the newsroom.* New York: Columbia University Press.

IV

JOURNALISM AND SOCIETY

17

Journalism and Democracy

Brian McNair

The histories of journalism and democracy are closely linked. The origins of journalism, as we recognize it today, parallel the turbulent birth of the first democratic societies nearly four hundred years ago. While the concepts of news, and the role of the correspondent as a professional dispatcher of newsworthy information, predate the bourgeois revolutions of early modern Europe, the modern notion of a political journalism which is adversarial, critical and independent of the state was first formed in the early seventeenth century, against the backdrop of the English Civil War and its aftermath. In that conflict, which pitted the forces of absolute monarchy against those in favor of democratic reform and the sovereignty of parliament, journalism played a key role (Conboy, 2004). It did so again during the French Revolution of 1789 (Popkin, 1991; Hartley, 1996), and also in the American War of Independence (Starr, 2004). Then, and since, the presence of a certain kind of journalism, existing within a functioning public sphere (Habermas, 1989), has been a defining characteristic of democratic political and media cultures. This chapter explores the role played by journalism in democratic societies, past and present, both from the normative and the pragmatic perspectives, and critically assesses its contribution to the development and maintenance of democratic political cultures.

JOURNALISM BEFORE DEMOCRACY—THE AUTHORITARIAN TRADITION

For the authoritarian feudal regimes of fifteenth and sixteenth century Europe, journalism was regarded as a useful if potentially dangerous instrument for more effective administration of, and control over, society. The capacity of information to upset and destabilize the authoritarian order of things was recognized from the invention of print in the late fifteenth century, by the monarchs of Tudor England as much as the Papacy in Rome. Early laws of libel, alongside restrictive licensing and copyright laws introduced in the late sixteenth century, sought to police information and neuter its potentially destabilizing effect on feudal power structures. The objective, as frankly stated in the first English law of copyright, was to prohibit, whether in journalism or other forms of printed public expression, "heresy, sedition and treason, whereby not only God is dishonoured, but also an encouragement is given to disobey lawful princes and governors."[1] Foreign news was banned in England in 1632 on the grounds that it was "unfit for popular view and discourse" (Raymond, 1996, p. 13).

JOURNALISM AND DEMOCRACY—BEGINNINGS

The foundations of modern political journalism lie in the seventeenth century struggle between the monarchy and parliament which led to the English Civil War and subsequent progress towards democratization. Before these events journalists, like all in feudal society, were subjects of the absolute monarch, subordinate to the demands of church and state. Early periodicals such as *Mercurius Gallobelgicus*, launched in 1594, provided coverage of politics, military affairs, economic trends and the like, but always within strict restrictions on content imposed by the feudal state.

But as capitalism developed and the legitimacy of feudal power began to be challenged by a rising bourgeoisie, journalists started to take sides in the intensifying class struggle. As conflict between crown and parliament grew into civil war in 1640s England, controls on the content of the press were loosened, and titles proliferated in response to the rising demand for news and analysis. The news books of this period—forerunners of the modern newspaper—were more than merely reporters of information but "bitter and aggressive instruments of literary and political faction" (Raymond, 1996, p. 13). Journalists took sides, becoming partisans and activists in the shaping of political reality, as opposed to mere reporters of it.

In the 1640s, too, journalism formalized the distinction between news and comment, or fact and opinion, in the form of the *Intelligencer*, a publication in which journalists "mediated between political actors and their publics" (Raymond, 1996, p. 168). By the end of that decade, "the detailed reporting of news was concomitant with strong interpretation and passionate persuasion" (Ibid.). The publication in 1644 of John Milton's defense of intellectual and press freedom, *Aeropagitica*, consolidated the emerging culture of critical, committed political journalism, and provided ideological legitimation for the early public sphere which it formed. Henceforth, there was growing demand for political coverage that was "free" from the restrictions of state and religious authority; the technological means of providing such coverage through print media; and growing numbers of literate readers, empowered as citizens and able to take advantage of this political coverage in individual and collective decision-making.

Following the execution of Charles 1 in 1649, there were many twists, turns and setbacks in the struggle for democracy in England, and universal suffrage was not achieved in advanced capitalist societies until the twentieth century, but by the early eighteenth century the principle of constitutional monarchy was established, a recognizably multi-party democracy was functioning, and a recognizably modern political media system alongside it. The first daily newspaper in English, the *Daily Courant*, appeared in 1703. Daniel Defoe's *Review*, described by Martin Conboy (2004, p. 60) as "the first influential journal of political comment" launched in 1704. By then, too, the normative expectations of political journalism in a democracy had been defined. I will outline them here under four headings.

JOURNALISM AS SOURCE OF INFORMATION IN A DELIBERATIVE DEMOCRACY

Democracy, it is generally accepted, contributes to good government only to the extent that it is reliably and accurately informed, and that the choices made by citizens in elections and other contexts are thus reasoned and rational (Chambers & Costain, 2001). In practice, of course, many democratic choices are founded on prejudice and ignorance. People vote for all kinds of reasons, as is their democratic right, and not always on the basis of rational thought or careful deliberation. But from the normative perspective the democratic ideal is one of informed choice, to which the outputs of political journalism are key contributors. Journalists provide the information on which citizens will be able to judge between competing candidates and parties. Journalists must be, in short, objective reporters of political reality, striving to be as neutral and detached as possible, even though they will hold their own political views. Partisanship in political journalism is permitted, but where it exists it should not pretend to be objective coverage, and should not crowd out of the public sphere the kind of detached, balanced reportage with which organizations such as the BBC, the *Financial Times* or the US TV networks are associated. As Peter J. Anderson (2007, p. 65) puts it in a recent study, "high-quality, independent news journalism which provides accurate and thoughtful information and analysis about current events is crucial to the creation of an enlightened citizenry that is able to participate meaningfully in society and politics."

JOURNALISM AS WATCHDOG/FOURTH ESTATE

An extension of the information function of political journalism in a democracy is the role of critical scrutiny over the powerful, be they in government, business or other influential spheres of society. This is the *watchdog* role of the journalist, who in this context becomes part of what Edmund Burke called the Fourth Estate. In order to prevent the abuses which characterized the feudal era, journalists in democracy are charged with monitoring the exercise of power. Are governments competent, efficient, and honest? Are they fulfilling their responsibilities to the people who elected them? Are their policies and programs based on sound judgments and information, and designed with the interests of society as a whole in mind? In its capacity as watchdog, political journalism oversees the activities of our governors, on our behalf, and with our permission.[2]

JOURNALISM AS MEDIATOR/REPRESENTATIVE

The watchdog function of journalism is undertaken on behalf of the citizenry. In this respect, the journalist is cast as a mediator between the citizen and the politician, the former's representative before power, who ensures that the voice of the public is heard.

This mediator/representative role can be performed in several ways. First, political media can give citizens direct access to the public sphere, in the form of readers' letters to newspapers, phone-in contributions to broadcast talk shows, and participation in studio debates about public affairs (for research on these forms of participatory political media Livingstone & Lunt, 1994; McNair, Hibberd, & Schlesinger, 2003). The representative function of political journalism is today enhanced by the availability of fast, interactive technologies such as email, text messaging and blogging, all of which provide new ways for citizens to communicate with political elites and participate in public debate. These technologies have fuelled the development of an unprecedentedly participatory democracy, in which more citizens now than at any other time in democratic history have regular access to the means of political communication. But from the journalistic perspective, the essence of the representative-mediator role remains as it was when readers' letters were the only practical form of participation in the public sphere for the great majority of citizens: to stand between the public and the political elite, and ensure that the voice of the people can be heard in the democratic process.

JOURNALISM AS PARTICIPANT/ADVOCATE

In the role of representative, the political journalist is positioned as advocate or champion of the people. Journalists can also advocate particular political positions, and be partisan with respect to the public debate, seeking to persuade the people of a particular view. As we have seen, journalistic partisanship (as opposed to mere propaganda) dates back to the English Civil war, where journalists participated in, as well as reported on, the conflict between the decaying aristocracy and the ascendant bourgeoisie. In the eighteenth century, writes Conboy (2004, p. 90), "adversarial politics engendered a partisan and often acrimonious press", while into the nineteenth century "the newspapers played an increasingly strident role in opinion formation and in the polarisation of popular political debate." Ever since, political media have taken sides, albeit in ways which aim to preserve the appearance of objectivity and factual accuracy in reporting. Reconciling these apparently contradictory goals is possible in the context of the separation of fact and opinion which is a structural feature of political journalism in a democracy, and of the distinction which exists in many countries between public and private media.

JOURNALISM AND DEMOCRACY—THE CRITICS

The normative expectations of political journalism in a democracy, as I have set them out above, are generally accepted to be: *information* (reportage); *critical scrutiny* (commentary, analysis, adversarialism); *representation and advocacy*; *partiality* (as long as it is clearly signaled as such, and commentary is distinguished from fact). The pragmatic performance of the political media in fulfilling these functions has, however, been criticized for as long as they have existed, from both left and right on the ideological spectrum.

The Critique of Liberal Pluralism and Objectivity

The Marxian critique, developed in the nineteenth century and still influential in media scholarship around the world, asserts that "freedom of the press," and the "bourgeois" notion of freedom in general, is essentially an ideological hoax, a form of false consciousness which merely legitimizes the status quo and distracts the masses from serious scrutiny of a system which exploits and oppresses them. The media are structurally locked into pro-systemic bias, and will rarely give "objective" coverage to anything which seriously threatens the social order of capitalism. The aspirations of objectivity, and of independence from the state, are masks for the production by the media of dominant ideology, or bourgeois hegemony, in the sphere of political coverage as elsewhere.

Marx and Engels developed this theory in the 1840s and after, in works such as *The German Ideology* (1976). It was then applied by the Bolsheviks to Soviet Russia, where journalists were required to renounce "bourgeois objectivism" and instead act as propagandists for the proletarian revolution and the dictatorship of the proletariat in particular. The Bolsheviks developed on this basis an entirely different theory of journalism from that which prevailed in the capitalist world, and exported it to other states with Communist Party governments. The classic *Four Theories of the Press* (Siebert, Peterson, & Schramm, 1963) set out the main differences between what it characterized as liberal pluralist theory on the one hand, and the authoritarian approach of the Communist-led states on the other (see *Journalism Studies* 3(1) for a retrospective on the *Four Theories* book). Though the Soviet Union is no more, the authoritarian approach continues to underpin the practice of political journalism in nominally socialist states such as Cuba and China. Journalism in these countries is institutionally part of the ideological apparatus of the state.

Comparable rationales to those traditionally adopted by the Soviet communists and their like-minded parties support the censorial media policies of Islamic fundamentalist states. In Saudi Arabia and Iran, for example, it will be argued that Islamic beliefs and truths are not reflected in secular, liberal notions of pluralism and objectivity, and that CNN, the BBC and others are promoting ideologically loaded accounts of global political events which can reasonably be censored in favor of state-sanctioned journalism. Here again, as in Cuba or China, the demand is for journalists to actively support a dominant ideology imposed by the ruling political faction, albeit one based on religious affiliation rather than notions of class domination. The extent to which liberal journalism can contribute to the establishment and maintenance of democracy in these countries, and also in post-Soviet countries such as Russia which have tended to veer between the authoritarianism of old and the stated objective of building democracy and free media, has informed a sizeable body of research. Kalathil and Boas (2003) have compared the role of the media—and emerging technologies such as the Internet in particular—in eight countries, including China, Cuba, Singapore and Egypt. They conclude, as does Atkins' (2002) comparative study of the role of journalism in Southeast Asia, that "overall, the Internet is challenging and helping to transform authoritarianism. Yet information technology alone is unlikely to bring about its demise" (Kalathil & Boas, 2003, p. x).

In advanced capitalist societies, meanwhile, scholars such as Chomsky and Herman have argued consistently against the validity of liberal journalism's claims to freedom and objectivity, implicating journalists in the maintenance of a "national security state" propped up by propaganda and attempts at "brainwashing" no less crude, they would assert, than that pursued by *Pravda* in the old Soviet Union (Chomsky & Herman, 1979). Others use different terminology and conceptualizations of the media-society relationship, but the core notion that political journalism is less about democratic scrutiny and accountability of the political elite than it is a vehicle for the "necessary illusions" (Chomsky, 1989) which prop up an unequal and exploitative capitalist system remains prevalent in media sociology, shaping a large body of research concerned with documenting the ways in which journalism contributes to the reinforcement and reproduction of dominant ideas and readings of events. The period since 9/11 and the invasions of Afghanistan and Iraq have seen an upsurge in scholarly work of this kind, as in for example Philo and Berry's *Bad News From Israel*. This critical content analysis of British TV news concludes that in coverage of the Israel-Palestine conflict, Israeli views receive "preferential treatment", and that there is "a consistent pattern on TV news in which Israeli perspectives tend to be highlighted and sometimes endorsed by journalists" (2004, p. 199). Although the BBC rejected allegations of systematic bias, its managers did accept that there was a difficulty in providing viewers of TV news, given the nature of the form and the limits on space, with the context and background required for making sense of current events. Similar controversies have surrounded public service journalism in Australia and elsewhere.

Other post-9/11 studies of news coverage of international politics include David Miller's edited collection of critical essays about news coverage of Iraq, *Tell Me Lies* (2004), and work by Howard Tumber, Jerry Palmer and Frank Webster (Tumber & Palmer, 2004; Tumber & Webster, 2006) which reaches less critical conclusions on the question of TV news alleged biases. A recent edited volume by Sarah Maltby and Richard Keeble (2008) explores the role of journalism in post-9/11 conflict situations from a variety of perspectives, both scholarly and practitioner-oriented.

Although the end of the cold war, and with it the global ideological division between communism and capitalism which dominated the twentieth century, has marginalized the Marxian critique of concepts such as pluralism and objectivity, the performance of the political media in the post-9/11 world continues to be the subject of debate and contention, with accusations of bias, propaganda and other deviations from the normative ideals of objectivity and balance being a regular feature of commentary by scholars, activists and also many journalists. The political media remain an arena of ideological dispute, not least on the issue of who—or which medium—

is telling the truth about political events, and whether such a thing as "objective truth" is even possible. There is bias, of course, in overtly partisan outlets such as Fox News and many newspapers, and this is usually apparent. As noted earlier, the blogosphere and online journalism in general have expanded the space available for opinionated, motivated journalism about politics to circulate, and this has encouraged at least some of the "old" media to wear their ideological preferences more overtly on their sleeves. On this all observers can agree, and choose their biases accordingly. On the deeper issue of political journalism's independence from the state and the political elite, and its capacity to be objective, individual conclusions tend to be premised on one's views about the nature of capitalism itself, its viability as a system, and the scope for serious alternatives. Believers in the fundamentally oppressive nature of capitalism, and its inevitable demise interpret journalism as part of the ideological apparatus without which it would collapse, and view its outputs with corresponding skepticism. Others are seeking to better understand the implications for politics, both domestically and internationally, of an increasingly globalised public sphere, in which elite control of information is being eroded (McNair, 2006). Building on the work of Castells and others on the network society, a number of contributors to the Maltby and Keeble collection cited above engage with what I in my own recent research have characterized as a chaos paradigm. Maltby's (2008, p. 3) introduction to the book, for example, notes that the multiple and diverse means of disseminating information in the public sphere have undermined the ways in which "states are able to control what is revealed, or concealed about their activities." In the same collection Tumber and Webster discuss the "chaotic information environment" which today confronts political elites, and observe "a growing awareness of human rights and democracy" on the part of the global audience (2008, p. 61).

As the Internet expands further, and real time news channels such as Al Jazeera proliferate and build audiences, scholarly focus on the relationship between globalised journalism and democratic processes is increasing (Chalaby, 2005). Al Jazeera itself has been the subject of several edited collections (see, for example, Zayani, 2005).

Commercialization, Dumbing Down and the Crisis of Public Communication

Another source of scholarly criticism on the relationship between journalism and democracy is the argument that competitive pressures on the media, and the consequent commercialization of journalism, have driven the standards of political journalism down, undermining democracy itself. Ever since the seventeenth century, the political media have been accused of deviating from the news agendas and styles required of democracy. In recent times, the intensifying commodification of journalism, it is argued, has favored the evolution of forms of political infotainment, a focus on sensation and drama in the political sphere, and the representation of democratic politics to the public as something akin to a soap opera. The popular vernacular for this process is "dumbing down," although this is more than a critique of the intellectual content of political journalism, but also of its increasing focus on matters deemed trivial from the normative perspective. Political journalism should be about economic policy, foreign affairs, and other matters of substance, it is argued, rather than the love lives of politicians, or their ability to look good on TV.

This set of arguments was prominent in the 1990s, exemplified by Blumler and Gurevitch's *The Crisis of Public Communication* (1995), Bob Franklin's *Packaging Politics* (1994) and other key texts of that decade. More recently, Anderson and Ward's (2007, p. 67) edited volume on *The Future of Journalism in the Advanced Democracies* laments the rise of "soft news" over "hard news," leading them to the pessimistic conclusion that "it is increasingly unlikely that much of the future news provision in the UK will meet the informational needs of a democracy." In addition to commercial pressures, they argue, the blogosphere and other developments arising from the emergence of Internet technology are squeezing out "hard" news. Anderson and Ward (2007, p. 8) define hard news as "journalism that can be recognized as having the primary intent to inform and encourage reflection, debate and action on political, social and economic issues," and journalism "that covers the issues that affect significantly people's lives." Against these criticisms and warnings of a degenerating public sphere, John Hartley (1996), Catharine Lumby (1999) and others (including this writer) have defended the evolving news agenda of political journalism as an intelligible and appropriate reflection of a popular democracy in which human interest issues have a role to play (if not to the exclusion of coverage of the more normatively preferred issues of public affairs). The blurring of traditional lines dividing the public from the private spheres is itself, from this perspective, a measure of the democratization of political culture, and its expansion to include the everyday concerns (and very human interests) of a mass citizenry.

Criticism has also been expressed of the extent to which coverage of politics has been subsumed within the broader category of celebrity culture, with its stress on personalities and image (Corner & Pels, 2003). Again, however, it is possible to argue that twenty first century politics is, inevitably, going to be about personality and its projection, and the judgments citizens make about the kinds of people who govern them. The 2004 election of Arnold Schwarzenegger as governor of California was covered at the time as symptomatic of this trend, condemned by some as evidence of the trivialization of politics and its colonization by the values of Hollywood and the entertainment industry. After the first wave of concern about the dire implications of Schwarzenegger's success, however, and in the face of the fact that the world did not end and life went on more or less as usual, the political media in the United States and elsewhere became accustomed to his governorship, and even the remote possibility of a future presidential campaign by the former action movie star (remote because of his Austrian roots, rather than his celebrity history, which was, of course, no obstacle to Ronald Reagan's rise from B movie status to governor and then two-term President).

Political Public Relations and the Rise of Spin

A key strand of both scholarly and public criticism of the journalism-democracy relationship has been the allegedly pernicious effect upon it of the growth of political public relations. While the conscious effort to shape media coverage of their declarations and actions by political actors is at least as old as political journalism itself, the twentieth century witnessed a qualitative transformation in both the intensity and the professionalism of the practice. The expansion of democracy on the one hand (with universal suffrage being achieved in most advanced capitalist societies by the outbreak of World War II), and of mass media on the other, created the need for purposeful communication between political actors and those who might vote or otherwise support them. Political public relations—the management of relations between politicians and their publics—became in the twentieth century a recognized sub-set of political communication, what I have characterized as a "Fifth Estate" evolving in parallel with the Fourth (McNair, 2001).

The emergence of political public relations has generated an extensive critical literature on "spin," which reads it as a deviation from or distortion of the normative public sphere. Political PR is viewed from this perspective as propaganda, in the negative sense of that term (i.e., as intentional deceit and dishonesty), and critiqued on that basis, alongside a critique of the extent to which political discourse and performance has changed in the media age. From Boorstin's (1962) seminal work on the pseudo-event to Aeron Davies (2007) recent book on *The Mediation of Power*, the concern with political communication practice, and its impact on journalism, has been central to journalism studies. So has the study of government communication, as in Sally Young's (2007) recent edited collection of essays on the Australian situation. Feeding into this work have been a growing collection of books by former "spin doctors" such as Alistair Campbell (2007), Bernard Ingham (1991) and Bill Clinton's communication adviser for much of his time in the White House, Dick Morris (1997). While media scholars have tended to be critical of the influence of public relations on the journalism-democracy relationship, these insider accounts, as one would expect, seek to justify and explain the rise of spin as a logical and in many ways necessary product of mediated democracy which facilitates elite-mass communication, to the benefit of the democratic process.

HYPERADVERSARIALISM

A recurring criticism of political journalism has focused on the rise of what James Fallows in the 1990s called *hyperadversarialism* (1996). Adversarialism, as we have seen, is widely regarded as a normative characteristic of journalism in a democracy, necessary for the effective exercise of critical scrutiny over political elites. Tough questioning, fearless criticism of falsehoods and mistakes, and readiness to go up against power, are essential attributes of journalism in a democracy. Less welcome, for many, is the aggressive, confrontational stance increasingly adopted by journalists allegedly seeking not elucidation and clarification of the pertinent facts of politics, but dramatic and crowd-pleasing contests. This trend is often associated with the increasingly competitive media environment, in which drama and confrontation are presumed to be more saleable in the news market place than quiet, considered reportage. Journalists, it is suggested by Fallows and like-minded critics, are under pressure to stand out, to make their political interviews newsworthy with provocative questions and answers, to set the agenda and become the story themselves.

These arguments have often co-existed with other, contradictory suggestions that far from being too critical of political elites, the media are insufficiently so. Barnett and Gaber (2001, p. 2), for example, identified the "twenty first century crisis in political journalism" as one of heightening economic, political and technological pressures combining "inexorably" to produce a "more conformist, less critical reporting environment which is increasingly likely to prove supportive to incumbent governments." By 2002, however, Barnett was complaining about the "increasingly hostile and irresponsible tenor of political journalism", and "the hounding of politicians" by a "cynical and corrosive media."[3] Political commentator Polly Toynbee shared his view, arguing that "journalism of left and right converges in an anarchic zone of vitriol where elected politicians are always contemptible, their policies not just wrong but their motives all self-interest".[4]

Writing in January 2005, constitutional historian Anthony Sampson argued that "journalists have gained power hugely [...and] become much more assertive, aggressive and moralizing in confronting other forms of power."[5] The changing style of political journalism, as this long-term observer of British democracy saw it, "reflects the declining role of other mediators, as much as the growing ambitions of the press." Echoing the views of James Fallows regarding political journalism in the United States, Sampson identified the competitive pressures on media organizations as the source of this unwelcome shift in the journalism-politician relationship.

> On the one hand they [journalists] are pressed towards more entertainment and sensation, to compete with their rivals, while the distinction between quality papers and tabloids has become less clear cut. On the other hand their serious critics expect them to take over the role of public educators and interpreters from the traditional mediators, including parliament.

This argument has driven the British debate around political journalism in recent years, as in John Lloyd's much-talked about *What's Wrong With Our Media*, published in 2004, which sparked a period of critical (and self-critical) journalistic reflection. Lloyd, himself a respected political journalist for many years, singled out the Andrew Gilligan affair of 2003 as an example of how reckless political journalism had become (Gilligan, for Lloyd, was reckless in suggesting that the government had lied about the threat posed to Britain by Iraqi weapons of mass destruction in order to mobilize public opinion behind invasion and removal of the Saddam Hussein regime). "If the best of journalism—the BBC", wrote Lloyd (2004, p. 14), "could both put out a report like that and defend it, and remain convinced that it had been unfairly criticised by [the Hutton inquiry, set up by the Blair government to investigate the circumstances of Gilligan's "sexed up" report and the subsequent suicide of his source, government scientist David Kelly] and traduced by government, then we have produced a media culture which in many ways contradicts the ideals to which we pay homage."

Political journalists cannot, of course, be both too conformist and too confrontational at the same time, and as ever in cultural commentary, one observer's "hyperadversarialism" is another's toadying favoritism. There *has* been a long term decline of journalistic deference towards political elites, as I and others have argued (McNair, 2000), rooted in wider socio-cultural trends and in itself very welcome from the perspective of what is good for democracy. Political elites have never been held more to account, more closely scrutinized, in both their public roles and their private lives, than today, a trend now exacerbated by the ubiquity of the Internet and satellite news media. The always-on, globalised news culture of the twenty first century makes journalists ever more dependent on the political sphere for stories, and less willing to accept traditional codes and conventions as to the appropriate subject matter and style of coverage. The Clinton-Lewinsky scandal is only the most infamous example of this trend, now echoed regularly in comparable scandals all over the world. There are reasonable objections to the growing journalistic fascination with personality and private life amongst the political class. And yet, as John Hartley (1996) and other have argued, this kind of political journalism reflects an evolving public sphere, in which the private as well as public affairs of politicians can have relevance to democratic decision-making. Issues of trust, personal morality and honesty *are* important in informing the judgments citizens make. If in the not-too-distant past they were generally excluded from public discourse, today they contribute to a broader picture of political life constructed by the media. Some politicians benefit from such exposure, while others suffer. The new rules of the game are widely understood, however, and contemporary politicians cannot claim ignorance as to the importance of image and personality. Indeed, an entire apparatus of public relations and promotional communication has developed precisely in order to manage media relations.

This brings us to a further defense of hyperadversarialism, related to the previous section's discussion of the rise of spin—that journalists today face politicians who are highly skilled in the communicative arts, supported by professional spin doctors, advisors and consultants. In response, political journalism has of necessity become more reflective and *metadiscursive*. This is the journalism of *political process*, which accepts as a given from the outset that politicians are engaged in spin and publicity, and actively seeks to expose and deconstruct it, in the interests of uncovering a deeper level of truth. So, yes, Jeremy Paxman asks a politician the same question fourteen times during a TV interview—as he did of the Conservative Home Secretary in the 1990s—and fourteen times he receives an evasive answer. If, as the critics of such gladiatorial journalism argue, the audience learns little or nothing about the substance of the issue under interrogation, it is left in no doubt that the politician has something to hide, or is insufficiently in command of his or her brief to answer the question with openness and confidence. That is useful knowledge in a modern mediated democracy, as long as it is set alongside information about policy.

In political journalism, as elsewhere, fashions change. The fashion for aggressive political interviewing of the type exemplified by Paxman, John Humphrys and others, which was prevalent in the BBC in the 1990s and came to exemplify hyperadversarialism and the "corrosive cynicism" of political journalists in the British context, has evolved into a more subtle approach which recognizes that there are other modes of interrogation than the one premised on the question, "Is that lying bastard lying to me?" That there are many interviewing styles which can extract information useful to the democratic process was always the case, as illustrated by David Frost's deceptively gentle sofa interview style. Today, perhaps, there is greater acceptance that the bulldog terrier approach to political journalism is not always the best way to maximize the delivery of useful information (although, as of this writing, Paxman and Humphrys remain the unchallenged titans of the political interview in the UK). Paxman himself, in a lecture given to the 2007 Edinburgh Television Festival, expressed sympathy with the view of Tony Blair, given in one of his final prime ministerial speeches, that the British press were like "a feral beast" in their approach to politicians.

CRISIS? WHAT CRISIS?

Criticisms of the agenda, content and style of political journalism are cyclical, often contradictory, and rarely resolvable in a definitive manner. As citizens make judgments about politicians according to changing fashions (Tony Blair was judged by many to be too smooth a communicator by far; his successor Gordon Brown is often accused, not least by the political media who railed about spin for the Blair decade, to be not smooth enough), scholars and other commentators make judgments about the perceived failings of political journalism, often linked to wider concerns about the health of democracy. Journalists have been blamed, for example—and the rise of hyperadversarialism, process journalism and political infotainment have all been implicated in this trend—for declining rates of democratic participation in Britain, the United States and comparable countries. Citizens, it is argued, are disillusioned, bored, and increasingly cynical about politicians whom the media continually attack and criticize for real or imagined failings. None dispute that coverage of financial corruption and other matters of relevance to the performance of public office is legitimate, and the more adversarial the better, but do our media really need to be so obsessed with style, personality and process? Are not these obsessions to blame for the historically low turn outs of the 2001 general election in the UK, or the 2000 presidential election in the United States?

The truth is, no one knows. There are competing explanations for changing levels of democratic participation across cultures and over time—economic affluence, the decline of ideology, the increase in the number of elections in which people have rights to vote (in this author's country, for example, Scotland—since devolution was introduced there have been elections for the European parliament, the Scottish parliament, the Westminster parliament, and local councils. Many citizens participate gladly in all of these. Others find their democratic energies dissipating before the regularity of campaigns, and the variety and complexity of voting systems). Journalism may be a factor in explaining trends in democratic participation, but it is beyond the current state of social scientific knowledge to say with certainty how important a factor.

Lewis, Inthorn and Wahl-Jorgensen's (2005, p. 141) study of political journalism, while "not blaming the news media for the general pattern of decline in voting and participation in electoral politics" argues that "the way ordinary people are represented in the news media does little to inspire active forms of citizenship." By representing people as consumers rather than citizens, they conclude on the basis of their analysis of US and UK news content, "news is part of the problem rather than part of the solution."

The political journalists have themselves adopted a number of strategies designed to engage audiences in the democratic process, such as more studio debates and other forms of public participation, utilizing the new technologies referred to above. The main commercial public service channel in the UK, ITV, experimented with reality TV techniques in *Vote For Me*, a series in which members of the public "stood" for selection as a parliamentary candidate in the 2005 election, chosen by studio audiences and viewers at home. The experiment failed to have significant impact, but was an honorable attempt to harness the demonstrable enthusiasm for public participation in decision-making demonstrated by the success of reality TV shows such as *Big Brother*.

One fact that can be stated with confidence is that, regardless of its agenda, content and style, there is more political journalism available to the average citizen in the average mature democracy than at any previous time in history. Newspapers are crammed with columnists and commentaries. Political editors and special correspondents are prominent in network news schedules. Twenty four hour news channels proliferate, while the Internet is crowded with blogs and online punditry. Much of this content is trivial, polemical, and ultimately disposable, as much political journalism always was. Much remains focused on the traditional agenda of political journalism—the economy, social affairs, the environment, and foreign policy, the latter having been boosted in newsworthiness by 9/11 and its aftermath. Amidst the arguments about the quality of political journalism, which come and go, this quantitative trend hints at a broad public appetite for information and news-based culture which must give some grounds for optimism about the future health of democracies.

FUTURE RESEARCH IN POLITICAL JOURNALISM STUDIES

Research on the content and contribution of journalism to the democratic process will continue. Political actors, scholars, and journalists themselves will continue to monitor the output of the political media, testing it against their expectations of what the journalism-democracy relationship should be. There is, however, a growing concern with the potential role of new digital media in enhancing participatory and interactive modes of political communication between the public as a whole and political elites. The European Union, for example, has begun consultations on how to ensure that the public service media of the future can be used to maximize democratic engagement and participation. In many countries, as the transition from analogue to digital media proceeds, and as media organizations adapt to emerging phenomena such as user generated content, blogging and social networking, the extent to which these new media can improve the performance of the political media as democratic assets remains a key question for scholars in both the political science and media studies fields. This concern extends to the role of new media in global conflicts.

CONCLUDING THOUGHTS: JOURNALISM AND DEMOCRACY IN THE TWENTY FIRST CENTURY

Political journalism of the modern type emerged in parallel with the first democracies, and the bourgeois revolutions of early modern Europe. Nearly 400 years later, the spread of democratic regimes across the planet, and the steady decline of authoritarian government since the fall of the Berlin Wall and the Soviet Union, has been accompanied by the growth of a globalised public sphere. In Latin America (Alves, 2005), Southeast Asia (Atkins, 2002), the former Soviet bloc, and the Middle East (Mellor, 2005, 2007), the end of authoritarianism and its replacement by democratic polities, hesitant and subject to resistance and reversal as that process remains, has been fuelled by the increasing availability of, and public access to, independent journalistic media such as Al Jazeera (Zayani, 2005), online sites, and other forms of digital journalism. Arab scholars and journalists now speak routinely of an "Arab public sphere," in which liberal principles of pluralism and political independence are pursued, even by a channel such as Al Jazeera which has a very different approach to the conflicts being played out in the Middle East than, say, CNN or the BBC. In China, half a billion people now use the Internet regularly, and the number grows steadily, presenting the Chinese communists with a deepening problem of legitimacy. That country's hybrid of "capitalism with Chinese characteristics" had of this writing avoided media freedom in the liberal pluralist sense, but the pressures to open access to media, up to and beyond the 2008 Olympics, were clear. In Putin's Russia, meanwhile, state restrictions on the political media, and intimidation of journalists across the country, were meeting resistance at home and abroad, widely interpreted as antithetical to the country's transition to mature democracy. In Russia, as in most other transitional societies in the early twenty first century, the establishment of genuine, lasting democracy was recognized to be inseparable from the establishment of free political media, a functioning public sphere and a pluralistic civil society. The emerging democracies differ in their form, as does the political journalism which supports them. Democratic political cultures will vary widely, and will always be rooted in specific histories and circumstances. There does now seem to be an acceptance, however, from the offices of Al Jazeera to the boardrooms of the BBC and CNN, that the normative principles of liberal journalism identified in this chapter have a general applicability. Whether the pragmatic realities of global politics will permit them to become universally entrenched remains to be seen.

NOTES

1. From the first ever law of copyright in England, enacted in 1556.
2. The exemplary case of this normative role being performed in practice is that of Carl Woodward and Edward Bernstein, and their exposure of the Watergate cover up which ultimately forced the resignation of President Richard Nixon. This famous case, and the book and the film which were based on it, provide a lesson in what journalistic scrutiny of democratic government means in reality, and the challenges it may require on the part of individual journalists and editors, who may have to overcome wilful evasion and cover-up of the facts, intimidation and harassment, and worse.
3. Barnett, S., "The age of contempt," *Guardian*, October 28, 2002.
4. Toynbee, P., "Breaking news," *Guardian*, September 3, 2003.
5. Sampson, A., "The fourth estate under fire," *Guardian*, January 10, 2005.

REFERENCES

Alves, R. (2005). From lapdog to watchdog: the role of the press in Latin America's democratisation. In H. De Burgh (Ed.), *Making journalists* (pp. 181-202). London: Routledge.

Anderson, P., & Ward, G. (Eds.). (2007). *The future of journalism in the advanced democracies*. Aldershot, UK: Ashgate.

Anderson, P. (2007). Competing models of journalism and democracy. In P. Anderson & G. Ward (Eds.), *The future of journalism in the advanced democracies* (pp. 39-49). Aldershot, UK: Ashgate.

Atkins, W. (2002). *The politics of South East Asia's new media*. London: RoutledgeCurzon.

Barnett, S., & Gaber, I. (2001). *Westminster tales: The twenty first century crisis in political journalism*. London: Continuum.

Blumler, J., & Gurevitch, M. (1995). *The crisis of public communication*. London: Routledge.

Boorstin, D. (1962). *The image*. London: Weidenfeld & Nicolson.
Campbell, A. (2007). *The Blair years*. London: Hutchinson.
Chalaby, J. (Ed.). (2005). *Transnational television worldwide*. London: Tauris.
Chambers, S., & Costain, A. (Eds.). (2001). *Deliberation, democracy and the media*. London: Rowman & Littlefield.
Chomsky, N. (1989). *Necessary illusions*. Boston: South End Press.
Chomsky, N., & Herman, E. (1979). *The political economy of human rights*. Boston: South End Press.
Conboy, M. (2004). *Journalism: A critical history*. London: Sage.
Corner, J., & Pels, D. (Eds.). (2003). *Media and the restyling of politics*. London: Sage.
Davies, A. (2007). *The mediation of power: A critical introduction*. London: Routledge.
Fallows, J. (1996). *Breaking the news*. New York: Pantheon.
Franklin, B. (2004). *Packaging politics* (2nd ed.). London: Arnold.
Habermas, J. (1989). *The structural transformation of the public sphere*. Cambridge, UK: Polity Press.
Hartley, J. (1996). *Popular reality*. London: Arnold.
Ingham, B. (1991). *Kill the messenger*. London: Fontana.
Kalathil, S., & Boas, T. C. (2003). *Open networks, closed regimes: The impact of the internet on authoritarian rule*. Washington, DC: Carnegie Endowment for International Peace.
Lewis, J., Inthorn, S., & Wahl-Jorgensen, K. (2005). *Citizens or consumers? What the media tell us about political participation*. Milton Keynes, UK: Open University Press.
Livingstone, S., & Lunt, P. (1994). *Talk show democracy*. London: Routledge.
Lloyd, J. (2004). *What is wrong with our media*. London: Constable.
Lumby, C (1999). *Gotcha: Life in a tabloid world*. St Leonards, UK: Allen & Unwin.
McNair, B. (2000). *Journalism and democracy: A qualitative evaluation of the political public sphere*. London: Routledge.
McNair, B. (2001). Public relations and broadcast news: an evolutionary approach. In M. Bromley (Ed.), *No news is bad n*ews (pp. 175-190). London: Longman.
McNair, B. (2006). *Cultural chaos:Journalism, news and power in a globalised world*. London: Routledge.
McNair, B., Hibberd, M., & Schlesinger, P. (2003). *Mediated access: Broadcasting and democratic participation in the age of mediated politics*. Luton, UK: University of Luton Press.
Maltby, S., & Keeble, R. (Eds.). (2008). *Communicating war*. Bury St Edmond, UK: Arima.
Marx, K., & Engels, F. (1976). *The German ideology*. London: Lawrence & Wishart.
Mellor, N. (2005). *The making of Arab journalism*. Boulder, CO: Rowman & Littlefield.
Mellor, N. (2007). *Modern Arab journalism: Problems and prospects*. Edinburgh: Edinburgh University Press.
Miller, D. (Ed.). (2004). *Tell me lies: Propaganda and media distortion in the attack on Iraq*. London: Pluto Press.
Morris, D. (1997). *Behind the oval office*. New York: Random House.
Philo, G., & Berry, M. (2004). *Bad news from Israel*. London: Pluto Press.
Popkin, S. (1990). *The reasoning voter.* Chicago: Chicago University Press.
Raymond, J. (1996). *The invention of the newspaper*. Oxford: Clarendon Press.
Siebert, F. S., Peterson, T., & Schramm W. (1963). *Four theories of the press: The authoritarian, libertarian, social responsibility, and Soviet communist concepts of what the press should be and do*. Champaign: University of Illinois Press.
Starr, P. (2004). *The creation of the media*. New York: Free Press.
Tumber, H, & Palmer, J. (2004. *The media at war.* London: Palgrave.
Tumber, H., & Webster, F. (2006). *Journalists under fire*. London: Sage.
Tumber, H., & Webster, F. (2008). Information war: Encountering a chaotic information environment. In S. Maltby & C. Keeble (Eds.), *Communicating war* (pp. 62–74). Suffolk, UK: Amira.
Young, S. (Ed.). (2007). *Government communication in Australia*. Melbourne: Cambridge University Press.
Zayani, M. (Ed.). (2005). *The Al Jazeera phenomenon: Critical perspectives on new Arab media*. Boulder, CO: Paradigm.

18

Journalism, Public Relations, and Spin

William Dinan and David Miller

INTRODUCTION

Public Relations (PR) is an expanding and increasingly significant feature of the contemporary media-scape. Despite academic and popular interest in propaganda, especially in times of armed conflict, understanding of routine domestic propaganda—PR or spin—is rather limited. The conventional view is that modern PR was invented in the United States in the early twentieth century, and later exported around the globe. A closer historical analysis suggests that spin was adopted as a strategic response by capital (and the state) to the threat of the extended franchise and organised labour (Miller & Dinan, 2008). The subsequent growth of the public relations industry is closely linked to corporate globalization (Miller & Dinan, 2003) and to forms of neoliberal governance, including deregulation and privatization (Miller & Dinan, 2000).

This chapter will outline an argument for rethinking the role of PR in contemporary society by critically examining popular theories of spin in the light of available evidence and trends. In particular this chapter offers a critique of the appropriation of Habermas (1989, 1996) by apologists for PR, and argues for a new synthesis of theories of communication, power and the public sphere, drawing on Habermas. This conceptualization problematizes the understanding of source studies as simply the communicative relationships between sources (e.g., spin doctors), the media and the public. Instead, we argue, the media are often by-passed by public relations as it seeks to speak directly to particular publics, such as elite decision-makers and power brokers. To be clear, we are not arguing that the media are unimportant, indeed we do see the role of the media in amplifying and helping to legitimate "systematically distorted communication" as a problematic function of journalism. However, it is also clear that elite communications have their own conditions of existence and outcomes.

We consider in particular the reshaping of the field of journalism in the UK and the US, and we argue that the potential of the new relations of journalism is to dissolve independent journalism in the fluid of commercial values, fake news and source originated content. Given the tendencies evident in the commercialization of news production and the ways in which professional public relations tends to serve powerful interests we could call this process the "neoliberalization of the public sphere." We also believe that while the tendencies we discuss below are most developed in the US and UK (home to the largest PR industries in the world), there is clear evidence of the same processes and practices in operation right across the globe.

HOW DID WE GET HERE?

Alex Carey (1995, p. 57) identifies three important inter-related developments that in many ways characterised the twentieth century:

> The growth of democracy, the growth of corporate power, and the growth of corporate propaganda as a means of protecting corporate power against democracy.

The twentieth century saw the birth and inexorable rise of modern spin. With the promise of a wider franchise, intellectuals and elites on both sides of the Atlantic began to worry about the "crowd" and how the newly "enthroned" masses (as PR pioneer Ivy Lee remarked in 1914) would impact on advanced liberal democracy (Hiebert, 1966). Important figures in journalism such as Walter Lippmann (1921, p. 158) began to see how the consent of the crowd could be manufactured by elites to ensure the best functioning of democracy: "Within the life of the generation now in control of affairs, persuasion has become a self conscious art and a regular organ of popular government." Those at the centre of this enterprise were the captains of industry and their appointed propagandists. Perhaps the most famous early pioneers of PR were Edward Bernays, Carl Byoir and Ivy Lee in the United States. They had their less celebrated counterparts in the UK, in figures like Basil Clarke and Charles Higham (see Miller & Dinan, 2008).

What united these people was their belief in the necessity of managing public opinion, and their efforts in the service of political and business elites seeking to thwart or manage democratic reform. All these early pioneers of PR were deeply influenced by their experiences of using propaganda in times of conflict and crisis: for British propagandists this meant their experiences of repressing Irish nationalists during and after the 1916 rising and the efforts to defeat the Germans in the first World War; for the founders of the US PR industry their experiences inside the Creel commission (which sought to promote the US entry into WWI and the subsequent war effort) were formative (Miller & Dinan, 2008). These propagandists emerged from the war acutely aware of the power of propaganda to shape popular perceptions and behaviours, and the strongly held conviction that the lessons of war-time propaganda could be applied to the management of democracy during more peaceful times.

World War II saw renewed and intense interest in the application of propaganda techniques. Joseph Goebbels, the chief Nazi propagandist, was inspired by Edward Bernays book, *Crystallising Public Opinion*, a fact about which Bernays kept quiet until much later in his life (Tye, 1998). In the wake of World War II, those involved in propaganda and intelligence also came out of the services with a strong sense of the power of propaganda. The rise of Nazism was understood in conventional wisdom as testament to the power of propaganda. But the history of propaganda and PR shows that much was learnt by the Nazi's from the Western powers (Miller & Dinan, 2008).

Where are we today? The current media ecology is characterised by the continuing expansion of media outlets and the increasing conglomeration of media industries (McChesney, 2004). These trends are evident across the promotional industries too, with the emergence of a number of mega corporations like Omnicom, Interpublic and WPP, each owning many global public relations consultancies and networks (Miller & Dinan, 2008). There has been very strong growth in professional PR (consultancy & in-house) in the past couple of decades. For instance, in 1963 there were "perhaps" 3,000 PR people in Britain (Tunstall, 1964). In 2005 a "conservative estimate" suggested some 47,800 people were employed in public relations in the UK (Chartered Institute for Public Relations [CIPR], 2005, p. 6).

As media outlets cutback on journalism, there is a growing reliance on "information subsidies"—press releases, video news releases, briefings, trails, and exclusives offered by spin doctors to increasingly pressurised journalists (Curran, 2002; Davis, 2007; Herman & Chomsky, 1988; Miller & Dinan, 2000, 2008). While these trends are most acute in the US and UK, the same dynamic is in play throughout the globe. The scale and scope of the modern PR industry is such that the idealised models of the investigative journalist, independent newsgathering and the institutional role of press as the critical fourth estate are increasingly unsustainable. Thus, it may be time to revisit some of the theories of public communication to better diagnose the current "communication crisis."

THE DEATH OF NEWS

The pressures unleashed by the shift to the market from 1979/80 onwards have had dramatic impacts on news. In the UK, writes Nick Cohen (1998), "the number of national newspaper journalists has remained the same since the 1960s, but the size of newspapers has doubled; the same number of people are doing twice the work. News is the chief victim." The emptying out of Fleet Street as newspapers re-housed themselves in Docklands in East London, was emblematic of the segregation of many journalists from first hand experience of the political process. As Cohen (1998) notes most journalists are now based "in the compounds of Canary Wharf and Wapping, where barbed wire and security patrols emphasise their isolation from a public whose lives they are meant to report. News comes on the telephone or from PRs; from the Press Association (which has itself cut back its once comprehensive coverage) or the temporary enthusiasms of a metropolitan media village."

The convergence between the media and PR business's is visible especially in companies like United Business Media, which owns CMP a provider of events, print and online publications. UBM is also a major shareholder of Independent Television News [ITN] (20 percent) and the Press Association (17.01 percent) (United Business Media [UBM], 2007). But UBM also owns PR Newswire, a publicity service for corporations and the PR industry which distributes content to news outlets such as ITN and the Press Association. PR Newswire is also the parent of another subsidiary, eWatch, a controversial internet monitoring agency which advertised a service to spy on activist groups and corporate critics. After it was exposed by *Business Week* in 2000, the page promoting this was removed from the eWatch Web site and PR Newswire even claimed that it had never existed. (Lubbers, 2002, p. 117)

The integration of the PR and media industries is in its early stages. But it is a tendency that undermines the possibility of independent media. This tendency is reinforced by the rise of "infomediaries" and "fake news." Amongst the developments is the trend towards the direct corporate control of information media. An early example of this was the joint venture between ITN and Burson Marsteller, one of the biggest and least ethical PR firms in the world. Corporate Television News was based inside ITN headquarters with full access to ITN archives and made films for Shell and other corporate clients. In 1999, one of the UK's leading lobbyists Graham Lancaster (then of Biss Lancaster, now owned by global communications giant Havas) expounded his view that PR firms "will increasingly" own their own channels for delivery to customers superceding "media." PR channels will become "infomediaries." But the important quality that they must have is apparent independence—they must be, in other words, fake news channels (G. Lancaster, personal communication, October 1999).

A new venture by one of New Labour's favourite PR people, Julia Hobsbawm, attempts to blur the lines between spin and journalism even further. Editorial Intelligence involves a range of professional communicators including journalists, PR people and lobbyists. Back in 2001 before its creation Hobsbawm (2001) had written that

> The role of PR is to provide information, to "tell the truth persuasively", and to allow journalism the right to interpret, for good or bad. [...] PR has nothing to hide. We send out press releases and give briefings openly (they are called press conferences and launches). With the exception of the mutually beneficial "off the record" quote, PR is transparent. But journalists' egos often make them demur when admitting the involvement of public relations, hence years of running doctored interviews rather than admit intervention.

Hobsbawm's argument attempts to "level" journalism and PR to suggest that one is, at least, no worse than the other. Journalist-source conflict is pointless and Editorial Intelligence is a kind of balm on the wound. Hobsbawm says that "ei" will combine "the consulting and analysis of a think-tank with the accurate data of a directory and the inside scoop of a newspaper." It aims to break down the "traditional hostility between journalism and PR by getting the two to mix at lunches, dinners and speaking events. 'Cynicism is so over,' she says" (Jardine, 2005). The venture came in for criticism from some in the mainstream. Alluding to the ei strapline—"Where PR meets journalism"—Christina Odone (2006) wrote:

> PR meets journalism in Caribbean freebies, shameless back-scratching and undeclared interests. A link to a PR firm should spell professional suicide for a journalist, rather than a place on a highfalutin advisory board. Journalists should meet PR in a spirit of hostility—treating the information passed on as suspect, scrutinising possible motives and investigating possible links. As it is, the Westminster village pens into a confined space politicos, hacks and PRs, making for an often unhealthy, if informal, proximity. An organised "network" such as EI's, where more than 1,000 hacks and PR figures formally join hands, risks institutionalising a clique where who knows who will influence who writes what.

In the domestic context efforts to dominate the information environment are furthest advanced in the United States, where there are extensive networks of think tanks, lobbying firms, and front groups associated with neoliberal and neoconservative tendencies. One pioneering example is Tech Central Station (TCS), which appears at first glance to be a kind of think tank cum internet magazine. Look a little deeper and it is apparent that TCS has "taken aggressive positions on one side or another of intra-industry debates, rather like a corporate lobbyist" (Confessore, 2003).

TCS is published by the DCI Group, a prominent Washington "public affairs" firm specializing in PR, lobbying, and "Astroturf" campaigning: "many of DCI's clients are also 'sponsors' of the site it houses. TCS not only runs the sponsors' banner ads; its contributors aggressively defend those firms' policy positions, on TCS and elsewhere" (Confessore, 2003). James Glassman, who runs Tech Central Station has:

> Given birth to something quite new in Washington: journo-lobbying [...] It's an innovation driven primarily by the influence industry. Lobbying firms that once specialized in gaining person-to-person access to key decision-makers have branched out. The new game is to dominate the entire intellectual environment in which officials make policy decisions, which means funding everything from think tanks to issue ads to phoney grassroots pressure groups. But the institution that most affects the intellectual atmosphere in Washington, the media, has also proven the hardest for K Street to influence—until now. (Confessore, 2003)

Such developments pose an enormous threat to independent journalism and proper scrutiny of public institutions and policy making. The PR industry certainly needs the appearance of independent media in order to sustain a patina of credibility, but the trajectory outlined above points to newly emerging political communication source strategies which aggressively seek to colonise or dominate the information environment. Thus, our models for understanding contemporary political journalism need to account for the spread of promotional culture and these new forms of spin.

THE PUBLIC SPHERE AND FORMS OF POLITICAL COMMUNICATION

The public sphere has become a very popular and influential model for analysing political communication. Perhaps part of the attraction of the concept is that it is elastic and sufficiently flexible to allow a variety of applications. As Garnham (2000, p. 169) suggests, the utility of Habermas's theory is that it seeks to "hold liberalism to its emancipatory ideals," by focusing on the links between institutions and practices in democratic polities, and "the necessary material resource base for any public sphere" (pp. 360–361). Much of the debate about the public sphere is media centric, in that it tends to focus on the role of the mass media in shaping public discourse. However, Habermas has a more nuanced understanding of political communication and the model allows for public and private communications, meaning a broader conception than simply the role of mass media and including also online and virtual communications, as well as elite communications and processes of lobbying. It is the latter which is a crucial element in our argument for the continuing utility of the model of the public sphere.

A repeated criticism of theories of the public sphere relates to its idealised (liberal-rational) model of public communication. Habermas champions forms of rational-critical debate, wherein argument and reason are paramount, and participations are truthful and consensus seeking. There is no place in this idealised model for strategic communication and the presentation of private interests as generalizable public interests. Therefore, much of the practice of PR has no place in a rational, deliberative democracy. Of course, in the real world PR is increasingly important in political and public communication, so the model of the public sphere needs to be revised to account for this empirical reality. To date the most developed area of research in political communications addresses political parties, their news management and spin tactics. It often excludes business and NGO media relations, and neglects the less public communicative activities of such groups, including lobbying and corporate social responsibility (CSR), think tanks and policy planning activities. This lacuna is partially explained by a tendency to focus on media rather than more broadly on communication. In our view this implicit model should be turned on its head and start with economic, social and political institutions, focusing on their attempts to pursue their own interests (including by communicative means). Seen from this vantage point, news and political culture are one part of wider communicative strategies employed. Starting from the media—all too often—results in a tendency to forget or ignore wider issues and (for some) a tendency to focus on media discourse as if it was divorced from other forms of communication, and most importantly from social interests and social outcomes (see Philo & Miller, 2002).

The model of the neoliberal public sphere proposed here is sensitive to the variety of communicative practices deployed by the array of competing interest groups and coalitions that form to seek social and political outcomes. It explicitly acknowledges the power and resource advantages in play in political communication and lobbying and how this fits into a wider power/resource context. It recognizes strategic communication and stresses those aspects of political communication not directly targeted at the mass media and the general public, but rather at specific decision-making, or "strong," publics. A strong public is a "sphere of institutionalised deliberation and decision making" (Eriksen & Fossum, 2000). Contrary to some discussions which see such "publics" as facilitating democratic (Habermasian) deliberation, they can equally be understood as undermining democracy by insulating decision making from popular pressures. The communicative strategies of social interests can be focused on a range of overlapping fields—mass media are one, intra-elite communications and policy planning another. But the point equally applies to all arenas of communication and socialization such as education, religion and science.

Any cursory review of the voluminous literature on collective political action and organised interest group politics indicates the centrality of business, particularly large corporations, as key participants in public policy debate. Even the literature on the collective action of new social movements (such as Beder, 1997; Crossley, 2002; Gamson, 1975; Klein, 2000; Sklair, 2002; Tarrow, 1998) which asserts a more fluid conceptualisation of political organisation, issue contestation, and agenda setting, often demonstrates the presence of organised private sector actors (be they individual corporations or collective business lobbies) in opposition to the demands and agendas of social movements, and local communities (Gaventa, 1982; Eliasoph, 1998, Epstein, 1991). Yet, very often journalism studies has turned its gaze away from these actors and their communicative agency.

For our purposes—theorising the role of spin as strategic political communication—we can draw upon aspects of Habermas's model, foregrounding interpersonal communication and those actors who are the prime movers of "systematically distorted communication" (Habermas, 1996) and allowing for questions of strategy and interest. However, before interrogating these dimensions of political communication it is necessary to offer an interpretation of the public sphere that proceeds from a broad framing of the concept to a more focused application of the theory to questions of PR and actually existing democracy. Thus a recent (re)definition by Habermas seems a useful point of departure:

> The public sphere is a social phenomenon just as elementary as action, actor, association, or collectivity, but it eludes the conventional sociological concepts of "social order" [...it] cannot be conceived as an institution and certainly not as an organisation. It is not even a framework of norms with differentiated competences and roles, membership regulations, and so on. Just as little does it represent a system...the public sphere can best be described as a network for communicating information and points of view [...] the public sphere distinguishes itself through a *communicative structure* that is related to a third feature of communicative action: it refers neither to the *functions* nor to the *contents* of everyday communication but to the *social space* generated in communicative action. (p. 360)

By attending to the importance of social spaces opened up through communicative activities Habermas is correctly emphasizing the significance of the networks and interactions of political actors. For Garnham (1992) a virtue of a Habermasian framing of the public sphere is the escape offered from binary debates about state and/or market control over public discourse. Indeed, the issues raised by Habermas and his critics are now pressing: "What new political institutions and new public sphere might be necessary for the democratic control of a global economy and polity?" (pp. 361–362).

PROMOTIONAL CULTURE, SPIN AND SYSTEMATICALLY DISTORTED COMMUNICATION

An integral characteristic of the idealised public sphere is its capacity to make the political process open and transparent. Habermas (1989, p. 195) emphasizes the "democratic demand for publicity" as fundamental to an accountable and democratic polity. Here the traditional watchdog role of the press as the fourth estate is clearly evident in the idealised model. The accessibility of the arena of politics, and thereby its participatory potential, seen through the optic of critical publicity, rests very much upon the communicative practices of those engaged in politics. How then does Habermas conceive of PR as political communication? Initially public relations is understood as a specialized subsystem of advertising, part of a wider "promotional culture" (Wernick, 1991), and it is noted that in class conscious society the "public presentation of private interests" must take on political dimensions; thus "economic advertisement achieved an awareness of its political character only in the *practice of public relations*" (Habermas 1989, p. 193).

The theory of the public sphere is clearly informed by an appreciation of the role of PR, particularly its early and persistent deployment by business interests. Habermas mentions pioneers of PR on behalf of corporate America, and notes that "in the advanced countries of the West they [PR practices] have come to dominate the public sphere [...] They have become a key phenomenon for the diagnosis of that realm" (p. 193). The notion that the public sphere is structured by power and money, and the assertion that those in the developed west live in societies of 'generalized public relations' points to the role of corporations, states and interest groups systematically distorting (public) communication to their own advantage. In essence this analysis chimes with other critical historical accounts of the development of corporate political power.

Corporate PR seeks to disguise the sectional private interests of powerful actors. Thus, the more PR ("the publicist self-presentations of privileged private interests") is involved in public affairs, the greater the likelihood of a collapse of rational-critical debate, undermined by "sophisticated opinion-moulding services under the aegis of a sham public interest" (Habermas 1989, p. 195). Such practices have profound consequences for democracy as "consent coincides with good will evoked by publicity. Publicity once meant the exposure of political domination before the use of public reason; publicity now adds up to the reactions of an uncommitted friendly disposition" (ibid.). So, for Habermas, PR is actually central to the refeudalisation (or, as we suggest, neoliberalisation) of the public sphere. Political discourse is driven toward the lowest common denominator:

> Integration of mass entertainment with advertising, which in the form of public relations already assumes a "political" character, subjects even the state to its code. Because private enterprises evoke in their customers the idea that in their consumption decisions they act in their capacity as citizens, the state has to "address" its citizens like consumers. As a result, public authority too competes for publicity. (Habermas 1989, p. 195)

This line of analysis complements historical scholarship on the entrance of commercial interests into the field of public policy (Carey, 1995; Cutlip, 1994; Ewen, 1996; Fones-Wolf, 1994; Marchand, 1998; Mitchell, 1989, 1997; Raucher, 1968; Tedlow, 1979). It suggests that realising liberal democratic theory in praxis is dependent on reforming governance so that systematically distorted communications cannot unduly influence the processes of deliberative democracy. The kinds of concrete steps necessary to secure such conditions for policy making must, at the minimum, be grounded in principles of openness and transparency. Journalism is integral to this model—fulfilling a watchdog function, defending and articulating the public interest and acting as a surrogate for disorganised publics. Critically, the example of lobbyists (a significant and under-researched area for communication studies) is seen by the sociologist Pierre Bourdieu as problematic for the realization of participatory democracy:

> The neoliberal vulgate, an economic and political orthodoxy so universally imposed and unanimously accepted that it seems beyond the reach of discussion and contestation, is not the product of spontaneous generation. It is the result of prolonged and continual work by an immense intel-

> lectual workforce, concentrated and organised in what are effectively enterprises of production, dissemination and intervention. (Bourdieu, 2003, p. 12)

Certainly, such interventions (or lobbies) are underpinned by "systems of information gathering, assessment, and communication. The problem is to open up both the actions and the related informational exchanges to processes of democratic accountability" (Garnham, 1992, p. 371). Under the conditions of neoliberal, or corporate-led, globalization it is clear that this model of the public sphere and political communication does not simply pertain to developed liberal democracies. The promotional impulse, and promotional agents, increasingly operate around the globe (Mattelart, 1991; Miller & Dinan, 2003; Taylor, 2001). There is now a well developed field of political communication studies examining the role of PR in election campaigning. But scholars and critics are beginning to turn their attention to the role of spin in routine corporate communications and governance.

POLITICAL COMMUNICATION, MEDIA STUDIES, AND SOURCE STRATEGIES

There has been a perceptible shift in media and journalism scholarship towards studying the activities and intentions of sources in seeking to shape perceptions and political agendas. Much of this work has been influenced, explicitly or implicitly, by theories of the public sphere in academic discourse.

> On account of its anarchic structure, the general public sphere is, on the one hand, more vulnerable to the repression and exclusionary effects of unequally distributed social power...and systematically distorted communication than are the institutionalised public spheres of parliamentary bodies. On the other hand, it has the advantage of a medium of unrestricted communication. (Habermas 1996, pp. 307–308)

On such a reading deliberative politics is shaped by the political economy of the mass media, processes of institutionalized will formation ('strong' publics), and the informal opinion formation of the 'wild' public sphere. This provides a point of intersection between dialogic approaches to political communication, and those informed by theories of capitalism and ideology. The former are favoured by advocates for PR who want us to see public communication as somehow free from material resources and interests; the latter is a necessary corrective to this. Taking each in turn let us examine writing on public relations, much of which adopts a Habermasian framework, and—in our view – somewhat perversely produces a normative justification for the increasing use of PR in public communication.

Grunig and Hunt's model of excellence in public relations (1984; see also Grunig, 1992) has become an obligatory point of reference for many studies of contemporary public relations. The model is particularly favoured by authors concerned with the professionalization and legitimation of PR. The Grunig and Hunt schema recommends a two-way symmetrical dialogue between organizations and their stakeholders. This model borrows from the Habermasian ideal speech situation, where notions of power and interests are evacuated to make way for consensus seeking and truth. The model identifies four different forms of PR. The most basic is "press agentry" which is essentially promotional media work; a more developed type of PR is "public information" which uses one way communication to promote messages; a more sophisticated model is two-way asymmetrical PR which allows feedback from audiences, using market research or public opinion polling, which of course can be used to refine messages and /or more effectively manipulate audiences. Finally there is the exalted two-way symmetrical model, which through dialogue is alleged to help "create mutual understanding between an organization and the public." This approach "is considered both the most ethical and most effective public relations model in current practice" (Grunig, 1996, pp. 464–465).

According to the dominant paradigms in communications studies, organizations must manage their relations with other actors and publics. It is recommended that two-way symmetrical communication between organizations and their publics, mediated by professional communicators, is the best form of communicative agency (Grunig & Hunt, 1984; Grunig, 1992). Such communication is characterised by openness, mutual trust and responsiveness. However, this theory is in effect an ideal type that has been used as an apologia or legitimation for the (mal)practice of public relations. It conspicuously avoids questions of strategy and interests in the political communication process, beyond the vacuous assertions that communication in itself is a positive virtue and that liberal democracy is based on the right to communicate, petition and make representations to governance actors. As many commentators have noted "organizations and their stakeholders may well be partners in two way communication, *but rarely will they be equals in terms of power*" (Coombs & Holladay, 2006, p. 37). Thus, one of the most influential models of PR in effect has little explanatory power. The model further suggests historical progression from bad to good.

Research and scholarship on public relations is a rather niche specialism across the social sciences and business disciplines. Within media and communication studies PR is usually located as a sub-category of work undertaken on production. In the business schools PR is but one, junior, element of the wider marketing mix. In many ways public relations research is still marked by its origins: "public relations grew out of a highly practical context and subsequently developed a theoretical apparatus to support the analysis and legitimation of its professional activity" (Cheney & Christensen, 2001, p. 167). Thus, there is a strong emphasis in the PR literature on issues of technique, efficacy, strategy and professionalization. Professional anxiety is manifest in the literature around the twin concerns of the status of PR vis-à-vis advertising and marketing (and securing a rightful seat on the corporate board as strategic counsel) and the dubious status of PR in society at large.

Research on PR technique, strategies and efficacy is often undertaken in terms of organizational goals and management objectives. In this line of work there has been considerable interest in questions of inter-cultural communication and how PR fosters relationships and facilitates communication in a globalised context. One strand of work in this area examines the interplay between the global communication strategies of transnational corporations and the local cultures where the publics, or audiences, for these communication programmes are located. Another approach to understanding contemporary corporate PR examines the aspects of globalisation from above and below. The former focuses on the role of PR in securing "license to operate" for business and promoting neoliberal governance (Beder, 2006), whereas the latter critically examines the role of corporate PR in managing debates about social responsibility and supply chain practices (Knight & Greenberg, 2002). What is striking about much of the contemporary research on PR is the fact that media-relations are but one aspect of corporate communication. This means that our understanding of PR must refocus from questions of media coverage and representation to source strategies and communicative power beyond the media.

Research into relations between sources and the media has moved away from the "media-centrism" (Schlesinger, 1990) of studies focused only on the view from media workers. Source-media studies examine the role of sources and their communications strategies aimed at the media and general public. Research examining contested media discourses, where official and oppositional (or institutional and non-institutional) actors struggle over policy debate in the mass media, is now well established. Recent reflections on this field of inquiry include Deacon (2003) and Davis (2002, 2003, 2007), both much more advanced than the PR apologists and both attuned to questions of power and ideology. Davis (2002, p. 3) suggests that:

> Behind the current media interest in a few key "spin doctors" a substantial layer of "cultural intermediaries" has evolved with a significant impact on news production and decision-making processes. Politics has become further "mediatized" as a form of public relations democracy has developed.

However, the framework Davis offered in his analysis of the UK's public relations democracy precluded investigation of some very significant PR activities—namely those *private* "public relations" in the form of lobbying, government relations, and regulatory affairs. Davis focuses on the news and media agenda (what Lukes,1974, terms the first face of power) largely neglecting how PR and lobbying can actually keep issues off the media and public agenda (the second face of power), and how corporate community relations, Corporate Social Responsibility (CSR) programmes, think tanks, elite policy planning groups and other such micro initiatives act to prevent grievances and issues being recognized as such by publics (the third dimension of power), and thus keeping legitimate interests disguised, dispersed and disorganized.

Davis does allude to corporate and state power, acknowledging the "conscious" attempts at control that can be pursued through ownership and management, and hinting that factors such as ideology and the economy play a role news production. He criticizes radical political economy accounts of media power as lacking "a substantial focus on micro-level influences and individual agency," objecting to research that is "too reliant on work that stresses macro and wider political and economic trends and have not adequately tested this thesis with micro-level empirical work that observes active agents" (Davis, 2002, p. 6). Research on source-media relations offers some redress to this problem. However, the central question for Davis is whether the expansion of PR undermines journalism, rather than the broader question of whether the expansion of PR undermines democracy.

SOURCE RELATIONS AND POLITICAL COMMUNICATIONS: SCOPING A NEW RESEARCH AGENDA

In a significant development of his position, Davis argues that "critical inquiry on the links between media, communication and power must look beyond the elite-mass media-audience paradigm" (Davis, 2007, p. 2). In particular he urges us, correctly, to consider intra-elite communication and the activities of sources at the key sites of power in contemporary society, placing proper emphasis on "the micro and less visible forms of communication at these sites, and on the private actions of powerful individuals" (p. 10) whose networked actions and decision making have wider social implications (p. 170). Davis applies this approach to his study of financial elites at the London Stock Exchange, the political village at Westminster and the policy networks of development NGOs. This approach is careful not to assume elite cohesion or unity of purpose, but is instead concerned with how elites use media and communication and also how elites, institutions and their networks are influenced by the media. In this scenario journalists don't simply report on the powerful, but are actually a resource for elites to draw upon in their scan of the policy and political horizon. Despite this orientation the emergence of professionalized communications, cultures and associated elite networks which exclude journalists appear to be increasingly significant (p. 174). Davis cites diplomatic, financial and international trade networks as displaying these "disembedded" tendencies. Davis' argument has moved a considerable distance. But in our view there is still further to travel. It is necessary to conceptualise this as a question of communications and power as distinct from the role of mass media institutions in power relations. The latter misses the wider questions about lobbying, think tanks and policy planning organisations in which communication and mediation play a key role. In our view these communications networks and fora are among the least visible, most exclusive and most politically significant spaces of the contemporary public sphere. There would appear to be an absence of critical publicity surrounding these spaces, which is somewhat puzzling given the emerging consensus in advanced liberal democracies of the declining important of the parliamentary complex.

Classic liberal pluralist conceptions of competition between policy actors can be revised to account for the resources devoted to lobbying and political PR by business and the observation that the state's interests regularly coincides with those of organized capital (Domhoff, 1990; Miliband, 1969; Offe, 1984, 1985; Sklair, 2002). In this respect the analysis resonates with some of Habermas's observations regarding the role of organized interests in the public sphere.

Organized interests (e.g., business groups) don't simply emerge from the public sphere, but "occupy an already constituted public domain…anchored in various social subsystems and affect the political system *through* the public sphere. They cannot make any manifest use in the public sphere of the sanctions and rewards they rely on in bargaining or non-public attempts at pressure" (Habermas, 1996, p. 364). This implies that business can only convert its social power into political power to the extent that it keeps policy negotiation private or convinces general opinion in the public sphere when issues gain widespread attention and become the subject of public will formation. The need for organized interests to convince the public doesn't arise in many day-to-day settings, which suggests the necessity of looking beyond the media for the locus of communicative power in our public relations democracy.

Davis (2003, p. 669) urges a "focus on processes of elite policy making and how media and culture affect elite decisions. From this perspective inter-elite communications and the culture of elites is […] significant for sustaining political and economic forms of power in society." This line of reasoning re-engages media studies with debates in political science and sociology that have kept the agency of elites in focus. Surprisingly perhaps, in so doing, Davis rejects theories of the public sphere as a useful way of developing this endeavour. It has been our argument that the public sphere is a useful concept both because of its normative dimension and because it recognizes the private communicative activities which have become increasingly important in the neoliberal period. In his own contribution to the debate, Deacon (2003, p. 215) identifies—we think correctly—a widespread failure to "appreciate how powerful institutions and individuals seek to exert influence and construct political discourse in arenas other than the media."

But, Deacon (2003, pp. 215–216) worries that "if the media are perceived as just one of the many arenas in which political and public discourses are formulated and contested, there is a risk of returning to the residual position of traditional policy analyses in which media systems are seen as subordinate to political systems, and a peripheral part of the 'environment' in which policy choices are formulated and implemented." For us it is not a question of returning to a confined model from the political science or sociology of yesteryear. We think that media and journalism studies have nothing to fear from empirical research or from orienting towards a wider picture. The communicative processes involved in reproducing or subverting power relations should be of interest wherever they occur. They are more pressing now because the world is changing. These changes have markedly affected the worlds of journalism and strategic communications. The neoliberalisation of the public sphere is threatening the basis on which independent journalism can exist and is providing at the same time new ways for social interests to interact with power elites, the defining characteristics of which are insulating power from democratic accountability.

Part of the future agenda for research on spin and information control should attend to the interests and communications strategies of powerful sources. This focus is of a piece with journalism that seeks to scrutinise democracy as practiced today. Both must, in our view, avoid the pit-falls of media-centrism. Critical media scholarship (and indeed investigative journalism) can make a considerable contribution to understanding and analysing communicative power by addressing the communicative strategies of organized interests alongside or outside the "strong publics" of governments and parliaments. There is much work to be done on elite communications such as lobbying, policy planning and the role of think tanks in terms of shaping information environments. The mass media may be a resource for such research, but equally grey literature such as trade, specialist and professional publications should be of interest. The World Wide Web also opens up possibilities for tracking communicative strategies, virtual ethnographies and accessing rather specialized discourses neglected by the mainstream media. In conjunction with standard social research techniques, the creative and determined researcher can find ways (admittedly rarely first-hand) of accessing and analysing elite communications.

CONCLUSIONS

In our view recent developments in strategic communication show a marked dislike for independent media. Recently authors like Davis (2003, 2007) have argued for media studies to reorient its attention toward the private communicative practices of the powerful. The value of public sphere theory in this context is firstly that, in Garnham's words, it seeks to hold liberal democracy to account and secondly that it is able to conceptualise the closed communicative processes of "strong" publics which are increasingly replacing democratic structures under neoliberalism. Combining a strong normative framework with a recognition of systematic distortion of public communication by powerful actors the public sphere offers fertile ground on which to build theories of elite communication, agency and spin, and its positioning in terms of countervailing forces emanating from civil society.

Habermas' theory of systematically distorted communication has been criticized on the grounds that it is an idealised model which is difficult to operationalize while holding to notions of power, interests and strategy (Crossley, 2004). Nevertheless, the diagnosis of public communication offered by Habermas remains cogent: public discourse is structured and shaped by power and money, this serves the interests of the powerful and acts against the realization of deliberative and participative democracy. By taking this ideal type—and the embedded challenge within critical theory to focus on emancipatory praxis—we are left with the empirical task of researching political communication within a framework that recognizes that, in essence, this is not what democracy is supposed to look like. It also retains some sense of how a rational democratic public sphere should operate. By focusing on spin and propaganda the heuristic power of the public sphere is clear. The rational foundations of claims making, the agency of claims-makers and the political economy of the public sphere (i.e., access to communicative power) all become central objects of analysis. The neoliberal tendencies within the public sphere are thus a key feature of political communication that must be analyzed in relation to their role in sustaining or undermining neoliberal governance.

REFERENCES

Beder, S. (1997). *Global spin: The corporate assault on environmentalism.* Totnes, Devon, UK: Green Books.

Beder, S. (2006). Corporate propaganda and global capitalism—Selling free enterprise? In M. J. Lacy & P. Wilkin (Eds.), *Global politics in the information age* (pp. 116–130). Manchester, UK: Manchester University Press.

Bourdieu, P. (2003). *Firing back: Against the tyranny of the market*. London: Verso.

Carey, A. (1995). *Taking the risk out of democracy—Corporate propaganda versus freedom and liberty* (series edited by A. Lohrey). Sydney: University of New South Wales Press.

Cheney, G., & Christensen, L. T. (2001). Public relations as contested terrain: A critical response. In R. L Heath (Ed.), *Handbook of public relations* (pp. 167–182). London: Sage.

CIPR (2005). *Reaching new heights*. Annual Review. London: CIPR.

Cohen, N. (1998). The death of news. *New Statesman*, 4386 (May 22), 18–20.

Confessore, N. (2003). Meet the press: How James Glassman reinvented journalism—as lobbying. *Washington Monthly*, 12. Retrieved June 11, 2007, from http://www.washingtonmonthly.com/features/2003/0312.confessore.html

Coombs, T. W., & Holladay, S. J. (2006). *It's not just PR: Public relations in society*. Oxford: Blackwell.

Crossley, N. (2002). *Making sense of new social movements*. Buckingham, UK: Open University Press.

Crossley, N. (2004). On systematically distorted communication: Bourdieu and the socio-analysis of publics. In N. Crosley & J. M. Roberts (Eds.), *After Habermas: New perspectives on the public sphere* (pp. 88–112). Oxford: Blackwell.

Curran, J. (2002). *Media and power: Communication and society*. London: Routledge.

Cutlip, S. (1994). *The unseen power: Public relations, a history*. Hillsdale, NJ: Erlbaum.

Davis, A. (2002). *Public relations democracy: Public relations, politics and the mass media in Britain*. Manchester, UK: Manchester University Press.

Davis, A. (2003). Whiter mass media and power? Evidence for a critical elite theory alternative. *Media, Culture & Society*, *25*(5), 669–690.

Davis, A. (2007). *The mediation of power: a critical introduction*. London: Routledge.

Davis, G. (2003). Selling their souls. *Press Gazette*, February 7, p. 18.

Deacon, D. (2003). Holism, communion and conversion: Integrating media consumption and production research. *Media, Culture & Society*, *25*(2), 209–231.

Domhoff, G. W. (1990). *The power elite and the state: How policy is made in America*. Hawthorne, NY: Aldine de Gruyter.

Eliasoph, N. (1998). *Avoiding politics: How Americans produce apathy in everyday life*. Cambridge: Cambridge University Press.

Epstein, B. (1991). *Political protest & cultural revolution: Nonviolent direct action in the 1970s and 1980s*. Berkeley: University of California Press.

Eriksen, E. O., & Fossum, J. E. (2000). Democracy through strong publics in the European Union? *ARENA Working Papers*. Centre for European Studies. University of Oslo. WP 01/16. Retrieved June 11, 2007 from http://www.arena.uio.no/publications/working-papers2001/papers/wp01_16.htm

Ewen, S. (1996). *PR! A social history of spin*. New York: Basic Books.

Fones-Wolf, E. (1994). *Selling free enterprise: The business assault on labor and liberalism, 1945–60*. Urbana: University of Illinois Press.

Gamson, W. A. (1975). *The strategy of social protest*. Homewood, IL: Dorsey.

Garnham, N. (1992). The media and the public sphere. In C. Calhoun (Ed.), *Habermas and the public sphere* (pp. 359–376). Cambridge, MA: MIT Press.

Garnham, N. (2000). *Emancipation, the media, and modernity: Arguments about the media and social theory*. Oxford: Oxford University Press.

Gaventa, J. (1982). *Power and powerlessness: Quiescence and rebellion in an Appalachian valley*. Urbana: University of Illinois Press.

Grunig, J. E., & Hunt, T. T. (1984). *Managing public relations*. Orlando, FL: Harcourt.

Grunig, J. E. (Ed.) (1992). *Excellence in public relations and communication management*. Hillsdale, NJ: Erlbaum.

Grunig, L. A. (1996). Public relations. In M. B. Salwen & D. W. Stacks (Eds.), *An integrated approach to communication theory and research* (pp. 459–477). Mahwah, NJ: Erlbaum.

Habermas, J. (1989). *The structural transformation of the public sphere: An inquiry into a category of bourgeois society.* Cambridge: Polity Press.

Habermas, J. (1996). *Between facts and norms: Contribution to a discourse theory of law and democracy.* Cambridge, MA: The MIT Press.

Herman, E., & Chomsky, N. (1988). *Manufacturing consent: the political economy of the mass media.* New York: Pantheon Books

Hiebert, R. E. (1966). *Courtier to the crowd: the story of Ivy Lee and the development of public relations.* Ames: Iowa State University Press.

Hobsbawm, J. (2001). PRs have nothing to hide. What about journalists? *The Independent*, November 27, 8. Retrieved June 11, 2007, from http://www.independent.co.uk/news/media/julia-hobsbawm-prs-have-nothing-to-hide-what-about-journalists-618200.html

Jardine, C. (2005). The rise and rise of the professional networker. *Daily Telegraph*, November 3, 27. Retrieved June 11, 2007, from http://www.telegraph.co.uk/arts/main.jhtml?xml=/arts/2005/11/03/lnet03.xml&page=3

Klein, N. (2000). *No logo.* London: Harper Collins.

Knight, G. & Greenberg, J. (2002). Promotionalism and subpolitics: Nike and its labor critics. *Management Communication Quarterly, 15*(4), 541–570.

Lippmann, W. (1921). *Public opinion.* New York: Free Press.

Lubbers, E. (Ed) (2002). *Battling big business.* Totnes, Devon, UK: Green Books.

Lukes, S. (1974). *Power: A radical view.* London: MacMillan.

McChesney, R. (2004). *The problem of the media: U.S. communications politics in the 21st century.* New York: Monthly Review Books.

Marchand, R. (1998). *Creating the corporate soul: The rise of public relations and corporate imagery in American big business.* Berkeley: University of California Press.

Mattelart, A. (1991). *Advertising international: The privatisation of public space.* London: Routledge.

Miliband, R. (1969). *The state in capitalist society.* London: Weidenfeld & Nicolson.

Miller, D., & Dinan, W. (2000). The rise of the PR industry in Britain 1979–1998. *European Journal of Communication, 15*(1), 5–35.

Miller, D., & Dinan, W. (2003). Global public relations and global capitalism. In D. Demers (Ed.), *Terrorism, globalization, and mass communication* (pp. 193–214). Spokane, WA: Marquette Books.

Miller, D., & Dinan, W. (2008). *A century of spin: How PR became the cutting edge of corporate power.* London: Pluto.

Mitchell, N. J. (1989). *The generous corporation.* New Haven, CT: Yale University Press.

Mitchell, N. J. (1997). *The conspicuous corporation.* Ann Arbor: University of Michigan Press.

Odone, C. (2006). EI seems a dangerous meeting of minds. *The Guardian*, March 27, Media Section. Retrieved June 11, 2007, from http://www.guardian.co.uk/media/2006/mar/27/mondaymediasection12

Offe, C. (1984). *Contradictions of the welfare state.* London: Hutchinson.

Offe, C. (1985). *Disorganised capitalism: Contemporary transformations in work and politics.* Cambridge: Polity Press.

Philo, G., & Miller, D. (2002). The circuit of mass communication. In M. Holborn (Ed.), *Developments in sociology* (pp. 1–21). London: Causeway Press.

Raucher, A. (1968). *Public relations and business, 1900–1929.* Baltimore, MD: Johns Hopkins University Press.

Schlesinger, P. (1990). Rethinking the sociology of journalism: Source strategies and the limits of media-centrism. In M. Ferguson (Ed.), *Public communication: The new imperatives* (pp. 61–83). London: Sage.

Sklair, L. (2002). *Globalization: capitalism and its alternatives.* Oxford: Oxford University Press.

Tarrow, S. (1998). *Power in movement.* Cambridge: Cambridge University Press.

Taylor, M. (2001). International Public Relations: Opportunities and challenges for the 21st century. In R. L. Heath (Ed.) *Handbook of public relations* (pp. 631–634). London: Sage.

Tedlow, R. (1979). *Keeping the corporate image: Public relations and business, 1900–1950.* Greenwich, CT: JAI Press.

Tunstall, J. (1964). *The advertising man in London advertising agencies.* London: Chapman & Hall.

Tye, L. (1998). *The father of spin: Edward L. Bernays & the birth of PR.* New York: Henry Holt.

United Business Media (2007). *Regulatory Announcements REG—United Business Media: Final Results Part 1.* March 2. Retrieved 11 June 2007 from http://www.unm.com/ubm/ir/rns/rnsitem?id=1172818830nPrr2FF3Ea&t=popup

Wernick, A. (1991). *Promotional culture, advertising, ideology and symbolic expression.* London: Sage.

19

Alternative and Citizen Journalism

Chris Atton

This chapter examines journalism that is produced not by professionals but by those outside mainstream media organizations. Amateur media producers typically have little or no training or professional qualifications as journalists; they write and report from their position as citizens, as members of communities, as activists, as fans. This chapter will show how key writers in the subject area have understood the activities of these amateur journalists. The chapter places these activities in three categories: social movement media and citizens' media; local alternative journalism; fanzines and blogs. It examines the major studies to show how different theoretical and ideological perspectives have influenced the nature of those studies. Examples will be drawn from the key texts in the area including Atton (2002), Downing, Ford, Gil and Stein (2001) and Rodriguez (2001).

The merits and limits of these and other studies will be examined. Methodological gaps will also be identified, such as the almost complete absence of research into audiences and the absence of any detailed, international comparative studies. Finally, proposals for future research will be made, in particular for studies that deal with alternative and citizen journalism as work and that examine how alternative and mainstream cultures of news production might be understood in complementary ways, rather than solely in opposition to one another.

DEFINITIONS AND CONCEPTS: SOCIAL MOVEMENTS AND CITIZENS' MEDIA

What are the features of this amateur journalism? What sets it apart from mainstream, professionalized practices? There have been many attempts to define and conceptualize it, vividly exhibited by the variety of terms employed to summarize its perspectives and practices: alternative journalism; citizen's media; citizen journalism; democratic media; radical media. This section will show how each term encapsulates a structuring philosophy that argues from a distinctive and ideological perspective. Nevertheless, they share a common foundation in their amateurism.

Raymond Williams (1980) highlights three aspects of communication that provide the material for this foundation. For Williams, public communication could only be rigorously understood by considering the process of "skills, capitalization and controls" (p. 54). To apply this principle to alternative media, James Hamilton (2000) argues that we need to talk of deprofessionalization, decapitalization and deinstitutionalization. In other words, alternative media must be available to "ordinary" people without the necessity for professional training and excessive capital outlay; they must take place in settings other than media institutions or similar systems. Such media will then have the potential to more closely reflect the practices of decentralized, directly democratic, self-managed and reflexive networks of "everyday-life solidarity" that Alberto Melucci (1996) finds at the heart of social movement activity. Similarly, John Downing (1984) considers radical media as the media of social movements, produced by political activists for political and social change. This signals an interest in considering media as radical to the extent that they explicitly shape political consciousness through collective endeavour (Enzensberger, 1976). Downing (1984) and Downing et al. (2001) argue that the media of these movements are important not only for what they say but for how they are organized. What Downing terms "rebellious communication" does not simply challenge the political status quo in its news reports and commentaries, it challenges the ways it is produced. This position echoes Walter Benjamin's (1934/1982) argument that, in order for political propaganda to be effective, it is not enough to merely reproduce the radical or revolutionary content of an argument in a publication. The medium itself requires transformation: the position of the work in relation to the means of production has to be critically re-aligned. This requires not only the radicalising of methods of production but a re-thinking of what it means to be a media producer.

If the aim of radical media is to effect social or political change, then it is crucial, Downing says, that they practice what they preach. He calls this "prefigurative politics" or "the attempt to practice socialist principles in the present, not merely to imagine them for the future" (Downing et al., 2001, p. 71). To achieve this, Downing proposes a set of "alternatives in principle" that draw on anarchist philosophy. This leads him to emphasize the importance of encouraging contributions from as many interested parties as possible, in order to emphasize the "multiple realities" of social life (oppression, political cultures, economic situations) (Downing, 1984, p. 17). Radical media thus come to constitute a major feature of an alternative public sphere (Downing, 1988) or, as the diversity of projects suggests, many alternative public spheres (Fraser, 1992; Negt & Kluge, 1972/1983). Thus, the global Internet-based news network, Indymedia, may be considered as a multiple of local alternative public spheres that together comprise a "'macro' public sphere [...which] offers geographically dispersed participants opportunities to debate issues and events [...and] to collaborate on activist initiatives of a global reach" (Haas, 2004, p. 118).

Downing privileges media that are produced by non-professionals, by groups that are primarily constituted for progressive, social change. He draws on an extremely wide range of forms drawn from two centuries of political activism. Whilst the most detailed examples come from leftist newspapers and radio in Italy and Portugal and from American access radio, reference is made to 18th and 19th century political cartooning in Britain, German labour songs of the 19th and early 20th centuries, and 19th century African American public festivals. Woodcuts, flyers, photomontage, posters, murals, street theatre and graffiti are also presented for their radical methods and messages.

Like Downing, Clemencia Rodriguez (2000) argues that independent media enable "ordinary" citizens to become politically empowered. For her, when people create their own media they are better able to represent themselves and their communities. She sees these "citizens' media" as projects of self-education. She draws particularly on Paulo Freire's (1970) theories of conscientization and critical pedagogy, and Chantal Mouffe's (1992) notion of radical democracy. Rodriguez argues, as does Downing, that alternative media do not only have a counter-information role. For Rodriguez, the term "citizens" is particular: it refers to those members of society who "actively participate in actions that reshape their own identities, the identities of others, and their social environment, [through which] they produce power" (Rodriguez, 2000, p. 19). Her studies of Latin American media (Rodriguez, 2000, 2003) demonstrate this. For example, Rodriguez notes how the production of a video by striking women workers in a Colombian maternity clinic led to "shifting power roles [...that] facilitate[d] a creative collective dynamic that [...] challenge[d] institutionalized leadership roles" (Rodriguez, 2001, pp. 123–124).

These "citizens' media" are aimed not at state-promoted citizenship but at media practices that construct citizenship and political identity within everyday life practices (de Certeau, 1984; Lefebvre, 1947/1991). Rather than relying on the mass media to set the boundaries of political involvement (Dahlgren, 2000), citizens use their own, self-managed media to become politically involved on their own terms (Norris, 1999). To become an active participant in the process of media production is a political education in itself. For Rodriguez, however, to become a producer seems at times to be more important than what is being produced. In her study of a Chilean community radio station she approvingly quotes a respondent: "It's more important to get five new people to participate than to get a thousand new listeners" (Rodriguez, 2003, p. 191). Downing too seems to privilege process over product, organization and engagement over words on the page and circulation figures. For both, political or civic self-transformation seems to be, if not the sole end of radical and citizens' media, at least its primary function.

Downing and Rodriguez demonstrate how such practices can create local, empowering public spheres. A study of Australian community broadcasting by Forde, Foxwell and Meadows (2003) similarly proposes that we should consider alternative journalism as a "*process* of cultural empowerment [...where] content production is not *necessarily* the prime purpose [and] what may be as (or more) important are the ways in which community media outlets facilitate the process of community organization" (p. 317, original emphases). Carroll and Hackett (2006) argue that such practices constitute "a reflexive form of activism that treats communication as simultaneously means and ends of struggle" (p. 96). This accounts for the building of identity (whether individual or collective) and of counter-publics, as well as the addressing of wider audiences. They do acknowledge, however, that media activists are "especially prone to 'getting stuck' at the first stage [...] with its own inherent satisfactions" (p. 98).

What do these studies tell us about journalism? Many of the media projects analysed by Downing and Rodriguez seem to have methods and ends so removed from the norms of mainstream journalism as to be unrecognizable. We learn little about these projects in terms of journalism practice: What do the participants do? How do they do it? How do they learn their practices? Do they even consider themselves as journalists? Hamilton is right to argue that amateur media production does not rely on professional training, large capital outlay and an "institution," but this is not to say that amateur journalism practices magically become independent, "free spaces" of the type idealized by Melucci (1995). Amateur media practices are always embedded in everyday life practices; they are therefore already located in broader political, economic, social and cultural contexts. For this reason, I use the terms "alternative media" and "alternative journalism" to describe these practices (Atton, 2002, 2003a, 2004). As Nick Couldry and James Curran (2003, p. 7) argue, "alternative" functions as a comparative term to indicate that "whether indirectly or directly, media power is what is at stake."

ALTERNATIVE JOURNALISM AND MEDIA POWER

We can examine amateur media practices for examples of how "naturalized" media frames and ideological codes may be disrupted. Nick Couldry (2000, p. 25) argues that alternative media projects result in the "de-naturalization" of media spaces, encouraging amateur media producers to rebalance the differential power of the media and to consider how "the media themselves are a social process organized in space." Pierre Bourdieu (1991) argues that symbolic power is the power to construct reality. Alternative media construct a reality that appears to oppose the conventions and representations of the mainstream media. Participatory, amateur media production contests the concentration of institutional and professional media power and challenges the media monopoly on producing symbolic forms. Therefore, to speak of alternative media and alternative journalism is to recognize the relationship between dominant, professionalized media practices and marginal, amateur practices. The struggle between them is for "the place of media power" (Couldry, 2000). Alternative journalistic practices present ways of re-imagining journalism and not only of adopting media practices for purposes of self-education and community empowerment. They offer a challenge to professional practices through their very recognition of those practices.

There is a further value in adopting the term "alternative journalism." No longer are we limited to thinking about amateur journalism solely as political projects, whose priorities are radical forms of organising, social movements, and individual or collective consciousness-raising. My own work has sought to explore the implications of what is both an expanded concept of amateur media and, at the same time, a more focused one: that of amateur journalism. Whilst not wishing to lose sight of any particular social relations that may be developed through amateur media production, I argue that any model of alternative media should consider equally processes and products (Atton, 2002); it should consider media content as journalism, not merely as accounts of self-reflexivity (Atton, 2003a). It is not only social relations (through organization) that can be transformed, but also the media forms themselves (discursively, visually, even distributively). There may also be a transformation of notions such as professionalism, competence and expertise. Alternative journalism may therefore include cultural journalism, such as we find in fanzines (Atton, 2001), as well as journalism published not by communities and movements, but by individuals (such as blogs). What happens, though, when "ordinary" people produce their own media? What are the features of alternative journalism? In the next section I explore this question by examining key studies in three areas: local alternative journalism, fanzines and blogs. Together they show the nature of the challenges that alternative journalism presents to the mainstream.

CHARACTERISTICS AND CHALLENGES OF ALTERNATIVE JOURNALISM

Studies of local alternative journalism will always be contingent upon particular geographic and demographic situations. They must be responsive to specific cultural and social contexts. Given the limits of the theories discussed earlier, such empirical studies can present valuable insights into journalism practice; insights that might well be missed by an over-emphasis on self-empowerment and radical citizenship.

In general, the commercial press relies on official sources as spokespeople not only for organizations and institutions, but as expert commentators on news events and issues as a whole. This specialist class is a social and political elite through which news values, newsworthiness and the very agenda of the news are defined (Hall, Critcher, Jefferson, Clarke, & Roberts, 1978). A hierarchy of access to the media is established that routinely marginalizes those without the social and political power to be deemed worthy of accreditation as sources (Glasgow University Media Group, 1976, p. 245). In mainstream news, these "ordinary" people are most often used as material for vox pop interviews and their opinions sought for human interest stories (Ross, 2006). By contrast, the local alternative press actively seeks out these people as expert sources. This does not only challenge mainstream sourcing practices. To bring the voices of the local community into the center of journalism is an ethical decision (Atton, 2003b). This decision not only considers the local community as important (after all, the commercial local press makes the same claim), it also places these voices "from below" at the top of the hierarchy of access, a practice that acknowledges ordinary people as experts in their own lives and experiences.

We find examples of this throughout the world. A study of the Bolivian miners' radio stations that flourished from 1963 to 1983 (but which first appeared in 1952, the year of National Revolution) emphasizes the value of participatory media production in highlighting the rights of workers in a politically marginalized region of a country (O'Connor, 2004). Similarly, the Movement of Popular Correspondents that developed in revolutionary Nicaragua in the 1980s and 1990s produced reports by non-professional, voluntary reporters from poor, rural areas that were published in regional and national newspapers alongside the work of professional journalists (Rodriguez, 2000). The Revolutionary Association of the Women of Afghanistan reported on the abuse of and execution of women under the rule of the Taliban, producing audio cassettes, videos, a Web site and a magazine (Waltz, 2005). Afghan women produced and distributed these clandestinely, using, for example, secretly-filmed camcorder footage of abuse. The South Korean *OhmyNEWS* (Kim & Hamilton, 2006) has adopted a hybrid approach to its Web site. Founded in 2000, the site relies on its network of hundreds of citizen reporters for contributions, though its editorial office is run by a small professional staff.

Participatory media production can be thought of as providing the constituents of an alternative public sphere, where agendas are set and discussion is developed through the journalism of social movements and communities. In his study of the German anti-nuclear media of the 1980s, Downing (1988) argues that they constitute, along with "bookstores, bars, coffee-shops, restaurants, food-stores," fora in which an alternative public sphere of discussion and debate may arise. He emphasizes social movement media that encourage "activity, movement and exchange [...] an autonomous sphere in which experiences, critiques and alternatives could be freely developed" (p. 168). Similarly, Jakubowicz (1991) adapts the concept of the public sphere to a more inclusive vision of communication and media. He identifies two alternative public spheres in his study of Poland in the 1980s, an alternative public sphere and an oppositional public sphere. These worked together against the Soviet-backed government of the day, "alternative" describing the activities of the Polish Roman Catholic Church, its newspapers and periodicals, whereas "oppositional" refers to the *samizdat* publications of the Solidarity movement.

Mathes and Pfetsch (1991) show how an alternative news agenda can spill over into mainstream media. In their examination of "counter-issues" from the mid-1980s in the former West Germany (the 1983 census, ID cards and a faked terrorist attack) they found a significant "inter-media" effect: the established West German liberal press tended to adopt both the topic of the issue from the alternative press as well as its frame of reference. Key to this process was *Die Tageszeitung* (or *taz*), a large-circulation, nationally-distributed alternative daily newspaper, founded in 1978. By the mid-1980s, *taz*'s reach went far beyond any alternative public sphere: it was read by prominent intellectuals and numerous mainstream journalists. It explicitly sought to "initiate a multiplier effect" (Mathes & Pfetsch, 1991, p. 37) by highlighting counter-issues to the mainstream media and actively moving these issues into wider public fora beyond the activist left.

There are two journalistic consequences of this ethos: the novel nature of many stories and the opportunity for sources to become journalists themselves. First, as Harcup (2006) shows, many stories in the local alternative press are unique to that medium (though the commercial press might subsequently report them). Stories tend to arise because of the highly varied pool of experts available to the alternative press. These experts might be factory, agricultural or shop workers, pensioners, working mothers, minor government officials or school children. This variety of sources might not only provide leads for stories, it can often bypass the event-driven routines of mainstream news practices: "[w]hereas mainstream media tended to notice health and safety stories only when there was a disaster [... *Leeds Other Paper*] exposed potential health risks before even the workers or their trade unions were aware of them" (Harcup, 2006, p. 133). This "investigative journalism from the grassroots" (p. 132) results from going beyond the typical "beats" of the local press (such as the emergency services, the courts and local council meetings) to privilege issues above events. The second consequence of this socially inclusive approach to reporting is that "ordinary" sources often become writers: "such journalism not only finds common cause with its community through advocacy; its explicit connections with the public sphere of that community serve as its rationale for seeking amongst that community for its news sources" (Atton, 2003a, p. 270).

These consequences may be used to build theory in the study of alternative journalism. Alternative journalism recognizes what might be achieved through challenging the rules and routines of normalized and professionalized practices. Its ethos of inclusiveness might well lead it to develop a network of "native reporters" (Atton, 2002). This is to expand the editorial group beyond the left-wing political activists who typically seem to be the initiators of such projects (Dickinson, 1997; Whitaker, 1981). Editorial inclusiveness also leads to organizational inclusiveness; Downing's prefigurative politics tend to be played out in anti-hierarchical, collective editorial groups. These methods, however, often work to the detriment of efficiency. Editorial copy might be argued over to such lengths that editions might be delayed and some reports might never appear due to lack of consensus. Comedia (1984) and Landry, Morley, Southwood and Wright (1985)—in an explicit echo of Jo Freeman's (1972) classic critique of structurelessness in the women's movement—argue that these methods, however "progressive" they might be, can only disadvantage the alternative press because they are adopted for ideological, rather than for instrumental, ends. Organizational problems are not universal, however. Blogs, for example, tend to be single-person operations, at least in their amateur form. Fanzines, too, tend to be run by individuals. Either they are overseen by one person, in the manner of an editor or, as is often the case, written entirely by one person.

FANZINES: ALTERNATIVE CULTURAL JOURNALISM

The fanzine shares much with its professional counterpart, popular cultural journalism. For instance, the roots of the popular music press in the UK and the US lie not in professionalized journalism but in the amateur, underground press of the late 1960s (Gudmundsson, Lindberg, Michelsen, & Weisethaunet, 2002). There is a significant similarity between the fan as amateur writer and the professional writer as fan. This says much about expert culture in popular musical criticism, where knowledge and authority proceed not from formal, educational or professional training but primarily from autodidactic, amateur enthusiasm. Simon Frith (1996, p. 38, n. 40) argues that "critics of popular forms (TV, film and to some extent pop) need know nothing about such forms except as consumers; their skill is to be able to write about ordinary experience." Once again, we see the privileging of the "ordinary" voice. In the case of fanzines, however,—and their online counterparts, ezines—these ordinary voices tend to be self-selected, rather than sought out and encouraged as in the alternative local press.

Fanzine journalism shares with its professionalized counterpart a perspective based on consumption. This is not to say that the two forms are identical. Fanzines often arise because the objects of their study (which may include football, film, comics and popular television series, as well as popular music) are ignored by mainstream journalism. This might be due to the novelty of the performer or genre (fanzines often draw attention to new and emerging cultural activities) or because they have become unfashionable (Atton, 2001). Fanzines also challenge critical orthodoxy; they may arise because their writers believe that "their" culture is marginalized or misrepresented by mainstream tastes. Consequently, fanzines and ezines become "cultural fora for the exchange and circulation of knowledge and the building of a cultural community" (Fiske, 1992a, pp. 44–45). The circulation of this knowledge within a like-minded community further develops expertise and cultural capital. Such a display of expert knowledge can challenge professional notions of expert authority (Atton, 2004, Ch. 6).

Unlike the local alternative press, fanzines offer opportunities to create, maintain and develop taste communities across geographic boundaries. They are less interested in reaching out to broader audiences, preferring to cultivate and consolidate a specialist audience. This consolidation often employs similar methods to mainstream cultural journalism such as interviews and reviews (or match reports, in the case of football fanzines). Fanzine writers, however, tend to write at much greater length than the "capsule" reviews that are now common in newspapers and specialist, commercial magazines. In some cases, particularly in ezines, a kaleidoscopic approach is obtained by publishing multiple accounts of the same event or product (Atton, 2001). The credibility and authority of a music fanzine will often enable it to obtain interviews from artists directly, bypassing public relations professionals. Newsgathering is a different matter. Fanzines will often have erratic publishing schedules; this infrequency militates against the timely reporting of news. My own study of football fanzines (Atton, 2006a) identifies three typical approaches to news: stories reproduced verbatim from professional news media; stories summarized from the professional media; and original journalism. The latter were in the minority and usually embedded in interviews. Hard news stories were usually sourced from commercial news providers. Unlike local alternative journalism, there was no evidence of original, investigative reporting. Instead, the fanzines drew mostly on local and national mainstream media, as well as press releases from the football clubs. There was little evidence of agenda setting. The lack of original news reporting is not necessarily a weakness, however. As John Hartley (2000) points out, public communication is becoming increasingly redactional, particularly through the proliferation of news providers on the Internet. The specialist audience might be well served by the news digests produced by football fanzines. These digests provide a backdrop against which the primary function of the fanzine is presented: expert, amateur commentary and opinion founded on the accumulation and display of detailed information.

BLOGS: PERSONAL-POLITICAL JOURNALISM

In its ideal form, the blog combines the individual approach often found in fanzines with the social responsibility of local alternative journalism. Blogging may be understood as a number of practices. These include the publishing of personal diaries by professionals (such as journalists and politicians), amateur investigative journalism, comment and opinion (such as American Matt Drudge's the *Drudge Report* and the British blogger, "Guido Fawkes") and eyewitness reporting by observers and participants. Amateur blogs have been credited with breaking news in advance of mainstream news organizations: for example, Trent Lott's resignation as the US Senate's majority leader in December 2002 followed his comments expressing "indulgence towards the racist policies of the Old South" (Burkeman, 2002). These comments, Burkeman notes, were first picked up and commented on by bloggers some days before the mainstream media ran the story. The Gulf War of 2003 saw a variety of bloggers supplementing mainstream media coverage. "Smash," the pseudonym of an American military officer serving in Iraq, posted chronicles of his experiences (Kurtz, 2003). Professional reporters used blogs to post commentaries that their employers would not be prepared to publish. A blog run by "Salam Pax" claimed to be written by a Baghdad resident and the US journal *New Republic* ran an online diary by Kanan Makiya, a leading Iraqi dissident. Blogs were posted from professional journalists "moonlighting" from their day jobs. The BBC and the British *Guardian* newspaper established "warblog" sites during the conflict. Blogs were also employed by NGOs such as Greenpeace.

The blog has become both an alternative and a mainstream practice; this demonstrates the contested nature of media power. Lowrey (2006) argues that the incorporation of blogs into professional journalism "repairs" the perceived vulnerabilities of professional journalists. Considering bloggers as occupational rivals, professional journalists reassess their professional processes. However, the incorporation of the blogs into news organizations and the use of bloggers as sources are not the only possible strategies: "the journalism community may try to redefine blogging as journalistic tool, and bloggers as amateur journalists or journalism wannabes (rather than as a unique occupation)" (Lowrey, 2006, p. 493). Lowrey does not develop this last point further, yet his claim offers an embryonic critique of the development of the present chapter.

Rodriguez's notion of citizens' media emphasizes media practices not as journalism, but primarily as projects of self-education. The community of professional journalists, Lowrey argues, might also consider practitioners of alternative media not to be journalists, but for different reasons. Their reasons would derive from the claim that it is only within professionalized and institutionalized media structures that journalists may practice. The ideology of such these structures places boundaries on what is to be considered as news, approaches to news gathering, decisions about who writes such news and how it is presented. We can characterize this ideology as the "regime of objectivity" (Hackett & Zhao, 1998, p. 86, cited in Hackett & Carroll, 2006, p. 33). Rather than acquiescing to this regime, alternative media practices challenge it. Their challenge has both a normative and an epistemological aspect. The normative ideal of professionalized journalism emphasises the factual nature of news. It is based on the empiricist assumption that there exist "facts" in the world and that it is possible to identify these facts accurately and without bias (the journalistic norm of detachment). The normative ideal of alternative journalism argues the opposite: that reporting is always bound up with values (personal, professional, institutional) and that it is therefore never possible to separate facts from values. This leads to the epistemological challenge: that different forms of knowledge may be produced, which themselves present different and multiple versions of "reality" from those of the mass media. These multiple versions demonstrate the social construction of news: there is no master narrative, no single interpretation of events. The regime of objectivity is only one of the many ways in we might construct news. Once we acknowledge the social construction of news, why should we then reject alternative journalism simply because it is not subject to the same normative and epistemological limits of mainstream journalism?

MERITS AND LIMITS

We have seen how alternative media have been characterized by their potential for participation (especially in Atton, 2002, Downing et al., 2001; Rodriguez, 2000). Rather than media production being the province of elite, centralized organizations and institutions, alternative media offer the possibilities for individuals and groups to create their own media from the social margins. Studies such as those by Downing and Rodriguez show how radical and citizens' media may be used to develop identity and solidarity within social movements and local communities. The democratic purpose of these kinds of media production is a valuable corrective to the "models of failure" of Comedia (1984) and Landry et al. (1985). Furthermore, they show how the notion of the "active audience" and its oppositional readings (Fiske, 1992b) can be developed radically into the notion of "mobilized audiences" (Atton, 2002, p. 25). To think about alternative media in this way is to consider them as far more than cultural aberrations or marginal practices. At a theoretical level such thinking encourages critiques of media production in general, to challenge what Nick Couldry (2002) terms "the myth of the mediated centre."

At an epistemological level, to consider the practices of alternative media producers as alternative journalism is to critique the ethics, norms and routines of professionalized journalism (Atton, 2003a; Atton & Wickenden, 2005; Harcup, 2003). Alternative journalism will tend, through its very practices, to examine notions of truth, reality, objectivity, expertise, authority and credibility (Atton, 2003b). Historical perspectives, such as those of James Hamilton (2003), and Hamilton and Atton (2001), may challenge the prevailing histories of journalism. Hamilton finds examples of alternative journalism that pre-date a notion of journalism centred on specialization, professional status and individual identity. In the place of this concept, he argues for a "'multidimensional' [view that] is meant to emphasize [...] a conception of media participation as varied, hybrid and, in many cases, not identifiable at all from within an evaluative framework that allows only producers and consumers" (Hamilton, 2003, p. 297).

Existing studies have their limits, however. The bulk of research into alternative and citizen journalism examines political media that are "progressive" in its ideology and aims. There is an emphasis on socialist and anarchist projects. To date there are few studies of what Downing et al. (2001, p. 88) term "repressive radical media" or of the use of alternative media forms for discriminatory ends (for example, Atton, 2006b; Back, 2002; O'Loan, Poulter & McMenemy, 2005). Even fewer studies critically examine "progressive" media in terms of their "repressive" aspects, such as the advocacy of violence (Atton, 1999, is an exception). Furthermore, there is a bias towards political projects in the United States and Western Europe. Rodriguez is the only researcher to consistently work in Latin America (though Huesca, 1995 and O'Connor, 2004 examine Bolivian miners' radio). Whilst there are numerous studies of the *Indymedia* network (such as Downing, 2002; Kidd, 2003; Platon & Deuze, 2003), they tend to ignore the network's specific regional and national practices. There are occasional studies from Asia, such as Kim and Hamilton's (2006) examination of *OhmyNEWS*. Studies of the Middle East, Africa and the Indian sub-continent are few: Gumucio Dagron's (2001) 50 brief "case stories" attest to diversity of citizen journalism projects in Africa and the Indian sub-continent. These cases focus on the use of participatory communication for social change. There is a need not only for these cases to be examined in greater depth, but also for comparative work to be undertaken. This is particularly important in regions where the writ of the western norms of journalism does not run, and where the challenges of alternative journalism might therefore be culturally and politically very different.

METHODOLOGICAL ISSUES

Studies of alternative media tend to employ qualitative approaches. This is especially appropriate given the perspectives of these studies. Qualitative methods emphasize the experience of media producers; an internal approach to understanding the culture of participants; and a search for the meaningfulness of production as a process (Jensen, 1991). However, whilst researchers have explicated their theoretical frameworks, concepts and epistemologies, they have devoted comparatively little attention (in their writings, at least) to the design of their methodologies and to the analytical apparatus they have employed in their methods. For example, whilst interviews comprise the dominant method (for example, Carroll & Hackett, 2006; Dickinson, 1997; Downing, 1984; Downing et al., 2001; Rodriguez, 2003), we have little detail about the style of these interviews; how subjects were selected; the contexts and conditions in which the interviews were conducted; and what questions were asked. Some studies (such as Atton & Wickenden, 2005; Rodriguez, 2000) use participant observation, but here too we have little detail of the methods. Lowrey's (2006) characterization of some alternative media studies as discursive is relevant here, at least in the sense that there is often no systematic display of methods, data and analytical procedures. In their place we find critical reflection that, whilst valuable, is often based on descriptive work, the methodological provenance of which is obscure.

These approaches make up the majority of studies in the area. On the other hand, the small number of studies that examine media content (such as news reports) tends to provide a more rigorous display of methods and analysis (for example, Atton & Wickenden, 2005; Harcup, 2003; Nelson, 1989). Generally, though, the paucity of methodological precision is an obstacle to understanding: it makes it difficult to verify, replicate, compare and refine investigations. Furthermore, the lack of methodological rigour in published work prevents the critical evaluation and development of methods. By contrast, the related area of community media studies offers case studies that, through their critical approach to methodology, enable tensions and blind spots to be identified (Jankowski, 1991).

CONCLUSION: DIRECTIONS FOR FUTURE RESEARCH

In general, the academic study of alternative media is dominated by an approach that focuses on progressive political value and, in particular, on the capacity of alternative media to "empower" citizens. This approach tends to celebrate alternative media and their achievements. Researchers have paid little attention to how alternative media are produced. They seem to know why practitioners do what they do, but less about what they do or why they do it in particular ways. What existing studies lack are examinations of what can be best termed "industrial practice." Despite its connotations from studies of the mass media, this term encourages us to consider alternative media practices as "work." It is surely this that is being lost—or at least marginalized—when we explore how alternative media come to be produced. The study of "work" in alternative media will include social and political processes such as decision-making processes, the structure of editorial meetings and ideological disputes. We will also need to examine the ways in which people work. How do they learn to become journalists or editors? How do they identify and choose their stories? How do they select and represent their sources? Are alternative journalists truly independent, or are their working methods influenced by the practices of mainstream journalists?

These are questions about media practice that require an understanding of its practitioners: their values, motivations, attitudes, ideologies, history, education, and relationships. They require what, in Bourdieusian terms, is an examination of practice that takes into account the relationship between habitus and field.

The privileging of participation in alternative media—as if it were the sole end of such media practices—is, as we have seen, often to the detriment of any consideration of how alternative journalism seeks its audiences and what use these audiences make of it. Perhaps this explains the enduring absence of audience studies in this area (Downing, 2003). We need audience studies not only to discover how alternative media are used (to what extent and in what ways do these media "mobilize" audiences?), but also to problematize the notion of audiences in contexts where they may take on the roles of producers and participants as well as "users."

Neither must we consider alternative media practices as entirely separate from the mainstream. Breaking television news frequently relies on camcorder footage, photographs taken on mobile phones and other forms of citizen journalism (Sampedro Blanco, 2005). Newspapers and broadcasters routinely incorporate blogs into their Web sites; some solicit advice and recommendations for stories and programmes from audiences. We might simply see this as the latest manifestation of what has been a longstanding practice in the local press (Pilling, 2006); alternatively, we might ask how amateur media practices might affect the epistemology of professional journalism through the "sheer *awkwardness*, of communication by 'fairly ordinary people'" (Corner, 1996, p. 174, original emphasis).

We need to consider alternative journalism practices as socially and culturally situated work, as well as processes of political empowerment. These practices might be drawn from mainstream practices, from history and from ideology. They might also challenge those practices or effect "new" forms of communication. These are important considerations if we are to take account of how alternative journalism is produced and how it connects to audiences.

REFERENCES

Atton, C. (1999). *Green Anarchist*: A case study in radical media. *Anarchist Studies, 7*(1), 25–49.

Atton, C. (2001). Living in the past?: Value discourses in progressive rock fanzines. *Popular Music, 20*(1), 29–46.

Atton, C. (2002). *Alternative media*. London: Sage.

Atton, C. (2003a). What is "alternative" journalism? *Journalism: Theory, Practice, Criticism, 4*(3), 267–272.

Atton, C. (2003b). Ethical issues in alternative journalism. *Ethical Space: The International Journal of Communication Ethics, 1*(1), 26–31.

Atton, C. (2004). *An alternative internet: Radical media, politics and creativity*. Edinburgh: Edinburgh University Press and New York: Columbia University Press.

Atton, C. (2006a). Football fanzines as local news. In B. Franklin (Ed.), *Local journalism and local media: Making the local news* (pp. 280–289). London: Routledge.

Atton, C. (2006b). Far-right media on the internet: Culture, discourse and power. *New Media and Society, 8*(4), 573–587.

Atton, C., & Wickenden, E. (2005). Sourcing routines and representation in alternative journalism: A case study approach. *Journalism Studies, 6*(3), 347–359.

Back, L. (2002). Wagner and power chords: Skinheadism, white power music, and the internet. In V. Ware & L. Back (Eds.), *Out of whiteness: Color, politics and culture* (pp. 94–132). Chicago: University of Chicago Press.

Benjamin, W. (1982). The author as producer. Edited translation in F. Frascina & C. Harrison (Eds.), *Modern art and modernism:A critical anthology* (pp. 213–216). London: Paul Chapman in association with the Open University. (Original work published 1934)

Bourdieu, P. (1991). *Language and symbolic power*. Cambridge: Polity Press.

Burkeman, O. (2002). Bloggers catch what *Washington Post* missed. *Guardian*, 21 December.

Carroll, W. K., & Hackett, R. A. (2006). Democratic media activism through the lens of social movement theory. *Media, Culture and Society, 28*(1), 83–104.

Comedia. (1984). The alternative press: The development of underdevelopment. *Media, Culture and Society, 6*, 95–102.

Corner, J. (1996). Mediating the ordinary: The "access" idea and television form. In J. Corner & S. Harvey (Eds.), *Television times: A reader* (pp. 165–174). London: Arnold.

Couldry, N. (2000). *The place of media power: Pilgrims and witnesses of the media age*. London: Routledge.

Couldry, N. (2002). Alternative media and mediated community. Paper presented at the International Association for Media and Communication Research, Barcelona, 23 July.

Couldry, N. & Curran J. (2003). The paradox of media power. In N. Couldry & J. Curran (Eds.), *Contesting media power: Alternative media in a networked world* (pp. 3–15). Lanham, MD: Rowman and Littlefield.

de Certeau, M. (1984). *The practice of everyday life*. Berkeley: University of California Press.

Dahlgren, P. (2000). Media, citizenship and civic culture. In J. Curran & M. Gurevitch (Eds.), *Mass media and society* (pp. 310–328). London: Arnold.

Dickinson, R. (1997). *Imprinting the sticks: The alternative press outside London*. Aldershot, UK: Arena.

Downing, J. (1984). *Radical media: The political experience of alternative communication*. Boston: South End Press.

Downing, J. (1988). The alternative public realm: The organization of the 1980s anti-nuclear press in West Germany and Britain. *Media, Culture and Society, 10*, 163–181.

Downing, J., Ford, T. V., Gil, G., & Stein, L. (2001). *Radical media: Rebellious communication and social movements*. Thousand Oaks, CA: Sage.

Downing, J. (2002). Independent media centres: A multi-local, multi-media challenge to global neo-liberalism. In M. Raboy (Ed.), *Global media policy in the new millennium* (pp. 215–232). Luton, Germany: Luton University Press.

Downing, J. (2003). Audiences and readers of alternative media: The absent lure of the virtually unknown. *Media, Culture and Society, 25*(5), 625–645.

Enzensberger, H. M. (1976). Constituents of a theory of the media. In *Raids and reconstructions: Essays on politics, crime and culture* (pp. 20–53). London: Pluto Press.

Fiske, J. (1992a). The cultural economy of fandom. In L. A. Lewis (Ed.), *The adoring audience: Fan culture and popular media* (pp. 30–49). London: Routledge.

Fiske, J. (1992b). British cultural studies and television. In R. C. Allen (Ed.), *Channels of discourse, reassembled* (2nd ed.; pp. 284–326). London: Routledge.

Forde, S., Foxwell, K., & Meadows, M. (2003). Through the lens of the local: Public arena journalism in the Australian community broadcasting sector. *Journalism: Theory, Practice and Criticism, 4*(3), 314–335.

Fraser, N. (1992). Rethinking the public sphere: A contribution to the critique of actually existing democracy. In C. Calhoun (Ed.), *Habermas and the public sphere* (pp. 109–142). Cambridge, MA: MIT Press.

Freeman, J. (1972). The tyranny of structurelessness. *Berkeley Journal of Sociology, 17*, 151–164.

Freire, P. (1970). *Pedagogy of the oppressed.* New York: Continuum.

Frith, S. (1996). *Performing rites: Evaluating popular music*. Oxford: Oxford University Press.

Glasgow University Media Group. (1976). *Bad news.* London: Routledge and Kegan Paul.

Gudmundsson, G., Lindberg, U., Michelsen, M., & Weisethaunet, H. (2002). Brit crit: turning points in British rock criticism, 1960–1990. In S. Jones (Ed.), *Pop music and the press* (pp. 41–64). Philadelphia: Temple University Press.

Gumucio Dagron, A. (2001). *Making waves: Stories of participatory communication for social change*. New York: Rockefeller Foundation.

Haas, T. (2004). Alternative media, public journalism and the pursuit of democratization. *Journalism Studies, 5*(1), 115–121.

Hackett , R. A., & Carroll, W. K. (2006). *Remaking media: The struggle to democratize public communication.* New York: Routledge.

Hall, S., Critcher, C., Jefferson, T., Clarke, J., & Roberts, B. (1978). *Policing the crisis: Mugging, the state, and law and order.* London: Methuen.

Hamilton, J. W. (2000). Alternative media: Conceptual difficulties, critical possibilities. *Journal of Communication Inquiry, 24*(4), 357–378.

Hamilton, J. W. (2003). Remaking media participation in early modern England. *Journalism: Theory, Practice, Criticism, 4*(3), 293–313.

Hamilton, J. & Atton, C. (2001). Theorizing Anglo-American alternative media: Toward a contextual history and analysis of US and UK scholarship. *Media History, 7*(2), 119–135.

Harcup, T. (2003). "The unspoken — said": The journalism of alternative media. *Journalism: Theory, Practice, Criticism, 4*(3), 356–376.

Harcup, T. (2006). The alternative local press. In B. Franklin (Ed.), *Local journalism and local media: Making the local news* (pp. 129–139). London: Routledge.

Hartley, J. (2000). Communicative democracy in a redactional society: The future of journalism studies. *Journalism: Theory, Practice and Criticism, 1*(1), 39–48.

Huesca, R. (1995). A Procedural view of participatory communication: Lessons from Bolivian tin miners' radio. *Media, Culture and Society, 17*(1), 101–119.

Jakubowicz, K. (1991). Musical chairs? The three public spheres in Poland. In P. Dahlgren & C. Sparks (Eds.), *Communication and citizenship: Journalism and the public sphere in the new media age* (pp. 155–175). London: Routledge.

Jankowski, N. W. (1991). Qualitative research and community media. In K. B. Jensen & N. W. Jankowski (Eds.), *A handbook of qualitative methodologies for mass communication research* (pp. 163–174). London: Routledge.

Jensen, K. B. (1991). Introduction: The qualitative turn. In K. B. Jensen & N. W. Jankowski (Eds.), *A handbook of qualitative methodologies for mass communication research* (pp. 1–11). London: Routledge.

Kidd, D. (2003). Indymedia.org: A new communications commons. In M. McCaughey & M. Ayers (Eds.), *Cyberactivism: Online activism in theory and practice* (pp. 47–70). New York: Routledge.

Kim, E.-G., & Hamilton, J. W. (2006). Capitulation to capital? *OhmyNews* as alternative media. *Media, Culture and Society, 28*(4), 541–560.

Kurtz, H. (2003). "Webloggers," signing on as war correspondents. *Washington Post,* 23 March.

Landry, C., Morley, D., Southwood, R., & Wright, P. (1985). *What a way to run a railroad: An analysis of radical failure*. London: Comedia.

Lefebvre, H. (1991). *Critique of everyday life. Vol. I: Introduction.* Translated by J. Moore. London: Verso. (Original work published 1947)

Lowrey, W. (2006). Mapping the journalism-blogging relationship. *Journalism: Theory, Practice, Criticism, 7*(4), 477–500.

Mathes, R., & Pfetsch, B. (1991). The role of the alternative press in the agenda-building process: Spill-over effects and media opinion leadership. *European Journal of Communication, 6*, 33–62.

Melucci, A. (1995). The new social movements revisited: Reflections on a sociological misunderstanding. In L. Maheu (Ed.), *Social movements and social classes: The future of collective action* (pp. 107–119). London: Sage.

Melucci, A. (1996). *Challenging codes: Collective action in the information age.* Cambridge: Cambridge University Press.

Mouffe, C. (1992). Democratic citizenship and the political community. In C. Mouffe (Ed.), *Dimensions of radical democracy: Pluralism, citizenship, community* (pp. 225–239). London: Verso.

Negt, O., & Kluge, A. (1972/1983). The proletarian public sphere. Translated from the German by S. Hood. In A. Mattelart & S. Siegelaub (Eds.), *Communication and class struggle, Vol. 2: Liberation, socialism* (pp. 92–94). New York: International General.

Nelson, E. (1989). *The British counter-culture, 1966–73: A study of the underground press.* London: Macmillan.

Norris, P. (1999). *Critical citizens: Global support for democratic governance.* Oxford: Oxford University Press.

O'Connor, A. (Ed.). (2004). *Community radio in Bolivia: The miners' radio stations.* Lewiston, NY: Edwin Mellen Press.

O'Loan, S., Poulter, A., & McMenemy, D. (2005). *The extent of sectarianism online.* Retrieved February 10, 2006, from http://www.cis.strath.ac.uk/research/lic/downloads/TESO_Full_04-05.pdf

Pilling, R. (2006). Local journalists and the local press: Waking up to change? In B. Franklin (Ed.), *Local journalism and local media: Making the local news* (pp. 104–114). London: Routledge.

Platon, S., & Deuze, M. (2003). Indymedia journalism: A radical way of making, selecting and sharing news? *Journalism: Theory, Practice and Criticism, 4*(3), 336–55.

Rodriguez, C. (2000). *Fissures in the mediascape: An international study of citizens' media.* Cresskill, NY: Hampton Press.

Rodriguez, C. (2003). The bishop and his star: Citizens' communication in southern Chile. In N. Couldry & J. Curran (Eds.), *Contesting media power: Alternative media in a networked world* (pp. 177–194). Lanham, MD: Rowman and Littlefield.

Ross, K. (2006). Open Source? Hearing voices in the local press. In B. Franklin (Ed.), *Local journalism and local media: Making the local news* (pp. 232–244). London: Routledge.

Sampedro Blanco, V. F. (Ed.). (2005). *13-M: Multitudes on-line.* Madrid: Catarata.

Waltz, M. (2005). *Alternative and activist media.* Edinburgh: Edinburgh University Press.

Whitaker, B. (1981). *News limited: Why you can't read all about it* (Minority Press Group Series No. 5). London: Minority Press Group.

Williams, R. (1980). Means of communication as means of production. In *Problems in materialism and culture: Selected essays* (pp. 50–63). London: Verso.

20

Journalism Law and Regulation

Kyu Ho Youm

INTRODUCTION

Journalism law, more widely known as media or mass communication law, centers on freedom of the press. What is the press? What makes the press free or not free? What purpose does or should press freedom serve? These and related questions guide the government in drawing the boundaries of journalism law. Over the years, the individual, societal, or political impact of the press as a social agency has animated journalism law. And new technology in media has added an interesting dimension to the mix. Where do we go from here? What is important at this juncture is examining research on journalism law in an international and comparative law light in order to better understand the realm of journalism law as it is and as it should be.

Freedom of the press is usually discussed in conjunction with freedom of speech. Thus, the theoretical framework of journalism law tends to be subsumed into freedom of speech (Barendt, 2005). Yet freedom of the press is distinguished from freedom of speech. The former concerns the "institutional press freedom from government control" (Merrill, 1989, p. 35), while the latter means an individual's freedom to speak and publish with no interference from the State. Hence, freedom of the press, more often than not, has been analyzed from an institutional perspective (Barron, 1973).

Press freedom as an institutional concept can be differentiated from *journalistic* freedom, which revolves around journalists' autonomy from the executives and editors of their news media (Merrill, 1989, p. 34). Few libertarian press systems recognize journalistic freedom as such, although some scholars argue for legal rules to protect the freedom of practicing journalists against the media owners (Gibbons, 1992).

Every country, whether governed by civil or common law, has its own set of journalism laws. The sources and objectives of these media laws reflect each society's political and sociocultural value judgments in weighing press freedom against its competing values. Some countries adopt special laws aimed directly at the press, while others choose indirect press laws. Those laws may or may not derive from a constitutional commitment to a free press. Regardless, a country's media law hinges not on a constitutional guarantee or a special press statute but on the "political philosophy" that underlies it (Lahav, 1985).

The tradition, culture, and norm of a free press can make a difference in journalism law. Not surprisingly, the authors of an early journalism law book, commenting on press law in France and Germany of the late 19th century, stated: "[I]n each country it is not so much the law itself as its administration that is complained of. The great central principle of the liberty of the press—freedom from previous restraint—stands unchallenged" (Fisher & Strahan, 1891, p. 204).

Journalism law is no different from other laws in that it remains in a state of flux. Indeed, journalism, in the sense of reporting, editing, and disseminating news, is changing in its structure and practice. The Internet revolution in communication enables anyone with a computer to communicate with a potential global audience in real time. The "new" journalism of bloggers and citizen reporters challenges the "old" journalism and its law (Gant, 2007).

The transformative process of journalism law goes beyond technology. It is intertwined with the accelerated globalization of media law (Winfield, 2006). International and comparative law has now taken on an added value as a framework for understanding press freedom. Yet it remains a theoretical challenge to formulate a transcultural media law model. Is media law so country-specific that its application to other countries is of limited relevancy? Or, because "media law and structures especially in increasingly international or global societies are so much a part of a transnational whole" (Price, 2002, p. 66), will their local differences likely be a nonissue?

It does seem that US media law remains relevant to other countries. This is not necessarily because it is better than other laws but because Americans' experience with freedom of speech and the press as a right is unusually rich (Smolla, 1992). However, the relevancy of the American law to the rest of the world will likely diminish in the future. As US telecommunication policy scholar Herbert Terry commented in August 2007, "Basically, there's good reason to suspect that (1) national media law will continue to erode, (2) [that] substantive transnational media law [...] will expand, and (3) that such expansion will fundamentally challenge the approaches to freedom of expression that have been pursued in the U.S. for over 200 years" (Terry, 2007).

With these thoughts in mind, let's turn to a discussion of the historical context of journalism law, the impact of the law on research, methodological issues, journalism law as a research discipline, and critical issues of journalism law.

HISTORICAL CONTEXT: SCHOLARLY AND PROFESSIONAL INTEREST

Noting the significance of teaching and research on freedom of speech and the press in the United States, journalism professor Charles Marler (1990, p. 179) observed:

> First Amendment studies—because of man's inherent tendency to attempt to control bad news, criticism, and dissent—made the legists—scholars who developed special knowledge in the law—one of the most dynamic journalism educator categories in the 20th century.

When compared with other fields of law, however, journalism law in the United States is a relatively new area of specialty for journalism and mass communication scholars and practitioners. The American history of education in mass communication law parallels the history of journalism education in the late 19th and early 20th century (Sutton, 1945).

The first book that focused on freedom of the press was James Paterson's *Liberty of the Press, Speech, and Public Worship* published in 1880. It was followed by Samuel Merrill's *Newspaper Libel* in 1888 and Joseph Fisher and James Strahan's *The Law of the Press* in 1891. The publication of Paterson's and Fisher and Strahan's books in England contributed to the emergence of "*a definite concept of journalistic law*" (Swindler, 1947, p. 8, emphasis in original), precipitated by the explosion of newspapers and the evolution of yellow journalism.

In the 1920s, *The Law of the Press* by Dean William Hale of the University of Oregon Law School, along with *Newspaper Law* (Loomis, 1924) and *The Law of Newspapers* (Arthur & Crosman, 1928), helped establish journalism law as an identifiable field of law. Dean Hale's 1923 book remained "a titan" among the American press law texts until the late 1940s. He explained why he wrote his book (Hale, p. iii):

> A few pamphlets and one or two brief books, devoted mainly, if not exclusively to the law of libel, have constituted the only specific contributions of American law writers to the field of journalism. An English volume by Paterson, entitled "Liberty of the Press, Speech, and Public Worship," is more comprehensive and scholarly than any of the American books; but it was published in 1880, and is now almost unobtainable. Moreover, it is not adapted to present-day needs in the United States.

Largely because freedom of the press, the central focus of Anglo-American media law, had long been part of free speech jurisprudence, a number of legal scholars played a prominent role in developing the theoretical and conceptual framework of press freedom. Harvard law professor Zechariah Chafee's 1919 article, "Freedom of Speech in Wartime," was expanded into his influential but controversial book, *Freedom of Speech* (1920). No less noteworthy is his majestic 1947 study of press-government relations as a member of the Hutchins Commission on Freedom of the Press (Chafee, 1947).

Other nonjournalism scholars have contributed substantially to media law literature by theorizing freedom of speech and reexamining the press clause of the First Amendment. Philosopher Alexander Meiklejohn (1948), for example, posited that political speech must be absolutely protected by the First Amendment, but nonpolitical speech can be regulated. It is not clear, however, how the Meiklejohnian theory on freedom of speech (protected) vs. freedom to speak (unprotected) would apply to the commercial media (McChesney, 2004). Historian Leonard Levy's provocatively revisionist *Legacy of Suppression* (1960) challenged the then widely accepted view on the First Amendment as an explicit rejection of seditious libel.

Not until the late 1960s and the early 1970s did journalism law emerge as a discrete major subject in journalism and mass communication and in law practice. The "contemporary period" of American journalism law for education started in 1960. Marler (1990, p. 183) described journalism law's contemporary period: "With a mass new constitutional law in hand, and more to come, the new legists' [sic] assigned themselves the research, writing, and tutorial burden to prepare media practitioners and their own successors to interpret and use properly the new dimensions of media law." University of Minnesota journalism professor Donald Gillmor and George Washington University law professor Jerome Barron published a new case law book, *Mass Communication Law*, in 1969. University of Wisconsin-Madison journalism professors Harold Nelson and Dwight Teeter authored their book, *Law of Mass Communications,* the same year. The two books were published at a time when journalism and mass communication as a discipline needed new texts and reference books on media law.

Guido Stempel III (1990, p. 280), formerly the editor of *Journalism Quarterly*, the premier scholarly journal for journalism educators in the United States, noted an increase in media law research during his editorship in 1973–1989 and attributed it in part to the use of computer databases such as Westlaw and Lexis and to the doctoral programs at Minnesota, Southern Illinois, and Wisconsin.

Perhaps the defining event of journalism and media law for American academics and practitioners was the founding of *Media Law Reporter* in January 1977 as a weekly loose-leaf service. *Media Law Reporter* aimed to meet an increasing need of, among others, educators, journalists, and lawyers for the timely reporting of the growing number of significant court decisions affecting the media. It continues to be the most comprehensive court reporter on US mass communication law and "virtually required reading" for the American communication law bar (Rambo, 1990).

In the meantime, foreign and international law on press freedom was more than a matter of passing interest in the early history of journalism law. *The Press Laws of Foreign Countries* was published in 1926 as a collection of laws in nearly 50 countries. It resulted from the UK Foreign Office's interest in compiling the "latest information" about press legislation around the world. The 328-page book was prepared for "general use" by media professionals, not as a press law manual for lawyers (Shearman & Rayner, 1926). Equally relevant is Eugene Sharp's *The Censorship and Press Laws of Sixty Countries* of 1936.

In comparative media law, Boston University law professor Pnina Lahav's *Press Law in Modern Democracies* stands out as pioneering legal scholarship. By comparing eight Western democratic press systems, including Japan and Israel, Lahav (1985, p. 1) explored several key questions about press freedom as a right:

- What makes the press "free"?
- Can there be a free press absent the inclusion of a commitment to press freedom in a constitution?
- Can a society have a statute that clearly defines the privileges and obligations of the press and still maintain a "free" press?
- Can the press be "free" under a regime of censorship?
- Can the state interfere with editorial discretion by providing for a statutory right of reply, for example, and still maintain a free press?
- Can the press fulfill its role as watchdog of the government and yet be sued for defamation by public officials?

LAW AND ITS IMPACT ON RESEARCH

American journalism law has its genesis in various court decisions on press freedom, including the *Zenger* case of 1735 in colonial America. The *Zenger* case set a precedent for Americans in demanding a Bill of Rights with a guarantee of freedom of the press. Equally influential is the 18th-century English jurist William Blackstone's definition of freedom of the press as absence of prior restraint (Blackstone, 1765–69). The more systematic development of journalism law for research in the United States started with *Near v. Minnesota* (283 U.S. 697, 1931), the landmark case of the US Supreme Court, which addressed prior restraint as a First Amendment issue for the first time in American history.

In the initial phase of journalism law, libel was the predominant topic for teaching and research, although contempt of court and copyright were also discussed. Nearly half of Hale's 1923 book, for example, was devoted to libel law, though privacy, newsgathering, and advertising were included, too.

More often than not, the scholarly research on journalism law was more expository than prescriptive. One notable exception, however, was Samuel Warren and Louis Brandeis's 1890 law review article, "The Right to Privacy." The two Boston lawyers proposed invasion of privacy as a new tort, and their article marked the beginning of the law of privacy. Its practical and conceptual impact has not been limited to US law. Privacy is now more widely accepted as a right in international and foreign law, too (Tugendhat & Christie, 2002).

During the "developmental period" of American journalism law (1944–1968), a number of major Supreme Court rulings bore directly on press freedom. Among the major press law issues the Court addressed were libel (e.g., *New York Times v. Sullivan,* 376 U.S. 254, 1964*),* privacy (e.g., *Time v. Hill*, 385 U.S. 374, 1967), free press vs. fair trial (e.g., *Sheppard v. Maxwell*, 384 U.S. 333, 1966), obscenity (e.g., *Roth v. U.S.,* 354 U.S. 476, 1957), contempt (e.g., *Pennekamp v. Florida*, 328 U.S. 331, 1946), and media distribution (e.g., *Associated Press v. U.S.*, 326 U.S. 1, 1945). A substantial amount of media case law from lower courts, both federal and state, led journalism law researchers to consider advertising and broadcasting in an in-depth way.

The traditional journalism law topics, such as prior restraint, still attracted attention from scholars. Yale law professor Thomas Emerson's (1970, p. 504) analysis of the prior restraint doctrine in free speech law remains a classic illustration:

> [G]overnmental restrictions cannot be imposed upon speech or other kind of expression in advance of publication. It does not touch on the question of what, if any, subsequent punishment can be administered for engaging in expression. The doctrine thus is solely concerned with limitations on the form of governmental control over expression. Even if the communication is subject to later punishment or can otherwise be restricted, it cannot be proscribed in advance through a system of prior restraint.

Significantly, the conventional negative concept of press freedom in American law has been challenged. Singularly significant was George Washington law professor Jerome Barron's (1967) proposal for access to the press as a new right under the First Amendment. "Private censorship can be as repressive and as pervasive as public censorship," Barron (2007, p. 938) recalled writing about his innovative First Amendment interpretation. "But I did not wish merely to call attention to the ways in which technology and media concentration have turned the possibility of private barriers to expression into a formidable reality. I wanted the law to respond to the reality of private censorship." Barron's access rights argument was rejected by the US Supreme Court (*Miami Herald Publishing Co. v. Tornillo,* 418 U.S. 241, 1974).

In contrast to the virtual nonexistence of access to the media in American law, except for political candidates, international and foreign law accommodates the public's right to participate in the media through the right of reply (Youm, 2008). The UN Convention on the International Right of Correction is an international treaty incorporating a version of the right of reply. The French-inspired right of correction was designed to establish a right of correction for officials, not for private individuals. To date, more than twenty nations have ratified the UN Convention.

Two regional human rights conventions—the American Convention on Human Rights and the European Convention on Human Rights (ECHR)—recognize the right of reply. Since 1974, the Council of Europe and the European Union have adopted various conventions and resolutions on the right of reply that apply to domestic and cross-border broadcasting. Most recently, the right of reply was extended to online factual allegations. The right of reply experience of European countries, individually and collectively, seems to prove that the right of reply is not fundamentally at odds with freedom of expression.

The right of reply varies from country to country. Although a limited number of countries provide for it as an express constitutional right, many others treat it as a statutory matter. France and Germany are the most influential countries that support the right of reply. When France and Germany made the right of reply a legal obligation in the nineteenth century and other countries followed them during the first half of the 20th century, they intended it to enable the defamed to respond to the defamer, i.e., the news media. In many of those right of reply countries in Africa, Asia, Europe, and Latin America, reputation and related personal interests continue to be a principal consideration in enforcing the right of reply.

During the past 40 years, the US Supreme Court has impacted journalism law as profoundly as in earlier periods, if not more. The Court has applied, fine-tuned, and at the same time created constitutional law on press freedom. Among the wide range of media law issues that the Court has ruled on since 1969 are prior restraint, the journalist's privilege, "burning the source" (i.e., breaking the confidentiality agreement with news sources voluntarily), the fairness doctrine, the right of reply, advertising, copyright, freedom of the student press, freedom of information, obscenity, indecent broadcasting, cable regulation, and Internet communication.

One of the most significant recent developments in US media law relates to commercial speech. The commercial speech exception to the First Amendment that the US Supreme Court accepted in the early 1940s was rejected in the mid-1970s. Most important, the turnabout for the Supreme Court in its commercial speech doctrine was based on the consumer's right to the "free flow of information," although the information was purely commercial advertising (*Virginia State Board of Pharmacy v. Virginia Citizens Consumer Council*, 425 U.S. 748, 1976).

Access to information as the right to know is widely recognized as an affirmative concept of freedom of speech and the press (Mendel, 2008). In the United States, however, only a limited number of journalists regularly use freedom of information (FOI) laws for their work. The mismatch between the lofty theory behind FOI laws and their actual use in the United States clamors for systematic research as a case study. In addition, the gap between theory and practice for journalism in FOI laws deserves a comparative examination. Further, scant attention has been paid to foreigners' extensive use of the federal FOI Act of the United States. Hence, it offers opportunities for research, whether quantitative or qualitative.

In contrast with freedom of information, which nearly seventy countries recognize as a right (freedominfo.org, 2007), "sunshine laws" regarding government meetings are few and far between. The United States seems to be a minority of one in its experience with open meetings laws since 1976. The enduring inertia among journalists, lawyers, and lawmakers on the public's right to attend government agency meetings is the rule, not the exception. Journalism law students and scholars might seek to explain the lack of attention to sunshine laws around the world.

The globalizing media have resulted in an array of challenges for journalism law. Academics and media lawyers are becoming more keenly aware of those challenges. As law professor David Kohler (2006, p. vii), the supervising editor of the *Journal of International Media and Entertainment Law*, noted:

> The media and entertainment businesses have become truly global. Companies that used to look to the United States for most of their revenue now look abroad for much of their growth. Lawyers representing media and entertainment companies now must confront not only the U.S. legal system, but also those of a host of other jurisdictions where their clients' products are distributed. Even products intended primarily for domestic consumption may find their way abroad through new technologies that facilitate seamless distribution across geographic borders.

Thus far, the US Supreme Court has yet to confront media law directly involving choice of law, jurisdiction, and enforcement of foreign court judgments. Several lower courts have adjudicated the First Amendment rights of the American media when they are sued abroad for defamation and other reasons. These still novel media law issues are likely to arise frequently in the Internet era, which compels journalism scholars and practitioners to better understand "the basic moral engine that drives each nation's media laws" (Glasser, 2006, p. xvi).

Up to now, research on international and comparative media law has been sporadic and less substantial. And media law has yet to emerge as a major scholarly topic for international and comparative law (see Reimann & Zimmermann, 2006). In recent years, however, it has gained traction with legal scholars and practitioners. The leading UK media law scholar, Eric Barendt, and others have examined freedom of speech and the press in international and comparative law.

Barendt's book *Freedom of Speech* (2005) exemplifies comparative scholarship in freedom of expression in examining the ECHR, England and Wales, the United States, France, Germany, and Australia. Equally important, the research and publications of ARTICLE 10 in London and other free speech organizations have addressed "a science of defective information" on comparative media law. For example, ARTICLE 19's *Press Law and Practice* (Coliver, 1993) informatively examines how freedom of the press is weighed against other social and individual interests in eight European countries (Austria, France, Germany, the Netherlands, Norway, Spain, Sweden, and the United Kingdom), as well as the United States, Canada, and Australia.

Several treatises on special media law topics have been published. Not surprisingly, libel and privacy have been the focus of book-length monographs. The enduring value of the leading British libel attorney Peter Carter-Ruck's *Carter-Ruck on Libel and Slander* (Carter-Ruck & Starte, 1997), whose first edition was published in 1952, is unmatched; the book discusses the domestic laws of more than 60 countries and international law on defamation. No less noteworthy is *International Privacy, Publicity, and Personality Laws* (Henry, 2001), which details the laws on privacy in 29 jurisdictions, including Hong Kong. Bloomberg News general counsel Charles Glasser's *International Libel & Privacy Handbook* (Glasser, 2006) is another welcome addition to the literature on international libel and privacy law. Although it turns to American law for its analytical framework, the book looks at 19 jurisdictions in addressing libel, privacy, and related issues.

The number of country-specific books on media law outside Anglo-American and European countries is growing. In this connection, the Asian Media Information and Communication Centre (AMIC) in Singapore deserves credit. Since the early 1990s, AMIC has published a series of English-language media law books on 10 Asian countries: Bangladesh, India, Indonesia, Malaysia, Nepal, Pakistan, the Philippines, Singapore, Sri Lanka, and Thailand. The AMIC Asian media law series was a concerted effort to respond to "the continuing call for a review of existing media laws and for press accountability and professionalism" in Southeast and South Asia (Carlos, 2006). Meanwhile, several journalism and legal scholars have published media law books about their countries since the mid-1990s. Among the countries whose press law was a general-interest subject for books were China (Fu & Cullen, 1996), Hong Kong (Weisenhaus, 2007) and South Korea (Youm, 1996). Still, there is an increasing need for research on country-specific media law because it will likely provide essential source material for those interested in international and comparative law.

Also of growing importance to journalism researchers is international law that comprises various world and regional covenants and treaties. Among the examples of international and regional agreements affecting freedom of the press are the International Covenant on Civil and Political Rights (ICCPR), the ECHR (see Thorgeirsdottir, 2005), and the American Convention on Human Rights. Likewise, the Berne Convention for the Protection of Literary and Artistic Works and the Agreement on Trade-Related Aspects of Intellectual Property Rights exert a significant impact on press freedom in the United States and other nations (see Goldstein, 2001).

METHODOLOGICAL ISSUES

Law deals with a matter of "substance knowledge," and its scholarship relates to "specific legal research methodologies" (Ugland et al., 2003, p. 386). Meanwhile, legal research on journalism should be contextual, not only for its target audience but also for researchers themselves. Thus, substantive media law issues and problems must be placed in the context of the law in general (Ibid.). As the noted communication law scholar Fred Siebert (1949, p. 26) stated in the late 1940s:

> Research in the field of legal problems of communication [...] cannot be sharply segregated either as to subject matter or as to methods. Almost every research project in the broad area of communications involves economic, political, or social as well as legal problems, and in many cases it is impossible to separate the strictly legal from the other aspects.

As Indiana University law professor Fred Cate (2006) noted, methodology is not a subject that legal scholars address in their classroom teaching and research publications. Nonetheless, he added, "Law is not as devoid of methodologies as generations of doctoral students and I may have surmised, although law's analytical tools may not be as clearly defined as in the social sciences" (p. 21).

The research methods in journalism law may vary according to the purposes of the legal research involved. However, they overlap when the research aims to provide "a means for *understanding* and for *explaining* communication and law" (Cohen & Gleason, 1990, p. 12). Furthermore, the interdisciplinary approach to communication law encourages more eclecticism in research methods, although the theoretical means are debatable (Bunker, 2001). Communication scholar Everette Dennis (1986, p. 10) wrote:

> We are witnessing the development of at least three strains of legal scholarship in mass communication today: first, the continued articulation of traditional, documentary research; second, socio-behavioral methods; and finally, the critical-qualitative method. There is much dissatisfaction with the singular focus in communication law studies and with the notion that media law scholars should be boosters for media industries.

Cate has identified the four most widely used research tools or methodologies in US journalism and communication law:

1. precedent: "How well does a current or proposed application of the law comport with past decisions?" (Cate, 2006, p. 16);
2. codified rules: "Did a court or other decision maker act as commanded by legislation or administrative rule?" (p. 16);
3. policy analysis: "[Is] the result of a particular legal decision or enactment [...] fair, efficient, or consistent with what the decision maker intended"? (p. 18);
4. procedural analysis: Cate calls this "the most important tool for legal practitioners, although the one least used by scholars" (p. 19), focusing on "a variety of questions involving the authority and competence of the decision maker, the process employed in arriving at the decision and the impact that process has on the substantive outcome of a legal question or dispute" (p. 19).

Although these research methods are directed at American law, they are easily applicable, with necessary modifications, to international and comparative law.

The traditional legal and historical methodologies are not the only means of conducting research on law. Legal questions are approached through social research methods to enhance scholarly insights. But they should not necessarily be used separately from legal and historical methods. Journalism law scholars Jeremy Cohen and Timothy Gleason (1990, p. 133) suggested that "communication scholars [...] use legal method *and* social research methods as tools in the process of building theories of communication and law."

Also, critical legal theory and cultural studies approaches to media law supplement the case-oriented doctrinal scholarship in journalism law. While the critical legal studies (CLS) approach challenges mainstream legalistic ways of understanding media law, the cultural studies approach emphasizes a broader analysis of media law by considering its cultural and social context. Thus, CLS informs the proposition that legislators and judges should view obscenity and pornography not simply as an individual right under a liberal concept of freedom of speech but as an unjust societal imposition perpetuated by male-oriented value judgments.

The cultural studies approach forces many free speech universalists to reconsider their rather simplistic position that the underlying values of freedom of speech and the press are impervious to cultural norms and traditions of a society. The differing ways of many nations to balance the culture-bound reputational interests with press freedom show how cultural studies can offer fresh insights into media law. Further, hate speech, pornography, and other culturally contingent expression lends credence to the argument that international law cannot dismiss culture as irrelevant to free speech jurisprudence.

Yet what Siebert (1942, p. 70) advised about research methods in journalism law is as relevant today as it was in 1942: "[T]hat we have *more case studies* and *fewer studies of cases.* By this I mean thorough analyses of individual instances rather than digests of a number of instances."

Regardless of whether one single method or a multitude of methods is used for legal research, the key question is this: Why should we do legal research from a journalism and mass communication perspective? The answer to this threshold question is that legal research on journalism provides a historical and current overview of the institutional and noninstitutional confrontations between the government and the media and between the media and the nongovernmental elements. The benefits of such research on journalism law are immediate and long-term.

If the research deserves to be called "good legal scholarship," however, it should contain a claim that is novel, nonobvious, useful, sound, and seen by the reader as such (Volokh, 2005).

No matter what tool or methodology is used for legal research in journalism, the research most likely will be an exercise in otiosity unless it serves one or more useful functions, whether theoretical or applicational. Five functions of legal research constitute a roadmap to various types of legal research in journalism (Ugland et al., 2003, pp. 393–394):

- Some research clarifies the law and offers explanation through an analysis of procedure, precedent, and doctrine;
- Some legal law research tries to reform old laws and suggest changes in the law;
- Research may be conducted to provide a better understanding of how law operates on society;
- Research may analyze the political and social processes that shape our communication laws;
- Research may furnish materials for legal and journalistic education in mass communication.

This typology of legal research in journalism and mass communication is somewhat similar to law professor Phillip Kissam's thoughtful discussion (1988, pp. 230–239) of the six purposes of legal scholarship, including "case analysis," "legal synthesis," "doctrinal resolution," "production of teaching materials," "understanding," and "critique."

STUDYING AND RESEARCHING JOURNALISM LAW

The widely accepted premise of studying journalism law in the United States and other similar free-press countries is that journalism students need to develop knowledge of the legal protections and restraints placed upon freedom of the press. That is, they should acquaint themselves with what may and may not be communicated to ensure that the injured have no legal ground for seeking redress.

Knowing media law by reading it is hardly adequate if it has no application in real life. It is one thing to be familiar with a relevant law on journalistic practices, but it is another to apply that law to specific situations. Knowing and applying journalism law is a significant challenge for students. Journalism law is not static. It is a living, evolving, changing set of formal principles, constantly subject to interpretation and application of the courts. This is especially true of American media law. Add the fact that American communication law carries global ramifications, which require journalism students to be less US-centric in examining press freedom.

In recommending media law as a course for any model journalism and mass communication curriculum in the United States, a 1984 comprehensive study suggested that the course focus on the system of free expression under which the media operate, the US communication law regime in a comparative context, the regulatory patterns as they affect the media, and the "survival kit" for the mass communicators in their self-protection (*Planning for Curricular Change*, 1984, p. 83).

The underlying issues addressed in undergraduate journalism law courses on the balance between freedom and control of the mass media in the United States can be framed as questions on three levels:

1. What are the legal limits on freedom of the press, and how does a journalism practitioner avoid legal problems?
2. Why have courts, legislatures, and administrative agencies established the existing limits?
3. How does US communication law interact with the laws of other countries in the era of globalizing media?

Closely related to teaching in journalism law is legal research in journalism, Media law has emerged as a topic of growing interest to scholars inside and outside the field of journalism. Indeed, there are more publication outlets for media law research now than ever. *Journalism and Mass Communication Quarterly* (*JMCQ*), the *Journal of Communication* (*JOC*), and other communication journals are not amenable to the kind of law review manuscripts that are voluminous, extensively documented, and doctrinally adversarial. *Communication Law and Policy* is an attractive alternative for journalism law scholars. The refereed journal of the AEJMC Law and Policy Division resulted from media law scholars' wish in the mid-1990s to address the long-standing strictures of *JMCQ* and other nonlaw journals on manuscript submissions (Youm, 2006).

The target audience of legal research published in refereed journalism and mass communication journals is significantly different from that of law reviews published by law schools. In particular, the practical impact of *JMCQ*, *JOC*, and other similar journals on the legal community is hardly noticeable when compared with law journals. Media law professor Clay Calvert (2002, p. 1), whose law journal articles have been cited by American courts, has noted: "Lawyers use them [law journal articles] to form legal arguments and often cite them in briefs to supplement case law and statutory authority. They also are constantly cited by courts and have greatly influenced the shape of the law."

CRITICAL ISSUES OF JOURNALISM LAW

Soon after World War II, Siebert (1946, p. 771) wrote that "[i]nformation and ideas know no physical boundaries, and their transmission by modern media such as radio, newspapers, news magazines, and mass literature of all types has already raised a host of intriguing legal problems." His 1946 "briefing on a few specific problems" in which the fields of law and journalism can collaborate to address was remarkably perceptive. The problems that Siebert identified remain, to varying degrees, central to journalism law. Law and journalism intersect with each other in, among other areas, libel, privacy, broadcasting, the reporter's privilege, diversity of jurisdictions, fair trial vs. free press, cameras in the courtroom, contempt of court, constitutional law, press freedom as a positive vs. negative right, and media monopolies and their "private censorship."

Siebert's listing of several journalism law problems was not necessarily confined to the United States. Libel law is one example. In US law, defamation, one of the earliest legal actions available against the press, is still the most common legal danger to the news media. Few dispute the fact that libel is an occupational hazard for American journalists. In American law, libel is mostly a matter of tort, i.e., a civil wrong. But the US Supreme Court has yet to repudiate criminal libel, although it cannot be squared with modern First Amendment principles (Media Law Resource Center, 2003).

This sets the United States in sharp relief to Mexico, which has abolished libel as a crime in 2007. The Mexican government's elimination of libel as a crime probably resulted from a 2004 landmark case of the Inter-American Court of Human Rights (IACHR) that overturned the criminal defamation conviction of Costa Rican journalist Mauricio Herrera Ulloa, a reporter with the daily *La Nación*. Mexico was not the only country in Latin America that embraced the IACHR's invitation to forgo criminal libel. El Salvador, Panama, and Peru preceded Mexico.

Further, journalism practitioners working for transnational media view libel as an exceedingly precarious challenge. This is largely because "media law around the world is a crazy patchwork quilt of laws, with each square reflecting a nation's cultural biases, political history, and economic structure" (Glasser, 2006, p. xiii). The international forum shopping by libel plaintiffs when suing in media-hostile countries pushes journalists to better understand foreign defamation law (Youm, 1994).

Privacy is similarly a critical issue in journalism law because it reflects the cultural values of each society. Conceptually, it is less definable than libel. It can refer to a right of autonomy from governmental restraint. It also can mean seclusion from trespassing or a right to control informational secrecy. Given that it is more amorphous and fluid than libel, privacy is "one of the most volatile and controversial subjects" in American free speech jurisprudence (Sanford & Kirtley, 2005, p. 273).

The journalist's privilege to protect news sources has recently emerged as a more difficult problem in US media law. More American journalists and news media are subpoenaed to identify their confidential sources or give up other information about stories they have covered. Under Ronald Dworkin's (1985) theoretical dichotomy, First Amendment law considers the privilege a matter of "policy," not "principle." The no-privilege quandary facing American journalists under their supposedly media-friendly law stands in marked contrast to the growing recognition of the journalist's privilege in international and foreign law.

The European Court of Human Rights (*Goodwin v. United Kingdom*, 1996) and the International Criminal Tribunal for the former Yugoslavia (*Prosecutor v. Brdjanin and Talic*, 2002) have accepted a journalist's privilege for news reporting as a right to press freedom. This leads some to wonder whether the United States can continue to claim its often touted "exceptionalism" in freedom of expression (Schauer, 2005a). In what way and to what extent is First Amendment exceptionalism a valid assertion or rhetorical hyperbole? More importantly, what explains the current US retrenchment on the journalist's privilege while international and foreign law are more willing than ever to recognize the privilege?

Freedom of the press has been debated in relation to its distinction—or lack thereof—from freedom of speech, especially since US Supreme Court Justice Potter Stewart (1975) argued extrajudicially that press freedom is not a redundancy of the speech clause of the First Amendment. The debate continues unabated (Anderson, 1983, 2002; Baker, 2007; Schauer, 2005b). Legal scholar Edwin Baker (2007, p. 1026) posited trenchantly:

> [F]ailure to acknowledge an independent status of the Press Clause of the United States Constitution is not only a theoretical mistake, contrary to the historical meaning of the Press Clause and contrary to the best normative interpretations of the Constitution and ... a potentially significant pragmatic mistake. It is also inconsistent with existing law.

On the other hand, the theoretical framework of press freedom as a positive (freedom for) vs. negative (freedom from) right is more strenuously argued in connection with the actual or perceived "private censorship" by the corporate media. Yale law professor Owen Fiss (1996, p. 46) favors an active role of the State in leveling the playing field: "We turn to the state because it is the most public of all our institutions and because only it has the power we need to resist the pressures of the market and thus to enlarge and invigorate our politics." Barron's theory on access to the media showcases the government's affirmative role in facilitating freedom of the press *in* the public interest.

Journalistic freedom, as distinct from freedom of the press from the State, is largely irrelevant in American law because the conflict between journalists and their media employers is not read into the press clause of the First Amendment. But the journalistic concept of press freedom is "not inconsistent" with the case law of the United States (Baker, 1989, p. 254). Certain countries ensure journalistic autonomy to protect journalists' freedom against abridgment by the media owners. For example, in South Korea, which boasts a libertarian press, several newspapers allow their reporters to participate in hiring and firing editors and also in setting the editorial policy of their newspapers.

The technological impact of the Internet and new media on journalism law is revolutionary. It transcends borders and makes the conventional common law approach to journalism law less resilient than assumed. Harmonization of the substantive law of media law among nations is patently urgent. But it will be a daunting challenge. It takes more than opting for an authoritarian (censorship-oriented) or libertarian (US-styled hands-off) approach to Internet law. As Daniel Solove, author of *The Future of Reputation* (2007, p. 193), observed: "There is [...] a limit to how much the law can do. The law is an instrument capable of subtle notes, but it is not quite a violin." Ergo, norms, markets, and "architecture" are equally powerful in restricting as well as encouraging speech in cyberspace (Lessig, 1999).

DIRECTIONAL AGENDA FOR FUTURE RESEARCH

Journalism law continues to be a major topic for teaching and research, and the role of the law, whether libertarian or authoritarian, in shaping or being shaped by journalism is undeniable. This entails an unending drawing of a line in the relationship between the press and the government. The theoretical, doctrinal, and methodological framework surrounding the State's authority (and obligation) to regulate the market-dictated media to expand the democratic values of society requires rethinking of the structural and individual dynamics of the press.

In the post-9/11 environment in the United States and beyond, the conflict between national security and freedom of speech and the press has reemerged with a greater sense of exigency (see, e.g., Stone, 2007). This historical moment represents an opportunity for more studies to test

Siebert's (1952, p. 10) proposition on freedom of the press: "The area of freedom contracts and the enforcement of restraints increases as the stresses on the stability of the government and of the structure of society increase."

These considerations are all the more pressing because communication law as a whole, which will affect journalism profoundly, is "one of the most rapidly evolving areas of the law today" (Farber, 2003, p. 225). Journalism law has expanded far beyond its modest parameters of the late 19th century and the early 20th century. Substantive legal topics such as libel, privacy, and free press vs. fair trial most likely will remain central issues.

The inexorable media convergence already creates ample opportunities for research in journalism law. Without a doubt the conceptual segregation of print from electronic media is an untenable proposition. Broadcasting is not limited to over-the-air broadcasting; it covers cable, satellite, and other new media technologies.

Cybercommunication is ubiquitous, and Internet media no longer constitute a fragile, nascent industry that needs government protection. In this connection, researchers might revisit the exceptionally libertarian policy of the United States, which exempts Internet intermediaries from liability for defamatory republication.

Amidst the accelerated globalization of the mass media in the 21st century, journalism law cannot be understood without its international context. For an examination of how other countries have reconciled freedom of the press with other competing values can provide telling insights into the balancing process that a society has chosen constitutionally or by custom (Krotoszynski, 2006).

Cultural and linguistic hurdles as well as substantive knowledge handicaps might remain considerable impediments to journalism scholars in internationalizing their media law teaching and research. Nonetheless, most of the challenges are becoming less formidable. The advent of the Internet and the predominance of English as the lingua franca have made access to international and foreign law sources a substantially less significant problem. Regardless, the critical but often ignored issue for journalism law scholars in placing their teaching and research in an international and comparative context is not whether they have more difficulty using foreign source materials but whether they can outgrow their often insular and culture-bound notion of press freedom.

REFERENCES

Anderson, D. (1983). The origins of the press clause. *UCLA Law Review, 30*(3), 455–541.

Anderson, D. (2002). Freedom of the press. *Texas Law Review*, *80*(3), 429–530.

Arthur, W., & Crosman, R. (1928). *The law of newspapers*. New York: McGraw-Hill.

Baker, C. (2007). The independent significance of the press clause under existing law. *Hofstra Law Review*, *35*(3), 955–1026.

Baker, C. (1989). *Human liberty and freedom of speech*. New York: Oxford University Press.

Barendt, E. (2005). *Freedom of speech* (2nd ed.). Oxford: Oxford University Press.

Barron, J. (1973). *Freedom of the press for whom?: The right of access to mass media*. Bloomington: Indiana University Press.

Barron, J. (1967). Access to the press: A new First Amendment right. *Harvard Law Review 80*(8), 1641–1678.

Barron, J. (2007). Access to the media—A contemporary appraisal. *Hofstra Law Review*, *35*(3), 937–953.

Blackstone, W. (1765–69). *Commentaries on the laws of England*. London.

Bunker, M. (2001). *Critiquing free speech: First Amendment theory and the challenge of interdisciplinarity*. Mahwah, NJ: Erlbaum.

Calvert, C. (Spring 2002). Should you publish in a law review? *Media Law Notes, 30*(3), 1.

Carlos, J. (2006). About this book. In L. Teodoro Jr. & R. Kabatay, *Mass media laws and regulations in the Philippines.* Singapore: Center for Research and Communication Foundation, Inc. and Asian Media Information & Communication Centre.

Carter-Ruck, P., & Starte, H. (1997). *Carter-Ruck on libel and slander* (5th ed.). London: Butterworths.

Cate, F. (2006). Method in our madness: Legal methodology in communication law research. In A. Reynolds & B. Barnett (Eds.), *Communication and law: Multidisciplinary approaches to research* (pp. 9–21). Mahwah, NJ: Erlbaum.

Chafee, Z. (1920). *Freedom of speech.* New York: Harcourt, Brace and Howe.

Chafee, Z. (1947). *Government and mass communications.* Chicago: University of Chicago Press.

Cohen, J., & Gleason, T. (1990). *Social research in communication and law.* Newbury Park, CA: Sage.

Coliver, S. (Ed.) (1993). *Press law and practice: A comparative study of press freedom in European and other democracies.* London: ARTICLE 19.

Dennis, E. (1986). Frontiers in communication research. *Communication and the Law*, *8*(4), 3–10.

Dworkin, R. (1985). *A matter of principle.* Cambridge, MA: Harvard University Press.

Emerson, T. (1970). *The system of freedom of expression.* New York: Vintage Books.

Farber, D. (2003). *The First Amendment* (2nd ed.). New York: Foundation Press.

Fisher, J., & Strahan, J. (1891). *The law of the press.* London: William Clowes & Sons.

Fiss, O. (1996). *Liberalism divided: Freedom of speech and the many uses of state power.* Boulder, CO: Westview Press.

Freedominfo.org. (2007). Retrieved December 31, 2007, from http://www.freedominfo.org/countries/index.htm.

Fu, H. & Cullen, R. (1996). *Media law in the PRC.* Hong Kong: Asia Law & Practice.

Gant, S. (2007). *We're all journalists now: The transformation of the press and reshaping of the law in the Internet age.* New York: Free Press.

Gibbons, T. (Summer 1992). Freedom of the press: Ownership and editorial values. *Public Law*, 279–299.

Glasser, C. (Ed.) (2006). *International libel & privacy handbook: A global reference for journalists, publishers, webmasters, and lawyers.* New York: Bloomberg Press.

Glasser, C. (2006). Understanding media law in the global context. In C. Glasser (Ed.), *International libel & privacy handbook: A global reference for journalists, publishers, webmasters, and lawyers* (pp. xiii–xxiii). New York: Bloomberg Press.

Goldstein, P. (2001). *International copyright: Principles, law, and practice.* New York: Oxford University Press.

Goodwin v. United Kingdom, 22 E.C.H.R. 123 (1996).

Hale, W. (1923). *The law of the press.* St. Paul, MN: West Publishing.

Henry, M. (Ed.) (2001). *International privacy, publicity, and personality laws.* London: Butterworths.

Kissam, P. (1988). The evaluation of legal scholarship. *Washington Law Review*, *63*(2), 221–255.

Kohler, D. (2006). Foreword. *Journal of International Media & Entertainment Law*, *1*(1), vii–viii.

Krotoszynski, R. (2006). *The First Amendment in cross-cultural perspective: A comparative legal analysis of the freedom of speech.* New York: New York University Press.

Lahav, P. (Ed.) (1985). *Press law in modern democracies: A comparative study.* New York: Longman.

Lessig, L. (1999). *Code and other laws of cyberspace.* New York: Basic Books.

Levy, L. (1960). *Legacy of suppression: Freedom of speech and press in early American history.* Cambridge, MA: Harvard University Press.

Loomis, W. (1924). *Newspaper law.* Salt Lake City, UT: Porte.

Marler, C. (1990). The legists. In W. Sloan (Ed.), *Makers of the media mind: Journalism educators and their ideas* (pp. 177–225). Hillsdale, NJ: Erlbaum.

McChesney, R. (Spring 2004). The Meiklejohn challenge. *Journalism & Mass Communication Educator, 59*(1), 24–30.

Media Law Resource Center. (March 2003). Criminalizing speech about reputation: The legacy of criminal libel in the United States after *Sullivan & Garrison. MLRC Bulletin* No. 1.

Meiklejohn, A. (1948). *Speech and its relation to self-government.* New York: Harper.

Mendel, T. (2008). *Freedom of information: A comparative legal survey* (2nd ed.). New Delhi: UNESCO, Regional Bureau for Communication and Information.

Merrill, J. (1989). *The dialectic in journalism: Toward a responsible use of press freedom.* Baton Rouge: Louisiana State University Press.

Planning for curricular change: A report of the project on the future of journalism and mass communication education. (May 1984). Eugene: School of Journalism, University of Oregon.

Price, M. (2002). *Media and sovereignty: The global information revolution and its challenge to state power.* Cambridge, MA: MIT Press.

Prosecutor v. Brdjanin and Talic, Case No. IT-99-36-AR73.9 (Dec. 11, 2002).

Rambo, C. (1990). Litigious age gives rise to media law. In K. Devol (Ed.), *Mass media and the Supreme Court: The legacy of Warren years* (4th ed., pp. 45–48). Mamaroneck, NY: Hastings House.

Reimann, M., & Zimmermann, R. (Eds.). (2006). *The Oxford handbook of comparative law.* Oxford: Oxford University Press.

Sanford, B., & Kirtley, J. (2005). The First Amendment tradition and its critics. In G. Overholser & K. Jamieson (Eds.), *The press* (pp. 263–276). New York: Oxford University Press.

Schauer, F. (2005a). The exceptional First Amendment. In M. Ignatieff (Ed.), *American exceptionalsm and human rights* (pp. 29–56). Princeton, NJ: Princeton University Press.

Schauer, F. (2005b). Towards an institutional First Amendment, *Minnesota Law Review, 89*(5), 1256–1279.

Shearman, M., & Rayner, O. (Eds.). (1926). *The press laws of foreign countries with an appendix containing the press laws of India.* London: H.M. Stationers' Office.

Siebert, F. (1952). *Freedom of the press in England, 1476–1776: The rise and decline of government controls.* Urbana: University of Illinois Press.

Siebert, F. (1942). Research in press law and freedom of the press. *Journalism Quarterly, 19*(1), 69–70.

Siebert, F. (1946). The law and journalism. *Virginia Law Review, 32*(4), 771–780.

Siebert, F. (1949). Research in legal problems of communications. In R. Nafziger & M. Wilkerson (Eds.), *An introduction to journalism research* (pp. 26–42). Baton Rouge: Louisiana State University Press.

Smolla, R. (1992). *Free speech in an open society.* New York: Alfred A. Knopf.

Solove, D. (2007). *The future of reputation: Gossip, rumor, and privacy on the Internet.* New Haven, CT: Yale University Press.

Stempel, G., III. (summer 1990). Trends in *Journalism Quarterly*: Reflections of the retired editor. *Journalism Quarterly, 67*(2), 277–281.

Stewart, P. (1975). "Or of the press." *Hastings Law Journal, 26(3),* 631–637.

Stone, G. (2007). *War and liberty: An American dilemma: 1790 to the present.* New York: W.W. Norton.

Sutton, A. (1945). *Education for journalism in the United States from its beginning to 1940.* Evanston, IL: Northwestern University.

Swindler, W. (1947). *A bibliography of law on journalism.* New York: Columbia University Press.

Terry, H. (2007). The future of media law and policy Part I: Telecommunications policy—Globalization and electronic media law and policy. Annual meeting of the Association for Education in Journalism and Mass Communication, Washington, DC.

Thorgeirsdottir, H. (2005). *Journalism worthy of the name: Freedom within the press and the affirmative side of Article 10 of the European Convention on Human Rights.* Leiden, Netherlands: Martinus Nijhoff.

Tugendhat, M., & Christie, I. (Eds.) (2002). *The law of privacy and the media.* Oxford: Oxford University Press.

Ugland, E., Dennis, E., & Gillmor, D. (2003). Legal research in mass communication. In G. Stempel III, D. Weaver, & G. Wilhoit (Eds.), *Mass communication: Research and theory* (pp. 386–405). Boston: Allyn & Bacon.

Volokh, E. (2005). *Academic legal writing: Law review articles, student notes, and seminar papers* (2nd ed.). New York: Foundation Press.

Warren, S., & Brandeis, L. (1890). The right to privacy. *Harvard Law Review, 4*(2), 193–220.

Weisenhaus, D. (2007). *Hong Kong media law: A guide for journalists and media professionals.* Hong Kong: Hong Kong University Press.

Winfield, R. (2006). Globalization comes to media law. *Journal of International Media & Entertainment Law, 1*(1), 109–116.

Youm, K. (1996). *Press law in South Korea.* Ames: Iowa State University Press.

Youm, K. (1994). Suing American media in foreign courts: Doing an end-run around U.S. libel law? *Hastings Communications and Entertainment Law Journal, 16*(2), 235–64.

Youm, K. (2006). Legal methods in the history of electronic media. In D. Godfrey (Ed.), *Methods of historical analysis in electronic media* (pp. 115–144). Mahwah, NJ: Erlbaum.

Youm, K. (2008). The right of reply and freedom of the press: An international and comparative perspective. *George Washington Law Review, 76*(4), 1017–1064.

21
Journalism Ethics

Stephen J. A. Ward

Journalism ethics, the norms of responsible journalism, can be traced back to the beginning of modern journalism in Europe during the seventeenth century. This chapter provides an overview of contemporary journalism ethics by following its evolution, by reviewing and critiquing major approaches, and by suggesting future work. The chapter begins with a view of ethics as practical normative activity that aims to solve problems, integrate values and help humans live rightly, as individuals and as societies. Journalism ethics is defined as a species of applied ethics that examines what journalists and news organizations should do, given their role in society. The main problem areas include editorial independence, verification, anonymous sources, the use of graphic or altered images, and norms for new forms of media.

The chapter identifies five stages in the development of journalism ethics and four approaches to its study today. First, the invention of ethical discourse for journalism during the seventeenth century. Second, a "public ethics" as the creed for the growing newspaper press, or Fourth Estate, of the Enlightenment public sphere. Third, the liberal theory of the press, during the nineteenth century. Fourth, development *and* criticism of this liberal doctrine across the twentieth century resulting in a professional ethics of objective journalism, bolstered by social responsibility theory; and an alternative ethics for interpretive and activist journalism. Fifth, today's current "mixed media" ethics which lacks consensus on what principles apply across types of media. These stages are used to explain four approaches: (1) liberal theory, (2) objectivity and social responsibility theory, (3) interpretive theory, and (4) an ethics of community and care.

The chapter then considers criticisms of current approaches by a range of disciplines, from critical and post-colonial theory to sociology of culture. The chapter concludes by arguing that the current media revolution and these new criticisms call for a fundamental re-thinking of journalism ethics. Journalism ethics needs a richer theoretical base, a more adequate epistemology, and new norms for the multi-platform, global journalism of today and tomorrow.

JOURNALISM ETHICS

Ethics is the analysis, evaluation and promotion of what constitutes correct conduct and virtuous character in light of the best available principles. Ethics does not simply ask how to live well. It asks how we should live well *ethically*, that is, in goodness and in right relation with each other, a task that may require us to forego personal benefits, to carry out duties or to endure persecution. Ethical reasoning is about how people interpret, balance and modify their principles in light of new facts, new technology, and new social conditions (Ward, 2007). The boundaries of ethics change. In our time, ethics has come to include such issues as animal cruelty, violence against women, the environment and the rights of homosexuals (Glover, 1999). Ethical reflection is *normative reason in social practice*. Ethics is the never-completed project of inventing, applying and critiquing the principles that guide human interaction, define social roles and justify institutional structures.

Therefore, ethics, especially journalism ethics, is essentially a practical activity (Black, Steele, & Barney, 1999) that seeks reasons to questions of how to act. Is it ethical for journalists to reveal their confidential sources to police? Is it ethical to invade the privacy of a much-admired politician to investigate alleged misconduct? Ethics includes the theoretical study of the concepts and modes of justification that provide ethical reasons for acting. But the purpose here is also practical: to clarify principles and improve deliberation so as to lead to well-considered ethical judgments. A stress on the practical in ethics assures us that "the problems we have followed into the clouds are, even intellectually, genuine not spurious" (Dworkin, 2000, p. 4).

Journalism Ethics as Applied

Applied ethics is the study of frameworks of principles for domains of activity, such as corporate governance, scientific research and professional practice (Dimock & Tucker, 2004). Journalism ethics is a species of applied media ethics that investigates the "micro" problems of what individual journalists should do in particular situations, and the "macro" problems of what news media should do, given their role in society. Journalists as members of news organizations have rights, duties and norms because as human beings, they fall under general ethical principles such as to tell the truth and minimize harm, and because as professionals they have social power to frame the political agenda and influence public opinion (Curd & May, 1984; Elliott, 1986).

Therefore, a question about journalism is an *ethical* question, as opposed to a question of prudence, custom or law, if it evaluates conduct in light of the fundamental public purposes and social responsibilities of journalism. A story that sensationalizes the personal life of a public figure may be legal—it may be legally "safe" to publish—but it may be unethical in being inaccurate and unfair. However, there is no necessary incompatibility between ethical values and other types of value. A story may be well-written, legal and career-enhancing, yet also ethical. What one regards as a question of journalism ethics depends, ultimately, on one's conception of the primary functions of journalism and the principles that promote those aims. Consequently, there is room for disagreement on the level of practice, in applying norms, and on the level of theory and principle.

Problem Areas

A major task of journalism ethics is to determine how existing norms apply to the main ethical issues of the day. Some current problem areas are:

- *Accuracy and verification*: How much verification and context is required to publish a story? How much editing and "gate-keeping" is necessary?
- *Independence and allegiances*: How can journalists be independent but maintain ethical relations with their employers, editors, advertisers, sources, police and the public. When is a journalist too close to a source, or in a conflict of interest?
- *Deception and fabrication*: Should journalists misrepresent themselves or use recording technology, such as hidden cameras, to get a story? Should literary journalists invent dialogue or create composite "characters"?

- *Graphic images and image manipulation*: When should journalists publish graphic or gruesome images? When do published images constitute sensationalism or exploitation? When and how should images be altered?
- *Sources and confidentiality*: Should journalists promise confidentiality to sources? How far does that protection extend? Should journalists go "off the record"?
- *Special situations*: How should journalists report hostage-takings, major breaking news, suicide attempts and other events where coverage could exacerbate the problem? When should journalists violate privacy?
- *Ethics across media types*: Do the norms of mainstream print and broadcast journalism apply to journalism on the Internet? To citizen journalists?

MAIN APPROACHES

The history of journalism ethics can be divided into five stages. The first stage is the invention of an ethical discourse for journalism as it emerged in Western Europe during the sixteenth and seventeenth centuries. Gutenberg's press in the mid-fifteenth century gave birth to printer-editors who created a periodic news press of "newssheets" and "newsbooks" under state control. Despite the primitive nature of their newsgathering, and the partisan nature of their times, editors assured readers that they printed the impartial truth based on "matters of fact." The second stage was the creation of a "public ethic" as the creed for the growing newspaper press of the Enlightenment public sphere. Journalists claimed to be tribunes of the public, protecting their liberty against government. They advocated reform and eventually revolution. By the end of the eighteenth century, the press was a socially recognized institution, a power to be praised or feared, with guarantees of freedom in the post-revolution constitutions of America and France. This public ethic was the basis for the idea of a Fourth Estate—the press as one of the governing institutions of society (Ward, 2005a, pp. 89–173).

The third stage was the evolution of the idea of a Fourth Estate into the liberal theory of the press, during the nineteenth century (Siebert, 1956). Liberal theory began with the premise that a free and independent press was necessary for the protection of the liberties of the public and the promotion of liberal reform. The fourth stage was the simultaneous development *and* criticism of this liberal doctrine across the twentieth century. Both the development and the criticism were responses to deficiencies in the liberal model. The "developers" were journalists and ethicists who constructed a professional ethics of objective journalism, bolstered by social responsibility theory. Objectivism sought to use adherence to fact and impartiality towards political party to restrain a free press that was increasingly sensational (or "yellow") and dominated by business interests (Baldasty, 1992; Campbell, 2001). The "critics" were journalists who rejected the restraints of objective professional reporting and practiced more interpretive, partial forms of journalism such as investigative reporting and activist (or advocacy) journalism.

By the late 1900s, the liberal and objective professional model was under attack from many sources as journalism entered its fifth stage, a stage of "mixed media." Not only were increasing numbers of non-professional citizen journalists and bloggers engaging in journalism, but these communicators used interactive multi-media that challenged the ideas of cautious verification and gate-keeping. As a result, journalism ethics was (and continues to be) fraught with disagreement on the most basic notions of what journalism is and what journalists are "for" (Rosen 1999).

With these stages in mind, we can better appreciate four normative theories of the press that are currently influencing this fifth stage: (1) liberal theory, (2) objectivity and social responsibility theory, (3) interpretive and activist theory, and (4) an ethics of community and care.[1]

Liberal Theory

Liberal theory continues to underpin current discussions, if only to act as a theory to be revised or criticized. Liberal press ideas, as espoused from John Milton and David Hume to J. S. Mill and Thomas Paine, were part of liberalism as a political reform movement for the surging middle classes.[2] Liberalism sought the expansion of individual liberties and an end to the privileges of birth and religion that marked non-liberal, hierarchical society. In economics, liberalism supported laisser-faire attitudes; in press theory it supported a free marketplace of ideas. Mill's *On Liberty* appealed to the individual *and* social benefits of freedom, within specified limits (Mill, 1965). This ascendant liberalism supplied the ethical ideology for both the elite liberal papers, such as *The Times* of London, and the egalitarian popular press, from the penny press to the mass commercial press of the late 1800s (Schudson, 1978). For liberal theory, journalists should constitute an independent press that informs citizens and acts as a watchdog on government and abuses of power. Today, the liberal approach continues to be used to justify arguments for a free press against media restrictions, such as censorship of offensive views, and the abuse of libel laws to curtain publication.[3]

Objectivity and Social Responsibility

As noted above, objectivism and social responsibility theory were liberal theories attempting to respond to a disillusionment with the liberal hope that an unregulated press would be a responsible educator of citizens on matters of public interest. That hope flagged in the late 1800s and early 1900s as a mass commercial press turned into a business of news directed by press barons. One response was to develop the ideal of an objective news press, with codes of ethics and other professional features. The liberal idea of a social contract (Darwall, 2003; Scanlon, 1982) was used to argue that society allowed professional journalists to report freely in return for responsible coverage of essential public issues (Klaidman & Beauchamp, 1987; Kovach & Rosenstiel, 2001).

From the early 1900s to the middle of the twentieth-century, objectivity was a dominant ethical ideal for mainstream newspapers in the United States, Canada and beyond, although it was less popular in Europe. By the 1920s, major journalism associations in the United States had adopted formal codes that called for objectivity in reporting, independence from government and business influence, and a strict distinction between news and opinion. The result was an elaborate set of newsroom rules to ensure that journalists reported "just the facts" (Schudson, 1978; Mindich, 1998).

The liberal social contract gave rise to two types of principles in professional codes of ethics: "proactive" and "restraining"[4] which were cashed out in terms of more specific rules, standards and practices. Pro-active principles assert that journalists do not simply have freedom to publish but they also have a *duty* to publish the most accurate and comprehensive truth on matters of public interest, and to report independently without fear or favor. "Seek truth and report it" and "act independently" are primary pro-active principles of most Western codes of ethics. Restraining principles call on journalists to use this freedom to publish in a responsible manner. Restraining principles include the duty to "minimize harm" to vulnerable subjects of stories, such as children or traumatized persons, and the duty to be accountable to the public for editorial decisions.

The professional model favors a holistic, contextual approach to the application of principles. For any situation, journalists are expected to weigh principles, standards, facts, expected consequences, rights and the impact on personal reputations (Black, Steele, & Blarney, 1999, pp. 29–30). When norms conflict, such as when reporting the truth conflicts with the desire to minimize harm, such as to *not* report a sensitive fact, journalists will have to decide which principles have priority. Reasoning in journalism ethics challenges journalists to reach a "reflective equilibrium" among their intuitions and principles (Rawls, 1993, p. 8).[5]

Another liberal response was social responsibility theory (Peterson, 1956), developed by scholars and journalists in the United States. While liberal theory recognized the idea of press responsibility and social utility, social responsibility theory underlined these neglected responsibilities. In the United States, the Hutchins Commission into the Freedom of the Press in the late 1940s gave the theory a clear and popular formulation.[6] In its report, *A Free and Responsible Press*, the commission stressed that the main functions of the press was to provide "a truthful, comprehensive, and intelligent account" of the news and events and "a forum for the exchange of comment and criticism." The press should provide a "representative picture of the constituent groups in society," and assist in the "presentation and clarification of the goals and values of society," and "provide full access to the day's intelligence" (Commission on Freedom of the Press, 1947, pp. 21–28). If journalistic self-regulation failed, social responsibility proponents warned that government regulators might intervene. Today, the ideas of social responsibility theory have "won global recognition over the last 50 years," such as in European public broadcasting (Christians & Nordenstreng, 2004, p. 4) and as far afield as Japan (Tsukamoto, 2006). Moreover, the theory continues to provide a basic vocabulary for new ethical approaches, such as feminist and communitarian theories, while providing standards by which press councils and the public can evaluate media performance.

Interpretation and Activism

The liberal ideal that a free press should inform citizens also has been embraced by the tradition of interpretive journalism that seeks to explain the significance of events and by the tradition of activist journalism that seeks to reform society. Both interpretive and activist traditions believe that journalists have a duty to be more than stenographers of fact. However, this stress on an active, non-objective press is not new. For most of modern journalism's history, journalists have been openly partisan, and their reporting has been biased towards political parties and funders. However, in the early 1900s, a less partisan interpretive journalism arose that sought to rationally and independently explain an increasingly complex world. For instance, Henry Luce's interpretive journalism was the model for *Time* magazine in the 1920s. In the 1930s and beyond, scholars, foreign reporters and journalism associations acknowledged the need to supplement objective reporting with an informed interpretation of world events, wars and economic disasters like the Great Depression (MacDougall, 1957). Newspapers in the 1930s and 1940s introduced weekend interpretations of the past week's events, beat reporters and interpretive columnists with bylines. This tradition of interpretive journalism would gather strength in the second half of the twentieth century in the hands of broadcast journalists, literary journalists and, then, online journalists.

Meanwhile, from the 1960s onward, activist journalists defined "informing the public" as challenging the status quo, opposing wars and promoting social causes. Activist journalists sought to organize public opinion against government and private sector misconduct, and unjust or unwise policies. Modern activist journalists were anticipated historically by the reform journalists of the late eighteenth century in England, and by the revolutionary journalists in America and France. Activist journalists also share many values with the muckraking magazine journalists in America during the first two decades of the 1900s (Filler, 1968; Applegate, 1997). In the 1990s, American journalists advocated a moderate reform journalism called "civic journalism" that saw the journalist as a catalyst for civic engagement (Rosen 1996).

Today, many journalists see themselves as some combination of informer, interpreter and advocate. Traditional values, such as factual accuracy, are not completely jettisoned. Even the most vocal muckraker or activist journalist insists that their reports are factually accurate, although they reject neutrality (Miraldi, 1990). Rather, they see their facts as embedded in interpretive narratives that draw conclusions. For both interpretive and activist journalism, the main ethical questions are: What are its norms and principles, if objectivity is not the ideal? What ethical theory can restrain the possible abuses or excesses of non-objective journalism?

Community and Care

The fourth influential approach to journalism ethics is the application of communitarian ethics (Christians, Ferre, & Fackler, 1993) and a feminist ethics of care to the practices of journalism (Gulligan, 1982; Noddings, 1984; Koehn, 1998).

Both approaches provide criticism of, and an alternative to, liberal theory. Both approaches emphasize the "restraining principles" of minimizing harm and being accountable while de-emphasizing the "pro-active" principles. The liberal perspective stress individual freedoms and rights; the communitarian and care perspectives stress the impact of journalism on communal values and caring relationships.[7]

Communitarianism in journalism ethics reflects a revival in communitarian ethical, legal and political theory over several decades (Peden & Hudson, 1991; Seters 2006). Communitarians stress the communal good and the social nature of humans. They argue that neither liberalism nor any theory can be liberal among different views of the good and therefore, journalists should support their community's commitment to substantive values and conceptions of the good life. Communitarian media ethicists, such as Clifford Christians, use the primacy of "humans-in-relation" to argue that the main function of the press is not a "thin" liberal informing of citizens about facts and events. The main function is the provision of a rich, interpretive dialogue with and among citizens that aims at "civic transformation" (Christians, 2006, pp. 65–66).

The communitarian approach is close in spirit to theories of care, developed by feminists and other scholars.[8] The promotion of caring human relationships, as an essential part of human flourishing, is a primary principle (Card, 1999; Pierce, 2000). Feminists promoted an ethics of care "founded on notions of community rather than in the rights-based tradition" (Patterson & Wilkins, 2002, p. 292). Gilligan (1982) criticized the moral development theory of Lawrence Kohlberg for ignoring gender.

An ethics of care attempts to restrain a news media that is often insensitive to story subjects and sources. As Jay Black has written, feminist scholars have argued that by paying attention to the tenets of an ethics of care, "a fuller, richer media system may emerge, on that can and will consider such concepts as compassion, subjectivity, and need" (Black 2006, p. 99). Ethicists have applied an ethics of care to cases in journalism, such as formulaic coverage of murders in Canada and the United States (Fullerton & Patterson, 2006). Steiner and Okrusch (2006) have argued that idea of professional responsibility in journalism can be re-interpreted in terms of caring.

All of these major approaches are informed by a significant increase in the empirical and theoretical analysis of journalism practice and ethics. The past half-century has seen an unprecedented rise in the study of media and culture and in the channels available for public discussion, from new books, journals, and Web sites to new associations and institutes for the rigorous study of journalism ethics and practice. Scholars, working in established academic departments of sociology or political science, or in expanding schools of journalism and communication, pursue vigorous lines of research such as the agenda-setting role of media (McCombs, Shaw, & Weaver, 1997), audience theory (McQuail, 1997), media economics and sociology (Picard, 1989; Albarran & Chan-Olmsted, 1998; McQuail, 1969), moral development among journalists (Wilkins & Coleman, 2005), and the history of journalism ethics (Spencer, 2007; Ward, 2005a). Journals and magazines publish ever new case studies and surveys using content analysis and other quantitative and qualitative methods of social science. These studies not only provide ethicists with data, they also enlarge the conceptual base of journalism ethics as a discipline by placing talk of principles and practices in a larger critical and theoretical framework. Of special note is the development of an international approach to the study of media communication and journalism. The studies provide a portrait of the "news people" around the world and how their media systems and values compare (Demers, 2007; Weaver, 1998). Discussions of ethics now take place against this growing body of literature on the relation of journalism ethics to economics, ideology, politics and global culture.

CRITIQUES OF TRADITIONAL JOURNALISM ETHICS

However, despite an increase in these studies, or perhaps partly because of them, the current climate of journalism ethics is one of fundamental disagreement about its nature and purpose. There are three main sources of debate. One source is a disagreement among the four approaches, outlined above, an internal debate within journalism ethics. A second source is a range of academic and critical perspectives from disciplines external to journalism and journalism ethics—political science, sociology, and culture and communication studies. These theories critique the project of journalism ethics by considering the relationship between ethical discourse and the exercise of power, Western economic and cultural dominance, and post-modern skepticism about truth and objectivity. The main questions raised are: (1) How can we interpret and practice journalism ethics so that we avoid turning ethical discourse into ethical ideology, a tool of Western dominance? (2) How can the universal principles of journalism ethics recognize political, social and cultural differences? A third source of debate is more practical. Changes to the technological and social conditions of journalism are creating a "new media" journalism with different values (Pavlik, 2001).

In this section, I summarize two "external" challenges to traditional journalism ethics: a post-modern questioning of the professional ideal of seeking the truth, objectively; and a "critical" analysis of journalism ethics.

Questioning Truth and Objectivity

Professional journalism ethics was built upon the twin pillars of truth and objectivity. By the late 1800s, mass commercial newspapers displayed a robust empiricism—an energetic pursuit of the news that amounted to a "veneration of the fact" (Stephens, 1988, p. 244). By the early 1900s, journalism textbooks, associations and codes of ethics attempted to restrain that robust empiricism by citing truth, objectivity and social responsibility as fundamental principles of the emerging profession. The adherence to truth and objectivity was part of an Enlightenment belief in a rational public—that humans would rationally seek and discern truth from falsehood, right from wrong, if they were provided with the facts, or objectively presented information. The heyday of traditional objectivity was from the 1920s to the 1950s in the mainstream broadsheet newspapers of North America. The doctrine was so pervasive that, in the 1956, press theorist Theodore Peterson said objectivity was "a fetish" (Peterson, 1956, p. 88). The second half of the century is a story of challenge and decline due to new forms of journalism, new technology and new social conditions.

The pillars of truth and objectivity show serious wear and tear due to a post-modern skepticism about objective truth and a cynicism about the claims of profit-seeking news organizations to be impartial informers. Therefore, any discussion of journalism ethics must include the *problem* of truth and objectivity in journalism, and the decline of the traditional doctrine of news objectivity to the point where it is, today, a spent ethical force (Ward, 2005a, pp. 261--264). There have been three types of complaint against news objectivity: First, objectivity is too demanding an ideal for journalism and hence objectivity is a "myth." Second, objectivity, even if possible, is undesirable because it forces writers to use restricted formats. It encourages a superficial reporting of official facts. It fails to provide readers with analysis and interpretation. Objectivity ignores other functions of the press such as commenting, campaigning and acting as public watchdog. Finally, objectivity restricts a free press. A democracy is better served by a non-objective press where views compete in a marketplace of ideas.

Objectivity was challenged from its inception. The magazine muckrakers of the early 1900s rejected neutrality in reporting. The emergence of television and radio created more personal forms of media. In the 1960s, an adversarial culture that criticized institutions, opposed war and fought for civil rights was skeptical of objective experts and detached journalism. Other writers, from Norman Mailer to Truman Capote, practiced a journalism that looked to literature for its inspiration.

In academia, philosophers, social scientists and others have challenged the notion of objective knowledge and objective science. Thomas Kuhn's influential writings were interpreted as showing that scientific change was a non-rational "conversion" to a new set of beliefs (Kuhn, 1962). All knowledge was "socially constructed" (Hacking, 1999). Philosopher Richard Rorty attacked the idea that objective knowledge was a "mirror of nature" (Rorty, 1979). Post-modernists such as Lyotard and Baudrillard questioned the ideas of detached truth and philosophical "meta-narratives"—large historical narratives that make sense of human experience (Connor, 1989). Butler describes the illusive sense of post-modernism as a "realism lost" where people live in a "society of the image" or "simulacra" (Butler, 2002). Some media scholars have treated objectivity as the tainted dogma of corporate media (Hackett & Zhao, 1998).

The questioning continues within journalism. Journalist Martin Bell rejected objectivity for a journalism of "attachment" (Bell, 1998). A lead article in the *Columbia Journalism Review*, entitled "Rethinking Objectivity," repeated the complaints cited above (Cunningham, 2003). A public policy center in the United Stated published a "manifesto for change" in journalism, which noted how objectivity is "less secure in the role of ethical touchstone" while norms such as accountability are increasing in importance (Overholser, 2006, pp. 10–11).

Yet skepticism about journalistic objectivity has not solved any serious ethical problems. It only leaves a vacuum at the basis of journalism ethics. If objectivity is abandoned, what shall replace it? Three options loom: Abandon objectivity and replace it with other principles; "return" to traditional objectivity in newsrooms; redefine objectivity. Returning to traditional objectivity is unrealistic. Abandoning objectivity, without a replacement, is not an option. A reform of news objectivity must explain how a non-positivistic notion of objectivity is possible if journalism is active inquiry into the world, involving choices, selection and interpretation. The central question is: If a news report involves (at least some) interpretation, how can it be objective? One option is to re-conceive objectivity as the testing of interpretations. On this view, objectivity is neither the reduction of reports to bare facts nor the elimination of all interpretation. Rather, objectivity is the testing of journalistic articles, regarded as interpretations, by a set of agreed-upon criteria appropriate to a given domain.[9]

Critical Theories of Media

Beyond the criticism of news objectivity, there are broad critiques of news media as social and political agents. These perspectives can be loosely collected under the term "critical theories," with one important type being post-colonial studies (Ahluwalia & Nursey-Bray, 1997; Shome & Hegde, 2002; Young, 2003).

The common starting point is a disenchantment with Western notions of rationality, universality, objective knowledge and progress. Wasserman (2007, p. 8) writes: "Postcolonialism shares with postmodernism the engagement with the failure of modernity to live up to its own ideals and ambitions." Critical theories resist attempts to impose a hegemonic system of Western ideas and values on other cultures, especially "neo-liberal" ideas. For some writers, the attempt to speak about universal values is suspect, since it suggests an "essentialism" that denies "difference."

From a critical perspective, the model of professional journalism ethics shares the same biases and limitations as the liberalism upon which it is based. Liberal press theory is said to be grounded in Enlightenment forms of thought that are male, Eurocentric, individualistic, and universal. Ethical discourse is not politically innocent but can be a political act of power, just as journalism can propagate Western propaganda (Chomsky, 1997). Critical theories warn that Western ideas can be used to justify imperialistic and "colonizing" purposes. Fourie writes: "It starts from the view that institutionalized knowledge and theories about issues such as race, class, gender, sexuality, and the media are/were subject to forces of colonialism" (Fourie, 2007, p. 4).

What are some specific implications of critical theory for journalism ethics? One implication is that scholars should "de-Westernize" journalism ethics. For example, some writers have examined whether the African tradition of *ubuntuism* should be the fundamental ethical value for African journalism, since *ubuntuism's* communal values are more in line with African society than a Western stress on a free and individualistic press (Fourie, 2007). De-Westernization also means using cross-cultural comparisons when discussing the principles of media ethics, and giving due weight to African, Indian and Eastern ethical systems.

Another implication is that journalism ethics should place more emphasis on the representation of others since mis-representation can spark wars, demean other cultures and support unjust social structures. Such issues go beyond factual accuracy. They require journalists to have a deeper cultural knowledge and a deeper appreciation of how language can distort "the other."[10] Paying attention to issues of representation also means questioning the everyday news practices that routinely exclude less powerful voices. This means defining "news" to include issues of social justice and their historical context, not just daily events and facts. It means seeking a greater diversity of sources in stories, and telling such stories from the perspective of non-dominant groups. Critical theories suggest that journalism ethics requires a commitment to social change that is more at home in the traditions of interpretive and activist journalism. In addition, journalism education should supplement the traditional emphasis on reporting skills and fact gathering with a more ethnographic approach that stresses cultural and international knowledge (Alia, 2004, p. 23, 26). The imperative to "seek truth and report" is transformed from a stenography of fact to an informed interpretation of the place that events have within a larger cultural and global context.

Finally, critical theories imply that the Western project of "media development" has to be re-thought. Western nations spend millions of dollars annually to send their journalists to struggling countries to develop their news media, as a step toward democracy (Coman, 2000; Howard, 2002, 2003). Many journalists attempt to teach the Western professional model, described above, to indigenous journalists, without sufficient consideration as to how appropriate these Western principles are to different cultures and different media systems. If such efforts are to be successful, and not accused of Western colonization, media developers need to re-consider their aims and guiding principles in light of the above discussed critiques of media theory.

In summary, these critical perspectives call for an enlargement of the conceptual base of journalism ethics. This entire range of thinking—feminist, post-modern, communitarian, and post-colonial—changes the basic discourse of journalism ethics and needs to be incorporated into ethics textbooks. The key theoretical debates extend beyond the traditional debate between liberal and social responsibility theory. The debate now includes such issues as the relationship of ethics and power, media representation and dominant cultures, the social construction of identities, differences in ways of knowing and valuing, and the relationship of the local and global. These far-reaching critiques expose a lack of theoretical depth in journalism ethics. As an applied discipline, journalism ethics too often falls back on simplistic appeals to general concepts such as "truth-seeking," "freedom," "serving the public," and "democracy." Recent academic and critical theories of news media note that such terms are contested (Berger, 2000). Clarification and reformulation of basic concepts is necessary.

However, something *more* than conceptual clarification is required. Journalism ethics should conduct its own critique of critical theories. The critical ideas canvassed above should not be accepted *verbatim*. These media critics have their own biases and blind-spots. Some theorists may set up an unproductive opposition between Western and non-Western cultures, or attack notions of truth and objectivity to the point where they undermine their own claims to truth. Critical theories may "romanticize" non-Western traditions or over-emphasize communal values at the expense of freedom of speech. Journalism ethics in its fifth stage needs to avoid a "stalemate" between Western and non-Western ideas by developing an ethical model that incorporates valuable norms from both traditions.

CONCLUSION: INTO THE FUTURE

Given this debate, whither journalism ethics? Positively, it is possible to regard the current media revolution as prompting a much-needed re-thinking of journalism ethics. The clash of ideas may lead to the invention of a richer journalism ethics.

The future of journalism ethics appears to depend on the successful completion of two large projects: (1) development of a richer theoretical basis for journalism ethics; (2) development of a "mixed media ethics"—a more adequate set of principles and norms for a multi-platform journalism with global reach.

As we have seen, the first project requires a more adequate epistemology of journalism, with a "believable concept of truth" and objectivity (Christians, 2005, p. ix). It also requires the enrichment of liberal theory with other approaches to media theory. Ethicists need to show how new theoretical approaches might change newsroom practice and journalism education.

The second project is a more practical task. It is the construction of rules, norms and procedures for newsrooms that tell stories in print, broadcast and online. What do the principles of truth-seeking and impartiality mean for mixed media? Do the norms and public aims of journalism change when embedded in "social media," that is, on Web sites where citizens share experiences, information and images (Friend & Singer, 2007). Is journalism ethics moving away from a professional emphasis on verification and gate-keeping to a non-professional emphasis on transparency, networking and unfiltered information?

Also, there is the practical question of how these ethical discussions are connected with the public monitoring of news organizations, and the reform of regulatory structures for media systems (Price, Rozumilowicz, & Verhulst, 2002). What new public mechanisms can be put in place to improve news media accountability, to make sure that journalism's age-old desire to "self-regulate" comes to include "public-regulation"?

Finally, journalism ethics should become more cosmopolitan in theory and practice (Gerbner, Mowlana, & Nordenstreng, 1993; Ward, 2005b). Historically, journalism and journalism ethics have been parochial. Journalism ethics was developed for a journalism of limited reach, whose public duties were assumed to stop at the border. The sufficiency of this parochial ethics has been undermined by the globalization of news media (Callahan, 2003). With global impact comes global responsibilities (Cooper, Christians, Plude, White, & Thomas, 1989; Morris & Waisbord, 2001). The violence that rippled around the world after the publication of the cartoons of Mohammed in a Danish newspaper is one example of global impact. Our world is not a cozy McLuhan village. News media link different religions, traditions and groups. Tensions propagate. A globally responsible journalism in needed to help citizens understand the daunting global problems of poverty and environmental degradation (Weaver, 1998; Price & Thompson, 2002; Seib, 2002).

Determining the content of a global journalism ethics is a work-in-progress. In recent years, ethicists have begun a "search" for the fundamental principles of a global media ethics.[11] This "search" faces the problem of how to do justice to both the particular and the universal (Ronning, 1994; Christians & Traber, 1997). Rao, for example, seeks ways to integrate "local" or "indigenous epistemologies" within global media ethics (Rao, 2007). But there are other questions, and other quandaries. How would a cosmopolitan ethics redefine the ideas of social responsibility or serving the public? Would a cosmopolitan ethics reject patriotism as a legitimate influence on journalists?

Despite these difficult questions and daunting problems, the future of journalism ethics requires nothing less than the construction of a new, bolder and more inclusive ethical framework for a multi-media, global journalism amid a pluralistic world.

NOTES

1. There are many ways to divide the field of normative journalism ethics. I divide the field into liberal, socially responsible, activist, and "care" because they identify fundamental ideas that are combined in all major forms of contemporary journalism.
2. See Milton (1951), Hume (1987), Mill (1965), and Foot and Isaac (1987).
3. Liberal theory is not identical with libertarian theories (Narveson, 1988). The latter is an extreme liberalism that argues that the press should have maximal freedom and few social duties.
4. For examples of pro-active and restraining principles, see major codes of ethics such as the code for the Society of Professional Journalists in the United States (www.spj.org) and the code for the Canadian Association of Journalists (www.caj.org).
5. For an example of a holistic approach to practical reasoning in media ethics textbooks see the "point-of-decision" model in Land and Hornaday (2006).
6. The core ideas of social responsibility theory were discussed years in advance of the Hutchins commission. See Cronin and McPherson (1992).
7. Code's feminist epistemology of care starts from the "feminist commonplace that the epistemologies of modernity, in their principled neutrality and detachment, generate an ideology of objectivity that disassociates itself from emotions and values" (Code, 1994, p. 180).
8. Interest in theories of care is shown by the fact that in 2000, a group of ethicists, philosophers, and others gathered for a colloquium at the University of Oregon on "Caring and the Media." The papers formed a special edition of the *Journal of Mass Media Ethics*, 21(2&3), 2006.
9. I develop a theory of "pragmatic objectivity" in Chapter Seven of Ward (2005a). For the idea of objective and intersubjective restraints on interpretation, see Denzin & Lincoln (2000) and Gadamer (2004). For the related idea of "interpretive sufficiency," see Christians (2005).
10. In his influential book, *Orientalism*, the post-colonial writer Edward Said (2003) critiqued Western culture's representation of the East by studying nineteenth-century French and British writers, travellers, and colonial administrators. More recently, geographer Derek Gregory (2004) has used Said's work to analyze how media mis-represent the Iraq war and other events (and ideas).

11. See "In search of a global media ethics," special edition of *Journal of Mass Media Ethics*, 2002, *17*(4).

REFERENCES

Ahluwalia, D., & Nursey-Bray, P. (Eds.). (1997). *Post-colonialism: Culture and identity in Africa.* Commack, NY: Nova Science Publishers.

Albarran, A., & Chan-Olmsted, S. (1998) *Global media economics: Commercialization, concentration and integration of world media markets.* Ames: Iowa State University Press.

Alia, V. (2004). *Media ethics and social change.* Edinburgh: Edinburgh University Press.

Applegate, E. (1997). *Journalistic advocates and muckrakers*. Jefferson, NC: McFarland and Company.

Baldasty, G. (1992). *The commercialization of the news in the Nineteenth Century.* Madison: University of Wisconsin.

Bell, M. (1998). The truth is our currency. *Harvard International Journal of Press/Politics, 3*(1), 102–109.

Berger, G. (2000). Grave new world? Democratic journalism enters the global twenty-first century, *Journalism Studies, 1*(1), 81–99.

Black, J. (2006). "Foreword." *Journal of Mass Media Ethics, 21*(2&3), 99–101.

Black, J., Steele B., & Blarney, R. (1999). *Doing ethics in journalism* (3rd ed.). Boston: Allyn and Bacon.

Butler, C. (2002). *Postmodernism: A very short introduction*. Oxford: Oxford University Press.

Campbell, W. (2001). *Yellow journalism: Puncturing the myths, defining the legacies.* Westport, CT: Praeger.

Callahan, S. (2003). New challenges of globalization for journalism. *Journal of Mass Media Ethics, 18*, 3–15.

Card, C. (Ed.). (1999). *On feminist ethics and politics*. Lawrence: University Press of Kansas.

Chomsky, N. (1997). *Media control: The spectacular achievements of propaganda.* New York: Seven Stories Press.

Christians, C. (1989). Ethical theory in a global setting. In T. Cooper, C., Christians, F., Plude, & R. White. (Eds.), *Communication Ethics and Global* Change (pp. 3–19). White Plains, NY: Longman.

Christians, C. (2005). Preface. In R. Keeble (Ed.), *Communication ethics today* (pp. ix–xiii). Leicester, UK: Troubador.

Christians, C. (2006). The case for communitarian ethics. In M. Land & B. Hornaday (Eds.), *Contemporary media ethic* (pp. 57–69). Spokane, WA: Marquette.

Christians, C., Ferre, J., & Fackler, P. (1993). *Good news: Social ethics and the press.* New York: Oxford University Press.

Christians, C., & Nordenstreng, K. (2004). Social responsibility worldwide. *Journal of Mass Media Ethics, 19*(1), 3–28.

Christians, C., & Traber, M. (Eds.). (1997). *Communication ethics and universal values.* Thousand Oaks, CA: Sage.

Code, L. (1994). Who cares? The poverty of objectivism for a moral epistemology. In A. Megill (Ed.), *Rethinking objectivity* (pp. 179–195). Durham, NC: Duke University Press.

Coman, M. (2000). Developments in journalism theory about media "transition" in Central and Eastern Europe 1990–99. *Journalism Studies, 1*(1), 35–56.

Commission on Freedom of the Press. (1947). *A free and responsible press.* Chicago: University of Chicago Press.

Connor, S. (1989). *Postmodernist culture*. Oxford: Blackwell.

Cooper, T., Christians, C., Plude, F., White, R., & Thomas, R. A. (Eds.). (1989). *Communication ethics and global change*. White Plains, NY: Longman.

Cronin, M., & McPherson, J. (1992). *Reaching for Professionalism and Respectability: The Development of Ethics Codes in the 1920s*. A paper presented at the annual conference of the American Journalism Historian's Association, October, at Lawrence, KS.

Cunningham, B. (2003). Rethinking objectivity. *Columbia Journalism Review, 4*, 24–32.

Darwall, S. (Ed.). (2003). *Contractarianism/contractualism*. Oxford: Blackwell.

Demers, D. (2007). *History and future of mass media: An integrated perspective*. Cresskill, NJ: Hampton Press.

Denzin, N., & Lincoln, Y. (Eds.). (2000). *Handbook of qualitative research* (2nd ed). Thousand Oaks, CA: Sage.

Dimock, S., & Tucker, C. (Eds.). (2004). *Applied ethics: Reflective moral reasoning*. Toronto: Thomson.

Dworkin, R. (2000). *Sovereign virtue: The theory and practice of equality*. Cambridge, MA: Harvard University Press.

Elliott, D. (Ed.). (1986). *Responsible journalism*. Beverly Hill, CA: Sage.

Foot, M., & Isaac K. (Ed.). (1987). *The Thomas Paine reader*. London: Penguin.

Filler, L. (1968). *The muckrakers*. Stanford, CA: Stanford University Press.

Fourie, P. (2007). *Moral philosophy as the foundation of normative media theory: Questioning African ubuntuism as a framework*. Paper presented to the International Roundtable on Global Media Ethics, Stellenbosch, South Africa, March 2007.

Friend, C., & Singer, J. (2007). *Online journalism ethics: Traditions and transitions*. Armonk, NY: M. E. Sharpe.

Fullerton, R., & Patterson, M. (2006). Murder in our midst: Expanding coverage to include care and responsibility. *Journal of Mass Media Ethics, 21*(4), 304–321.

Gadamer, H. (2004). *Truth and method*. (2nd rev. ed.). London: Continuum.

Gerbner, G., Mowlana, H., & Nordenstreng, K. (Eds.). (1993). *The global media debate*. Norwood, NJ: Ablex.

Glover, J. (1999). *Humanity: A moral history of the twentieth century*. London: Jonathan Cape.

Gregory, D. (2004). *The colonial present: Afghanistan, Palestine, Iraq*. Malden, MA: Blackwell.

Gilligan, C. (1982). *In a different voice: Psychological theory and women's development*: Cambridge, MA: Harvard University Press.

Hackett, R., & Zhao, Y. (1998). *Sustaining democracy? Journalism and the politics of objectivity*. Toronto: Garamond Press.

Hacking, I. (1999). *The social construction of what?* Cambridge, MA: Harvard University Press.

Howard, R. (2002). *An operational framework for media and peacebuilding*. Vancouver: IMPACS.

Howard, R. (2003). *Conflict sensitive journalism: A handbook by Ross Howard*. Copenhagen, Denmark: IMS and IMPACS.

Hume, D. (1987). *Of the liberty of the press. Essays: Moral, political and literary* (rev. ed.). Indianapolis: Liberty Fund.

Koehn, D. (1998). *Rethinking feminist ethics: Care, trust and empathy*. London: Routledge.

Kovach, B., & Rosenstiel, T. (2001). *The elements of journalism: What newspeople should know and what the public should expect*. New York: Crown.

Klaidman, S., & Beauchamp T. (1987). *The virtuous journalist*. Oxford: Oxford University Press.

Kuhn, T. (1962). *The structure of scientific revolutions*. Chicago: University of Chicago Press.

Land, M., & Hornaday, B. (Eds.). (2006). *Contemporary media ethics*: Spokane, WA.: Marquette Books.

MacDougall, C. (1957). *Interpretive reporting* (3rd ed.). New York: MacMillan.

McCombs, M., Shaw, D., & Weaver, D. (1997). *Communication and democracy*: *Exploring the intellectual frontiers in agenda-setting theory*. Mahwah, NJ: Erlbaum.

McQuail, D. (1969) *Towards a sociology of mass communications*. London: Collier-Macmillan.

McQuail, D. (1997). *Audience analysis*. Thousand Oaks: Sage.

Mill, J. S. (1965). On liberty. In M. Lerner (Ed.), *Essential works of John Stuart Mill* (seventh printing, pp. 255–360). New York: Bantam Books.

Milton, J. (1951). *Areopagitica*. (Ed. George H. Sabine). New York: Appleton-Century-Crofts.

Mindich, D. (1998). *Just the facts: How "objectivity" came to define American journalism*. New York: New York University Press.

Miraldi, R. (1990). *Muckraking and objectivity*. New York: Greenwood Press.

Morris, N., & Waisbord, S. (Eds.). (2001). *Media and globalization*: *Why the state matters*. New York: Rowman and Littlefield.

Narveson, J. (1988). *The libertarian idea*. Philadelphia: Temple University Press.

Noddings, N. (1984). *Caring: A feminine approach to ethics and moral education*, Berkeley: University of California Press.

Overholser, G. (2006). *On behalf of journalism: A manifesto for change*. Annenberg Public Policy Center. Philadelphia: University of Pennsylvania.

Patterson, P., & Wilkins, L. (2002). *Media ethics: Issues and cases* (4th ed.). New York: McGraw-Hill.

Pavlik, J. V. (2001). *Journalism and the new media*. New York: Columbia University Press.

Peden, C., & Hudson, Y. (Eds.). (1991). *Communitarianism, liberalism and social responsibility*. Lewiston, NY: E. Mellen Press.

Peterson, T. (1956). The social responsibility theory of the press. In F. Siebert, T. Peterson, & W. Schramm, *Four theories of the press* (pp. 73–103). Urbana: University of Illinois Press.

Picard, R. (1989). *Media economics: Concepts and issues*. Newbury Park, CA: Sage.

Pierce, C. (2000). *Immovable laws, irresistible rights: Natural Law, moral rights, and feminist ethics*. Lawrence: University Press of Kansas.

Price, M., & Thompson, M. (Eds.). (2002). *Forging peace: Intervention, human rights and the management of media space*. Edinburgh: Edinburgh University Press.

Price, M., Rozumilowicz, B., & Verhulst, S. (Eds.). (2002). *Media reform: Democratizing the media, democratizing the state*. London: Routledge.

Rao, S. (2007). *Postcolonial theory and global media ethics: A theoretical intervention*. Paper presented to the International Roundtable on Global Media Ethics, Stellenbosch, South Africa, March 2007.

Rawls, J. (1993). *Political liberalism*. New York: Columbia University Press.

Ronning, H. (1994). *Media and democracy: theories and principles with reference to an African context*. Harare, Zimbabwe: Sapes.

Rorty, R. (1979). *Philosophy and the mirror of nature*. Princeton, NJ: Princeton University.

Rosen, J. (1996). *Getting the connections straight: Public journalism and the troubles in the press*. New York: Twentieth Century Fund Press.

Rosen, J. (1999). *What are journalists for?* New Haven, CT: Yale University Press.

Said, E. (2003). *Orientalism*. London: Penguin. (Original work published 1978)

Scanlon, T. M. (1982). Contractualism and utilitarianism. In A. Sen & B. Williams (Eds.), *Utilitarianism and beyond* (pp. 103–128). Cambridge: Cambridge University Press.

Schudson, M. (1978). *Discovering of news: A social history of American newspapers*. New York: Basic Books.

Seib, P. (2002). *The global journalist: News and conscience in a world of conflict*. Lanham, MD: Rowman and Littlefield.

Seters, P. (Ed.). (2006). *Communitarianism in law and society*. Lanham, MD: Rowman and Littlefield.

Shome, R., & Hegde, R. (2002). Postcolonial approaches to communication: Charting the terrain, engaging the intersections. *Communication Theory, 12*(3), 249–270.

Siebert, F. (1956). The libertarian theory of the press. In F. Siebert, T. Peterson, & W. Schramm, *Four theories of the press* (pp. 39–71). Urbana: University of Illinois Press.

Siebert F., Peterson T., & Schramm W. (1956). *Four theories of the press*. Urbana: University of Illinois Press.

Spencer, D. (2007). *The yellow journalism: The press and America's emergence as a world power*. Evanston, IL: Northwestern University Press.

Steiner, L., & Okrusch, C. (2006). Care as a virtue for journalists. *Journal of Mass Media Ethics, 21*(2 & 3), 102–122.

Stephens, M. (1988). *A history of news: From the drum to the satellite*. New York: Viking.

Tsukamoto, S. (2006). Social responsibility theory and the study of journalism ethics in Japan. *Journal of Mass Media Ethics, 21*(1), 54–68.

Ward, S. J. A. (2005a). *The invention of journalism ethics: The long path to objectivity and beyond*. Montreal: McGill-Queen's University Press.

Ward, S. J. A. (2005b). Philosophical foundations for global journalism ethics. *Journal of Mass Media Ethics, 20*(1), 3–21.

Ward, S. J. A. (2007). Utility and impartiality: Being impartial in a partial world. *Journal of Mass Media Ethics, 22*(2-3), 151–167.

Wilkins, L., & Coleman, R. (2005). *The moral media: How journalists reason about ethics.* Mahwah, N.J.: Erlbaum.

Wasserman, H. (2007). *Finding the global in the particular: Media ethics and human dignity in the post-colony.* Paper presented to the International Roundtable on Global Media Ethics, Stellenbosch, South Africa, March 2007.

Weaver, D. H. (Ed.). (1998). *The global journalist.* Cresskill, NJ: Hampton Press.

Young, R. (2003). *Post-colonialism.* New York: Oxford University Press.

22

Journalism and Popular Culture

John Hartley

INTRODUCTION: POPULAR CULTURE AND JOURNALISM STUDIES

This chapter identifies popular culture as the true origin of modern journalism, taking "origin" to refer both to empirical historical beginnings, in revolutionary France and industrializing Britain, and also to theoretical first principles, where popular culture is the subject (source) of journalism, not its object (destination). Therefore, I argue, the relations between journalism and popular culture, and between journalism studies and cultural studies, are best studied historically. Within such histories can be discerned the working through of two contrasting underlying models of communication and determination. In one the consumers of news are an effect of media; in the other they are a source of meaning. One model leads to a representative, expert journalism; the other to emancipationist self-representation (see Table 22.1). Both are present throughout the history of modern media, although during the long reigns of the press barons and broadcast monopolies the top-down version has predominated. This predominance is currently in crisis; my argument is that scholarly attention to the historical relations between journalism and popular culture can help to explain what is at stake in that crisis.

There are two methodological lessons that may be drawn from this history. First, journalism as such is not the fundamental point of difference. The practice of journalism has evolved through both the expert and the emancipationist traditions. Second, the "popular culture" model, based as it is on the underlying notion of an "active audience," has received an immense boost in recent times, owing to the growth of user-led innovation, consumer-generated content, self-made media, DIY culture, citizen-journalism, the blogosphere and peer-to-peer social networks.

HISTORICAL ORIGINS OF JOURNALISM AS SOCIETY-WIDE COMMUNICATION

Historically, journalism is a creature of the popular classes that were thrown together and massively expanded by urbanization, industrialization and the intellectual ferment of Enlightenment and Revolutionary Europe (from the 1790s to the 1830s). It is true that newspapers and therefore journalists predate this period. The first *Intelligencers* and *Mercuries* dated from the seventeenth century; *The Times* (the first proper daily paper) from the eighteenth. However, the early press had neither the technical means nor the political desire to create what remains journalism's most important "product," namely a national *reading public*; the "republic of letters" as Tom Paine called it, that extended to the popular classes.

TABLE 22.1
Two Paradigms for the Study of Journalism

Journalism studies	*Cultural studies*
Object(-ive)	Subject(-ive)
Supply side	Demand side
Popular culture as effect	Popular culture as cause
Producer-provider perspective	Consumer-agent perspective
Representative	Self-representation
Professional Expertise	Popular Emancipation

The empirical origin of modern, mass-mediated journalism is to be found in the Parisian revolutionary press and even more importantly in the so-called "pauper press" in Britain that fought for popular emancipation and democratization over the ensuing fifty years. The public was not a product of the "respectable" press that served existing status-groups (the *ancien regime* and the "gentry"). These latter may have been technical innovators and influential on the opinions and policies of the already-enfranchised classes (perhaps only three percent of men and no women during much of the nineteenth century). But they were not the champions (indeed they were among the opponents) of the fraught and contested development of *mass communication* among the popular classes on a national scale. The circulation of even the most successful stamped (officially authorized) papers like *The Times* remained in the low thousands while that of the unstamped "pauper press" regularly spiked to the hundreds of thousands, from the incendiary works of early popular agitators like Tom Paine and William Cobbett, to the radical-popular press of the industrial revolution (e.g., the *Republican, Poor Man's Guardian*, *Northern Star*) and on to the first commercial-popular newspapers with circulations in the millions—all of which came from radical origins (e.g., *Lloyd's Weekly News*, *Reynold's News*, *News of the World*) (Conboy, 2002; Hartley 1992, 1996).

THE POPULAR EXTENSION OF THE READING PUBLIC

As for theoretical first principles, these gradually clarified in the flux of practice. Modern journalism and the mass reading public were unplanned outcomes of efforts directed to other ends. It was only after their scale and adaptability had been demonstrated that their general importance to a complex open system like modernity could be discerned. But to establish a reading public that could be taken to be coterminous with "the nation," or with "society" in all its populous unenfranchised multifariousness, was not a straightforward process. Nor did it go uncontested. Inventing, extending and stabilizing the "mass" reading public took longer than a generation. Nor was it achieved by the press alone. The pulpit took printed form too, and so did fictional entertainment. But *journalism* could not have developed without the pauper press, and the "reading public"—*the* public of modernity—could not have developed without journalism.

From the point of view of production and distribution, establishing "the public" required technology, capital, industrious enterprise both collaborative and competitive, a network of agents for newsgathering and vending, a creative imagination, "popular address" (discursive and rhetorical populism), fast distribution (railways), and a willingness to persevere in the face of official suppression and frequent incarceration. From the point of view of the readership, it required non-instrumental literacy, sufficient disposable income, and a desire to keep up with events as they unfolded, resulting in the habit of re-consumption. This could only occur when "consumers" liked what they read and wanted to be part of the movement or community "hailed" by their paper, believed they had a personal stake in the outcomes for which it campaigned, and were willing to be represented by their own "organ of enlightenment" in the competitive contestations of opinion in "the public sphere." In this sense the pecuniary nexus that laid the foundation for the commercialization of the press (i.e., myriad individual artisans and their families, exchanging a penny for an unstamped paper) was also a "vote" by each of them for the political program espoused within its pages. They had no other vote.

Here, then, over a fifty-year period (1790s to 1840s), was the beginning of that peculiarity of modernity; the marketization of democratic representation. The market came into play only after a two-way connection had been firmly established. In other words, the representation came first. Representation was also two-way. The paper *represented to* the readership their co-subjectivity with a "class action" cause or movement; and the paper was *representative of* its readership (the larger the better) in the political arena. Purchasers received not only a regular dose of information and entertainment, but also access to a "global" textual system and resources for autodidactic political and social education. The vendors received not only myriad pennies but also ongoing confirmation that they were leading a campaign, not simply exploiting a market.

And thus, out of this combination of economic enterprise, political emancipation, personal hazard, and via a laborious process of contested construction, journalism won a place as an essential mechanism of modern societies. Its importance remains not so much as an industry or economic sector but as a general enabling "social technology," that is just as important as (say) the law and the financial system. It is the *textual system* of modernity (Hartley, 1996). It has only achieved this condition because it actually does, or at least it is taken to, reach the whole population of a given ethno-territorial polity, creating for the first time on a mass scale what is now called the "collective intelligence" of social networks. In short, modern journalism is embedded within, representative of, and speaking both for and to, *popular culture*. It was in place by the "year of revolutions," 1848.

This was a new invention on an unprecedented scale, an "imagined community" of nevertheless real co-subjects, attending together in the here and now to the same events or issues, and occasionally capable of concerted action too. It reached across demographic boundaries of class, gender, age-group, region and ethnicity, to forge a national public for modern industrialized countries. Popular culture provided a new, secular means of public communication for changing societies. Instead of binding "the people" to authority and tradition, as had the only hitherto "mass medium," i.e., the pulpit, it focused public attention on contemporary life and future possibilities. It took the quotidian measure of competitive political, economic and personal development ("scandal"). It brought to everyone's attention the specialist knowledge distributed across a highly differentiated complex social system ("muckraking"). Equally it was a vehicle for various interests, associations and ideologies to contend for popular support, taking the oratorical traditions of the pulpit into the service of politics ("rabble-rousing").

TRUTH AND TEXTUALITY (A SHORT HISTORY OF "TRUTHINESS")

Popular culture is often taken to be a domain of leisure entertainment and fictional narrative, while journalism is often taken to be a part of the democratic process. The lesson of history is that these are not conflicting attributes, but part of the same generative process, the same *realist* textual system. Popular journalism predated popular democracy by decades. The agitation for popular emancipation required masses of potentially activist readers, and in order to attract and retain them the pauper press had to learn the tricks of textuality, or what US television comedian Stephen Colbert—reminding us of the central role of the comic satirist in the politics of truth (and the truth of politics)—has called "truthiness."

The radical papers pioneered the union of entertainment and emancipation, narrative and nationhood, realism and representation. They sought to propagate commanding truths in the form of compelling stories. They spoke directly to the experience and in the language of those whom they wanted to represent; drawing together and encapsulating the identities and aspirations of myriad individuals in an imagined commonality of which the paper itself was the voice. They did not baulk at using fiction as a means to this end, as well as fact, and indeed the line between the two was not clear. For instance a personalized account of the privations of a family, a worker, or a region, often in the form of a letter, might stand in for a sociological truth, whether the featured family or correspondent actually existed or not. Conversely, imagined human frailties were clothed in the garb of truth, with petty criminals, pretty girls and attractive victims in an incessant parade across the page as personifications of imaginary fears and desires.

The *most* popular journalism remained that which tapped into human conflict (i.e., drama): "true crimes" and scandalous disclosure (news); ferocity, exploit, and arrested development (sport); marriageability and its vicissitudes (human interest). In fact and fiction alike, "truthiness"—the *impression* of truth in the mind and emotion of consumers—shifted from medieval revelation to modern competition, and journalism's special contribution to this shift was to fuse truth with violence (Hartley, 1999; Hartley, 2008b, p. 28). Furthermore, these longstanding elements of popular narrative were newly combined with the great fantasies of the modern imagination—narratives of progress and equality, of both competitive individualism and class consciousness; of the power of knowledge, and of the emergence of the ordinary as a positive social value. And let it not be forgotten that straightforward fiction—thrillers, romances and crime stories—was a staple of journalism and remained prominent even in the daily press at least until the arrival of television. The "story magazine" survives still in *The People's Friend*, founded in 1869 and published by D.C. Thomson (see: www.jbwb.co.uk/pfguidelines.htm).

Popular culture was the nutrient of democratic action; it succeeded in (and by) combining the rationalist, secular progressivism of the Enlightenment with the emotionalist, narrative "sensationalism" borrowed from the popular dramatic and musical traditions. It gave both individual agency and systematic shape to "the public." Democracy was precipitated out of popular journalism rather than a being a precondition for it, and the admixture was saturated with potent concentrations of fiction, fun and faith, as well as realism, righteousness and reason. Catalyzed by simple, well-told stories, this incendiary mixture of journalism and popular culture generated much more political energy than either "rational" journalism or "emotional" popular culture taken alone, and it was capable occasionally of causing a truly explosive reaction.

"THE POPULAR": RADICAL VS. COMMERCIAL

The *study* of the relationship between journalism and popular culture, and the *conduct* of that relationship in everyday life and enterprise, have both pivoted about the question of what is at stake in the word "popular" (Dahlgren, 1992, pp. 5–6). Early cultural studies theorists including Raymond Williams (1976), Richard Hoggart and E.P. Thompson, in different ways, were interested in the relationship between popular culture and class. The main problem here was a conflict between "popular culture" construed as a "whole way of life," a life literally *made by* the working class for and by itself, the classic statement of which is Thompson (1963), and "popular culture" construed as pleasures and entertainments laid on for the enjoyment of working class people by commercial enterprises, the classic critique of which is Hoggart (1957). Out of the former came the labor movement, trade-unionism and other collective mechanisms for self-representation (popular culture as subject). Out of the latter came commercial media including the press, television, cinema, magazines and the like (popular culture as object).

Journalism occurred on both sides of this conflict: it could be "radical popular" or "commercial popular" (Hartley, 1992, pp. 177–181), and the two types could co-exist, although the commercial popular press did not take off until the second half of the nineteenth century, after a popular reading public had been established by the pauper press. Indeed, it may be argued that commercial popularity systematically supplanted the radical popular (Conboy, 2002, pp. 80–86). Increasingly the commercialization of the entire media sector tended to exclude all but a few radical popular voices, in favor of commercial properties owned by "press barons" whose own political views were more likely to be reactionary than revolutionary.

The "radical popular" retracted to a committed readership that was eventually far from "popular" in number, while the "commercial popular" remained dominant numerically but treated the populace as a mass market, the object of campaigns both political and commercial. Not surprisingly, observers from the radical side of politics continuously criticized these developments, berating the commercial popular media for "dumbing down" as well as "demagoguery." They objected to the fact that "popular" journalism had stopped speaking *for* or even *as* "the people," and instead spoke *to* them, seeking to manipulate their behavior rather than to represent their voice. Thus, by the time the serious academic study of *popular culture* began in Britain in the 1960s and 1970s, there was felt to be a need to understand how "radical" communicative action by oppositional classes, which themselves were proliferating beyond the industrial proletariat to include identity groups based on gender, ethnicity, nationality, sexual orientation and the like, might survive and even prosper in an era of commercial media.

The answer to this problem took two forms; one practical and the other theoretical. In practice, radical communicative action abandoned the field of formal journalism almost entirely, emerging instead within the "whole way of life" associated with counter-cultural alternatives, especially those associated with music and subcultures, from flower power to the hippies; from blues to punk. In the era of identity politics and the "politics of the personal," self-representation was carried on largely through the entertainment aspect of popular culture, by musicians and artists who combined commercial success, entrepreneurial acumen and an image of freedom. Successive singers—Pete Seeger, Bob Dylan, Jimmy Hendrix (Gilroy, 2006), John Lennon, Bob Geldof, Bono—seemed to speak on behalf of a global, anti-war, pro-ecology "constituency" that saw mainstream journalism as part of the problem, not as their representative voice. Lennon in particular was willing to use his mass-mediated fame to put items on the political agenda that were entirely consonant with the "radical popular" media of a previous century—opposition to state control, advocacy of peace, and pursuit of an alternative lifestyle, all conducted through popular media, in which journalism was simultaneously an adversary, a foil, and an ally (see www.theusversusjohnlennon.com/).

Accompanying such efforts, entirely new forms of journalism arose in the spaces between music, counterculture, politics and identity, including what was called the New Journalism, and exemplified in the "underground" press and "alternative" magazines, such as *Oz, Ink, Rolling Stone, Spare Rib* among many others; continuing through the punk period via fanzines like *Sniffin' Glue*; and into the era of DIY culture and digital media. These models of self-representation and in-group distribution left the mainstream media looking distinctly flat-footed: a rich vein of journalism which is simply invisible in journalism studies, in J-school curricula, or in discussions of the "democratic process" and "professional journalism."

Meanwhile, the theoretical attempt at a "solution" to the conflict between radical communicative action and commercial media was the Marxist concept of the "national popular" (Gramsci, 1971; Laclau & Mouffe, 1985), which substituted "nation" for "class" and "popular" for "proletariat" in an attempt to identify the "alliance" needed to win power by constitutional rather than revolutionary means (Forgacs, 1993). Many countries in Europe and Latin America, for example, built "national popular front" parties or alliances to pursue that goal. Such political efforts influenced the study of journalism. Researchers sought to identify what the prospects were for building a "radical popular" media in the context of "commercial popular" media dominance (Hall, Critcher, Jefferson, Clarke, & Roberts, 1978). Since the diffusion of cultural studies into the academic mainstream following its internationalization in the 1980s, this specifically political agenda for popular journalism studies has also dissipated somewhat, although vestiges of the "class war in language" approach survive in many studies of the "capitalist" press and media (for an interesting reworking of this trope see Lewis, 2005). At the same time, interest in the radical possibilities offered through music and other forms of countercultural consciousness has remained a central concern of cultural studies.

However, the basic proposition, that *popular journalism is a creation of popular culture*, just as the labor movement is, has been almost entirely forgotten in journalism studies. J-schools have tended to focus on journalism as an occupation, one moreover linked to the formal political process and the specialist needs of business, not to the myriad-voiced expression of popular aspiration. Indeed, the most recent commentators judge that "bottom-up" journalism is literally unthinkable. Martin Conboy (2007, p. 2), for instance, introducing a special issue of *Journalism Studies* on "Popular Journalism," admits defeat:

> In our contemporary capitalist consumer culture, it is hard to envisage much in the way of journalism which is produced entirely by ordinary people and consumed by sufficient numbers of them to maintain regular production as journalism given the institutional and financial demands of the genre.

Such a view clearly requires the restriction of what is meant by "journalism" to its highly capitalized "industrial" form (i.e., "the press"; or "the media"). It does not admit *as journalism* the self-representations characteristic of Web 2.0 applications, including e-zines, the blogosphere, citizen journalism and "collaborative" online news production. Here it is at odds with those analysts who see journalism not as an industry but in terms of its ability to "help enable, extend, and enhance public discovery, discussion and deliberation of the news" (Bruns, 2005, p. 317)—a function that can be performed by anyone and indeed everyone (Hartley, 2008a), despite professional misgivings about the "cult of the amateur" (Keen, 2007).

TABLOIDIZATION AND CELEBRITY

Within the converse "cult of the expert," as it were, the excision of "bottom-up" popular and countercultural journalism from the equation leaves only "commercial popular" forms. Here the chief problem associated with popularity is what has come to be called *tabloidization* (Hargreaves, 2003; Lumby, 1999; Turner, 2005; Bird, 2003; Langer, 1998) and *celebrity culture* (Ponce de Leon, 2002; Turner, 2004; Rojek, 2004). The nature of the "problem of the popular" changes from a debate about *representation* ("by" or "for" the people?) to a debate about *reason*. Popular culture has come to be associated with emotion, irrationalism, affect, sensation, and embodied experience. As mentioned above in relation to the nineteenth-century pauper press, journalism was first popularized with the aid of these dangerous allies, which were harnessed in the cause of popular emancipation. But as time wore on, and as popular sovereignty became routine and the popular press commercial, the use of sensation in the service of truth began to jar the modern sensibility.

As a child of the Enlightenment with strong investment in the liberal values of reason, truth, science, progress and realism, journalism has had a tough time coming to terms with the corporeal basis of knowledge. Despite the empirical fact that no journalistic enterprise has ever succeeded in separating reason and emotion, information and entertainment, the real and the imagined, the facts and the story, nevertheless the idea persists that journalism *should not* deal with the "naughty bits." Reason fends of its opposite number with revealing squeamishness (Lumby, 1999); a combination of lust and loathing (not excluding self-loathing), which divides the profession of journalism itself.

But the problem remains as it was in the beginning, when the pauper press attracted readers with rapes, murders and pugilism in order to hold them for radical reform. How do you get uncommitted ordinary people (voters, citizens, consumers, audiences) to take an interest in things they do not know or care about? How can you impart information to the public if they do not pay attention to you? How can you confine journalism to the doings of one elite (the politico-business decision-makers) while scorning those of another (celebrity-entertainment role models). Why fetishize facts when journalism deals in stories? Why is it acceptable to write about Monica Lewinsky's encounter with cigars, or Camilla Parker-Bowles' with tampons, on the grounds that these raise constitutional issues, but to declare "a vacancy at the Paris Hilton" (Sconce, 2007) in relation to popular celebrities, on the grounds that citizens *ought not* to be interested in, or told about, the sex life (or the *Simple Life*, or the prison life) of the rich and famous (Lumby, 1999, p. 65)? Why lament a generation that does not vote while lambasting the same group for its devotion to peer-to-peer social networking and self-expression through entertainment? Trying to hold a middle line in this environment is more difficult than it may seem, despite the very obvious fact that any form of communication must appeal to those addressed in order for them to attend to it (Lanham, 2006); and despite the less obvious one that even the most "low-brow" entertainment may carry important information, teach some truth, and engage with real experience. For instance, Liz Nice (2007, p. 132), former editor of *Bliss*, writes:

> Teenage magazines are not big on social and political debate so may not encourage their readers [...] to do something about social problems and start campaigns. But editors insist that they do empower them to deal with peer pressure, teenage pregnancy, bullying and drugs. And through continuing interactivity, via text messaging, letters pages, e-mail and the magazine's website, they offer readers a forum which helps editors to understand them better and give them a voice.

Such sentiments are not confined to editors of consumer magazines. Ian Hargreaves, former deputy editor of the *Financial Times*, editor of the *Independent* and the *New Statesman*, and director of news and current affairs at the BBC, put the same case in his book *Journalism: Truth or Dare* (2003, pp. 134–135):

> It is a difficult line to tread between appealing to the audience's natural point of interest and emotional pressure points, without trivializing events. It cannot be denied that there is plenty of bad tabloid journalism [...] But there is also brilliant tabloid journalism, in newspapers, magazines, television and radio, that brings issues alive and broadens popular engagement.

Indeed, Rupert Murdoch himself has claimed that his most famous tabloid title is in fact a *radical* newspaper: "The *Sun* stands for opportunities for working people and for change in this society. It's a real catalyst for change, it's a very radical paper" (Murdoch cited in Snoddy, 1992).

The problem of the popular returns unchanged; except that now the "radical popular" is conflated with the "commercial popular" (Allan, 1999).

CITIZENSHIP AND SELF-REPRESENTATION

The current research environment is one of furious convergence among many different and previously contending positions on the problem of the popular. Despite their disciplinary, ideological, professional and geographical diversity, a common focus has emerged, centered on the idea of cultural citizenship. The question that was once posed at the level of class is now posed at the level of the individual consumer-citizen: What are the prospects for informed, embodied self-representation (Bird, 2003; Hermes, 2005; Bruns, 2005; Rennie, 2006)?

The very idea would have horrified the pioneers of "commercial popular" journalism, for whom the salient fact about individual bodies was that there were multitudinously too many of them; and that if left to their own devices they would destroy knowledge rather than share and expand it (Bagehot, 1867). This tension between democratization and dumbing down still infuses the study of journalism (Rushbridger, 2000). A question for future research, then, is how do divergent but overlapping energies—for instance globalization, economic growth and competition, Internet affordances, the commercialization of culture, and the agency of myriad individuals located in diverse contexts—enable or inhibit popular self-representation?

METHODOLOGICAL CONSIDERATIONS

Popular culture has featured in journalism studies largely as an "other," associated not with freedom, truth, power and organized news-making, but with entertainment, consumerism, persuasion and personal identity. As a result, especially in English-speaking countries, the research field of journalism studies is frequently at loggerheads with cultural studies (Windschuttle, 1998; Zelizer, 2004). This methodological stand off is debilitating to a proper understanding of the relationship between the two fields. The gap that is now evident between journalism (studies) and popular culture (studies) is real, but it is also a link. They are linked because they are at opposite ends of the same information supply chain; at one end the "writer" (producer) and at the other the "reader" (consumer). Journalism studies in the US, UK and other countries like Australia have tended to focus on the occupation of the news reporter, often with scant regard for the readership (beyond an interest in its scale). Cultural studies, conversely, has had more to say about the cultural form of journalism, investigated from the point of view of the reader or audience, giving no special status to journalists themselves. The often strained relations between those who study them may be "referred pain"—an expression of a real but indirectly experienced conflict of interest between producers and consumers of news in modern societies.

MODEL 1: THE VALUE CHAIN (OBJECTIVE, SUPPLY-SIDE JOURNALISM)

Journalism (the modern occupation) is at one end of the supply chain while popular culture (the modern experience) is at the other:

Journalist → News → Public

That linear chain is superimposed on another one; a commonsensical model of communication:

Sender/addresser → Message/text → Receiver/addressee

The apparent homology of these two models (as in Table 22.2) seems almost naturally to explain the relative position of journalists and their readers at opposite ends of a "value chain of meaning" (Hartley, 2008b, p. 28; Porter, 1985):

Producer/originator → Commodity/distribution → Consumer/user

This "value chain" model, through which journalism is both practiced and studied, seems also to show causal sequence: A causes B; B affects C, therefore C is an effect of A (where → = direction of causation):

A	→	B	→	C
Firm	→	Entertainment	→	Popular culture

The doctrine of causation by agents further up the communication/value chain generates the familiar "media effects" model. Despite criticism of it in cultural and media studies (e.g., Gauntlett, 1998, 2005), "media effects" thinking continues to exert force in both academic (e.g. political economy) and journalistic accounts of journalism. It implies that journalists are congregated at the powerful producer end of the value/causal chain, while popular culture is massed down at the consumer end, a behavioral effect of corporate processes which have their explanation, and their pleasures and powers, elsewhere.

Government	("makes")	Decisions	("that affect")	Citizens ("voters")
Journalist	→	Copy/script	→	Reader/audience

Finally, all of these linked sequences express an underlying presumption (shared by Marxists and liberals alike) about causation in contemporary society:

Economy → Politics → Culture

The mainstream tradition of university-based journalism studies has been dedicated to the producer/publisher/provider, or supply side. Cultural studies is dedicated to the consumer/audience/user, or demand side. Both phenomena (journalism and popular culture) can be studied without reference to the other, because each is associated with a different version of the "chain" metaphor. Nevertheless the two chains are versions of a homologous relationship within the same overall system. Table 22.2 sums up what is at stake, which becomes clear when the terms introduced so far are read "vertically" as well as horizontally.

This homology among different commonsensical models of communicative relationship demonstrates two things. First, the three-link structure of the model is extremely robust, embedded in common sense as a kind of retained resource of intellectual capital, a generally available means to make unreflecting sense of modern experience. In this respect the model itself is a component of popular culture; it has the reassuring appeal of "truthiness." And second, it is a serviceable model in practice. It works.

End of story? Not quite. The "effects" model cannot help but cast consumers—and therefore

TABLE 22.2
Supply-Side Journalism and the Value-Chain Model of Communication

Model	*Supply side*		*'Medium'*		*Demand side*
	Economy	→	**Politics**	→	**Culture**
Value chain	Producer/originator	→	Commodity/ distribution	→	Consumer
Communication	Sender (agent)	→	Message	→	Receiver (behavior)
Public affairs	Government ('makes')	→	Decisions ('that affect')	→	Citizen ('voters')
Journalism (form)	Writer/news-gatherer	→	Copy/script	→	Reader/audience
Journalism (occupation)	**Journalist**	→	News	→	Public
Commerce	Firm	→	Entertainment	→	**Popular culture** (experience)
Power	Cause	→	'Media'	→	Effect

by homology audiences, readers and citizens—in a poor light; as behavioral "effects" of media, dumbed-down dupes and distracted dopes, manipulated or worse by firms or state agencies. Small wonder that journalists, understood as those employed in newsrooms at the causal end of the information supply chain, literally "in the know," do not want to be associated with them, even "in theory." Instead of fraternizing with the punters, journalism research has focused on "professional" practice, construing news-consumers as behavioral effects of journalistic causes. Tellingly, this is the journalistic culture that Prasun Sonwalkar (2005) dubs "banal journalism," predicated on a deeply assimilated "us-them" binary.

Even as this way of modeling communication took hold in empirical social science, James Halloran (1981, p. 22) warned of the inherent danger of such a turn:

> It is now suggested that research...should be shifted away from such questions as "the right to communicate" to "more concrete problems." But what are these "concrete problems"? They are the same as, or similar to, the safe, "value-free" micro-questions of the old-time positivists who served the system so well, whether or not they intended or understood this. All this represents a definite and not very well disguised attempt to put the clock back to the days when the function of research was to serve the system as it was—to make it more efficient rather than to question it or suggest alternatives.

While positivist accounts of "the system as it was" continued to gain strength in journalism studies despite Halloran's worries (e.g., Donsbach, 2004, 2007; Löffelholz & Weaver, 2008), the pioneers of cultural studies were also interested in "concrete problems," but saw them in terms of political rights not supply-chain efficiencies, and analyzed them from a perspective grounded in the humanities not the social sciences. They approached both journalism and the study of popular culture from a true "alternative": the point of view of the "consumer."

MODEL 2: SELF-REPRESENTATION (SUBJECTIVE, DEMAND-SIDE JOURNALISM)

From this perspective, neither audiences nor popular culture are the end-point of a chain; they are the source of productive labor, of action (especially collective political action) and of language and culture. Early cultural studies was an amalgam of (Leavisite) literary history and (leftist or Marxist) emancipationist politics, brought together in 1950s New Left activism in Britain through such figures as Richard Hoggart (1957, 1967), Raymond Williams (1968) and Stuart Hall (UWI, n.d.). From this perspective, consumers were "ordinary people," and cross-demographic communication was not a three-link chain but an antagonism between opposed structural positions. Thus, the study of news media was part of a larger project in cultural politics (see Lee, 2003; Hartley, 2003; Gibson, 2007).

In this schema, ordinary people were—among other things—a "reading public" (Webb, 1955); a social network constructed historically, held together by cultural affinities, and grown to popular scale during more than a century of industrialization, the growth of the press, mass literacy, and both democratic and class politics ("struggle"). A reading public is a deliberative agent of knowledge, not a behavioral effect of media. It is the locus of "cultural citizenship"; the place where "we" engage with textual systems to "reflect on, and reform, identities that are embedded in communities" (Hermes, 2005, p. 10).

JOURNALISM IN CULTURAL STUDIES: YOU HAVE NOTHING TO LOSE BUT YOUR VALUE CHAINS

Where the cultural-studies pioneers were interested in journalism, it was to understand its role in a "system of representation," and to show that such a system was determined by economic forces and political power. Raymond Williams wrote about the need for "a recognition of the social reality of man in all his activities, and of the consequent struggle for the direction of this reality by and for ordinary men and women" (Williams, 1968, p. 16). We can now recognize that "recognition" as the project of cultural studies. By 1968 Williams was ready to name the "struggle for the direction of this reality": he called it "socialism."

Thus cultural experience was seen as the ground upon which both class consciousness (socialism) and ideology (e.g., consumerism) were propagated. Later, Stuart Hall (1981, p. 239) made very clear why he thought popular culture was worthy of study:

> [Popular culture] is one of the sites where this struggle for and against a culture of the powerful is engaged: it is also the stake to be won or loss in the struggle. It is the area of consent and resistance. It is partly where hegemony arises, and where it is secured [...] it is one of the places where socialism might be constituted. That is why "popular culture" matters. Otherwise, to tell you the truth, I don't give a damn about it.

Popular culture was an arena of struggle, and to the extent that power was concentrated in the hands of the owners and managers of the means of production and their hired experts, including journalists, such a circumstance called for change, not passive consent, so that "ordinary men and women" might gain power over the "direction of this reality" by their own collective efforts, guided by analysis from intellectuals working in the tradition of the rational left.

Among the issues that had divided those working in that tradition was whether to focus organized popular action on the economic sphere (the worker) via the labor movement and revolutionary parties, or on the political sphere (the voter) via reformist social-democratic parties and representative government. Cultural studies posed a third alternative: if change was not secured by direct struggle in the economic and political spheres, then perhaps attention needed to turn to the cultural sphere (the audience, consumer). Was there something about the experience of culture that impeded (or might encourage) popular (or "national-popular") political and economic

TABLE 22.3
Cultural Studies as the Continuation of Class Struggle By Other Means

Sphere (determination):	Economy →	Politics →	**Culture + Society (Williams)**
Site (of struggle):	Factory	Parliament/government	**Home + Neighborhood (Hoggart)**
Representation:	Labor movement	Labor Party	**Media + Ideology (Hall)**
Leadership	Revolutionaries	Reformists	**Intellectuals (New Left/CCCS)**
Subjectivity	**Worker**	**Voter**	**Audience + Consumer**

action? This was the founding question of cultural studies, which turned out to be as much a challenge to existing dispositions of knowledge as it was to extra-mural action (Lee, 2000, 2003; Wallerstein, 2001, 2004, pp. 18–22). Quite a few analysts feared, and still do, that in this context journalists were part of the problem, not the solution. Table 22.3 shows why. The entry for "media + ideology" in Table 22.3 may appear to be an odd-one-out; conceptually different from the other terms in the field. Where the class-based organizations of the labor movement were seen as "bottom-up" agencies of self-representation for working people (e.g., Thompson, 1963), the media were seen as "top-down" and invasive, speaking to and for "ordinary people" while actually representing the interests of the "power bloc." One of the important innovations of early cultural studies was its interest in how the media ought to be understood both as a system of representation and as a means of popular expression. This work was initiated by Richard Hoggart (1957, 1967), and taken up by Raymond Williams (1974), but it was most fully elaborated by Stuart Hall (often working with colleagues), who had built up over thirty media-related publications by the time the capstone *Policing the Crisis* was published in 1978 (UWI, n.d.). As cultural studies turned from the "worker" (economics) and "voter" (politics) to the "consumer"' (culture) in order to investigate how modern subjectivity was formed, attention was inevitably drawn to the media, both the "radical popular" press of self-representation and the "commercial popular" press of expansive capitalist culture. Was the latter responsible for helping or hindering the process of self-representation by modern subjects?

To answer this question, cultural studies turned to a different model of determination, the Marxist concept of base and superstructure, within which both politics and culture appear as effects (in the last instance) of causal determinations generated in the economic sphere. In such a structure, the media are not simply a system of representation but more to the point an ideological system; they cannot help but express "ruling ideas" no matter how popular they are. It was within this model of determination that Stuart Hall proposed the "Encoding/Decoding" model (1973), to "answer back" to the naturalistic three-part value-chain/communication model inherited from common sense (see Table 22.4).

TABLE 22.4
Journalism as an Ideological System of Representation

Economy (**base**)	[Politics + Culture] (**superstructure**)
Determination	Ideology
Encoding	Decoding (Hall)
Objective	Subjective

CONCLUSION

The seemingly inexorable tendency in current "professional" journalism studies towards a top-down functionalist account of journalism as public communication, where journalists provide communication *to* the public, is not simply a choice between otherwise neutral models or paradigms. Historically, it errs by putting the cart before the horse, which ought to be recognized if only to honor those whose struggle *against* the social leadership of their day produced the means for today's practitioners to grasp professional autonomy and social leadership for themselves. But more importantly, putting the cart before the horse is an error of theoretical principle. It reverses the true *flow of causation*. The flow of causation in journalism is not *from* a professional provider *to* popular culture, but the other way round. Popular culture is the cause, the subject, the agent, the origin, of journalism, no matter how professionalized, industrialized and bureaucratized the latter may become.

This is what journalism studies neglects to its cost. It has fetishized the producer-provider (individual journalist and proprietor or firm); it ignores the agency of the consumer, except as a "micro" or individualized behavioral *effect* of causation by professional-industrial expertise. It has no concept of a "macro" textual system, which is shared among a large-scale social network of attention-paying co-subjects, and which forms the condition of possibility (the "demand") for journalism to be practiced at all.

The importance of this blind-spot in journalism studies and among journalists is that as a result they have diminished means to explain what happens when shifts occur in the reading public and evolution occurs in the textual system. For example, *systemic* changes are under way at the present time, in the shift from "read-only" participation in public affairs and popular representation to a "read-and-write" mode of socially networked mass digital literacy in which information, news, and representation are self-made but simultaneously socially scaled. This is where popular culture is currently most energetically concentrated, around Myspace, Facebook, YouTube, the Wikipedia. Here also is where enterprise, capital investment and marketization have followed, just as was the case with the initial invention of the mass reading public in the nineteenth century. A model of journalism that focuses unduly on the professional provider, and sees self-propagating social networks as somehow irrelevant to that calling, will have little understanding of (and less sympathy with) this emergent social technology. As a result, journalism is being reformed from the outside, without the help of journalism studies, because in the end the social functionality of public communication belongs to the public, not to an autonomous caste of self-appointed representatives in the pay of corporate monopolies, no matter how "popular" their work may seem for the time being. The relationship between journalism and popular culture is in flux, again, so it is important to understand the direction of causation. That is why it is necessary to analyze journalism from the perspective of popular culture, which may be taken as its subject, not its object.

REFERENCES

Allan, S. (1999). *News culture*. Milton Keynes, UK: Open University Press.

Bagehot, W. (1867). *The English constitution* (1872 rev. ed.). Retrieved July 19, 2008, from http://www.gutenberg.org/etext/4351

Bird, S. E. (2003). *The audience in everyday life: Living in a media world*. New York: Routledge.

Bruns, A. (2005). *Gatewatching: Collaborative online news production*. New York: Peter Lang.

Conboy, M. (2002). *The press and popular culture*. London: Sage.

Conboy, M. (2007). Permeation and profusion: Popular journalism in the new millennium. *Journalism Studies*, *8*(1), 1–12.

Dahlgren, P. (1992). Introduction. In P. Dahlgren & C. Sparks (Eds.), *Journalism and popular culture* (pp. 1–23). London: Sage.

Donsbach, W. (2004). Psychology of news decisions: Factors behind journalists' professional behavior. *Journalism, 5*(2), 131–157.

Donsbach, W. (October 2007). *What Professional Journalists Should Know About Communication Research.* Keynote address to "Harmonious Society, Civil Society and the Media", conference held by the Communications University of China and the International Communication Association, Beijing, China.

Forgacs, D. (1993). National-popular: genealogy of a concept. In S. During (Ed.), *The cultural studies reader* (pp. 210–219). London: Routledge. (Original work published 1984)

Gauntlett, D. (1998). Ten things wrong with the "effects model." In R. Dickinson, R. Harindranath, & O. Linné (Eds.), *Approaches to audiences—A reader.* London: Arnold. Retrieved July 19, 2008, from http://www.theory.org.uk/david/effects.htm

Gauntlett, D. (2005). *Moving experiences, 2nd edition: Media effects and beyond.* London: John Libbey.

Gibson, M. (2007). *Culture and power: A history of cultural studies.* Oxford: Berg.

Gilroy, P. (2006). *Bold as love? On the moral economy of blackness in the 21st century.* W.E.B. Du Bois Lectures, Harvard University. Retrieved July 19, 2008, from http://www.news.harvard.edu/gazette/2006/10.12/09-gilroy.html

Gramsci, A. (1971). *Selections from the prison notebooks.* London: Lawrence & Wishart.

Hall, S. (1973). *Encoding and decoding in the media discourse.* Stencilled Paper no.7, Birmingham: CCCS.

Hall, S. (1981). Notes on deconstructing the popular. In R. Samuel (Ed.), *People's history and socialist theory* (pp. 227–40). London: RKP.

Hall, S., Critcher, C., Jefferson, T., Clarke, J., & Roberts, B. (1978). *Policing the crisis: Mugging, the state and law & order.* London: Macmillan.

Halloran, J. D. (1981). The context of mass communication research. In E. McAnany, J. Schnitman, & N. Janus (Eds.), *Communication and social. structure* (pp. 21–57). New York: Praeger.

Hargreaves, I. (2003). *Journalism: Truth or dare.* Oxford: Oxford University Press.

Hartley, J. (1992). *The politics of pictures: The creation of the public in the age of popular media.* London: Routledge.

Hartley, J. (1996). *Popular reality: Journalism, modernity, popular culture.* London: Arnold.

Hartley, J. (1999). Why is it scholarship when someone wants to kill you? Truth as violence. *Continuum: Journal of Media & Cultural Studies, 13*(2), 227–236.

Hartley, J. (2003). *A short history of cultural studies.* London: Sage.

Hartley, J. (2008a). Journalism as a human right: The cultural approach to journalism. In M. Löffelholz & D. Weaver (Eds.), *Global journalism research: Theories, methods, findings, future* (pp. 39–51). Oxford: Blackwell.

Hartley, J. (2008b). *Television truths: Forms of knowledge in popular culture.* Oxford: Blackwell.

Hermes, J. (2005). *Re-reading popular culture.* Oxford: Blackwell.

Hoggart, R. (1957). *The uses of literacy.* London: Chatto & Windus.

Hoggart, R. ed. (1967). *Your Sunday paper.* London: University of London Press.

Keen, A. (2007). *The cult of the amateur: How today's Internet is killing our culture.* New York: Doubleday.

Laclau, E., & Mouffe, C. (1985). *Hegemony and social strategy: Towards a radical democratic politics.* London: Verso.

Langer, J. (1998). *Tabloid television: Popular journalism and the "other news."* London: Routledge.

Lanham, R. A. (2006). *The economics of attention: Style and substance in the age of information.* Chicago: University of Chicago Press.

Lee, R. E. (2000). The structures of knowledge and the future of the social sciences: Two postulates, two propositions and a closing remark. *Journal of World Systems Research, 6*(3), 786–787.

Lee, R. E. (2003). *Life and times of cultural studies: The politics and transformation of the structures of knowledge.* Durham, NC: Duke University Press.
Lewis, J. (2005). *Language wars: The role of media and culture in global terror and political violence.* London: Pluto Books.
Löffelholz, M., & Weaver, D. H. (Eds.). (2008). *Global journalism research: Theories, methods, findings, future.* Oxford: Blackwell.
Lumby, C. (1999). *Gotcha! Life in a tabloid world.* Sydney: Allen & Unwin.
Nice, L. (2007). Tabloidization and the teen market: Are teenage magazines dumberer than ever? *Journalism Studies, 8*(1), 117–136.
Ponce de Leon, C. L. (2002). *Self-exposure: Human interest journalism and the emergence of celebrity in America 1890–1940).* Chapel Hill: University of North Carolina Press.
Porter, M. (1985). *Competitive advantage: Creating and sustaining superior performance.* New York: The Free Press.
Rennie, E. (2006). *Community media: A global introduction.* Lanham MD: Rowman & Littlefield.
Rojek, C. (2004). *Celebrity.* London: Reaktion Books.
Rushbridger, A. (2000). Versions of seriousness. *Guardian Unlimited.* Retrieved July 19, 2008, from http://www.guardian.co.uk/dumb/story/0,7369,391891,00.html
Sconce, J. (2007). A vacancy at the Paris Hilton. In J. Gray, C. Sandvoss & C. L. Harrington (Eds.), *Fandom: Identities and communities in a mediated world* (pp. 328–343). New York: New York University Press.
Snoddy, R. (1992). *The good, the bad and the unacceptable: The hard news about the British press.* London: Faber & Faber.
Sonwalkar, P. (2005). Banal journalism: The centrality of the "us-them" binary in news discourse. In S. Allan (Ed.), *Journalism: Critical issues* (pp. 261–73). Milton Keynes, UK: Open University Press.
Thompson, E. P. (1963). *The making of the English working class.* London: Victor Gollancz.
Turner, G. (2004). *Understanding celebrity.* London: Sage.
Turner, G. (2005). *Ending the affair: The decline of current affairs in Australia.* Sydney: University of New South Wales Press.
UWI (n.d.). *Stuart Hall, publications and papers.* University of the West Indies at Mona, Jamaica: Library. Retrieved July 19, 2008, from http://www.mona.uwi.edu/library/stuart_hall.html.
Wallerstein, I. (2001). *Unthinking social science: The limits of nineteenth-century paradigms* (2nd ed.). Philadelphia: Temple University Press.
Wallerstein, I. (2004). *The uncertainties of knowledge.* Philadelphia: Temple University Press.
Webb, R. K. (1955). *The British working class reader 1790–1848.* London: George Allen & Unwin.
Williams, R. (Ed.). (1968). *May Day manifesto.* Harmondsworth, UK: Penguin Special.
Williams, R. (1974). *Television: Technology and cultural form.* London: Fontana.
Williams, R. (1976). *Keywords.* London: Fontana.
Windschuttle, K. (1998). Journalism versus cultural studies. *Australian Studies in Journalism, 7,* 3–31.
Zelizer, B. (2004). When facts, truth, and reality are god-terms: On journalism's uneasy place in cultural studies. *Communication and Critical/Cultural Studies, 1*(1), 100–119.

23

Audience Reception and News in Everyday Life

Mirca Madianou

> To calm myself, I turned to that evening clinic of referred pain, the TV news. Tonight, a mass grave in a wood in central Bosnia, a cancerous government minister with a love-nest, the second day of a murder trial. What soothed me was the format's familiarity: the war-beat music, the smooth and urgent tones of the presenter, the easeful truth that all misery was relative, then the final opiate, the weather. (McEwan, 1998, pp. 46–47)

Although most research on news is ultimately concerned with its impact on society, the question of the news audience has often remained an implied category. News is a heavily researched genre but, comparatively, its audience has not always received as much attention as other aspects: For example, questions of the economy of production, newswork, news sources and representation have been studied intensively as is manifested in the chapters of the present volume. Such observations led researchers to note that what is missing from the sociology of news is an account of its audiences (Schudson, 2000, p. 194). This is not exactly correct, however, as there is a growing body of studies, some of them path-breaking, on the interpretation of news (see Gamson, 1992; Morley, 1980; Lewis, 1991; Philo, 1990; Liebes, 1997). According to Silverstone, what is missing is not research on news viewers, but rather a more ritual and mediational approach to news as a dynamic component of social and cultural life (2005, p. 17).

This chapter, after presenting the historical context in which audiences for news have been studied, will mainly focus on two important traditions in the study of the news audience. The first approach is linked to the emergence of British Cultural Studies and in particular the work of Stuart Hall (1980) and his seminal "Encoding/Decoding" model. The emphasis here is on audiences' interpretation of the news. The second approach that I will discuss evolved out of the "exciting phase of audience research" that Hall's work inspired. The studies in this group approach news consumption as a ritual (Carey, 1989) and adopt an ethnographic perspective in their investigation.

After considering the merits and limitations of each approach, the chapter will discuss the present challenges in the study of the news audiences. These include new communication technologies and the blurring of boundaries between consumption and production; the concern with the emotional; the need for comparative research. All these point to directions for future research and compel us to reconsider (yet again) the usefulness of the term "audience."

PENDULUM SWINGS AND IMPLIED AUDIENCES

Perceptions about audiences for news have followed a series of pendulum swings parallel to those concerning media effects. From the early ideas about omnipotent media during the interwar period to the paradigm of "limited effects" (Klapper, 1960) and then on to the current orthodoxy, what is often described as the *media malaise* thesis, audiences have been construed as either passive recipients of media messages and thus vulnerable, or as active agents capable of producing their own meanings. The *media* or *video malaise* thesis—a bit of a misnomer as it is hardly a thesis but rather a group of studies that point to the adverse effects of television news—has gained currency from the late 1960 and 1970s. Several authors (Lang & Lang, 1966; Gerbner, Gross, Miorgan, & Signorelli,1986; Robinson, 1976) argued that the exposure to television news, by emphasizing conflict and exaggerating the negative, cultivates a negative way of looking at the world (Gerbner, 1986) and even political disaffection (Robinson, 1976) especially amongst heavy viewers (Lang & Lang, 1966; Gerbner et al., 1986). More recently the debate has been taking place between two well known authors: Robert Putnam (2000), who in his influential *Bowling Alone* has argued that television viewing contributes to civic disengagement and Pippa Norris (2000), who conversely made a case for news consumption as contributing to a virtuous circle of civic participation.

Putnam, using an impressive amount of data from the US General Social Survey, argued that mass media, and television in particular, have contributed to the decline of civic engagement and the disintegration of community bonds. Although historically, newspaper reading made an important contribution to American democracy, according to Putnam this has now been replaced by television news, which is also in decline and contaminated, if not replaced, by the rise of entertainment culture. Norris, in her extensive study of US and European Surveys[1] found little evidence to support the *media malaise* thesis. On the contrary, she found that the news media are positively associated with increased levels of political knowledge, trust and mobilization. She argued that people "who read more newspapers, surf the net, and pay attention to campaigns are consistently more knowledgeable, trusting of government and participatory" (Norris, 2000, p. 17). Norris explained this by suggesting that people who use the news media are already predisposed to civic participation. Furthermore, and this is where the "virtuous circle" begins, people's engagement with the news media increases their interest in politics and reduces the barriers to further civic engagement.

It is fair to say that in much of this influential literature, the audience remains an implied category (Livingstone, 1998a), and conclusions are extracted with certainty from the relationship between abstracted message content and equally abstracted individual or aggregate responses. It was only through the development of the field of audience research in the 1980s that audiences received attention and acquired visibility.

NEW AUDIENCE RESEARCH

The turning point not only for the study of news audiences, but media studies more broadly, was Stuart Hall's "Encoding/Decoding" model, initially published as a working paper of the Centre for Culture Studies in Birmingham in 1973 and republished in 1980. A theoretical convergence of previously antagonistic traditions, the critical and administrative, Hall's (1980) intervention signaled the beginning of an "exciting phase of audience research." Hall, who wrote his piece as a critique of positivist media sociology (Hall, 1994, p. 203), which had been the dominant paradigm of communication research (Gitlin, 1978), brought together the agenda of the critical tradition (the concerns with power and ideology) and the empirical focus on audiences which had traditionally been associated with the positivist tradition of media sociology and the study of media effects. Hall's model thus attempted to "incorporate both the vertical and the horizontal dimension of the communication process" (Hall, 1988 cited in Morley, 1996, p. 323). Hall understood communication as a dynamic circuit. He argued that the same event can be encoded in different ways; encoding and decoding need not be symmetrical. Even though Hall argued that there is a preferred meaning, messages are inherently polysemic. Drawing on Parkin's (1971) political sociology, Hall identified three hypothetical decoding positions: the dominant-hegemonic, the negotiated and the oppositional. Morley's (1980) *Nationwide* study has widely been seen as the empirical application of the "Encoding/Decoding" model. Morley examined the different interpretations of the popular current affairs program, *Nationwide*, by audience groups. Each group was homogenous, representing a distinct demographic profile. The study demonstrated that readings of the text were based on "cultural differences embedded within the structure of society [...] which guide and limit the individual's interpretation of messages" (Morley, 1992, p. 118). Thus the "meaning" of a text or message was understood as being produced through the interaction of the codes embedded in the text with the codes inhabited by the different sections of the audience (Morley, 1992).

The "Encoding/Decoding" model and Morley's study have been criticized for class determinism, linearity and for introducing two problematic terms, the "preferred reading" and the "negotiated decoding" (all points discussed by Morley himself in a later (1992) reflexive piece). The model has also been criticized for emphasizing interpretation and underplaying other processes such as comprehension, which play an important part in the decoding of the news. Morley has noted himself that it is conceivable that the rejection of the dominant message by members of the audience can, on some occasions, be attributed to a lack of comprehension (because of limited literacy and educational capital) and not to an oppositional interpretation (Morley 1999, p. 140), in which case there is nothing celebratory about it. However, despite these criticisms, Hall's model and Morley's study have been pivotal in opening the field of audience research and making "visible an audience which has hitherto been devalued, marginalized and presumed about in policy and theory" (Livingstone, 1998b, p. 240). As Livingstone (1998a, p. 195) has remarked, this visibility matters theoretically, empirically and politically.

Following Hall (1980) and Morley (1980) numerous other studies investigated audience interpretation (Gamson, 1992; Lewis, 1991; Liebes, 1997; Kitzinger, 1993; Neuman, Just, & Crigler, 1992; Philo, 1990). Members of the Glasgow University Media Group, well known for their study of news production and content, became involved in audience research (Eldridge, 1993). An exemplary study was the one by Philo (1990) who examined the reception of news about the 1984–85 miners' strike in Britain. Philo and his colleagues interviewed a number of audience groups following a similar methodology to the *Nationwide* study. The groups were shown 12 pictures taken from the reporting of the strike and were asked to comment upon them. What Philo found was that belief in the dominant media frame was highest amongst those who were most dependent on the media. Those who were highly reliant on television news believed that most picketing was violent, thus reflecting the fact that violence was a major theme in the news coverage. Conversely, those who rejected the media account either had direct experience of the events, knowledge of the strikers and their families or access to alternative sources of information (Philo, 1990, p. 47).

Similarly, research from Greece points to the importance of direct personal experience in challenging news content (Madianou, 2007). The study examined the reception of two events (an incident in Greek-Turkish relations and an international crisis, namely the Kosovo conflict in 1999) as part of a larger ethnography of news consumption (Madianou, 2005b). The study observed that whilst the news discourse both in the national incident and the Kosovo crisis remained largely ethnocentric, the viewers' responses were evidently differentiated. During the national incident viewers questioned the dominant news discourse, while in the Kosovo case study some of the interviewees reverted to an ethnocentric discourse in line with the content of the news. One explanation for the discursive shifts is that of personal experience. Most interviewees who challenged the content of national news did so by drawing on their own personal experiences (for example, their experience of compulsory military service) which gave them confidence to question the dominant discourse presented in the news. Conversely, the events in Kosovo were largely mediated as people had no direct experience of the conflict and were therefore less prepared to be critical of the news reports. The study (Madianou, 2005b) also identified another explanation for the viewers' discursive shifts: by interpreting the news reports about an incident in Greek-Turkish relations as an internal, "family" affair, viewers felt comfortable to criticize the dominant discourse found in the news. During the Kosovo war, however, many interviewees felt they had to embrace the dominant nationalistic discourse and assert their identity in responding to an international conflict which they interpreted as a threat to their culture and identity from the outside. This last observation points to the fact that news reception is a relational and dynamic process that involves not only national news and their local audiences, but which is also, inevitably, transnational (Madianou, 2005b, 2007).

Liebes (1997), in her study of the reception of news about the 1990s Intifada in Israel, found that the news reinforced pre-existing ideas. As news programs tended to reflect the dominant viewpoint, they were in agreement with hawkish positions in Israeli society. Liebes, who studied the reception of news in family contexts, observed how the news provided a tool for the ideological socialization of the children. In such a fraught socio-political environment, oppositional readings were scarce and dependent on the viewers' media literacy skills and educational capital.

The literature on news audiences points to a number of findings. Research confirms that although interpretation cannot be predetermined, it is constrained by a number of factors including the text itself—and the ideological climate which has shaped it—(Lewis, 1991; Liebes, 1997; Morley, 1980; 1992; Philo 1990), comprehension and the educational capital that this implies (Morley, 1999; Liebes, 1997; Madianou, 2005b), pre-existing beliefs and tastes (Bird, 1992; Liebes, 1997; Kitzinger, 1993), social class and other demographic determinants (Morley, 1980), the existence of alternative sources and the degree of exposure to and dependency on the news media (Madianou, 2007; Philo, 1990).

It thus becomes apparent that far from celebrating the popular and some form of "semiotic democracy" (Fiske, 1987) as has often been the criticism (Curran, 1990; Murdock, 1989), most studies of news audiences have grappled with notions of power and tried to map how it is played out in the context of news reception. Moreover, audience researchers have acknowledged that "the power of viewers to reinterpret meanings is hardly equivalent to the discursive power of centralized media institutions to construct the texts which the viewer then interprets" (Morley, 1992, p. 31), a comment echoed by other researchers within the same tradition (Ang, 1996, p. 140).

The studies within this paradigm are mainly text-based: news audiences are studied in relation to news content. News is understood as a text and the audiences as readers and interpreters of that text. Perhaps the intensive preoccupation with the text is both the merit and the weakness of this approach. On the one hand, the text provides an immediate link to questions of ideology and power; on the other hand, the limitation is that reception is investigated in isolation, without knowledge of the social context and the extent to which it may be affected by the media.

CONSUMPTION AND THE PLACE OF NEWS IN EVERYDAY LIFE

What happened in the late 1980s and 1990s was a gradual increase of interest in television, not just as content, but also as a technology and object (Silverstone, 1989; Morley, 1995).[2] Television news was therefore not only a text, but also a social phenomenon, and its viewing a ritual. The key term for understanding this aspect of television was consumption, a more encompassing term than reception. Consumption was beginning to receive a lot of attention in the cognate fields of social anthropology and material culture (Miller, 1987).

Silverstone (2005, p. 19) suggested that research should focus on news as a social phenomenon that has become an indispensable component of everyday life. He observed that:

> [news'] particular, and remarkably globally homogenous, structures of story-telling, accounts of heroism and disaster, narrative closure, construction of the newsreader as the nightly reader of tales, and its fixed position in the radio and television schedules together define the genre as crucial in this subject.

In the above quote news form is almost more significant than content (the most heavily researched aspect of the news). How something is said is as, if not more, important than what is said. Moreover, Silverstone (1994) observed an ostensible tension between news content (which is often about conflict and crisis) and news as a ritual and fixed markerpoint in people's everyday lives (something which evokes reassurance). Silverstone saw the news as the "key institution in the mediation of threat, risk and danger" from the outside world (p. 17). For Silverstone (1994, p. 16), it is "the dialectical articulation of anxiety and security" that results in the creation of trust:

> Our nightly news watching is a ritual, both in its mechanical repetitiveness, but much more importantly in its presentation, through its fragmentary logic, of the familiar and the strange, the reassuring and the threatening. In Britain, no major news bulletin will either begin without a transcendent title sequence [...] nor end without a "sweetener"—a "human story" to bring viewers back to the everyday. (Silverstone, 1988, p. 26)

It can be argued that the seeds for a ritual approach to news consumption can be found in Anderson's *Imagined Communities* (1991[1983]). Anderson is one of the few political theorists who wrote on the role of the print media and their contribution to the emergence of nationalism. He saw "the convergence of capitalism and print technology" as the catalyst for the emergence and consolidation of the imagined community that became the modern nation (p. 46). Print capitalism allowed for a simultaneous mediated communication across the nation-state as people read the same newspapers or novels and began to recognize themselves as part of an imagined community. The simultaneity made possible by the print media gave "a hypnotic confirmation of the solidity of a single community, embracing characters, authors and readers" (p. 27).

Of course, Anderson's argument is theoretical and historical. His aim was not to investigate the newsreading public to establish whether indeed an imagined community was formed. But his argument can be applied to an empirical context and indeed research findings suggest that television news often provides a common point of reference amongst its audiences (Madianou, 2005b). This happens not only by the simultaneous consumption of the same news stories, but also through the fact that television news is a fixed markerpoint in people's daily routine and punctuates time and activity. News watching often coincides with family meal times, as studies from the UK (Gauntlett & Hill, 1999) and other countries have shown (for a US example, see Jensen, 1995; for Greece, see Madianou, 2005b). Pointing to the power of television news,

Jensen notes that these daily rhythms are naturalized as nobody questions the time of the news: it is the viewers who schedule their activities around the news and not the other way around (Jensen, 1995). These observations echo the "structural" uses of television whereby television news acts a regulative source within the household (Lull, 1990).

It emerges then, that news is much more than just information. Early evidence about the non-informational uses of the newspaper can be found in the insightful study by Berelson who conducted innovative research during the 1945 newspaper strike in New York City (Berelson, 1949). What Berelson found is that during the strike his interviewees did not miss the newspaper content (for example, information about political and economic matters) as much as the pleasure of reading. Moreover, he identified other non-informational uses of the newspaper—the fact that it provided topics of everyday conversation—which the interviewees reported to miss. Further research has also confirmed the importance of news as a social resource (Jensen, 1995; Madianou, forthcoming).

Recent research has revealed other non-informational uses of television news. For example, it has emerged that for some people, television news is the vehicle for voicing complaints or criticisms. Canclini (2001) has observed that in Mexico people resorted to radio and television to obtain recognition and justice that the traditional citizen institutions did not provide. Similar examples from an ethnography of news consumption in Greece have shown that television news programs often become, quite literally, the mediators between public institutions and private interests (Madianou, 2005c). People aimed to appear on television news and radio broadcasts in order for their complaints to be taken seriously by public institutions.

Research also points to news viewing as linked to the performance of identity. For British Asian teenagers in London's Southall, watching the news is associated with entering adulthood (Gillespie, 1995). Better educated than their parents' generation, the teenagers in Gillespie's study would translate British news for their parents, thus acquiring an elevated status of respect and responsibility within the household. For members of an ethnic minority in Greece, the viewing of Greek news was a way to make a symbolic statement about their citizenship and being part of the "country they live in" (Madianou, 2005a). "Watching the news" therefore becomes much more than merely "watching": it can be a statement for one's identity, an aspiration, a desire to participate in a cultural or political narrative, a habit, or a resource that helps people cope with the demands of everyday life. Perhaps these are some of the reasons which explain why people express the "need to keep up" (an almost universal finding as the comparative studies in Jensen (1998) suggest) and even become "addicted to the news" often describing themselves as "news junkies" (Madianou, 2005b, forthcoming).

Interestingly, despite compelling evidence for the non-informational uses of news, research has also highlighted that news audiences often express a strong sense of duty about watching the news. News viewing has been associated with the civic duty of being informed, as research from the United States (Graber, 1984) and Norway (Hagen, 1997) has shown. This normative viewing is so internalized (Graber, 1984) that people express anxiety or embarrassment (Hagen, 1997; Madianou, forthcoming) when they are seen not to be in touch with current affairs. Such observations point to the extent to which the presence of news in everyday life is naturalized and taken for granted. This, perhaps, is the strongest evidence of the power of news.

METHODOLOGICAL ISSUES

Interviewing and focus groups have been particularly popular in the study of news reception (Gamson, 1992; Lunt & Livingstone, 1996; Morley, 1980; Neuman et al., 1992; Philo, 1990).

There are many advantages to the group discussion approach, the main one being that it allows the researcher to gauge the social formation of opinions, justifying the idea that group discussions are a miniature of the thinking society (Moscovici, 1984). At a more practical level, group interviews allow for the inclusion of more interviewees into the research design—a significant advantage given how expensive and time consuming qualitative research is. Individual interviews, on the other hand, can allow for more probing and depth. A concern about group discussions is whether a false consensus is imposed on the group, thereby silencing dissent—this is obviously not a problem in the case of semi-structured interviewing. One to one interviews may be more suitable for sensitive topics and, some argue, when the respondents are recruited from disadvantaged backgrounds.

Interview-based approaches tend to be largely text-centered, that is, they explore the audiences' reaction to the news text, whether a whole broadcast, a news report, or images from the news (Philo, 1990). Predictably, the emphasis is on interpretation, although there have been interview-based studies which have explored consumption (Morley, 1986). However, in order to understand consumption as a process of practices, an ethnographic approach is most suitable. Through participant observation, the researcher can have access to the sphere of everyday life practices. The television text (the news) is not presumed important (as it is in a text-centered approach), but rather, it is investigated as part of a range of media (and, ideally, even non-media related) practices. The bottom up perspective allows for the categories of analysis to be derived from the data.

Crucially, because it can include both interviews and participant observation, ethnography allows for the observation not only of people's discourses (what people say in an interview context), but also of their practices (what they actually do in their everyday lives) (Miller, 1998). These two are not always in agreement and such discrepancies can be very revealing about the processes of consumption and media power in everyday life (Madianou, 2005b, forthcoming). For example, and to return to a point made earlier, people will claim in an interview that they watch the news because it is their duty to be informed, but their actual practices may reveal myriad other uses.

Through the immersion in the research field, ethnographers develop a long-term rapport with the informants. This in-depth perspective into people's lives allows for the development of a relationship of trust and empathy which is vital for the understanding of the intimate dimensions of everyday life of which the media are part. Through trust, the ethnographer can gain access in people's households and develop the necessary rapport which is crucial, especially if the research has a sensitive dimension.[3] Through empathy the ethnographer can understand nuances that may otherwise be left unnoticed.

Finally, an ethnographic perspective on news consumption "can inform our understanding of media power as it operates in the micro-contexts of consumption—without divorcing those issues from those of macro-structural processes" (Morley, 1992, p. 40). Drawing on Giddens' (1984) structuration theory, Morley argues that "macro structures can only be reproduced through micro processes" (p. 19). Because of the openness of the approach, ethnography allows for the inclusion of different levels of inquiry (depending on the research question). Thus one can study the news text, its reception, and the context of the reception. By integrating the different levels of analysis, one can aim to achieve empirical confirmation (Livingstone 1998a, p. 206) and unpack the riddle of media power.

So far I have only focused on qualitative methods because these have been the main approaches for the study of the audience in the traditions established within the context of British cultural studies. Quantitative methods, still widely used in effects research, can be very useful and, of course, add the much desired representativeness to a sample. There have been some studies that have collected impressive data relating to patterns of media (including news) consumption. One such study was by Gauntlett and Hill (1999) who made perceptive observations regarding British news viewing habits based on a large scale survey. Triangulating qualitative and quantitative methods can work very well, as the latter approach lends representativeness and breadth, and the former depth and detail. One study which has combined both approaches admirably (although the focus is not exclusively on news) looked at media consumption and public engagement, and was conducted by Couldry, Livingstone, and Markham (2007).

TOWARDS A THEORY OF MEDIATION?

We noted earlier that the "Encoding/Decoding" model was a reaction against the dominant paradigm of media effects in which communication was understood as a model of transmission. The criticism then that the "Encoding/Decoding" model does not radically depart from a linear model of communication is perhaps surprising. Morley, in his 1992 reflexive account, referred to the model as "the conveyor belt of meaning" (p. 121). Through their intensive orientation towards news content, reception analysts found it hard to investigate how audiences' interpretations feed back into the communication process, thus demonstrating the dynamic nature of communication.[4] Ethnographies of news consumption, albeit more holistic in their approach, run the danger of being too preoccupied with the context whilst losing sight of the question of power. Silverstone (1999, 2005) proposed the concept of mediation as a means of overcoming the above limitations and capturing the dynamic character of communication. He defined mediation as a:

> fundamentally dialectical notion which requires us to understand how processes of communication change the social and cultural environments that support them as well as the relationships that participants, both individual and institutional, have to that environment and to each other. At the same time it requires a consideration of the social as in turn a mediator: institutions and technologies as well as the meanings that are delivered by them are mediated in the social processes of reception and consumption. (Silverstone, 2005, p. 3)

Such a holistic approach requires that the focus of research extends beyond the point of contact between texts and audiences (the traditional focus of reception research) in order to follow instead the "circulation of meaning" (Silverstone 1999, p. 13). In this vein, audiences need to be examined together with the other moments that constitute the mediation process, namely media production, the media texts, the media as technologies and objects and the social and cultural context. Arguments for a theory of mediation echo the cultural or ritual model of communication (Carey, 1989) and some of the existing developments which have already been discussed in the previous paragraphs in the field of media consumption and media anthropology (Ginsburg, Abu-Lughod, & Larkin, 2002). However, Silverstone's contribution is that he urges researchers to systematize a holistic approach. Methodologically, this can be achieved through the development of a multisited ethnography (Marcus, 1995). Multisited ethnographic research—developed within the context of the postmodern turn in anthropology (Clifford & Marcus, 1986; Marcus & Fischer, 1986)—moves from single sites and local situations of conventional ethnographic research "to examine the circulation of cultural meanings, objects and identities in diffuse time-space" (Marcus, 1995, p. 96). Note the emphasis on the "circulation of meanings" which was also at the heart of the definition of mediation (Silverstone, 1999, p. 13). Multisited ethnography can allow the study both of production and reception, thus integrating the levels of analysis (Livingstone, 1998a). Given the diffuse nature of media power (Couldry, 2000), the ethnographic approach is well suited to identify the moments of media influence, but also of audience resistance.

UBIQUITY AND FRAGMENTATION, AFFECT AND MORALITY: DIRECTIONS FOR FUTURE RESEARCH

News programs are undergoing rapid changes, the two most significant being the rise of rolling news channels and 24/7 news, and the emergence and popularity of blogs and citizen journalism (Allan, 2006). These fundamental changes in news production and form have immediate implications for news consumption. First of all, new media and technological convergence are blurring the boundaries between producers and consumers, begging us to reconsider whether the term "audience" is valid. In the last couple of years we have witnessed an explosion of blogs as well as independent news fora (like Indymedia) which is often described as the emergence of citizen journalism. At the same time, international news corporations such as the BBC and CNN have encouraged their audiences to participate in the news gathering process by sending in their images and texts, which are then used as part of the reporting. This has proved particularly successful at times of crisis. For instance, in the aftermath of the London bombings in 2005, the response was extraordinary: people started sending images "within minutes of the first problems" and in the hours following the events, the BBC received "more than 1000 pictures, 20 pieces of amateur video, 4000 text messages and around 20,000 emails [...] many of which were first hand accounts" (Allan, 2006, pp. 147–148). Of course, whether such grassroots contributions challenge the core values of news production and news content is often questionable (especially when they are appropriated by journalists to complement the regular reporting). What is undeniable is that there is a fundamental shift in the identity of the audience: people are not only viewers, potential sources and witnesses of events, but also reporters of events. Never before were audiences able to "talk back" in such an immediate and visible way. Now that the initial enthusiasm and excitement about the democratic effects of blogs is beginning to settle, it remains to be seen what their impact is in the field of information: are they going to live up to the expectation of grassroots independent and possibly radical media, or will there be a process of consolidation during which blogs will succumb to market pressures with the attendant consequences for their content.

The rise of rolling news channels challenges our traditional conceptions of the "national audience" and the ritual viewing of the evening news. Even though evening news programs continue to enjoy popularity, they are no longer the exclusive outlets to the cultural narrative that is news. News has become ubiquitous (through 24/7 news channels, transnational news channels (such as Al Jazeera), internet news sites and blogs and the development of mobile television and mobile news updates) and the implications for the audience remains to be investigated. The discussion so far has emphasized the fragmentation of the audience, but there is still a need to understand the new place of news in everyday life. It can be argued that news is more ubiquitous than ever before.

The above developments point to the need for more research on news consumption, ideally within a "mediational" (Silverstone, 2005) or "multisited ethnographic" (Marcus, 1995) perspective that will help understand both the fragmentation and the ubiquity of news. The call for more research is also underlined by the increasing presence and visibility of transnational news networks and audiences. News is the main means for the mediation of conflict and war, as well as for the mediation of otherness (Chouliaraki, 2006; Silverstone, 2007). Understanding the process through which audiences make sense of the other (as well of themselves) is crucial in any attempts to change and improve any prejudiced and essentialist views. There is a moral and ethical argument to be made about researching the place of news in a transnational world.

All the above developments conjure up images of audiences—the blogger, who passionately offers his views in a public diary, the news junkie, who checks the news online and through rolling news channels several times a day, the member of the public, who becomes angry with the way s/he is represented in the dominant media—that point to how central the news is to everyday life. Moreover, people's engagement with the news emerges as an affective process that remains to be fully understood. Most research has hitherto focused on either audiences' comprehension or their interpretation reflecting the "often unwitting normative view that the news' primary function is to serve society by informing the general population in ways that arm them for vigilant citizenship" (Schudson, 2000, p. 194). It is no surprise then that when it comes to the news the term that is often used is not audiences, but rather public—a term that evokes seriousness and the link to politics and citizenship (see Madianou, 2005c). In recent years we have witnessed an affective turn in the social sciences in general and media studies are no exception. Existing work on the ritual uses of television points to the capacity of television news to soothe and catalyze feelings of belonging. It could be argued that the ritual tradition has placed too much emphasis on the capacity of television to include. As much as it includes, television news also excludes, and it is compelling to also investigate negative emotions and in particular anger, shame and embarrassment in relation to processes of exclusion (Madianou, 2005a). The research on emotions can also cast light on the relationship between media and political engagement and disengagement. Political participation involves affective elements (Marcus, 2002), notably passion, which is also the driving force behind much online civic participation and blog writing.

It becomes clear that the range of practices and habits associated with the term "audience" have diversified to the extent that questioning the usefulness of the term audience seems justified (yet again). Audiences for news have often been set apart from those for other genres, often described as "the public," thus giving away the seriousness with which news is often associated. The ritual perspective on news consumption might support the view that instead of audiences, viewers and readers we ought to be using the more encompassing term consumers. But what about the bloggers who produce alternative news content? Perhaps no other term is laden with more implicit normative aspirations than that of citizen journalists. Suddenly, the term "audiences," despite its limitations, seems a useful and rather neutral shorthand for the range of practices associated with the cultural and social phenomenon that the news is. Alternatively, of course, there is people.

NOTES

1. Norris analysed multiple datasets: data from UNESCO since 1945; 30 series of Eurobarometer surveys; US National Election Surveys (1948–1998).
2. Note that the distinction between content and form as well as content and technology is an analytical one as many studies in this paradigm have sought to combine a concern with content, form and technology.
3. For example, in my past research on news consumption with members of an ethnic minority in Greece, given the sensitivity surrounding minority issues in Greece, it was only through a long term immersion and participation in my informants' everyday lives that I managed to gain people's trust and access to their homes. The initial resistance that I encountered in the field forced me to reconsider what was a interview-based research design and move towards an ethnographic perspective (Madianou, 2005b).
4. Hall (1994, p. 255) was aware of the model's limitations and has reminded us that the model was not intended as a "grand model." Hall's aim in the 1973 talk, the basis for the published text (1980), was to criticise what was then the dominant paradigm and not to develop a mode "of theoretical rigor, internal logic and conceptual consistency" (Hall, 1994, p. 255). The fact that the model achieved a canonic

status thereafter was certainly not the intention of its author; rather canonization was thrust upon it (Gurevitch & Scannell, 2003).

REFERENCES

Allan, S. (2006). *Online news*. Maidenhead, UK: Open University Press.

Anderson, B. (1991). *Imagined communities*. London: Verso. (Original work published 1983)

Ang, I. (1996). *Living-room wars: Rethinking audiences for a postmodern world.* London: Routledge.

Berelson, B. (1949). What missing the newspaper means. In P. Lazarsfeld & F. Stanton (Eds.), *Communications research 1948–9* (pp. 111–128). New York: Harper and Brothers.

Bird, E. S. (1992). *For inquiring minds: A cultural study of supermarket tabloids.* Knoxville: University of Tennessee Press.

Canclini, N. G. (2001). *Consumers and citizens: Globalization and multicultural conflicts.* Minneapolis: University of Minnesota Press.

Carey, J. (1989). *Communication as culture: Essays on media and society.* New York: Routledge.

Chouliaraki, L. (2006). *The Spectatorship of suffering*. London: Sage.

Clifford, J., & Marcus, G. (Eds.). (1986). *Writing culture: The poetics and politics of ethnography.* Berkeley: University of California Press.

Couldry, N. (2000). *The place of media power: Pilgrims and witnesses in a media age.* London: Routledge.

Couldry, N., Livingstone, S., & Markham, T. (2007). *Media consumption and public engagement: Beyond the presumption of attention.* London: Palgrave.

Curran, J. (1990). The new revisionism in mass communication research. *European Journal of Communication, 5*(2/3), 135–164.

Eldridge, J. (Ed.). (1993). *Getting the message: News, truth and power.* London: Routledge.

Fiske, J. (1987). *Television culture*. London: Routledge.

Gamson, W. (1992). *Talking politics*. Cambridge: Cambridge University Press.

Gauntlett, D., & Hill, A. (1999). *TV living: Television culture and everyday life*. London: Routledge.

Gerbner, G., Gross, L., Miorgan, M., & Signorelli, W.. (1986). Living with television: The dynamics of the cultivation process. In J. Bryant & D. Zillman (Eds.), *Perspectives on media effects* (pp. 17–40). Hillsdale, NJ: Erlbaum.

Giddens, A. (1984). *The constitution of society: Outline of the theory of structuration.* Cambridge: Polity.

Gillespie, M. (1995). *Television, ethnicity and cultural change.* London: Routledge.

Ginsburg, F., Abu-Lughod, L., & Larkin, B. (2002). *Media worlds: Anthropology on new terrain.* Berkeley: University of California Press.

Gitlin, T. (1978). Media sociology: the dominant paradigm. *Theory and Society*, *6*(2), 205–253.

Graber, D. A. (1984). *Processing the news: how people tame the information tide*. New York: Longman.

Gurevitch, M., & Scannell, P. (2003). Canonization achieved? Stuart Hall's encoding/decoding. In E. Katz, J. D. Peters, T. Liebes, & A. Orloff (Eds.), *Canonic texts in media research* (pp. 231–247). Cambridge: Polity.

Hagen, I. (1997). Communicating to an ideal audience: News and the notion of the "informed citizen." *Political Communication, 14*, 405–419.

Hall, S. (1980). Encoding/decoding. In S. Hall, D. Hobson, A. Lowe, & P. Willis (Eds.), *Culture, media, language* (pp. 128–138). London: Hutchinson,.

Hall, S. (1994). Reflections upon the encoding-decoding model: An interview with Stuart Hall. In J. Lewis & J. Cruz (Eds.), *Viewing, reading, listening: Audiences and cultural interpretation* (pp. 253–274). Boulder, CO: Westview.

Jensen, K. B. (1995). *The social semiotics of mass communication.* London: Routledge.

Jensen, K. B. (Ed.). (1998). *News of the world: World cultures look at television news.* London: Routledge.

Klapper, J. (1960). *The effects of mass communication.* New York: Free Press.

Kitzinger, J. (1993). Understanding AIDS: Researching audience perceptions of the acquired immune deficiency syndrome. In J. Eldridge (Ed.), *Getting the message: News, truth and power* (pp. 271–304). London: Routledge.

Lang, K., & Lang, G. (1966). The mass media and voting. In B. Berelson & M. Janowitz (Eds.), *Reader in public opinion and communication* (pp. 455–472). New York: Free Press.

Lewis, J. (1991). *The ideological octopus: An exploration of television and its audience.* London: Routledge.

Liebes, T. (1997). *Reporting the Israeli-Arab conflict: How hegemony works.* London: Routledge.

Livingstone, S. (1998a). Audience research at the crossroads: the "implied audience" in media and cultural theory. *European Journal of Cultural Studies, 1*(2), 193–217.

Livingstone, S. (1998b). Relationships between media and audiences: Prospects for audience reception studies. In J. Curran & T. Liebes (Eds.), *Media ritual and identity* (pp. 237–255). London: Routledge.

Lull, J. (1990). *Inside family viewing: Ethnographic research on television's audience.* London: Routledge.

Lunt, P., & Livingstone, S. (1996). Rethinking the focus group in media and communication research. *Journal of Communication, 46*(2), 79–98.

Madianou, M. (2005a). Contested communicative spaces: identities, boundaries and the role of the media. *Journal of Ethnic and Migration Studies, 31*(3), 521–541.

Madianou, M. (2005b). *Mediating the nation: News, audiences and the politics of identity.* London: UCL Press/Routledge.

Madianou, M. (2005c). The elusive public of television news. In S. Livingstone (Ed.), *Audiences and publics: When cultural engagement matters to the public sphere* (pp. 99–114). Bristol: Intellect Press.

Madianou, M. (2007). Shifting identities: banal nationalism and cultural intimacy in Greek television news and everyday life. In R. Mole (Ed.), *Discursive constructions of identity in European politics* (pp. 95–118). London: Palgrave.

Madianou, M. (forthcoming). Ethnography and news audiences. In S. Allan (Ed.), *The Routledge companion to news and journalism studies.* Abingdon, UK: Routledge.

Marcus, G. E. (1995). Ethnography in/of the world system: The emergence of multi-sited ethnography. *Annual Review of Anthropology, 24*, 95–117.

Marcus, G. E. (2002). *The sentimental citizen: Emotion in democratic politics.* Philadelphia: Penn State University Press.

Marcus, G. E., & Fischer, M. (1986). *Anthropology as cultural critique: An experimental moment in the human sciences.* Chicago: University of Chicago Press.

McEwan, I. (1998). *Enduring love.* London: Vintage.

Miller, D. (1987). *Material culture and mass consumption.* Oxford: Blackwell.

Miller, D. (1998). Introduction: Why some things matter. In D. Miller (Ed.), *Material cultures* (pp. 3–24). London: UCL Press.

Morley, D. (1980). *The Nationwide audience: Structure and decoding.* Television monograph. London: BFI.

Morley, D. (1986). *Family television.* London: Comedia.

Morley, D. (1992). *Television, audiences and cultural studies.* London: Routledge.

Morley, D. (1995). Television: Not so much a visual medium, more a visible object. In C. Jenks (Ed.), *Visual culture* (pp. 170–189). London: Routledge.

Morley, D. (1996). The geography of television: Ethnography, communications and community. In J. Hay, L. Grossberg, & E. Wartella (Eds.), *The audience and its landscape* (pp. 317–342). Boulder, CO: Westview.

Morley, D. (1999). Finding about the world from television news: Some difficulties. In J. Gripsrud (Ed.), *Television and common knowledge* (pp. 136–158). London: Routledge.

Morley, D., & Brunsdon, C. (1999). *The Nationwide television studies.* London: Routledge.

Moscovici, S. (1984). The phenomenon of social representations. In R. Farr & S. Moscovici (Eds.), *Social representations* (pp. 3–69). Cambridge: Cambridge University Press.

Murdock, G. (1989). Critical inquiry and audience activity. In B. Dervin, L. Grossberg, & E. Wartella (Eds.), *Rethinking Communication* (Vol. 2, pp. 226–249). Newbury Park, CA: Sage.

Neuman, R., Just, M., & Crigler, A. (1992). *Common knowledge: News and the construction of political meaning.* Chicago: University of Chicago Press.

Norris, P. (2000). *A virtuous circle: Political communications in the post-industrial democracies*. New York: Cambridge University Press.

Parkin, F. (1971). *Class inequality and political order*. New York: Praeger.

Philo, G. (1990). *Seeing and believing: The influence of television*. London: Routledge.

Putnam, R. (2000). *Bowling alone: The collapse and revival of American community*. New York: Simon and Schuster.

Robinson, M. (1976). Public affairs television and the growth of political malaise: The case of "the selling of the president." *American Political Science Review*, *70*(3), 409–32.

Schudson, M. (2000). The sociology of news production revisited (again). In J. Curran & M. Gurevitch (Eds.), *Mass media and society* (3rd ed., pp. 175–200). London: Edward Arnold.

Silverstone, R. (1988). Television, myth and culture. In J. Carey (Ed.), *Media, myths and narratives* (pp. 20–47). Newbury Park, CA: Sage.

Silverstone, R. (1989). Television and everyday life: Towards an anthropology of the television audience. In M. Ferguson (Ed.), *Public communication: The new imperatives: Future directions for media research* (pp. 173–189). London: Sage.

Silverstone, R. (1994). *Television and everyday life*. London: Routledge.

Silverstone, R. (1999). *Why study the media?* London: Sage.

Silverstone, R. (2005). Mediation and communication. In C. Calhoun, C. Rojek, & B. Turner (Eds.), *Handbook of sociology* (pp. 188–207). London: Sage.

Silverstone, R. (2007). *Media and morality*. Cambridge: Polity.

V

JOURNALISM STUDIES IN A GLOBAL CONTEXT

24

Journalism and Globalization

Simon Cottle

We live in an increasingly inter-connected, interdependent and inegalitarian world. In recent social theory parlance, a globalizing world that has both accelerated and shrunk though processes of "time-space compression" (Harvey, 1989) and stretched social relations (enabling action at a distance) through "time-space distanciation" (Giddens, 1990). These globalizing tendencies, moreover, have become increasingly *mediated* through communication flows that are now capable of circumnavigating the globe 24/7 in real-time. New digital technologies and satellite delivery systems disseminate a daily multitude of images, ideas and information to distant countries and disparate cultures. And mobile telephony and the Internet provide hitherto unimaginable opportunities for new forms of connectivity that are now being realized by vast numbers of people around the globe. This new communications-based "space of flows" underpins influential ideas of the rise of the "network society" and serves today's global geometry of power (Castells, 1996, 2007). The central role of communications and flows of information and culture in processes of globalization are no less central to the thinking of other contemporary social theorists, whether embedded in influential ideas of "reflexive modernization" (Beck, Giddens, & Lash, 1994), "world risk society" (Beck, 1999), "liquid modernity" (Bauman, 2007) or "global complexity" (Urry, 2003). Each, in their own distinctive terms, endorses the discourse and reality of globalization.

Scholars and students of journalism, for their part, are no less interested in globalizing communication flows and have been for some time, though here the ideas of major contemporary social theorists have yet to take root. Concerns about transnational media corporations and the dominance of Western news agencies, news values and news flows, for example, have long been taken as characteristics of homogenizing world media (Galtung & Ruge, 1965; McBride, 1980), and more recent regional media formations, emergent contra-flows and the cacophony of views and voices emanating from the World Wide Web are today often seen as the more contradictory and uneven expressions of globalization. Clearly, much still hangs on what exactly is understood by this most contested "'G'-word" (Giddens, 2005) and, as we shall hear, "sceptics," "globalists" and "transformationalists" (Held & McGrew, 2003) all stake out the contested field of international and global journalism research today.

This chapter sets out to review the contemporary field of journalism studies approached through the theoretical and conceptual prisms of international communications and media globalization. Specifically, it seeks to map the principal orientations and theoretical debates now structuring the research field as well as pointing to emergent trends and new research departures. The theoretical approaches that variously orient the study of journalism in international and global contexts have long proved contentious and are destined to remain so. Whether approached through the paradigms and perspectives of "modernization" or "dependency," "cultural imperialism" or "information society," "global dominance" or "global public sphere," "international communications" or "media globalization," these competing frameworks structure the field as inherently contested. It is certainly theoretically disputatious and how could it not be given the essentially contested terrain of international relations, geo-political power and opposing interests and ideological outlooks that both shape and become struggled over in the formations and flows of international and global news. Recent discourses of media globalization, as we shall hear, have only exacerbated this tendency and their infusion into the world of journalism research has played a major part in unsettling entrenched theoretical positions. The following now seeks to provide an overview map of the overarching paradigms, principal approaches and salient debates currently structuring the research field of international and global journalism studies before briefly noting some productive research departures.

INTERNATIONAL COMMUNICATIONS AND MEDIA GLOBALIZATION

Two research paradigms, one long established in international communications research, the other still emerging in the wider field of media and globalization studies, currently set the parameters for much of the work undertaken in the field today. Each has its own disciplinary antecedents, leading exponents, distinctive ontologies and epistemologies and characteristic research agendas. Studies within the "global dominance" paradigm generally work within and update the critical tradition of political economy while those conducted under the "global public sphere" paradigm represent a more diffuse group of recent disciplinary infusions from cultural studies, anthropology and approaches to the global "network society." At their respective cores are deep-seated differences of theoretical orientation towards international and global communications as well as questions about the mechanisms and meanings of power. Whereas studies conducted under the "global dominance" paradigm generally approach questions of power in terms of the structures and interests of geo-political dominance and market determinations rooted in political economy, those coalescing under the "global public sphere" paradigm tend to pursue the emergence of world cosmopolitan citizenship and a global public sphere theorized in terms of transnational cultural flows, fluids, mobilities and networks (see Figure 24.1). Global dominance theorists are paradigmatically and methodologically inclined, therefore, to investigate the operations of markets and corporate interests in the structural conditioning of today's cultural industries; global public sphere theorists are disposed to explore the flows of cultural meanings and discourses of identities that circulate around the globe. These essentially different theoretical orientations and outlooks can be elaborated on further.

News Media as Emissaries of Global Dominance

Under the global dominance paradigm, researchers observe news and journalism through a lens of geo-political economy that sees transnational media corporations and Western-dominated global news agencies positioned by history and market ascendancy to capitalize on contemporary internationalizing market processes (Boyd-Barrett & Rantanen, 1998; McChesney 1999; Thussu 2003). In an era of economic liberalization marked by de-regulation, privatization and transnational corporate expansion, fuelled in part by the market exploitation of digitalization and new communications delivery technologies (Murdock, 1990), processes of media corporate

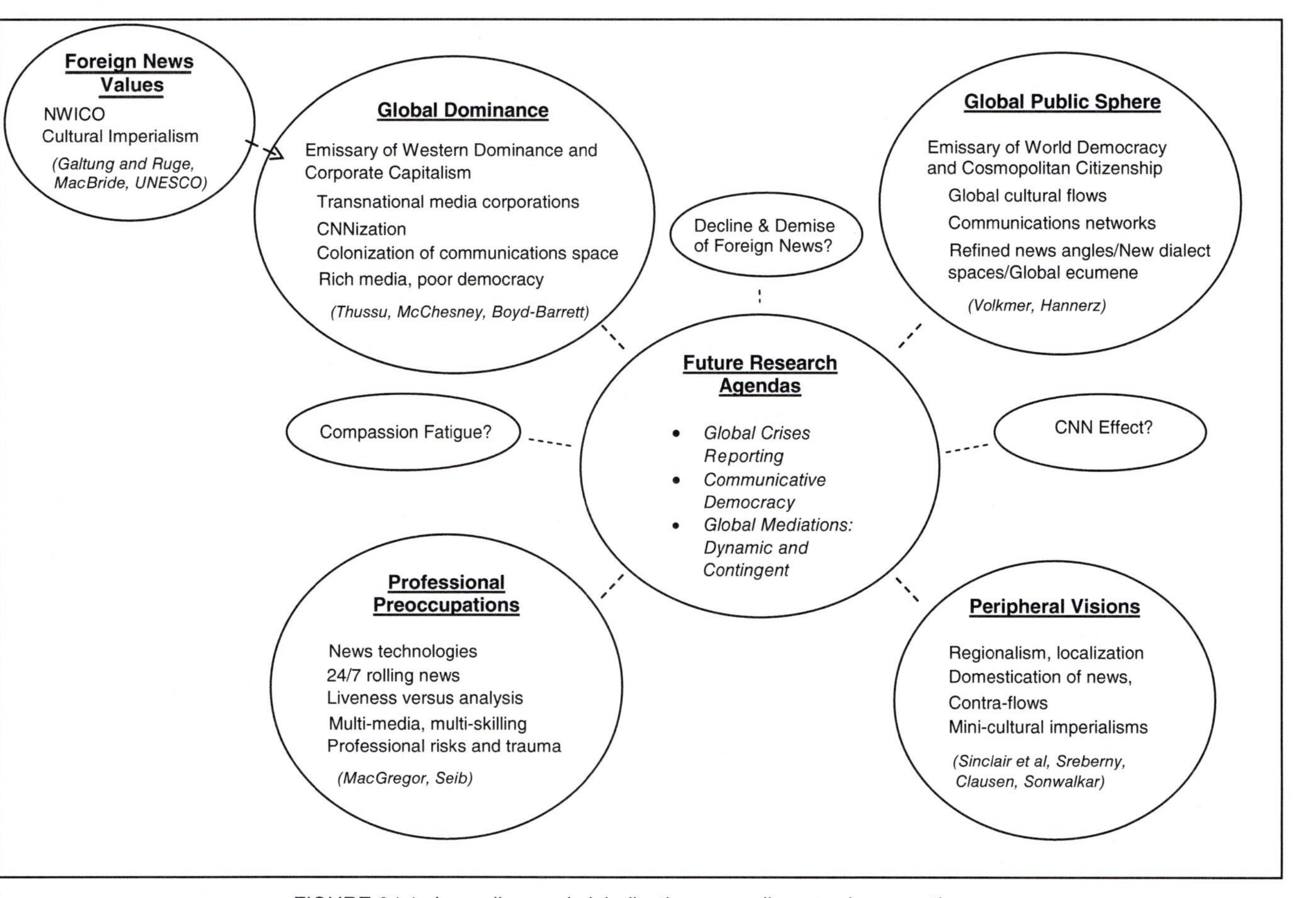

FIGURE 24.1 Journalism and globalization—paradigms and perspectives.

concentration and conglomeration have become exacerbated (McChesney, 1999). It is in this context that transnational corporations and regional formations of capital seek to "colonize communications space" (Boyd-Barrett, 1998). From this contemporary political economy perspective the cultural imperialism thesis underlined by the 1974 UNESCO report on international media flows (Nordenstreng & Varis, 1974), essentially still holds firm (Schiller, 2005) and this is so notwithstanding developed critiques across the years (Tomlinson 1991, 1999; Sreberny, 2000, Mackay, 2004).

Daya Thussu (2003) argues that a "CNNization" of television news is taking place with leading US and other Western networks such as CNN and the BBC effectively setting the agenda in the global news market where smaller, regional players monitor their content and adopt their models of production. Rather than contributing to a diversified "global public sphere," then, new regional news channels represent a universalisation of "US-style" journalism and an increasing homogenization of news structures and content around the world. In such ways, these theorists are skeptical about the validity of ideas of the "global" and globalizing news formations and news flows which, more accurately, reflect the relentless capitalist expansion and worldwide "Westernization" of culture and commerce. Here discourses of globalization are likely to be rejected as little more than an ideological smokescreen concealing the continuing geo-political realities of Western power, corporate interests and neo-liberal economics. From this critical vantage point, "corporate transnationalism" not "globalism" best describes the "swelling global flows of the cultural industries" (Schiller, 2005), global media are perceived as the new "missionaries of corporate capitalism" (Herman & McChesney, 1997), and Western "rich media" are destined to produce "poor democracy" around the world (McChesney, 1999).

News Media as Emissaries of a Global Public Sphere

Global public sphere theorists challenge the pessimistic accounts of the geo-political economists above. Building on Marshall McLuhan's notion of a "global village" (1964) and refashioning Habermas' well-known concept of the public sphere (1989), Ingrid Volkmer, for example, argues that world satellite news channels are engendering the emergence of a mediated "global public sphere" (1999, 2003) and thereby laying foundations of cosmopolitan citizenship. CNN, she argues, "invented a new form of international reporting, which extended the narrow, 'national' journalistic concept by including new political contexts and enlarging the political horizon beyond a single-nation-state" (Volkmer, 2002, p. 245). News angles are thus seen to have become "refined" and CNN is said to have played "an important role in the global public sphere by reconfiguring journalistic styles and formats" (p. 245). The complex communications cross-traffic and counter-flows around the world today, she argues, underpins the network society and this helps to constitute "a new concept of (world) citizenship" (Volkmer, 2003, p. 15). Much is made, for example, of CNNI's *World Report*, a distinctive programme in which journalists from around the world can broadcast their own stories and story angles on CNNI's platform. But to what extent *World Report* is truly representative of CNNI news reporting or global news flows more widely and opens up "new dialectical spaces" has yet to be fully explored (Rai & Cottle, 2007).

Volkmer's emphasis on today's mediated global interconnectedness is nonetheless important and encourages a deeper appreciation of how news can display cultural differences as well as communicate conflicts around the world. The anthropologist Ulf Hannerz (2000, p. 112) similarly observes in a study of contemporary foreign correspondents how a "conspicuous part of reporting [...] is not devoted to hard news and unique events but to a continuous thematization of difference itself." Here in-depth news features and the subjunctive style of news writing contribute, he suggests, to "thick cosmopolitanism" or feelings of being at home within a culturally heterogeneous world. The work of Volkmer, Hannerz and others invites us, therefore, to re-examine the cultural flows of global news and discover to what extent cultural disjuncture and difference are valorized in today's global "mediascape" (Appadurai, 1996) and consider how global media contribute to a new "global ecumene" (Hannerz, 2000) or sense of global belonging and world citizenship. For these globalists the contemporary international configuration of news delivery represents real changes in the global news landscape; processes that exemplify the spatial-temporal transformations that lie at the heart of globalization, namely: stretched social relations, intensification of flows, increasing interpenetration and global infrastructure (Held, 2004).

QUALIFYING PERSPECTIVES IN THE FIELD: PERIPHERAL AND PROFESSIONAL

The contemporary field of international and global journalism studies also hosts a number of "peripheral visions" and "professional preoccupations" that serve to qualify, whether theoretically or on more pragmatic grounds, the generalizing tendencies and global claims of these two overshadowing paradigms.

Peripheral Visions

A number of disparate studies collectively termed here "peripheral visions" (Sinclair, Jacka, & Cunningham, 2002) are now beginning to qualify the overarching claims of Western media dominance and they also exhibit a more theoretically circumspect or cautious stance towards claims of an emergent global public sphere—whether advanced in the field of news and journalism study or media globalization studies more widely. Included here are studies of new regional media formations and regional media production (Chalaby, 2002; Sinclair et al., 2002; Sonwalkar, 2004; Sreberny, 2000), contra-flows from new regional players (Azran, 2004; El-Nawawy & Iskander, 2003), discerned "mini-cultural imperialisms" enacted by former colonies and new regional powers (Sonwalkar, 2001, 2004), the national "domestication" of news exchange materials and news reports of global events (Clausen, 2003; Cohen, Levy, Roeh, & Gurevitch, 1996), and studies of world news audiences (Jensen, 2000). Together these open up a host of new dynamics and complexities in the study of global communication formations and news flows. This more complex, variegated and regionalist perspective, sensitive to the specificities and dynamics of production and flows both within as well as across the international communications environment, qualifies Western-led and Western-centric accounts of contemporary journalism. Processes of news "domestication," both in respect of global news exchange materials and their cultural inflection by national broadcasters (Cohen et al., 1996) and processes of national construction of major global events such as the UN's world conference on women (Clausen, 2003), for example, point to the constitutive role of culture in processes of news mediation and manufacture. Studies of world news audiences also suggest that "varied local cultures manifest themselves in the interpretation of foreign as well as domestic news" and that "culture shines through" in processes of audience news reception (Jensen, 2000, p. 190). These studies seemingly dent presumptions about the Western news media's capacity to export ideological frames and impose meanings on local cultures and, in this respect, news remains "a potential resource for action in a specific time and place."

Prasun Sonwalkar (2001, 2004) also encourages a less Western-centric understanding of today's news media; post-colonial societies exhibit their own powered geometry in terms of media formations and markets and cannot adequately be theorized through a prism of "West to the rest" communications.

> In large multicultural settings such as India, for the first time, local cultures and politics are being presented and represented within the country and to the rest of the world in ways that not only enhance local democratisation, a sense of nationalism and regional cohesion, but also a greater awareness and integration with global cultures and global politics [...] the proliferation of television since the mid-1980s has further enhanced India's cultural appeal in the region and created commercial opportunities to reach out to the 25 million strong South Asia diaspora across the globe [...] at the regional level, Indian cultural industries have the makings of "little cultural imperialism." (Sonwalkar, 2004, pp. 112–113)

These disparate studies of contemporary global journalism, then, each in their own way contribute to a more multi-faceted, less Western-led and deterministic theorization and in these respects entertain a more *transformationalist* (Held, 2004) view of the nature of contemporary news organizations, journalist practices, news output and processes of news reception around the globe. None, however, has sought to ignore the market conditioning of political economy or fails to acknowledge something of the democratizing impulses that sometimes register in the contra-flows and regional dynamics of contemporary media formations. These peripheral visions are less inclined nonetheless, on grounds of global complexity, to simply accept totalizing theoretical claims of either Western global dominance or global public sphere theorists.

Professional Preoccupations and Practices

Also informing the academic field of journalism and globalization studies are professional journalist discourses about the changing nature of news production and practices. Concerns here are frequently raised about how new technologies of production and delivery are impacting journalists practices and their professional standing. These professional preoccupations often tend toward the technologically determinist and are generally a-theoretical in their conceptualization, contextualization and explanations of changing news practices and performance (such views often surface, for example, in UK trade publications such as *Press Gazette, Broadcast* and *British Journalism Review*). Their concerns are normatively framed and frequently point, as I say, to the changing technologies and infrastructure that are thought to facilitate or restrict the professional practices and performance of journalists working in international and global contexts. Specifically, these expressed concerns include: 1) the industry's fetish of "live" 24/7 news from around the globe facilitated by cable and satellite delivery systems; 2) the potential threat of the Internet to, respectively, traditional news forms, the use of accredited sources and established journalist norms of impartiality, detachment and balance; 3) the role of mobile telephony and camcorders in the rise of citizen journalism, freelance (often at risk) "war correspondents" and underpaid and casualized "video journalists"; and 4) the impact of new electronic systems of news production in reconfiguring newsrooms and facilitating multi-media news production and multi-skilled (or "deskilled") journalism.

Changes in news technology, then, are often at the heart of these and other professional preoccupations. Academics have pursued many of them more sociologically in methodologically informed and systematic studies. "Breaking news" as well as "live two-ways" and "hotel stand-ups" are professionally often regarded as a poor substitute for in-depth reportage delivered by knowledgeable correspondents based in the field and have received detailed academic commentary (MacGregor, 1997; Seib, 2004). A study of BBC World and other 24/7 UK channels has also put to the test the industry's claim to be providing live, breaking news documenting how significant "breaking news" (that is, up-to-the-moment news and live reporting as the story happens) is in fact a rarity on these channels—granting credence to professional concerns over the sacrifice of in-depth news analysis for superficial, content-thin, immediacy (Lewis, Cusion, & Thomas, 2005).

An ethnographic study of the introduction of new production technologies and multi-skilling at the BBC has further demonstrated how technological developments are today incorporated and deployed for strategic and competitive advantage but do not, in and of themselves, dictate corporate policy much less determine how they are incorporated and shaped in practice (Cottle, 1999; see also Marjoribanks, 2000). Based on observations and interviews with newsroom personnel and decision makers the study paints a more nuanced picture of multi-skilling within the changing and pressurized corporate context of the BBC. Here "the problem is professionally perceived and experienced as one of increased pressures of work informed by an impinging context of cost reduction and management's sought efficiency gains through multi-skilled, multi-media working practices" and it is in this context that "Professional status, traditional hierarchies, career opportunities and traditional medium demarcations have all become unsettled" (Cottle, 1999, pp. 38–39).

Such studies, then, help to go behind the professional and normative concerns of journalists working with new technologies to reveal something of the complex mediations "at work." Professional and normative concerns also feature in at least three major debates about the changing nature and impact of contemporary international and global journalism, discussed next.

DEBATES OF OUR TIME

Our two overarching paradigms and qualifying perspectives also feed into current debates about the nature and impacts of international and global journalism. These debates have a relatively independent standing in the field though each is also subject to the distinctive "takes" of surrounding theoretical positions and perspectives. This is clearly demonstrated in the debate surrounding the demise or redefinition of foreign correspondence, a debate that is positioned between the explanatory logic of political economy and global dominance on the one side and new forms of global interconnectedness and claims for an emergent global public sphere on the other (see Figure 24.1).

The Demise or Redefinition of Foreign Correspondence?

Amidst claims of "dumbing down" in the journalism field are specific concerns about the shrinkage of foreign news both in the press and on TV (Pew Centre, 2002; Utley, 1997). Garrick Utley (1997), for example, charted the shrinkage of foreign news (specifically, foreign bureau reports, foreign policy coverage and overseas news) over an eight year period and across the three main US networks, ABC, CBS and NBC, and found that foreign news had been generally reduced by half across this period. More recently research conducted by the Pew Centre (2002) has pointed to the US audiences' need for more informed understanding of the world following the attacks of 9/11. Systematic studies of international issues in the news and general factual programming in the UK have also documented a decline in the public representation of serious issues over recent decades (DFID, 2000; Dover & Barnett, 2004; Stone, 2000). Foreign coverage in factual programming, for example, is now much more likely to be concerned with wildlife and travel than development, environment and human rights (Stone, 2000). The decline in international journalism documented by Utley and others clearly goes to the heart of concerns about an informed citizenry and its capacity for understanding today's global world, its interdependencies and inequalities. In this context, so-called "parachute journalism" is a poor substitute for correspondents based in countries overseas with their on-the-ground knowledge and source contacts built up over time (Pedelty, 1995). Whether accenting "the economic" in explanations based on market imperatives and the economic costs of supporting correspondents overseas or "the political" in terms of the influence of geo-political interests and outlooks inhibiting "foreign news" reports from politically remote places, political economy approaches are paradigmatically disposed to see such developments in terms of "business as usual." When approached through an optic of globalization seen as intensified interdependencies and cultural flows, however, a less pessimistic account comes into view.

> But do these perceived declines accurately measure the quantity and quality of foreign reporting that actually exists? We think not. The alarm, we propose, is based on an anachronistic and static model of what foreign correspondence is and who foreign correspondents are. (Hamilton & Jenner, 2004, p. 303)

For these authors, in a world of increasingly porous borders, the lines between foreign and domestic news have become blurred, just as they have in the world of commerce, health, culture and the environment. In this interconnected and interpenetrating context, they maintain, "Local reporters can find sources for foreign news among those they interact with daily" (p. 306) and "the new media landscape that undermines the old news flow structures allows foreign events to be covered in entirely new ways" (p. 313). On these grounds they question the use of numbers of traditional foreign correspondents and even the numbers of "overseas news stories' as the appropriate yardstick for measuring "foreign news." It is not entirely clear, however, how this redefinition of foreign correspondence manages to address, if at all, the mainstream news media's "forgotten humanitarian disasters" and "hidden wars" as well as other major concerns of development and human rights abuses around the globe—which brings us to two further debates in the current field of international journalism and global communications research: the CNN effect and compassion fatigue.

The CNN Effect?

Claims about the "CNN effect" and "compassion fatigue" circulate widely today, are essentially contradictory and suffer from a similar lack of robust empirical evidence. Adherents to the so-called "CNN effect" maintain that global broadcasting corporations like CNN, which can transmit scenes and news reports of human suffering around the globe, prompt changes in foreign policy and galvanize the momentum for humanitarian interventions. The opposite effect is alleged by the compassion fatigue thesis, which argues that media reports and televised scenes of human suffering have a diminishing capacity to mobilize sentiments, sympathy and humanitarian forms of response.

Research about the "CNN effect" can usefully be situated in descent from the so-called "Vietnam war syndrome." This refers to the US military and US State Department's belief that media scenes of US military casualties and the carnage of the Vietnam War sapped public morale on the home front and undermined the resolve to continue the war. Daniel Hallin (1986) effectively rebuts this "myth" and does so on the basis of a detailed historical account of the changing trajectory of the war, the growing elite dissensus that this produced within the US administration and the belated opportunities only that this created for a more challenging and questioning journalism. In other words, he argues, the US media followed rather than led the establishment view. Though the "Vietnam syndrome" may be based on a myth, it has proved no less consequential in its effects; military commanders and governments around the world continue to impose tight media controls on this basis (Knightly, 2003; Lewis et al., 2006). The point here, however, is that Hallin's study as well as other models of media-elite "indexing" (Bennett, 1990) prompt a more historically contingent and politically dynamic approach to the role of media in conflict reporting and humanitarian emergencies. As such, they qualify the generalizing claims of a media-led causality built into the notion of the CNN effect. Even so, some commentators have argued that in exceptional cases such as the humanitarian intervention to support the Kurdish refugees following the US invasion of Iraq, the media can and do exert influence on decision makers.

> The central agencies of global civil society in the Kurdish crisis, the institutions which forced the changes in state policies which constituted "humanitarian intervention," were in fact television news programmes. Television—not newspapers, not social movements, certainly not the traditional representative institutions—took up the plight of the Kurds and in an unprecedented campaign successfully forced governments' hands. [...] Television news' role in the Kurdish crisis is all the more surprising, at first sight, since it contrasted so clearly with the managed medium which they had represented during the Gulf War. (Shaw, 1999)

Others, even in this seemingly strong case, are less convinced and point to underlying geopolitical interests as the most likely cause precipitating US humanitarian involvement in the Kurdish crisis and many other humanitarian interventions.

> It is contended [...] that, given Turkey's membership of NATO, its loyalty (particularly during the Gulf War) to the US and its on-going "problem" with Kurdish separatists in southern Turkey, geo-strategic concerns rather than media-inspired humanitarian intent or media-public relations are sufficient to explain the intervention. At the very most the critical and empathy-framed coverage would have had an enabling effect, helping to explain and justify the deployment of ground troops in Iraq to the US public, but the decision itself was most likely motivated by non-media related concerns. In short, the claim that ground troop intervention in northern Iraq was a case of the strong CNN effect is not born out by this case study. (Robinson 2002, pp. 70–71)

Across recent years a number of scholars have sought to develop more analytically nuanced accounts of the CNN effect (for a review, see Gilboa, 2005). Notable amongst them is Piers Robinson (2002) who, through detailed and comparative case studies, seeks to establish the precise conditions under which a CNN effect may, very occasionally, take place. He argues that this occurs when there is elite dissensus, a high degree of policy uncertainty and when preceding media coverage has involved emotive pictures and empathetic and critical framing. Even under these exact conditions however, as we have just pointed out, the operation of strategic and geo-political interests as well as other possible factors "behind the scenes," may be the key determinants of humanitarian intervention and today's new "military humanism" (Beck, 2005, p. 65). Too often claims about CNN effects are deduced from policy outcomes and based on a simple correlation with empathetic media coverage (Shaw, 1996), rather than in-depth study of policy making personnel, institutions and processes (Gilboa, 2005). Some theorists also suggest that the CNN effect essentially misses the point (Hawkins, 2002; Jakobsen, 2000). Victor Hawkins, for example, argues that by focusing its gaze on particular conflicts, the media ignores many others (and the massive amount of human suffering that they cause) and thereby exclude these as possible influences on public and policy agendas, though implicitly thereby granting the CNN effect some residual validity. The debate continues.

Compassion Fatigue?

The notion of "compassion fatigue" (Moeller, 1999) has also gained popular (and media) currency across recent years—which is not to say, of course, that the media phenomenon the idea purports to explain is real. In fact, the concept exhibits a distinct lack of analytical precision in terms of the complex interactions between humanitarian organizations, news media and audiences.

> Compassion fatigue is the unacknowledged cause of much of the failure of international reporting today. It is at the base of many of the complaints about the public's short attention span, the media's peripatetic journalism, the public's boredom with international news, the media's preoccupation with crisis coverage. (p. 2)

As this all-encompassing statement signals, the concept of compassion fatigue is often asked to do a great deal, from explaining the failures, practices and forms of international news reporting to audience-based questions about levels of news engagement and interests. As we know however, matters are a good deal more complicated on all these fronts. Humanitarian aid organizations, interestingly, generally prefer to use the term "media fatigue" rather than the more generalised "compassion fatigue," and they do so on the basis of their understanding of the news media and its operations (Cottle & Nolan, 2007). The debate about "compassion fatigue" also tends to produce speculative statements rather than empirically sustained argument and theorisation. Michael Ignatieff (1998, pp. 11–12) has written, for example, that, "Through its news broadcasts and spectaculars like 'Live Aid,' television has become the privileged medium through which moral relations between strangers are mediated in the modern world" and he suggests "Images of human suffering do not assert their own meaning; they can only instantiate a moral claim if those who watch understand themselves to be potentially under obligation to those they see." Keith Tester (1994, p. 130), no less eloquently, takes a more media-centric and less historically progressive view. "Certainly the media," he says, "communicate harrowing representations of others, but the more the face of the other is communicated and reproduced in this way the more it is denuded of any moral authority it might otherwise possess ... Increased visibility of the gaze seems to go hand in hand with increasing invisibility from the point of view of the responsibility of moral solidarity." Speculative views on the role of televised images of human suffering and their capacity to move us, such as these, demand further empirical investigation.

Here recent work on the news media's "spectacle of suffering" (Chouliaraki, 2006) and discourses of global compassion (Höijer, 2004) help to recover something of the complexities buried beneath the nebulous term of "compassion fatigue" and also point to the need for more refined analytical distinctions. Brigita Höijer (2004) observes in her audience-based study how "compassion" is often dependent on visuals, involves ideal victim images and can also be analytically disaggregated into different forms of "tender-hearted," "shame-filled," "blame-filled" and "powerlessness-filled" compassion. In such ways, she argues, audience responses to reports of human suffering exhibit their own complexities and contingencies, just as with the complex dynamics and determinants that we know shape international news reporting. These complexities, then, are not usefully collapsed under the catch-all concept of "compassion fatigue" especially when masquerading as an "explanation" for all things international and global news.

WHERE TO NEXT? EMERGENT AND NEW TRAJECTORIES

The foregoing, in broad outline only, has mapped the principal paradigms, perspectives and debates currently structuring the field of international and global journalism studies and these no doubt will continue to shape much of the work undertaken in this field in the foreseeable future. Even so, it is possible to detect other research trajectories as well as prominent silences that must now be addressed if the field of international and global journalism study is to continue to engage with pressing real-world concerns and developments. The following simply signals three possible trajectories, each of which chimes with contemporary social theoretical concerns and more nuanced positions now emerging in the field of international communications and media globalization.

Global Issues and World Risk Society

The unprecedented nature of many of today's global threats has yet to be taken seriously by journalism scholars—theoretically, methodologically and substantively. Many of the conflicts and crises reported on in the world today are global in their nature, scope, and potential impacts. The fall-out from Chernobyl, as well as the potential effects of new virulent pandemics and market crashes, can all, for example, migrate at speed round the globe and with indiscriminate effects on distant populations as can new forms of transnational terrorism and its deadly twin, the "global war on terror." Global warming and other ecological threats confront us all and do so notwithstanding the distributional inequalities of impact and response. There is something unprecedented about these global threats which go to the core of contemporary arguments about global cosmopolitanism and a possible global public sphere (Beck, 2006). They demand concerted responses from researchers working in the field of international and global journalism studies (Cottle, forthcoming).

According to Ulrich Beck (2005, pp. 38–39), it is the common and increasingly mediated perception of global threats, not universalizing statements about shared humanity, that serve to underpin and mobilize global cosmopolitan citizenship and an emergent global public sphere:

> [...] it is the *reflexivity of world risk society* that creates the reciprocal relationship between the public sphere and globality. Regardless of all the borders and rifts that separate nations, the constructed and accepted definition of planetary threat and its global mass-media-projected omnipresence create a common arena of values, responsibility and action which, analogously to the national arena, *can* (though need not necessarily) give rise to political action among strangers. This is the case when the accepted definition of threat leads to global norms, agreements and common action. (original emphasis)

Today's crises of "World Risk Society" signal the necessity for a theoretical reorientation that deliberately moves beyond the confines of the nation state and "methodological nationalism." This is warranted by the global nature of the perceived threats as well as their elaboration and engagement within and through the formations and flows of today's global media ecology. This is not an argument therefore for simply more comparative research but the necessity to take "global issues" seriously—theoretically, methodologically, ontologically. Important studies of "race" and migration, the global war on terror, environment and ecology, for example, continue to be conducted *inside* particular national contexts and *through* national prisms, but how many have sought to track and theorize these global phenomena beyond the nation state and with reference to the wider flows and formations of globalizing communications? Where are the studies today of journalism and international governance, journalism and international law, journalism and the normative discourse of global human rights, journalism and migration flows, journalism and ecology—all conceived and approached globally? A call, then, for new research agendas deliberately setting out to study today's major global issues and crises and how these become constituted and contested within global media formations and communication flows around the world and exploring what part these may perform in *re-imagining the political* within an increasingly interconnected, inter-dependent and *threat-filled* world.

Communicative Democracy

Notwithstanding generalizing statements about the emergence of a democratizing "global public sphere" as well as its claimed opposite of "poor democracy" manufactured by corporate news media, there is in fact a democratic lacuna at the heart of major theoretical approaches to the study of international and global journalism (Cottle & Rai, 2008), as there is in the study of national news outlets more widely (Cottle & Rai, 2006). This concerns the failure to interrogate the complexities of the public elaboration of conflicting interests and identities in news presentation and delivery and how these become conditioned and shaped, enabled and disabled, within the communicative structures of their mediation. How global news providers, for example, mediate conflicts and imagined communities to wider audiences around the world is crucial for any serious evaluation of how news media are implicated in reproducing structures of dominance or processes of enhancing democracy. These complexities have generally been occluded by the theoretical generalizations and political expectations of both the global dominance and global public sphere paradigms. Conditions are now propitious for a re-examination of the news media's possible contribution to processes of mediated democracy.

In late modern societies, traditional beliefs, political institutions and scientific and other authorities must seek public legitimacy on the media stage and they do so at a time of diminishing deference and a global profusion of migrating ideas, beliefs and values (Beck, 1999; Castells, 1997; Giddens, 1990, 1994). New social movements and different cultural identities compete and contend for media attention along with the "public relations state" and the "argumentation craftsmen" of corporate interests (Beck, 1999). And, as parliamentary democracies become perceived by many as moribund, civil societies have become increasingly agonistic and conflicted (Mouffe, 1996) and calls for the "democratizing of democracy" (Giddens, 1994), "democratic deepening" and "deliberative democracy" are made (Benhabib 2002, Habermas 1996). In today's globally interconnected and inegalitarian world, democracy is not best conceived as "genteel conversation" but rather as a series of embattled fields of contention, insurgency and reflexivity that are local to transnational in scope (Dryzek, 2000, 2006).

In today's mediated world, we also need to acknowledge and better theorize the contribution that image as well as ideas, rhetoric as well as reason, affect as well as analysis can play in the public enactment and elaboration of "communicative democracy." Visualized narratives, experiential accounts and emotive testimonies can all contribute to processes of recognition and understanding of competing world outlooks (Cottle, 2006b, pp. 167–184) as can more traditional forms of information conveyance, claims-making and argumentation by contending interests. The communicative architecture of international and global journalism draws on both these communicative modes of *display* and *deliberation*—often consequentially so. As well as addressing "global issues" in the news, then, we also need to attend much more closely to the forms of "communicative democracy" embedded in their news mediation and how these become naturalised and professionally produced through time and across different news organisations.

Global Mediations: Dynamic and Contingent

The ideas of "communicative democracy" referenced above are premised on ideas of social formations and processes of globalization as inherently contested and conflicted. How these contests of interest and identity are conducted and play out through space and time generates unpredictability, contingencies and political opportunities and these increasingly become enacted and performed in the media. Too often these dynamics and contingencies, the *stuff* of politics in action, become theoretically minimised by a priori expectations. So here, finally, is a claim for the necessity to theoretically bring politics back into the field of international and global journalism research and by this I mean into the study of how conflicts and contention are strategically pursued and performed in the media by contending interests and across time—challenging static theoretical frameworks and deterministic models in the field. There are good empirical grounds on which to develop a more dynamic and contingent understanding of international and global news mediations and its theorisation. Contrary to the "propaganda model" elaborated in Herman and Chomsky's *Manufacturing Consent* (1988), for example, studies of war reporting (and peace reporting) are increasingly sensitive to the changing nature of reporting through time and in relation to shifts of political and public opinion (Entman, 2004; Hallin, 1986; Tumber & Palmer, 2004; Wolfsfeld, 1997, 2004). The *stuff* of politics is here enacted in and through processes of journalistic mediation and this demands fine-grained empirical analyses and refined theoretical elaboration. Only then will we be in a position to better theorise the complexities and contingencies involved and avoiding the heavy determinisms and ideological dominance of "manufacturing consent" (Herman & Chomsky, 1988) approaches on the one hand, and the recent tendency to theorise global journalism in terms of radical indeterminacy and chaos, on the other (McNair, 2006).

The study of mediatized rituals and global media events also challenges entrenched theoretical views about media power, its locations and determinations and the role of media in processes of manufacturing consent (Cottle 2006a; Alexander et al., 2006). Some mediatized rituals, contrary to both Durkheimian and neo-Marxian traditions (still the dominant traditions in the field of ritual study), appear to open up productive spaces for social reflexivity and critique and can be politically disruptive or even transformative in their reverberations within civil and wider societies. The media's performative use of resonate symbols, dramatic visualization, narrative and embedding of emotions into ritual forms sometimes confront the strategic power of institutions and vested interests and can even lend moral gravitas to the projects of challenger groups within society. These sometimes disruptive phenomena and their globalization through the news media demand comparative empirical analysis and further theorization. Mediated disasters, whether Hurricane Katrina or the Asian Tsunami, for example, represent an important sub-class of potentially politically disruptive and globalised media events.

> In contradistinction to media events, the shared collective space created by disaster time-out, zooming in on victims and their families, is the basis not for dignity and restraint but for the chaotic exploitation of the pain of participants on screen, and for the opportunistic fanning of establishment mismanagement, neglect, corruption, and so on. Whereas the principle of broadcast ceremony is to highlight emotions and solidarity and to bracket analysis, a disaster marathon constitutes a communal public forum where tragedy is the emotional motor which sizzles with conflict, emphasizing anxiety, argument and disagreement. (Liebes, 1998, pp. 75–76; see also Katz & Liebes, 2007)

How these, and other, major media events become circulated and consumed, contested and challenged in the global flows and forms of journalism and with what impact on political elites and the formations of publics around the world are important questions now deserving increased attention.

CONCLUSION

The contemporary field of international and global journalism research, as we have seen, is inherently contested and theoretically disputatious—sometimes productively so. The above has done no more than sketch something of this structuration by overshadowing paradigms, different perspectives and salient debates and has moved to offer three further possible research trajectories for the future. We live in a global age and journalism and processes of globalization are inextricably intertwined (though the role of journalism within these processes is often undertheorised by contemporary social theorists). Researchers need to rise to the significant challenge of studying journalism and continuing processes of globalization in all their multifaceted complexity and interpenetration. Guiding theoretical frameworks, empirical engagement and debate remain as indispensable as ever to this task.

REFERENCES

Alexander, J., Giesen, B., & Mast, J. (2006). *Social performance: Symbolic action, cultural pragmatics and ritual.* Cambridge: Cambridge University Press.

Appadurai, A. (1996). *Modernity at large: Cultural dimensions of globalization.* Minneapolis: University of Minnesota Press.

Azran, T. (2004). Resisting peripheral exports: Al Jazeera's war images on US television. *Media International Australia, 113*, 75–86.

Bauman, Z. (2007). *Liquid times.* Cambridge: Polity.

Beck, U. (1999). *World risk society.* Cambridge: Polity.

Beck, U. (2005). *Power in the global age.* Cambridge: Polity.

Beck, U. (2006). *Cosmopolitan vision.* Cambridge: Polity Press.

Beck, U., Giddens, A., & Lash, S. (1994). *Reflexive modernization.* Cambridge: Polity.

Benhabib, S. (2002). *The claims of culture.* Princeton, NJ: Princeton University Press.

Bennett, L. (1990). Towards a theory of press-state relations in the United States. *Journal of Communication, 40*(2), 103–25.

Boyd-Barrett, O. (1998). Media imperialism reformulated. In D. K. Thussu (Ed.), *Electronic empires: Global media and local resistance* (pp.157–176). London: Arnold.

Boyd-Barrett, O., & Rantanen, T. (Eds.). (1998). *The globalization of news.* London: Sage.

Castells, M. (1996). *The rise of the network society.* Oxford: Blackwell.

Castells, M. (1997). *The power of identity.* Oxford: Blackwell.

Castells, M. (2007) Communication, power and counter-power in the network society. *International Journal of Communication*, (1), 238–266.

Chalaby, J. (2002). Transnational television in Europe: The role of pan-European channels. *European Journal of Communication, 17*(2), 183–203.

Chouliaraki, L. (2006). *The spectatorship of suffering.* London: Sage.

Clausen, L. (2003). *Global news production.* Copenhagen: Copenhagen Business School Press.

Cohen, A., Levy, M., Roeh, I., & Gurevitch, M. (1996). *Global newsrooms, local audiences: A study of the Eurovision news exchange.* London: John Libby.

Cottle, S. (1999). From BBC newsroom to BBC news centre: On changing technology and journalist practices. *Convergence, 5*(3), 22–43.

Cottle, S. (2006a). Mediatized rituals: Beyond manufacturing consent. *Media, Culture and Society, 28*(3), 411–432.

Cottle, S. (2006b). *Mediatized conflict: Developments in media and conflict studies.* Maidenhead, UK: Open University Press.

Cottle, S. (forthcoming). *Global crisis reporting: Journalism in the global age.* Maidenhead, UK: Open University Press.

Cottle, S., & Rai, M. (2006). Between display and deliberation: Analyzing TV news as communicative architecture. *Media, Culture and Society, 28*(2), 163–189.

Cottle, S., & Nolan. D. (2007). Global humanitarianism and the changing aid field: "Everyone was dying for footage." *Journalism Studies, 8*(6), 862–878.

Cottle, S., & Rai, M. (2008). Global 24/7 news providers: Emissaries of global dominance or global public sphere? *Global Media and Communication, 4*(2), 157–181.

Department for International Development (2000). *View the world: A study of British television coverage of developing countries*. London: DFID.

Dover, C., & Barnett, S. (2004). *The world on the box: International issues in news and factual programmes on UK television 1975–2003*. London: Third World and Environmental Broadcasting Project.

Dryzek, J. (2000). *Deliberative democracy and beyond*. Oxford: Oxford University Press.

Dryzek, J. (2006). *Deliberative global politics*. Cambridge: Polity Press.

El-Nawawy, M., & Iskandar, A. (2003). *Al-Jazeera*. Cambridge MA: Westview.

Entman, R. (2004). *Projections of power*. London: Sage.

Galtung. J., & Ruge. M. (1965). The structure of foreign news: The presentation of the Congo, Cuba and Cyprus crises in four newspapers. *Journal of International Peace Research, 1*, 64–90.

Giddens, A. (1990). *The consequences of modernity*. Cambridge: Polity Press.

Giddens, A. (1994). *Beyond left and right*. Cambridge: Polity Press.

Giddens, A. (2005). Giddens and the "G" Word: An interview with Anthony Giddens. *Global Media and Communication, 1*(1), 63–78.

Gilboa, E. (2005). The CNN effect: The search for a communication theory of international relations. *Political Communication, 22*, 27–44.

Habermas, J. (1989). *The structural transformation of the public sphere*. Cambridge: MIT Press.

Habermas, J. (1996). *Between facts and norms*. Cambridge: Polity Press.

Hallin, D. (1986). *The "uncensored war?': The media and Vietnam*. New York: Oxford University Press.

Hamilton, J. M., & Jenner, E. (2004). Redefining foreign correspondence. *Journalism, 5*(3), 301–321.

Hannerz, U. (2000). *Foreign news: Exploring the world of foreign correspondents*. Chicago: The University of Chicago Press.

Harvey, D. (1989). *The condition of postmodernity*. Oxford: Blackwell.

Hawkins, V. (2002). The other side of the CNN factor: The media and conflict. *Journalism Studies, 3*(2), 225–240.

Held, D. (Ed). (2004). *A globalizing world?* London: Routledge.

Held, D., & McGrew, A. (2003). The great globalization debate: An introduction. In D. Held & A. McGrew (Eds.), *The global transformations reader* (pp.1–50). Cambridge: Polity.

Herman, E., & Chomsky, N. (1988). *Manufacturing consent: The political economy of the mass media*. London: Vintage.

Herman, E., & McChesney, R. (1997). *The global media: The new missionaries of corporate capitalism*. London: Cassell.

Höijer, B. (2004). The discourse of global compassion: The audience and media reporting of human suffering. *Media, Culture and Society, 26*(4), 513–531.

Ignatieff, M. (1998). *The warrior's honor: Ethnic war and the modern conscience*. London: Chatto and Windus.

Jakobsen, P. V. (2000). Focus on the CNN effect misses the point: The real media impact on conflict management is invisible and indirect. *Journal of Peace Research, 37*(5), 547–562.

Jensen, K. (Ed.). (2000). *News of the world: World cultures look at television news*. London: Routledge.

Katz, E., & Liebes, T. (2007). "No more peace!": How disasters, terror and war have upstaged media events. *International Journal of Communication, 1*(1), 157–166.

Knightly, P. (2003). *The first casuality*. London: Andre Deutsch.

Liebes, T. (1998). Television's disaster marathons: A danger for democratic processes? In T. Liebes & J. Curran (Eds.), *Media, ritual and identity* (pp. 71–84). London: Routledge.

Lewis, J., Cusion, S., & Thomas, J. (2005). Immediacy, convenience or engagement? An analysis of 24-hour news channels in the UK. *Journalism Studies, 6*(4), 461–477.

Lewis, J. , Brookes, R., Mosdell, N., & Threadgold, T. (2006). *Shoot first and ask questions later: Media coverage of the 2003 Iraq war*. New York: Peter Lang.

MacGregor, B. (1997). *Live, direct and biased? Making television news in the satellite age*. London: Arnold.

Mackay, H. (2004). The globalization of culture? In D. Held (Ed.), *A globalizing world?* (pp. 47–84). London: Routledge.

Marjoribanks, T. (2000). *News corporation, technology and the workplace*. Cambridge: Cambridge University Press.

McBride, S. (1980). *Many voices, One world*. Oxford: Rowman and Littlefield.

McChesney, R. (1999). *Rich media, poor democracy: Communication politics in dubious times*. Illinois: University of Illinois Press.

McLuhan, M. (1964). *Understanding media: The extensions of man*. New York: McGraw Hill.

McNair, B. (2006) *Cultural chaos: Journalism, news and power in a globalised world*. London: Routledge.

Moeller, S. (1999). *Compassion fatigue*. London: Routledge.

Mouffe, C. (1996). Democracy, power and the "political." In S. Benhabib (Ed.), *Democracy and difference* (pp. 245–256). Princeton, NJ: Princeton University Press.

Murdock, G. (1990). Redrawing the map of the communication industries: Concentration and ownership in the era of privatization. In M. Ferguson (Ed.), *Public communication: The new imperatives*. (pp. 1–17) London: Sage.

Nordenstreng, K., & T. Varis (1974). *Television traffic: A one-way street?* Paris: UNESCO.

Pedelty, M. (1995). *War stories*. London: Routledge.

Pew Research Centre for the People and the Press (2002). *Public news habits little changed by September 11: Americans lack background to follow International News*. Washington, DC: Pew.

Rai, M., & Cottle, S. (2007). Global mediations: On the changing ecology of satellite television news. *Global Media and Communication, 3*(1), 51–78.

Robinson, P. (2002). *The CNN effect*. London: Routledge.

Schiller, H. (2005). Not yet the post-imperialist era. In M. Durham & D. Kellner (Eds.), *Media and cultural studies: Key works* (pp. 318–333). Oxford: Blackwell.

Seib, P. (2004). *Beyond the front lines*. Houndmills, UK: Macmillan.

Shaw, M. (1996). *Civil society and media in global crises*. London: St Martin's Press.

Shaw. M. (1999). Global voices: Civil society and media in global crises. Retrieved 28/6/07 from http://www.sussex.ac.uk/Users/hafa3/voices.htm

Sinclair, J., Jacka, E., & Cunningham, S. (2002). Peripheral vision. In J. Sinclair, E. Jacka, & S. Cunningham (Eds.), *New patterns in global television: Peripheral vision* (pp.1–32). Oxford: Oxford University Press.

Stone, J. (2000). *Losing perspective: Global affairs on British Terrestrial Television 1989–1999*. London: Third World and Environmental Broadcasting Project.

Sonwalkar, P. (2001). India: Makings of little cultural/media imperialism? *Gazette, 63*(6), 505–519.

Sonwalkar, P. (2004). News imperialism: Contra view from the South. In C. Paterson & A. Sreberny (Eds.), *International news in the twenty-first century* (pp. 111–126). Eastleigh, UK: John Libby.

Sreberny, A. (2000). The global and the local in international communications. In J. Curran & M. Gurevitch (Eds.), *Mass media and society* (pp. 93–119). London: Edward Arnold.

Tester, K. (1994). *Media, culture and morality*. London: Routledge.

Thussu, D. K. (2003). Live TV and bloodless deaths: War, infotainment and 24/7 news. In D. K. Thussu & D. Freedman (Eds.), *War and the media: Reporting conflict 24/7* (pp. 117–132). London: Sage.

Tomlinson, J. (1991). *Cultural imperialism*. London: Pinter Press.

Tomlinson, J. (1999). *Globalization and culture*. Chicago: University of Chicago Press.

Tumber, H. & Palmer, J. (2004). *Media at war: The Iraq crisis*. London: Sage.

Urry, J. (2003). *Global complexity*. Cambridge: Polity.

Utley, G. (1997). The shrinking of foreign news: From broadcast to narrowcast. *Foreign Affairs* 76(2), 1–6.

Volkmer, I. (1999). *News in the global sphere: A study of CNN and its impact on global communication*. Luton, UK: University of Luton Press.

Volkmer, I. (2002). Journalism and political crises in the global network society. In B. Zelizer & S. Allan (Eds.), *Journalism after September 11* (pp. 235–246). London: Routledge.

Volkmer, I. (2003). The global network society and the global public sphere. *Development, 46*(1), 9–16.

Wolfsfeld, G. (1997). *Media and political conflict: News from the Middle East*. Cambridge: Cambridge University Press.

Wolfsfeld, G. (2004). *Media and the path to peace*. Cambridge: Cambridge University Press.

25
Development Journalism

Xu Xiaoge

Development journalism debuted in Asia in the late 1960s when the idea of communication for development was garnering support academically and politically, especially among the newly independent nations. Theoretically equipped with the proliferating development communication paradigm, journalism was believed and expected to play a key role in facilitating and fostering national development. Such a belief and expectation constituted the driving forces behind the rising popularity of development journalism among developing nations in Asia, Africa and Latin America. And it remains vital and vibrant as a journalism practice despite criticisms and prejudices.

Having been practiced for more than four decades across three continents, development journalism has generated diverse principles and practices. Ironically, such diversity has not been duly captured in journalism studies. What is more disturbing is the absence of systematic and theoretical constructs and corresponding models to describe, explain and predict its different practices and performances. The situation is largely caused by the fact that development journalism has long been neglected by the journalism research community.

To serve as a stepping-stone for further research, the current chapter begins with a scan of conceptual components and empirical practices of development journalism, followed by a review of its contextual origins, including the indigenization efforts and the Asian values debate. Readers will also be introduced to its major schools of thought, scholars and publications. Further investigation is made into its pending issues. Last but not least, the chapter identifies key areas for further academic studies.

CONCEPTUAL COMPONENTS

The concept of development journalism emerged at a workshop for economic writers in the Philippines in the late 1960s (Gunaratne, 1996; Stevenson, 1994). At the workshop, the British journalist, Asia-hand and champion of development journalism, Alan Chalkley, told the participants that journalists should alert news audiences to development problems and open their eyes to possible solutions (Chalkley, 1968). Without claiming to be "a new kind of journalism," development journalism represented "a new attitude towards the treatment of certain subjects" in relation to development. It was designed to serve the ordinary people, not the elite (Chalkley, 1980, p. 215).

Key components of development journalism include the following five aspects:

1. to report the difference between what has been planned to do and what in reality has been achieved as well as the difference between its claimed and actual impact on people (Aggarwala, 1978);
2. to focus not "on day-to-day news but on long term development process" (Kunczik, 1988, p. 83);
3. to be independent from government and to provide constructive criticisms of government (Aggarwala, 1978; Shah, 1992; Ogan, 1982);
4. to shift "journalistic focus to news of economic and social development" while "working constructively with the government" (Richstad, 2000, p. 279) in nation building;
5. and to empower the ordinary people to improve their own lives and communities (Romano & Hippocrates, 2001).

EMPIRICAL PRACTICES

One of the early practices of development journalism can be traced back to Depthnews (Development Economic and Population Themes News), a regional development news agency intended to provide model stories for the Asia's press. Depthnews focused on coverage of women, science, health, rural development and environmental concerns, avoiding news of political, military and natural disasters. Addressing topics that were less covered by Western news agencies, and relying on sources and actors from the Third World, Depthnews constituted a force in advancing South-South communication and understanding (McKay, 1993).

At the national level, development journalism was practiced with variations in different countries as its practice was influenced by different social, economic, cultural and political conditions and situations (Chen, 1991; Maslog, 1985; Shah, 1989; Verghese, 1976; Vilanilam, 1975, 1984). Although development journalism was enthusiastically promoted first in the Philippines, it did not win ready acceptance from mainstream journalists largely because few of them bothered to get involved in its conceptualization or application (Shafer, 1998). After reaching its height in the mid-1980s, development journalism lost its momentum when most journalists reverted to traditional and libertarian Western approaches after the Epifanio de Los Santos Avenue (EDSA) Revolution (Shafer, 1998). Development journalism did not enhance the press's watchdog function but resulted in the press being the tool of the authoritarian Marcos government (1965–1986). Also, economic constraints on the press have prevented an effective, independent, and critical form of journalism from emerging (Shafer, 1991). Although development journalism is not widely practiced in the Philippines, it remains a vibrant course in journalism education in the country, indicated by the active operation of the department of development journalism at the University of the Philippines, Los Banos.

Development journalism is also enthusiastically advocated and promoted in India where it has been practiced since the late 1960s. Experiments were also carried out to promote it, such as the project "Our Village, Chhatera" conducted by *Hindustan Times* (Verghese, 1976). Even though, according to some scholars, news coverage of development was neither significant nor encouraging (Murthy, 2000; Vilanilam, 1975), development journalism remains highly respected in India. The Institute of Mass Communication runs a prestigious Diploma Course in Development Journalism for mid-career journalists and information service officers from non-aligned and developing countries in Asia, Africa, Latin America, and Europe.

Being strategically linked to the government, the press in Singapore has played a major role in nation-building and economic construction. As a small, young, developed, and multiracial country, Singapore is highly concerned about social stability, racial harmony, and relations with neighboring countries. Such concerns have constituted the major rationale for its press to adopt elements of development journalism (Latif, 1998; Xu, 2005). This is also true for the press in Malaysia (Ali, 1980, 1990). In these two countries, the constructive partnership between the press and government is highly expected in theory and respected in practice.

Development journalism has also been incorporated in journalism training, education and practice in China, where development has become a national priority, especially since China started its economic reform and opened to the outside world in the late 1970s. Development journalism has played an increasingly important role in boosting economic, cultural and political development in China (Chen, 1991; Fang, 1983; Wu, 1987; Zhou, 1992;).

Just like in Asia, the socio-economic conditions, the desperate needs for economic development, and nation building in Africa and Latin America created a favorable environment for the adoption and growth of development journalism (Domatob & Hall, 1983; Edeani, 1993; Isiaka, 2006; Mwaffisi, 1991). Poverty-stricken and underdeveloped, many countries in those parts of the world have become experimental venues for development journalism since the late 1960s. Governments in these areas continue to use development journalism to maintain their powers and influences, and to aid national political, economic, and cultural development. The ready adoption of development journalism was originally legitimatized by the neo-colonial reality in Africa, which remained in the grip of colonial domination, inequality and dependence (Domatob & Hall, 1983).

The African press is expected to play a major part in informing, educating, motivating, mobilizing, and entertaining the people. In practice, although the press has contributed to health, nutrition, family planning, and agriculture education programs in countries like Nigeria, Ghana, Cameroun, Zaire, and Kenya, it has largely been used by "most African ruling groups to consolidate and perpetuate power in the name of development journalism" (Domatob & Hall, 1983, p. 18). Consequently, it is the elite, not the ordinary people who have benefited most from the practice of development journalism.

CONTEXTUAL ORIGINS

Historically, development journalism emerged out of the urgent need for social, economic and political development in Asia in the "chaotic aftermath of the Pacific War and colonialism in many Asian countries" (Richstad, 2000, p. 279). It was situated in "the growing number of independent economies in the world, the sharp rise in sophistication and modernization among them—and, most of all, the soaring aspirations of the people" in the post 1945 years (Chalkley, 1980, p. 215). Its mission lied "in furthering the emancipation of such deprived groups as the urban poor, the rural people, women and so on and helping them actively to participate in the political process, that is actively influence their destinies" (Quebral, 1975; as cited in Kunczik, 1988, p. 85).

Development journalism also grew out of the special role of journalism played by "former journalists who became leaders of newly independent states" in Africa, including "Ghana's Kwame Nkrumah, founder and publisher of the 'Accra Evening News,' Nigeria's Nnandi Azikiwe, 'West Africa Pilot,' Kenya's Jomo Kenyata, founder and publisher of a Kikuyu newspaper influential in the independence struggle and Tanzania's Julius Nyerere, publisher of 'Uhuru,' the TANU party newspaper" (Kunczik, 1988, p. 85). These journalists-turned politicians emphasized the importance of journalism in shaping national identities and promoting national cohesion (Kunczik, 1988).

Theoretically, development journalism was strongly supported by modernization and development communication theories. In the logic of these approaches, for the developing or underdeveloped countries to modernize themselves, they should learn from the West, importing communication technologies along with ways of doing things from the West including concepts like press freedom and the watchdog function of the media. These approaches also emphasized the effectiveness of the mass media in developing and modernizing a nation (Lerner & Schramm, 1967; Pye, 1963; Rogers, 1962, 1976; Schramm, 1964).

Development journalism was also inspired by dependency theory, which has two variants: structural imperialism (Galtung, 1971) and cultural imperialism (Schiller, 1976). Both were deeply rooted in the theoretical foundations of development journalism, in that they provided strong theoretical support and guidelines for the battle against Western cultural invasion and the promotion of national cultural values and identities through development journalism (Kunczik, 1988).

Systems theory demonstrated the relationships between interrelated and interdependent subsystems, i.e., between journalism and its social, economic, cultural and political environments. In the perspective of the systems theory, different and interdependent relationships between the press and its various environments would produce different perceptions of the press and different types of press models in developing countries (Akahenda, 1983; Edelstein, 1982; Kunczik, 1988; Ogan, 1982).

Ideologically, development journalism was closely connected to the movements of the New International Economic Order (a 1974 UN declaration), and the New World Information Order (called for in 1980 by MacBride Commission). UNESCO-sponsored projects like Radio Rural Forums in India, Ghana and Costa Rica (Hornik, 1988) provided further ideological support to the growth of development journalism.

INDIGENIZATION EFFORTS AND THE ASIAN VALUES DEBATE

Another major component of its contextual origin was a widely shared concern in Asia that the traditional Western model of news reporting, which emphasized events rather than processes that produced the events (Ali, 1980), was inadequate for developing countries in Asia. Such a concern led to efforts to reform the reporting and editing practices of the Asian press (Abundo, 1986) to replace the Western practice of emphasizing sensationalism and commercialism, which produced little coverage of socially important news about the ordinary people, community projects, rural developments, and efforts to address poverty (Wong, 2004).

Development journalism was also boosted by the de-Westernization efforts in the region. At the 1985 Bangkok Symposium, media scholars and practitioners gathered to explore Asian perspectives on communication and to assess the relevance and applicability of Western communication theory in the Asian context. At the seminar, proposals were put forth to explore Asian perspectives on communication theory from Chinese, Islamic, Japanese, and Indian perspectives. More efforts were also made to indigenize Western communication theories to suit Asian cultures and adapt their operationalization to the constraints of multi-ethnic, pluralistic Asian societies (Asian Media Information and Communication Centre, 1985).

The indigenization efforts continued when media practitioners and scholars gathered at the 1988 Jakarta Consultation to re-examine the role and responsibility of the press in ASEAN countries (Singapore, Malaysia, Thailand, Indonesia, Philippines, and Brunei Darussalam). At the meeting, ASEAN government officials sent out a clear message in their respective remarks tAnwar Ibrahim described the cultural domination of alien values and standards as “the biggest obstacle to the media development of Asian countries" (as cited in Menon, 1988, p. 2). It was agreed at the meeting that the main priority of the ASEAN press was to promote and preserve political stability, rapid economic growth, social justice, and greater regional cohesion (Mehra, 1989).

Government officials' call for Asian models of journalism also echoed among journalists in Asia. For instance, at the 1987 Asian-Pacific Conference of the International Federation of Journalists held in Hong Kong, journalists proposed to build an Asian model of journalism in which the press worked with the government to build a national consensus. Under the assumption that Western-style press freedom and confrontation with authorities would conflict with traditional Asian cultural values, the press in developing countries should promote consensus and teamwork necessary for economic, cultural and political development of a nation (Asian Media Information and Communication Centre, 1988).

One of the most powerful and influential movements in de-Westernization efforts is the Asian Values debate, which was initiated in the 1970s. Being more widely shared and emphasized in Asia (Xu, 1998), values were believed to have contributed to the economic miracle achieved first in Japan, and then in Singapore, South Korea, Taiwan, and Hong Kong in the 1970s (Berger & Hsiao, 1988; Seah, 1977; Xu, 1998, 2005). Some Asian leaders like Lee Kuan Yew in Singapore and Mahathir Mohamad in Malaysia used Asian values to defend their own principles and practices in modernization, development, human rights, and democracy to safeguard against perceived threats to Asian cultural identities and diversities from the domination of Western cultures and values (Xu, 2005).

By the 1990s, Asian values were also used in journalism to advocate national stability, racial harmony, nation building, and national development as major national considerations to guide journalism practices in Asia (Xu, 2005). This has strongly supported the practice of development journalism in the region.

Although media practitioners and scholars were widely divided over Asian values and their existence in journalism, a consensus was reached regarding the need to identify certain universal values deeply rooted in the Asian context and to promote them in the professional sphere (Masterton, 1996). These values are truth, objectivity, social equity, and nonviolence. Although universal, these values have been prioritized in Asia when Asian countries confront the following issues: (a) market practices in conflict with journalistic integrity and professional standards, (b) interference by the boardroom in the newsroom, (c) lack of adequate dialogue and network mechanisms to allow journalist in Asian countries to exchange news and information independent of existing Western or government agencies, and (d) government interference in editorial functioning through various forms of censorship in the name of nation-building and national security (Masterton, 1996, p. 172).

All de-Westernization efforts pointed to upholding the journalistic values suitable for the Asian contexts and searching for Asian normative theories of the press. Such efforts have contextualized the emergence and growth of the development-oriented practice of journalism, i.e., development journalism.

SCHOOLS OF THOUGHT

In the early 1980s, there were largely only two major approaches within development journalism: investigative and authoritarian-benevolent (Kunczik, 1988). The investigative type focused on "critical questioning and evaluation of the usefulness of development projects" (Kunczik, 1988, p. 86). In covering the development newsbeat, journalists were expected to critically examine, evaluate and report (a) the relevance of a development project to national, and most importantly, to local needs; (b) the difference between a planned scheme and its actual implementation; and (c) the difference between its impact on people as claimed by government officials and as it was actually experienced by the people (Aggarwala, 1978, p. 200). The authoritarian-benevolent style of development journalism was strongly advocated by authoritarian governments who believed that journalism should cooperate with governments in nation-building and overall social, economic and political development.

Since the early 1980s, however, great social, economic and political changes have taken place in the world. Consequently, further changes also occurred in development journalism principles and practices. Reflecting these changes, Romano (2005) divided development journalism perspectives into the following five categories: (a) journalists as nation builders, (b) journalists as government partners, (c) journalists as agents of empowerment, (d) journalists as watchdogs, and (e) journalists as the guardians of transparency.

Journalists as Nation Builders: Strongly influenced by modernization theory, the nation-building approach advocates that news reporting should be aimed at maintaining social stability, building social harmony and strengthening national economy. It also holds that news reporting should be solution-oriented instead of sensational (see Ali, 1994).

Journalists as Government Partners: This perspective is closely related to the nation-building approach but differs from the former insofar as it holds that press freedom should be subjected to the overriding national interests of social, economic and political development priorities (Hatchten, 1999; Lent, 1979; McQuail, 1987; Romano, 2005). The two closely interrelated approaches are widely shared in much of Asia.

Journalists as Agents of Empowerment: This approach holds that journalism should empower the ordinary people, not the elite, to participate in public life and human development (Dagron, 2001; Shah, 1996, as cited in Romano, 2005).

Journalists as Watchdogs and Guardians of Transparency: The last two perspectives are also interrelated and difficult to separate from one another. They both advocate that journalism should monitor the performance of the government and make it as transparent as possible to the public. Without free press and other civil liberties, good governance and economic development will be undermined (Romano, 2005, p. 11).

As products of different perspectives and expectations in different environments and different periods of time, different approaches are actually interlinked vertically and horizontally by three major schools of thought: (1) Pro-Process, (2) Pro-Participation, and (3) Pro-Government.

According to Pro-Process thinking, journalism should support and contribute to the process of development, which is the name of the game in development journalism (Chalkley, 1980). And the process of economic development and nation building, whether it comes in the form of progress or problem, has to be told in simple language and in a humanizing fashion. Since development journalism is not meant for the elite but for the ordinary people, pictures and charts should be used in news stories (Chalkley, 1980). And what matters in development journalism is to facilitate and foster social, economic and cultural developments.

When scholars and journalists enthusiastically advocate development journalism, they focus on the ordinary people, not the elite. By and large, the term "ordinary people" refers to farmers, women, children, the elderly, the less fortunate, etc. It is these people who development journalists care most about. Moreover, these people determine the development journalists' choice of subjects, style of storytelling, and even diction. The whole point of development journalism is to engage and empower the people and to involve them actively in the process of economic, cultural and political development. The fundamental principles of the pro-process approach were actually adopted by Depthnews (McKay, 1993) as well as community or rural newspapers in Asia, Africa and Latin America (Edeani, 1993; Maslog, 1985; Verghese, 1976).

Pro-participation scholars or journalists would place more emphasis on participation of the ordinary people instead of stressing the number of people who actually receive assistance. They advocate that ordinary people should be empowered to participate in the process of development instead of being the passive recipients of development news.

Pro-participation recommendations have been made, too. For instance, Wilkins (2000) proposed that we need to situate the discourse and practice of development communication within contexts of power as the political, economic and cultural power of the lower-status segments of the population is severely lacking. Servaes (1999) suggested that power should be given to the ordinary people to allow them to participate in collective decisions at all levels of society. Melkote and Steves (2001) highlighted empowerment as a process in which individuals and organizations can control social, political, economic and cultural conditions and outcomes. Viewing development as the cultural and political acceptance of human rights, White (2004) argued that power should be viewed as a source of social responsibility and service, and that the rights of all in society should be respected. As mass media have not played an effective role in development journalism, Isiaka (2006) proposed a group media approach to development journalism practice by decentralizing and localizing broadcast media, narrow casting, and setting up radio groups, information centers, video/TV viewing centers, and cyber cafés to engage and empower rural populations.

The Pro-Government camp is dominant in terms of geographical spread as well as political and professional impact. Driven by de-Westernization efforts, the Pro-Government school emphasizes the constructive cooperation between the press and the government, the education role of the press in nation building and economic construction, and the responsible exercise of press freedom (Xu, 2005).

The press is expected to support government if governance is clean, good and effective in enhancing the well-being of citizens (Cheong, 1995; Latif, 1996). Further, the press ought to operate within the parameters of government policies, regulations and expectations for the sake of nation-building and economic development. When social stability, racial harmony, economic growth, and political stability are at stake, the relationship between the press and the government is expected to be co-operative rather than adversary (Xu, 2005), and the press is expected to operate "in close conformity with government regulations and expectations" (Kuo, 1999, p. 232).

Within the parameters of the government-press partnership, the role of the press is to promote and preserve political stability, rapid economic growth, social justice, and greater regional cohesion in ASEAN countries (Mehra, 1989). The press is also expected to facilitate nation building, partnership in national development, social harmony amid diversity, and cooperation among member states of South Asia Association for Regional Cooperation (SAARC).

The press in Asia is expected to play the role of "a catalyst of social and political change" rather than act as an adversarial institution (Shim, 1995). It should also avoid excessive criticism and defend cultural identity, preserve national unity, and enhance economic growth (Katoppo, 1995). Asian journalists are educators, rather than mere entertainers (Datta-Ray, 1995). In Asia, nation building is still "a critical process," which "unfortunately, not many Western journalists fully understand or appreciate." The role of the press in promoting nation building remains a priority in many Asian countries, which "colours Asian priorities and perceptions of journalistic values" (Menon, 1996, vii).

The catalytic role of the press in Asia does not necessarily mean that it becomes less critical of government. Criticism of government remains part of development journalism practice, although it tends to be more mild than wild. The fundamental role of the press is to "get involved in the process of interaction between farmers, workers, scientists, teachers, planners and decision-makers on the one hand and the government on the other, among various sections of society" (Bandyopadhyay, 1988, p. 40).

The role of the press in society advanced by the pro-government camp can be summarized as follows: (a) the advocacy of a co-operative role for the press in nation building and national development, (b) the role of the press as a catalyst for social and political change; and (c) the duty of the press to (i) educate instead of merely entertaining, (ii) maintain social stability and racial harmony, and (iii) aid in economic development and nation building. These roles are prioritized in Asia largely in line with (a) social structures, (b) political systems, (c) cultural sensitivity and traditions, (d) economic conditions, and (e) historical experiences in Asia (Xu, 2005, p. 53).

Another principle is the pro-government camp's notion of press freedom as relative and contingent. Press freedom should be promoted in light of different social structures, political systems, cultural values, historical backgrounds, and national conditions (Kuo, 1997; Latif, 1998; Menon, 1998; Mahathir, 1989; Mahbubani, 2002). The press should be more socially responsible when it exercises its freedom and more mindful of causes of events and consequences of news coverage (Xu, 2005).

KEY SCHOLARS AND STUDIES

Although limited in its literature, development journalism has its own key scholars and studies. Some provided their observations and insights of what development journalism was expected to be and do in various societies while others investigated what development journalism was and did.

As a passionate champion of development journalism, Alan Chalkley elaborated his notion and expectations of development journalism in *A Manual of Development Journalism* (1968) and "Development Journalism—A New Dimension in the Information Process" (1980). His publications are valuable in understanding the original concepts and expectations of development journalism.

Floyd J. McKay (1993) investigated the practice of development journalism in Depthnews through a content analysis of its news coverage. The results showed that "the original idea of development news survived" (p. 237) as indicated by its sustained focus on news about rural development, health, population, science and women; its reliance on non-institutional sources and subjects and its avoidance of direct government ties. However, in his examination of media and development issues in Asia, Guy de Fontgalland (1980, p. 156) concluded that "the overall record of Asian newspapers is dismal in its treatment of the very developmental issues surrounding it."

Angelo Romano (1999) offered observations and insights on development journalism in "Normative theories of development journalism: State versus practitioner perspectives in Indonesia," which contained the results of a survey of Indonesian journalists regarding their views on Indonesia's New Order Government (1966–1998). The results showed that "although the New Order attempted to establish a coherent press model, suited to local cultures and economic prerogatives, respondents conceived their role in markedly different terms" (p. 183).

In his pioneering study on the legitimacy of Asian-based development journalism, Kokkeong Wong (2004) opened up a new domain for research on development journalism. Looking into three major newspapers' coverage of the 1999 general elections in Malaysia, Wong found that the newspaper coverage of the election "could hardly be described fair and independent", thus "calling into question the legitimacy of Malaysia's Asian-based development journalism" (p. 37). Lacking in legitimacy, Wong argued, "development journalism could be dismissed as no more than a modern version of the traditional authoritarian approach of the feudal past" (pp. 37–38).

For African perspectives on development journalism, the article "Development Journalism in Black Africa" by Jerry Komia Domatob and Stephen William Hall (1983) is another must-read piece. These scholars observed that African notions of development journalism were largely grounded in the neo-colonial realities of modern Africa, that is, colonial domination, inequality and dependence. They also found that development journalism was "a relatively vague concept charged with political rhetoric" (p. 15) and that the press in Africa was largely elite-oriented with little relevance to the interests of the masses.

As one of the breakthroughs in development journalism studies, Hemant Shah's (1996) article "Modernization, Marginalization, and Emancipation: Toward a Normative Model of Journalism and National Development" represented one of the few torches that attempted to lead development journalism research out of the tunnel. In his article, Shah argued that efforts at reforming journalism practice ought to avoid being structured around Western notions of press freedom, which diverted attention from how journalism could contribute to participatory democracy, security, peace and other humanistic values. Therefore, the concept of "emancipation" and its related concept of "emancipatory journalism" should be used to replace that of development journalism. As "a localizing power," emancipatory journalism should be able to "help people establish local control over their immediate social conditions," "providing people immediately with resources to mount a challenge to the equations of power" (p. 160).

In another attempt, B. T. Isiaka (2006) proposed a paradigm shift in development journalism practices; from mass media to group media approaches. Group media approaches tend to be more effective than mass media approaches since they involve a more extensive use of audio-visual aids at meetings, seminars, workshops, demonstrations, exhibitions, discussions, visits etc. to harness groups for reception of vital information for development. Specifically, seven strategies were identified in highlighting the group media practices of development journalism: (a) decentralization and localization of broadcast media, (b) rural radio, (c) radio groups, (d) video/TV viewing centre, (e) cyber café, (f) information center, and (g) narrow casting.

PENDING ISSUES

Development journalism faces several pending issues that have hindered its further development, acceptance or recognition as a journalism practice and a branch of journalism studies. These issues have been neglected for quite a long time. The first pending issue lies in the prejudice against development journalism and its studies. Despite its four-decade-long practice across three continents, development journalism is not even listed in the volume *Key Concepts in Journalism Studies* (Franklin, Hamer, Hanna, Kinsey, & Richardson, 2005). As a matter of fact, development journalism and scholarship around it have long been belittled or neglected by the journalism research community. One indication can be found in the limited output of academic studies in the literature of journalism studies. In the past four decades, only 34 articles have been published in academic journals (see Table 25.1), which is totally out of proportion when compared to its four-decade-long practice on three continents.

Among the 34 research articles, one article was published in the 1960s, five in the 1970s, 11 in the 1980s, 14 in the 1990s, but only three since 2000. Some articles were devoted to the examination of what constitutes development news (e.g., McKay, 1993; Ogan, Fair, & Shah, 1984), while others focused on the quantity rather than quality of development news (e.g., Mustapha, 1979; Sutopo, 1983). Several papers examined conceptual issues, principles or functions of development journalism (e.g., Chalkley, 1980; Gunaratne, 1996; Isiaka, 2006; Romano, 1998, 1999; Romano & Hippocrates, 2001; Shah, 1996).

Early studies were based primarily on print media in Asia and Africa. Few studies were published on development journalism in Latin America. Electronic media and new media were

TABLE 25.1
Development Journalism Research Articles

Name of Journal (year of creation)	*60s*	*70s*	*80s*	*90s*	*Since 2000*	*Total*
Journal of Communication (1951)		1				1
(International Communication) Gazette (1955)		2	3	2	1	8
Journal of Development Communication (1990)				3	2	5
Asian Journal of Communication (1990)				1		1
Media Asia (1974)		2	5	1		8
AsiaPacific MediaEducator (1996)				1		1
Communication Theory (1991)				1		1
Journalism (and Mass Communication) Quarterly (1928)	1		3			4
World Communication (1971-2001)				1		1
Africa Media Review (1986)				2		2
Australian Journalism Review (1978)				2		2
Total	1	5	11	14	3	34

Note: Articles were generated (using development journalism as key word) on June 1, 2007, from "Communication & Mass Media Complete" database (covering all academic journals in the field) at Nanyang Technological University library in Singapore.

examined only in a small number of papers. Many studies have been conducted on the digital divide, but few of them have examined the impact of new media on development journalism. New media technologies can greatly facilitate the functions of development journalism in encouraging more participation from the ordinary people in the process of development and also in empowering them to have their voices and views heard and felt in an enlarging public sphere. Unfortunately, these areas have not been adequately examined.

Further neglected areas include cultural and political aspects of development, such as freedom from foreign cultural and political control and influence. Few studies have examined how, and to what extent, the press can support the process of developing a nation culturally and politically.

Another missing area examines how effective development journalism is in disseminating development news to ordinary people, empowering them to participate in the process of economic, cultural and political development. Also needed are studies that assess the different factors that shape how development journalism operates in different countries.

Furthermore, the gap between what is advocated and what is actually practiced in development journalism has not been adequately addressed. Little research has been done to locate different factors that work to narrow or widen this gap in different countries, as well as to explain how and why influential factors are differently prioritized in different situations.

MAJOR AREAS FOR FURTHER STUDIES

The first important area is to standardize conceptualization of fundamental components of development journalism and to build a set of theoretical constructs explaining different relationships and interactions among its components on the basis of its different practices in different cultures and countries.

Another major area to examine involves two sets of principles that influence the way development journalism operates in the case of most developing countries. The first set of principles are those that journalists uphold: (a) to focus on the ordinary rather than the elite, (b) to stay independent and free from government control, (c) to emphasize the process of local development, and (d) to engage and empower local people. The second set of principles are those that governments in developing or newly developed countries would use in regulating the press: (a) social stability and racial harmony, (b) regional/cultural/religious sensibilities, (c) nation building, and (d) national identity. How do these two sets of principles interact and interplay with each other? How can they be reconciled when compromises need to be made for the benefit of overall national development? What is the impact of that interaction or reconciliation between the two different sets of principles on society?

There is always a gap between what the press is expected to be and do in society, and what it actually is and does. This gap is vulnerable to changes in social, economic, cultural, and political conditions and situations. How do social, economic, cultural and political factors influence and shape the way development journalism is expected to operate and the way it actually operates? How should the narrowing or widening of the normative-empirical gap in practicing development journalism be measured and explained? And what models can be developed to describe, explain and predict the changing gap?

Another major area for further studies lies in the use of new media in development journalism to cater to the interests and needs of farmers, women, children, the elderly, the minorities, and other sectors of the population that have been marginalized by the traditional mass media. How can we take advantage of the new media to bridge the information divides between the haves and the have-nots?

As different priorities are assigned to different dimensions of development, and as countries develop at different levels in different contexts, further studies should take note of these different priorities. How effectively do different prioritizations guide development journalism practices, and what is their impact on the people?

As development has its economic, cultural and political dimensions, further research should cover these different dimensions instead of focusing on the economic aspects only. Development journalism is practiced differently in different countries. Journalism studies needs to explain the different practices and develop models to describe, explain and predict the way development journalism operates.

For further studies on development journalism, combinations of research methods instead of one single method should be employed to generate more comprehensive and reliable data for comparative examinations. While further country studies are urgently required to capture the latest developments and new phenomena, cross-medium and cross-country comparative studies are equally imperative.

REFERENCES

Abundo, R. (1986). Training population and development reporters: The PFA experience. *Populi, 13*(3), 17–23.

Aggarwala, N. K. (1978). News with Third World perspective: A practical suggestion. In P. C. Horton (Ed.), *The third world and press freedom* (pp. 197–209). New York: Preager.

Akahenda, E. F. (1983). The imperative of national unity and the concept of press freedom: The case of East Africa. *Gazette, 31,* 89–98.

Ali, O. A. (1994). Roundtable, *Media Asia, 21*(2), 90.

Ali, S. M. (1980). Notes on the changing role of the press in Asia's economic development. *Media Asia, 7*(3), 153–155.

Ali, S. M. (1990). Asian journalism in the 1990s: And the challenges ahead. *The Journal of Development Communication, 1*(2), 52–56.

Asian Media Information and Communication Centre. (1985). *AMIC-Thammasat University symposium on mass communication theory: The Asian perspective*. Singapore: Asian Media Information and Communication Centre.

Asian Media Information and Communication Centre. (1988). *AMIC consultation on press system in ASEAN*. Singapore: Asian Media Information and Communication Centre.

Bandyopadhyay, P. K. (1988). Values and concepts of news. *Journal of the Northwest Communication Association, 23*, 40–42.

Berger, P. L., & Hsiao, H. H. M. (Eds.). (1988). *In search of an East Asian development model*. New Brunswick, NJ: Transaction Books.

Chalkley, A. (1968). *A manual of development journalism*. Manila: Thomson Foundation and Press Foundation of Asia.

Chalkley, A. (1980). Development journalism—a new dimension in the information process. *Media Asia, 7*(4), 215–217.

Chen, L. (1991). The door opens to a thousand blossoms: A preliminary study of communication and rural development in China (1979–88). *Asian Journal of Communication, 1*(2), 103–121.

Cheong, Y. S. (1995). Speech excerpts. In Freedom Forum (Ed.), *Asian values and the role of media in society* (p. 6). Arlington, VA: The Freedom Forum.

Dagron, A. G. (2001). *Making waves: Stories of participatory communication for social change*, New York: Rockefeller Foundation.

Datta-Ray, S. K. (1995). Speech excerpts. In Freedom Forum (Ed.), *Asian values and the role of media in society* (pp. 12–13). Arlington, VA: The Freedom Forum.

Domatob, J. K., & Hall, S. W. (1983). Development journalism in black Africa. *Gazette, 31*, 9–33.

de Fontgalland, G. (1980). Asian media and development issues: From confrontation to cooperation. *Media Asia, 7*(3), 156–158.

Edeani, D. O. (1993). Role of development journalism in Nigeria's development. *Gazette, 52*, 123–143

Edelstein, A. S. (1982). *Comparative communication research*. Sage: Beverly Hills, CA:.

Fang, G. (1983). The role of China's rural publications in the development of agriculture. *Media Asia, 10*(4), 183–185.

Franklin, B., Hamer, M., Hanna, M. Kinsey, M., & Richardson, J. (Eds.). (2005). *Key concepts in journalism studies*. London: Sage.

Galtung, J. A. (1971). Structural theory of imperialism. *Journal of Peace Research, 8*, 81–118.

Gunaratne, S. A. (1996). Old wine in a new bottle: Public journalism versus developmental journalism in the US. *AsiaPacific Media Educator, 1*(1), 64–75.

Hatchten, W. A. (1999). *The world news prism* (5th ed.). Ames: Iowa State University Press.

Hornik, R. (1988). *Development communication: Information, agriculture and nutrition in the third world*. New York: Longman.

Isiaka, B. T. (2006). Paradigm shift in development journalism practices for effective dissemination of agricultural information. *The Journal of Development Communication, 17*(1), 56–71.

Katoppo, A. (1995). Speech excerpts. In Freedom Forum (Ed.), *Asian values and the role of media in society* (pp. 6–7). Arlington, VA: The Freedom Forum.

Kunczik, M. (1988). *Concepts of journalism: North and South*. Bonn: Friedrich-Ebert-Stiftung.

Kuo, E. C. Y. (1997). Viewpoints and comments. *The Mass Media and Press Freedom International Symposium*, Taipei.

Kuo, E. C. Y. (1999). The role of the media in the management of ethnic relations in Singapore. In A. Goonasekera & Y. Ito (Eds.), *Mass media and cultural identity: Ethnic reporting in Asia* (pp. 223–255). Sterling, VA: Pluto Press.

Latif, A. (1996). Asian values in journalism: Idle concept or realistic goal? In M. Masterton (Ed.), *Asian values in journalism* (pp. 152–157). Singapore: Asian Media Information and Communication Centre.

Latif, A. (1998). The press in Asia: Taking a stand. In A. Latif (Ed.), *Walking the tightrope: Press freedom and professional standards in Asia* (pp. 3–15). Singapore: Asian Media Information and Communication Centre.

Lent, J. A. (1979). *Topics in third world mass communication: Rural and development journalism, cultural imperialism, research and developments.* Hong Kong: Asian Research Service.

Lerner, D., & Schramm, W. (Eds.). (1967). *Communication and change in the developing world.* Honolulu: East-West Center Press.

Mahathir, M. (1989). The social responsibility of the press. In A. Mehra (Ed.), *Press system in ASEAN states* (pp. 115–116). Singapore: Asian Media Information and Communication Centre.

Mahbubani, K. (2002). *Can Asians think?* (2nd ed.). Singapore: Times Books International.

Maslog, C. C. (1985). Case studies of four successful Asian community newspapers. *Media Asia, 12*(3), 123–130.

Masterton, M. (Ed.). (1996). *Asian values in journalism.* Singapore: Asian Media Information and Communication Centre.

McKay, F. J. (1993). Development journalism in an Asian setting: A study of Depthnews. *Gazette, 51*, 237–251.

McQuail, D. (1987). Mass communication theory: An introduction (2nd ed.). London: Sage.

Mehra, A. (1989). *Press system in ASEAN states.* Singapore: Asian Media Information and Communication Centre.

Melkote, S. R., & Steves, H. L. (2001). *Communication for development in the Third World: Theory and practice for empowerment.* London: Sage.

Menon, V. (1988). Welcome Address. In *AMIC consultation on press system in ASEAN.* Singapore: Asian Media Information and Communication Centre.

Menon, V. (1996). Preface. In M. Masterton (Ed.), *Asian values in journalism* (pp. vii–ix). Singapore: Asian Media Information and Communication Centre.

Menon, V. (1998). Foreword. In A. Latif (Ed.), *Walking the tightrope: Press freedom and professional standards in Asia* (p. ix). Singapore: Asian Media Information and Communication Centre.

Mustapha, H. D. (1979). A comparative analysis of the use of development news in three Malaysian dailies during 1974. In J. Lent & J. Vilanilam (Eds.), *The use of development news* (pp. 56–70). Singapore: Asian Media Information and Communication Centre.

Murthy, D. V. R. (2000). Developmental news coverage in the Indian press. *Media Asia, 27*(1), 24–29, 53.

Mwaffisi, S. (1991). Development Journalism: How prepared are Tanzanian journalists? *Africa Media Review, 5*(2), 85–94.

Ogan, C. L. (1982). Development journalism/communication: The status of the concept. *Gazette, 29*(1-2): 3–13.

Ogan, C. L., Fair, J. E., & Shah, H. (1984). A little good news: The treatment of development news in selected third world newspapers. *Gazette, 33*, 173–191.

Pye, L. W. (Ed.). (1963). *Communication and political development.* Princeton, NJ: Princeton University Press.

Richstad, J. (2000). Asian journalism in the twentieth century. *Journalism Studies, 1*(2), 273–284.

Rogers, E. M. (1962). *Diffusion of innovations.* New York: Free Press.

Rogers, E. M. (1976). Communication and development: The passing of the paradigm. *Communication Research, 3*, 121–133.

Romano, A. (1998). Normative theories of development journalism: State versus practitioner perspectives in Indonesia. *Australian Journalism Review, 20*(2), 60–87.

Romano, A. (1999). Development journalism: State versus practitioner's perspectives in Indonesia. *Media Asia, 26*(4), 183–191.

Romano, A. (2005). Asian journalism: News, development and the tides of liberation and technology. In A. Romano & M. Bromley (Eds.), *Journalism and democracy in Asia* (pp. 1–14). London: Routledge.

Romano, A., & Hippocrates, C. (2001). Putting the public back into journalism. In S. Tapasall & C. Varley (Eds.), *Journalism theories in practice* (pp. 166–184). Melbourne: Oxford University Press.

Schiller, H. I. (1976). *Communication and cultural domination.* New York: International Arts and Sciences Press.

Schramm, W. (1964). *Mass media and national development: The role of information in the developing nations*. Stanford, CA: Stanford University Press.

Seah, C. M. (Ed.). (1977). *Asian values & modernization*. Singapore: Singapore University Press.

Servaes, J. (1999). *Communication for development: One world, multiple cultures*. Cresskill, NJ: Hampton Press.

Shafer, R. (1991). *Journalists for change: Development communication for a free press*. Manila: Philippine Press Institute.

Shafer, R. (1998). Comparing development journalism and public journalism as interventionalist press models. *Asian Journal of Communication, 8*(1), 31–52.

Shah, H. (1989). A preliminary examination of journalistic roles and development reporting at three Indian newspapers. *Media Asia, 16*(3), 128–131.

Shah, H. (1992). Development news: Its potential and limitations in the rural United States. *The Journal of Development Communication, 3*, 9–15.

Shah, H. (1996). Modernization, marginalization, and emancipation: Toward a normative model of journalism and national development, *Communication Theory, 6*(2), 143–166.

Shim, J. H. (1995). Speech excerpts. In Freedom Forum (Ed.), *Asian values and the role of media in society* (p. 5). Arlington, VA: The Freedom Forum.

Stevenson, R. L. (1994). *Global communication in the twenty-first century*. New York: Longman.

Sutopo, I. (1983). *Development news in Indonesia dailies*. Singapore: Asian Media Information and Communication Centre.

Verghese, B. G. (1976). Project Chhatera—an experiment in development journalism. *Media Asia, 3*(1), 5–11.

Vilanilam, J. V. (1975). Developmental news in two leading Indian newspapers. *Media Asia, 2*(1), 37–40.

Vilanilam, J. V. (1984). Rural press for development. *Media Asia, 11*(4), 183–187.

White, R. A. (2004). Is "empowerment" the answer*? Gazette, 66* (1), 7–24.

Wilkins, K. G. (Ed.). (2000). *Redeveloping communication for social change: Theory, practice and power*. Lanham, MD: Rowman and Littlefield.

Wong, K. (2004). Asian-based development journalism and political elections: Press coverage of the 1999 general elections in Malaysia. *Gazette, 66*(1), 25–40.

Wu, Y. (1987). Rural development leads to a press boom. *Media Asia, 14*(2), 63–66.

Xu, X. (1998). Asian values revisited in the context of intercultural news communication. *Media Asia, 25*(1), 37–41.

Xu, X. (2005). *Demystifying Asian values in journalism*. Singapore: Marshall Cavendish Academic.

Zhou, L. (1992). Education in development journalism and communication: Asia Pacific cooperation and China scenario. *The Journal of Development Communication, 3*(1), 74–81.

26

Advocacy Journalism in a Global Context

Silvio Waisbord

INTRODUCTION

This chapter reviews historical and contemporary advocacy journalism in a global context, and identifies future directions for research. The intention is not to offer a comprehensive survey, a rather ambitious scope given the diversity of journalistic practices worldwide, but rather to review conceptual definitions and historical developments to locate advocacy journalism as a specific form of journalistic practice.

According to Morris Janowitz (1975), advocacy journalism assigns journalists the role of active interpreters and participants who "speak on behalf" of certain groups, typically those groups who are denied "powerful spokesmen" (p. 619) in the media. Journalists are representatives for specific interests, and are motivated by the desire to redress power imbalances in society. They are guided by a "reformist impulse" to promote perspectives that are typically under or misrepresented in the media. Advocacy journalism is the opposite of the "gatekeeper" model, the notion of professional journalism guided by the ideals of objectivity and public service (also see Emery, 1972; Johnstone, Slawski, & Bowman, 1972–1973).

Here I present the argument that contemporary advocacy journalism is not limited to Janowitz's concept of the "advocate-journalist." Another form is the civic model of advocacy journalism. It refers to organized groups that use the news media to influence reporting, and ultimately, affect public policies. It belongs to forms of political mobilization that "seek to increase the power of people and groups and to make institutions more responsive to human needs." It attempts "to enlarge the range of choices that people have by increasing their power to define problems and solutions and participate in the broader social and policy arena" (Wallack, Dorfman, Jernigan, & Themba, 1993, p. 28). Through advocacy journalism, civic organizations aim to raise awareness, generate public debate, influence public opinion and key decision makers, and promote policy and programmatic changes around specific issues.

This chapter explores similarities and differences between the "journalist" and the "civic" model of advocacy journalism, and discusses their significance for journalism and democracy.

ADVOCACY JOURNALISM IN HISTORICAL PERSPECTIVE

Ever since someone decided to launch a publication to disseminate personal views, the "journalist" model of advocacy has been historically an integral part of the press. One could argue that until the ascendancy of ideals of objectivity and "professional reporting," journalism was largely "advocacy journalism," a propaganda tool for political organizations, a platform for press entrepreneurs with political ambitions, a path for political activism for reporters. This kind of reporting is what Max Weber described in his *Politics as Vocation*, when he observed that journalism "remains under all circumstances one of the most important avenues of professional political activity" (in Gerth & Mills, 1946, p. 98). Weber's statement remains as applicable to journalism around the globe as it was in early twentieth-century Germany. It is the kind of journalism that Janowitz and other defenders of the "professional" model of reporting criticize for undermining the prospects for the press to serve "the public interest" in a democracy.

Advocacy journalism evolved through different paths on both sides of the Atlantic. Reasons are found in the different evolution of press systems and journalistic ideals. In established European democracies, advocacy journalism traditionally found room in newspapers and publications that openly embraced partisan positions particularly in pluralist and corporatist media systems (Hallin & Mancini, 2004). Its evolution has been inseparable from the communication history of political parties. Because parties have historically held noticeable influence on the press, partisan viewpoints were often inseparable from news reporting. Editorial standings impregnated news coverage and the overall treatment of information. The structural linkages between parties and the press coupled with the existence of strong partisan identities in society at large underpinned the affirmation of journalistic identity strongly tied to partisan views. Across European democracies, journalists typically approached news reporting as a way to get politically involved, and to promote viewpoints generally associated with political parties.

In recent decades, the ascendancy of market forces in media systems coupled with the weakening of partisan identities has weakened the historical grip of parties on political communication. Although this process has happened across the region with different intensity and at different pace, political parties do not wield the same media power they once had. Studies, however, have found that the notion of advocacy remains a desirable journalistic ideal among European journalists (Patterson & Donsbach, 1996; Köcher, 1986). Notwithstanding the gradual loosening of party-media connections, the notion of the "journalist as advocate" continues to capture the professional imagination of journalism (Hallin & Mancini, 2004).

In the United States, the historical trajectory of advocacy journalism has been quite different. Between the mid-1800s and 1920s, the gradual demise of the partisan press and the concomitant rise of the commercial press set different conditions for advocacy journalism. The adoption of objectivity as the normative ideal of professional reporting displaced advocacy journalism to the margins of the press system. Unlike in European democracies, advocacy journalism was not strongly linked to organized parties. This was a byproduct of the perennial communication weakness of the two dominant political parties, and the untrammeled power of the market. Instead, advocacy journalism has been historically associated with nineteenth-century movements that promoted women's voting, abolitionism, and workers' rights (Ostertag, 2006), and turn-of-the-century muckrakers who criticized political corruption and business practices. They unabashedly fused facts and politics, and championed the idea of the journalist as social advocate. Advocacy journalism remained marginal throughout the twentieth century as mainstream media organizations embraced the notion of objectivity, and neither major political party maintained organic relations with large media organizations. The most influential newspapers largely restricted advocacy journalism to editorials and op-ed pages. Alternative publications remained the flag-carriers of advocacy journalism such as the publications of anti-war, feminist, gay, environmental, and ethnic rights movements, particularly during the 1960s and 1970s. They broadly expressed the political views of a disparate array of social movements, opinion groups and activists-turned-publishers.

Advocacy journalism historically found a more receptive environment in Western Europe than in the United States. In the latter, the adoption of the ideal of objectivity as the preeminent journalistic norm functioned as a bulwark against alternative views including the notion of "journalists as advocates." Even today, a professional imaginary strongly attached to notions of objectivity and political detachment (Schudson, 2001) continues to be the reference point to assess the merits of advocacy journalism. In Western Europe, instead, the lack of consensus around journalistic norms coupled with the stronger grip that political parties historically had on national political communication offered propitious conditions for advocacy journalism.

Because advocacy journalism historically has had a different presence in the mainstream press in the United States and Western Europe, questions about the desirability of advocacy journalism for public life and democratic rule received different answers. While advocacy journalism has found supporters among European publishers and journalists, it has been vigorously criticized by the mainstream US press. In the United States, publishers and journalists' associations have remained strongly opposed to any alternatives to the ideal of objectivity and political detachment. In the early 1970s, for example, debates in newsrooms and academia about journalistic norms showed the reluctance of editors and academics to admit advocacy journalism into the newsroom. Leftist analysts argued that objectivity is not feasible when political-economic interests influence news coverage, questioned its appropriateness to produce comprehensive and critical news reports of powerful interests, and considered it as a mere discursive justification for professional legitimacy (Bagdikian, 1973). They considered that the norm of "objectivity" effectively functioned as a subterfuge for advocacy for *status quo* policies and ideologies. In contrast, scholars and practitioners who championed objectivity firmly believed that the latter was the best alternative to fend off advocacy journalism. For them, the latter was undistinguishable from propaganda, which they identified as contradictory with the essential values of the democratic press such as fairness and truth-telling. Furthermore, they found advocacy journalism problematic in a context of agitated politics and growing political distrust during the Vietnam war and Watergate scandal. Janowitz (1975) argued that advocacy journalism fueled distrust of authority and undermined the professional status of journalism. Similar arguments were expressed during the recent controversy about civic journalism. While its defenders called journalists to act as facilitators of community dialogue, critics considered that civic journalism mistakenly assigned journalists the role of community advocates (McDevitt, 2003; Ryan, 2001).

Despite the opposition by defenders of the canon of US journalism, advocacy journalism has recently found a home in the mainstream media, as expressed in the strident conservative views of Fox News, the outspoken partisan positions of cable news anchors and commentators, and the editorializing of news content in some tabloids. Journalists and news organizations with right-wing sympathies, rather than progressive reporters as Janowitz and other press scholars feared in the 1970s, have sneaked advocacy journalism into the corporate press. Unlike the advocacy journalism practiced by the alternative press, advocate-journalists are ubiquitous in news organizations that do not challenge basic premises of the current political-economic system, but unequivocally champion some of its central ideological underpinnings. In summary, advocacy journalism remains visible in mainstream news organizations with clear right-wing editorial sympathies, as well as in progressive publications that continue the tradition of alternative and radical news.

ADVOCACY JOURNALISM IN THE GLOBAL SOUTH

Outside the West, the trajectory of advocacy journalism broadly resembles the European more than the US experience. In countries with weak democratic history, the notion that the press should champion specific political standpoints has been widespread. In some cases, advocacy journalism expressed the views of official parties, much along the lines of classic big party machines in Western democracies. In other cases, advocacy journalism reflected the views of individual publishers and journalists allied with specific governments and other political interests.

Reasons for the persistence of the "journalist" model of advocacy journalism are found in the political economy of the press. As long as governments and politicians continue to wield substantial power on press economies, news organizations are likely to act as vehicles for promoting their political interests. This basic arrangement remains largely unchanged even when globalization and market forces have refashioned media systems in the past decades. Government and personal funds are still the lifeblood of media finances in many countries across the globe. Access to government monies, party coffers, and individual fortunes are crucial to maintain news organizations running. Often, the weakness of market and public funding concedes tremendous power to government officials, politicians, and large business to affect news coverage. In such situations, it is unthinkable that journalism is anything *but* advocacy journalism. Buffering mechanisms that could temper the influence of editorial politics on newsrooms are weak, if not completely absent. The need to maintain a wall between "the church" and "the state" in newsrooms is simply impracticable when publishers conceive news organizations as instruments for promoting politics and are economically dependent on political favors.

The fact that governments and political financiers continue to wield power in press finances coupled with the inclination of governments to bulldoze any signs of press independence continues to favor advocacy journalism. As understood in the tradition of the Anglo-American press, a cornerstone of the ideal of professional journalism is that considerations such as newsworthiness, fairness, audience interest, and public service should trump personal politics. Professional ideals do not eliminate, but rather, restrain personal sympathies; they are the safeguard against the intrusion of "the personal" into news. Pure professional considerations should determine the news value of information, news-gathering methods, news frames, the selection of sources, and so on. In the global South, however, observing such principles in actual practice has been generally difficult. The combined pressures of publishers and owners who conceive news organizations as "house organs" and political and business interests shaping content through subtle and open mechanisms frequently cut off the oxygen of professionalism.

Despite signs of increased professionalization, a disjuncture between ideals and practice persists. As long as basic political-economic conditions are missing, keeping reporting above the political fray is not feasible. Back in the heyday of authoritarian and totalitarian rule, news organizations and reporters had to follow the official party line or stand in the opposition and suffer persecution. Keeping reporting and politics at a safe distance was elusive when expectations dictated that newsrooms had to dance to the official tune. Norms to standardize professional practice were unnecessary when control was imposed "from above" through direct ownership, official censorship, and blunt repression.

The collapse of military dictatorships and one-party regimes opened opportunities to redefine journalistic norms. The recent literature on journalistic norms shows that professional identities and roles are in transition in Asia, Africa, and the Americas (Donsbach & Klett, 1993; Gross, 2003; Hanitzsch, 2005; Hasty, 2005; Hughes, 2006; Nyamnjoh, 2005; Pan & Chan, 2003; Ramaprasad, 2001; Ramaprasad & Hamdy, 2006; Rampal, 1996; Richstad, 2000; Sakr, 2006). Consensus on journalism norms is still lacking. Neither objectivity nor partisanism holds a tight grip. Just as objectivity remains a troubling and contested norm, old-fashioned advocacy journalism is constrained by editorial politics (Mano, 2005; Mwesige, 2004; Waisbord, 2000). Reporters remain skeptical about the applicability of objectivity as well as the notion of "journalists as social mobilizers." More than impartial reporters of reality or passionate political advocates, journalists often perform balancing acts between personal politics and newsroom *Realpolitik*, clutching to professional principles and observing editorial expectations. When the norm of impartiality does not command strong allegiances among journalists nor is expected enforced in daily practice, advocacy journalism has fewer restrictions.

THE GLOBAL RISE OF CIVIC ADVOCACY JOURNALISM

Neither in the North nor in the global South is contemporary advocacy journalism limited to the "journalist" model. The recent growth of the "civic" model of advocacy journalism has been significant. Unlike the "journalist" model which expresses the political interests of journalists, the "civic" model represents advocacy efforts by civic groups that promote social change. Through advocacy journalism, groups that traditionally have had limited access to the news media aim to raise awareness and provide information, and affect public opinion and policy debates. Civic advocacy journalism is driven by the notion that the news media should be a tool of social change. Because the press contributes to both raising awareness among the public and setting policy priorities and agendas, civic actors aim to shape news coverage. They approach journalism as another mobilization strategy to affect the definition of "public problems" (Gusfield, 1981; Hilgartner & Bosk, 1988). Civic advocacy is the product of a growing consciousness among civic groups about the importance of the media in the construction of public problems, and the need to approach the press as a tactical ally.

Civic advocacy journalism is associated with the recent professionalization of media tactics of social movements and interest groups. Until recently, it has been limited to liberal democracies in the North where assorted social movements and interest groups have consciously tried to affect news coverage on health issues (Morgen, 2002; Wallack et al., 1993), tobacco control (Petrschuk, 2001), environmental policies (Vliegenthart, Oegema, & Klandermans, 2005), and policies against domestic violence (Berns, 2005). Lately, similar movements have also gained strength across the global South. From environmental to land rights movements, there is no shortage of organizations that have utilized advocacy journalism to promote their goals.

How to explain this phenomenon? Civic advocacy journalism reflects remarkable changes in the overall political and media environment in vast regions in the global South. First, the collapse of military authoritarianism and one-party regimes has paved the way for the intensification of civic mobilization in political contexts with, at best, weak traditions of democratic rule. In new democracies, the crisis of modern political ideologies has given way to the emergence of civic movements whose demands and identities fall outside traditional political divisions. Social mobilization around health, the environment, domestic violence, immigration, global poverty, and children's rights hardly fit in conventional ideological and partisan packages. Old dividing lines that characterized national politics and articulated identities are insufficient to capture multiple concerns that articulate civic mobilization. Distinctions between conservatives and liberals, capital and labor, or urban and rural interests that have historically defined the basis for political mobilization and identity, do not capture the multiplicity of issues that spark civic actions.

Second, the move to democracy brought new conditions for journalistic practice. Doubtlessly, conditions vary among news organizations, and from country to country. From the pressures of business and government to statelessness (Waisbord, 2007a), journalists continue to face numerous obstacles. News organizations, particularly if critical of dominant political and economic powers, face enormous obstacles. The end of formal state censorship and the climate of repression, however, facilitated a gradual opening to different perspectives in news reporting, including civic organizations that had been disregarded or actively suppressed. The combination of new forms of public mobilization coupled with the improvement of the conditions for journalism have ushered a context that is more conducive for civic organizations to shape news coverage.

Recent media changes have also facilitated civic advocacy journalism. Because media economics and systems are different across countries, this process has happened at a different pace. The expansion of cable and satellite radio and television, the consolidation of specialized sections (e.g., science, health, food, environment, education) in both print and broadcast news; the popularity of news and talk-shows, the growth of "niche" publications, and the emergence of endless news sites on the Internet have contributed to the multiplication of media offerings. In turn, the increase in the volume of news has opened new opportunities for civic advocacy.

These changes resulted from the combination of legal changes, technological innovations, and economic calculations. First, the combination of privatization, deregulation, and technological changes has enlarged the number of news outlets. In most of the global South, the news media landscape is considerably different in countries where governments had historically controlled news mainly through direct media ownership or direct censorship. Today's media systems are dotted with a variety of commercial, religious, semi-public, and community radio and television stations with a diversity of agendas and interests. Second, a wide variety of innovations in information technologies have also contributed to the multiplication of media offerings as represented by cable and satellite television stations and Internet Web sites. New information technologies offer novel avenues for advocacy and social activism (Bennett, 2003). Third, the process of news segmentation has resulted in the opening of "niche" news directed to specific audiences. Although profit-seeking, rather than a commitment to social justice, has been driving this process forward, it has opened opportunities for civic advocacy journalism by creating platforms for news coverage on issues related to social justice.

These processes have mixed consequences for media democratization. On the one hand, the unbridled power of business interests and the absence of strong countervailing forces raise concerns about whether recent changes are leveling opportunities for public expression or, instead, are tilting the balance further in favor of the powerful. On the other hand, the multiplication of news outlets, particularly in countries with a long tradition of government media monopolies and manipulation of news content, offer justifiable reasons for moderate optimism. Today's media landscape may not be a "brave new world" of unrestricted speech and equal opportunities, but it is important to recognize the innovations brought about by the explosion of news platforms, particularly in countries where "the news" had been, basically, government propaganda through public and privately-owned media. What matters for advocacy journalism is that a wide set of transformations in media systems have made it possible for civic movements to influence news content, and reach different publics.

THE PRACTICE OF CIVIC ADVOCACY JOURNALISM

Two questions need to be considered to examine civic advocacy journalism. One set of questions are related to how civic organizations aim to affect news coverage. Another set of questions deal with the impact of such efforts in expanding the range of voices and opinions reported. This section delves into the first issue; the next section examines the impact of civic advocacy.

Civic organizations are often in a disadvantageous position for "getting in the news." Because they are not official sources, they have neither newsmaking clout nor easy access to newsrooms. Unlike government sources, they lack "definitional power" (Schlesinger & Tumber, 1994). Because they are not well-heeled businesses, they lack the resources to hire public relations firms to secure favorable and continuous news coverage. Because many organizations are concerned with social issues that either are not covered regularly or have only been recently included in news beats, they often find it difficult to make news. Because they often challenge powerful political and economic actors, they are likely to confront timid newsrooms, and at times, outright opposition.

The predicament of civic organizations as both "news sources" and "news subjects" has long been a concern among social movements promoting social change. Whether the media are allies or obstacles for social movements has been a perennial point of debate. Protest movements traditionally either interacted cautiously or simply refuse to engage with mainstream news organizations. Asymmetrical power relations and the political agenda of the corporate media explain why news coverage typically offers a warped view of oppositional movements. Such concerns have not disappeared (Carroll & Ratner, 1999; Downing, 2005; Smith, 2001). In fact, they have inspired the explosion of alternative news and the ongoing democratic media movement (Hackett 2000) to develop alternatives to corporate news. Such decisions follow a tradition of oppositional movements who, facing silence or prejudice from mainstream news, prioritized strengthening their own means of expression for advocacy. They embrace the notion that the alternative press has a preeminent role through voicing concerns, debating ideas, building identity, and mobilizing publics.

In the context of this tradition, civic advocacy journalism signals a different sensibility among organizations engaged in social change. It reflects the realization that media publicity is central to advance political causes in an age of "mediated" politics. It expresses the decision to approach the mainstream media as a potential "strategic ally" in the struggle to promote changes, and the realization that communication strategies need to integrate conventional news biases. Unlike oppositional movements that radically question the prevailing order, civic advocacy groups pragmatically engage with the mainstream media, mainly, because they value the reach and influence of the media to affect specific actors (e.g., decision makers, funders) and society at large (Cullinan, 2003). Instead of focusing exclusively on their own media, they work through a variety of news outlets. Rather than opposing the mainstream media, they deal with them in their own terms.

At a time when public relations are responsible for producing a substantial portion of daily news, civic organizations have adopted public relations principles in the service of social change (Bennett & Lawrence, 1995). They hold news conferences, issue press releases particularly around established "news hooks," stage "media events" featuring political and entertainment celebrities, take advantage of standard "news events" (e.g., accidents, official announcements, natural disasters) and "media panics," and line up experts to provide assessments and news facts. The media repertoire of civic advocacy journalism is not limited to standard public relations practices. Straddling the traditions of news management orthodoxy and radical politics, it combines news management with savvy street theater. From protest movements, it borrows rallies, sit-ins, parades, and other forms of public theater (e.g., dramatic representations, music shows) to attract media coverage. Some social movements, most notably AIDS and environmental groups (Anderson, 1997; Smith, 2000), have incorporated street theater into sophisticated forms of media management. This includes the orchestration of stunts and dramatic visuals intended to disrupt or hijack official events such as G8 summits and meetings of international financial organizations. Such actions are examples of communication jujitsu as they use media attention focused on official events for their own purposes. These media strategies are often identified with the activities of Greenpeace (Dale, 1996) and ACT UP (Gould, 2002; Gross, 2001) that have influenced, respectively, the advocacy repertoire of environmental movements opposing whale-hunting, nuclear plants, and deforestation (Anderson 2003), and the Treatment Action Campaign and the Sexual Rights Campaign in South Africa (Msimang, 2003).

While aiming to promote social changes, civic advocacy journalism strictly adheres to standard reporting practices and codes. Rather than pushing to revolutionize journalism, it follows conventional news routines and norms to raise media attention. The "institutionalization" of media advocacy (Gillett, 2003) among mobilized publics reflects the acceptance of established news-gathering routines and news conventions such as dramatic, conflict-driven, sensationalist, event-centered, and celebrity news. Such characteristics of media coverage have increasingly become widespread in newsrooms across the South (Natarajan & Hao, 2003; Ryfe, 2006; Tomaselli, 1996). Because "what is news" seems to be increasingly similar despite political, economic and cultural differences, strategies are similar across the globe. Civic advocacy journalism hardly represents a breakthrough in newsmaking; it is rather a conservative approach with a dash of creativity to news management that capitalizes on the biases of contemporary journalism to further social justice goals.

BRINGING NEW VOICES IN

What is the impact of civic advocacy journalism on news coverage? Although it regularly observes conventional news-gathering and production routines, civic advocacy journalism contributes to widening news coverage by spotlighting issues and featuring voices that are typically ignored in the mainstream media. In doing so, it makes positive contributions to democratic debate. It neither aims to overthrow the current news order nor opt out to set up independent media. Instead, it introduces important innovations by bringing the voices of actors who are typically excluded or misrepresented, challenging powerful sources, and offering alternative news frames (Benford & Snow, 2000).

Consider the case of health news and HIV/AIDS reporting. Across the global South, Ministries of Health and other government agencies typically have the upper hand in news management through making information available, promoting policies and initiatives, and so on. As it has been observed in news reporting of HIV/AIDS in the North, particularly in earlier phases of the epidemic (Colby & Cook, 1991; Lupton, 1994; Peterson, 1998), the news media in the South also largely relies on government information for health reporting. When official sources wield unmatched power in setting news agendas and content, government positions on specific health and other social issues are extremely important for news coverage. Because public agencies are often the "primary definers" of news narratives, they set the news frames in ways that determine, for example, whether health issues are presented as matters of public health, moral breakdown, protection of human rights, or national security. This explains why when government officials are divided on a given subject, reporters can tap into sources with different positions, and thus, produce news featuring different views. News coverage of tobacco control in several countries shows that differences inside governments facilitated critical coverage of tobacco consumption and manufacturers (Durrant, Wakefield, McLeod, Clegg-Smith, & Chapman 2003; Pertschuk, 2001). In contrast, when officials close ranks around a certain issue, then, it becomes exceedingly difficult for reporters to find sources willing to provide different testimonies.

As the strength of local groups promoting or opposing specific causes and policies varies from country to country so, too, the content of advocacy journalism. When publics mobilize around specific issues, such as HIV/AIDS or reproductive rights, it is more likely that the news media can tap into alternative sources of information. In contrast, weak local mobilization reduces the chances for civic advocacy to bring in other voices. Around the world, activists' groups have achieved important goals through advocacy journalism. The mobilization of people living with HIV/AIDS across countries is perhaps one of the best illustrations of this process. It has forced the news media to pay serious attention to a broad set of issues including government policies, treatment costs, and prevention programs. This has been particularly noticeable in countries where governments lacked adequate policies to provide preventive and care services, or simply, suppressed information. HIV/AIDS activists have offered counter opinions to governments that denied the existence of HIV in Malawi, South Africa, and Zimbabwe (Robins, 2004; Stein, 2002; Traquina, 2004). Also, HIV/AIDS activism has put pressure on news organizations to scrutinize the functioning of government programs in South Africa (Butler, 2005). In Uganda, criticism of government management of anti-retroviral drugs has contributed to raising media attention about the distribution of expired drugs for treatment (Diop, 2000). In many countries, activist groups have also contributed to shifting public discourse about disease and health by framing key issues (e.g., access to treatment, anti-discrimination actions, biomedical research) as a matter of human rights (Schoepf, 2004). By using the language of international human rights, they have made significant inroads in a matter of social justice that had been dominated by medical and business discourses.

Likewise, grassroots movements have helped to put women's health in the media agenda across the globe. Without their efforts to reach out to journalists, it is difficult to imagine that the media would have put the spotlight on issues such as reproductive health and female genital cutting in countries where such issues are politically sensitive and women largely disempowered. Women's movements have offered alternatives to medical and individualistic frames used by governments and health experts. News reports have featured reproductive health organizations and feminist activists who criticize official views on abortion and family planning and HIV prevention methods (Brookman-Amissah & Moyo, 2004). By emphasizing environmental factors and gender inequalities, breast cancer groups have politicized issues that had remained limited to the "apolitical" sphere of medical expertise and framed in terms of individual responsibility (Kolker, 2004). Women's groups have also contributed to reframing news coverage of domestic battering that prioritized individualistic narratives (Silveirinha, 2007). Reframing issues and news has also been a key concern for movements working on gender-based violence. Rights-based discourse is central to their efforts to raise awareness about different forms of violence against women and girls (e.g., female genital mutilation, custodial rape, "dowry deaths," early marriage).

WHERE CIVIC AND JOURNALIST ADVOCACY MEET

The global ascendancy of civic advocacy journalism throws into sharp relief questions about professional norms and identity, and the position of journalism vis-à-vis movements promoting social justice. How do journalists balance personal commitment with newsroom constraints? Do reporters refrain from infusing stories with personal positions? If not, how do they put personal politics in everyday reporting? What discursive frames are used to negotiate personal and organizational politics? How do journalists deal with the "whats" and the "whys" of social justice? How do they negotiate with governments and advocacy groups the selection of news frames for different stories?

These questions need to be addressed by placing both journalist and civic advocacy within specific contexts of journalistic practice. In countries where the ideal of objectivity remains prevalent, responses may fall into established, normative arguments about the role of journalism in society. Those who defend objectivity frown upon advocacy reporting, no matter its goals or whether it is initiated by journalists or sources. Maintaining journalistic fairness and integrity should be a priority, regardless of the motivations and identities of sources and news subjects. A different set of arguments and reactions is expected in countries where neither objectivity nor other principles associated with the professional norms of journalism are prevalent. As mentioned previously, the transition and consolidation of democratic rule has not ushered in a consensus on professional ideals in most of the global South. Rather than a consensus around one set of hegemonic norms, journalistic norms are the subject of debate in new democracies and transitional regimes.

In those contexts, it is not surprising that journalists and civic organizations actively collaborate in advocacy journalism. Across the South, a myriad of journalists' organizations actively try to increase the volume of reporting and widening news perspectives on social issues. In contrast to traditional institutions that bring together publishers and/or journalists that are interested in promoting "press issues" (e.g., freedom of expression, protection of reporters, press laws), this new breed of advocacy organizations are primarily interested in promoting news coverage of issues related to social change. Examples include African journalists who promote HIV/AIDS issues, such as Nigeria's Journalists Against AIDS and Tanzania's AGAAT (Falobi & Banigbetan, 2000), and women's rights, including Kenya-based FEMNET, Media Women's Associations in Tanzania, Uganda and other East African countries, and South Africa's Gender and Media Network. Others aim to stir up interest in a variety of social and political issues such as Nairobi-based MESHA, and the Media Institute of Southern Africa. In Latin America, journalists have formed associations to promote reporting of children's issues (e.g., Brazil-based *Agência Not'cias de Direitos da Infancia*), women's issues (e.g., Mexico's *Comunicación e Información de la Mujer*), environment (e.g., *Red de Comunicación Ambiental de América Latina y el Caribe*) and social issues in general (Argentina's *Red de Periodismo Social*, Ecuador's *Agencia Latinoamericana de Información*). These organizations feed information to newsrooms, provide logistical support to facilitate coverage, bring journalists together through virtual networks, form alliances with news organizations, organize training workshops, produce articles and series for publication, and so on.

Aside from editorial politics, advocates-journalists frequently confront the disinterest of their news organizations. They have meager resources and space for their work. Also, they often clash against editors who are reluctant to publish "depressing" and "soft" stories that are "not relevant to audiences," show interest only in sensationalistic coverage of social issues, and fail to ensure minimal resources to gather information (PANOS, 2007). Amidst the litany of justifications for limited news space and resources and pressures not to antagonize governments and sponsors, practicing advocacy journalism is extremely difficult. Journalists' advocacy networks aim to persuade editors to provide room for social issues, and present alternative news frames. Here it is important to mention the transnational dimensions of these networks. They often collaborate with regional and global institutions working on similar social issues, and partner with colleagues in other countries. They tap into a vast array of global organizations, including both experts' and activists' groups, that devote considerable resources and time to influence local news through sponsoring training programs, journalism grants, and awards.

SUGGESTIONS FOR FURTHER RESEARCH

Because the historical trajectory of journalism varies across countries, universal generalizations about advocacy journalism can easily fall into flat-footed abstractions. The dearth of comparative studies makes it difficult to draw broad conclusions. The danger of reducing journalism to unique local processes, however, should be equally avoided. Dissolving all explanations into "localisms" is rather unhelpful for sound concept building. With this goal in mind, and from the evidence presented in this chapter, I advance three propositions for further exploration.

First, we can identify a set of conditions that favor advocacy journalism. Despite substantial historical differences across press systems, contemporary advocacy journalism requires similar conditions: the absence of a consensus around journalistic norms and ideals, and media-savvy civic organizations. When these conditions prevail, it is more likely that journalists would openly act as advocates for specific causes, and that mobilized publics use mainstream media to influence news agenda and public opinion, and achieve policy goals. Both reporters and sources act as advocates, and at times, closely collaborate. Different scenarios are found when neither of these conditions exists. In countries where journalists are constrained by the ideals of objectivity, fairness, and other "God-terms" of modern journalism (Zelizer, 2004), and organized groups mobilize to advocate for media coverage and policies, then, advocacy journalism is more likely to be civic advocacy journalism. When journalists are not held by norms of impartiality, and collective action around specific social causes is weak or non-existent, then, advocacy journalism is likely to be associated with advocate-journalists.

Second, the fact that civic movements in the global South use similar media advocacy strategies suggests the increasing use of similar journalistic criteria in the definition of news across the world. While important differences remain across press systems and journalistic cultures, journalists share similar definitions of "what is news." Although work in newsrooms that may not necessarily expect journalists to balance sources, properly document facts, and observe other principles that are often identified with the conventions of modern Anglo-American journalism, similarities about "who, what, when, and why is news" are perceptible around the globe. In this sense, the global emergence of the ideal of "professional" journalism seems to be tied to the adoption of certain rules-of-thumb to determine newsworthiness. A growing homogeneity about "what is newsworthy" across newsrooms worldwide explains why global and local organizations use a common set of "source strategies" worldwide to practice advocacy journalism. The cases of Greenpeace and ACT UP are perhaps some of the best-known cases of advocacy groups that mix street theater and public relations to get in the news in distant corners of the globe. Anti-tobacco groups in Japan use media strategies that are not substantially different from their counterparts in the United States and Europe (Hajime, 2003). In the Ukraine, the media strategies of women's groups in support of family planning and abortion policies are similar to the one used by similar movements elsewhere (Bishop, Kovtun, Okromeshko, Karpilovskaya, & Suprun, 2001). The mobilization strategies of anti-vaccination groups in the United Kingdom and Nigeria reflected different forms of political participation and decision making, but they appealed to news media with a similar appetite for sensationalist news and dramatic images (Petts & Niemeyer, 2004; Waisbord, 2007b). In summary, global civic advocacy increasingly relies on a common set of newsmaking strategies because similar criteria are used to determine news, a phenomenon that, perhaps as a result of globalization, deserves further attention.

Third, the cases of advocacy journalism presented in this chapter raise questions about the linkages between global and local advocacy. Much has been recently discussed in the literature on collective action and social movements about the vitality of global forms of civic action (della Porta, 2006; Keck & Sikkink, 1998). On these issues, it is important to highlight aspects that are directly relevant to advocacy journalism and the uses of communication and the media in global social change. Does global advocacy effectively shape news coverage when it dovetails with local actions, considering journalism's preference for local news hooks? What happens when global advocacy clashes with the interests of national and local governments, the preeminent definers of daily news? How global advocacy movements effectively support local advocacy needs to be understood by analyzing local reporting practices. One could approach this subject by studying how transnational networks affect governments, civic movements, and news organizations which, in turn, set the boundaries for what and how is reported. Another possibility is to review the trajectory of specific issues in national and local public spheres to determine how local and global forces have contributed to focusing attention and framing issues. Because both journalism and civic movements are subjected to the influence of globalizing forces, advocacy journalism is at crossroads of the global and the local. In this sense, it offers an opportunity to explore how media and politics interact at both global and local levels.

Engaging with questions about the professional identity of journalists and the impact of global efforts on local news is important not only to understand contemporary advocacy journalism and its contributions to social justice, but also to inform current theoretical debates in the field of journalism studies. Comparative research on advocacy journalism can shed light on journalistic practice and norms in a globalized world.

REFERENCES

Anderson, A. (1997). *Media, culture and the environment.* Piscataway, NJ: Rutgers University Press.

Anderson, A. (2003). Environmental activism and news sources. In S. Cottle (Ed.), *News, public relations and power* (pp. 63–79). London: Sage.

Bagdikian, B. (1973). Shaping media content: Professional personnel and organizational Structure. *Public Opinion Quarterly, 37*(4), 569–579.

Benford, R. D., & Snow, D. A. (2000). Framing and social movements: An overview and assessment. *Annual Review of Sociology, 26*(1), 611–639.

Bennett, W. L. (2003). New media power: The Internet and global activism. In N. Couldry & J. Curran (Eds.), *Contesting media power* (pp. 17–38). Lanham, MD: Rowman and Littlefield.

Bennett W. L., & Lawrence, R. G. (1995). News icons and the mainstreaming of social change. *Journal of Communication, 45*(3), 20–39.

Berns, N. (2005). *Framing the victim: Domestic violence, media, and social problems.* Glenside, CA: Aldine.

Bishop, A., Kovtun, A., Okromeshko, S., Karpilovskaya, S., & Suprun, N. (2001). Lives renewed: The emergence of a breast cancer survivor movement in Ukraine. *Reproductive Health Matters, 9*(18), 126–134.

Brookman-Amissah, E., & Moyo, J. B. (2004) Abortion law reform in Sub-Saharan Africa: No turning back. *Reproductive Health Matters, 12*(24), 227–234.

Butler, A. (2005). South Africa's HIV/AIDS policy, 1994–2004: How can it be explained? *African Affairs, 104*(417), 591–614.

Carroll, W. K., & Ratner, R. S. (1999). Media strategies and political projects: A comparative study of social movements. *Canadian Journal of Sociology, 24*(1), 1–34.

Colby, D. C., & Cook, T. E. (1991). Epidemics and agendas: The politics of nightly news coverage of AIDS. *Journal of Health Politics, Policy, & Law, 16*(2), 215–49.

Cullinan, K. (2003). The media and HIV/AIDS: A blessing and a curse. *AIDS Bulletin, 10*(2), 35–39.

Dale, S. (1996). *McLuhan's children: The Greenpeace message & the media.* Toronto: Between the Lines.

della Porta, D. (2006). *Globalization from below: Transnational activists and protest networks.* Minneapolis: University of Minnesota Press.

Diop, W. (2000). From government policy to community-based communication strategies in Africa: Lessons from Senegal and Uganda. *Journal of Health Communication, 5,* 113–118.

Donsbach, W., & Klett, B. (1993). Subjective objectivity: How journalists in four countries define a key term in their profession. *Gazette: International Journal for Communication Studies, 51*(1), 53–83.

Downing J. D. H. (2005). Activist media, civil society and social movements. In W. de Jong, M. Shaw & N. Stammers (Eds.), *Global activism, global media* (pp. 149–164). London: Pluto Press.

Durrant, R., Wakefield, M., McLeod, K., Clegg-Smith, K. & Chapman, S. (2003). Tobacco in the news: an analysis of newspaper coverage of tobacco issues in Australia, 2001, *Tobacco Control, 2*, 1175–1181.

Emery, E. (1972). *The press and America*. Englewood Cliffs, NJ: Prenctice-Hall.

Falobi, O., & Banigbetan K. (2000). When can journalists become advocates? Media networking in the area HIV/AIDS and the experience of Journalists Against AIDS (JAAIDS) Nigeria. *International Conference on AIDS*, July 9–14, 13.

Gerth, H. H., & Mills, C. W. (Eds.). (1946). *From Max Weber: Essays in sociology*. New York: Oxford University Press.

Gillett, J. (2003). The challenges of institutionalization for AIDS media activism. *Media, culture and society, 25*(5), 607–624.

Gould, D. B. (2002). Life during wartime: Emotions and the development of Act Up. *Mobilization, 7*(2), 177–200.

Gross, L. (2001). *Up from invisibility*. New York: Columbia University Press.

Gross, P. (2003). New Relationships: Eastern European media and the post-Communist political world. *Journalism Studies, 4*(1), 79–89.

Gusfield, J. R. (1981). *The culture of public problems: Drinking-driving and the symbolic order*. Chicago: University of Chicago Press.

Hackett, R. A. (2000). Taking back the media: Notes on the potential for a communicative democracy movement. *Studies in Political Economy, 63*, 61–86.

Hajime, S. (2003). Agenda setting for smoking control in Japan, 1945–1990. *Journal of Health Communication, 8*(1), 23–40.

Hallin, D., & Mancini, P. (2004). *Comparing media systems: Three models of media and politics*. Cambridge: Cambridge University Press.

Hanitzsch, T. (2005). Journalists in Indonesia: Educated but timid watchdogs. *Journalism* Studies, *6*(4), 493–508.

Hasty, J. (2005). *The press and political culture in Ghana*. Bloomington: Indiana University Press.

Hilgartner, S., & Bosk, C. L. (1988). The rise and fall of social problems: A public arenas model. *American Journal of Sociology, 94*(1), 53–78.

Hughes, S. (2006). *Newsrooms in conflict: Journalism and the democratization of Mexico*. Pittsburgh, PA: University of Pittsburgh Press.

Janowitz, M. (1975). Professional models in journalism: The gatekeeper and the advocate. *Journalism Quarterly, 52*(4), 618–626.

Johnstone, J. W. C., Slawski, E. J., & Bowman, W. W. (1972–1973). The professional values of American newsmen. *Public Opinion Quarterly, 36*(4), 522–540.

Keck, M. E., & Sikkink, K. (1998). *Activists beyond borders: Advocacy networks in international politics*. Ithaca, NY: Cornell University Press.

Köcher, R. (1986). Bloodhounds or missionaries: Role definitions of German and British journalists. *European Journal of Communication, 1*(1), 43–64.

Kolker, E. S. (2004). Framing as a cultural resource in health social movements: Funding activism and the breast cancer movement in the US, 1990–1993. *Sociology of Health & Illness, 26*(6), 820–844.

Lupton, D. (1994). *Moral threats and dangerous desires: AIDS in the news media*. London: Taylor & Francis.

Mano, W. (2005). Press freedom, professionalism, and proprietorship: Behind the Zimbabwean media divide. *Westminster Papers in Communication and Culture*, November, 56–70.

McDevitt, M. 2003. In defense of autonomy: A critique of the public journalism critique. *Journal of Communication, 53*(1), 155–160.

Morgen, S. (2002). *Into our own hands: The women's health movement in the United States, 1969–1990*. Piscataway, NJ: Rutgers University Press.

Msimang, S. (2003). HIV/AIDS, globalization and the international women's movement. *Gender and Development, 11*(1):109–113.

Mwesige, P. G. (2004). Disseminators, advocates and watchdogs: A profile of Ugandan journalists in the new millennium. *Journalism, 5*(1), 69–96.

Natarajan, K. & Hao, X. (2003). An Asian voice? A comparative study of channel News Asia and CNN. *Journal of Communication, 53*(2), 300–314.

Nyamnjoh, F. B. (2005). *Africa's media: Democracy and the politics of belonging*. London: Zed Books.

Ostertag, B. (2006). *People's movements: The journalism of social justice movements*. Boston: Beacon Press.

Pan, Z., & Chan, J.M. (2003). Shifting journalistic paradigms: How China's journalists assess "media exemplars." *Communication Research, 30*(6), 649–682.

PANOS. (2007). What the papers aren't saying: How can we enhance media coverage of TB? Retrieved April 20, 2007, from http://www.panos.org

Patterson, T., & Donsbach, W. (1996). News decisions: Journalists as partisan actors. *Political Communication, 13*, 455–468.

Pertschuk, M. (2001). *Smoke in their Eyes: Lessons in movement leadership from the tobacco wars*. Nashville, TN: Vanderbilt University Press.

Peterson, M. A. (1998). The rhetoric of epidemic in India: News coverage of AIDS. *Alif: Journal of Comparative Poetics, 18*, 237–268

Petts, J., & Niemeyer, S. (2004). Health risk communication and amplification: Learning from the MMR vaccination controversy. *Health, Risk and Society, 6*(1), 7–23.

Ramaprasad, J., & Hamdy, N. N. (2006). Functions of Egyptian journalists: Perceived importance and actual performance. *Gazette: International Journal for Communication Studies, 68*(2), 167–185.

Ramaprasad, J. (2001). A profile of journalists in post-independence Tanzania. *Gazette: International Journal for Communication Studies, 63*(6), 539–555.

Rampal, K. R. (1996). Professionals in search of professionalism: Journalists' dilemma in four Maghreb states. *Gazette: International Journal for Communication Studies, 58*(1), 25–43.

Richstad, J. (2000). Asian journalism in the twentieth century. *Journalism* Studies, *1*(2), 273–284.

Robins, S. (2004). "Long live Zackie, long live': AIDS activism, science and citizenship after Apartheid. *Journal of Southern African Studies, 30*(3), 651–672

Ryan, M. (2001). Journalistic ethics, objectivity, existential journalism, standpoint epistemology, and public journalism. *Journal of Mass Media Ethics, 16*(1), 3–22.

Ryfe, D. (2006). The nature of news rules. *Political Communication, 23*(2), 203–214.

Sakr, N. 2006. Foreign support for media freedom advocacy in the Arab Mediterranean: Globalization from above or below? *Mediterranean Politics, 11*(1), 1–20.

Schlesinger, P., & Tumber, H. (1994). *Reporting crime*. New York: Oxford University Press.

Schoepf, B. G. (2004). AIDS, history, and struggles over meaning. In E. Kalipeni, S. Craddock, J. R. Oppong, & J. Ghosh (Eds.), *HIV and AIDS in Africa: Beyond epidemiology* (pp. 15–28). Oxford: Blackwell.

Schudson, M. (2001). The objectivity norm in American journalism. *Journalism, 2*(2), 149–170.

Silveirinha, M. J. (2007). Displacing the "political": The "personal" in the media public sphere. *Feminist Media Studies, 7*(1), 65–79.

Smith, J. (2001). From protest to agenda building: Description bias in media coverage of protest events in Washington, D.C. *Social Forces, 79*(4), 1397–1423.

Smith, J. (2000). *The daily globe: Environmental change, the public and the media*. London: Earthscan.

Stein, J. (2002). *What's news: Perspectives on HIV/AIDS in the South African media*. Johannesburg: Centre for AIDS Development, Research and Evaluation.

Tomaselli, K. (1996). "Our culture" vs. "foreign culture": An essay on ontological and professional issues in African journalism. *Gazette: International Journal for Communication Studies, 57*(1), 1–15.

Traquina, N. (2004). Theory consolidation in the study of journalism: A comparative analysis of the news coverage of the HIV/AIDS issue in four countries. *Journalism*, 5(1), 97–116.

Vliegenthart, R., Oegema, D., & Klandermans, B. (2005) Media coverage and organizational support in the Dutch environmental movement. *Mobilization, 10*(3), 265–381.

Waisbord, S. (2000). *Watchdog journalism in South America*. New York: Columbia University Press.

Waisbord, S. (2007a). Democratic journalism and statelessness. *Political Communication*, *24*(2), 115–130.

Waisbord, S. (2007b). Missed opportunities: Communication and the polio eradication initiative. *Communication for Social Change*, *1*(2), 145–165.

Wallack, L., Dorfman, L., Jernigan, D., & Themba, M. (1993). *Media advocacy and public health: Power for prevention*. Thousand Oaks, CA: Sage.

Zelizer, B. 2004. When facts, truth, and reality are God-terms: On journalism's uneasy place in cultural studies. *Communication & Critical/Cultural Studies*, *1*(1), 100–119.

27

Covering War and Peace

Howard Tumber

The reporting of war and peace has been of unique importance and fascination to communication, media and journalism scholars. This is due in part, to the dramatic nature of war and conflict, its importance to states and its publics, and the amount of time and money devoted to it by media and news organizations. The examination of media and conflict has spawned many important theoretical and conceptual debates within the academy that have implications for other aspects of communications analysis. These debates include: definitions of war and (more recently) terrorism, conflict resolution, the public sphere, political economy, information management, definitions and role of media sources, the occupation of journalism, and objectivity.

In modern times, from the Napoleonic wars in the mid-eighteenth century onwards, reporting from the frontline of conflict became less of a rarity. The British *Oracle and public Advertiser's* John Bell visited the front and sent back reports of the battles. The mid nineteenth century saw a larger transformation of conflict reporting with the start of cooperative news gathering, field reporters and new technologies especially the telegraph and the railway. Previously to this, the only information from the front came from soldiers' letters home and military dispatches from commanders in the field. Undoubtedly, the most famous reporter of the time was the Irish journalist William Howard Russell. He reported on the Crimean War for the *London Times* for nearly two years. He is regarded as the first of the modern war correspondents and his dispatches from the front enabled the public, for the first time, to read about the reality of warfare. The public outcry resulting from his reports led the British Government of the time to reassess the treatment of soldiers in the battlefield and eventually led to the downfall of the Government of the day and the resignation of the Prime Minister, Lord Aberdeen. Russell was seen by some as a traitor for denigrating Britain's competence in its conduct of the war and he was also accused of providing secrets to the enemy. Antagonism from the military to Russell's reports led to some British commanders and officers refusing to speak to him. Phillip Knightley (1975) in his book about the rise of the war correspondent as hero, propagandist and mythmaker describes Russell as "the miserable parent of a luckless tribe."

During World War II, journalists wrote stories about soldiers' experiences in battle and about the more mundane tasks soldiers undertook during their time at the front. Similar stories were a feature of the reporting of some embedded journalists during the recent Iraq War. The prominence of radio as a medium was another feature of World War II. The public was kept informed about events happening from the front through reports from correspondents stationed in the battle zones, and governments used radio for public information announcements on the home front.

World War II also witnessed the beginnings of the "cult" of the journalist. As the war progressed, many journalists became famous with the public through their dispatches and some, such as Ernie Pyle, became highly esteemed by their readers. Many journalists who reported from the front during World War II returned to "action" for the Korean War.

War reporting has always been regarded as a glamorous specialism of journalism. Journalists who cover war and conflict relate exciting stories about their dangerous work and life in memoirs and autobiographies providing poignant and interesting reflections (see Pedelty, 1995, pp. 29–30; Tumber, 2006). However, the work of the frontline correspondent is getting more difficult and dangerous. Boundaries between combatants can be vague, journalists can be on the receiving end of friendly fire, and are often targets for kidnapping and death. Despite news organization cuts in foreign coverage in recent years and the closing of foreign bureaus, many journalists congregate in conflict zones equipped with lightweight technologies enabling them to transmit via satellite with immediacy unimaginable in past conflicts. Through use of the Internet, larger audiences than ever before can easily access their reports. They can be challenged almost immediately by critics elsewhere and even by the subjects on whom they are reporting. Despite the dangers, journalists are still motivated to report from conflict zones in dangerous places.

Conditions in Iraq for journalists, for example, deteriorated so dramatically after the fall of Baghdad in April 2004 that they found it virtually impossible to work. Veteran journalists found conditions in Iraq some of the worst they had to face in decades of foreign affairs reporting, with only Chechnya rivaling it for risk. Journalists are regularly becoming targets making the job harder than ever to complete. The situation remains so dangerous that journalists no longer feel able to do a proper reporting assignment, with many of them unable to travel inside the country, walk in the streets or look for stories (see The Committee to Protect Journalists, 2007). There is huge reliance on local journalists, fixers, translators and drivers to get any kind of story. This was the major reason why, when the US assault on Fallujah took place in November 2004, there was hardly any independent reporting. Reports came only from the handful of journalists embedded with the Marines (themselves in hazardous circumstances), and they were highly constrained in what they could report. Consequently, it was several weeks after the event that the scale of physical destruction of Fallujah began to be made known—and the numbers and identities of Iraqi dead and injured were never reported (Tumber & Webster, 2006, p. 21).

DEFINITIONS OF WAR AND CONFLICT

After World War II, the emergence of a number of smaller conflicts led to the questioning of the conventional categorization of conflict (Gray, 1997, p. 156). The concept of "total war," more adequate for the characterization of World Wars I and II since they involved the mobilization of entire national populations both civilians and military, seemed inappropriate for describing later conflicts such as those in the Falklands, Bosnia and Kosovo, Rwanda and Somalia, and the two Gulf wars. Whilst civilian populations are not mobilized in the same way as they were during the two world wars, the development of communications technologies has led the public to become witnesses to war.

There is a distinction between the terms "our wars" and "other people's wars." The media coverage of "our wars" involving "our troops" fighting alongside "our allies" against the enemy and "other people's wars" where conflicts that do not involve our armies or are not involved as allies of one side of the conflict, is different in relation to the degree of engagement (Taylor, 1997, p. 130). In the first case, the media coverage supports "our" side and the audiences' emotional involvement is much greater. In the second scenario, the coverage and the media involvement is more detached. In many instances, the dividing line between "their conflict" and "our conflict" can be blurred.

One reason for the increasing attempts to place any military action within the political discourse of one's nation is the increasing realization that political preparation and political justification at home play an important role in winning over public opinion. The important decisions that define the outcome of any war action are not only taken at the field of battle but increasingly in the political arena (Gray, 1997, pp. 169–170). The reporting of "other people's wars" may be less engaged until the dominant political discourse is transformed and "their war" becomes "our war."

Following September 11, 2001, a further characteristic evident of modern-day war has been the increasing blurring between terrorism and war. Despite the "smart" weapons and the "distant" targets, terrorism brings war back home. As a dominant form of international conflict, terrorism rejects civilian immunity and agreed warfare conventions, thus accelerating emotional responses (Carruthers, 2000, pp. 163–164). The September 11 attack, due to its aim and proximity for the Western World, put the traditional conceptions of warfare under question. In the twenty-first century, political violence has become the primary means to communicate political messages, and terrorist attacks have taken a leading position in world news since the beginning of the new millennium. As early as the end of the 1960s, the concept of "international terrorism" became a common currency. During this period, the common method of looking at international terrorism was through trying to connect the phenomenon with the Soviet Union and the left in general, leading to the simplification of the terrorist objectives. In the early 1980s, the US government adopted this view as the main orthodoxy, while at the same time, violent repressive and authoritarian regimes that were deemed friendly to the United States and Western interests were not associated with terrorism.

Terrorism has now become a major issue in the post-cold war era for a number of reasons. First, the collapse of the Soviet Union has fostered anti-American political violence whereas previously it was able to restrain countries that belonged to the Eastern bloc or were affiliated to it, thus keeping terrorism beneath a certain threshold. Second, the end of the old world order unleashed a number of religious and nationalist forces emerging from the new states that were formed following the breakdown of the Soviet Union. In particular, the religious groups engaged in political violence are prepared to engage in terrorist attacks not bound to the moral imperatives of previous groups like the Italian Red Brigades or the German Red Army Faction (Nacos, 2002, pp. 21–26).

New communication technologies delivered to larger audiences provide new avenues of publicity for terrorist groups. New media markets and concentration of media ownership has created the possibility of international and global coverage as well as national. The "news media have become unwitting accomplices of media savvy terrorists" (Nacos, 2002, p. 29). Extensive news reporting and public attention, even if the actual identity and the motives of the terrorist remain unknown, has already made cases of "propaganda of the deed" highly successful (Nacos, 2002, pp. 8–10; Tuman, 2003, p. 120). As the demand for increasingly more dramatic and "bloody" events guarantees increased coverage, the threshold for a successful terrorist attack is also raised (Tuman, 2003, pp. 119, 135–136; Nacos, 2002, pp. 28–29). The centrality of communications for terrorism has also lead to increased sophistication on the part of the terrorists. As a deviant branch of political communications professionals, terrorists try to by-pass the journalists by actively engaging in their own broadcast production. The Bin Laden tapes, for example, although amateur by Western standards, are relatively sophisticated in terms of their rhetoric targeting an Arab as well as a global audience (Tuman, 2003, pp. 136–137). Furthermore, the choice of Al Jazeera as the outlet indicates a logic that operates on the "exclusivity" lines that Western political candidates have capitalized on for decades. The bypassing of traditional media by terrorist groups reached an apotheosis with the use of internet broadcasts to show the beheading of hostages in Iraq (see Tumber & Webster, 2006).

PROPAGANDA AND POLITICAL ECONOMY

The Vietnam War fought in the 1960s and early 1970s set the tone for all the subsequent scholarly debate regarding the media coverage of conflict. Hallin's (1986) study of the US media and the Vietnam War was a key work in analyzing the way that the government and military behaved during the conduct of a relatively long conflict. Hallin challenged the "radical" political economy or propaganda model espoused by Herman and Chomsky (2002) in their analysis of US foreign policy as being overly deterministic. He argued that the way the media report events is closely tied to the degree of consensus among the political elite, the "sphere of consensus." Hallin's (1986, p. 11) view also contrasted with the conservative analysis of the media at that time as "anti-establishment" institutions which were "undermining the authority of governing institutions." Hallin's (1986, pp. 63–69) explanation for the media's "volte face" in its support for/rejection of the war was that the media was grounded in its "commitment to the ideology and the routines of objective journalism." From the beginnings of the Vietnam conflict up to 1967, there was relatively little disagreement among the policy elite and reflecting this official viewpoint for the media did not "seem to violate the norms of objective journalism" (1994, pp. 52–53). However, during the period 1963–1967 reporters in Vietnam itself were given accounts of the war by serving officers in the US military which were not compatible with the largely optimistic accounts coming out of Washington. This gap between the realities of the position on the ground and the official line emanating from the US capital lead to stormy news conferences particularly in Saigon. During this period, both versions of the state of the war were reported (1986, pp. 38–39).

Later, according to Hallin, the media coverage reflected the gradual breaking down of the national security consensus and the cold war ideology amongst the political elite together with concern over the conduct of the war. The media was able to respond to the growing strains and divisions within the foreign policy elite by producing far higher amounts of critical news coverage "without abandoning objective journalism for some activist and anti-establishment conception of their role." As opposition to the war moved into the mainstream, the news media reflected this movement of debate into "the sphere of legitimate controversy." The media reflect the prevailing pattern of political debate: "when consensus is strong, they tend to stay within the limits of the political discussion it defines; when it begins to break down, coverage becomes increasingly critical and diverse in the viewpoints it represents, and increasingly difficult for officials to control" (1994, pp. 53–55). As the policy debate moves from the "sphere of consensus" to the "sphere of legitimate controversy," governments and administrations become concerned at the possible loss of control over the news agenda. Censorship and attacks on the media consequently become prominent features of their response to the increase in media activity as journalists begin to question government statements and become more sensitive to other official and non-official viewpoints (Hallin, 1994, p. 71; see also Morrison & Tumber, 1988, p. 228).

Mermin (1996) suggested a further development of Hallin's thesis. During the period of the "sphere of consensus" the major media try to maintain the illusion of fulfilling the journalistic ideals of balance and objectivity "by finding conflicting possibilities in the efforts of officials to achieve the goals they have set" (Mermin 1996, p. 191). When there is no policy debate in Washington, "reporters offer critical analysis *inside the terms of the apparently settled policy debate*, finding a critical angle in the possibility that existing policy on its own terms might not work" (p.

182). Focusing on this "critical angle" helps to explain the perception among politicians and business leaders that journalists are overly independent and critical of government, and to illustrate that there is a significant element of present-day conflict in the news. Some journalism can find conflicting possibilities in the effectiveness of the government of achieving its own goals while still not presenting "the policy decision that set those goals in the first place as open to critical analysis and debate" (p. 191).

INFORMATION POLICY AND MILITARY MEDIA RELATIONS

William Russell's efforts at the frontline of the Crimean War and those of other reporters who followed him later in the nineteenth and then twentieth centuries provoked governments and military to adopt strategies for restricting media access to the frontlines and managing the flow of information. The United States government attempted to censor and manage the flow of information during the Civil War and the later Spanish-American War—although on both occasions these efforts were largely unsuccessful. The British government proved more adept at controlling information flow during the Boer War through the ruse of turning reporters into commissioned military officers and hence making them subject to military regulations. The government also restricted publication of information that could be valuable to the enemy. It was from the twentieth century onwards though, that war was experienced as a mass phenomenon. The French and British governments restricted access for journalists to the frontlines at the beginning of World War I. This strategy changed once these governments realized that morale at home was detrimentally affected and that the German government encouraged correspondents from neutral countries to visit the frontlines. The general consensus regarding the reporting of World War I was that reporters, out of a sense of patriotism, generally cooperated with the military and offered little criticism of the official "line." The media coverage during World War II saw a sea change in a number of ways. Journalists often lived with the troops with the consequent inevitability of identification and attachment—a problem analyzed in more recent times following reporters' reliance on the military for access during the Falklands Conflict 1982 (see Morrison & Tumber, 1988) and in discussion of the embedding of journalists with the military in the Iraq War 2003 (see Tumber & Palmer, 2004).

Despite the formulations devised by scholars of the media and conflict, for governments and military, the lesson of the Vietnam War was that the media and television in particular, was to blame for the United States defeat in South East Asia. Commanders and politicians were convinced that the years of uncensored reporting, unrestricted access, and the mismanagement of military briefings in Saigon (known as "Five o'clock Follies"), were directly responsible for providing information and succor to the enemy, for lowering morale at home and for losing the battle for public opinion. It was a scenario that they believed must not be repeated in future conflicts. Since then they have experimented with different methods of "controlling" and "managing" the media with stricter controls imposed on the media in order to contain information and ultimately win the battle for the hearts and minds of the public.

It was these sentiments that governed Britain's attitude to the media during the Falklands/ Malvinas conflict. The information policy adopted by the British government and the military during the Falklands was poorly organized and lacked planning. There was an absence of agreed procedure or criteria, no centralized system of control and no co-ordination between departments. But whatever seemingly "on the hoof" measures the British introduced were based on the "myth" of Vietnam. During the Falklands conflict, the battle for public opinion was fought under the guise of "operational security," an all-embracing term used as an excuse for delaying and censoring information and disseminating misinformation (see Morrison & Tumber, 1988, pp. 189–190). But whatever the outcomes of the reporting, it was not due to astute planning by the British. The news was controlled by the very location—a windswept archipelago eight thousand miles from the UK in the South Atlantic. Journalistically speaking, it was in the wrong place. There were no means for the journalists to get their reports back to their news organizations in London other than through the military's communications network. Copy had to be taken to one of the ships that possessed a Marisat satellite system for transmission. Although it was not known if the Argentineans possessed the capability to access the Marisat system, it was not totally secure, even though some of the journalists considered it so. Twenty-five years on, today's mobile personal satellite communications systems make it impossible to control the flow of information, as it was possible then.

Military and defense officials in the United States noted with alacrity the experience of the Falklands. The uses of both military and civilian minders, the stationing of reporters in military units, and pooling arrangements were all adopted in various guises in future conflicts. In the 1980s, discussions took place between news organizations and the United States Department of Defense in order to establish some ground rules for co-operation. The first "test" of this new détente occurred in the invasion of Granada (known as operation "Urgent Fury") in 1983. However rather than setting a tone for harmonious relations between the military and the media, it provoked an outcry from news organizations as over six hundred reporters were left stranded in Barbados unable to report what was occurring in Grenada. It was two days later, when the initial assault was over, that fifteen reporters and photographers selected as pool reporters were allowed onto the island. The military had been logistically unresponsive to the needs of news organizations. The intense criticism that followed led to the setting up in 1984 by the United States Joint Chiefs of Staff of a commission headed by General Winant Sidle to look into future media operations. One of the main recommendations proposed that a national media pool should be created to cover future operations where full media access was not available. These proposals were implemented during the operation to maintain freedom of navigation in the Persian Gulf in 1988 (known as Operation Earnest Will) and then in Panama (1989) when US troops were engaged. This latter operation proved a disaster for the "new" pooling system because Dick Cheney, then Secretary of Defense, obstructed the mobilization of the pool and journalists were unable to cover the engagement. The sixteen-member press pool arrived in Panama four hours after US troops invaded and were only allowed to send their first reports after ten hours. Sidle was critical of the exercise and the manner in which his recommendations were implement. Further discussions between military commanders and news organizations followed the Panama fiasco and eventually led to all future battle plans containing a section on dealing with the media. To some extent, this worked reasonably well in the military engagements in Somalia in the early 1990s and in Haiti in 1994 although the pool system remained unpopular with the news organizations.

By the time of Gulf War I in 1991 (known as Operation Desert Shield), reporters covered military events via organized pools and formal briefings. Journalists were restricted in their travel movements and had to subject their copy to formal security review. The problem for the military became a logistical one of how to cope with hundreds of reporters flocking to the region. Ad-hoc press pools were organized but many journalists decided to ignore them and instead to move about independently. The outcome was frustration on behalf of news organizations and continuing bewilderment on behalf of the military about how journalists operate.

Coverage of the Gulf War in 1991 revealed especially effective perception management, since it achieved massive media attention yet was antiseptic in substance (Bennett & Paletz, 1994; Kellner, 1992; Mowlana, Gerbner, & Schiller, 1992; Taylor, 1997). As one *New York Times* reporter reflected some years later,

> The [1991] Gulf War made war fashionable again [...] television reporters happily disseminated the spoon-fed images that served the propaganda effort of the military and the state. These images did little to convey the reality of war [...] It was war as spectacle. War as entertainment. (Hedges, 2002, pp. 142–143)

Military-media relations went through a further downturn during the Kosovo campaign in 1999, a conflict where journalists had little access to the province and relied on the military for information about the bombing campaign. For the invasion in Afghanistan (2001), many editors, bureau chiefs, and correspondents regarded the Pentagon's reporting rules as some of the toughest ever (see Hickey, 2002). The main grievances consisted of the lack of reasonable access to land and sea bases from which air attacks on Taliban positions were launched, and the restrictions on access and information emanating from the Pentagon.

The US bombing campaign of Iraq in 2003, consciously and accurately titled "Shock and Awe," and the lack of an Iraqi air force to offer any resistance, led to a victory inside four weeks, with few allied casualties and unknown and unreported Iraqi military deaths. When asked about Iraqi casualties, the US Commander Tommy Franks observed that "we don't do body counts" (of the enemy). Not surprisingly, then, estimates of Iraqi losses varied widely, most suggesting between 15,000 and 35,000 military deaths (Conetta, 2003), though a cluster analysis undertaken in September 2004 by a team of researchers from Johns Hopkins University, based on death rate measures, suggested 100,000 excess Iraqi deaths due to the war (Roberts, Lafta, Garfield, Khudhairi, & Burnham, 2004). Securing the occupation for the United States, though, has been much more problematic, and American casualties escalated through 2003–2005 as the occupying troops faced the Iraqis on the ground rather than from the air.

The mythical legacy of Vietnam still leads to apprehension on the part of the military and government that the public will react badly to pictures of casualties. Commanders and politicians are anxious about the effects of displays of bloodied bodies of civilians rather than ones of "precision strikes on legitimate targets," or the media reproduction of photographs showing Iraqi prisoners in Abu Ghraib being abused by American guards as occurred in April 2004. In the United States, there remains a particular fear that body bags containing dead servicemen from Iraq or Afghanistan would sap domestic support for the war. This explains why the US military transported home in secrecy the bodies of those killed while on duty, with no photographs allowed throughout 2003–2004. It also explains the military's acute embarrassment when pictures were obtained by newspapers of flag-draped coffins in a cargo plane.

Inevitably, apprehension about domestic public opinion impels military leaders into careful rehearsal and management of information from and about the war, whilst at the same time making assiduous efforts to avoid the charge of censorship. Failing to do this would diminish the "free media" claim of the democratic state and undermine the persuasiveness of what is reported. Perception management has to combine methods of ensuring a continuous stream of positive media coverage that is ostensibly freely gathered by independent news organizations.

EMBEDDING AND OBJECTIVITY

An important feature of the Falklands War, unusual among recent conflicts, was that it involved an intense closeness between journalists and troops. There were no journalists present from countries not party to the conflict who might have offered a more "removed" perspective. This was not a war zone where the journalists might accompany troops or insurgents and then leave them to file their copy down the line from a hotel. Instead, it involved living with the troops day in and day out for months, sharing a common discomfort, and depending upon them for protection. It was a shared world, and as with all shared worlds, the meanings attributed to it came to be held in common. In reporting events in Northern Ireland, which some of the same journalists had done, the definition given to what was happening and the deaths and injuries witnessed came through civilian perspectives. This was not the case in the Falklands, where civilian understanding of reality was exchanged for a military one. As the journalists gained more insights into the military world, they became more sympathetic to it, expressing admiration for the professionalism of the British troops. The reporting of the Falklands War saw a tension develop between two competing sentiments. On the one hand, the journalists carried with them the occupational ideology of impartiality and objectivity, whilst on the other they faced a situation in which they passed from the traditional role of journalist-as-observer to that of journalist-as-participant (see Morrison & Tumber, 1988, chapter 6). The result was that journalists not only shared the moods of the troops through collective experience, but also began to identify with them by being part of the whole exercise.

> Consequently, although some of the journalists disagreed with the decision to send the Task Force to the South Atlantic, once it seemed that conflict was inevitable, they felt an affinity with the troops, a shared determination to see the venture through to the end. (p. 97)

The Iraq War of 2003 was the most heavily covered war in recent times. Over three thousand journalists were assigned to the region. Of these, five hundred were embedded with various military units and the other "independents" scattered over the area working for news organizations as staffers or freelancers. Attempts by the US government and military to control and manage news during the invasion phase of the 2003 Iraq conflict involved a number of different measures and procedures. Using familiar techniques of censorship, misinformation, obfuscation and psychological operations to varying degrees, the United States was able to frustrate journalists and news organizations in their search for information. But it was the process of embedding journalists with military units that became the topic of intense discussion.

The embedding of journalists with the military was different to the situation during the Falklands conflict when journalists were "embedded" with the British Task force almost by accident. This time there was a deliberate plan set out by the US Department of Defense in consultation with news organizations for journalists to be "situated" with various parts of the military. The thinking behind this "innovation" had been developing for some time. A number of briefings took place in Washington between Pentagon officials and news organizations to discuss the process and journalists began attending military training courses in November 2003 in preparation for the impending invasion. Neither the military nor the news organizations relished the idea of a return to the pool system or the sole reliance on official briefings employed in previous wars. Some journalists expressed concern about the embedding process, particularly about the ability to maintain their impartiality. Others embraced the opportunity to go to the front line whilst the news organizations looked forward to continuous live broadcasting. A second concern to emerge in the days following the invasion was that the embedded journalists were only providing a snapshot of the war. Both US and UK governments complained that the public was receiving a distorted picture of the conflict (Tumber & Palmer, 2004, p. 7).

The organization of the embedded process was based on a plan of allocating places to news organizations, rather than individual reporters. This made it difficult for freelancers to gain accreditation unless contracted to a news organization. It also enabled the US Department of Defense to "control" the process more easily through possible sanctions on news organization for "misbehavior" on the part of their correspondents. The journalists embedded with the troops were given special procedures and guidelines for how they could operate. Journalists and news organizations were required to sign documents complying with the rules set out at the beginning about what they could or could not report. For example, they could not report on details of future operations, hold private satellite telephones or cell phones, travel in their own vehicles whilst in an embedded status, take photographs showing level of security or ones showing an enemy prisoner of war or detainee's face, nametag or other identifying feature. Reporters also had to agree to honor news embargos that could be imposed to protect operational security (Tumber & Palmer, 2004, p. 16).

The initial enthusiasm by news organization editors for the embedded reporters program was very marked since the process allowed reporting in virtually real time with no censorship from the military, although sandstorms and rapid troop movements had caused a few delays. The Pentagon's agreement to allow large numbers of journalists to be embedded with the troops enabled news organizations and outlets not normally on the Pentagon's top priority list to gain access to the war. It gave smaller locally based newspapers a presence in the conflict and a prestigious—"we were there"—with their audiences, something which was rare in previous conflicts (Tumber & Palmer, 2004, p. 19).

Whilst the process of embedding started with a wave of enthusiasm from both the military and the news organizations, it was not long before tensions began to emerge. Some journalists were frustrated that they were embedded with units that were not seeing any action. Consequently, some left their units or were told to leave by their news organizations. For the larger news organizations who had other journalists working independently of the embedding process, this was not as great a problem as it was for some of the smaller ones who did not have the resources to base reporters all over the conflict area. Some journalists complained about their reliance on military communications for sending their copy back. Another major issue to arise was the safety of the journalists. Those embedded with the troops could rely on the protection of their units with the risk, like their military protectors, of injury or death. But there was also the potential problem of capture and if that happened whether they would be regarded as prisoners of war under the protection of the Geneva Conventions or treated as spies and therefore not entitled to the same protections. For those operating independently of the military ("unilaterals," as they came to be called) the dangers were all too obvious. Not only did the military often treat them as second class citizens compared to the embeds by refusing access, transport and communications but many of them were killed or injured in the conflict (see Tumber & Palmer, 2004, p. 7).

CONFLICT RESOLUTION AND PEACE JOURNALISM

Over the last ten years or so, scholarly and journalistic attention has shifted towards an interest in developing new concepts and paradigms of conflict coverage. Books and articles devoted to "peace journalism" as opposed to "war journalism" have emerged. Much of the literature deals with how the media and journalists can play a "more" constructive role in reporting and resolving conflict. Other interesting literature has looked at the media's role in public diplomacy and conflict resolution.

If the Vietnam War was known as the first television war, Gulf War I was known for the arrival of twenty-four hour news, and in particular, the entrance of CNN to the world of news reporting, providing a challenge to the three established US networks. CNN scored a major coup by being the only broadcaster to broadcast from Baghdad during the initial American bombing campaign. It also made household names of journalists such as Peter Arnett and Christine Amanpour. CNN also has the distinction of having its name used to describe the phenomenon of twenty-four hour news effects. The CNN effect, a term used to describe the perceived impact of real time twenty-four hour news coverage on the foreign policy decision-making processes of states in the post cold war is thought to have been first coined by a Pentagon official. Saturation coverage of particular events is viewed as being strongly influential in bringing images and issues to the immediate forefront of public political consciousness and hence influencing Governments' foreign policy decision making (see Livingston, 1997; Robinson, 2002). The high emotional content of a news report or series of reports "may capture the attention of the public which may then put pressure on policy makers" (Seib, 2002, p. 27). Criticism leveled at the CNN effect is that it is unpredictable and is only one of many factors contributing to policy making. In most cases, the CNN effect will gain purchase only if a policy vacuum exists. Other concepts of the media's role provide greater insights into policy, particularly conflict resolution.

Wolfsfeld's (2003) political contest model, for example, concentrates on the role the media may play in the possible resolution of conflict. The ability of powerful sources to manage the news tends to vary over time and circumstance with the key variable being the degree of monopoly over the information environment. The "news media are more likely to play an independent role when the powerful lose control because it allows the weaker side a better platform for the promotion of its frame of the conflict and increase the probability for third parties to intervene" (p. 228). Wolfsfeld uses the analysis of sources to examine the extent to which the press becomes an active agent in a given conflict rather than a passive conveyor of political information (see also Wolfsfeld, 2004; Weiman, 1994; Gilboa, 1998). Peace journalism advocates, though, are suggesting a different kind of agenda—a manifesto rather than a theory.

Two of the advocates of peace journalism describe it as what happens "when editors and reporters make choices—about what stories to report and how to report them—which create opportunities for society at large to consider and to value non-violent responses to conflict" (Lynch & McGoldrick, 2005, p. 5). They see peace journalism as "a fund of practical options for editors and reporters to equip readers and audiences to decode propaganda and produce their own negotiated readings, thereby holding power to account" (Lynch, 2006, p. 75). From this definition it is clear why peace journalism has been criticized for concentrating on individual and voluntary perspectives rather than structural ones (see Hanitzsch, 2007; Phillips, 2006; Tehranian, 2002).

The accepted norm for the individual journalist, based on their professional values, is that they should adopt a neutral role in reporting conflict, avoiding bias and striving for objectivity, thus refraining from advocating or defending the position of either side. This perspective, however, does not assist with understanding the reality and the dynamics of covering a conflict. Even unintentionally, the mere presence of the media may alter the behavior of conflicting parties. For example, in the case of Bosnia, it has been argued that the presence of reporters prevented or postponed some of the atrocities (Botes, 1996, p. 6) Others, though, have criticized journalists in Bosnia for being partial and embarking on crusades against Serbian aggression. The human rights perspective, adopted by sections of the media alongside calls for humanitarian intervention, was further in evidence in the lead-up to and duration of the Allied bombing of Kosovo (see Hammond & Herman, 2000, p. 124).

The danger for journalists is that they can become the third party, a role that is legitimately reserved for conflict mediators rather than reporters. Journalists' attempts to get to the "heart of the conflict" may lead to "reframing," a standard process in conflict resolution where the conflicting parts identify their shared problems that lead to the conflict. Within this picture, the media become forums of direct or indirect exchange of viewpoints and debate over possible avenues toward conflict resolution. Radio talk shows, television discussion programs and round tables all could play a peacemaking role as mediating forums (Botes, 1996, p. 7; Tehranian, 1996, p. 3).

However, unlike conflict mediators, journalists' professional aims and objectives are quite different and subject to different constraints. As employees of news organizations, they produce a commodity that is supposed to generate profit. Conflict sells and the emphasis on violence, and simplification of the conflict, increases the value of their commodity. Media interest in conflicts focuses on the high points of the dispute, dramatic or violent incidents, events that can be interpreted as focal points in the course of the conflict (Botes, 1996, pp. 7–8). Peace journalism advocates believe that the news media over value violent responses and under value non-violent ones. They argue for "co-operative exchange and deliberation which is not based on claims to universal moral judgments, or even shared language and assumptions, but instead on a concept of impartiality which consists in a diversity of perspectives" (Lynch, 2003). Their view of impartiality rests on "giving peace a chance in national and international debate" (Lynch & McGoldrick, 2005, p. xxi).

REFERENCES

Bennett, W., & Paletz, D. (1994). *Taken by storm: The media, public opinion and the Gulf War*. Chicago: University of Chicago Press.

Botes, J. (1996). Journalism and conflict resolution. *Media Development, 43*(4), 6–10.

Carruthers, S. L. (2000). *The media at war*. Basingstoke, UK: Macmillan Press.

Conetta, C. (2003). The wages of war: Iraqi combatant and non-combatant fatalities in the 2003 conflict. *Project on Defence Alternatives Research Monograph*, 8, 20 October. Retrieved January 4, 2008, from http://www.comw.org/pda

Gilboa, E. (1998). Media diplomacy: Conceptual divergence and applications. *Harvard International Journal of Press/Politics, 3*, 56–75.

Gray, H. C. (1997). *Postmodern war*. London: Guilford.

Hallin, D. C. (1986). *The "Uncensored" war: The media and Vietnam*. Oxford: Oxford University Press.

Hammond, P., & Herman, E. S. (Eds.). (2000). *Degraded capability: The media and the Kosovo crisis*. London: Pluto.

Hanitzsch, T. (2007). Situating peace journalism in journalism studies: A critical appraisal. Retrieved August 6, 2008, from http://www.cco.regene-online.de

Herman, E. S., & Chomsky, N. (2002). *Manufacturing consent*. New York: Pantheon Books.

Hickey, N. (2002). Access denied. *Columbia Journalism Review*, 1. Retrieved August 6, 2008, from http://cjrarchives.org/issues/2002/1/afghan-hickey.asp

Kellner, D. (1992). *The Persian Gulf TV war*. Boulder, CO: Westview.

Knightley P. (1975). *The first casualty: From the Crimea to Vietnam—The war correspondent as hero, propagandist and myth-maker*. New York: Harcourt Brace Jovanovich.

Livingston, S. (1997). *Clarifying the CNN effect: An examination of media effects according to type of military intervention*. Research, John F. Kennedy School of Government's Joan Shorenstein Center on the Press, Politics and Public Policy at Harvard, Paper R-18, June 1997.

Lynch, J. (2003). BBC's best defence is diversity. *UK Press Gazette*, August 29, 12–13.

Lynch, J. (2006). What's so great about peace journalism? *Global Media Journal*, Mediterranean Edition, *1*(1), 74–87.

Lynch J., & McGoldrick, A. (2005). *Peace journalism*. Stroud, UK: Hawthorn Press.

Mermin, J. (1996). Conflict in the sphere of consensus? Critical reporting on the Panama Invasion and the Gulf War. *Political Communication, 13*(2), 181–194.

Morrison, D. & Tumber, H. (1988). *Journalists at war*. London: Sage.

Mowlana, H., Gerbner, G., & Schiller, H. I. (Eds.). (1992). *Triumph of the image*. Boulder, CO: Westview.

Nacos, B. L. (2002). *Mass media and terrorism*. Lanham, MD: Rowman & Littlefield.

Pedelty, M. (1995). *War stories: The culture of foreign correspondents*. London, Routledge.

Phillips, A. (2006). Review of *Peace journalism*, by Jake Lynch and Annabel McGoldrick, *Global Media and Communication*, 2(2), 236–239.

Roberts, L., Lafta, R., Garfield, R., Khudhairi, J., & Burnham, G. (2004). Mortality before and after the 2003 invasion of Iraq: cluster sample survey. *The Lancet, 364*(9445), 30 October, 1–8.

Robinson, P. (2002). *The CNN effect: The myth of news, foreign policy and intervention.* London: Routledge.

Seib, P. (2002). *The global journalist: News and conscience in a world of conflict.* Oxford: Rowan and Littlefield.

Taylor, P. (1997). *Global communications, international affairs and the media since 1945.* London: Routledge.

Tehranian, M. (1996). *Communication and conflict. Media Development, 4*(3), 3.

Tehranian, M. (2002). Peace journalism: Negotiating global media ethics. Harvard *International Journal of Press/Politics, 7,* 58–83.

Tuman, J. S. (2003). *Communicating terror: The rhetorical dimensions of terrorism.* Thousand Oaks, CA: Sage.

Tumber, H. (2006). The fear of living dangerously: Journalists who report on conflict. *Journal of International Relations, 20*(4), 439–452.

Tumber, H., & Palmer, J. (2004). *Media at war: The Iraq Crisis.* London: Sage.

Tumber, H., & Webster, F. (2006). *Journalists under fire: Information war and journalistic practices.* London: Sage.

Weiman, G. (1994). Can the media mediate? Mass mediated diplomacy in the Middle East. In G. Ben Dor & D. Dewitt (Eds.), *Confidence building measures in the Middle East* (pp. 291–307). New York: Westview.

Wolfsfeld, G. (2003). The role of the news media in unequal political conflicts: From the 1987 Intifada to the 1991 Gulf War and back again. In N. Palmer (Ed.), *Terrorism, war, and the press* (pp. 223–257). Hollis, NH: Hollis.

Wolfsfeld, G. (2004). *Media and the path to peace.* Cambridge: Cambridge University Press.

28

Researching Public Service Broadcasting

Hallvard Moe and Trine Syvertsen

INTRODUCTION

Public service broadcasting is in no sense a precise analytical term.[1] It was originally used to describe the state broadcasting corporations set up in Europe in the 1920s and 1930s, of which the BBC is the most well known example. Since then, the term has been used to describe a variety of institutions, regulatory arrangements, social obligations and types of programming.

In this chapter, the term "public service" is used in a rather general sense, referring to forms of political intervention into the media market with the purpose of ensuring that broadcasters produce programs deemed valuable to society (Syvertsen, 2003, p. 156). Most governments intervene into the media market in some way or another, but the degree and type of intervention vary. On the basis of several recent classifications of broadcasting systems (Hallin & Mancini, 2004; Hoffman-Riem, 1996; Humphreys, 1996; McKinsey & Company, 2004; Mendel, 2000), we can identify three main types of public service broadcasting arrangements:

Broad interventions, strong public service broadcasting systems: Although Western Europe historically has been the heartland of traditional public service broadcasting, the support for it varies from north to south. Its traditional stronghold is in Northern Europe: Scandinavia, the UK, Germany, Belgium and The Netherlands. In these countries governments intervene on a broad front, public broadcasters are reasonably well funded and have a strong position. Most of these countries have retained the licence fee as a way of funding public service broadcasters.[2] In this category we may also place Japan and its broadcaster NHK, which is perhaps the best funded public service broadcaster in the world (Mendel, 2000).

Some public service intervention, usually in order to stimulate domestic programming, a lower level of public funds available for public service broadcasting: In several countries the main purpose of government intervention into broadcasting is to secure a high level of domestic production. In countries such as France, Australia, Canada and South Africa substantial regulation is imposed to secure programming that reflects national cultural and social issues, but the level of public funding remains low. In Australia, Canada and South Africa there is no licence fee; public service broadcasters are funded through public grants and varying degrees of advertisement, and the services are perpetually underfinanced (Mendel, 2000).

Minimalist intervention, low level of public funding, marginal public service broadcasters: In some countries public service broadcasters are mainly seen as a supplement to commercial services, and not as core national broadcasters. In southern European countries like Greece, Italy, Portugal and Spain, as well as in New Zealand and the United States, there is a lower degree of public intervention, a low level of public funding and considerably less public support for public service broadcasting. In Greece, public service broadcasting is funded through a tax on electricity, and both Portugal and Spain have abolished the licence fee (Mendel, 2000). It seems unlikely that public service broadcasters will regain a strong position in any of these countries without substantial regulatory intervention.

Since public service broadcasting is dependent on decisions within the political realm, it should come as no surprise that much research have focused on political issues, whether in the form of regulatory questions, or broader issues of democracy or nation-building. In this chapter we identify four different strands of research on public service broadcasting. First, there is a strand of *policy* studies: analyses of the changing conditions for public service broadcasting in the wake of increased competition, new technologies, privatization and globalization. Second, there is the related strand of *institutional* studies; studies of how traditional public service companies have responded and adapted to changing circumstances. A third strand focuses more explicitly on the role of public service *in social and democratic life of modern nation-states.* Fourth, and more tentatively, we wish to suggest that there is an emerging strand of *post-modern* approaches, which are critical of the modernist stance prevalent in most public service broadcasting studies and more explicitly inspired by the transformative potentials of new communication technologies.

We begin by outlining the origins of public service broadcasting and broadcasting research. Next, we in turn discuss the four strands of research, concentrating on the merits and limitations of different approaches. Throughout, we draw particularly on literature from Scandinavia, the UK and German-speaking countries, but also include key works from other countries with distinct public service broadcasting traditions. The discussion leads us to point to remaining tensions, and suggest directions for further research.

THE ORIGINS OF PUBLIC SERVICE BROADCASTING AND BROADCASTING RESEARCH

The growth of *research* on public service broadcasting must be understood in relation to the development of public service broadcasting *institutions*. The first public service corporation was established in Britain in 1926, and the BBC and British researchers have since played a prominent role in research and debates about public service broadcasting. This position is also due to John Reith, the first Director of the BBC, and the influence of his broadcasting ideology—later to be called "Reithianism." In his 1924 book *Broadcast over Britain*, Reith takes stock of opponents claiming broadcasting should give people "what they want". Few know what they want, and very few what they need, Reith proclaimed, and continued to say that "our responsibility is to carry into the greatest possible number of homes everything that is best in every human department of knowledge, endeavour and achievement, and to avoid the things which are, or may be hurtful" (Reith, 1924, p. 34).

Public corporations were set up all over Europe in the inter-war period, and in most cases, retained their monopoly positions until the 1980s. In the 1950s and 1960s television was implemented into this structure without much change, except in Britain, where a so-called Independent Television (ITV) network was set up alongside the BBC in 1955. However, ITV was also subject to public service content and ownership restrictions. In this period there was little actual research on public service broadcasting (cf. Moe & Syvertsen, 2007). Notwithstanding some studies of the history of the original institutions, such as the early history of the BBC (e.g., Briggs, 1961), research did not flourish until the late 1970s and 1980s. At that time, media research institutions began to be set up in response to increased social demand for knowledge about media influence.

The last two decades have seen a tremendous change in the broadcasting market and a corresponding expansion of research. Although the process of change is continuous, two distinct waves can be identified. The first wave was in the 1980s and early 1990s when the monopolies were broken, and traditional broadcasters met competition from commercial operators. The second wave is linked to digitalization and convergence in the late 1990s and 2000s. In this era competition has been increased on all platforms, prompting public service broadcasters to venture into new markets and explore services beyond radio and television broadcast.

POLICY STUDIES

The first strand of studies may be labelled *policy studies.* Over the last two decades there has been a range of studies on the changing broadcasting market and the responses to these changes by policy makers and governments. Many studies—whether comparative or case studies—have tried to grasp the complex interplay of technological, economic, political and cultural forces that separately and together have produced a new situation for public service broadcasters. The studies are similar across national boundaries, often discussing the changes in policy and the challenges to public service broadcasting under broad headlines such as new technology, globalization, privatization and commercialisation.

The Euromedia research group, with members from all over Europe, has shown a persistent interest in this field since the early 1980s. Since their first book appeared in 1986, the group has published a series of comparative, as well as country studies, on the "new media order" in Europe (McQuail & Siune, 1986, p. 197; see also McQuail & Siune, 1998; Truetzschler & Siune, 1992). The group has painted the challenges to the public service broadcasters with a relatively broad brush, portraying them mainly as cultural institutions threatened by the expansion of "the market", and discussing in detail the many different policy challenges they have encountered over the years. This kind of general cultural policy approach contrasts somewhat with the more specific studies of broadcasting regulation emerging from the fields of political science and law. One prominent example is Wolfgang Hoffman-Riem's (1996) comparative study of the licensing and supervision of broadcasting in six countries, which go more into detail on the nature of actual government interventions (see also Levy, 1999). Hoffman-Riem's study also identifies a move from "culture" to "market", or more specifically: "(f)rom special culturally based broadcasting regulation to general economic regulation" (p. 344), but he also pinpoints contradictory tendencies. After surveying two decades of regulatory change, he concludes that the public service philosophy "continue to be praised" (p. 356) and that there are many examples of public service regulation "that were maintained despite considerable resistance by the broadcasting industry" (e.g.; advertising restrictions and production quotas) (p. 355).

Those studying the changes in European media policy increasingly reflect over the role played by the European Union. Since a common market for television was set on the agenda with the establishment of a trans-European television directive in 1989, the European Commission has concerned itself with two policy issues that both remain highly relevant for public service broadcasters. These are the on-going concern to develop an information economy in Europe, and the recurring conflict between private and public service broadcasters over whether the licence fee constitute a form of illegal subsidy (Levy, 1999). Although studies agree that these issues have significant implications, they differ as to whether they see the actions of the EU as detrimental to or supportive of public service broadcasting. On the sceptical side is Jakubowicz (2004), who argues that the Union has allowed the agenda-setting role to be taken by opponents of public service broadcasting. Papathanassopoulos (2002) argues that the EU (among others) "only rhetorically support the real future of public broadcasters" (p. 86), while Coppens and Saeys (2006, p. 261) state that the EU, along with private broadcasters, "have taken the lead in the latest upsurge in fault-finding" with regard to public service. David Ward (2003), on the other hand, takes a more positive view of the EU's role in policy making. Ward's analyses of the cases where private broadcasters have challenged the privileges of public service broadcasters suggest that "the commission has generally been supportive of public broadcasting and their perceived role in public and democratic life" (p. 248).

Based on close reading of both comparative and case studies, it seems clear that both national and EU policy makers remain divided over the issue of public service. On the one hand, the social role of public service broadcasters is acknowledged and supported, but on the other hand, policies are put in place intending to limit their range and scope. This is not least seen in studies of how policy makers approach the issue of convergence and digitalisation (cf. Donges & Puppis, 2003; Marsden & Verhulst, 1999). Moe's (2008) comparative study of public service broadcasters' Internet activities shows for example that Western European governments differ profoundly in how far they are willing to go in letting the corporations develop services on digital platforms, and that the EU takes a rather restricted view. Nevertheless, as Storsul and Syvertsen (2007) point out in their study of European convergence policies, the pro-public service broadcasting lobbies in the EU have been gaining strength over the last decade, and restrictive policies are as a rule met with counter-actions from public service supporters. Not least due to skilful lobbying from the public service broadcasters themselves, there is strong support for the view that publicly funded corporations should be allowed to diversify their activities in the digital age (Levy, 1999, pp. 95–97; Siune & Hultén, 1998, pp. 34–35).[3]

In general, policy studies often portray public service broadcasters as vulnerable to pressures from competitors and regulators. However, there is much to be gained from a perspective that perceives broadcasting institutions as active, resourceful and adaptable to changing circumstances. As we shall see in the next section, the public service broadcasters have over the last decades taken the challenges to their existence very seriously indeed, and have done a great deal to improve relations with policy-makers, industry and the public at large.

STUDIES OF PUBLIC SERVICE BROADCASTING INSTITUTIONS

The new and difficult climate brought on by the technological and political transformations of the 1980s meant that public service broadcasters had to change. After an initial period of resistance and confusion, the 1990s became a decade of massive reorientation within the original corporations. New transformations followed from the late 1990s as public service broadcasters increasingly began to define themselves as multi-media conglomerates. The second strand of research deals with these changes within the public service institutions.

From the early 1980s, public service broadcasters in Europe and elsewhere have been facing increased competition from private and commercial channels. Many viewers and listeners were dissatisfied with the public service programming policies, and welcomed more choice and, in particular, more entertainment. Public service broadcasters were fearful of loosing audiences to the new services, and responded with changes in programming and scheduling. This again led to discussion about whether the public service broadcasters were becoming too similar to their commercial counterparts and loosing sight of their public service mission.

These (political) questions were quickly picked up by media research. In the 1994 article *Public service television and the tendency towards convergence,* Hellmann and Sauri revitalised a method originally used by Raymond Williams (1975)[4] to determine to what degree programming on commercial and public service broadcasters was becoming more similar. Hellmann and Sauri contrasted two hypotheses: one of *constancy* (programming on the two types of channels would remain distinct) and one of *convergence* (programming on different channels would become more similar). The authors found both hypotheses to be confirmed: while the overall composition of programming remained quite stable, the public and commercial broadcasters were clearly becoming more similar in prime time. Prime time "has become a set of rules," the authors concluded (p. 63), an observation that pointed to the fact that although public service broadcasters continued to show more factual, cultural and serious programming, they had adopted similar scheduling principles to their commercial competitors.

These findings were largely replicated in other countries, for example in Denmark (Søndergaard, 1994), Sweden (Edin, 2000) and Norway (Syvertsen, 1997; Ytreberg, 1999). Indeed, the finding that the public service broadcasters were changing, while still remaining distinct from commercial services, also permeated studies of individual programme genres. A range of comparative studies of journalism have shown, for example, that competition has led to more human interest, less foreign news, more crime and sport, shorter news stories and more formats mixing news and entertainment. Nevertheless, as Hjarvard (1999, pp. 253–258) summarises after having reviewed comparative news studies from several countries, differences in content and style remain between commercial and public service channels.

Studies of programming and scheduling mainly use (simple) quantitative and qualitative analysis, often combined with analyses of documents and interviews with broadcasters. Much rarer is the use of observational methods, especially the kind of long term fieldwork that characterises anthropological studies. Georgina Born's comprehensive study of the BBC, *Uncertain vision* (2004), is one astute example of a study that uses ethnographical methods to dig deeper into structural changes within the broadcasting organisations. The study paints a detailed picture of the changes that have taken place in many public service broadcasting institutions over the last decade: the adoption of new public management principles, the creation of larger organisational units, the amplification of audience research and commercial scheduling principles, and the strengthening of planning, branding and customer relation functions. Born perceives the combination of external and internal pressures to be exceedingly harmful for the BBC, and characterises the situation in the late 1990s as "widespread cynicism" and "a devastating erosion of morale and of belief in management's commitment to, and its ability to secure, the BBC's public service purposes" (p. 109). Although Born is critical of the strategies adopted, particularly under Director-General John Birt, the picture she paints contrasts sharply with a view of public service broadcasters as passive and vulnerable. Born rather suggests that the corporation was becoming "over-managed" (p. 6), being so eager to adjust to external expectations that creativity was compromised.

A similar picture of pro-active and strategy-driven institutions emerges in studies examining how public service broadcasters are meeting the digital challenge (cf. Donges & Puppis, 2003; Lowe & Jauert, 2005). Studies have in particular pointed to four areas where public service broadcasting has been eager to expand the use of digital technology. This is first the area of *distribution* where the organizations' pro-active stance in the so-called switch-over (to terrestrial digital networks) has been analyzed in several national contexts (cf. Brown & Picard, 2004; Galperin, 2004). The second is the creation of *thematic channels*, where the aim has been to exploit the increased distribution capacity on digital channels and create bonus services within news, film, sport and children's programming (Papathanassopoulos, 2002). The third strategy is to expand to *new platforms*, including online media such as the Internet and mobile telephony. Studies have identified a move among public service broadcasters to proclaim the Internet a "third pillar" in addition to radio and television services, although the regulatory basis for incorporating this new platform remains unclear (Degenhart, 2001; Moe, 2008). The fourth area represents a combination of the above; there has been a number of attempts to *combine platforms*—television, Internet, mobile phones—in order to enhance choice and create richer and more participatory broadcasting services. In an interview survey with Norwegian media executives, Maasø, Sundet, and Syvertsen (2007) demonstrated that the three main motivations cited for combining traditional and new media were to increase customer loyalty, establish new sources of revenue, and create new spaces for experimentation and innovation. These motivations cut across commercial and public service media, although the public service broadcasters remained more concerned about establishing services where audiences could participate also in a non-commercial setting.

The move to digital has brought out a fresh round of pessimism concerning the future of public service. In his study of television in the digital era, Papathanassopoulos (2002, pp. 79–80) claims that "public broadcasters face the most difficult challenge in their long history." Digitalisation will, in his view, lead to a further fragmentation of the audience, increasing costs, loss of revenue, and additional competition because of the commercial actors' capacity to acquire and derive direct benefit from rights to popular programming such as soccer and films. Richeri (2004, p. 192) echoes this sentiment, claiming that "it is unlikely that public broadcasters will be able to maintain the same investment and quality standard of scheduling when audience size declines." He believes that "in the past few years a number of different factors have been coming together in a way that creates a crisis in public television services and also marks the beginning of their final marginalization or their end" (p. 178). While these two authors, both from Southern Europe, may well be accurate in their dystopian visions of some public service channels, others are more optimistic. Writing from Britain, Born shows, for example, that the BBC's Internet and new media services were launched to almost universal acclaim, and cites figures showing that the BBC's Web site rapidly became the most visited non-portal Web site outside the United States (p. 9). In her view, the BBC's digital strategies show "subtle and imaginative thinking about the digital future and the BBC's role in optimising that future for contemporary Britain" (p. 482).

The massive changes in public service broadcasting over the last decades imply that the traditional services have moved quite some distance away from their origins. Nevertheless, in many countries, the commitment to publicly funded broadcasters remains strong, and this is reflected in public support, government funding and viewer statistics.[5] In countries with less strong public broadcasting traditions, however, support is less forthcoming. Here, researchers remain more pessimistic about securing a sound base for public service interventions in the future.

PUBLIC SERVICE BROADCASTING, DEMOCRACY AND SOCIAL LIFE

Above, we have argued that many viewers and listeners were critical of the paternalist policies of the original public service institutions. The institutions were, however, also criticized from a different angle, that of Marxist theorists and radical activists. Among these were several of the young media scholars that entered the scene from the late 1970s onwards. Inspired by Marxist thought on ideology and Gramsci's concept of hegemony, cultural studies pioneers like Stuart Hall attacked the idea that public service broadcasting represented a neutral force in society. Rather, Hall (1977, p. 346) argued, public service along with other media performed "the critical ideological work of 'classifying the world' within the discourses of the dominant ideologies." Hall's argument was echoed by others, among them the young political economist Nicholas

Garnham, who called for a fundamental reshaping of the British public service system. In 1978 he wrote about the ITV and the BBC:

> What in fact we have is a system in which two powerful institutions responsible not to the public but to the real, though hidden, pressures of the power elite, government, big business and the cultural establishment, manipulate the public in the interest of that power elite and socialise the individual broadcaster so that he collaborates in this process almost unconsciously. (p. 16)

These criticisms were voiced in the late 1970s. In only a few years, however, much more powerful threats were coming to public service broadcasting from new media moguls and the economic liberalist governments of the 1980s. As these interests made public service broadcasters one of their main targets, radical critics began more explicitly to defend public service. A strand of thought developed from the mid-1980s and argued more explicitly in favour of public service broadcasting as a key democratic force in society. Among the contributors to this third strand of public service research were Nicholas Garnham, Paddy Scannell, Graham Murdock, and John Keane; Nicholas Garnham being perhaps the most outspoken convert from the earlier critical perspective. In a much-cited 1986 article, Garnham confronted a view of public service broadcasting commonly held by leftists as either a "smokescreen" for "the coercive or hegemonic nature of state power," or as "occupied from within by commercial forces" (p. 40). Garnham wanted to change the situation whereby the Left had merely provided "mealy-mouthed support" for public service (p. 40), and set out to reformulate its value base by way of the concept of the public sphere.

In his *Habilitationsschrift*, Jürgen Habermas ([1962] 1989) described historically the rise and decline of a public sphere in Western European nation-states. In this sphere, detached from state and market, men could deliberate freely over politically relevant issues, aiming at reaching consensus. In Garnham's (1986, p. 41) reading, it was a "space for rational and universalistic politics" which in modern societies could only be embodied by public service broadcasters, removed as they were from direct state or market control. In his defence of public service broadcasting, Garnham wanted to "build upon the potential of its rational core" (p. 53), while still suggesting improvements in terms of higher accountability, better training of journalists and more participation from the public.

Garnham's defence should be understood in the context of a concerted political and industrial attack on public service broadcasting. The same backdrop is crucial to understand the contribution of another key figure, Paddy Scannell. His interests lay in the history of radio and television and in the role of broadcasting in everyday life. Like Garnham, Scannell (1989, p. 136) attacked arguments from the left that devalued broadcasting as "a form of social control, or of cultural standardization or of ideological (mis)representation." Also building on Habermas, Scannell argued that radio and television had made available a new kind of access to the public sphere for all citizens: "By placing political, religious, civic, cultural events and entertainment in a common domain, public life was equalized in a way that had never before been possible" (p. 140). Broadcasting had profoundly contributed to democratization from its inception, Scannell argued, and pointed to public service broadcasting as "perhaps the only means" by which common knowledge in a shared public life as a social good for all could be maintained (p. 164). "As such," he concluded, public service broadcasting "should be defended against its enemies" (p. 164).

Academic analyses of the relationship between public service broadcasting and democracy have been carried out in several countries (e.g., Langenbucher, 1990; Lucht, 2006; Skogerbø, 1996). Nevertheless, the British contributions stand out as key works, and have had a significant influence on both broadcasting research and political thought. These contributions introduced continental public sphere theory to Anglophone broadcasting research, and in so doing, helped to bridge the gap between media studies and political theory. While the policy studies (above) were normative on a more implicit level, these latter studies provided an outspoken defence for public service and had significant impact on actual policy discussions in a period of tremendous change. By extension, the early contributions yielded a line of elaborate and sophisticated studies in the years that followed, several of which comprised scrutiny of media outside broadcasting (e.g., Blumler, 1992; Curran, 2002; Garnham, 1992; Keane, 1991). Later studies of broadcasting and democracy also offered original input to public sphere theory itself (e.g., Dahlgren, 1995; Gourd, 2002). Still, this strand of broadcasting research has been criticised; the main points of this criticism can be discussed under the heading of post-modern approaches.

POST-MODERN APPROACHES TO PUBLIC SERVICE BROADCASTING

The three above approaches are fairly easy to identify and separate from each other. Finally, and more tentatively, we wish to include a fourth strand of research which we have labelled post-modern. Here we have included rather diverse contributions from recent years, which reach beyond the rationale of the original broadcasting institutions and explore new options and conceptions of public service. The studies placed under this—admittedly wide—heading are in part critical of the modernist pro-public service stance of the above approaches and in part inspired by the potential for playing, participating and embracing the popular which new technologies and platforms make possible.

While the public sphere/public service approach spearheaded by Nicholas Garnham has been influential, it has also had its critics. The application of abstract normative theory to actual media practices is a daunting task, and the leap requires an operationalization of the ideals which is not always properly undertaken. Further, the early Habermasian public sphere concept had its problematic sides even as an ideal type, and these have been pointed out repeatedly by critics ranging from feminist theory and popular culture to globalization studies (cf. Calhoun, 1992; Crossley & Roberts, 2004; Habermas, [1992] 1996). The somewhat limited focus on rational thought and discourse, found in the early studies, could be seen to neglect the importance of other forms and modes of communication, and the approach seems "at times oddly removed from the everyday sociological realities" (Dahlgren, 2004, p. 16). The early contributions portrayed public service broadcasting as the "institutional guarantor and instrument of the modern public sphere", in the words of Richard Collins (2002, p. 66), but practices of public service broadcasting have historically never corresponded to the ideal public sphere, nor do they automatically fit a future realization or approximation. Finally, and crucially, there was a tendency to perceive the market and public service as incompatible principles of organization. Especially early works by British scholars stressed market organization as irreconcilable with democracy (cf. Collins, 2002, p. 69), but such a stark dismissal is highly problematic.

Concerned with the development of the Australian public service broadcaster ABC, Elizabeth Jacka (2003, p.178) has declared the public sphere-based defence—represented by Garnham's work—as sounding "more and more tired" (see also Nolan, 2006). Her alternative builds on cultural studies scholar John Hartley's (1999) notion of post-modern television, and also refers to political theorist Chantal Mouffe's concept of agonistic democracy. According to Mouffe (2005), the ideal of deliberation in the public sphere in order to reach political consensus is both undesirable and impossible; instead, the public sphere should provide channels for expression of collective passions and confrontation between hegemonic political projects. On this basis, Jacka positions herself in opposition to Garnham's Habermasian stance, which, in her view, remains too focused on consensus-building, the superiority of state- over private-owned broadcasting, and the primacy of high modern journalism in the media mix (Jacka, 2003, p. 179).

In Jacka's view, Garnham's position neglects the key contributions made by commercial media to modern democracies—such as distribution of information, fostering of identities and provision of arenas for public debate.[6] Many other contributors have pointed to popular journalism and commercial entertainment formats as crucial for individual well-being and collective experiences in modern societies. For example, Stuart Hall has hailed the advertising-funded public service broadcaster Channel 4's remit as "a genuinely novel and original way of rethinking the 'public service idea' outside of the BBC," and claimed that Channel 4 enfranchised the audience and granted representation to marginalised groups (Hall, 1992, p. 30). Others have pointed to the historical role that entertainment and popular genres have played in legitimating public service broadcasters, and claimed that it is time to embrace the popular more explicitly as part of the public service remit (Enli, 2008; Syvertsen, 2004; van Zoonen, 2004).

Contributions within this strand of thought also explicitly address the fragmented and pluralistic nature of the audience, and the failure by traditional public service broadcasters to address it fully and adequately. In the 1992 article titled "Which Public, Whose Service" (above), Stuart Hall claimed that the united national public has always been a construct and that public service could only survive if it adapted by "pluralising and diversifying its own interior worlds" (p. 34). Broadcasting needed to be turned in to "the open space, the 'theatre' in which this cultural diversity is produced, displayed and represented" (p. 36). This call seems to be at least partly answered by the recent endeavours of public service broadcasters to involve more audience activity. Enli (forthcoming) has pointed to how early public service broadcasting was reluctant to involve common people, but that this is changing with the onset of digital technology. In a survey of Scandinavian, British and US public service broadcasters, she identifies public participation and the inclusion of user-generated programming as a key strategy for public service broadcasters to regain their position as a national arena in a highly competitive situation.

Critics within this strand of research have also positioned themselves against the "crisis discourse" which has characterised much of the literature on public service broadcasting (cf. Enli, 2008, p. 2). Pro-public service-scholars have had a tendency to view all new developments with suspicion as the beginning of a new and sharp decline for public service, but in reality, the broadcasters have often managed to use new technologies to revitalize their services and address new audiences. Rather than seeing current developments in public service and democracy as a recurrent set of crises, it is argued that these may represent fruitful starting points for new—and more inclusive—understandings of public service and democracy (Jacka, 2003, pp. 181–183). A similar point is made by Geoffrey Craig (1999). Establishing that the Australian ABC exists in a state of perpetual crisis, he suggests embracing conflicts as the best defence: public service broadcasters should "generally provide spaces for, and in turn articulate, the ongoing 'crisis' which always constitutes the public life of a society" (Craig, 1999, p. 113)—a public life "characterised by difference and incommensurability" (p. 112).

Craig's argument is explicitly located within an agonistic model of democracy, and according to him irreconcilable with a Habermasian model. One might argue that such a rejection is neither necessary, nor desirable: it is possible to conceive public service media as a meeting point for conflicting ideas and perspectives also from a Habermas-inspired public sphere approach. Nevertheless, the value of an agonistic model is its focus on the ever-present issues of exclusion, as well as a richer understanding of the range of communicative modes and features present in the public sphere.

LIMITATIONS AND FURTHER DIRECTIONS

As pointed out in the introduction, much research on public service broadcasting has focused on *political* questions—partly questions of policy, organization and management and partly questions of democracy and the public sphere. While the two first strands comprise studies that are mostly descriptive and analytical, studying changes within and around public service broadcasting, the latter two comprise more normative approaches. The key emphasis within these latter two strands is on the question: What exactly is the point of public service broadcasting in modern societies?

On this count, research on public service broadcasting and actual broadcasting debates converge. The positions held by scholars mirror the divisions in the debate over the future of public service broadcasting in society. Almost a decade into the 21st century, three main positions can be clearly identified both in the academic and public debate:

The first position holds that public service broadcasting is rapidly becoming an anachronism. Following those enthusiastic on behalf of the democratic potential of the new media (e.g., Coleman & Gøtze, 2001; Froomkin, 2004), public service broadcasting appears to be both unnecessary and outdated. If the Internet facilitates direct dialogue between citizens, as well as an abundance of differentiated content, why continue to pour large subsidies into state-owned broadcasting institutions?

The second position is at the opposite end of the scale, holding that public service broadcasting is more important than ever before. As the public sphere gets more fragmented and it gets increasingly easy to exclude information, opinions and perspectives inconsistent with personal likes or conceptions, observers fear a "balkanization" of public debate (Sunstein, 2001). In this situation, some call for sustaining and strengthening the traditional national broadcasting systems "for they preserve the principle and practice of a common public life against all those contemporary forces that fragment it" (Scannell, 2005, p. 141).

The final position is closer to the second, but may be seen as an attempt to carve out a compromise, a third way. The idea here is to reformulate the traditional concepts of public service to make it less restricted and limited. Graham Murdock (2005, p. 227) has, for example, sought to redefine public service remits within what he calls a "digital commons": "a linked space defined by its shared refusal of commercial enclosure and its commitment to free and universal access, reciprocity, and collaborative activity." The space is imagined as potentially global in scope, built on computer-mediated communication, where public service broadcasting institutions making up "the central node" in the network.

This third approach may seem attractive to many observers, since it attempts to combine traditional values with new applications. Nevertheless, in order to develop such a position academically and intellectually, some thorny questions remain. One question concerns the *centrality* of traditional public service broadcasters in the years to come: What is really meant by the suggestion that public service broadcasters should make up a central node in a larger network, and what are the implications for structure and funding? How does it relate to the idea proposed for example by the British regulator Ofcom (2007) to set up a "Public Service Provider" to cater for new media content outside the established institutions?

Another issue concerns the *distinctiveness* of public service broadcasters in the digital era. Public funding rests on the idea that public service broadcasting to some extent remains distinct from commercial services, and it continues to be a task for researchers to demonstrate exactly how distinct these services are. Research may also be able to validate whether there is any truth to the claim that public service functions might as well be taken care of by other institutional arrangements, including institutions more akin to community media (Harrison & Wessels, 2005).

A final issue concerns the relationship between ideal conceptions of public service broadcasting and the historical specificity of actual institutions. A large majority of the works reviewed in this chapter relates to very particular situations: the transformation of specific institutions at a certain point in time. The reasoning is far from universal, and may only with great caution be transferred to other contexts. Too often, arguments in discussions about public service broadcasting are lifted without due consideration from one setting to another—disregarding the role of concrete media systems' historical developments, the specificity of language areas and demography, or the size and structure of different markets. This poses a great challenge for researchers, and should stimulate efforts to carry out more comparative studies. One may also learn from historians whose studies demonstrate that large public organizations as a rule are surrounded by internal and external tensions, and exist within a web of conflicting interests. A case in point is Burns (1977, p. 9) who claims that the establishment of public service broadcasting was visible as "a superb example of accomodatory politics, spreading satisfactions and dissatisfactions fairly evenly among the interest groups concerned." This may indeed be the best public service can hope for also in the years to come.

NOTES

1. Many studies have pointed out that "the concept of public-service broadcasting" is "extremely difficult to define" (Feintuck, 1999, p. 66), that it "is not a precise scientific term" (Kuhn, 1985, p. 4), that "[t]here is no easy answer to the question of what public service broadcasting is" (Raboy, 1996, p. 6). There have been several attempts at eliciting a list of public service principles such as "the broadcasting institution is a public body," "the service is provided to all [...] in return for a basic initial payment, usually in the form of an annual license fee" and "a commitment to balanced scheduling across the different programme genres," to mention some of the criteria listed by Kuhn (1985, see also Scannell, 1990). As Raboy (1996, p. 7) points out, however, "The real problem around ... is not to improve the list but rather how to apply any such set of principles." Syvertsen (1999) points to the number of definitions and argues that the term public service broadcasting is "too vague to be used successfully as an analytical term" (see also Bolin, 2004). Others claim that the similarity across institutions makes it possible to identify core public service values (Born & Prosser, 2001; Moe, 2003).
2. The license fee has recently been abolished in the Netherlands and the Flemish community of Belgium. A public grant has replaced the fee (European Audiovisual Observatory, Press release, Strasbourg 9. April 2002. Retrieved March, 16, 2007, from: http://www.obs.coe.int/about/oea/pr/service_public.html.)
3. See for example, the EU's so-called Amsterdam protocol on public broadcasting, which acknowledges national governments' right to determine the funding and mandate of public service broadcasting in their respective states (EU, 1997, protocol no. 32).
4. The method was developed by Williams in order to discuss the differences between US and UK programming. Programming was divided into two main types in order to determine the proportion of typical public service programming on each channel.
5. In the countries identified above as having strong public service traditions, public service television have, as a rule, retained more than one third of the viewing time. (Figures by email from EBU/Nordicom, table 22.4.c)
6. In a reply, Garnham (2003) agrees to the value of commercial broadcasting, while maintaining that the British system had advantages over the American. He argues, however, for a more conservative definition of politics as being about making decisions that affect us as citizens. His main concern is to ensure that the decisions made—the effect of politics—are in the best way possible controlled by the people:

"within a structure of representative democracy informed by a widely accessible public debate" (p. 196). Public service broadcasting remains a guarantor for this debate.

REFERENCES

Blumler, J. G. (Ed.) (1992). *Television and the public interest. Vulnerable values in West European broadcasting*. London: Sage.

Bolin, G. (2004). The value of being public service: The shifting of power relations in Swedish television production. *Media, Culture & Society*, *26*(2), 277–287.

Born, G., & Prosser, T. (2001). Culture and consumerism: Citizenship, public service broadcasting and the BBC's fair trading obligations. *The Modern Law Review*, *64*(5), 657–687.

Born, G. (2004). *Uncertain vision—Birt, Dyke and the reinvention of the BBC*. London: Secker & Warburg.

Briggs, A. (1961). *The birth of broadcasting. The history of broadcasting in the United Kingdom. Vol 1.* London: Oxford University Press.

Brown, A., & Picard, R. G. (Eds.). (2004). *Digital terrestrial television in Europe*. London: Lawrence Erlbaum.

Burns, T. (1977). *The BBC: Public institution and private world*. London: Macmillan.

Calhoun, C. (Ed.). (1992). *Habermas and the public sphere*. Cambridge, MA, London: The MIT Press.

Coleman, S., & Gøtze, J. (2001). *Bowling together: Online public engagement in policy deliberation*. London Hansard Society.

Collins, R. (2002). *Media and identity in contemporary Europe: Consequences of global convergence*. Bristol: Intellect Books.

Coppens, T. & Saeys, F. (2006) Enforcing performance: new approaches to govern public service broadcasting. *Media, Culture & Society*, *28*(2), 261–284.

Craig, G. (1999). Perpetual crisis: The politics of saving the ABC. *Media International Australia—Incorporating Culture and Policy*, *94*, 105–116.

Crossley, N., & Roberts, J. M. (Eds.). (2004). *After Habermas: New perspectives on the public sphere*. Oxford: Blackwell.

Curran, J. (2002). *Media and power*. London, New York: Routledge.

Dahlgren, P. (1995). *Television and the public sphere—Citizenship, democracy and the media*. London: Sage.

Dahlgren, P. (2004). Theory, boundaries and political communication: The uses of disparity. *European Journal of Communication*, *19*(1), 7–18.

Degenhart, C. (2001). *Der Funktionsauftrag des öffentlich-rechtlichen Rundfunks in der «Digitalen Welt.»* Heidelberg: Verlag Recht und Wirtschaft.

Donges, P., & Puppis, M. (Eds.). (2003). *Die Zukunft des öffentlichen Rundfunks—Internationale Beiträge aus Wissenschaft und Praxis*. Köln, Germany: Halem.

Edin A. (2000). *Den föreställda publiken: programpolitik, publikbilder och tiltalsformer i svensk public service-television*. Stockholm/Stehag: Brutus Österlings bokförlag Symposion.

Enli, G. S. (2008). Redefining public service broadcasting: Audience participation and multi-platform formats. To be published in *Convergence*.

European Union (EU). (1997). Treaty of Amsterdam. *Official Journal of the European Communities*, C 340.

Feintuck, M. (1999). *Media regulation, public interest and the law*. Edinburgh: Edinburgh University Press.

Froomkin, A. M. (2004). Technologies for democracy. In P. M. Shane (Ed.), *Democracy online: The prospects for political renewal through the internet* (pp. 3–20). New York: Routledge.

Galperin, H. (2004). *New television, old politics—The transition to digital TV in the United States and Britain*. Cambridge: Cambridge University Press.

Garnham, N. (1978). *Structures of television*. London: British Film Institute.

Garnham, N. (1986). The media and the public sphere. In G. Murdock, P. Golding, & P. Schlesinger (Eds.), *Communication politics* (pp. 37–54). Leicester: Leicester University.

Garnham, N. (1992). The media and the public sphere. In C. Calhoun (Ed.), *Habermas and the public sphere* (pp. 359–77). Cambridge, MA: The MIT Press.

Garnham, N. (2003). A response to Elizabeth Jacka's "democracy as defeat." *Television & New Media, 4*(2), 193–200.

Gourd, A. (2002). *Öffentlichkeit und digitales Fernsehen*. Wiesbaden, Germany: Westdeutscher Verlag.

Habermas, J. (1989). *The structural transformation of the public sphere: An inquiry into a category of bourgeois society.* Cambridge, MA: Polity Press. (Original work published 1962)

Habermas, J. (1996). *Between facts and norms: Contributions to a discourse theory of law and democracy.* Cambridge, MA: The MIT Press. (Original work published 1992)

Hall, S. (1977). Culture, the media and the "ideological effect." In J. Curran, M. Gurevitch, & J. Woolacott (Eds.), *Mass communication and society* (pp. 315–349). London: Edward Arnold.

Hall, S. (1992). Which public, whose service? In W. Stevenson (Ed.), *All our futures. The changing role and purpose of the BBC* (pp. 23–38). London: British Film Institute.

Hallin, D., & Mancini, P. (2004). *Comparing media systems—Three models of media and politics*. Cambridge: Cambridge University Press.

Harrison, J., & Wessels, B. (2005). A new public service communication environment? Public service broadcasting values in the reconfiguring media. *New Media & Society, 7*(6), 834–853.

Hartley, J. (1999). *Uses of television*. London: Routledge.

Hellman, H., & Sauri, T. (1994). Public service television and the tendency towards convergence: Trends in prime-time programme structure in Finland, 1970–92. *Media, Culture & Society, 16*(1), 47–69.

Hoffman-Riem, W. (1996). *Regulating media. The licensing and supervision of broadcasting in six countries*. New York: Guilford.

Hjarvard, S. (1999). *TV-nyheder i konkurrance*. Frederiksberg, Denmark: Samfundslitteratur.

Humphreys, P. J. (1996). *Mass media and media policy in Western Europe*. Manchester: Manchester University Press.

Jacka, E. (2003). "Democracy as defeat"—The impotence of arguments for public service broadcasting. *Television & New Media, 4*(2), 177–191.

Jakubowicz, K (2004). A square peg in a round hole: The EU's policy on public service broadcasting In I. Bondebjerg & P. Golding (Eds.), *European culture and the media* (pp. 277–301). Bristol: Intellect Books.

Keane, J. (1991). *The media and democracy*. Cambridge: Polity Press.

Kuhn, R. (Ed.). (1985). *The politics of broadcasting*. London: Croom Helm.

Langenbucher, W. R. (1990). Braucht eine demokratische Gesellschaft öffentlichen Rundfunk? *Media Perspektiven, 11*, 699–716.

Levy, D. A. (1999). *Europe's digital revolution. Broadcasting, the EU and the nation state*. London: Routledge.

Lowe, G. F., & Jauert, P. (Eds.). (2005). *Cultural dilemmas in public service broadcasting*. Göteborg, Sweden: Nordicom.

Lucht, J. (2006). *Der öffentlich-rechtliche Rundfunk: ein Auslaufmodell? Grundlagen—Analysen—Perspektiven*. Wiesbaden, Germany: VS Verlag.

Marsden, C. T., & Verhulst, S. G. (Eds.). (1999). *Convergence in European digital TV regulation*. London: Blackstone.

Maasø, A., Sundet, V. S., & Syvertsen, T. (2007). "Fordi de fortjener det." Publikumsdeltakelse som strategisk utviklingsområde i mediebransjen. *Norsk Medietidsskrift, 14*(2), 125–153.

McQuail, D., & Siune, K. (Eds.). (1986). *New media politics: Comparative perspectives in Western Europe*. London: Sage.

McQuail, D. & Siune, K. (Eds.). (1998). *Media policy: Convergence, concentration and commerce*. London: Sage.

McKinsey & Company. (2004). *Review of public service broadcasting around the world.* Retrieved April 10, 2007, from: http://www.ofcom.org.uk/consult/condocs/psb2/psb2/psbwp/wp3mck.pdf

Mendel, T. (2000). *Public service broadcasting. A comparative legal survey.* Kuala Lumpur: UNESCO, Asia Pacific Institute for Broadcasting Development. Retrieved April 10, 2007, from: http://www.unesco.org/webworld/publications/mendel/jaya_index.html

Moe, H. (2003). *Digitaliseringen av fjernsyn og allmennkringkastingens skjebne.* Department of Media Studies, University of Bergen, Norway.

Moe, H. (in press). Public service media online? Regulating public broadcasters' internet services — a comparative analysis. *Television & New Media, 9*(3). 220–238.

Moe, H., & Syvertsen, T. (2007). Media institutions as a research field: Three phases of Norwegian broadcasting research. *Nordicom Review, 28,* 149–167.

Mouffe, C., (2005). *On the political.* Abingdon: Routledge.

Murdock, G. (2005). Building the digital commons. In G. F. Lowe & P. Jauert (Eds.), *Cultural dilemmas in public service broadcasting* (pp. 213–231). Göteborg, Sweden: Nordicom.

Nolan, D. (2006). Media, citizenship and governmentality: Defining "the public" of public service broadcasting. *Social Semiotics, 16*(2), 225–242.

Ofcom (2007). *A new approach to public service content in the digital age,* London: Ofcom

Papathanassopoulos, S. (2002). *European television in the digital age.* Cambridge: Polity Press.

Raboy, M. (Ed.). (1996). *Public broadcasting for the 21st century. Academia research monograph, 17.* Luton, UK: University of Luton Press.

Reith, J. (1924). *Broadcast over Britain.* London: Hodder and Stoughton.

Richeri, G. (2004), Broadcasting and the market: The case of public television. In A. Calabrese & C. Sparks (Eds.), *Toward a Political Economy of Culture: Capitalism and Communication in the Twenty-First Century* (pp. 178–193). Lanham, MD: Rowman & Littlefield.

Scannell, P. (1989). Public service broadcasting and modern public life. *Media, Culture & Society, 11*(2), 135–66.

Scannell, P. (1990). Public service broadcasting: the history of a concept. In A. Goodwin & G. Whannel (Eds.), *Understanding television* (pp. 11–29). London: Routledge.

Scannell, P. (2005). The meaning of broadcasting in the digital era. In G. F. Lowe & P. Jauert (Eds.), *Cultural dilemmas in public service broadcasting — RIPE@2005* (pp. 129–143). Göteborg, Sweden: Nordicom.

Siune, K., & Hultén, O. (1998). Does public broadcasting have a future? In D. McQuail & K. Siune (Eds.), *Media policy: Convergence, concentration and commerce* (pp. 23–37). London: Sage.

Skogerbø, E. (1996). *Privatising the public interest — conflicts and compromises in Norwegian media politics 1980–1993.* PhD dissertation. Department of Media and Communication. Oslo: University of Oslo.

Sunstein, C. R. (2001). *Republic.com.* Princeton, NJ: Princeton University Press.

Storsul, T., & Syvertsen, T. (2007). The impact of convergence on European television policy: Pressure for change Luton forces of stability. *Convergence, 13*(3), 275–291.

Syvertsen, T. (1997). *Den store TV-krigen.* Bergen, Norway: Fagbokforlaget.

Syvertsen, T. (1999). The many uses of the "public service" concept. *Nordicom Review, 20*(1), 5–12.

Syvertsen, T. (2003). Challenges to public television in the era of convergence and commercialization. *Television & New Media, 4*(2), 155–175.

Syvertsen, T. (2004). Citizens, audiences, customers and players — a conceptual discussion of the relationship between broadcasters and their publics, *European Journal of Cultural Studies, 7*(3), 363–380.

Søndergaard, H. (1994). *DR i tv-konkurrencens tidsalder.* Frederiksberg, Denmark: Samfundslitteratur.

Truetzschler, W., & Siune, K. (Eds). (1992). *Dynamics of media politics: Broadcasting and electronic media in Western Europe.* London: Sage.

Ytreberg, E. (1999). *Allmennkringkastingens autoritet: endringer i NRK Fjernsynets tekstproduksjon, 1987–1994.* Department of Media and Communication, University of Oslo.

Van Zoonen, L. (2004). Popular qualities in public service broadcasting. *European Journal of Cultural Studies, 7*(3), 275–282.

Ward, D. (2003). State aid or band aid? An evaluation of the European Commission's approach to public service broadcasting. *Media, Culture & Society*, *25*(2), 233– 255.
Williams, R. (1975). *Television: Technology and cultural form*. London: Fontana.

29

Comparative Journalism Studies

Thomas Hanitzsch

GEARING UP FOR CROSS-NATIONAL RESEARCH

International studies of journalism have demonstrated that the onward march of globalization coincides with a convergence in journalistic orientations and practices. The ideals of objectivity and impartiality dominate many newsrooms around the world, indicating a "diffusion of occupational ideologies," or "transfer of ideology," from the West to the East (Golding, 1977, pp. 292–293). Similarities in professional routines, editorial procedures and socialization processes exist in countries as diverse as Brazil, Germany, Indonesia, Tanzania and the United States (Hanitzsch, 2005; Herscovitz, 2004; Ramaprasad, 2001; Weaver, Beam, Brownlee, Voakes, & Wilhoit, 2007; Weischenberg, Malik, & Scholl, 2006). At the same time, research has shown that substantive differences continue to prevail, and that professional views and practices of journalists are deeply colored by national media systems (e.g., Berkowitz, Limor, & Singer, 2004; Deuze, 2002; Esser, 1998; Golding & Elliott, 1979; Patterson & Donsbach, 1996; Shoemaker & Cohen, 2006; Splichal & Sparks, 1994; Weaver 1998b). Hence, the attempt to probe deeper into these similarities and differences in journalistic cultures around the world has become one of the most fascinating sub-domains in the field of journalism studies, and researchers in this area increasingly adopt a comparative perspective.

Over the years, comparative research has not only yielded valuable insights beyond a mere description of similarities and differences, but also contributed to our understanding of specific countries. A tradition of almost 40 years of research has revealed that news production is contingent on the cultural, political and historical contexts that shape the journalist's work. International studies have raised awareness of the fact that the Western conception of journalism in a free-press system does not reign supreme in many parts of the world, and may not even be desirable in some. Comparative research is, therefore, not only indispensable for establishing the generalizability of theories and findings, it also forces us to test our interpretations against cross-cultural differences and inconsistencies (Kohn, 1989).

Political changes and technological advancements have supported a trend towards cross-cultural research. The end of the cold war and the advent of a globalizing world gave a fresh impetus to the mobility of researchers, with academics finding more and more opportunities to meet their colleagues from afar. New communication technologies triggered the rise of institutionalized global networks of scientists, including sections devoted to the study of journalism in the International Communication Association and the European Communication Research and Education

Association. Moreover, it has become much easier to acquire funding for international studies, as sponsoring institutions become aware of the virtues of comparative research. The European Framework Programme for Research and Technological Development, for instance, has created unprecedented opportunities for those who seek funding for multi-national and interdisciplinary research projects.

This chapter provides an overview of the growing field of comparative research in journalism studies, as well as a critical examination of this field. It begins with a historical introduction to comparative research and continues with the discussion of key studies. Subsequent sections elaborate on critical and methodological issues, and the chapter concludes with a discussion of directions for further research.

CONCEPTUAL ISSUES IN COMPARATIVE RESEARCH

Historical Backgrounds and Definitions

The origins of cross-cultural research can be traced back to the work of Edward Tylor, who is generally credited as the "father" of anthropology. In his book *Primitive Culture* (1958[1871]), which became a milestone in English-speaking anthropology, Tylor proposed the first known formal definition of culture as the "complex whole which includes knowledge, belief, art, morals, law, custom, and any other capabilities and habits acquired by man as a member of society" (p. 1). The first major comparative study was probably Emil Durkheim's (1897) research on suicide and social anomy, but it was not until the Second World War that comparative research became common in the social sciences and humanities. It rapidly influenced psychology, sociology, history and political science and led to the creation of a number of academic journals devoted to cross-cultural studies, most notably the *International & Comparative Law Quarterly* (founded in 1952), *Comparative Studies in Society and History* (1958), *Comparative Politics* (1968), *Journal of Cross-Cultural Psychology* (1970) and *Journal of Intercultural Communication Research* (2006).

However, terminology in comparative research still tends to be ambiguous and confusing. Labels such as "cross-country," "cross-national", "cross-societal", "cross-cultural", "cross-systemic" and "cross-institutional," as well as "trans-national", "trans-societal" and "trans-cultural" are used both as synonymous with "comparative" research, and to denote specific kinds of comparisons (Øyen, 1990, p. 7). There is also a considerable disagreement on the kinds of research that the term "comparative" refers to, or should refer to. Some scholars have limited it to the comparison of two or more *nations* (Edelstein, 1982), others argue that *all* social research is comparative (Beniger, 1992). The latter is certainly true to the extent that all new evidence needs to be tested against, and thus compared with, the existing stock of knowledge. Cross-cultural studies, on the other hand, entail several specific conceptual and methodological challenges that make them distinct from mono-cultural research. For the purposes of this chapter, I will refer to a study as comparative if two or more *a-priori*-defined cultural populations are compared according to at least one functionally equivalent concept. This formula, however, excludes the temporal aspect of comparative research, that is, the comparison between different points in time.

Paradigms

The historical evolution and development of comparative journalism research can be divided into four broad paradigms:

- *The US and the rest*: This paradigm has dominated communication and media studies from the 1950s to the 1960s, and is exemplified by the influential work of American scholars such as Daniel Lerner (*The Passing of Traditional Society*, 1958) as well as that of Fred S. Siebert, Theodore Peterson and Wilbur Schramm (*Four Theories of the Press*, 1956). US-centrism and the juxtaposition of the "modern" West and the "traditional" East were particularly prevalent in this period of time. In the field of journalism studies, Jack McLeod is generally credited with having pioneered comparative research. He invented a scale to measure the level of professionalism among journalists, which was first applied to news workers in the United States (McLeod & Hawley, 1964) and later to Latin American journalists (McLeod & Rush, 1969a, b). Other researchers followed suit, including Wright (1974) in Canada, Donsbach (1981) in Germany and Henningham (1984) in Australia. The paradigm slowly faded away in the mid 1970s when researchers begun to realize its ideological bearings (see below).
- *The North and the South*: This period was primarily shaped by major political processes that took place within UNESCO and the European Community. In the mid 1970s, the growing recognition of uneven communication flows between the industrialized North and developing South fuelled a controversy, staged at UNESCO, on the need for a New World Information and Communication Order. This debate inspired a 29-nation study on foreign images that was replicated in the 1990s on a sample of 38 countries (Sreberny-Mohammadi, Nordenstreng, & Stevenson, 1984; Wu, 2000). These studies are, to date, the largest concerted research endeavors in the field of communication and media studies. At the same time, as the European Community became further integrated during the 1970s, the political processes that took place within its institutions attracted the interest of several European researchers. Foremost among them was Jay G. Blumler (1983), who coordinated a nine-country study on the role of television in the campaigns that led up to the 1979 European Parliamentary elections.
- *The West and the West*: This paradigm dominated the field between the mid 1980s to the late 1990s. It was very much driven by European scholarship and also marks the beginning of methodologically more advanced comparative research. Scholars became more cautious in selecting countries, turning their attention to mostly Western countries due to their similarities and, hence, their comparability. Köcher (1986) and Esser (1998) investigated journalists and newsrooms in Germany and the UK, while Chalaby (1996) compared the histories of journalism in France, Great Britain and the United States. A more recent example is the comparison of online journalists in Germany and the United States (Quandt, Löffelholz, Weaver, Hanitzsch, & Altmeppen, 2006). The most deliberate comparative design to date was employed by Patterson and Donsbach (1996) who administered identical questionnaires to 1,361 journalists in Germany, Great Britain, Italy, Sweden and the United States.
- *The West and the Global*: Within this most recent paradigm, researchers are interested in the universal and the specific in journalistic cultures around the world, though most studies still rely on Western-grown concepts. One of the first studies within this strand of research was Golding and Elliott's (1979) analysis of broadcasting organizations in Sweden, Ireland and Nigeria, but it was not until the 1990s that this paradigm gained popularity. Splichal and Sparks (1994) coordinated a survey of first-year journalism students in 22 nations, while journalists in the United States have been compared to their counterparts in China and Taiwan (Zhu, Weaver, Lo, Chen, & Wu, 1997), Russia (Wu, Weaver, & Johnson 1996), as well as Australia, Great Britain, Germany and the Netherlands (Deuze, 2002). David Weaver (1998c), in his seminal collection *The Global Journalist*, reported evidence

from surveys of an unmatched body of 20,280 journalists from 21 countries. Pamela Shoemaker and Akiba Cohen (2006) recently published their findings from the *News Around the World* project that involved ten countries from all inhabited continents. At the same time, theoretical and methodological reflections on comparative research have become much more common in the field (e.g., Chang et al., 2001; Johnson & Tuttle, 2000; Livingstone, 2003; Wirth & Kolb, 2004).

Units of Analysis

In theory, the units of analysis in comparative research can be selected from various social levels, but in practice, journalism researchers tend to compare two or three, rarely more, countries to which they happen to have access. Nations, however, may not always be proper units of comparison since they are far from self-contained but rather comprise multiple cultures (Livingstone, 2003). National borders do not necessarily correspond to cultural, linguistic and ethnic divisions, nor do they correspond to a common sense of identity (Hantrais, 1999). However, nations also offer a convenient shorthand for comparative studies since they possess clearly-defined boundaries and are often the only kinds of units available for comparison (Hofstede, 2001). Even more importantly, news production is still strongly geared towards news agendas that prioritize domestic news, as well as media coverage that champions national actors, and journalists speaking to national or local audiences.

Despite the overwhelming dominance of cross-national research, comparisons of units on the sub-national level have found their niche. Several studies have compared language areas within countries, exemplified by surveys of journalists in Canada (Pritchard & Souvageau, 1998) and Switzerland (Marr, Wyss, Blum, & Bonfadelli, 2001). Other studies explored similarities and differences between (former) states within a particular nation (East and West Germany: Schoenbach, Stuerzebecher, & Schneider, 1998), or ethnic groups within a country (Indonesia: Hanitzsch, 2006). In addition to the sub-national level, there are other options for a creative selection of units for comparison, most notably cross border regions, such as the European Union, the ASEAN, or culturally cohesive regions like Latin America. Other possibilities are news organizations that operate transnationally, such as the *International Herald Tribune*, Euronews or Al Jazeera.

KEY STUDIES

Professionalism and Professionalization

Early comparative research in journalism studies focused on professionalism and processes of professionalization. These two terms were often used interchangeably, although they clearly have conceptually different meanings. Professionalism is something that journalists embrace or pursue, while professionalization refers to a process of an occupation gradually becoming a true profession.

The first truly comparative study in journalism research was carried out by Jack M. McLeod in the late 1960s. McLeod, together with Searle E. Hawley Jr. (1964), developed a 24-item scale to measure the level of professionalism among US journalists. Data were gathered from 115 journalists working for two local newspapers based in Milwaukee, Wisconsin. Five years later, McLeod and his former doctoral student Ramona R. Rush (1969 a, b) published two articles based on data from the original Wisconsin study and an additional sample of 46 Latin American journalists. In their comparative study, McLeod and Rush (1969a) found greater similarity than dissimilarity between Latin American and US journalists in all areas. The only major difference occurred in the greater desire of Latin American journalists for prestige in the organization and the community, and for respect regarding their newspapers and co-workers. They were also less satisfied with their jobs. American journalists, on the other hand, gave relatively more emphasis to the enjoyment of the job, availability of support on the job and having a job that is valuable to the community.

In a subsequent paper, McLeod and Rush (1969b) reported that those journalists in Latin America who were more likely to be professionally oriented tended to be younger, male and had journalistic training in their university backgrounds. Consistent with the findings from the US study, they found that the "professional" Latin American journalists were more critical of the content of their own newspapers. Those who had newspaper reporting or editing jobs in newspapers were also found to be more professional than their colleagues who had newspaper managerial positions or other media jobs. Contrary to what was commonly believed, McLeod and Rush (1969b) concluded that professional journalists seem no more likely to have come from the developed countries or from countries with lesser restriction on press freedom than do those who are less professional.

Drawing on McLeod's work on US and Latin American journalists, as well as on Wright's (1974) study of 77 Canadian journalists and his own data from 261 West German journalists surveyed in 1974, Donsbach (1981, pp. 55–56) found that relationships with colleagues played a considerably less important role among Latin American journalists than for their counterparts in the developed countries. Also, the possibility of exercising social influence seemed substantially less central to Latin American journalists, while they regarded career and prestige as more important. German journalists, on the other hand, were characterized by their desire to influence political and social processes, a strong aspiration to increase their own chances for participation, as well as a relatively firm peer orientation. Given the sometimes striking differences between journalists from the countries he had compared, Donsbach (p. 64) concluded that "professionalization is neither a universal nor a value-neutral concept."

Concepions of professionalization and professionalism, however, have received substantial criticism from scholars arguing that these notions have evolved in a Western context, and the application of these concepts to non-Western societies has been inadequate (Starck & Sudhaker, 1979, p. 34). Birkhead (1982, p. 130) also noted that "there is no clearly defined counter-concept, no alternative focus for looking at occupational behavior and structure in a different light." In a forceful critique of the professionalization concept, Starck and Sudhaker (1979, p. 41), somewhat pessimistically, concluded that "[s]tudies in comparative professionalism so far have yielded findings narrow in dimension, short on insight."

News Decisions

Another tradition in comparative journalism studies emerged when German researchers turned their attention to the political views and professional roles of journalists, and how these influence their news decisions. The interest in journalists' political orientations was largely driven by the fact that German newspapers were much stronger aligned with particular ideological positions than, for instance, US newspapers. Such an orientation, it was speculated, makes it more likely that the political views of the journalists substantially shape their news decisions. The emphasis on political roles was very much informed by Cohen's (1963) and Janowitz's (1975) work on professional role models.

Renate Köcher's (1986) dissertation on German and British journalists was the first deliberate comparative attempt to tap into this area. Her study was based on face-to-face interviews with

450 German and 405 British journalists in print and broadcast media. The findings confirmed Köcher's initial expectation that German and British journalists differ in their perception of roles, their professional motivation and their evaluation of work norms. German journalists were in favor of a more active role of advocacy, whereas their British counterparts were inclined to embrace a more neutral reporter role. The roles of criticizing abuses and of spokesman for the underdog, which stand for value judgments and advocacy, tend to be accepted by German journalists more than by their British colleagues.

British journalists, by way of contrast, outdid their German colleagues in terms of claiming a political influence. This finding, however, together with British journalists embracing an instructor or educator role more than the Germans, ran somewhat counter to the evidence presented earlier. Both inconsistencies were not convincingly resolved by Köcher. Her claim that the responses indicated that German and British journalists would "tend to act differently" (p. 59) was also not warranted by her findings since she did not look at the actual practice but relied on the journalists' responses to the questionnaire. The somewhat sweeping conclusion—that British journalists viewed themselves as "bloodhounds" or "hunters of news," while their German colleagues perceived themselves as "missionaries" (p. 63)—was an over-interpretation of what was actually ambiguous evidence. This, to the credit of the study's author, has been admitted by Köcher, when she conceded that German and British journalists interpreted their roles more as a conglomerate of neutrality and advocacy.

Some of Köcher's results were, a few years later, confirmed by the findings from the *Media and Democracy Project* coordinated by Thomas E. Patterson and Wolfgang Donsbach (1996). A mail survey was administered to journalists in Germany, Great Britain, Italy, Sweden and the United States sequentially from 1991 to 1993. In each country, 600 journalists were contacted, but varying response rates (between 51 and 36 percent) produced a total sample 1,361 respondents. Patterson and Donsbach asked the respondents to make 24 news decisions about four hypothetical situations. The news decisions were developed from actual news stories, with 17 framed in a way that favored a partisan view and the remaining seven news stories framed neutrally.

Asking the journalists about their political orientations, Patterson and Donsbach found that all journalists—in the broadcast and newspaper industries at both the national and local levels—were somewhat left of center in their political beliefs. Journalists also viewed themselves as more liberal than the news organizations for which they worked. In addition, in all five countries, journalists positioned themselves to the left of where they perceived their news audience to be. One of the main findings of the study was that the journalists' partisanship was significantly related to their news decisions, although the actual correlations were rather weak. Patterson and Donsbach nonetheless claimed that their survey provided "substantial evidence" (p. 465) that partisan beliefs intrude on news decisions. The authors concluded that "the hues of journalists' partisanship tend to shade the news rather than coloring it deeply. Partisanship is a measurable but not a robust influence on journalists' news decisions."

Among the five countries, the German news system was found to be the most partisan, and the British and American news systems the least. In all countries, journalists were motivated primarily by the task of gathering and disseminating information. US journalists, however, liked to exert political influence, though not by championing their subjective values and beliefs, as did their German and Italian colleagues (Donsbach & Patterson, 2004). The differences between German and American journalists were seen as resulting from specific newsroom structures, most notably the division of labor. This molded news production in the two respective countries to become "two very different professional worlds" (Donsbach, 1995, pp. 25–26): US newsrooms were dominated by a strict role-division of reporter, editor and commentator roles, while German journalists tended to mix these different roles.

Another interesting finding of the *Media and Democracy Project* was the different perception of the objectivity norm in at least four of the countries. Journalists in the United States and Great Britain seemed to prefer a more retained notion of objectivity by stressing the news media's function to act as a common carrier between interest groups and the public. News people in Germany and Italy, on the other hand, were more inclined to investigate the assertions of interest groups, and try to get to the hard and "true" facts of the political scene. Donsbach and Klett (1993, p. 80) concluded from their analysis that there are "partially different 'professional cultures' where the boundaries can be drawn between the Anglo-Saxon journalists on the one, and the continental European journalists on the other side."

Considerable similarities, on the other hand, were found recently in the *News around the World* project, led by Pamela J. Shoemaker and Akiba A. Cohen (2006). The study was conducted in ten countries that cut across different cultures and political systems, including Australia, Chile, China, Germany, India, Israel, Jordan, Russia, South Africa and the United States. The selection was made to represent large, medium-sized and small nations. It covered countries from the West and the East, the North and the South, as well as the developed and the developing world. The study combined a quantitative content analysis with qualitative focus group discussions: A total of 32,000 news items were investigated from newspapers and television and radio news programs. Focus group discussions were conducted with journalists, public relations practitioners and audience members.

In their analysis of news topics, Shoemaker and Cohen found a remarkable agreement across the ten countries on what kinds of events, ideas and people should constitute news: An event, person or idea is most likely to become news "if it deals with sports, international or internal politics, cultural events, business, internal order, or human interest" (p. 45). Science and technology, the environment, labor relations and trade unions, energy, fashion and beauty, and population, on the other hand, are least likely to make it into the news. Shoemaker and Cohen also discovered a substantial agreement among the focus group participants in terms of the perceived newsworthiness of news items. The correlations between the perceived newsworthiness and the actual newspaper coverage, on the other hand, were much lower. Particularly perplexing was the fact that the relationships between the journalists' individual views on news values and the actually produced content were unexpectedly weak and even negative at times. This may be seen as an indication that organizational imperatives of the news media override the journalists' individual preferences. Shoemaker and Cohen concluded that, across the board, people tend to agree more with each other about the newsworthiness of the stories than with the news decisions made by their cities' newspaper editors. The authors therefore speculated about a "general sense of malaise or disappointment with the media as expressed by citizens—both media professionals and laypeople—around the world" (p. 89).

Global Journalists

One of the major sources in comparative journalism research to date is David Weaver's (1998c) meticulous compilation, *The Global Journalist*. The key assumption behind this volume was that "journalists' backgrounds and ideas have some relationship to what is reported (and how it is covered) in the various news media around the world, in spite of various societal and organizational constraints, and that this news coverage matters in terms of world public opinion and policies" (Weaver, 1998a, p. 2). The book reports evidence from surveys of a total of 20,280 journalists from 21 countries, with remarkable methodological variation among the 25 studies: Some studies have used either mail surveys, telephone or personal interviews, others have combined different methods of data collection. Sample size ranged from 5,867 obtained questionnaires in

China to 100 interviewed journalists in Mexico; and response rates varied from a low of 32 percent in Brazil to a high of 95 percent among Canadian women journalists. The compared body of data stretched across ten years, with the first study conducted 1986 in Algeria and the last one 1996 in Canada.

Given the methodological constraints posed by this kind of data, Weaver (1998b, p. 455) noted that "[c]omparing journalists across national boundaries and cultures is a game of guesswork at best." He concluded that the "typical journalist" is mostly a young college-educated man who studied something other than journalism and who came from the established and dominant cultural groups in his country. In terms of professional roles, Weaver found a remarkable consensus among journalists regarding the importance of reporting the news quickly and some agreement on the importance of providing access for the people to express their views. There was much less support for providing analysis and being a watchdog of the government. Weaver also reported much disagreement on the importance of providing entertainment, as well as reporting accurately and objectively. It remains questionable, however, if the strong support expressed by Chinese journalists for investigating government claims stands up to closer scrutiny.

Weaver also found considerable national differences in the journalists' ethics of reporting. With the exception of the case of revealing news sources that have been promised confidentiality, journalists generally disagreed on whether some ethically questionable reporting practices might be justified in the case of an important story. They differed in the extent to which they would pay for information, pretend to be someone else, badger news sources, use documents without permission, as well as get employed to gain inside information. In light of these very large differences with respect to the justification of ethically questionable reporting methods, Weaver concluded that it seems "there are strong national differences that override any universal professional norms or values of journalism around the world" (p. 473). Many of these heterogeneities seemed related to differences in political systems, more than to the influences of news organizations, journalism education and professional norms. However, cultural norms and political values did appear to have at least some influence on journalists' views of their values and ethics.

Weaver's attempt to get added value from survey data that were not tailored to cross-national comparison can certainly be contested on methodological grounds. Varying conceptualizations and research methodologies make this kind of "second-hand comparison" problematic, if not inadequate. However, the book is still the most comprehensive collection of findings from studies of news people around the world, and it continues to be a major reference for journalism researchers who engage in comparative research.

Historical Studies

Weaver's conclusion that influences stemming from political systems may be most important in shaping a given country's journalistic culture is also supported by a historical study authored by Daniel C. Hallin and Paolo Mancini (2004). Their research focused on media systems in North America and Western Europe, due to their relatively comparable levels of economic development and their common culture and political history. Although Hallin and Mancini did not limit their analysis to journalism, many of their conclusions are of immediate relevance to journalism studies, since the study's main concern was political communication.

Hallin and Mancini identified four major dimensions according to which media systems in Western Europe and North America can be usefully compared: (1) the development of media markets, with particular emphasis on the strong (or weak) development of a mass circulation press; (2) political parallelism, or the extent to which the media system reflects the major political divisions in society; (3) the development of journalistic professionalism; and (4) the degree and nature of state intervention in the media system. With these four factors in mind, Hallin and Mancini distinguished between three models of media and politics. The *Mediterranean* or *Polarized Pluralist Model* (e.g., France, Greece, Italy, Portugal and Spain) is characterized by an elite-oriented press with relatively small circulation and a corresponding centrality of broadcasting media. In countries that fall under this model, the news media tend to have a strong political leaning, and professionalization of journalism is rather weak, as journalism is not particularly strongly differentiated from political activism. The press is marked by a strong focus on political life in which opinion-oriented or advocacy journalism has a bolder presence compared to other models.

The *Northern European* or *Democratic Corporatist Model* (e.g., Austria, Belgium, Denmark, Finland, Germany, the Netherlands, Norway, Sweden and Switzerland) is characterized by early development of the newspaper industry and very high newspaper circulation. Another attribute of this model is the history of strong party newspapers which coexisted with the commercial press throughout much of the 20th century. Opinion-oriented journalism still persists in this system, though it is of diminishing importance, while journalists increasingly embrace neutral and information-oriented roles. Journalistic professionalism is above average and is marked by a high degree of formal organization. The *North Atlantic* or *Liberal Model* (Canada, Great Britain, Ireland and the United States), on the other hand, is distinguished by the early emergence of a mass-circulation press, although circulation today tends to be lower than in Democratic Corporatist societies. With the exception of the highly partisan British press, newspapers do not show a strong political leaning, thus information-oriented journalism predominates. Journalism is highly professionalized in this model, even though journalistic autonomy is more likely to be limited by commercial pressures.

While Hallin and Mancini's study was primarily geared towards the understanding of the interplay between media and politics, the work of Jean K. Chalaby (1996) tapped into the relationship between journalism and culture. Chalaby's well-cited main argument is that "journalism is an Anglo-American invention" (p. 303). He based his thesis on a historical comparison of French, British and US journalism between the 1830s and the 1920s. Chalaby's contention is that American and British journalists invented the modern conception of news, that Anglo-American newspapers contained more news and information, and that they had much better organized news-gathering services. Among the factors that contributed to the rapid development of journalism in Great Britain and the United States were the independence of the press from the literary field, parliamentary bipartism, the ability of newspapers to derive substantial revenues from sales and advertising, the dynamics of the English language, as well as the Anglo-Saxon central and dominant position in the world. Another difference between Anglo-American and French journalism has to do with the way news reports are structured. In the Anglo-Saxon tradition, news accounts place the most newsworthy first and are constructed around "facts." In French newspapers, on the other hand, the organizing principle of many articles is the mediating subjectivity of the journalist. However, French journalists do not only wrap information into their own observations but construct their articles according to their own interpretation of the related events. Here, Chalaby's conclusions resonate with findings from survey researches that emphasize the more interpretative style of news reporting found in many continental-European media cultures.

CRITICAL ISSUES AND METHODOLOGICAL PITFALLS

Although comparative research is currently a rapidly growing subdomain of journalism studies, its rising significance has not been accompanied by adequate development in theory and methodology. While new technologies have made it possible to conduct extensive surveys, process enormous quantities of data and then make this data available to researchers working in various countries, a sophisticated discussion about theories, concepts, designs and methods in comparative communication research has only just begun (Hantrais & Mangen, 1996; Wirth & Kolb, 2004).

Major Challenges to Comparative Research

One of the major challenges in comparative research lies in the epistemological domain. Since cross-cultural studies often implicitly assume methodological and theoretical universalism, they are vulnerable to the production of out-of-context measurement (Livingstone, 2003). It is still common that investigators conduct their research, at least partly, in a cultural context different from their own. In this kind of "safari research" (Hantrais & Mangen, 1996, p. 4), they mostly compare other nations to their own countries by evaluating other cultures through the lens of their own cultural value-systems. If they then focus on differences between the units of analysis, they tend to understate heterogeneities within the examined cultures, ignoring the fact that, occasionally, variances within cultures may be greater than those across cultural boundaries (Blumler, McLeod, & Rosengren, 1992; Øyen, 1990). This is, for instance, the case in the analysis of professional orientations of journalists across nations, as the diversity of journalistic cultures within nations often remains unaddressed.

When very different systems or time periods are analyzed, the extent of the differences may overwhelm any meaningful comparison (Blumler, McLeod, & Rosengren, 1992). These differences may not only be large and multidimensional, but may also vary by domain. What we treat as a similarity at one level of analysis may reveal myriad differences at more detailed levels of analysis (Kohn, 1989). Furthermore, differences and similarities, for instance between British and American journalists, may be "caused" by the genuine features of the two media systems, but they may also result from diffusion across national boundaries. Diffusion is particularly likely when countries share a common cultural origin. It can also be accelerated by ongoing globalization processes. The professional ideology of objectivity, for example, has spread from the United States to many parts of the world. An analysis that does not address these processes of diffusion, therefore, may be inadequate.

Ideological Bearings and Western Bias

Another problem in comparative journalism research is Western bias. According to Josephi (2006), the Anglo-American dominance in journalism studies has resulted from the long tradition of journalism studies in America, accompanied by the concentration of academic and textbook publishers in Great Britain and the United States, and the fact that English has developed into a world language. Colonial history is another important factor, as mass media in Africa, Latin America and Asia have developed as derivatives of those in the West (Golding, 1977). With the gradual decolonization of the Third World, however, Western scholars have failed to realize that the normative expectations of their models have biased their interpretations. If standards of developed nations are applied to developing countries, the result can only be a fundamentally unsympathetic view of the problems of journalism and journalists in those societies (Starck & Sudhaker, 1979).

This Western bias in journalism studies had some notable ideological implications. News people in the Third World were portrayed as needing to "catch up" with journalistic norms in the developed world, while the ideology of "professionalism" was transferred from the North to the

South (Golding, 1977, p. 292). For Halloran (1998, pp. 44–45), this "research imperialism" legitimized and reinforced established order, while strengthening the Third World's economic and cultural dependence on the West. However, there is a growing awareness among Western media researchers who "feel embarrassed about viewing the rest of the world as forgotten understudy" (Curran & Park, 2000, p. 3).

The Problem of Equivalence

Weaver's (1998c) international compilation of studies is a case in point for this Western bias in journalism research. The measurement of professional roles in the surveys conducted in Brazil, China, Hong Kong, Korea, Taiwan, and the Pacific Islands almost exclusively relied on translations of the original US questionnaire. With other role conceptions, most notably the concept of development journalism, only rudimentarily included or even entirely excluded, this measurement may well turn out to be inappropriate for many of these countries. Hence, if researchers speak of "professional roles" as a concept, they need to ensure that it covers its functional equivalents—that is, all relevant aspects in a given cultural realm—in every single culture included in a comparative study. Equivalence should therefore be seen as the major problem in comparative research (van Vijver & Leung, 1997; Wirth & Kolb, 2004). Researchers should not only make sure they apply concepts equivalently in all cultures, but they also ought to use equivalent research methods and administrative procedures. Furthermore, researchers need to invest considerable effort in the development of research instruments which must be thoughtfully developed, consequently pre-tested, carefully adjusted and strictly applied.

Selection of Cultures

Another important consideration in comparative research is the selection of cases. Hantrais (1999, pp. 100–101) rightly noted that "[a]ny similarities or differences revealed by a cross-national study may be no more than an artifact of the choice of countries." Geddes (2003) has convincingly demonstrated how case selection can affect, or even render unreliable, outcomes of a comparative study. Whatever considerations serve as the rationale for the sampling, the units of analysis should be chosen within a conceptual framework that justifies their comparison (Chang et al., 2001). In reality, however, investigators in comparative journalism researches have often failed to present a rationale for their mix of countries.

Related to this issue is the question of how many cases should be selected in a comparative study. There is no general answer to this. Most common in journalism research are small-sample designs with two or three countries being compared. Medium-sample studies, which range between five to 60 countries, are rare but increasingly proliferating (e.g., Patterson & Donsbach, 1996; Shoemaker & Cohen, 2006; Splichal & Sparks, 1994; Weaver 1998b), whereas large-sample designs are still nonexistent in our field. While medium-sample and large-sample studies certainly have their advantages in terms of causal inference and generalization, it is not necessarily true that the more cultures included in the analysis, the more we learn (Kohn, 1989).

DIRECTIONS FOR FUTURE RESEARCH

As comparative research is proliferating in most fields of the social sciences and humanities, journalism scholars need not to reinvent the wheel. They can take advantage of the rich literature and theoretical and methodological advances in other disciplines that have an established tradition in cross-cultural studies; most notably sociology, anthropology, psychology, and political science. The problem of equivalence should be taken much more seriously; it needs to be addressed in every comparative study. In this respect, the insight that "[e]quivalence should be established and cannot be assumed" (van de Vijver & Leung, 1997, p. 144) should guide any comparative work.

Journalism studies needs to develop concepts that deliberately serve a comparative purpose, and extend beyond Western-grown models. Some reconceptualization of professional roles ("media roles") has been done by Donsbach and Patterson (2004), Pan and Chan (2003) and Ramaprasad (2001). Pfetsch (2001) developed the concept of a "political communication culture," while Hanitzsch (2007) proposed a universal theory of "journalism culture" for the purpose of comparative analysis. Shoemaker and Reese's (1996) levels-of-analysis approach has also proven to be a useful heuristic tool for a cross-cultural look into the factors that shape the similarities and differences in the news.

Another important deficiency is the lack of sophisticated explanatory analyses that assess the relative contribution of contextual factors (such as gender, media ownership, cultural values, political and economic structures) to the variations among journalistic cultures around the world. Such studies should make optimal use of the potentials of quasi-experimental designs by purposefully selecting countries or other cultural units so as to attribute similarities and differences to their underlying causal factors. These similarities and differences ought to be addressed at different and multiple levels of analysis in order to take account of the diversity of journalistic cultures that cut across and nest within countries.

Finally, collaborative research should be a principal venue in comparative journalism studies since it is the most powerful approach to overcome ethnocentrism in research. While it is true that collaborative research often requires enormous resources and, most importantly, willingness to compromise among the participating scholars, it has, in fact, turned out to be efficient and advantageous in many scientific disciplines.

REFERENCES

Beniger, J. R. (1992). Comparison, yes, but—the case of technological and cultural change. In J. G. Blumler, J. M. McLeod, & K. E. Rosengren (Eds.), *Comparatively speaking: communication and culture across space and time* (pp. 35–50). Newbury Park, CA: Sage.

Berkowitz, D., Limor, Y., & Singer, J. (2004). A cross-cultural look at serving the public interest: American and Israeli journalists consider ethical scenarios. *Journalism, 5*(2), 159–181.

Birkhead, D. (1982). Ideological aspects of journalism research on professionalism. *Journal of Communication Inquiry, 7*(2), 121–134.

Blumler, J. G. (Ed.). (1983). *Communicating to voters: Television in the first European parliamentary elections*. London: Sage.

Blumler, J. G., McLeod, J. M., & Rosengren, K. E. (1992). An introduction to comparative communication research. In J. G. Blumler, J. M. McLeod, & K. E. Rosengren (Eds.), *Comparatively speaking: Communication and culture across space and time* (pp. 3–18). Newbury Park, CA: Sage.

Chalaby, J. K. (1996). Journalism as an Anglo-American invention: A comparison of the development of French and Anglo-American journalism, 1830s–1920s. *European Journal of Communication, 11*(3), 303–326.

Chang, T.-K. with Berg, P., Fung, A. Y.-H., Kedl, K. D., Luther, C. A., & Szuba, J. (2001). Comparing nations in mass communication research, 1970–97: A critical assesment of how we know what we know. *Gazette, 63*(5), 415–434.

Cohen, B. C. (1963). *The press and foreign policy*. Princeton, NJ: Princeton University Press.

Curran, J., & Park, M.-J. (2000). Beyond globalization theory. In J. Curran & M.-J. Park (Eds.), *De-Westernizing media studies* (pp. 3–18). London: Routledge.

Deuze, M. (2002). National news cultures: a comparison of Dutch, German, British, Australian and U.S. journalists. *Journalism & Mass Communication Quarterly, 79*(1), 134–149.

Donsbach, W. (1981). Legitimacy through competence rather than value judgments: The concept of journalistic professionalization reconsidered. *Gazette, 21*(1), 47–67.

Donsbach, W. (1995). Lapdogs, watchdogs and junkjard dogs. *Media Studies Journal, 9*(4), 17–30.

Donsbach, W., & Klett, B. (1993). Subjective objectivity: How journalists in four countries define a key term of their profession. *Gazette, 51*(1), 53–83.

Donsbach, W., & Patterson, T. E. (2004). Political news journalists: partisanship, professionalism, and political roles in five countries. In F. Esser & B. Pfetsch (Eds.), *Comparing political communication: theories, cases, and challenges* (pp. 251–270). New York: Cambridge University Press.

Durkheim, E. (1897/1973). *Der Selbstmord.* Neuwied: Luchterhand.

Edelstein, A. S. (1982). *Comparative communication research.* Beverley Hills, CA: Sage.

Esser, F. (1998). Editorial structures and work principles in British and German newsrooms. *European Journal of Communication, 13*(3), 375–405.

Geddes, B. (2003). How the cases you choose affect the answers you get: Selection bias in comparative politics. In B. Geddes (Ed.), *Paradigms and sand castles: Theory building and research design in comparative politics* (pp. 89–129). Ann Arbor: University of Michigan Press.

Golding, P. (1977). Media professionalism in the Third World: The transfer of an ideology. In J. Curran, M. Gurevitch, & J. Woollacott (Eds.), *Mass communication and society* (pp. 291–308). London: Arnold.

Golding, P., & Elliott, P. (1979). *Making the news.* London: Longman.

Hallin, D. C., & Mancini, P. (2004) *Comparing media systems: Three models of media and politics.* New York: Cambridge University Press.

Halloran, J. D. (1998). Social science, communication research and the third world. *Media Development,* (2), 43–46.

Hanitzsch, T. (2005). Journalists in Indonesia: Educated but timid watchdogs. *Journalism Studies, 6*(4), 493–508.

Hanitzsch, T. (2006). Mapping journalism culture: a theoretical taxonomy and case studies from Indonesia. *Asian Journal of Communication, 16*(2), 169–186.

Hanitzsch, T. (2007). Deconstructing journalism culture: Towards a universal theory. *Communication Theory, 17*(4), 367–385.

Hantrais, L. (1999). Cross contextualization in cross-national comparative research. *International Journal of Social Research Methodology, 2*(2), 93–108.

Hantrais, L., & Mangen, S. (1996). Method and management of cross-national social research. In L. Hantrais & S. Mangen (Eds.), *Cross-national research methods in the social sciences* (pp. 1–12). London: Pinter.

Herscovitz, H. G. (2004). Brazilian journalists' perceptions of media roles, ethics and foreign influences on Brazilian journalism. *Journalism Studies, 5*(1), 71–86.

Hofstede, G. (2001): *Culture's consequences. Second edition: Comparing values, behaviors, institutions and organizations across nations.* Thousand Oaks, CA: Sage.

Janowitz, M. (1975). Professional models in journalism: The gatekeeper and the advocate. *Journalism Quarterly, 52*(4), 618–626, 662.

Johnson, J. D., & Tuttle, F. (2000). Problems in intercultural research. In M. K. Asante & W. B. Gudykunst (Eds.), *Handbook of international and intercultural communication* (pp. 461–483). Newbury Park, CA: Sage.

Josephi, B. (2006). Journalism in the global age: Between normative and empirical. *Gazette, 67*(6), 575–590.

Köcher, R. (1986). Bloodhounds or missionaries: Role definitions of German and British journalists. *European Journal of Communication, 1*(1), 43–64.

Kohn, M. L. (1989). Cross-national research as an analytic strategy. In M. L. Kohn (Ed.), *Cross-national research in sociology* (pp. 77–102). Newbury Park, CA: Sage.

Lerner, D. (1958). *The passing of traditional society: Modernizing the Middle East.* Glencoe: The Free Press.

Livingstone, S. (2003). On the challenges of cross-national comparative media research. *European Journal of Communication, 18*(4), 477–500.

McLeod, J. M., & Hawley, S. E. (1964). Professionalization among newsmen. *Journalism Quarterly, 41*(4), 529–539.

McLeod, J., & R. R. Rush (1969a). Professionalization of Latin American and U.S. journalists. *Journalism Quarterly, 46*(3), 583–590.

McLeod, J., & R. R. Rush (1969b). Professionalization of Latin American and U.S. journalists: Part II. *Journalism Quarterly, 46*(4), 784–789.

Marr, M., Wyss, V., Blum, R., & Bonfadelli, H. (2001). *Journalisten in der Schweiz. Eigenschaften, Einstellungen, Einflüsse*. Konstanz, Germany: UVK.

Øyen, E. (1990). The imperfection of comparisons. In E. Øyen (Ed.), *Comparative methodology: theory and practice in international social research* (pp. 1–18). London: Sage.

Pan, Z., & Chan, J. M. (2003). Shifting journalistic paradigms: How China's journalists assess "media exemplars." *Communication Research, 30*(6), 649–682.

Patterson, T. E., & Donsbach, W. (1996). News decisions: Journalists as partisan actors. *Political Communication, 13*(4), 455–468.

Pfetsch, B. (2001). Political Communication Culture in the United States and Germany. *Harvard International Journal of Press/Politics, 6*(1), 46–67.

Pritchard, D., & Souvageau, F. (1998). The journalists and journalisms of Canada. In D. H. Weaver (Ed.), *The global journalist: news people around the world* (pp. 373–393). Cresskill, NJ: Hampton Press.

Quandt, T., Löffelholz, M., Weaver, D. H., Hanitzsch, T., & Altmeppen, K.-D. (2006). American and German online journalists at the beginning of the 21st century: A bi-national survey. *Journalism Studies, 7*(2), 171–186.

Ramaprasad, J. (2001). A profile of journalists in post-independence Tanzania. *Gazette, 63*(6), 539–556.

Schoenbach, K., Stuerzebecher, D., & Schneider, B. (1998). German journalists in the early 1990s: East and West. In D. H. Weaver (Ed.), *The global journalist: News people around the world* (pp. 213–227). Cresskill, NJ: Hampton Press.

Shoemaker, P. J., & Cohen, A. A. (2006). *News around the world: Content, practitioners and the public*. New York: Routledge.

Shoemaker, P. J., & Reese, S. D. (1996). *Mediating the Message: Theories of Influence on Mass Media Content*. White Plains, NY: Longman.

Siebert, F. S., Peterson, T., & Schramm, W. (1956). *Four theories of the press: The authoritarian, libertarian, social responsibility and Soviet communist soncepts of what the press should be and do*. Champaign: University of Illinois Press.

Splichal, S., & Sparks, C. (1994). *Journalists for the 21st century: Tendencies of professionalization among first-year students in 22 countries*. Norwood, NJ: Ablex.

Sreberny-Mohammadi, A., Nordenstreng, K., & Stevenson, R. L. (1984). The world of the news study. *Journal of Communication, 34*(1), 134–38.

Starck, K., & Sudhaker, A. (1979). Reconceptualizing the notion of journalistic professionalism across differing press systems. *Journal of Communication Inquiry, 4*(2), 33–52.

Tylor, E. B. (1871). *Primitive culture: researches into the development of mythology, philosophy, religion, art, and custom*. London: J. Murray.

van de Vijver, F. J. R., & Leung, K. (1997). *Methods and data analysis for cross-cultural research*. Thousand Oaks, CA: Sage.

Weaver, D. H. (1998a): Introduction. In D. H. Weaver (Ed.), *The global journalist: News people around the world* (pp. 1–4). Cresskill, NJ: Hampton.

Weaver, D. H. (1998b). Journalist around the world: Commonalities and differences. In D. H. Weaver (Ed.), *The global journalist: news people around the world* (pp. 455–480). Cresskill, NJ: Hampton.

Weaver, D. H. (Ed.). (1998c). *The global journalist: news people around the world*. Cresskill, NJ: Hampton.

Weaver, D., Beam, R., Brownlee, B., Voakes, P., & Wilhoit, G. C. (2007). *The American journalist in the 21st century. U.S. newspeople at the dawn of a new millenium*. Mahwah, NJ: Erlbaum.

Weischenberg, S., Malik, M., & Scholl, A. (2006). *Die Souffleure der Mediengesellschaft. Report über die Journalisten in Deutschland.* Konstanz, Germany: UVK.

Wirth, W., & Kolb, S. (2004). Designs and methods of comparative political communication research. In F. Esser & B. Pfetsch (Eds.), *Comparing political communication: Theories, cases, and challenges* (pp. 87–111). New York: Cambridge University Press.

Wright, D. K. (1974). An analysis of the level of professionalism among Canadian journalists. *Gazette, 20*(3), 132–144.

Wu, H. D. (2000). Systemic determinants of international news coverage: a comparison of 38 countries. *Journal of Communication, 50*(1), 110–130.

Wu, W., Weaver, D., & Johnson, O. V. (1996). Professional roles of Russian and U.S. journalists: a comparative study. *Journalism & Mass Communication Quarterly, 73*(3), 534–548.

Zhu, J.-H., Weaver, D., Lo, V., Chen, C., & Wu, W. (1997). Individual, organizational, and societal influences on media role perceptions: a comparative study of journalists in China, Taiwan, and the United States. *Journalism & Mass Communication Quarterly, 74*(1), 84–96.

30

Towards De-Westernizing Journalism Studies

Herman Wasserman and Arnold S. de Beer

HISTORICAL AND PRESENT CONTEXT

The accelerated globalization of media and its increasingly participatory possibilities in the twentieth and twenty-first centuries as a result of technological advances has raised pertinent questions regarding the definition of journalism and journalists. In an era where media have become "environmental" to the extent that the world is becoming a "mediapolis," (Silverstone, 2007), the task of empirically and normatively defining "who is a journalist"; "what is journalism" (cf. Wyatt, 2007); deciding what is meant by journalism studies education (Fröhlich & Holtz-Bacha, 2003; Murray & Moore, 2003) and how it could be researched (see Löffelholz & Weaver, 2008) has become urgent—even while there is not agreement on evidence pointing to the relative "newness" of the current epoch of media globalization (Sparks, 2007).

Globalization opens the way for the study of journalism and media in their hybrid, regional and global-local manifestations (McMillin, 2007, p. 2), increasing the need to take a global perspective on the study of journalism (which, as a fundamental theoretical point of departure, is something different from incorporating diverse perspectives from around the world). This need springs not only from the momentum of globalization, but also from a global "political realignment" that has resulted in the deconstruction of discourses of global democracy after 9/11 (Josephi, 2005, p. 575). In the field of journalism studies this realignment has led to a questioning of the link between journalism and a particular form of political organization, opening the way for a definition of journalism that is more inclusive of global political differences. As more comparative studies are being done (see Hanitzsch, 2007, for a summary), the dominant Anglo-American view of journalism is being challenged by studies showing up the gap between theory and practice (Josephi, 2005, p. 576). Institutionally, the increased internationalization of the field of journalism is evident, for example, from the constituents of the International Communication Association's Journalism Studies Division (with more than half of its members coming from outside the United States; ICA, 2007) and international conferences on Journalism Studies being held outside major centers in the North (e.g., in Brazil 2006 and Singapore 2007).

Yet globalization of media and journalism and of the scholarly study thereof, remains a highly uneven and heterogeneous phenomenon. If it has to have analytical usefulness as well as critical potential for de-Westernizing the field, journalism studies has to extend beyond descriptive comparative studies of journalism. A critical journalism studies would also turn the gaze upon itself and the normative assumptions underlying comparative work, by locating comparative studies within global power relations both epistemologically and politically. Unless comparative analyses lead to a re-examining of the theoretical foundations of journalism studies, such studies will remain an exercise in curiosity rather than result in a far-reaching de-Westernizing of the field.

A related question, and one which we will not attempt to answer here, is whether "Western journalism" in itself exists (cf. Hanitzsch, 2007, p. 368), even if the historical origins of modern mass media are rooted in the West (Couldry, 2007, p. 247). While several studies have found commonalities in the professional ideologies of journalists in countries around the world, significant differences have also been noted (see Hanitzsch, 2007, for an overview of these studies). Attempting to contribute more non-Western perspectives to the field of journalism studies should therefore not rest on the assumption that journalism in "The West" can be homogenized, or that a binary opposition between "West" and "non-West" can (or should) be drawn in any uncomplicated fashion. In this chapter it will be argued that a global approach to journalism studies should start at a fundamentally epistemological level. Theories about how journalism should be defined, what its relationship with society is, how it should be taught and how it should be practiced ought to be constructed within a globally inclusive, dialogic setting. The difference between a dialogic and an inclusive approach is important. Even if diverse journalisms are *included* in a global purview, some of them could still be marginalized or ghettoized as "alternative" journalisms or as belonging to geographically specific areas, and therefore unable to exert pressure on the dominant mainstream to change like they would in a truly *dialogic* approach (see Mowlana, 1996). Inclusive approaches thus far have resulted in the "reluctant" acceptance of models that differ from Anglo-American ones. Normative assumptions like the equation of journalism and liberal democracy, however, remain largely unquestioned (Josephi, 2005).

What is needed, therefore, is a global approach to journalism studies that is "comprehensively and mutually comparative" (Couldry, 2007, p. 247): one which can "disrupt" existing paradigms. Linked to such an approach is an understanding of how the political economy of scholarly production and distribution impacts on the field of journalism studies. Not only the inclusion of "other" perspectives on journalism studies is important—at stake are also the conditions under which these "other" perspectives are allowed to enter the academic discourse.

In other words, a project to de-Westernize journalism studies would have an epistemological as well as a political-economic dimension. While these two aspects are interrelated, they should also be unpacked in terms of their implications for knowledge production in journalism studies. Part of a de-Westernizing approach to journalism studies would entail the realization that all theory is situated somewhere—there is no such thing as a decontextualized theory.

In this chapter, we want to connect the epistemological and political-economic dimensions of a de-Westernizing approach to journalism studies by focusing on one specific area where these two aspects become clearly visible: that of journalism studies knowledge production in sub-Saharan English speaking Africa.

Our position as researchers of African, especially South African, media, also informs the preliminary remarks about "de-Westernizing" journalism studies that we would like to offer here. With our focus on Africa, we cannot presume to speak on behalf of the Global South[1] as a whole, but we anticipate that at least some of what we discuss will have a bearing on journalism studies in other developmental contexts. While the political-economic context of journalism studies in Africa might differ considerably from some non-Western contexts like Asia, it might correspond with, for instance, Latin America, for both historical (such as the history of colonialism) and economic (as developing regions in the global economy) reasons. But just as there is no one Western journalism even if similarities exist (Hanitzsch 2007), the project of de-Westernizing journalism studies cannot be seen as one-dimensional and should be conducted on multiple levels. With reference to Zelizer's (2004) seminal book on journalism studies and the academy, we would like to argue that for journalism studies to be a truly global project, African journalism studies approaches should be taken seriously as part and parcel of a globalizing world, and not as an "area study," isolated from broader debates.

While the focus on Africa to illustrate some of the key issues in de-Westernizing journalism studies is primarily chosen for practical reasons, such a focus can also be justified in terms of its neglect or relative minor position even in comparative studies (e.g., that of Hallin & Mancini, 2004).

Furthermore, a study of African journalism will illustrate the contested nature of the epistemologies, professional ideologies and value systems that mark journalisms worldwide. Journalism in Africa often displays an uneasy relationship between its colonial heritage and post-colonial appropriation, between globalized, Western influence and local resistance. As such, African journalism studies itself is marked by heterogeneity and ambivalence.

KEY ELEMENTS

Key to understanding attempts to de-Westernize journalism studies is the realization that this process has to take place on several levels. Addressing imbalances in journalism scholarship is firstly an epistemological issue, dealing with the origin and nature of knowledge about journalism and assumptions regarding its universality and generalizability. The production, canonization and distribution of knowledge do not take place in a vacuum, however. Epistemologies are produced and attain their validity within social relations, which in turn are embedded in political and economic conditions. These relations often remain hidden but can become visible in a critical analysis of the manifestation of knowledge in the form of scholarly output. To illustrate the above dimensions of journalism studies from a non-Western perspective, they are discussed below with a specific focus on the African context.

Epistemological Issues

An epistemology of global journalism, as a study of knowledge systems and their justification (Hanitzsch, 2007, p. 375), will be invalid if it rests upon evidence gathered from a "tiny handful of countries" made to represent the whole of the world (Curran & Park, 2000, p. 3). While the Western bias of journalism and media studies is increasingly acknowledged and refuted, the question remains how exactly this situation should be rectified. A mere comparative study of how different dimensions of journalism are being understood or implemented around the world may be more inclusive, but would not necessarily de-Westernize the field. This is because the very categories within which such comparisons are made, are often deduced from concepts that have historically been central to Western, liberal-democratic normative notions of journalism, like objectivity, truth-telling and the need for a "free" press. The result is that "other" journalisms, be they African, Asian or Latin American, are then presented in terms of their correspondence with or deviation from established categories, with the normative category itself remaining unchanged even if deviance is not viewed negatively. (Often, however, a negative evaluation of "other" journalisms or the relation between media and state in non-Western countries has more to do with legitimating or repairing the Western paradigm "at home" than with an attempt to get to grips with the situation elsewhere. In this regard, the "othering" of non-Western journalism can serve the construction of the occupational identities of the Western self.) One way around this would be to work inductively from non-Western contexts, through "thick descriptions," to re-establish epistemological dimensions for global journalism. Such an approach might lead us to discover that claims to truth and knowledge, as these are understood in Western societies, might be made differently (e.g., through performativity or subjectivity rather than objectivity and rationality), or that such claims might not even be central to journalistic identities in the non-West and the central category would therefore have to be rethought.

De-Westernizing the epistemology of journalism studies would also mean that the research agenda is constructed more inclusively. Instead of constructing research questions in the West and then attempting to answer them in a globally comparative, inclusive manner, the research agenda itself should be conceived of in global terms. Too much theorization about journalism studies is done in ignorance of/or an apparent disinterest in the situation outside Northern academic centers and media institutions. The recent shift towards participatory journalism brought on by technological advancement such as blogging and video-blogging, leading to either celebratory declarations (e.g., *Time* magazine's awarding of their "Person of the Year" in 2006 to "You," i.e., everyone using computers to create a new information commons) or to doom-mongering (e.g., about the future of older media like newspapers or television) as if the trajectory of media evolution in the West is universally inevitable, is one example. While journalism theory is being revised and questions raised around the definition of journalism, journalism ethics and audience preferences, scant attention is paid to the situation in parts of the world where these technologies are less pervasive, but where journalism producers and consumers are finding more and more creative ways of dealing with lack of access in order to compete in a globalized media world. The very fact that these specific sets of questions, predicated as they are on the situation in media-saturated societies, dominate the journalism studies research agenda indicates the need to de-Westernize the field of enquiry.

Some critical comments have been sounded against this "self-absorption and parochialism of much Western theory" (Curran & Park, 2000, p. 3). They point to several events and trends (globalization, the end of the Cold War, the rise of the Asian economy, the emergence of alternative centers of media production and the world-wide growth of media studies) that have made the existing "narrowness" of media theory "transparently absurd."

Similarly, John Downing (1996) has called for more comparative work on a theoretical level. Influential, yet outdated and biased, models for comparative media systems such as that of Siebert, Peterson and Schramm (1956) have been revisited (e.g., by Hallin & Mancini, 2004), and global comparative projects undertaken (e.g., Weaver, 1998). Nevertheless, some areas of the world (notably Africa) remain either ignored or occupy a marginal position in these works. African scholars and media practitioners themselves also often uncritically measure their own media institutions and practices against Western-biased frameworks rather than engaging with them critically and creatively.

When the global South enters the dominant Northern scholarship, it is much less often as a critical interlocutor succeeding in bringing about self-reflexivity in the center than as a terrain for "modernization" according to the dominant Western developmental model that remains prevalent even in the era of globalization (Curran & Park, 2000, pp. 4–5, Sparks, 2007, p. 28). The end-result is too often that the Western democratic model of liberal democracy remains the implicit or explicit normative ideal against which journalism in non-Western societies is measured, with media-state relations as a primary determinant of journalistic standards.

If it is then acknowledged that journalism and media theories need to include more non-Western perspectives, what are the impediments in the way of a more inclusive, global approach to journalism studies? To answer this question, the political economy of knowledge production in the field of journalism studies has to be considered.

Political-Economic Issues

Journalism studies is gaining ground as a research field at a time when the globalization paradigm has become the dominant one for the study of media and communication, even if there is disagreement about the evidence to support this paradigm and what it means (Sparks, 2007, p. 149). Critical political economists have tended to see globalization in a negative light, as a "capitalist victory that is dispossessing democracies, imposing policy homogenization, and weakening progressive movements rooted in working-class and popular political organizations" (Curran & Park, 2000, p. 11). The weakening of the nation-state under pressure of globalization has implications for the type of approach to be followed in a de-Westernizing of journalism studies. Nation-states can no longer unproblematically be used as the only or main units for comparison, but media should be seen in terms of the "translocal" (Couldry, 2007, p. 248). That nation-states have not lost all relevance, however, has become especially clear in the post-9/11 era, when journalism has been awash with nationalist and xenophobic discourses (Pludowski, 2007; Berenger, 2004).

Comparative frameworks classifying media according to political and economic systems (e.g., Curran & Park, 2000) or regional media traditions (e.g., Hallin & Mancini, 2004) could both be useful in comparing journalistic ideologies, norms and practices around the world, since they acknowledge respectively the influence of political and economic systems on the practice of journalism as well as the historical development of professional culture in different regions of the world. The acceleration of globalization has meant, however, that even if the conceptual framework of nations or regions might be retained for practical or other reasons (De Beer & Merrill, 2004, p. xv), what is becoming increasingly important is global interdependence between them.

But because of increasing global media flows on these various levels, Couldry (2007, p. 249) has also suggested that comparative media studies should focus more on the difficult and "fuzzy" notion of "media cultures," rather than the more fixed and clearly delineated media systems. Couldry's cultural approach suggests a closer look at the appropriation and creative agency exercised by media users outside of the dominant centers. This is a valid point, as long as the attention to "fuzzy" exchanges includes a scrutiny of the structural inequalities (like the so-called Digital Divide) within which these exchanges take place.

Studies of journalism outside of the dominant Western centers (and often taken up in debates among professional journalist elites within non-Western countries themselves) focus mostly on press freedom (or the lack of it) as the central characteristic of journalism. There is a predictability in the regularity with which the state features as the central object of scrutiny in such studies which suggests that liberal democratic assumptions of politics and economy remain the dominant perspective on journalism globally (cf. Nyamnjoh, 2005).

A comparative approach that would focus more on cultural exchanges than structural dimensions like media: state relations would take into account the flow and counter-flow (see Thussu, 2007) of media content globally. Ironically, however, a nuanced and thickly textured picture of the way these "fuzzy" trends of appropriation and redirection are playing out in regions like Africa still eludes journalism studies scholarship exactly because of structural obstacles in the way of wider knowledge about journalism and media in Africa (De Beer, 2007, 2008). One such aspect is the political economy of scholarship, to which we now turn.

Knowledge Capacity Building and Publishing

While there is a clear need for more inclusive and dialogic studies of journalism worldwide, the extent to which this can be done is dependent on more than scholarly interest and openness alone. Knowledge production and theory building takes place within structural constraints, and these become especially evident when scholarly publication is considered. Nyamnjoh (2005, p. 29) points out how economic considerations impact negatively on the plurality and diversity of content, with the result that scholarship rarely strays beyond the boundaries of the usual:

> If he who pays the piper calls the tune, then the cultural capital most likely to inspire investment is that which is familiar to the paymaster's race, place, class, gender or generation; that into which s/he has been schooled to the point of second nature and which, instinctively, s/he expects every piper worth the name to internalize and reproduce. [...] This makes publishing a very conservative industry where despite rhetoric to the contrary, the emphasis is less on creativity than mimicry, and less on production than reproduction.

African scholars (and this could equally apply to scholars from other non-Western regions) are, according to Nyamnjoh (2006), left with an impossible choice: On the one hand, they may write for an African audience in order to remain socially relevant, but sacrifice wider recognition in the scholarly community and miss out on the opportunity to influence global debates. On the other hand, they can choose scholarly recognition in the wider international academic circle but—because their colleagues in the developing world lack the means to access scholarly work produced in costly journals or books elsewhere—forego the opportunity to engage with local audiences that would benefit from the relevance of such scholarly work.

The global political economy of scholarly publication and distribution has a normative effect: The dominance of especially American academic publishing houses and journals has, over the last half-century, become so all-encompassing that generations of journalism students in English-speaking African countries have become inculcated in the American "way of doing things." American textbooks on journalism have become the major, and often the sole, published source for journalism students in Africa. From Wolseley and Campbell (1959) in the 1950s, Bond (1961) in the 1960s, through Metz (1977), Harriss, Leiter, and Johnson (1992), to the latter authors' updates in the 2000s, American textbooks became the conduit for English speaking African students to learn journalism.

Against the avalanche of available American journalism textbooks, preciously little was produced in Anglophone Africa in terms of journalism textbooks (and exception to the rule was for instance the work done by Francis Kasoma (e.g., 1994) and various authors in South Africa (e.g., Greer, 1999; Nel, 2002), although in some areas of journalism studies like ethics, local authors by and large just took over paradigms developed elsewhere. Journalism training programs conducted by well-meaning NGOs also sometimes assume a certain universality of journalism ideology and practice. These programmes often follow a type of developmental journalism based on a generic understanding of the relation between journalism, society and democracy, rather than a participatory approach where the parameters for training would be set by local journalists and audiences. Murphy and Rodriguez (2006) argue in a special edition of *Global Media and Communication* that questions of globalization and hegemony compel mass communication scholars in the North to rethink the theoretical constructs and praxis of the media industries in Latin America. The same reasoning could apply to Africa, where, as in Latin America,

> a cultural landscape [is] increasingly defined by the conspicuous markers of technology and global capitalism (e.g. cybercafés, cell phones, cineplexes, etc.) embedded in social struggles (e.g. democratization, armed conflict, racism, poverty, resource control, immigration) and framed by the thick residues of indigenous, colonial, revolutionary, and pre-capitalist pasts. (p. 268)

For such a rethink to happen within the field of journalism studies, a more inclusive dialogue in the sphere of scholarly publication has to take place. This, in turn, requires that the asymmetry within the publishing industry and its patterns of distribution be addressed (see Zegeye & Vambe, 2006, pp. 333–334).

JOURNALISM STUDIES IN AFRICA: SCHOLARS AND TEXTS

Given the political economy of scholarly publishing, it is not surprising that journalism studies in sub-Saharan Africa has not produced a strong corpus of home-grown theoretical approaches and key texts.

The exception in this regard is South Africa (others to an extent being Kenya and Nigeria), due to, amongst other elements, its relatively strong economic position that has enabled it to develop a significant publication industry. The academic boycott during the apartheid years isolated the scholarly community in that country, contributing to the establishment of several journals to serve as publication outlets. After the end of apartheid, some of these journals have entered the international arena when they were acquired by international publishing groups (e.g., *Communicatio* and *Critical Arts* now published by Taylor and Francis) or university publishers (e.g., *Ecquid Novi: African Journalism Studies*, published by University of Wisconsin Press).

Whereas the historical isolation of South Africa has contributed to the development of a domestic academic publishing industry, an extensive body of journalism studies scholarship and publications has been produced by scholars from the rest of the continent residing in the diaspora. The global political economy of publishing has therefore led to the irony that African scholars working at universities in Northern America and Europe have contributed to a relatively stronger position for African journalism studies globally, due in part to their access to publication and dissemination opportunities in the North.

The same Northern influence is found even in the African peer-reviewed journal devoted to journalism studies research in Africa: *Ecquid Novi: African Journalism Studies.*[2] Published since 2008 by University of Wisconsin Press, in association with the Department of Journalism, Stellenbosch University, the research articles published in this journal show a strong influence from American scholars, although contributions from African authors are encouraged. An exception to this trend was *Africa Media Review*, a journal of the now apparently defunct African Council of Communication Education (ACCE) based in Nairobi, Kenya, with recent efforts by the Council for the Development of Social Science Research in Africa, based in Dakar, Senegal, to resurrect the journal.

However, the strong influence of authors from the North writing on African journalism studies might be changing. For instance, Boafo and George's (1992) book has been published under the auspices of the ACCE in Nairobi. Ansu-Kyeremeh (2005) from Ghana gathered, for his book on *Indigenous communication in Africa*, ten authors of whom seven are from Africa. Francis Nyamnjoh, based at Codesria in Dakar, Senegal, received international acclaim for his book *Africa's Media* (2005).

For a broad overview of the work dealing with African journalism and media, certain recurring topics or trends can be identified. These themes have started to characterize the field of journalism studies in Africa (although they often address journalism as part of a broader discussion of media and communication). To illustrate the kind of work done within these broad rubrics, some recent texts in the respective areas can be noted. This should not be seen as an exhaustive list or a "who's who" of seminal texts, but as a brief attempt to map the field:

- *Journalism, democracy and press freedom* (Berger & Barratt, 2007; Hachten & Giffard, 1984; Hasty, 2005; Hydén et al., 2002; Jackson, 1993; Kasoma, 2000; Tomaselli & Dunn,

2002; Nyamnjoh, 2005; Ocitte, 2005; Olorunnisola, 2006; Switzer, 1997)

- *Media systems and political economy of media* (Bourgault , 1995; Horwitz, 2001; M'Bayo et al., 2000)
- *Journalism ethics* (Kasoma, 1994; Rønning & Kasoma, 2002; Oosthuizen, 2002)
- *Journalism/media and development* (Okigbo & Eribo, 2004)
- *Journalism education and training* (Greer, 1999; Boafo, 2002; Steenveld, 2002)

Caveat and Critique

While the literature from and about African media and journalism provide perspectives that can contribute to what one could call the "de-Westernizing" of journalism studies, such perspectives should not be elided with so-called "Afrocentric" positions (Tomaselli, 2003, cites Ziegler & Asante, 1992, and Kasoma, 1996, as representative of this position). Afro-centric approaches to journalism can be rather problematic, especially when it takes a normative position premised on essentialist African identity and culture. A static notion of "African culture" can legitimize an approach to journalism that rejects Western values wholesale, which is not a helpful analytical position in a globalized era where the dominant mode is that of interdependency and exchange.

Given the struggle for press freedom and democracy in many African countries (to which some of the literature listed above attests), Afro-centric positions that may lead to an uncritical acceptance of authority, undemocratic exclusion of minority voices and the stifling of free speech should be guarded against. Recent work by Tomaselli (2003) and Fourie (2007) has criticized Afro-centered journalistic practices on these grounds. They point to the danger that the very notion of "de-Westernizing" or "indigenization" or "African values" can be oppressive and lead to the stifling of critical debate (Tomaselli, 2003, p. 435; Blankenberg, 1999, p. 61).

The argument advanced in the current chapter is for a dialogic, interdependent approach to global journalism studies. Such an approach to the "de-Westernization" of the field would avoid crude notions of "African values" or "indigenization," but would be based on an awareness of structural inequalities regarding scholarly production and the concomitant effect it has on epistemology. The emphasis should therefore fall on the contemporary experience of African journalism in a global context (which often is the experience of marginalization, exclusion and ignorance), rather than on a supposed static, pan-African cultural traits, or claims of "authenticity."

CONCLUSION

The fact that epistemological as well as political economic factors exclude journalism practices, frameworks and ideologies in large parts of the world from scholarly research and debate should not be viewed in deterministic terms. Scholars located outside of dominant centers (in the case of this chapter, in Africa) or working in areas (like African journalism) that are marginalized in global journalism studies have found ways to overcome limitations. While the publication of journals on African journalism or media studies through an established publisher in the North may provide one way of overcoming limitations on publication and distribution, this increases the need for scholars to remain in touch with what is happening "on the ground" in African contexts and incorporate the lived experience of journalists and audiences outside of the metropolitan context.

The inroads made into metropolitan centers are, however, not enough to ensure that journalism studies become a truly global and de-Westernizing project. Attempts should be made to divert funding to scholars working in Africa and other areas outside the dominant centers; to provide financial support to publications in these areas; to provide scholarships and travel grants to enable scholars in poorer countries to attend conferences. Such economic intervention should complement a willingness and openness by journalism scholars to continually question the assumptions and theoretical foundations upon which they build, in order to develop a truly global study of journalism.

NOTES

1. In keeping with the terminology of "de-Westernizing" as it has gained currency within scholarly debates especially after Curran and Park's (2000) well-known book, this chapter will refer to the "West" and the "non-West." However, it is acknowledged that in a post-Cold War geopolitical and geo-economic context, it would make more sense to speak of the Global North or South, or, even more appropriately, the Tri-Continent (Africa, Asia and Latin America) (McMillin, 2007, p. 1, 222).
2. Disclosure: The current authors are respectively editor and managing editor of the journal.

REFERENCES

Ansu-Kyeremeh, K. (Ed.). (2005). *Indigenous communication in Africa: Concept, applications and prospects.* Accra: Ghana Universities Press.

Berger, G. & Barratt, E. (2007). *Fifty Years of Journalism. African media since Ghana's independence.* Grahamstown: Highway Africa, The African Editors Forum and the Media Foundation West Africa.

Blankenberg, N. (1999). In search of a real freedom: Ubuntu and the media. *Critical Arts, 13*(2), 42–65.

Boafo, K. (Ed.). (2002). *Communication training in Africa: Model curricula.* Paris: UNESCO

Boafo, S. T. K., & George, N. A. (Eds.). (1992). *Communication research in Africa. Issues and perspectives.* Nairobi, Kenya: ACCE.

Bond, F. F. (1961). *An introduction to journalism—A survey of the Fourth Estate in all its forms.* New York: Macmillan.

Bourgault, L. M. (1995). *Mass media in sub-Saharan Africa.* Bloomington: Indiana University Press.

Couldry, N. (2007). Researching Media Internationalization: Comparative research as if we really meant it. *Global Media and Communication, 3*(3), 247–271.

Curran, J., & Park, M-J. (2000). Beyond globalization theory. In J. Curran & M.-J. Park (Eds.), *De-Westernizing media studies* (pp. 3–8). London: Routledge.

De Beer, A. S. (2008). South African journalism research: Bridging the schisms. In. M. Löffelholz & D. H. Weaver (Eds.), *Global journalism research: Theories, methods, findings, future* (pp. 185–196). Oxford: Blackwell.

De Beer, A. S. (2007). *Looking for journalism education scholarship in some unusual places: The case of Africa.* Paper read at the 1st World Journalism Education Conference, Singapore.

De Beer, A. S. & Merrill, J. C. (Eds.). (2004). *Global journalism. Topical issues and media systems.* New York: Pearson.

Downing, J. (1996). *Internationalizing media theory.* London: Sage.

Fourie, J. P. (2007). Moral philosophy as the foundation of normative media theory: The case of African Ubuntuism. *Communications, 32,* 1–29.

Fröhlich, R., & Holtz-Bacha, C. (Eds.) 2003. Journalism education in Europe and North America: An International Comparison. Cresskill, NJ: Hampton.

Greer, G. (1999). *A new introduction to journalism.* Cape Town: Juta.

Hachten, W. A., & Giffard, C. A. (1984). *Total onslaught. The South African press under attack.* Johannesburg: Macmillan.

Hallin, D., & Mancini, P. (2004). *Comparing media systems: Three models of media and politics.* New York: Cambridge University Press.

Hanitzsch, T. (2007). Deconstructing journalism culture: Toward a universal theory. *Communication Theory, 17*(4), 367–385.

Hasty, J. (2005). *The press and political culture in Ghana.* Bloomington: Indiana University Press

Horwitz, R. B. (2001). *Communication and democratic reform in South Africa.* Cambridge: Cambridge University Press

Hydén, G., Leslie, M., & Ogundimu, F. F. (Eds.) (2002). *Media and democracy in Africa.* Uppsala, Sweden: Nordiska Afrikainstitutet.

ICA (2007). Journalism Studies Division homepage. Retrieved 11 November 2007 from http://www.icahdq.org/divisions/JournalismStudies/jsdweb/index.html

Jackson, G.S. (1993). *Breaking story. The South African press.* Boulder, CO: Westview.

Josephi, B. (2005). Journalism in the Global Age: Between Normative and Empirical. *Gazette, 67*(6), 575–590.

Kasoma, F. (1994). *Journalism ethics in Africa.* Nairobi: ACCE.

Kasoma, F. (1996). The Foundations of African Ethics (Afri-ethics) and the professional practice of journalism: The case for society-centred media morality. *Africa Media Review, 10*(3), 93–116.

Kasoma, F. (2000). *The press and multiparty politics in Africa.* Tampere, Finland: University of Tampere.

Leiter, K., Harriss, J., & Johnson, S. (1992). *The complete reporter: Fundamentals of news gathering, writing, and editing.* Boston: Allyn and Bacon.

Löffelholz, M., & Weaver, D. (Eds.) (2008). *Global journalism research: Theories, methods, findings, future.* Oxford: Blackwell.

M'Bayo, R. T., Onwumechili, C., & Nwanko, R. N. (Eds.). (2000). *Press and Politics in Africa*: Lewiston, NY: Edwin Mellen

McMillin, D. C. (2007). *International media studies.* Malden, MA: Blackwell.

Metz, W. (1977). *Newswriting: From lead to "30".* Englewood Cliffs, NJ: Prentice-Hall.

Murphy, P. D., & Rodriguez, C. (2006). Between Macondo and McWorld: Communication and culture studies in Latin America. *Global Media and Communication, 2*(3), 267–277.

Murray, M. D., & Moore, R. L. (Eds.). (2003). *Mass communication education.* Ames: Iowa State Press.

Nel, F. (2002). *Writing for the media in South Africa.* Cape Town: Oxford.

Nyamnjoh, F. B. (2004). From publish or perish to publish and perish: What "Africa's Best Books" tell us about publishing Africa. *Journal of Asian and African Studies, 39*(5), 331–355

Nyamnjoh, F. B. (2005). *Africa's media, democracy and the politics of belonging.* London: Zed.

Ocitte, J. (2005). *Press, politics and public policy in Uganda.* Lampeter, Wales: Edwin Mellen Press.

Okigbo, C. C., & Eribo, F. (Eds.). (2004). *Development and communication in Africa.* New York: Rowman & Littlefield.

Olorunnisola, A. A. (2006). *Media in South Africa after apartheid: A cross-media assessment.* Lampeter, Wales: Edwin Mellen Press.

Oosthuizen, L. M. (2002). *Media ethics in the South African context.* Lansdowne, South Africa: Juta.

Rønning, H., & Kasoma, F. (2002). *Media Ethics: An introduction and overview.* Lansdowne, South Africa: Juta & Nordic SADC Journalism Centre

Siebert, F., Peterson, T., & Schramm, W. (1956). *Four theories of the press.* Urbana: University of Illinois Press.

Silverstone, R. (2007). *Media and morality:Tthe rise of the mediapolis.* Cambridge: Polity.

Sparks, C. (2007). *Globalization, development and the mass media.* London: Sage.

Steenveld, L. (2002). *Training for media transformation and democracy.* Johannesburg: South African National Editors' Forum.

Switzer. L. (Ed.). (1997). *South Africa's alternative press. Voices of protest and resistance, 1880s–1960s.* Cambridge: Cambridge University Press.

Thussu, D. (Ed.). (2007). *Media on the move: Global flow and contra-flow.* London: Routledge.

Tomaselli, K. G. (2003). "Our Culture" vs "Foreign Culture": An essay on ontological and professional issues in African journalism. *Gazette, 65*(6), 427–441.

Tomaselli, K .G., & Dunn, H. S. (Eds.). (2002). *Media, democracy and eenewal in Southern Africa.* Denver, CO: International Academic Press.

Weaver, D. H. (Ed.). (1998). *The global journalist: News people around the world.* Cresskill, NJ: Hampton Press.

Wolseley, R. E., & Campbell, L. R. (1959). *Exploring journalism. With emphasis on its social and professional aspects.* Englewood Cliffs, NJ: Prentice-Hall.

Wyatt, W. (Ed.). (2007). Foreword. *Journal of Mass Media Ethics*, 22(4), 239–240 (special Issue on "Who is a Journalist?").

Zegeye, A., & Vambe, M. (2006). Knowledge production and publishing in Africa. *Development Southern Africa*, *23*(3), 333–349.

Zelizer. B. (2004). *Taking journalism seriously: News and the academy.* Thousand Oaks, CA: Sage.

Ziegler, D., & Asante, M. K. (1992). *Thunder and silence: The mass media in Africa.* Trenton, NJ: Africa World Press.

Author Index

Subject Index